Britain Since 1945

Making Contemporary Britain Series

General Editor: *Anthony Seldon*
Consultant Editor: *Peter Hennessy*

Published

Northern Ireland Since 1968
Paul Arthur and Keith Jeffery

The Prime Minister Since 1945[†]
James Barber

British General Elections Since 1945[†]
David Butler

The British Economy Since 1945
Alec Cairncross

Britain and the Suez Crisis*
David Carlton

Town Planning in Britain Since 1900
Gordon Cherry

The End of the British Empire[†]
John Darwin

Religion in Britain Since 1945
Grace Davie

British Defence Since 1945[†]
Michael Dockrill

British Politics Since 1945
Peter Dorey

Britain and the Falklands War*
Lawrence Freedman

Britain and European Integration Since 1945[†]
Stephen George

British Social Policy Since 1945 (second edition)
Howard Glennerster

Judicial Politics Since 1920: A Chronicle*
John Griffith

Britain Since 1945
Jonathan Hollowell (ed.)

Sport in Britain Since 1945
Richard Holt and Tony Mason

Consensus Politics from Attlee to Major
Dennis Kavanagh and Peter Morris

The Politics of Immigration*
Zig Layton-Henry

Women in Britain Since 1945*
Jane Lewis

Britain and the Korean War*
Callum Macdonald

Culture in Britain Since 1945*
Arthur Marwick

Crime and Criminal Justice Since 1945*
Terence Morris

Electoral Change Since 1945
Pippa Norris

Youth in Britain Since 1945
Bill Osgerby

The British Press and Broadcasting Since 1945
Colin Seymour-Ure

The Labour Party Since 1945
Eric Shaw

Third Party Politics Since 1945*
John Stevenson

The Trade Union Question in British Politics*
Robert Taylor

The Civil Service Since 1945
Kevin Theakston

British Science and Politics Since 1945*
Thomas Wilkie

British Public Opinion*
Robert M. Worcester

Local Government Since 1945
Ken Young and Nirmala Rao

Forthcoming

British Industry Since 1945
Margaret Ackrill

The Conservative Party Since 1945
John Barnes

Education in Britain Since 1945
David Crook

Parliament Since 1945
Philip Norton

*Indicates title now out of print
[†]Indicates title available through print-on-demand. To order our print on demand titles: **Individuals:** please order through your favorite local or on-line bookseller. **Retailers, wholesalers, and libraries:** please place your order with Ingram Book Company. **For US customers:** 1-800-937-8000, this number has options to follow, to place an order, press #1. **Canada:** 1-800-289-0687. **All other international callers:** (+) 1-615-793-5000 ext 27501.

The series *Making Contemporary Britain* is essential reading for students, as well as providing masterly overviews for the general reader. Each book in the series puts the central themes and problems of the specific topic into clear focus. The studies are written by leading authorities in their field, who integrate the latest research into the text but at the same time present the material in a clear, ordered fashion which can be read with value by those with no prior knowledge of the subject.

THE INSTITUTE OF CONTEMPORARY BRITISH HISTORY *Senate House, Malet Street, London WC1E 7HU*

Britain Since 1945

Edited by Jonathan Hollowell

Blackwell
Publishing

350 Main Street, Malden, MA 02148-5018, USA
108 Cowley Road, Oxford OX4 1JF, UK
550 Swanston Street, Carlton South, Melbourne, Victoria 3053, Australia
Kurfürstendamm 57, 10707 Berlin, Germany

First published 2003 by Blackwell Publishers Ltd

Library of Congress Cataloging-in-Publication Data

ISBN 0-631-20967-0 (hardback); ISBN 0-631-20968-9 (paperback)

A catalogue record for this title is available from the British Library.

Set in 10/12pt Sabon
by Kolam Information Services Pvt. Ltd, Pondicherry, India
Printed and bound in the United Kingdom
by MPG Books Ltd, Bodmin, Cornwall

For further information on
Blackwell Publishers, visit our website:
http://www.blackwellpublishing.com

Contents

Notes on Contributors

Jon Agar is a writer and lecturer based in London. From 1994 to 2001 he taught at the Centre for History of Science, Technology and Medicine, University of Manchester. His publications include *Turing and the Universal Machine* (2001) and *The Government Machine* (forthcoming).

Stephen Broadberry is Professor of Economic History in the Department of Economics at the University of Warwick, and has also taught at the universities of Oxford, Cardiff and British Columbia. He is an editor of the *European Review of Economic History*, and has published widely on nineteenth- and twentieth-century economic history. Recent publications include *The Productivity Race: British Manufacturing in International Perspective, 1850–1990* (1997) and articles in the *Journal of Economic History* (1998), *Business History* (2000) and the *Economic History Review* (2002).

Michael Bromley is Professor and Head of Journalism at Queensland University of Technology, Brisbane, Australia. A former daily newspaper journalist, he has taught at a number of universities in the UK and USA and has published widely on journalism and the media in the nineteenth and twentieth centuries. He is a founder co-editor of the journal *Journalism: Theory, Practice and Criticism*, and in 2001 edited *No News is Bad News: Radio, Television and the Public*.

Tarani Chandola is a Senior Research Fellow at the Department of Public Health and Epidemiology, University College London. He is currently working on the Whitehall II Study investigating the effect of the social environment on health and the causes of social inequalities in health.

Christopher Coker teaches in the International Relations Department at the London School of Economics. He is the author of a number of books, including *Waging War Without Warriors: The Changing Dynamic of Military Conflict* (2002), *Humane Warfare* (2001) and *War and the Twentieth Century* (1994). In the 1980s he wrote a number of books on defence including *British Defence Policy in the 1990s: A Guide to the Defence Debate* (1987).

Keith Dowding is Professor of Political Science at the London School of Economics and Political Science. He has published *Rational Choice and Political Power* (1991), *The Civil Service* (1995), *Preferences, Institutions and Rational Choice* (edited with Desmond King) (1995), *Power* (1996) and *Challenges to Democracy* (edited with James Hughes and Helen Margetts) (2001), as well as numerous articles in the fields of political philosophy, political theory, social choice, urban politics, public administration and British politics. He is co-editor of the *Journal of Theoretical Politics*.

Roger Eatwell   is Professor of Politics in the Department of European Studies at the University of Bath, where he teaches British politics at both the undergraduate and Master's level (together with comparative European politics and fascism). His main interests are political parties and social movements, covering both their ideologies and support. Recent publications include (as editor) *Contemporary Political Ideologies* (2nd ed. 1999) and various articles and chapters on issues such as the extreme right and charismatic leadership.

Helen Fawcett   is Jean Monnet Fellow and Lecturer in Government at Strathclyde University. Her research focuses on comparative welfare state development. She is currently principal investigator on a project in the ESRC's Devolution and Constitutional Change Programme that examines the development of policies to combat social exclusion in the UK. She has written extensively on the development of state and private pension policy, and has worked on unemployment policy and social exclusion in the European Union.

Ray Fitzpatrick   is Professor of Public Health and Primary Care at the University of Oxford and Fellow, Nuffield College, Oxford. Previously he taught at London University. He is the author of over two hundred publications on social aspects of health, illness and health care. Recently he co-edited *Social Studies in Health and Medicine* (2000) and *Methods in Evidence Based Healthcare* (2001). He is currently a member of the Council of the UK Medical Research Council and a Governor of the BUPA Research Foundation.

Duncan Gallie   is an Official Fellow of Nuffield College and a Professor of Sociology at the University of Oxford. He is a fellow of the British Academy. His research has included studies on changes in employment experience and on the social consequences of unemployment. Recent publications include *Restructuring the Employment Relationship* (1998), co-authored with Michael White, Yuan Cheng and Mark Tomlinson and *Welfare Regimes and the Experience of Unemployment in Europe* (2000), co-edited with Serge Paugam.

Wyn Grant   is Professor of Politics at the University of Warwick. He has written extensively on pressure groups, including *Pressure Groups and British Politics* (2000).

Anthony Heath   is Head of the Sociology Department at Oxford University. His research interests include sociology of education and ethnicity, social mobility, political sociology, and cross-national research with a special interest in India. He is editor of (with R. Breen and C. T. Whelan) *Ireland North and South: Perspectives from Social Science* (1999).

Jonathan Hollowell   is an independent scholar living in New York. Educated at Cambridge University, the London School of Economics and Political Science, the University of Rochester (USA), and Oxford University, he was formerly a tutor for St. Peter's College, Oxford. He is a former research fellow at the Institute for Contemporary History in London and an assistant to former

Prime Minister Edward Heath for his memoirs, *Course of My Life* (1998). He is co-editor of *The European Review of History/Revue européenne d'histoire*, and among his publications are *Twentieth-Century Anglo-American Relations* (2001) and a forthcoming text on twentieth-century Europe.

Simon James is based at the OECD in Paris. His books include *British Government: A Reader in Policy-Making* (1997) and *British Cabinet Government* (second edition, 1999).

Jane Lewis is Barnett Professor of Social Policy at the University of Oxford. She has written widely on gender, family change and family policies. Her most recent contributions are (with K. Kiernan and H. Land) *Lone Motherhood in Twentieth Century Britain* (1998), and *The End of Marriage? Individualism and Intimate Relations* (2001).

Arthur Marwick was Professor of History at the Open University from 1969 to 2001. His recent publications are *The Sixties: Cultural Revolution in Britain, France, Italy and the United States, c.1958–c.1974* (1998), *The New Nature of History: Knowledge, Evidence, Language* (2001), *The Arts in the West since 1945* (2002) and *A History of the Modern British Isles, 1914–1999: Circumstances, Events and Outcomes* (2000).

Jim McGuigan is Reader in Cultural Analysis and Programme Director for Sociology in the Department of Social Sciences at Loughborough University. He has worked for both the Arts Council and BBC Television and published widely in cultural studies and sociology. His books include *Cultural Populism* (1992), *Culture and the Public Sphere* (1996), *Cultural Methodologies* (1997) and *Modernity and Postmodern Culture* (1999). He has recently completed a study of the Millennium Dome for the Arts and Humanities Research Board and is currently writing a book on cultural policy.

James Mitchell is Professor of Politics, University of Strathclyde, Glasgow. He is the author of many articles and chapters on Scottish and British politics. He is author of *Conservatives and the Union* (1990), *Strategies for Self-Government* (1996) and *Governing Scotland* (2002) and co-author of *Politics and Public Policy in Scotland* (1991), *How Scotland Votes* (1997) and '*Scotland Decides': The Devolution Issue and the 1997 Referendum* (2000). He is currently completing a book on devolution in the UK.

Kenneth O. Morgan, D.Litt. (Oxon.) was Fellow in Modern History and Politics at Queen's College, Oxford (1966–89), Vice-Chancellor of the University of Wales, Aberystwyth (1989–95), Senior Vice-Chancellor of the University of Wales (1993–5) and Visiting Professor at Witwatersrand University, South Africa (1997–2000). The most recent of his 25 books are *Modern Wales: Politics, Places and People* (1995), *Callaghan: A Life* (1997), *The Twentieth Century* (2000) and *The People's Peace: British History since 1945* (new ed. 2001). He has edited *The Welsh History Review* since 1965, was elected a Fellow of the British Academy in 1983 and was made a Labour peer in March 2000.

Henry Patterson is Professor of Politics at the University of Ulster at Jordanstown. He has published widely on Irish politics and the Northern Ireland conflict. Among his publications are *The Politics of Illusion: A Political History of the IRA* (1997) and a forthcoming book, *Ireland since 1939*. He is director of an ESRC-funded research project on 'The Decline of The Loyal Family? Popular Unionism and the Devolution Process', which is part of the ESRC's Devolution and Constitutional Change programme.

Nirmala Rao is Reader in Politics and Head of the Department of Social Policy and Politics at Goldsmiths' College, University of London. She formerly held posts at the Policy Studies Institute and Queen Mary and Westfield College. She is the author of numerous publications in the field of local politics, including *Towards Welfare Pluralism* (1996), (co-author) *Local Government since 1945* (1997), *Reviving Local Democracy: New Labour, New Politics?* (2000) and *Governing London* (2002).

Shamit Saggar is Reader in Electoral Politics at Queen Mary, University of London. He is presently on secondment to the UK Cabinet Office (Performance and Innovation Unit) and is also head of strategic review of ethnic minority labour market achievements in the UK. He is the author of *Race and British Electoral Politics* (1998), *Race and Representation* (2000), and editor of *Minority Ethnic Groups in Britain and Social Change* (forthcoming).

Raymond Seitz was born in Hawaii and educated at Yale University. He was Assistant Secretary of State for Europe from 1989 to 1991 and US Ambassador to Great Britain from 1991 to 1994. Currently he is Vice-Chairman of the American investment bank Lehman Brothers.

Alan Sked is Senior Lecturer in International History and formerly Convener of European Studies at the London School of Economics. His books include *Post-War Britain: A Political History, 1945–1992* (with Chris Cook, 1990), *An Intelligent Person's Guide to Post-War Britain* (1997), *Britain's Decline: Problems and Perspectives* (1986), *The Decline and Fall of the Habsburg Empire, 1815–1918* (1989) and *The Survival of the Habsburg Empire. Radetzky, the Imperial Army and the Class War, 1848* (1979). He is presently writing the Penguin History of Post-War Europe. He is a Fellow of the Royal Historical Society.

Rebecca Surender is a social policy lecturer in the Department of Social Policy and Social Work, University of Oxford. She worked in Washington, DC between 1987 and 1993 as a Project Evaluator for the US government. Past research has focused on GP fundholding and the introduction of market mechanisms into the NHS. Recent research includes an evaluation of a National Clinical Effectiveness Initiative in Wales, a study of the health status and needs of people in Russia, and a Health Poverty Index Study for the Department of Health. She is currently involved in a study examining the impact of recent health-care reforms in South Africa.

Chris Wrigley   is Professor of Modern British History and Head of the School of History and Art History, Nottingham University. His books *include David Lloyd George and the British Labour Movement* (1976), *Lloyd George and the Challenge of Labour* (1990), *Arthur Henderson* (1990) and an edited, three-volume *History of British Industrial Relations* (1982–97). He was President of the Historical Association, 1996–9.

General Editor's Preface

The Institute of Contemporary British History series, *Making Contemporary Britain*, is aimed at school students, undergraduates and others interested in learning more about topics in post-war British history. In the series, authors are less concerned with breaking new ground than with presenting clear and balanced overviews of the state of knowledge on each of the topics.

The ICBH, which produces the series, was founded in October 1986 with the objective of promoting the study at every level of British history since 1945. To that end it publishes books and a quarterly journal, *Contemporary Record*, it organizes seminars and conferences for sixth-formers, undergraduates, researchers and teachers of post-war history, and it runs a number of research programmes and other activities.

A central belief of the ICBH's work is that post-war history is too often neglected in British schools, institutes of higher education and beyond. The ICBH acknowledges the validity of the arguments against the study of recent history, notably the problems of bias and of overly subjective teaching and writing, and the difficulties of perspective. But it believes that the values of studying post-war history outweigh the drawbacks, and that the health and future of a liberal democracy require that its citizens know more about the most recent past of their country than the limited knowledge possessed by British citizens, young and old, today. Indeed, the ICBH believes that the dangers of political indoctrination are higher when the young are *not* informed of the recent past of their country.

The dawning of the new millennium, and the funeral of the Queen Mother in April 2002, brought the twentieth century into a clearer historical focus. Suddenly, we are no longer part of the century, and we can begin to view it with greater clarity. As a result, more history of the century is being written than ever before. The danger is that we over-specialise in our knowledge, and see the history only through narrow spectacles.

The great virtue of *Britain since 1945*, edited with real acumen by Jonathan Hollowell, is that it allows one to comprehend the whole waterfront of the history since 1945 in a single volume. It is very good, for example, to have chapters on science, race relations and on political thought in the same book. The more one comes to understand post-war history, the more one realises that all the various branches of history interlink. Economic performance affects defence policy, which influences foreign policy, which helps determine the actions of pressure groups, which are influenced by, and which influence, the media. And so on.

No one can read this book without becoming substantially wiser and better informed about the decades of rapid change that followed the ending of the Second World War.

Anthony Seldon

Foreword

The Hon. Raymond G. H. Seitz

Some observers would have transposed the words in the title of this series and, rather than calling it 'Making Contemporary Britain', might have instead suggested 'Making Britain Contemporary'. Well beyond the end of the Second World War there was, to many commentators, an appealing aspic quality to the United Kingdom. Even when things did change in Britain they were supposed to look as if they hadn't. Certainly many outsiders, but many British as well, assumed that the nation would simply flow onwards, rippling gently like a Somerset brook, sunlit and dappled, along its unalterable course of destiny.

Once the relief and exhilaration of wartime victory had settled down, however, a much gloomier interpretation emerged, and this different and darker view eventually became the popular norm. Tradition, once an undeniable British strength, was seen to have exerted too strong a grip on the national psyche and created an inert land for the fuddy-duddy. The national history had accumulated too much drag. More critically, the economy failed to respond no matter how often it was kicked. And social differences in Britain had become so impacted that the stereotypical class system of bowler hats and cloth caps was blamed for everything. The British way of doing things, it seemed, had become a kind of sociological cul-de-sac from which there was no discernible exit. By the early 1970s, pundits were predicting the onset of national rigor mortis.

Things did seem pretty bleak a quarter-century ago. At the end of that decade, in fact, it was hard for a foreigner to find anyone British, of whatever political persuasion or social identification, who had a good thing to say about the place. Britain was yesterday's nation, doomed to a gradual, irreversible decline.

As things turned out, the fatalists were wrong. Debate about the nation's future remains today as intense as ever, and so is the controversy about Britain's essential national identity. But the country has changed dramatically in the last quarter-century. Some of the change has been specifically engineered: some has simply happened. Much of the change has been positive: some of it less so.

What is important, however, is that the United Kingdom has become accustomed to change, and more confident about it. In fact, even the concept of change has changed.

Perhaps the most graphic alteration has been in the boundaries of Britain's international governance. In scarcely more than a generation, the brilliant British pink that until recently covered much of the globe has been transformed into a multicoloured, post-imperial palette. The Empire, which for centuries had done so much to define Britain's role and scope in the world, and which was basic to the British image of themselves, is now a part of historic recollection which only the most senior of British citizens can recall. All that an imperium implied – controlled trade, military reach, diplomatic sway – has dwindled. The Suez crisis of 1956 sounded the excruciating death knell. Few nations have gone through such a dramatic reversal of international fortune in so short a time, and it is a testimony to British ingenuity that this imperial upheaval has been managed with so little violence.

With the end of the Empire, Britain came face to face with the question of how to connect with the rest of the world. As Dean Acheson, the former American Secretary of State, once commented, 'The British have lost an empire but not yet found a role.' Acheson's stinging remark was a little premature. Britain did develop a role during the hard years of the Cold War, when London became the junior partner in a close security relationship with Washington. As a nuclear power and permanent member of the UN Security Council, Britain remained a major player in international events, though not a dominant one.

Reluctant at first, and then stymied for a while, Britain also became a participant in the great European experiment, and though it joined the European Community late in the day it nonetheless came to play a significant role in European councils. In fact, Britain's close relations in America and Europe considerably enhanced London's international stature because London acted as a two-way ambassador and interpreter between the two continents. It was the best of both worlds.

With the end of the Cold War, this position is more ambiguous. Security issues count for less in the post-Cold War era, and Europe's continuing consolidation has strained Britain's willingness to keep up the pace. Britain today struggles with the question of where its future lies: across the Atlantic or across the Channel? There is more economic and cultural affinity with America; there is more geographic and social affinity with Europe. There are debits and credits on both sides of the ledger, and the truth is probably that Britain must prosperously manage both relationships, as difficult as this may be, rather than seeming to choose between the two. But at least the strategic issue is clear and the subject of animated political debate.

The enormous change in Britain's external role has run parallel with domestic change. In the last two decades Britain seems to have found answers to many of the nagging problems of its post-industrial economic decline. In a far less regulated environment, there is a new entrepreneurial spirit in the country which has driven the transition to a modern services-based economy. The trade unions, once the bad boy of British economic development, have assumed a more proportionate and constructive role. Always an outward trading and investing nation, Britain has prospered in the atmosphere of globalisation. It is the largest foreign investor in the United States, for example, and the financial services of the City of London are the most international and sophisticated in the world. Ironically, Britain's economic reform has now become the model for other European nations, and the kingdom's profound economic restructuring is the envy of many.

The social atmosphere is also different. The trappings of the old division between working class and upper class are still evident, but they mean much less than they used to. Britain is no longer two nations, but many nations. Immigration has contributed to this and so has devolution. The overwhelming rise of the media is also an important factor, especially the electronic media, and so is the dramatic expansion of education, particularly at university level. The truth is that Britain today is largely a middle-class nation with middle-class hopes and middle-class anxieties. There is surely a social scale in the country, as there is in any country, and there are still many pretensions abroad in the land; but on the whole these have little effect on the day-to-day conduct of the affairs which matter to people.

The change is not complete. It never is. Britain has rarely indulged in revolution, and change here will always be gradual and sometimes imperceptible. But looking over the last half-century, change is indisputable. This is the real value of the present series of Making Contemporary Britain. By examining different areas of national life, this survey takes the measure of Britain today and will help us understand Britain tomorrow.

Introductory Note and Acknowledgements

The chapters in this text are divided into three broad themes involving British government and politics, society, and the economy, in which contributors aim to discuss the prominent developments in their subjects in the period from 1945 to the end of the millennium, presenting to the reader a reliable source of historical fact in concise form. As such, *Britain Since 1945* is intended to serve as an introduction for both the student and general reader as well as a reference source for all those with an interest in contemporary Britain. While designing this text to cover Britain on a comprehensive basis, I was unable to include every topic I would wish to, simply for reasons of limiting the work to its prescribed length. Thus while others would not have included certain fields in a survey of Britain, I have included chapters on such important areas as gender, culture, and the media. However, it is my regret that I could not also include a separate chapter entirely devoted to the role and position of the monarchy since 1945 (though Simon James has touched uopn this in his discussion of the constitution in chapter 2); but alas, the limitations of length. For any oversights in conception and design of the text, as well as in all other respects, I accept full responsibility.

I would like to express my gratitude to Tessa Harvey, commissioning editor at Blackwell, for accepting my proposal for the inception of this text, and for allowing me free rein in fashioning its contents as I would wish and commissioning its contributors, and for the patience of everyone as the final manuscript slowly emerged. From beginning to end, the process unfolded as a number of contributors changed institutions, positions, and even countries of residence while respective manuscripts trickled in; and I thank Blackwell for the additional time for my completing the editing of the entire manuscript, in between my undertaking postgraduate research in the Modern History Faculty of Oxford University, my teaching duties at St. Peter's College and elsewhere, and my activities as a research fellow at the ICBH, where the indefatigable Peter Catterall, former Director, was a constant source of encouragement.

Jonathan Hollowell
Empire State College
State University of New York

Part I
Government and Politics

1 Foreign and Defence Policy

Christopher Coker

Britain emerged from the Second World War one of the Big Three: perhaps not a superpower like the United States and the Soviet Union, but the third wealthiest power in the world. Of the three victors it had been the first to enter the war, and unlike the other two it had the distinction of having declared war on Germany first.

Britain's reputation was higher than perhaps at any time in the twentieth century. But it was clearly exhausted from its efforts. Even in the closing months of the war its strength was visibly declining. In June 1944 British Empire troops deployed in Normandy had equalled those of the Americans; by March 1945 only about a quarter of the troops under the command of the Supreme Allied Commander General Eisenhower were British. By the end of the conflict the British wartime debt stood at £22 billion (about $2,000 per capita). The post-war debt of the United States was in per capita terms much the same, but the American national income had doubled during the war, and went on in the next five years to double again. The British emerged from the war almost bankrupt. Both countries had learned that the cost of victory comes high, but for the British the cost was so high that it threatened to lower permanently their economy and their standard of living.

British power was so rapidly eclipsed during the last months of the war that the United States became convinced that, together with the Soviet Union, it could construct a post-war order largely without British assistance. And yet the United Kingdom spent the next 25 years as a major world power. The British retained conscription, maintained a relatively large force in uniform (800,000 men and women in 1951) and spent about 10 per cent of their GNP on defence (as opposed to 3 per cent in pre-war years). This was a remarkable effort at a time when they continued to be beset by shortages, rationing and austerity measures at home. Not until the late 1960s did they begin to see themselves as a medium-sized power.

In short, in the 25 years that followed the surrender of German forces at Lüneberg Heath, Britain continued to play the role of a world power, tracing a path that had seemed questionable even at the turn of the century. Inevitably, historians have been prompted to ask whether it might have been better to have accepted the inevitable, to have reduced defence spending, to have played a diminished role in world affairs. In fact, when we look at the period closely, we will see that the option was remote for reasons that were all too clear at the time.

To begin with, the next challenge to the European balance was already identifiable. The reality, real or perceived, of the Soviet threat meant there could be no Ten-year Rule as there had been in the 1920s, when the government had based its defence spending on the assumption that there was no immediate prospect of war with any power or combination of powers. As an occupying power in 1945, Britain was persistently reminded that there had been no peace settlement. Germany might be divided but the division was meant to be temporary; its permanence served to underline the impermanence of the peace.

Secondly, Britain may have emerged from the war economically weak but it was by far the strongest European power. In 1948 British defence spending exceeded that of all other European countries. Even as late as 1952 Britain's arms production was greater than that of all the other European North Atlantic Treaty Organization (NATO) members combined. As a result the British believed they could not confine their interests to Europe. As the first post-war Foreign Secretary, Ernest Bevin, remarked, 'Europe is not enough; it is not big enough.'

Thirdly, the prestige of the armed forces was never higher in the nation's history. Twenty-five military conflicts won unqualified public support for the professionalism of the services, who seemed to show a certain élan sadly missing in British society at large. Even if the contours of that society were changing fast, the armed forces maintained public esteem.

When looking at Great Britain's post-war role it is also important to recognise that it operated in a 'permissive environment' in terms of public opinion at home. In the 1920s Britain had to rapidly demobilise. Expenditure on the army was cut by half every year between 1919 and 1923. By 1922 social spending equalled 26 per cent of all government expenditure. Where large numbers of troops were deployed this was in Britain itself. The government called upon 43 infantry battalions during the railway strike of 1919; 56 battalions and 6 cavalry regiments were used to deal with the national coal strike two years later, almost the same number of troops that the British believed were necessary to keep down India.

These trends threw up new opportunities in British politics, as well as new challenges. The regional basis of unemployment and unrest turned the Labour Party from a clique into the official Opposition and propelled it into government for the first time in 1924. The decision to enfranchise not only women, but a third of all adult males who had been denied the vote ten years earlier, created a political climate of great uncertainty. In the 1923 election 79 per cent of those entitled to vote had never voted before.

It is against this background that Britain's decision to disarm, and later pursue a distinctively unheroic policy of appeasement towards the dictators, should be seen. After the Second World War, these circumstances did not apply.

Despite the traditional picture of a nation that emerged from the war exhausted and dispirited, the British people were very different from 1919. The voters had voted before, and although they voted Churchill out of office they expected Britain to remain a great power. The British remained an intensely international people. If the historian A. J. P. Taylor was right to claim that the Battle of Britain was the last great moment in British history, the British people lived off its memory for years afterwards.[1] After the war they clearly felt they had made too many sacrifices to be reduced 'to a cold and unimportant little island, where we should all have to work very hard and live mainly on herrings and potatoes', as George Orwell remarked in *The Road to Wigan Pier*. Even if this was a fate they could not escape indefinitely, the British people seemed willing to pay the price of protracting their decline as long as possible. It was a feat which their political leaders in the end accomplished with consummate skill.

Churchill, in fact, continued to inspire a generation even after he had passed from the political scene. The sense of heroic destiny he painted survived him. The British people did not seem ready to turn their backs entirely on history, even if they did not expect greater triumphs to come. They were not disappointed.

Embarrassed by appeasement in which they had connived with the politicians, the British people made no demands for a drastic reduction in defence spending. Even though the country struggled to get back to its pre-1938 levels of prosperity, the British did not consider themselves overtaxed when it came to defence spending. According to an opinion poll conducted in the early 1980s, only 13 per cent of those polled knew that Britain spent less than 10 per cent of its GNP on defence. Considering that throughout the 1970s up to 10 per cent of those canvassed believed the country should spend more, they clearly considered that the cost of remaining a great power, though high, was at least an investment in the future.

Finally, one of the most striking features of British political life in the immediate post-war years was the extent to which both Labour and Conservative governments succeeded in maintaining a solid bipartisan consensus on security policy which was strikingly different from the lack of consensus in the 1930s. The left wing of the Labour Party may have cast negative votes on peacetime conscription, membership of NATO, and the deployment of British forces overseas, justifying its dissent by reference to such socialist principles as internationalism, anti-capitalism and anti-militarism, but on all major issues the Labour Party steered the same course as the Conservatives. The special relationship with the United States became a predominant theme of Labour politics, even when the relationship turned increasingly on nuclear cooperation between the two countries.

On the right of British politics a similar pragmatism held sway. Gaullism did not gain a hold. If successive Tory governments expected Britain to play a major role, they also expected it to do so in association with the United States. So too did the British electorate, which consistently accepted high defence spending in every election except one (1951). The reasons for that support were many, but the most telling was undoubtedly the post-war environment in which the country found itself in 1945.

East of Suez

Reviewing the entry of British troops into Tunis in 1943, Harold Macmillan recorded in his memoirs: 'these men seemed on that day masters of the world and heirs of the future'.[2] Any decision to have reduced the commitments prematurely and adopted a Little England stance would have been seen as an abdication of the country's international responsibilities. That those responsibilities were taken seriously by the political elite and even the public at large became clear from Britain's role in the defence of South Korea (1950–3), which involved a substantial number of casualties, the great majority of whom were national servicemen. As late as 1966 the British still deployed a force of over 60,000 men in South-East Asia, as well as a naval task force of 80 ships. As late as 1968 large numbers of British soldiers were serving in the Middle East, mostly in Aden.

It was fortunate, perhaps, that Britain did not face a challenge to its world position in the immediate post-war period at all comparable to the threats it faced in the 1930s. Of its two pre-war rivals east of Suez, Japan had been defeated and the United States co-opted. As for the Soviet Union, it figured hardly at all in British military planning. It took almost no role in any of the challenges which faced Britain in the Middle East, and none in South-East Asia. The British 'moment' in the Middle East was brought to an end not by Moscow but by Arab nationalism. These challenges were very different from the strategic headaches the British had to face before the Second World War. So, even if they clung to a status which had lost much of its meaning, even if British power was in decline, even if the withdrawal from east of Suez represented what Laurence Martin once called 'a long recessional', at least it was not a headlong retreat. With one exception, it never provoked a hasty and ill-advised last stand.

The exception was Suez. The Suez crisis was provoked in 1956 by the decision of the Egyptian leader Abdul Nasser to unilaterally nationalise the Suez canal in order to pay the costs of the country's biggest development programme, the Aswan Dam. In response, Britain and France decided to seize control of the canal. But they were unable to act quickly enough. They also wavered in their objectives and did not have a clearly defined political purpose. For the first time, too, they faced opposition from both the United States and the Soviet Union, and even at home public opinion was bitterly divided. The military campaign was successful, but it came too late, and in the face of overwhelming international condemnation the British and French were forced to withdraw, leaving Nasser's authority in the Middle East higher than ever, and their own lower than ever before.

Suez demonstrated British weaknesses in other ways. There was a rapid decline in the country's foreign currency reserves as foreign governments withdrew funds from British banks, and as US speculators and the Federal Reserve Bank tried to get rid of their sterling. The Suez war convinced the British establishment that Britain could no longer exercise world power without the support of the United States. The crisis, in fact, reminded the political establishment that the relationship was not one between equals. The British recognised that they should never again engage in a military operation without America's open or tacit encouragement and, better still, day-to-day support. The lesson the French learned, by contrast, was never again to find themselves in a situation in which they could be overruled by the United States, as well as never again to rely on the British as an interlocutor between Paris and Washington.

It would be wrong to conclude, however, that the British ceased to be of account internationally after 1956. On a famous occasion in December 1962 Dean Acheson, a former American Secretary of State, said that Britain had 'lost an empire and not yet found a role'. The remark drew a swift response in London, and many were quick to point out that, far from clinging to a post-imperial role, the British government had applied to join the European Economic Community 16 months earlier. What annoyed his critics both in Britain and the United States was his assertion that 'the attempt to play a separate role – that is, a role apart from Europe' had failed.

In the event, British policy in the world at large was still successful. In 1961 it successfully dissuaded Iraq from invading Kuwait. Between 1963 and 1966 it fought and won an extensive conflict against Indonesia which wanted to undermine the Malay Federation by detaching the island of Borneo from it. The campaign fought by the British in 'the Indonesian Confrontation' was a classic of its kind.

In the end, what forced the British to withdraw from east of Suez was a weak economy. When they were forced to devalue sterling in 1967 they had to summon the legions home. But if the Suez crisis had effectively displaced it as the main Western power in the Middle East, it did not displace it in the Persian Gulf until much later. Indeed, it was not until 1973 that an American aircraft carrier, *Task Force*, visited the region for the first time since the Second World War, and not until three years later that the US navy established its first base in the region, in Bahrain.

After 1973, however, the British were able to operate only on limited contract. They were still able to engage in occasional exercises, of which the largest was 'Operation Swift Sword' (1986), in which the UK's rapid reaction force, the Fifth Airborne Brigade, was deployed to Oman within 36 hours. But its forces had no heavy equipment and only a minimum of light armour. By the 1980s, in fact, it had already become clear that, short of an unexpected crisis which would call for an extraordinary response (notably the war in the South Atlantic in 1982 – of which more anon), the British would only be involved in that or any other region as partners of the United States. They went to Sinai in 1981 as part of a five-power peacekeeping force to underwrite the American-brokered Camp David agreement. They went to Lebanon in 1984 as part of another five-power force, this time in the shadow of the 16-inch guns of the US Navy. Unlike the exercises conducted with the Dutch and French navies in the Gulf in 1972, the two British patrol vessels which operated in the area in 1984 co-ordinated their activities with a US carrier force group led by the USS *Midway*. By necessity, as much as choice, Britain's role was restricted to areas where the United States could provide protection or reinforcement or the promise of assistance if needed. This was a principal theme of the Strategic Defence Review of 1998.

Ironically, the only major war Britain fought in this period was not east, but west of Suez. For most of the 20 years before the Falklands War of 1982 it had been engaged in negotiations with Argentina over the future of its colony in the Falkland Islands in the South Atlantic, some 500 kilometres off the Argentinian mainland. In late 1981 negotiations over the future of the colony collapsed and there seemed little prospect of their revival. Sovereignty over the islands – called the Malvinas in Argentina – had been an emotive issue for several decades.

On 2 April 1982 Argentina invaded and occupied the islands. Britain's response was to despatch a task force on the 13,000-kilometre journey to the South Atlantic. The British war effort proved to be an admirable feat of organisation and logistics, sustained by seaborne air power and surface and submarine naval forces. Eventually about 12,000 troops were landed in the islands and, following a successful but bloody campaign onshore, the Argentinian forces surrendered. The outstanding performance of British forces illustrated the superiority of regular, professional, fit and well-led forces over a largely conscript army.

It was probably the last encounter of its kind. Never again will Britain have such a stage or such a military task to perform. With the massive defence cuts which followed the end of the Cold War, it is also doubtful whether it would still have the arms to perform it.

The Anglo-American Relationship

One of the enduring problems of the Anglo-American Partnership (Britain's 'special' ally, America's 'closest') was caught by Ian McEwan's novel *The Innocent* (1990), with its ironic alternative title 'The Special Relationship'. The Englishman Leonard Marnham and the American Bob Glass are working together on 'Operation Gold' (1955/6), the tunnel under East Berlin, a joint CIA/ MI6 venture that was undertaken in real life. The work is fraught with mutual irritation. The British find the Americans exasperating in their self-confidence and ignorance. 'What's worse, they won't learn, they won't be told. It's just how they are.' The Americans, for their part, find the British amateurish and proud of their amateurism. 'They're so busy being gentlemen.'

The real source of irritation, however, is what has dogged the partnership from the first. 'I really don't understand why we let you people in on this,' declares Glass. 'Collaboration leads to errors, security problems, you name it.' Britain simply cannot keep up with the superpowers. Marnham's reply captures one of the enduring themes for the British of their partnership with the United States, their wish to perpetuate the wartime alliance. 'We're in on this because we have the right. No one fought Hitler for as long as we did. We saw the whole war through.' Glass's response is equally telling. 'Don't get me wrong . . . you guys were great in the war, you were formidable. It was your moment. And this is my point . . . that was your moment, now this is ours.'[3]

Judging a historical moment is clearly a delicate matter when two or more countries are involved. How do you get the most out of someone else's historic moment? Clearly, by being useful. With the Lend-Lease programme in 1940 (when it agreed to sell 50 old warships in return for base rights in British colonies in the Caribbean) the United States took part in Britain's moment in history. With the Atlantic Charter in August 1941 Britain served notice that it was about to take part in America's. True to their first principles, the British have always seen the relationship in historical terms. True to their own principles, the Americans have been far more pragmatic. 'The relationship was not particularly special in my day,' reflected Henry Kissinger a few years ago. 'It was normal.' Britain was important because 'it made itself so useful'.[4]

There were those who argued that the special relationship was becoming more symbolic than real with every year, that it encouraged Britain's preoccupation with its past and made it uncertain about its future, that it was, at best, the sole consolation of a nation which found itself increasingly on the margins of history. Others argued that it contributed to much higher defence expenditure than Britain could afford, that it distorted its scientific effort in the direction of research and development and encouraged it to act as a non-European power.

The British establishment, however, also believed it derived much from being what the Americans themselves called their 'closest' ally. In the post-war period the Foreign Office set out with the clear intention of forging an interdependent set of links which would firmly couple the United States and Britain. As one official put it in March 1946, the Soviet Union knew which of its former allies had become its most implacable opponent, not the strongest but the most astute: 'the one quality which most disquiets the Soviet government is the ability which they attribute to us to get others to do our fighting for us.... They respect, not us, but our ability to collect friends.'[5]

Twenty years later the British continue to derive unique advantages from the relationship, particularly in defence, including a direct input into American strategic thinking. 'There was no other government', the American Secretary of State Henry Kissinger later recalled, 'which we would have dealt with so openly, exchanged ideas so freely, or in effect permitted to participate in our deliberations.'[6]

Even if the relationship was not quite as exclusive or as wide-ranging as many British officials thought at the time, the close ties engendered by similar historical and cultural bonds, the close relationship between the scientific and military establishments of the two countries, created a special understanding of each other's position. The writer Coral Bell once described the relationship as a capacity, not a construction, 'a capacity to see the elements of common interest in whatever international storms the times may bring'.[7]

It is interesting that in commemorating the special relationship, the former Secretary of State, Henry Kissinger, chose to speak of values rather than interests, reminding those present at a conference in London in 1982 that it was beyond the psychological resources of the United States 'to be the sole, even the principal centre of initiative and response in the non-communist world'. In that respect, it may well have counted for much that Britain was never seen in Washington to have a defence identity incompatible with its membership of NATO; it was important that there was never a British problem, which was not true of France. The fundamental dependability of the United Kingdom remained beyond question for over forty years, as different governments came and went.

Who can overestimate the immense importance this had in reconciling different American administrations to the commitments to defend what, from an American perspective, often seemed to be querulous and ungrateful allies? As the alliance became more fractious and discontented in the 1980s the British perhaps played a larger role than they imagined.

The apotheosis of that partnership was the Gulf War. It was Britain's 'finest hour'. For it was able to produce the second largest allied contingent in a war directed by a US commander for the first time since sending a lamentably small and embarrassingly underequipped force to Korea. A comparison of the two campaigns is instructive. In Korea the British contingent was woefully under-manned and underequipped. 27 Brigade had no gear for warfare in either hot or cold climates; no sleeping bags for its troops and only a handful of vehicles. A US signals division in the Commonwealth Division posted a sign outside its camp which read 'Second to None'. A British radio relay station a few hundred yards down the road put up a sign which defiantly stated 'None'.[8] No wonder Dean Acheson, on reading a State Department memo in 1950, insisted on striking out a reference to Britain as a 'partner' of the United States.

In the Gulf War, by contrast, Britain was able to contribute forces as and when it felt able to fill a gap that its other allies could not meet, as well as according to its own perception of what the United States itself would find most useful. It upgraded the naval patrol that was already in the area. Later it despatched an infantry battalion and then an armoured brigade. In the final months of the build-up the British were able to further upgrade that commitment to an armoured division.

In Korea the British were entirely subordinate to American command, despite the misgivings about the quality of American troops whom the British commander-in-chief complained were badly trained, led by inexperienced commanders, would not stand and fight and disliked night combat. Some of these opinions were also expressed by American officers, including MacArthur's replacement General Ridgeway. The British contribution, however, was so small that its government had little if no influence over MacArthur's eventual dismissal or Truman's decision to authorise dummy air runs over China in preparation for a nuclear attack.

In the Gulf the British contribution was large enough for them to carve out an independent command. It provided it with an opportunity to also influence American thinking. The size of the UK's commitment enabled it to fight the war it wanted to fight and in the way it wanted to fight it. It did not have to conform to the plans of a US divisional commander, or to fight under a US divisional command – something which no British government has welcomed since the experience of Korea.

The century ended with continued British support for American actions in the Gulf, this time for keeping on the defensive the defeated but still dangerous Saddam Hussein. In December 1998 the two countries launched a joint air strike against Iraq, 'Operation Desert Fox'. Fifty-five years on from the Second World War Britain and America were still coordinating military policies in an attempt to police regional order. This was something that Roosevelt would not have imagined possible, even when Britain was a member of the Big Three.

Nuclear Policy

Britain's attempt to retain its independent manoeuvre between the nuclear superpowers was predicated, in part, on its becoming a nuclear power itself. Nuclear policy was at the heart of British security thinking throughout the Cold War.

It was the Attlee government which first decided to allow nuclear weapons to be based in the United Kingdom when acceding to America's request to station three groups of B29 bombers, without insisting on a formal treaty. The Americans were so surprised by the informality of the arrangement that their ambassador was instructed to ask Ernest Bevin whether he was fully live to the likely effects on public opinion of the arrival of the first US aircraft. James Forrestal, the US Secretary of Defense at the time, recorded in his diary: 'We have the opportunity now of sending these planes and once they are sent they would become something of an accepted fixture whereas a deterioration of the situation in Europe might lead to a condition of mind under which the British would be compelled to reverse their present attitude.'[9]

A formal agreement was not, in fact, concluded until the last months of the Attlee government, and the first months of the incoming Churchill administration. The Attlee–Churchill Understandings, as they subsequently became known, were bound to invite controversy once the situation in Europe did begin to deteriorate as Forrestal had foreseen, and more to the point, perhaps, once the United States lost its own monopoly of nuclear weapons.

The situation arose in 1957 with the deployment of a new generation of American intermediate-range ballistic missiles. To the cynically minded it now appeared possible for the Americans to pre-empt an attack upon the continental United States by what was called at the time 'a diversified means of delivery'. By launching a nuclear strike from Britain they could confine a nuclear exchange to Europe. The same questions were to arise much later in 1983 when a new, updated generation of theatre nuclear missiles arrived in Britain. By then, however, the issue had become subsumed in a much broader debate about the ethical and economic costs of maintaining Britain's own deterrent.

A second feature of Attlee's nuclear programme was the decision to develop an independent nuclear force. For Attlee, as for every other Prime Minister who succeeded him, an independent deterrent represented a necessary investment in Britain's future as a great power. When the Americans suspended nuclear co-operation in 1948 (when the US Congress passed the MacMahon Act) the British government was forced to press ahead on its own. It did not consider this a desirable option. Even at the eleventh hour it offered to transfer all weapons production to the United States in exchange for a small stock of bombs under British control, a concession the Americans rejected.

One of the ironies of the Cold War was that despite immediate post-war attempts to stifle Britain's nuclear programme, the United States eventually ended up underwriting it. In May 1959 Britain was able to buy component parts for its nuclear weapon systems. Soon this understanding extended to delivery systems. When Prime Minister Harold Macmillan offered the United

States a forward base for its new Polaris submarine fleet, Eisenhower reciprocated with an offer to sell the land-based Skybolt missile. After Skybolt was cancelled, the United States agreed to sell Polaris submarines instead.

During the 1960s that support was extended. America provided Britain with a launching system, the critical components of a system of inertial navigation and even the high-stress steel for the submarine hulls of the Polaris fleet. Much of this was kept secret at the time to spare the government political embarrassment at home. A case in point was the agreement to pool nuclear research and development; another was the arrangement to waive the research costs charged to the United Kingdom in the agreement reached in Nassau in 1962 between John F. Kennedy and Harold Macmillan.

As Defence Minister Francis Pym admitted in the 1980s, eight successive governments (both Labour and Conservative) 'declined to make public their nuclear targeting policy and plans, or to define precisely what minimum level of destructive capability they judged necessary for deterrence'. During the last Labour government of the Cold War era secrecy was taken to excessive lengths. In 1974 the party had promised the British people that it had 'renounced any intention of moving towards a new generation of strategic nuclear weapons', a manifesto pledge later repeated in the 1975 Defence White Paper. Yet the government decided to opt for the development of the Chevaline Programme, an update of Polaris, within days of its return to office. It also resumed nuclear testing. The Chevaline programme went ahead as planned, despite its expense. Indeed, the Americans were informed that the British government was not particularly concerned about its rapidly rising costs since they were hidden in the defence budget and did not need to be publicly justified.

At Nassau Britain agreed to build the submarines itself and to provide the warheads but to use US test-base facilities and expertise. It was mainly these advantages which persuaded Mrs Thatcher to opt for the next-generation American submarine, Trident, and an agreement that Britain would buy the system was reached during her first visit to Washington in December 1979. Until the very end of the Cold War the United States continued to underwrite the British nuclear deterrent. And for Britain the system was cheap. Even when the United Kingdom discovered halfway through the 1980s that it had to buy the more expensive Trident 2 system, the costs still seemed reasonable, 3 per cent of the defence budget over 20 years, 6 per cent of the equipment budget overall.

As a counterforce system, however (i.e. a system designed to take out military targets and bases), Trident was less convincing. In the highly unlikely event that all the missiles would have been at sea, the British would only have been able to have taken out 9 per cent or less of the Soviet land-based missile force. Even before the Cold War came to an end there were questions whether Britain should remain in the nuclear business at all. At the heart of the Trident issue lay the suspicion that it was still play-acting, in the hope not of deterring the Soviet Union so much as bluffing the world that it was still a power of importance, playing its hand well, indeed with confidence, without quite convincing itself.

As the twentieth century drew to a close, however, the terms of the debate changed. Russian nuclear weapons were no longer targeted on the British Isles. What concerned the government most was the threat of nuclear proliferation, the threat that 'rogue' states like Libya or Iraq might gain nuclear forces in the future, and thus be able to strike at the United Kingdom for the first time. It is a challenge which is likely to be viewed with concern well into the twenty-first century.

Context of Decline

Throughout the post-war years the majority of commentators looked at Britain's foreign and security policies in the context of its economic decline. There was one school of thought that the United Kingdom had declined because it pursued a role which was clearly beyond its resources. The historians of decline in these years spoke of the 'collapse of British power', the 'long recessional', the 'descent from power' (to cite the title of three books), terms which conjured up the ghosts of opportunities lost and choices avoided.[10]

Many critics argued that a whole generation of civil servants and politicians had preferred to parade a series of commitments which could not be honoured and to issue a series of promissory notes which could not be cashed. Sir Richard Clark, one of the Foreign Office 'mandarins' concerned, who was involved in overseas financial policy in the late 1940s when Attlee decided that Britain would remain a great power whatever the cost, appeared to confirm this diagnosis in his own reminiscences: 'Thirty years later, when one sees the relative success of Germany, Japan and France, which were forced to make great social and economic changes, one cannot be absolutely sure that our right long-term cause was to display remarkable ingenuity and to retain the status quo.'[11] Over the years critics pursued this line of argument with remarkable consistency, charting the various turning points when choices might have been made, such as the aftermath of Suez, or the decision of Britain's partners in Europe to forge a Common Market in 1957.[12]

The other point of view, put equally cogently, argued that in real terms Britain did not decline in this period; that manpower cuts were dictated by defence inflation and structural disarmament which the country was not alone in fighting; that the British armed forces were more professional and better equipped than at any time in their history. One only has to compare the success of 1982 with the military shambles of Suez to see the improvements actually made. Instead of declining, Britain's armed forces were merely restructured in these years.

More recently still, some historians have begin to argue that the management of Britain's decline was an exemplary lesson in how to retain political influence as long as possible by evading radical choices, and electing politicians who preferred continuity to discontinuity, soft rather than hard-nosed men who were singularly adept in not taking tough decisions. As the historian Paul Kennedy remarks, 'Keeping a declining British . . . omnibus going along the road for such a long time is a fair art, and not one that should be entrusted to persons who are liable to shoot the passengers, who don't know how to service and oil the machine, and who have the nasty habit of trying to crash into oncoming vehicles.'[13]

It does indeed seem that even in the 1950s the best the out-and-out reformers could have done was to have introduced piecemeal administrative reforms making choices within roles rather than choosing between them, an endeavour which, while worthy in itself, would have altered attitudes in the services in Whitehall very little, and in the nation at large even less. A number of more radical measures, if applied in happier circumstances, might have yielded better results. If implemented, however, radical measures might have wrought greater damage on the services than any they were designed to repair. There is little evidence, anyway, that British society was ready to act on them.

Setting an example by unilaterally disarming or revising the transatlantic bargain, or entering Europe in 1957 at the expense of other commitments, might only have brought the decline to a head much faster than carrying on as Britain did. The Left would doubtless have welcomed such an outcome, seeing it as an emancipation from the dead weight of the past, perhaps more imagined than real. The Right might have seen it as a relatively painless adjustment to a Little England posture, painful only if carried out too abruptly, inevitable in the context of a much wider development, the marginalisation of Europe in an age of the superpowers. As it was, the bipartisan consensus with which I began this chapter was not so bad, looking back. Britain emerged from the Cold War one of the victors. Only a preoccupation with our uncertain and insecure times obscures the importance of that victory.

One of the ironies, of course, is that since the mid-1980s the debate on decline has largely come to an end. Rightly or wrongly, the British seem to have arrested, and perhaps even reversed it. The economy ended the 1990s one of the strongest in Europe, with one of the lowest rates of inflation and unemployment, and an apparently strong entrepreneurial culture. Britain ended the twentieth century the fifth richest country in the world. The question is, was Britain still holding on to many of the myths that had been necessary to cushion its long recessional, its retreat from great-power status?

Was it ready for new thinking at a time when its national identity was being questioned from within the United Kingdom itself, as the Celtic fringe sought greater autonomy, with perhaps, one day, independence? Was Britain any more reconciled to its European future at a time when the pace of integration had quickened? If British foreign and security policy in the post-war years can be considered a much greater success than it was seen at the time, had that very success delayed coming to terms with a new post-Cold War environment?

The issues before Britain in the next century: its complicated relationship with Europe; a special relationship with the country that looks less to Europe than at any other time than in recent years; a world in which Asia will play an important part; a world of proliferating nuclear powers, the most dangerous on the outskirts of Europe: these are all new problems requiring new solutions. But they were not part of the British foreign policy agenda during the Cold War; it is only now that they have become part of the post-Cold War debate.

Defence Estimates and White Papers

One of the best ways to gauge the strength of British forces after the Second World War is to look at the numerous defence reviews which followed the

Duncan Sandys exercise of 1957. Most of the reviews were the residual reflex of people who, with the end of the war, felt that history had in some puzzling way delivered far less than it had promised.

It was probably inevitable that significant cuts would be made throughout the post-war period. The extraordinary effort Britain made to rearm during the Korean War which dwarfed its efforts in the inter-war years had claimed no less than two years' real economic growth. It was largely for this reason that the Labour Minister for Health, Aneurin Bevan, chose to resign in 1951 from Attlee's Cabinet. He did not object in principle to rearmament being granted a prior claim on national output; he resigned because he objected to the scale of the defence increases. He thought them 'unrealisable', which they were.

As early as 1952 the new Conservative government had announced the need to 'adjust' the Labour government's rearmament programme by spreading planned expenditure over a much longer period than three years. After they came to power in 1951, they put forward a review, the first of many, but by far the most radical, and the most substantial change ever made in peacetime. It reduced the strength of the British Army of the Rhine (BAOR) from 77,000 to 64,000 men, and then again to 50,000 a few years later, at which it remained pegged for the next 30 years. The second Tactical Air Force in Germany was cut by half. The decision was taken to abandon conscription in the early 1960s and revert to an all-professional force.

The cuts may have been substantial but they were not enough. The 1965 Defence White Paper criticised the previous government for making no real attempts to match political commitments to military resources, still less to relate the resources made available for defence to the economic circumstances of the nation. When it came to the crunch, of course, the Labour government found the exercise equally difficult. Course corrections were made, but British forces still found themselves ill-equipped and sometimes overextended. The story of the 1966–7 Defence Reviews, which were important for permanently reducing Britain's commitments east of Suez, is that of a government desperately trying to ensure that Britain remained a great power in all but name. The cuts were presented as a decision over force levels rather than a fundamental change of policy. Only the devaluation of sterling in 1967 forced the government's hand.

The 1975 Defence Review followed the same pattern. On this occasion the Wilson government preferred to cut costs, often by stealth. The Chevaline Nuclear Programme was absorbed into the defence budget, in order to avoid a debate on whether Britain still needed an independent nuclear deterrent. Co-operation with allies in programmes such as the Tornado multi-purpose aircraft spread the cost of procurement while allowing Britain to avoid having to specialise in certain roles. The country's amphibious capability had to be confined to the defence of NATO's northern flank, not its southern. In 1978 the Royal Navy pulled out of the Mediterranean for the first time in 300 years.

The final review of the Cold War years by the Defence Secretary John Nott in 1981 was conducted in the same atmosphere of short-term financial crisis. It tackled the problem of costs from three different angles. First the government expressed a perhaps unfounded hope that technological developments in the field of electronics might reduce costs substantially. It also saw ways of maintaining its many commitments with a less sophisticated mix of assets, such as fewer aircraft types for the air force. Finally, it also proposed a greater degree of specialisation by working with its NATO allies. What it proposed to do, however, was to cut the strength of the Royal Navy substantially. Perhaps what is most interesting about the debate is that it was very short in duration. It was a measure of the declining importance of defence in government thinking that the 1981 Review was completed in 12 weeks and involved only one three-hour meeting of the Cabinet. The 1967 Review, by comparison, had taken 12 months to prepare and involved 30 separate full Cabinet meetings.

In short, during the Cold War the British maintained a deterrent posture and spent more than any other NATO ally, Turkey and the United States excepted, but did so at the same time as substantially reducing its capabilities. The normal response of government in these years was to go for cuts which stretched Britain's forces to breaking point, followed by major retrenchment in its strategic responsibilities, followed by another bout of cuts – a debilitating progress which left the country and possibly the Alliance weaker with every cycle. The increasing contraction of Britain's force strength also brought an end to certain features of its role as a military power: it lost the capacity to maintain a large standing army in 1959, an independent strategic missile deployment in 1960, an independent tactical missile development two years later, and, in 1965, an indigenous military aircraft procurement. The following year also saw the end of a fully capable blue-water navy, and later still an amphibious capability outside Europe (1975).

On the other hand, Britain's armed forces were more professional than they had been in the 1950s, as both the Falklands War and the Gulf War were to show. The Royal Air Force was much better equipped, and defence budgets, far from shrinking, actually increased – they merely bought less.

With the end of the Cold War the situation changed dramatically. In pursuit of an illusive 'peace dividend' (a significant reduction in defence spending made possible by the disappearance of the Soviet threat), the British reduced their forces significantly. An exercise called 'Options for Change' was adopted in 1991. By the end of the 1990s the services had been cut by 25 per cent. As a percentage of GNP, spending on defence was reduced from 5 per cent to 2 per cent. Perhaps the most significant aspect was the cut in manpower levels. The armed forces were reduced to a size that had not been seen since 1938. The army was reduced to a little over 100,000 men (small enough to fit into Wembley Stadium); the navy was cut back to just over thirty ships; the air force was substantially reduced. By the end of the 1990s the British were spending on defence, in per capita terms, only three times more than the nation spent on the National Lottery, or about what it spent on package holidays in the sun.

The consequences of this reduction in force strengths, the largest since the 1920s, came home in the Kosovo War in 1999. In a 78-day campaign NATO was able to defeat Serbia and occupy the province. But it was essentially a US-led and financed war. Even before the firing began the British found that, even in partnership with the French, their combined air forces were not large enough to deny the Serb air force control of its own airspace. And once Kosovo was occupied the British forces (the spearhead of NATO's forces on the ground) had to be substantially cut back before winter because of severe manpower problems. Britain's forces were simply undermanned and overstretched to maintain the force commitments required in the post-Cold War era. The conclusion reached by the Blair government was to coordinate defence with its European partners, a decision taken at the NATO summit meeting in April 1999. It was a radical break with 40 years of British policy by Labour and Conservative governments alike. It was a seminal moment in the country's foreign policy debate, a significant break with Cold War thinking.

Notes

1 Harold Macmillan, *The Blast of War, 1939–45*, London, 1969, p. 269.
2 Cited in *The Times*, 22 March 1991.
3 Ian McEwan, *The Innocent*, London, 1990.
4 *The Times*, 13 March 1995.
5 The *Guardian*, 12 February 1986.
6 *The Times*, 22 March 1991.
7 Coral Bell, 'The Special Relationship', in Michael Leifer (ed.), *Constraints and Adjustments in British Foreign Policy*, London, 1972, p. 119.
8 Max Hastings, *The Korean War*, London, 1988, p. 167.
9 Cited in John Baylis, *Anglo-American Defence Relations: The Special Relationship*, London, 1981, p. 34.
10 Correlli Barnett, *The Collapse of British Power*, London, 1984; Fred Northedge, *Descent from Power*, London, 1973; Laurence Martin, 'British Defence Policy: The Long Recessional', Adelphi Paper 61, London, 1969.
11 Cited in Malcolm Chalmers, *Paying for Defence: Military Spending and Britain's Decline*, London, 1985, p. 40.
12 For a discussion of Britain's relationship with Europe, see chapter 4 in this volume.
13 Paul Kennedy, 'Why Did the British Empire Last So Long?', in *Strategy and Diplomacy 1870–1945*, London, 1983, p. 218.

Further Reading

General and historical questions

Bartlett, C. J., *British Foreign Policy in the Twentieth Century*, London, 1989.
Curtis, Mark, *The Ambiguities of Power: British Foreign Policy since 1945*, London, 1995.
Kennedy, Paul, *The Realities Behind Diplomacy: Background Influences on British External Policy, 1865–1980*, London, 1985.

Relations with Europe

Brivati, Brian and Jones, Harriet (eds), *From Reconstruction to Integration: Britain and Europe since 1945*, London, 1993.
George, Stephen, *An Awkward Partner: Britain in the European Community*, Oxford, 1998.
Greenwood, Sean, *Britain and European Co-operation since 1945*, Oxford, 1992.

Kitzienger, Uwe, *Diplomacy and Persuasion: How Britain Joined the Common Market*, London, 1973.

Relations with the United States

Cameron Watt, Donald, *Succeeding John Bull: America in Britain's Place, 1900–1975*, Cambridge, 1984.
Dillon, G. M., *Dependence and Deterrence: Success and Civility in the Anglo-American Special Nuclear Relationship 1962–1982*, London, 1983.
Louis, William and Bull, Hedley, *The Special Relationship: Anglo-American Relations since 1945*, Oxford, 1986.

Defence and foreign policy

Bartlett, C. J., *The Long Retreat: A Short History of British Defence Policy, 1945–70*, London, 1972.
Baylis, John, *Anglo-American Defence Relations, 1939–84*, London, 1984.
Croft, Stuart (ed.), *British Security Policy: The Thatcher Years and the End of the Cold War*, New York, 1991.
Freedman, Laurence, *Britain and the Falklands War*, Oxford, 1988.
Freedman, Laurence, *Britain and Nuclear Weapons*, London, 1980.
Ovendale, Ritchie, *British Defence Policy since 1945*, Manchester, 1994.

Chronology

1947	Dunkirk Treaty.
1948	Brussels Pact.
1949	NATO Treaty.
1952	UK becomes a nuclear power.
1954	Collapse of European Defence Community.
1955	Formation of Western European Union.
1956	Suez crisis.
1957	UK does not enter European Common Market.
1962	Nassau Conference (UK gets Polaris programme).
1963	De Gaulle rejects UK membership of EEC.
1967	Devaluation of sterling and decision to withdraw east of Suez.
1967	UK rejected for second time for membership of EEC.
1973	UK enters EC.
1978	Chevaline update of Polaris programme.
1982	Falklands War.
1987	UK joins the EC's single market.
1989	Collapse of Berlin Wall and end of Cold War.
1990–1	Gulf Crisis and War – Operation Desert Shield and Operation Desert Storm.
1992	Maastricht Treaty.
1993	UK leaves European Exchange Rate Mechanism.
1998	Operation Desert Fox.
1999	UK decides not to join European Monetary Union.

2 The Constitution, Government and Parliament

Simon James

The history of post-war British constitutional development is very uneven. From 1945 to the late 1960s there was little change, apart from some tinkering with the House of Lords. The 1970s saw a spell of frenetic activity, whose only (but very significant) concrete result was membership of the European Union (EU). Then for almost two decades the Thatcher and Major governments ruled out almost any change – to be followed in 1997 by the Blair government's blizzard of constitutional reform legislation.

This chapter begins with a brief definition of what we mean in Britain by 'the constitution', then details the history of, and reasons for, change and failure to change since 1945. It then examines the development of three of the main institutions of the constitution: the monarchy, Parliament and government; and concludes by examining two major issues: the implications of EU membership and the problems of political accountability. Inevitably, such a synoptic piece paints with a broad brush, and more detailed treatment of certain topics will be found in later chapters in this volume, notably those dealing with European integration, Scotland, Wales, Northern Ireland, the civil service and local government.

Defining the Constitution

The conventional observation is that Britain does not have a written constitution and that most other countries do. This is inaccurate. Much of our constitution is written down, in the form of Acts of Parliament (for example, Acts specifying the succession to the throne and the powers of the House of Lords), of secondary legislation (e.g. governing the conduct of elections), of charters (bits of Magna Carta are still operative), legal judgements (many restrictions on state power were actually imposed by the courts in the seventeenth century) and international treaties such as those governing the EU. So it is more accurate to say that while much of the constitution is written down, it is not systematically codified. There is a heavy reliance on unwritten conventions to fill in the gaps between these records, and often these conventions are expressed in documents, such as the Blair government's 'Code for Ministers', which have a quasi-constitutional status. The overall picture is of an archipelago of fragmentary writings, in a sea of conventions and customs.

By the same token, it is untrue to say that in other countries the entirely of their constitution is to be found in the document marked 'Constitution'. That document will set out the main principles and mechanisms governing the conduct of political and public life, but of itself this is rarely self-sufficient. Usually it will be supplemented by subsidiary laws, such as those detailing the electoral system. Of equal importance is practice. Any constitution is more than just the mechanisms prescribed in the rule book; it consists also of the working practices, habits and values of those who daily translate the constitution into reality, which in turn are influenced heavily by the political environment. These are often taken for granted and not reduced to writing. For example, the relative roles of the French President and Prime Minister are very different to those which a strict reading of France's written constitution might suggest – not least in recent periods of *cohabitation*.

None of this is to glorify or belittle the particular constitutional practice of Britain or any other country. The point is that in all countries the constitution consists of what people think and do, as well as consisting of what is written down. Consequently there is nothing illogical in examining, as this chapter does, both practice and written constitutional law.

Pressures for Reform

Although opinion polls since at least the 1970s have consistently shown public support for such changes as a Bill of rights, proportional representation and reform of the House of Lords, the polls have also shown that people are far more concerned with economic and social issues. Constitutional reform has been mainly the preoccupation of a rarefied circle of parliamentarians, politicians, journalists, academics and a small number of pressure-group activists. Their activities since 1945 fall into five chronological stages, which can be characterised individually as torpor; mild reformism; frenetic but futile activity; utter refusal to change; and frenetic activity leading to achievement.

1945–1964: torpor

In the aftermath of the Second World War, the Labour government was not interested in changing the constitution. With a shattered economy, a programme of nationalisation and a welfare state to build, Labour had bigger fish to fry. It had long before shed its early commitment to Scottish home rule and (once it started to benefit from first-past-the-post) electoral reform. Its only radical com-

mitment was to abolishing the Lords. But Conservative peers were wisely restrained under the Attlee government, their leader, Salisbury, propounding the
doctrine that the Lords should not reject or wreck with amendments any Bill
that the electorate had implicitly approved at the election. The upshot was that
Labour confined itself to reducing the Upper House's powers to delay a Bill
from three successive sessions to two – and even that was done only because of
fears that the Lords would attempt to block the nationalisation of steel until
after a general election. Otherwise the only major constitutional legislation was
the ending of additional votes for businessmen and university graduates.

If Labour were not interested in radical change, the Conservatives were not
going to outbid them. The 1950s were a dull decade, nowhere more so than in
constitutional law. The consensus that the constitution was in fine shape reflected a wider sense of satisfaction with public institutions: our police and civil
service were wonderful, our constitution a model for the Commonwealth. A
rare dissident voice came from the Liberals, who as early as the 1940s called
for devolution to Scotland and Wales, reform of the Lords and electoral reform,
but at this time their fortunes were at their nadir.

The exception to this complacency was again the House of Lords, its membership still entirely hereditary. A study in the 1950s recorded that attendance
was low – perhaps thirty after 5.30 p.m. – and there were scarcely enough
Labour peers (mostly elderly and infirm) to staff the Opposition front bench.[1] It
was embarrassing. The idea of life peers had been around since Victorian times,
and an all-party conference in 1948 (in the run-up to the Attlee reform) had
actually agreed on reorganising the membership, but had deadlocked on reducing the Upper House's powers. Macmillan now seized the initiative and life
peers were introduced by an Act of 1958, opposed by Labour on the prescient
grounds that it would undermine more radical plans for Lords reform. As a
postlude, in 1963 the Labour MP Anthony Wedgwood-Benn (later to restyle
himself Tony Benn) persuaded Parliament to allow peers not to take up their
seats in the Lords (he wished to disclaim the unwelcome peerage inherited from
his father which had forced him out of the Commons). This change was soon
used by two senior Conservatives, Lord Hailsham and Lord Home, to transfer
to the Commons.

1964–1970: mild reformism

With the Labour government elected in 1964 we enter a period of slightly
greater activism. It had no reliable majority until after the 1966 election, but
the Prime Minister, Harold Wilson, made some changes of a non-legislative
kind. In 1965, UK citizens were given the right to petition the European Court
of Human Rights in Strasbourg if they felt that their rights under the European
Convention on Human Rights (ECHR) had been infringed. A Department of
Economic Affairs was created as a rival to the Treasury's power (it failed); later
the Fulton Commission on the Civil Service led to the creation of a separate and
longer-lived Civil Service Department, also carved out of the Treasury (although
the civil service notoriously sank the rest of the Fulton Report). And the Home

Secretary Roy Jenkins famously engineered the liberalisation of the law on censorship, abortion and homosexuality, although the words 'civil rights' were not used at the time and these issues were not seen as having a constitutional character or implication.

After gaining a large majority in the 1966 election, the Labour government showed a modest interest in legislation: the voting age was lowered from 21 to 18; an ombudsman was introduced; and in 1968 the government made a shot at reforming the composition of the Lords. The first two were popular; the last was a fiasco. The proposal for a new House composed wholly of nominated and salaried peers, although supported by the Conservative front bench, was fiercely resisted by a combination of Labour abolitionists led by Michael Foot and Conservative mavericks led by Enoch Powell. Their brilliant guerrilla campaign blocked the Bill for months in committee until the government gave up in disgust.

The 1970s: frenetic but futile activity

The next decade saw at last a genuine interest in constitutional reform. High inflation and union militancy seriously frightened many people in the mid-1970s, and a line of reasoning developed amongst moderate Labour and Conservative politicians that proportional representation was necessary, both to head off a Cabinet dominated by the Labour left, and because they perceived the confrontational nature of British politics as actually encouraging economic dislocation. This was reinforced by the famous split over Common Market membership, in which moderates from both major parties united with the Liberals against their own respective anti-EU colleagues, to the extent of fighting and defeating them in the 1975 referendum campaign.

Reformist thought cut little ice with the Labour and Conservative front benches, however. They were not going to give away power – indeed, in the mid-1970s, the main perception was that governments needed to reassert themselves in the face of frightening events. They also contrived to ignore the implications of simultaneous changes in Northern Ireland and the European Community (EC). When Northern Ireland burst into violence in the 1960s the Labour government made little effort to remedy the underlying political and social injustices and left the Unionist government at Stormont more or less in charge. After further violence, the Heath government in 1972 belatedly remedied 50 years of neglect by abolishing the Northern Ireland Parliament, and created a new assembly led by a mixed executive of Nationalists and Unionists, which, however, was overthrown by a Unionist strike within months. (A subsequent constitutional convention achieved nothing.) Yet British politicians stubbornly depicted Northern Ireland as a matter wholly apart from the rest of the United Kingdom, and as such not possessing any implications for constitutional arrangements on the mainland. The assembly was elected by proportional representation, and a referendum was held on the future of the border, but such outlandish devices were depicted by mainland politicians as necessary aberrations with no relevance to the constitution of the rest of the UK. Similarly, leading politicians contrived (with singular dishonesty) to pretend that the UK's accession to the EC in 1973 had no great constitutional ramifications (a point explored further below).

Instead, the only attempts at constitutional change by the Labour government of 1974–9 were wrung from it by political necessity: the threat of nationalism. This had been seen as a fringe phenomenon of limited electoral importance until the Scottish Nationalists won the sensational Hamilton by-election of 1967, terrifying Labour in its heartland. Wilson set up a Royal Commission on the constitution, with a strong steer to look at devolution for Scotland and Wales. Its report in 1973 favoured just that, and Labour promptly adopted the policy, with Heath following suit. In 1975, its slender majority wiped out at by-elections, the Labour government wooed Nationalist MPs – and sought to win back their voters – by introducing devolution legislation. The whole business proved infinitely more complex than anybody had expected, not least because many ministers communicated to officials their deep dislike of devolution, so that the Devolution Unit at the Cabinet Office faced enormous opposition and procrastination from departments from the Treasury down. There was resistance from some English Labour MPs who saw devolution as favouritism for Scotland and Wales, and who compelled the government to hold referenda in both Scotland and Wales. A backbench rebellion eventually imposed amendments requiring 40 per cent of registered voters to support the proposals for them to take effect. In 1979 the Welsh referendum rejected the proposals by four to one, and while there was a majority in Scotland, it fell short of the 40 per cent threshold. The Nationalists and Liberals then withdrew their support from the Labour government, which lost a vote of confidence in May.

Equally unproductive were the other constitutional proposals that the Liberals pressed on the government. Proportional representation for elections to the European Parliament was the price of their support for the minority Labour administration, but in 1978 sufficient Labour backbenchers joined the Opposition to defeat the proposal. The Liberals were furious, but powerless. Nor could they salvage the Freedom of Information Bill promoted by the Liberal MP Clement Freud in 1978, which had much cross-party support but was lost at the 1979 dissolution.

So the scorecard for the 1970s, after huge upheaval, was failure on all fronts except accession to the EC – a change that, almost unbelievably, few perceived in constitutional terms.

1979–1987: utter refusal to change

Then came the era of Mrs Thatcher, when constitutional reform was ruled out completely. She was a stubborn Unionist in Scottish, Welsh and Irish contexts, and loathed devolution almost as much as she loathed separatism. She was not going to change an electoral system or a House of Lords that served her purposes well, nor did she have the remotest interest in human rights or freedom of information. The 1979 manifesto had promised the latter, but the Protection of

Official Information Bill introduced was so restrictive that an outcry forced its withdrawal and the issue was not reopened. Besides, Mrs Thatcher's priorities lay elsewhere, in economic and industrial change. Most senior Conservatives probably shared her lack of enthusiasm, not least recalling the hours devoted to constitutional legislation in the 1960s and 1970s, most of which had turned out to be wasted.

The Major government from 1990 to 1997 showed itself a little more adventurous, although (like the 1964–6 government) preferring to avoid legislation. It introduced a parliamentary committee to oversee the security services; inaugurated (on a non-statutory basis) a modest measure of freedom of information; and published the previously secret list of Cabinet committees and the Cabinet handbook *Questions of Procedure for Ministers* (one suspects here the influence of the liberal-minded Foreign Secretary, Douglas Hurd). But changes to the 'big architecture' of the constitution were strongly resisted: if anything, Major hated devolution more than his predecessor did.

1997 onwards: activity and achievement

The Labour Party that came to power in 1997 was committed to a programme of constitutional reform without parallel since Gladstone's 'great feats of political engineering' of the mid-nineteenth century. It executed its promises swiftly and wholeheartedly. In the 1997–8 session of Parliament alone, Bills were pushed through to establish a Scottish Parliament, a Welsh Assembly, regional development agencies for England (which could prove the forerunners of regional assemblies if that is the local wish), to incorporate the ECHR into domestic law, to introduce proportional representation for elections to the European Parliament and to hold referenda on devolution in Scotland, Wales and London. In addition, the Good Friday settlement in Northern Ireland, an unexpected bonus, required several constitutional Bills. In the following session, Bills followed to create an elected mayor and assembly for London and to remove hereditary peers from the Lords. The government also published a White Paper on freedom of information, and received – but sat on – a report from an independent commission (the Jenkins Commission) recommending the introduction of proportional representation for Westminster elections.

How do we explain the stop-go nature of constitutional reform since 1945, the alternating periods of torpor and frenzied activity? This might just be the natural rhythm of constitutional change. In the previous 100 years, constitutional reform had tended to come in spasms: the great extension of the franchise in the 1860 and 1870s; and the constitutional strife of 1909–18 over the House of Lords, home rule for Ireland and Scotland, and women's suffrage. In between there had come long bouts of constitutional somnolence, with a few adjustments made by consensus, such as lowering the voting age for women from 30 to 21 in the late 1920s. Seen against this background, the last phase of Conservative government, 1979 to 1997, was the real aberration: atypical because of the utter refusal to countenance legislative change of any sort. This caused problems because the upheavals of the 1970s had led to no change whatsoever, and had left a mass of unresolved questions – whither Northern Ireland? where would European union lead? – and frustrated aspirations, nowhere more than in Scotland where, after all, a simple majority of those voting in 1979 had favoured devolution. And because the Thatcher governments genuinely altered the configuration of the state by a centralisation of power – notably by the debilitation of local government and the proliferation of quangos – a sense of an unbalanced constitution arose.

By the mid-1980s there were various currents of reformist thought, mostly articulated by single-issue advocacy groups, the most important of which were:

- The Campaign for Freedom of Information, a small but professional pressure group which successfully promoted legislation for freedom of information in local government, and for the right of access by the public to medical and other files. It advanced cogent arguments for similar reforms in central government.
- A loose coalition of lawyers who wanted a bill of rights. This group included Lord Scarman, who had first articulated the call in the early 1970s, supported by a gamut of intensely respectable lawyers from the Law Lords downwards. By the late 1980s the consensus amongst them was that the best way of achieving this was by incorporating the ECHR into domestic UK law. In the early 1990s the distinguished Liberal Democrat lawyer Anthony Lester twice steered a Bill to effect this through the Lords, only to see it blocked in the Commons.
- The devolution enthusiasts. In the 1980s a Scottish constitutional convention was established with the support of a large spectrum of Scottish business and social opinion. It drew up a 'Scottish Claim of Right' and devised plans for a devolved Parliament. Its well-publicised deliberations fostered a consensus in Scotland around the desirability of devolution. In Wales the debate on devolution was largely internal to the Labour Party, which dominated the politics of the principality and was frankly divided on the question. In England, the debate was even more muted, again conducted largely among Labour Party members, and not many of those. But the experience of the 1970s had shown that no government could legislate for Scotland without considering Wales and England: Callaghan in the 1970s had been forced to publish a Green Paper on English regional devolution, and to set up development agencies for the north-east and north-west of England.
- Electoral reform had long been advocated by the Liberals, and by the Electoral Reform Society, whose publications on different proportional electoral systems ensured that there was no excuse for an under-informed debate. This attracted minority interest in both Labour and Conservative parties, both of which, from the 1970s, had their own pressure groups in favour of proportional representation.

These different strands were combined into a coherent programme by Charter 88, partly an umbrella group and partly an elite pressure group, which gave their disparate objectives a common philosophical basis, and highlighted their common cause by skilful publicity. But pressure groups achieve nothing until they capture the support of the front bench of a major party. The Liberals had long been enthusiasts, but the crucial turning point was the conversion of Labour. In 1987 Neil Kinnock had been edging that way, taking the party into the election committed to a Scottish Assembly. The decisive shove, however, was given by his successor as leader, John Smith, an Edinburgh MP keen on devolution but who saw constitutional reform as little short of a moral issue, and committed his party to supporting, in essence, the whole Charter 88 programme. This was the decisive moment, and while his successor Tony Blair was accused by some of his party of less wholehearted enthusiasm – insisting, for example, on referenda before devolution[2] – his government delivered faster and more fully than their most optimistic supporters had hoped.

The sudden explosion of reform in 1997 requires explanation. The various pressure groups described above certainly had considerable impact on the content of Labour's manifesto. One can point to the importance of personalities: the legacy of Smith, and the presence in charge of Blair's reform programme of Lord Irvine, the energetic Lord Chancellor who used his position as the Prime Minister's trusted lieutenant and as controller of the legislative programme to push reform through quickly. One can point to short-term political attractions: as Labour moved closer to the post-Thatcherite socio-economic consensus, constitutional reform was the big issue that clearly defined it from the Conservatives. And, in an era of retrenchment, it was cheaper than, say, social reform.

All true, but insufficient as an explanation for so radical a programme. The 1997 reforms were in truth no more than an overdue response to a colossal backlog of maintenance accumulated during the sterile 1970s and the subsequent 18 years of 'no pasarán' constitutional Conservatism. Had government remained after 1997 in the hands of a party opposed to reform, the expectations generated by the Scottish constitutional convention would most likely have erupted from the bottle at some point (after the 1992 election, the Scottish Secretary had been frightened enough by suppressed expectations to urge Major, unsuccessfully, for a referendum in Scotland on independence. Once Scotland sprang free, consequences for Wales and England had to follow). Another genie – much less easily controlled by government or Parliament – lay in developments in the courts. From the 1970s onwards, with embarrassing and increasing frequency, the government lost cases brought in the European Court of Human Rights by British citizens unable to enforce those rights in the domestic courts. The UK was committed to observe the Convention and so – usually with ill grace – legislated to remedy the defects identified. The illogicality of failing to incorporate the Convention into domestic law became near- intolerable. And from the 1980s onwards the domestic courts, ever pragmatic and increasingly willing to overrule government decisions, inched towards incorporating the ECHR by the back door: for example, they would 'have regard' to the Convention when domestic law was unclear. The courts also edged ever closer to requiring public authorities to give reasons for decisions – a clear precursor of a judge-made requirement for greater access to information.

These twin pressures – regional sentiment and judicial creativity in defence of individual rights – would most likely have forced constitutional change whether the government of the day liked it or not. And the point would have come when government and Parliament would have had to ask themselves: are we to let this be imposed on us, or are we to harness and mould these forces into a national constitutional settlement as a whole? Certain elements – Lords reform, PR – would probably have been left in touch. But it is difficult to resist the conclusion that long-term and probably irresistible constitutional currents were at work.

This, then, was the overall picture. The next section of this chapter looks at three key institutions of the constitution, which were not directly the objects of much of this reform, but were affected by it. Their activities were, on the whole, not regulated by law but by unwritten convention or executive direction. They are the monarchy, Parliament and the central executive.

The Role of the Monarch

In the 1940s and 1950s, textbooks dealt at unnecessary length with the role of the Queen. Today, they tend to neglect it unduly. The monarch remains constitutionally important for three reasons. First, she has the right to be consulted by, and to advise, her ministers. Used discreetly, this amounts to a marginal but high-level influence which the present monarch has used to prudent effect.[3] Second, the Queen has 'reserve powers' to choose a Prime Minister and to grant or refuse a dissolution of Parliament. Choosing a premier is necessary only when a general election fails to generate a clear winner, which has happened only once since the war: in February 1974, when the Prime Minister, Edward Heath, was unable to secure a workable minority and resolved the problem by advising the Queen to call on the Labour leader to form a government. It can also happen when a party has no machinery for electing a leader, as was true of the Conservatives after the resignations of Anthony Eden and Harold Macmillan, leaving the Queen to await the result of party infighting. Now that all parties elect their leaders, this contingency is remote. The power to grant or refuse a dissolution poses a problem only if a Prime Minister with a working majority seeks a dissolution at a relatively early stage of a Parliament that is still viable. In practice, the only premature dissolutions have been sought by prime ministers leading minority administrations (namely, Harold Wilson in 1966 and October 1974).

The third and most significant role of the monarch is as national symbol, exemplified by her annual leadership of the act of remembrance at the Cenotaph, or her addresses to the nation before the Falklands and Kuwait campaigns. This is constitutionally important not because of the role it bestows on the Queen, but because it prevents politicians from taking the role of national symbol on themselves. It limits the extent to which party politicians can wrap themselves in the national flag for partisan purposes – as happens in France or the United States, where the head of government is also head of state. And in the (hopefully remote) contingency of a prime minister becoming as paranoid as, say, President Nixon was in his last days in office, it is rather important that the Queen, not the premier, should hold the ultimate, failsafe authority as head of state, not to mention the final authority as commander-in-chief of the armed forces. The constitutional role of the Crown is marginal, and likely to be invoked only in rare and extreme circumstances. But in those rare circumstances, it remains of primary importance.

Parliament

The term 'parliamentary government' is thoroughly misleading. Parliament has never governed: rather, its role has been to act as commentator and critic on the actions and proposed legislation of the government and, as a consequence of this, to influence to some extent future government action.

The track record of Parliament since 1945 has been decidedly mixed. Government activity has grown immensely in scope and complexity, but while there have been reforms to parliamentary procedures, these have at best been unsystematic tinkering at the margins. Parliament determines its own procedures and the Commons in particular have proved surprisingly resistant to any systematic or radical reform. The House of Lords, on the other hand, has become markedly more effective. Because the two houses differ in character and purpose, it makes sense to consider them separately.

The House of Commons

The composition of the Commons has changed markedly since 1945. The immediate post-war house had a sizeable proportion of manual workers and trade unionists on the Labour benches, and many knights of the shires and MPs with service backgrounds on the Conservative side (although of course many Labour MPs had seen wartime service). In contrast, in the Parliament elected in 1997, 76 per cent of Conservative MPs and 54 per cent of Labour MPs had a professional or business background: overall there were 126 teachers or lecturers (most of them Labour) and 64 lawyers. Only one Conservative MP and 54 Labour MPs had a background as manual workers. Almost three-quarters of MPs had a university education. There were more women, although still underrepresented: 120 in 1997 compared to only 28 as recently as 1964. Ethnic minorities, with only 9 MPs in 1997, remained under-represented.[4] Still, the degree of change since 1945 has been considerable.

Equally significant, however, and less easy to quantify, is the change in the motivation of MPs. There have always been plenty of ambitious politicians in the Commons, but until at least the 1970s there was a ballast of solid, unambitious MPs, the height of whose ambition was to represent their constituents, support their party and voice dissent only discreetly. Tory backbenchers of the ilk of Sir Arnold Gridley and Rear-Admiral Sir Giles Morgan found fulfilment in supporting, and sometimes restraining, their front benches; and they had their counterparts (perhaps with less evocative names) on the Labour benches. Today, as the journalist and historian Peter Riddell has observed, politics has become professionalised.[5] MPs are not interested in sitting on the backbenches for twenty years. They want to become ministers.

Yet, paradoxically, backbenchers have over the same period also become more independent-minded. This first became a noticeable phenomenon in the late 1960s, when mass backbench opposition compelled the Labour government to abandon industrial relations legislation, and backbench guerrilla warfare killed Lords reform. It really took hold in the 1970s with the rise of issues that split parties and aroused strong emotions: economic and industrial policy (on which Heath faced revolts as serious as those which subsequently plagued his Labour successors), the Common Market and devolution. This may have reflected broader social trends: just as society became less deferential towards authority, MPs became less afraid of their front benches. Ambitious MPs may have seen political advantage to themselves in the occasional rebellion: if the issue was right, it gained them publicity, a reputation for taking a stand on principle, and kudos with their constituents. A 1985 survey of two-thirds of backbenchers showed a widespread independence of thought: only half agreed that their primary loyalty was to their party, and over four-fifths said that their electors expected them to use their judgement on issues, and that they would be prepared to vote against their party on a three-line whip.[6] And it also became apparent that the influence of party whips was much exaggerated, since ultimately their only sanction was the 'nuclear option' of withdrawing the whip, thereby losing all control over the rebellious MPs.

Essentially the functions of the House of Commons are threefold: to scrutinise and restrain the actions of government; to legislate; and to influence the future policy of government.

As an agent of scrutiny, the Commons has proved rather effective over the past half-century or so. Long-established mechanisms of scrutiny have been better used, and new mechanisms devised. The use of parliamentary questions has blossomed. Michael Ryle, a Commons clerk for 38 of the post-war years, recalled that at the end of the 1950s 'we thought we had had a busy day if we received a hundred Questions; in 1989–90, over 66,000 Questions appeared on the Order Paper – an average of nearly 400 Questions a day'.[7] Admittedly only 15 to 20 questions are answered orally each day (questions not reached are answered in writing), but it still means that each department's ministers are regularly and by rota exposed to fierce questioning. Ministers prepare elaborately for their regular ordeal: their reputation and chances of promotion depend on giving a convincing defence of their policies. And in the best publicised of exchanges, since the early 1960s the Prime Minister has faced half an hour of questions (originally in two 15-minute sessions on Tuesday and Thursday, since 1997 in one session on Wednesday).

Also potent is the Commons' ability to criticise government actions. Every month provides examples of debates in which the government must justify and defend its actions. The government will usually win the vote, but cannot avoid explaining itself. There are numerous procedures to permit this: e.g. there are days on which the opposition parties select the topic for debate; backbench members may ask the Speaker for an emergency debate; the government may provide time for debate. And if they fail to persuade their backbenchers, ministers must climb down – again, a development particularly visible since the 1970s. Notable examples of successful backbench rebellions have been the

1978 vote that destroyed the Callaghan government's pay policy, the 1985 rebellion which forced the Thatcher government to abandon the proposed sale of British Leyland to General Motors, and a similar revolt six years later which forced ministers to reduce the scale of proposed mines closures.[8]

A third means of scrutiny is the select committee system. This evolved slowly.[9] The post-war Estimates Committee was rather ineffectual, but a Nationalised Industries Select Committee, operating from 1957 onwards, carried out pioneering work in taking evidence not just from ministers and officials, but from a wider spectrum of interested parties, and in producing substantial reports. The Labour governments of 1964–70 extended the experiment, with committees on such subjects as race relations and science and technology. Even so, there was much resistance; the Commons was sluggish and reluctant to recognise the inadequacy of the floor of the House for scrutinising an ever more complex administration. Traditionalists led by Michael Foot and Enoch Powell argued that the whole House was the proper forum for holding government to account, while harder-headed realists like Edward du Cann and John Mackintosh pointed to the sheer impossibility of this. The realists won. Norman St John Stevas, Leader of the Commons in Mrs Thatcher's first administration, re-engineered the system to create a network of 14 committees shadowing individual departments; in the subsequent 20 years the committees have become an established part of the landscape. Their effectiveness and impact varies, and opportunities for debating their reports on the floor of the House are limited, but they are established, irremovable, and moderately effective. To quote Ryle again: 'the House is a much more lively and politically significant body than it was fifty years ago and, in particular, is far more effective today as a critical body than it has been for a very long time'.[10]

However, one aspect has remained woefully inadequate throughout the post-war period: the scrutiny of estimates – essentially, the government's future spending proposals. A review by a special committee in the early 1980s described Commons control of finance as 'a myth'.[11] Matters have not improved since. *Post hoc* scrutiny by the venerable and energetic Public Accounts Committee, which uncovers inefficiency and misdoing retrospectively, is still highly effective: this committee is feared by Whitehall. But it only acts after the event.[12]

The legislative function may be examined more briefly. The government controls the timetable, its business takes priority, and the whips ensure that the government usually gets what it wants. There is limited time for backbenchers' bills (for a brief while after the war the press of government business squeezed them out altogether) and the only ones with a prospect of success are those whose promoters win a high place in the annual ballot, and who propose something to which the government does not object. For practical purposes, therefore, legislation means government legislation, which takes up some 30 per cent of the Commons' time.

Scrutiny is inadequate. It is not for want of rebellions, because here too backbenchers have shown greater independence since the 1970s. Famous revolts include the 'Rooker–Wise' amendment that compelled the Callaghan government to index-link tax allowances; the Commons' rejection at the second reading in 1986 of the Shops Bill, and the 1994 refusal to double VAT on fuel. And for every government defeat, there are dozens of government concessions in the face of backbench warnings. Rather, the failure lies in the scrutiny of the bulk of bills that do not excite political passions. Partly this is because at committee stage government backbenchers often just act as lobby fodder and take little interest in the business. Partly it is that the opposition's main weapon is delay, so that the typical pattern is over-long scrutiny of early clauses, followed by a 'guillotine' motion to cut short debate, so that the later clauses of the bill are steamrollered through with minimal scrutiny. Only in 1997 did the Commons begin experimenting with a more rational system for 'timetabling' bills. It is true that many bills are extensively amended, but almost every successful amendment is proposed by the government, sometimes to meet opposition suggestions, more often just to tighten up drafting.

If scrutiny of bills is weak, that of secondary legislation is risible. Virtually every Act of Parliament gives ministers power to make legal regulations filling in the detail. As early as 1949 there were some 23,000 pages of secondary legislation in operation.[13] Post-war deregulation pruned this somewhat in the 1950s, but then it started growing again. The year 1996 – a typical one – saw 3,291 additional statutory instruments, adding 10,274 extra pages to secondary legislation; every year the ratio of secondary to primary legislation, in terms of pages, is roughly four to one. Not all regulations need parliamentary approval; if they do, they receive cursory debate; and there is no provision for amending them. In the 1990s both Commons and Lords established committees to vet secondary legislation to ensure that the powers bestowed on ministers were not excessive. But this still perpetuates the fault identified by a shrewd Commons clerk, Kenneth Mackenzie, back in 1949: it focuses on the legislative aspect, not on the merits of the proposal.[14] These woeful deficiencies are all the more surprising because a good model exists in the arrangements for scrutinising EU legislation introduced in 1974, under which a scrutiny committee, meeting weekly, sifts out important proposals from the EU and refers them to a special standing committee which may question the responsible minister, hold a debate and pass a resolution.[15]

The third function of the Commons is to influence future government policy. Here the Commons' effectiveness is difficult to gauge. Some of this influence is public: MPs publicly badgering the government for a change in government policy, either to favour their constituents (build the bypass, support this industry) or because the MP has a bee in his bonnet. Famous personal campaigns include Sir Gerald Nabarro's persecution of successive Chancellors over the illogicalities of Purchase Tax and Jack Ashley's tireless championing of the rights of disabled people. Much of this is done by speeches in debate, written and oral questions, and the like. However, throughout the post-war period a semi-public conduit has also greatly developed, by which MPs either take deputations of constituents to see ministers, or forward constituents' letters to ministers and ask for their response. This activity is difficult to quantify, but as a rough indicator, in the 1940s the volume of such letters appears to have been slight; by the early 1980s MPs were writing approximately 120,000 letters a year to ministers on behalf of constituents; and by the end of the decade the figure was closer to 180,000.[16]

Also influential is the private lobbying of ministers by MPs that goes on in the margins of everyday parliamentary life: 'a word in the lobby', as it known. Civil servants are familiar with the morning telephone call from the minister's office: 'He was told X by backbenchers in the House last night: could you please let him have a note on the problem?' The impact of such influence cannot be measured, but this author's experience in Whitehall is that it is significant.

The House of Lords

What of the Lords? The introduction of life peers after 1958 slowly transformed the House. The number and length of sittings increased; the quality of debate rose; respected select committees on Europe and on science were established; and the quality of expertise improved. Consequently, the Lords demonstrated growing self-confidence, which they exercised most tellingly in the area where the Commons was weakest: close scrutiny of government legislation. The first serious stirrings were in the 1970s, especially in resistance to shipbuilding nationalisation. But it was in the 1980s that the Lords determinedly ran up the flag of critical resistance against the Thatcher government, particularly – but not uniquely – against its seemingly endless legislation on local government. In the early 1970s, governments lost roughly 2 per cent of divisions in the Lords; in the early 1980s, between 5 per cent and 7 per cent; by the early 1990s, between 7 per cent and 10 per cent.[17] If the Commons disagreed with the Lords' amendments the Upper House would usually back down, but there were moments of obstinacy. And often the peers won – for example, forcing the government in 1996 to accept the splitting of pensions between couples at the time of divorce. On two occasions – the War Crimes Bill of 1990 and the bill introducing proportional representation for European parliamentary elections in 1997 – the Commons had to resort to the override provisions of the Parliament Act.

In short, the Commons has been slow to change and, while highly effective in calling ministers to account for their actions and moderately influential in shaping future ministerial policy, remains woefully defective as a scrutineer of legislation. The Lords, in contrast, has revived to become an effective revising chamber.

The Government

As with Parliament, so with the executive: it is striking that the extensive changes of the past half-century have made so little difference to the way in which the centre of government operates. To a suprising extent, ministers and their ministries operate much as they did under the Attlee government. There are, however, some differences worth cataloguing.

First, from the 1960s onwards there was greater interest in the way in which government worked. Until quite recently governments of all parties preferred to keep their *modus operandi* secret. Until well into the 1970s, for lack of facts, academic textbooks were long on platitudes and short on hard information, and there was little journalistic investigation – indeed, when *The Times* appointed a Whitehall correspondent in the 1960s, the Prime Minister ordered that no minister or official should speak to him. But exercises like the 1968 Royal Commission Report on the civil service inevitably lifted the lid, and in 1975 came the publication (despite government attempts to ban it) of Crossman's *Diaries of a Cabinet Minister*: gossipy, prejudiced and inaccurate, but vividly depicting Whitehall life in human terms. Better diaries followed – notably those of Barbara Castle – and were supplemented by the investigative work of Peter Hennessy, first as journalist, later as academic. It was this prising open of the black box that made possible the television series *Yes, Minister*, which popularised the question of the relationship between ministers and officials.

Second, this interest was partly fuelled by a wholly misleading debate as to whether the Prime Minister had become a president, as Crossman claimed he had. This greatly exaggerated the contemporary power of the premier, and underestimated his power in the past: no post-war premier until Mrs Thatcher achieved the dominance enjoyed by Lloyd George or Chamberlain between the wars.

Third, the debate over the Prime Minister overshadowed a significant change in the operation of the Cabinet. Attlee markedly changed the system by deliberately delegating as much as possible to Cabinet committees. These had existed on quite a large scale before 1939, but had not been systematically used. Attlee insisted that every issue should be considered by a committee first, and should only go on to Cabinet if the committee could not agree or the issue was extremely important. Consequently, the Cabinet served principally as a court of appeal from 1945 to 1979. After this latter date Mrs Thatcher was reluctant to let the Cabinet discuss or decide any significant matter at all, and committees became the true locus of decision- making. The Cabinet became instead more of a weekly meeting of political colleagues, which discussed issues of the moment, especially forthcoming parliamentary and European business, but ceased to take decisions as such.

Fourth, the dominance of the Treasury has diminished. From the 1920s to the 1960s it was the premier department, controlling civil service pay and promotions as well as finance and the economy. This drew flak from radical critics in the early 1960s, who claimed (probably wrongly) that the Treasury was a brake on economic expansion. Wilson mistrusted it and sought to weaken its influence, first by creating a rival Department of Economic Affairs – a duplication which led to confusion and rivalry and was soon axed – and later by splitting off the personnel functions into a more durable Civil Service Department. Also significant in the Treasury's loss of primacy was the economic trauma of the 1970s, which deeply shook its collective self-confidence. From the 1970s onwards, Whitehall increasingly recognised the Cabinet Office as an alternative centre of power: its previous influence had certainly been underestimated, but it took over the more significant civil service management functions in the 1980s, with the Cabinet Secretary becoming head of the civil service. Certainly in the last twenty years or so civil servants have not regarded the Treasury as the all-powerful overlord that it was well into the 1960s.

Fifth, there was the rise and fall of the machinery of 'hands-on' economic intervention. This took two forms. First, from the 1940s to the 1980s government was preoccupied with the nationalised industries, notably coal, gas, electricity and the railways, which were run at arm's length by public corporations, but whose management and financial problems still made great demands on ministers and officials, and raised serious political waves. Second, from the early 1960s to the late 1970s government, in an effort to control inflation, created endless commissions and mechanisms to control prices and incomes. Such issues merit essays to themselves: for immediate purposes it is sufficient to note that a colossal amount of time and energy was given over to creating and guiding state machinery for this purpose.

The Impact of the European Union

The United Kingdom's membership of the EU has had a profound effect on the constitution, yet here again the impact on the day-to-day government of the country has been limited. Parliament and the executive work much as they did before entry in 1973. There are certain mechanical changes. Parliament has developed the new arrangements for scrutinising EU legislation mentioned above. The Cabinet system has developed new arrangement for coordinating EU policy, although these have evolved within the traditional structure of inter-departmental coordination of policy, with a network of Cabinet committees to transact the business and an additional secretariat in the Cabinet Office. Ministers and civil servants have spent much time in Brussels negotiating with European partners, and have had to adapt themselves to a different structure of policy-making, for the EU has a very different structure of law and policy-making. Some departments – most notably the Ministry of Agriculture, Fisheries and Food – have had to reorient themselves almost entirely to EU concerns. A few ministers, notably the Foreign Secretary and Agriculture Minister, reputedly see more today of their European counterparts than they do of their UK Cabinet colleagues. Yet the overall shape and dynamics of the parliamentary and governmental systems remain as they were before 1973, when Britain entered the then European Community.[18]

Nonetheless, a profound change has been wrought. The British constitution was – still is – founded on the principle of parliamentary sovereignty: that is, that there is no limit to parliamentary power, and that the scope of Acts of Parliament is restricted only by the physical frontiers of the state and the political tolerability of laws. In particular, the tradition has been that there is no superior body of law. This principle is seriously infringed by the UK's membership of the EU, for the Treaty of Rome explicitly provides that EU law is superior to the domestic law of a member state. At the time of the UK's accession, opponents of membership – notably Enoch Powell and Tony Benn – warned of this implication. They were right. Euro-enthusiasts, rather dishonestly, played it down. Admittedly, in the context of the EU's limited scope of operation in the 1970s its significance was limited. But as the EU extended its field of competence, so the scope for conflict between Community and domestic law expanded. The courts tactfully skirted round the issue for as long as possible, but in 1991 they were compelled to rule that parts of British merchant shipping legislation were illegal because it effectively restricted the right of Spanish fishermen to trawl in British waters. Three years later they declared part of an Act of Parliament on part-time working unlawful for the same reason. The upshot is that Parliament must voluntarily draw in its horns when it wants to legislate in a certain way but is warned, usually by ministers, that it would be violating EU legislation. If Parliament presses ahead anyway, it is liable to be overruled in the European Court of Justice, should a suit be brought there by an individual in the UK claiming the protection of European law over UK law.

Similarly, the character of government decisions has changed. In fields of EU competence, ministers now decide not what will happen, but what they will urge the EU Council of Ministers to agree. For example, the government used to decide annually on farm prices. Today it can only agree a negotiating position to be adopted by its minister in Brussels. Admittedly, while in one sense this restricts the autonomous sovereignty of the British polity, in another but vaguer sense it extends it, since Britain can now, via the EU, influence the law operating in other countries; for example, to stop French and Italian hunters from shooting migratory birds. For present purposes, however, the fact is that the much-vaunted principle of the sovereignty of the UK Parliament has been infringed – a truth that British politicians are most unwilling to admit.

A further constitutional problem is that, because ministers no longer take decisions but participate in meetings of the Council of Ministers (which meets in private), it is difficult to hold them politically accountable for the final decision. The minister can claim that a decision was not his fault, because EU colleagues overruled him. This was, for example, the defence of British agriculture ministers in the early 1990s when they were criticized for failing to secure tighter controls on the conditions in which animals are transported across Europe.

The Problem of Political Accountability

This last point brings us to another major constitutional question that underlies post-1945 constitutional development: the accountability of the executive to the legislature. As the span of government activity grew, it obviously became more difficult for ministers to be accountable to Parliament for everything done in their name.

Accountability can mean two things: one, being answerable for decisions, and two, if they are unpopular, being punished for them. The first type of accountability has grown stronger, the second weaker. As mentioned above, Parliament has become, if anything, more effective as a scrutineer of government action. This has been supplemented by, and probably reinforced by, the far more assertive and inquisitorial role of the news media. In the 1940s and 1950s, journalists were deferential to politicians to an extent quite unbelievable today. The development of a more critical and searching form of journalism has forced ministers to work harder to justify their policies to the public. In this sense, ministers are more 'answerable'.

But they are less easy to punish if things go wrong. Here the core question is: to what extent are ministers responsible for the acts of their officials? In 1954, the great constitutional panjandrum Sir Ivor Jennings was happy to recite the doctrine – hallowed since at least Victorian times – that the minister alone was responsible to Parliament for all acts by officials within his department.[19] Coincidentally, in the same year a crisis blew up over the Ministry of Agriculture's use of land at Crichel Down in Dorset. Land acquired compulsorily during the war, instead of being returned to its original owner, was instead used for experimental agriculture. There was a row, the minister resigned, and several officials were punished. Much legend surrounds this episode: myth holds that the minister resigned as a scapegoat for his officials' actions, whereas he actually tried to reassure the Commons that he had smoothed it all over, and only resigned when Tory backbenchers reacted with fury. And in a subsequent debate the Home Secretary, David Maxwell-Fyfe, promulgated the famous rules that bear his name, which effectively hold that a minister is responsible for decisions that he has taken or which flow from his policy, but not for misdeeds of which he is ignorant.[20]

The trouble is that ministers seem to have been reluctant to accept even this restricted notion of responsibility. In 1981 Lord Carrington resigned over the Falklands invasion, but principally because he felt that Britain could not fight a war with a Foreign Secretary under criticism – and he was cleared by the subsequent Franks enquiry. More serious was the series of prison escapes in the 1990s in which Home Secretaries – first Kenneth Baker, then Michael Howard – refused to accept responsibility for what they claimed were 'operational' matters, even when it became clear that they had themselves been involved in detail in operational decisions. Instead they blamed officials, and Howard sacked the chief executive of the Prison Service, who promptly sued, forcing the government to settle out of court. The position in law may be clear – ministers, not civil servants, are accountable to Parliament – but something has gone adrift in practice.

The whole question of the political neutrality of the civil service is dealt with in more detail by Keith Dowding's chapter 9 in this volume. Here I will simply flag the constitutional headline: that the traditionally anonymous civil service is becoming more visible. As early as 1949, the sagacious Mackenzie observed that because the Estimates Committee called evidence from civil servants, and not just ministers,

> The House has virtually admitted that, though in principle the minister is responsible for every action of his department, however small, and must be prepared to defend it, in actual practice the work of the department is the work of his permanent officers and they, as the real authors of administrative decisions, are in the best position to explain them.[21]

Officials now speak to public audiences, and their names and telephone numbers are published in the *Civil Service Yearbook*. Most significant, the hiving off of government activities into 'executive agencies' has made their chief executives responsible *de facto* when something goes wrong. When the ill-fated

Child Support Agency attracted criticism in the 1990s, it was the chief executive, not the minister, who was forced to resign. Fifty years on, the strains are
showing.[22]

Conclusion

Post-war constitutional development has been very British: incremental, pragmatic, and unphilosophical. The mildly reformist, episodic history of the period
1945–79 was consistent with this. The aberration was the attempt in 1979–87
to slam on the lid and prevent any change at all. At any time this would have
been difficult; given near-irresistible pressure for Scottish devolution, it dammed
up the pressure, providing by the mid-1990s a politically attractive issue for the
Opposition to exploit. Yet Labour's constitutional revolution is operating essentially within the traditional constitutional framework. The British constitution
is rather like an ancient building of which parts have been demolished, others
remodelled, and new sections added until it has become an eclectic and even
bewildering mix – which, however, remains fairly serviceable as a place to live.

Notes

1 P. Bromhead, *The House of Lords in Contemporary Politics*, London, 1958.
2 See P. Anderson and N. Mann, *Safety First: the Making of New Labour*, London,
   1997, ch. 8.
3 P. Hennessy, *The Hidden Wiring: Unearthing the British Constitution*, revised ed.,
   London, 1996.
4 P. Silk and R. Walters, *How Parliament Works*, 4th ed., London, 1998, p.11.
5 Peter Riddell, *Parliament Under Pressure*, London, 1998.
6 A. Mitchell, 'Consulting the Workers: MPs on Their Job', *The Parliamentarian*,
   January 1985.
7 M. Ryle, 'The Changing Commons', in F. F. Ridley and M. Rush (eds), *British
   Government and Politics since 1945: Changes in Perspective*, London, 1995, p. 652.
   See also Public Information Note 46, from the House of Commons Public Information Office, 1997.
8 Both detailed in S. James, *British Government: A Reader in Policy-Making*, London,
   1997.
9 See J. Garrett, *Does Parliament Work?*, London, 1992, ch. 4; G. Drewry, *The New
   Select Committees*, 2nd ed., Oxford, 1989.
10 M. Ryle, 'The Changing Commons', p. 648.
11 Select Committee on Procedure (Supply), 1st Report Session 1982–3, HC 118.
12 For a critical history of this deficiency see J. Garrett, *Does Parliament Work?*, esp.
   ch. 5.
13 *The Statutory Rules and Orders and Statutory Instruments*. Revised to December
   1949. London, HMSO, 1951.
14 K. Mackenzie, *The English Parliament*, London, 1950, pp. 201–3.
15 House of Commons Information Office, Factsheet No. 56: The House of Commons
   and European Legislation, 1994.
16 A. Mitchell MP, 'The Constituency Role of MPs', in Ridley and Rush, *British Government*, p. 711.

17 Derived from Written Answer in Lords, *Hansard*, 16 October 1995, col. 90.
18 For Britain's entry to and relations with the EC, see Jonathan Hollowell's chapter 4 in this volume.
19 Sir Ivor Jennings, *The Queen's Government*, London, 1954, pp. 108–13.
20 House of Commons Debates 20 July 1954, especially cols, 1286–7.
21 Mackenzie, *English Parliament*, pp. 199–200.
22 For a detailed study of this subject, see D. Woodhouse, *Ministers and Parliament: Accountability in Theory and Practice*, Oxford, 1994.

Further Reading

An admirable if polemical book on the British constitution and its problems, with sections on all the main institutions, is Ferdinand Mount's *The British Constitution Now* (London, 1993) – lively, scholarly and readable. The collection of essays edited by F. Ridley and M. Rush, *British Government and Politics since 1945: Changes in Perspective* (London, 0000), covers many of the themes treated above. In a more academic mould are Vernon Bogdanor's *Power and the People: A Guide to Constitutional Reform* (London, 1997) and Rodney Brazier's *Constitutional Reform* (Oxford, 1998). Anything by the Constitution Unit at University College London is worth reading, particularly 'Constitutional Futures' edited by Robert Hazell (Oxford University Press, 1999); their website at http://www.ucl.ac.uk/constitution-unit/ is always worth a browse.

On the monarchy, Bogdanor's *The Monarchy and the Constitution* (Oxford, 1995) is a pretty definitive study, and the opening chapters of Peter Hennessy's *The Hidden Wiring: Unearthing the British Constitution* (revised ed., London, 1996) are an excellent study of the monarch's reserve powers and the use of her advisory powers.

On Parliament, an admirable comprehensive introduction is the fourth edition of P. Silk and R. Walters, *How Parliament Works* (London, 1988). Do not be put off by the fact that the authors are parliamentary administrators: they write with a light touch and know their subject backwards. The established expert on Parliament is Phillip Norton, who now himself sports a peerage: start with his *Does Parliament Matter?* (London, 1993). There are plenty of 'reformist' tracts by academics and MPs: I recommend the one by J. Garrett, a management consultant turned MP who offers a comprehensive programme of reform – *Does Parliament Work?* (London, 1992).

On central government, I immodestly offer my own *British Cabinet Government* (2nd ed., London, 1999) as a student's best guide to the Prime Minister and Cabinet. For historical studies of the premiership, see James Barber, *The British Prime Minister since 1945* (Oxford, 1991). A fuller study by Peter Hennessy is imminent.

Additional suggestions for reading will be found in later chapters in this volume, notably those on the EU (4), Scotland (5), Wales (6), Northern Ireland (7), the civil service (9) and local government (10).

Chronology

1948 Business and university franchise abolished.
1949 Parliament Act, reducing delaying powers of the House of Lords.
1958 Legislation introduces life peers to House of Lords and allows female hereditary peers to take their seats.

1963	Peerage Act allows peers to renounce seats in Lords.
1967	Ombudsman created.
1969	Government legislation to transform Lords into an entirely nominated and salaried body abandoned after strong backbench opposition.
1972	European Communities Act. Northern Ireland Parliament suspended.
1974	Northern Ireland Assembly and power-sharing executive established, but brought down by Unionist strike.
1975	Referendum approves continued membership of EC. Legislation for devolution to Scotland and Wales introduced.
1977	Commons rejects proportional representation for European Parliament.
1978	Commons adds requirement for referenda in Scotland and Wales before devolution is implemented and imposes requirement that 40 per cent of electorate must vote in favour.
1979	Devolution heavily defeated in Welsh referendum and fails to reach 40 per cent threshold in Scotland. After general election, Thatcher government creates the modern system of select committees.
1982	New Northern Ireland Assembly elected; gets nowhere and is eventually dissolved.
1984–6	Legislation to abolish GLC and metropolitan councils extensively amended by House of Lords. Commons defeats Shops Bill at second reading.
1991	Parliament Act invoked to overrule Lords' rejection of War Crimes Bill.
1992	Government publishes *Questions of Procedure for Ministers* and details of Cabinet Committees.
1997	Labour government returned with extensive commitment to constitutional reform. Human Rights Act incorporates European Convention on Human Rights into UK law.
1998	Good Friday Agreement in Northern Ireland, approved by referendum. Legislation to implement it immediately passed; elections to Northern Ireland Assembly. Acts passed to introduce devolution to Scotland and Wales, Regional Development Agencies in England, and proportional representation by list system for European Parliament. Government publishes proposals for freedom of information. Referendum in London approves plans for a directly elected mayor and Assembly.
1999	Parliament Act invoked to overrule Lords' rejection of proportional representation by list system for elections to European Parliament; first such elections held (June). First elections by proportional representation to Scottish Parliament and Welsh Assembly lead to no overall majority in either.

3 The Political Parties

Alan Sked

The history of Britain's political parties since 1945 has been one of consensus.[1] The famous 'post-war consensus', based on a mixed economy, the welfare state, Keynesian economic policy and economic corporatism in domestic affairs was complemented by a consensus over foreign policy that included support for the North Atlantic Treaty Organization (NATO), a special relationship with the United States, the peaceful transformation of empire into Commonwealth, an independent nuclear deterrent, and – eventually – membership of the EEC/EC/EU.[2] Around the middle of the 1970s this consensus came under strain, but with the Thatcher era a new consensus emerged based on free-market economics, the privatisation of the nationalised industries and the abandonment of corporatism and Keynesianism. In foreign affairs the consensus over NATO and the Comonwealth survived, as did support for an independent nuclear deterrent and the special relationship with the United States. The relationship with the EC after the fall of Mrs Thatcher, on the other hand, became much more controversial.

For most of the period after 1945 Britain also witnessed the operation of a 'two-party system', insofar as the first-past-the post electoral system made it very difficult for third parties to win seats, far less elections. No voter could doubt that *only* the Conservative Party or the Labour Party would form a government after each general election. In most cases the winning party would also be sure of a working majority, although the results were very close in 1950, 1964, 1974 (after both elections that year) and even 1992. From the 1960s onwards there were a series of 'Liberal revivals', but the two-party system was only seriously challenged with the formation of the Social Democratic Party (SDP) in 1981 following the split within the Labour Party. Thereafter the electoral alliance of the SDP and the Liberals, culminating in the formation of the Liberal Democratic Party in 1988, kept the threat to the two-party system alive. This threat was strengthened by the growth in political support for the Welsh and Scottish Nationalist Parties (particularly the latter), especially after the general election of 1997 which saw the Conservative Party lose all its parliamentary seats in Scotland and Wales. Despite that, the 1997 general election did not provide evidence that the two-party system in England was about to end. In Scotland and Wales, on the other hand, after the first elections for the new Assemblies/Parliaments there, it looks as if *new* two-party systems could emerge, based on the Labour Party and the local Nationalists.

If the history of British political parties during this period began and ended with huge Labour parliamentary majorities after landslide election victories in 1945 and 1997, this should not obscure the fact that the party in power for most of the time was the Conservative Party. Labour, in fact, was out of office from 1951 to 1964; from 1970 to 1974 and from 1979 to 1997; i.e. in the 55 years from 1945 to 2000, Labour has been in power for only 20, the Tories, 35. Indeed, until Blair's massive victory in 1997, Labour was experiencing longer and longer periods out of office as the century wore on: 1931–40; 1951–64; 1979–97. The twentieth century may not have ended as a Tory one in Britain, but there can be little doubt that, politically, it was dominated overwhelmingly by the Conservative Party.

Indeed, Tony Blair seems determined to obliterate the legacy of his predecessors as Labour leader by referring constantly to his party as 'New Labour' and hinting that he is the heir to Mrs Thatcher rather than to Mr Callaghan. His aim seems to be to create a political alliance of the centre-right, based on New Labour, but absorbing the Liberal Democrats and pro-European Tories, allowing the rest of the Tory Party to follow the trade unions into the political wilderness. His main weapon in this plan may yet turn out to be the electoral system. Whether he will emerge as the agent of permanent political change or whether – like Attlee or Wilson – he will do little in the long term to undermine Tory dominance, despite a landslide election victory, remains to be seen. Events – as Harold Macmillan famously complained – can alter the best-laid plans, so that developments in Northern Ireland, Scotland, Wales, Europe and, not least, the Balkans, will be eagerly followed by all those critical of the New Labour Prime Minister's progress. On the other hand, events could make him the first President of a United States of Europe, given his continued political popularity and the lack of any obvious charismatic European rival, should he decide, as seems likely, to back the case for European union.

The interpretation of post-war British politics as a period of a developing and therefore changing consensus has not been universally accepted; nonetheless, it seems difficult to refute. After the war the consensus was based primarily on Keynesian economics, the mixed economy and the welfare state, all supervised by a system of political cooperation between the political parties, the leaders of industry and the trade unions. This cooperation, or corporatism, as some would have it, never approached the degree of institutionalisation, say, of the *Sozialpartnerschaft* of post-war Austria,[3] but it was certainly one of the unspoken assumptions of British politics that, given the record of trade union cooperation during the Second World War – or myth of trade union cooperation, if Correlli Barnett[4] is to be believed – governments should not go out of their way to upset the trade unions. In any case, the post-war consensus was being laid down by a Labour government, one of whose leading members, the Foreign Secretary, Ernest Bevin, was the country's most distinguished trade unionist; while it was the trade unionists inside the party that controlled both Labour's finances and the block votes at the Labour Party Conference. Sir Winston Churchill, the Tory leader, was also determined to befriend the unions after his return to power in 1951, and all governments between the early 1960s and 1979 felt compelled to draw the trade unions into official structures of one kind or another in order to secure their agreement to incomes (often prices and incomes) policies designed to combat inflation or balance of payments crises or, more usually, both.

These institutional innovations were a consequence of the belief that the government had a duty to 'manage the economy', something which was based on so-called 'Keynesian' economics, although whether Keynes himself would have believed in boosting demand in an inflationary economic environment has been doubted by his distinguished biographer, Robert Skidelsky.[5] In any case, in the age of 'Butskellism' – the term coined by *The Economist* to describe the indistinguishable policies of the Labour and Tory Parties by the 1950s, both parties convinced themselves that they were being faithful to Keynes's theories of demand management. Indeed, Butler himself wrote of Gaitskell: 'We both spoke the language of Keynes but with different accents.'[6]

Keynes's greatest treatise on economics was his work of 1936 *General Theory of Employment*. In this he argued, as opposed to the economic orthodoxy current at the time, the primacy of *demand* over *supply*. (Mrs Thatcher's later supporters would be known, significantly, as *supply-siders*.) Instead of reacting to unemployment by using the traditional remedy of deflation, Keynes argued that unemployment was more likely to be cured if the governments pumped more money into the economy, thus allowing people to buy goods and create jobs. Deflation, on the other hand, by reducing government expenditure and raising interest rates and taxes, merely added to the numbers of the un-employed. Keynes, almost certainly, believed that he had found the key to curing unemployment at a time of falling prices and reduced demand. The trouble was that after the war, under very different economic circumstances, this remained the key, if not the magic wand, for governments facing economic difficulties at times when demand was growing and prices were rising. Yet both major parties stuck to the Keynesian formula like glue, with Harold Macmillan, for example, sacking his whole Treasury team in 1958 when his Chancellor, Peter Thorneycroft, demanded expenditure cuts. Macmillan dismissed their op-position as 'a little local difficulty'.

In contrast to Peter Thorneycroft, Enoch Powell and Nigel Fisher – Macmil-lan's Treasury team – Tory Keynesians believed that high public expenditure would get them out of economic difficulties. Reginald Maudling attempted to do this before the 1964 election, creating instead a huge balance of payments problem – the reverberations of which were to necessitate a devaluation of the pound in 1967 – while Anthony Barber, Chancellor in Edward Heath's disas-trous government of 1970–4, reacted to a million unemployed in 1971 by insti-tuting the 'Barber boom', with equally unpleasant results, most notably a huge surge in inflation, something which was exacerbated in turn by the Organiza-tion of Petroleum-Exporting Countries (OPEC) price rise of 1973 and other international factors.

Adherence to Keynesian nostrums, however, brought not merely a predisposition to high public expenditure, but also an assumption that governments had the ability to 'manage the economy', 'go for growth' or 'sustain' or 'create demand' by direct intervention. The idea that the economy might get along better by itself without such government action, or indeed, the realisation that government information might simply be too inaccurate, out of date, or incomplete to constitute the basis for rational policy, was something that never seemed to engage the minds of public policy-makers, whether in government or in the civil service. Their desire to do good overwhelmed whatever difficulties their goodness encountered.

The need to do good, of course, was felt by everyone. Just in case it was not, the need to share responsibility for policies that might go wrong was certainly felt by governments. This need to avoid rocking the boat then led to forms of corporatism that became more and more complicated over time. It all began in 1961, however, with the establishment of the NEDC, or National Economic Development Council, presided over by the Chancellor of the Exchequer, at which representatives of government, industry and the trade unions reviewed the problems of the economy. In 1964 Labour then set up the Department of Economic Affairs, with the task of 'planning the economy', using the techniques of 'indicative planning' supposedly employed with great success by the then highly intellectually fashionable *Commissariat Général du Plan* in France. Eventually a series of targets were set, but the whole venture was such an embarrassing exercise in make-believe that it was soon consigned to oblivion. Corporatism, therefore, quickly degenerated into a desperate attempt to get the trade unions in an inflationary age to rein in their pay demands. This process became known as 'having an incomes policy' and began under the Tories in 1962 with the setting up of the National Incomes Commission. It continued under Labour after 1964 with the National Board for Prices and Incomes and then, under the Tories again, after 1972, with the Pay Board. By now, however, true corporatism – or true blue corporatism, one might say – had broken down with the trade union revolt against Heath's Industrial Court and other legislative initiatives taken to counter trade union power. Yet Labour, having dismantled Heath's stillborn reforms, themselves became a victim of the trade unions. The final example of government desperation to secure a public agreement on incomes policy was the 'social contract' of 1975–9, which only undermined credibility in the economy and led to the International Monetary fund (IMF) taking control in 1976. The end result was another trade union revolt, the 'winter of discontent', and Mrs Thatcher's resounding victory at the 1979 election with a mandate to sort out the trade union barons. By now, therefore, at least one part of the consensus had collapsed.

The most obvious form of post-war direct government intervention in the economy, of course, was the nationalisation of about 20 per cent of the British economic base after the Second World War. In 1946 the Bank of England, the coal industry and civil aviation were nationalised; 1947 saw the railways and gas join the list; iron and steel followed in 1949; while most of Britain's hospitals were nationalised in 1946 when the National Health Service (NHS) was created. The Tories offered little opposition after their 1945 election defeat: the

NHS was not opposed on principle but over a number of practical matters (e.g. the status of doctors; in fact, real opposition was left to the British Medical Association), while only the nationalisation of the steel industry (still profitable) roused real resentment from Conservative spokesmen. In fact, if Labour had been in power ten years earlier, the list would have been a great deal longer, the Labour Party's 1934 programme entitled *For Socialism and Peace*, for example, having called for the nationalisation of banking and credit, transport, fuel and power, agriculture, iron and steel, shipping, textiles, chemicals and insurance. It had also promised employees 'the right acknowledged in law to an effective share in control and direction of industry'. The programme had been modified after the 1935 election and, after the war, was modified further.

One reason was that, although Labour had talked a great deal about nationalisation, it had never bothered to plan in any detail exactly what the concept would mean if and when it was ever implemented. In the end no experiments in workers' control or shareholding were tried and models such as the pre-war BBC, the Port of London Authority, the London Passenger Transport Board the Central Electricity Generating Board were utilised to run the new industries. The result was that ownership of the nationalised industries was simply taken over by the State which set up boards of the good and the great (including ennobled trade union leaders) to supervise the largely loss-making activities of the managers and workers whose lives remained unchanged by the legislation. Certainly, the workers received no new powers under the State's dispensation, and management structures remained the same.

As early as the 1950s, therefore, nationalisation was seen as a failure, since quite clearly the only beneficiaries from the process had been the owners of the dud companies which had been taken over, capitalists, who could now invest the money they had been paid as compensation in profitable enterprises. Workers naturally became very cynical about nationalisation as a tool for change, since as far as they could see, nothing had changed. The Labour Party, out of loyalty to old ideals, nonetheless insisted on including token nationalisation proposals in its election manifestos, and Harold Wilson, after 1964, did renationalise the steel industry which the Tories had denationalised. This was a symbolic gesture, however, despite the fact that Labour's 1959 general election manifesto had promised to nationalise industries 'which failed the nation'. After all, in terms of efficiency and profitability, all nationalised industries failed the nation.

By the 1950s, as the American economist John Kenneth Galbraith pointed out, it was less the owners than the managers of industry who determined the profitability of a company. This insight was adopted by the Labour intellectual Anthony Crosland in his influential book of 1956, *The Future of Socialism*, which argued that socialism had much more to do with equality and moral solidarity between the classes than with the nationalisation of industry. Nationalisation, nonetheless, had led to what was known as the 'mixed economy', which was part of the Keynesian consensus. It was, after all, a monument to government intervention based on a motive of improvement and social solidarity and therefore fitted the post-war consensus. The Tories, for their part, provided little theoretical opposition. Indeed, Anthony Eden could state in 1947:

'we are not a party of unbridled capitalism and never have been...we are not the political children of the *laissez-faire school*. We opposed them decade after decade.'[7] Quintin Hogg averred: 'Modern Conservatism inherits the traditions of Toryism which are favourable to the activity and authority of the state.'[8] Thus, although the steel industry was denationalised by the Tories after their return to power in 1951, Edward Heath, despite much *laissez-faire* rhetoric before the 1970 election, in 1971 saved both Rolls-Royce and the Upper Clyde Shipyard from looming bankruptcy by taking both into public ownership. And even today politicians can always be found clamouring, if not for the public ownership of, at least for government subsidies for, local firms that are in danger of going under. Today, of course, inward investors are also given massive public subsidies to attract them, something which arouses no public debate.

Full-scale nationalisation, on the other hand, became an embarrassment for Labour during the 1950s when it lost three general elections in a row. Clause Four of Labour's 1918 constitution seemed to call for the nationalisation of all British industry (at the very least, 'the means of production, distribution and exchange') and was held by Hugh Gaitskell, the party's leader, to be a vote loser. However, he failed to get the party to drop it after its 1959 defeat and it was left to Tony Blair to replace it after his election landslide in 1997 with a new Clause Four that committed the party to work for 'a dynamic economy...enterprise of the market...the rigour of competition...a just society' – and 'an open democracy'.[9] This change was endorsed by the party as a whole.

The other obvious manifestation of government intervention was of course the welfare state, founded on these two solid pillars of post-war Labour legislation: the National Insurance Act and the National Health Service Act of 1946, which constituted Labour's response to the Beveridge Report of 1942.[10] Thereafter, Britons enjoyed health care, free at the point of use, not to mention an ever-growing array of social benefits and services. Today, contributory benefits include old-age pensions, invalidity and unemployment benefit, with a cost to the taxpayer of £40 billion annually; income-related benefits include income support, housing/council tax benefits, family credit and others costing £27 billion annually; while non-contributory benefits include child benefit, disability, attendance and care allowances and cost £13 billion annually. The overall cost of social welfare is approaching £100 billion annually. In 1960 the share of GDP devoted to social expenditure was 13.9 per cent; in 1970, it was 18.6 per cent; and in 1980, 22.1 per cent. Of the welfare state, Julian Le Grand has written: 'For many people it was the crowning achievement of the post-war consensus: a public edifice constructed through the efforts of altruistic people to help the disadvantaged and promote social justice.'[11] Moreover, it seemed to work. Before 1979, the homeless were given homes; the number of overcrowded homes fell; and the percentage increases in numbers of hospital doctors, consultants, nurses, midwives, general practitioners and health visitors between 1950 and 1980 were 146, 218, 116, 88, 26 and 288, respectively. People assumed that public welfare was economically useful; better-educated people were more likely to perform better in industry than ill-educated ones; education would reduce resistance to new ideas and improve information and choice; increased education would lead to a more rational labour market and would allow workers to master more complicated technology. The case for a healthy workforce seemed self-evident.

There were also arguments that by taking care of the elderly and the very young, the sick and others, public services, by replacing the extended family, would make more adults available for employment, particularly women, who had traditionally been limited to household work and raising families. By providing minimum standards of living, it was also argued that social services would reduce public apathy and dejection and thus maintain the will to work. In a more positive way, by raising public expectations, social services might reinforce, for better or worse, the general belief that economic growth was and must remain a paramount objective of any government. (This indeed, had been one of Crosland's main points, i.e. that higher standards of welfare provision required continuous economic growth.)

For a long time, therefore, the welfare state remained an object of political veneration. Nor was it seen in any way as a challenge to the work ethic. Reviews in 1951, 1956, 1958, 1961 and 1964 by the National Assistance Board found no evidence of work-shyness. A report by the Supplementary Benefits Commission in 1978 concluded:

> the proportion of unemployed who actually get more money in benefit than in work is very small. They are mainly men in the early months of unemployment for whom higher unemployment benefits have been deliberately designed and when the disincentive effect seems very small anyway; or men on supplementary benefit with low earnings potential and large families.[12]

In November 1979 the Labour MP, Frank Field, claimed that benefit fraud amounted to only 0.273 per cent of all claims and 0.027 per cent of all expenditure. Research on earnings-related benefits and family income supplements during the 1980s also failed to find any disincentive effects.

The Tories were only too happy to agree. In the years after 1945, as Peter Lilley would point out in 1999, government spending on health rose by 4 per cent per annum under the Tories and only by 3.2 per cent under Labour. The Tories pointed to Disraeli and 'the politics of sewage', to the social reforms of the 1930s under the National Government, while Churchill gave Harold Macmillan the daunting task, which he successfully completed in 1953, of building over 300,000 council houses a year. Mrs Thatcher, despite her supposed opposition to welfare spending, presided over the largest welfare budget in history, and when she left office the percentage of GDP taken by the state was higher than it had been under Callaghan. She never ceased proclaiming that the 'National Health Service is safe in our hands', although towards the end of her premiership she did introduce reforms into it which were seen by many, rightly or wrongly, as paving the way for privatisation. Whatever Thatcher's real intentions towards the NHS may have been, the popular appeal of high state spending on social services remained strong. Thus an opinion poll carried out as late as 19 May 1996 for the *Sunday Times* discovered that 36 per cent of the population wanted higher benefits still, while 26 per cent were satisfied with current levels and only 18 per cent favoured radical cuts. Moreover, 68 per cent were opposed to replacing the state old-age pension with private schemes. After their general election defeat of 1997 the Tories seemed in no mood to disagree. On 20 April 1999 Peter Lilley, the deputy Leader of the Tory Party, explained to the party faithful in his Butler lecture that in order to prove its commitment to the welfare state, the party had to accept that private enterprise had only a limited role to play in health and education.

Some critics have argued that there was no consensus – that in the 1950s class voting was at its height,[13] that there was great controversy over the creation of the NHS[14] and that on the right wing of the Tory Party and on the Labour left there were many who opposed consensus politics with vigour. None of these arguments carries much weight, however; no one is suggesting that the consensus was monolithic or that class voting did not exist or that the NHS was not highly controversial when it was introduced. The point is that governments in power after the war pursued the same type of policies and accepted most of what their predecessors had. Again, others have argued that the consensus actually began during the war itself or indeed even before it.[15] This seems more convincing as a criticism, but does not actually refute the idea that the post-war years were indeed ones of consensus.

It should be remembered that consensus also involved foreign affairs. NATO soon became the sheet anchor of British foreign policy in the era of the Cold War and it was taken for granted that a 'special relationship' existed with the United States. Decolonisation went ahead under the Tories (indeed, at phenomenal speed under Macmillan) and Labour refused to decommission Britain's Polaris submarines after coming into office in 1964. In fact, under Labour they were technologically upgraded under the Chevaline programme of 1974. It was left to the Tories in 1980, however, to announce that Britain would buy Trident nuclear missiles from the USA as replacements for Polaris. Yet Labour, in office again in 1997, accepted this without demur. There were times when Labour departed from the consensus in opposition – opposing nuclear weapons briefly in 1960 and again in the 1980s or advocating withdrawal from the EC under Foot and Kinnock. This departure from the consensus, however, only made the party unelectable. The result was that Kinnock abandoned these polices and eventually ended up as EU Transport Commissioner. Mrs Thatcher's growing opposition to the EC meanwhile helped bring about her political downfall, split her party, and defeat it in the 1997 general election.

The consensus over foreign policy, therefore, was not only fairly apparent but popularly supported. As early as the 1950s, for example, one satirist had written:

> The Bevin or the Churchill touch
> Seem both alike to Danes and Dutch;
> If Socialist or Tory speaks,
> It's all the same to French and Greeks.[16]

Meanwhile, in 1953, Edward Hyams had written a novel, entitled *Gentian Violet*, in which the hero managed to get elected to Parliament as both a Labour and Tory MP without anyone noticing. By the 1970s, on the other hand, the consensus was under strain. Nationalisation was no longer part of it. The mixed economy no longer seemed a blessing since, economically, Britain was seen as 'the sick man of Europe'. Corporatism had broken down under the strain of trade union militancy and the welfare state was absorbing so much of the country's economic resources that the budget seemed out of control. In 1976 the IMF had to be called in to bail out the Labour government and the package of measures it dictated to the Prime Minister, James Callaghan, and the Chancellor, Denis Healey, made clear that government spending would have to be radically cut. In the words of one minister: 'the party [was] over'.[17] Callaghan himself told Labour Party activists at their 1976 party conference:

> We used to think you could spend your way out of recession and increase employment by boosting government spending. [Unemployment had risen from 1 per cent in the early 1960s to 4 per cent of the labour force by 1976.] ... that option no longer exists, and insofar as it ever did exist, it only worked on each occasion since the war by injecting a bigger dose of inflation into the economy, followed by a higher level of unemployment as the next step.[18]

Healey, instead, under IMF supervision, brought in expenditure cuts as well as monetary targets, now used for the first time since the war as an instrument of economic policy. Indeed, Tony Benn was later to condemn Healey as the first and most effective monetarist Chancellor. The Keynesian, high tax-and-spend, interventionist attitude to the economy was therefore also clearly breaking down by the mid-1970s.

The economic failures of the 1960s and 1970s – growing unemployment, rising inflation, balance of payments crises, the 1967 devaluation and the 1976 IMF crisis – had forced almost everyone interested in the fate of the country to re-examine the assumptions behind the consensus. The behaviour of the trade unions – now largely seen as the main cause of 'Britain's relative decline' – also helped the process. Their refusal to co-operate with Wilson's *In Place of Strife* proposals of 1969; their opposition to Heath's industrial courts and other pieces of legislation designed to bring them within the law; Arthur Scargill's emergence as a would-be maker and breaker of governments after the miners' strikes of 1972 and 1974; and, finally, the 'winter of discontent' of 1978–9 which completely undermined the Callaghan government, meant that Thatcher could campaign openly against them in the general election of 1979 and succeed in winning a mandate to reform them and to sort out the economy.

Did Thatcher's election victory, therefore, mark some kind of political revolution? This was certainly thought so at the time and for several years afterwards, as the country adjusted to the sheer force of her personality. Many of the first books written about her either explicitly announced the 'end of consensus' or raised it as an issue.[19] Peter Jenkins entitled his book *Mrs Thatcher's Revolution;* John Cole's study had the title *The Thatcher Years: A Decade of Revolution;* while Dennis Kavanagh's *Thatcherism and British Politics* was subtitled *The End of Consensus?* There was certainly reason to believe that the new government would pursue a different course, under the influence of free-market think-tanks like the IEA (the Institute of Economic Affairs, established and run by Arthur Seldon and Ralph Harris) and the CPS (the Centre for Policy Studies, founded by Thatcher's intellectual mentor and Tory colleague, Sir Keith Joseph, and Alfred Sherman). Indeed, Thatcher's election as leader of the Tory Party in 1975 was self-evidently a repudiation by the Conservative Party of Heath's legacy of U-turns and of his failure to tame the trade unions and inflation. The Tory policy document of 1976 entitled *The Right Approach* therefore emphasised supply-side economics, the free market, and the need for private enterprise. The need for a sound monetarist policy was also stressed. Here the influence of Milton Friedman, the American economist who saw the money supply as the key to inflation, was apparent. Friedman argued that inflation was caused by a surplus of money in the economy and advocated restricting the money supply as the means of containing it. The means of doing this was to set monetary targets and to stick to them. (The difficulty, of course, was how to measure the money supply.) Friedmanism, however, seemed to undermine the very basis of post-war economic policy, based as it had been on increased growth and increased government spending as the means to create jobs and to bankroll the welfare state. Friedman, on the other hand, argued that workers merely 'priced themselves out of jobs' if their pay rises caused inflation and undermined competitiveness.

The New Right, as those Conservatives who upheld such theories came to be labelled collectively, also stressed the need for individual liberty under a strong framework of law. Much of this kind of thinking was due to the influence of the Austrian philosopher, Friedrich Hayek, whose seminal work, *The Road to Serfdom*, had been published as long back as 1944. Hayek preached that the state should provide merely an impartial legal framework for its citizens, who should be accorded the greatest possible liberty to order their own lives. If it tried to control industry and welfare, it would end up making them socially and economically dependent on bureaucrats and government handouts. This was the road to serfdom. Instead, the policies to be pursued were those that stimulated self-reliance, independence and private enterprise, virtues which Mrs Thatcher herself had learned from her father while working in his grocery shop in Grantham.

These ideas undoubtedly influenced the legislative record of the Thatcher years, whose main policies – trade union reforms, privatisation of the nationalised industries, income tax and corporation tax cuts, the setting of monetary targets, the sale of council houses and the creation of a 'property-owning democracy', the creation of an internal market in the NHS, the linking of state pensions to rises in the cost of living rather than the average wage, and even the ill-fated poll tax – all reflected them. Still, Thatcher had her critics inside the Tory Party ranging from Ian Gilmour, on the left, who argued that without support from the state, citizens would end up losing any loyalty to it, through pragmatists in the centre who, like Burke in the 1790s, feared that the pursuit of any ideologically oriented policy would threaten the organic development of society, to those on the right, like Roger Scruton, John Casey and Peregrine Worsthorne, who believed that the real task of conservatism in the 1980s was to restore the authority of government after the chaos of the 1970s (strikes, inflation, economic failure) caused principally by the trade unions. In Worsthorne's words, the main priority was 'for the state to regain control over the people, to re-exert its authority, and it is useless to imagine that this will be helped by some libertarian mish-mash drawn from the writings of Adam Smith and John Stuart Mill'.[20]

In the end, Thatcher's record was not merely one of a reformed economy but of a stronger state. Local government, doctors and hospitals, universities, schools, the legal profession and even the police were subjected to unprecedented government inspection and control, while Arthur Scargill's miners – 'the enemy within' in Thatcher's revealing phrase – were defeated in the Armageddon of the miners' strike of 1984–5 which spelled the end of the trade union movement as an influence on British government. Little wonder that one influential analysis of the Thatcher era was entitled *The Free Economy and Strong State*.[21]

Thatcher herself always condemned the idea of consensus, declaring that instead she was a 'conviction politician' whose task was to lead rather than follow. On the other hand, she owed her election victory in 1979 to the shifting consensus of the 1970s: the growing feeling that the trade unions had become selfish and dangerous; the lack of faith in Keynesianism to cure inflation or unemployment; the realisation that change was necessary. Her own policies, although always controversial, consolidated this shift in the consensus, if and when they were seen to work. In a sense she both reacted to a changing consensus and created a new one. The twin proofs of this were, first, her series of election victories – all of them with sound majorities – and secondly, the changes that occurred within the Labour Party, which by 1997 was campaigning under the title New Labour. For it, too, had had to adjust to the changing consensus.

This was a painful process, since in the aftermath of Thatcher's 1979 election victory the party leadership had gone to the old warhorse of the Labour left, Michael Foot, who was a passionate believer in unilateral nuclear disarmament. The party's constitution had also been changed to allow for the reselection of MPs between elections by party constituency activists and for the leader and deputy leader to be elected by an electoral college voting system that gave 40 per cent of the vote to the trade unions and only 30 per cent each to party members and MPs. In 1981, therefore, the party split, with David Owen, Shirley Williams, Roy Jenkins and Bill Rodgers, 'the gang of four', forming a new Social Democratic Party (SDP), which was soon able to challenge Labour in the polls. Labour, however, did its best to undermine its own position by breaking with the new consensus. Its 1983 election manifesto – dubbed by Gerald Kaufman the 'longest suicide note in history' – advocated withdrawal from NATO and the EC, a huge increase in public ownership, and Britain's economic isolation behind a tariff wall, as part of its 'New Economic Strategy' (the brainchild of Stuart Holland, MP). The result was the electoral disaster of 1983 when it took merely 28 per cent of the vote. (The SDP–Liberal Alliance was only 2 per cent behind).

Foot was replaced by his left-wing and unilateralist protégé, Neil Kinnock, who had the task of restoring the party's fortunes. His main problems were that many local authorities and constituency parties were in the grip of the 'hard left': the Trotskyite Militant Tendency took control of Liverpool; Ken Living-stone and what became known as 'the loony left' were in control of the Greater London Council (GLC) and several London boroughs; while Arthur Scargill, the Marxist leader of the National Union of Mineworkers, was spoiling for the chance to bring down the Thatcher government by instituting a miners' strike. Luckily for Kinnock, Thatcher solved many of his problems for him. She defeated the miners' strike in 1984–5 and abolished the GLC. She also curbed the amount of money that local councils could spend. Eventually, the Liverpool Militants overreached themselves as well and were expelled from the Labour Party. Yet Kinnock's 1987 election manifesto still advocated unilateral disarma-ment, although by now Labour seemed to be reconciling itself with free-market economics (the New Economic Strategy had disappeared). Great care was taken with election presentation, but as the result of the 1987 election was hardly better than in 1983 (30.8 per cent of the vote), clearly more radical measures had to be taken to make the party politically more respectable. The result was that a Policy Review Committee which met between 1987 and 1989 committed the party to co-operating with the EC (including membership of the exchange-rate mechanism, or ERM) and to accepting Thatcher's trade union reforms. The Tory Party's own troubles after 1988 – disputes between Thatcher and her Chancellor, Nigel Lawson, the problem of relations with the EC, the introduc-tion of the poll tax and the introduction of the internal market into the NHS – also helped Labour. Indeed, by 1990 the Tories were so appalled by their low ratings in the opinion polls that they decided to save their skins by the most ruthless act of ingratitude in the history of modern democratic politics: they ditched Thatcher as leader before she could lose an election and replaced her with the unknown and unimpressive John Major, who, unexpectedly, went on to win the 1992 general election. This was largely the fault of Kinnock, whose notorious verbosity and intellectual shallowness meant that he simply was not trusted to lead the country at a time when party politics was becoming more and more presidential in presentation.

After 1992 Major continued to pursue Thatcherite policies domestically, but his party was split down the middle over the Maastricht Treaty and relations with the EC, the issue which had offered Thatcher's opponents (Howe and Heseltine) the opportunity to get rid of her. The Labour leadership, meanwhile, had gone to John Smith, a rather dour Scottish QC, who was no unilateralist and who promised further party reforms in the direction of 'one member, one vote'. In practice this meant reducing the block vote of the trade unions in constituency selection committees and at Labour Party conferences. However, Smith died in 1994 and was replaced by the young, handsome and articulate Tony Blair, who pursued the same policies, but with real style and panache. Blair also emphasised that Labour was in favour of the EU and NATO, wel-comed the free-market approach to economics, and was business-friendly. The trade unions, he made clear, could expect no special treatment from a Labour government. Insofar as socialism meant anything, it involved a commitment to the European Social Chapter and a minimum wage, neither of which was regarded as having major policy implications, but which allowed the party to appear more European than the Tories. In fact, Blair was happy to praise Mrs

Thatcher and to hint that he was more the heir to her achievements than to Callaghan's or Wilson's. Memories of Labour's past, in any case, were largely obliterated and the party adopted the title of New Labour as a conscious means of disassociating itself with the failures of the 1960s and 1970s.

Today, therefore, a new consensus appears to be in place. The welfare state is to be preserved and at greater cost. The Blair government has got rid of the internal market in the NHS, but, after struggling unsuccessfully to reform the social security system, has left it largely alone (there are rumours, however, of US firms running parts of it privately on an experimental basis). The economic policy of the Tories has been little changed, with Gordon Brown sticking to the same spending targets as his Tory predecessor as Chancellor, Kenneth Clarke. The Tories have recommitted themselves to the welfare state and have reluctantly accepted Labour's policy on Scotland, Wales and Northern Ireland – the Blair government's most radical breaks with the past – while both parties have taken a cautious attitude towards adopting the euro, although the prospect is that Labour will support and the Tories oppose accepting the new single European currency. Meanwhile both parties proclaim their desire to be parties of business, free enterprise and market-led economics. If the consensus breaks down in future, it is almost certain that foreign policy and constitutional issues will be the causes.

The consensus was upheld, of course, not merely by 'the two main parties', but by the Liberals and their successors at the centre of the British political spectrum, first the Social Democrats (who immediately formed an electoral alliance with the Liberals) and then the Liberal Democrats, when the two parties combined. The Liberals had been the dominant party in Britain during the second half of the nineteenth century and the period before the First World War. Thereafter, however, they rapidly declined and were replaced by Labour as the main opposition to the Conservatives. In 1945 they took only 9 per cent of the vote and in 1951 almost disappeared with only 2.5 per cent. Churchill asked their leader, Sir Archibald Sinclair, to join his Cabinet, and had the offer been accepted, the party might well have been absorbed by the Conservatives. However, Sinclair declined and his successor, the charismatic Jo Grimond, managed, in the aftermath of Suez, to capture some of the renewed radicalism apparent in the country and to double the party's vote in 1959. He did the same in 1964, by which time the party had won an astounding by-election success at Orpington in 1962. After the 1964 election, the party held nine seats, and after the 1966 general election twelve seats. Yet although membership grew, the election of Harold Wilson as Labour Party leader meant that Grimond became eclipsed as the voice of the moderate, radical left. At the 1970 election, the party's share of the vote dropped to 7.5 per cent and the number of seats held was cut to six. Heath's difficulties again enabled the party – which, despite distinctive policies on industrial partnership and a programme calling for a federal Britain in a federal Europe, was used by the electorate mainly as a 'party of protest' – to make headway. Five seats were won in by-elections between October 1972 and November 1973, and in the February 1974 election the Liberals won 19.3 per cent of the vote, their highest since 1929. They were now led by another charismatic leader, Jeremy Thorpe, who, if he lacked Grimond's intelligence and gravitas, made up for it in wit and showmanship. Unfortunately, the party lacked any real strategy for a hung Parliament, so, despite the Liberals' strong showing in a situation where there was no overall parliamentary majority, Harold Wilson was allowed to return to power. Thereafter, the Liberals declined, with Thorpe being arrested for the attempted murder of his alleged male lover, while his dour successor, David Steel, rather overreached himself by telling Liberal delegates at their party conference in 1976 that they should return home 'and prepare for government'.

The truth seemed to be that any Liberal revival would depend first on the obvious incompetence of the party in government, and secondly a polarisation of the two major parties, allowing the Liberals to occupy the middle ground. Grimond had also believed that the embourgeoisement of the working classes would ultimately undermine Labour, leading to a realignment of the Left under Liberal leadership. Certainly, Steel made it clear by his 'Lib-Lab Pact' with Callaghan between 1977 and 1978, which brought no Cabinet posts for his party, but did help bring about a referendum on devolution for Scotland and Wales in 1979 and direct elections to the European Parliament the same year, that, like Grimond before him, he also looked for a realignment of the Left that would unite moderate reformers on a radical platform without relying on a class base. The trouble was that when the supposed conditions for a Liberal revival occurred – the obvious incompetence of the Callaghan government with Thatcher as head of the Tories polarising the parties – the Liberals were identified with the Callaghan government and the middle ground was overrun by voters following Thatcher's lurch to the right. The party's vote in 1979 fell to 13.8 per cent – not as bad as in the 1950s, but a considerable fall from the level of 1974 general elections. The formation of the SDP and its alliance after 1981 with the Liberals did seem to presage Grimond's hoped-for realignment of the Left. Yet quarrels between David Owen and Roy Jenkins over the leadership of the SDP, Thatcher's victory over Argentina in the 1982 Falklands War, followed by the economic upswing of the mid-1980s, meant that the chance was lost. When Steel, immediately after the 1987 election, called for the merger of the two parties, Owen refused to back it. He thought the Liberals too ill-disciplined, too left-wing, too much in favour of nuclear disarmament, and too likely to submerge the SDP in any merged party. He himself had grown more Thatcherite in his economic policies. He thus led a rump SDP for a while before abandoning politics altogether, accused of having split, first, Labour and then the SDP. If the Alliance had secured 25.4 per cent of the vote in 1983 and 22.6 per cent in 1987, by 1992 the Liberal Democrats were down to 17.8 per cent. Their share of the vote would fall again in 1997 to 16.8 per cent, although the collapse of the Tories would give them extra seats. Yet the two-party system remained. The mould of British politics had not been broken.

It would certainly change, however, with the rise of Scottish and Welsh nationalism. Scotland did very well economically and politically out of the Union.[22] She was over-represented in the Commons and Scottish affairs were administered from Edinburgh; economically she was over-subsidised by the Treasury on the basis of her population, while by the mid-1990s the average Scot was better off than the average Englishman. Yet during the late 1960s and the 1970s the failure of the Heath and Wilson governments channelled political protest in Scotland towards the Scottish National Party (SNP), which until then had been viewed as part of the political lunatic fringe (it had never received even 5 per cent of the vote until 1966). Very quickly, however, with the aid of the separate Scottish media, it transformed itself into a highly efficient vote-winning machine, attracted the support of young people, and, capitalizing on the discovery of North Sea Oil, characterized as 'Scotland's oil' which the London government had stolen, it managed to secure 22 per cent of the Scottish vote at the February 1974 election, winning seven seats and coming second in about thirty more. Further, in October 1974 the SNP was to capture 30 per cent of the Scottish vote and eleven seats. This opened up the prospect of it taking a majority of Scottish seats in 1979, causing the Labour Party to panic. Until then Labour had followed the line that workers in Scotland and England had the same socialist needs and that nationalism was a bourgeois device designed to divide them. Now the Scottish Labour Party was force-fed a diet of devolution or home rule and James Callaghan, as Prime Minister (who only panicked in a crisis), promised a referendum on the matter.

Wales also benefited, although Welsh nationalism was politically weaker and much more based on cultural factors, given that 20 per cent of the population spoke Welsh, something which worried the 80 per cent who did not and feared that they might be forced to learn it under a Plaid Cymru government. When the referenda were held in 1979, therefore, the Welsh rejected the rather moderate proposals involved by four to one, while the Scottish proponents of devolution failed to get the necessary 40 per cent of the electorate to vote for them, despite a slim majority of 52 per cent to 48 per cent of votes cast in favour. Thereafter, the issue lost its urgency and the SNP lost seats in 1979. However, having performed such a public U-turn on devolution and having campaigned for it in the referendum, Labour could hardly drop the issue. Thus a few months after the 1997 election – in which devolution figured as eighth in the list of topics which Scots felt concerned about, according to opinion polls – Tony Blair capitalised on the rout of the Tory Party in Scotland to hold another referendum on devolution which, this time, was won. (There was practically no time for any opposition to reorganise after the Tory election massacre.) The policies that were usually administered from St Andrew's House in Edinburgh by the Scottish Secretary were henceforth to be legislated by a Scottish Parliament to which a new Scottish Prime Minister and Cabinet would be responsible. The financing of these policies would be principally through a block grant from Westminster, although the Scots did receive the right to raise an additional income tax of 3p in the pound (the tax-varying powers). Meanwhile, Scottish MPs remained at Westminster, with the right – indeed the duty – to vote on English affairs. In fact, the British Cabinet was dominated by Scots, with a Scottish Prime Minister (Blair, albeit representing an English seat), a Scottish Foreign Secretary (Cook), a Scottish Chancellor (Brown) and a Scottish Defence Secretary (Robertson), to name just the most obvious ones. Welsh MPs would also have the right to vote on English affairs, although a new Welsh Assembly would remove Welsh affairs from the purview of the House of Commons. (The Welsh were denied extra tax-raising powers, however, and their assembly was a watered-down version of the Scottish one.) The new system amounted to the wanton destruction of the British constitution with separate assemblies/parliaments for Scotland and Wales, but not England; with different electoral systems for all of these (plus a different one again for the new Assembly in Northern Ireland, not to mention the European elections, which were boycotted by the vast majority of voters, with only 8 per cent of the voters in Liverpool, for example, turning out for the first European parliamentary by-election in 1996).

The reform of the House of Lords revealed the same mindless desire for change. No thought was given to any coherent review of the constitution or to the need to make the various parts fit a workable whole. The only rationale for the constitutional mess created was Blair's desire to be seen to fulfil election promises as soon as possible and to give Labour a vaguely modernising appeal. In the end, when elections were held for the new assemblies in May 1999, only 46 per cent of the Welsh electorate bothered to turn out, while in Scotland, despite all the hype about a new era there, only 58.8 per cent took the trouble to vote. As critics of Blair had warned, the whole process merely allowed the Nationalists to claim the real credit for these developments and this factor, along with the new voting systems, served to deprive Labour of the overall majorities it had taken for granted. In Scotland, Labour secured only 56 seats out of 129, with the SNP taking 35, while in Wales, Labour took 28 out of 60 seats, with Plaid Cymru taking 17. In both assemblies the Tories came a poor third, with 18 seats in Scotland and 9 in Wales. They had not recovered from their general election performance and the outlook must be that the Nationalists will form the other half of new two-party systems in Scotland and Wales. Given that Blair's purpose in introducing devolution was 'to strengthen the Union', his policies may yet prove to be counter-productive. His critics will no doubt be watching events in Northern Ireland, the Balkans and Europe to discover whether a similar verdict might be in order generally.

All in all, therefore, until very recently, the history of British politics seemed a fairly straightforward tale of a two-party consensus that evolved and changed over time. With the advent of the Blair government, however, the political system – or at least its constitutional framework – has been changed, albeit haphazardly. What this will lead to, given the virtual destruction of the Tory Party in Scotland and Wales, not to mention its inability since 1997 to present a united front or to find the confidence to oppose Blair effectively, is anyone's guess. Yet nothing can be taken for granted. Labour after all secured only 28 per cent of the vote in 1983, 3 per cent less than the Tories in 1997, and still returned from the dead. The Tories, it should also be remembered, have been the most successful political party in history. It is much too early, therefore, to write them off or to conclude that Britain's political system is incapable of throwing up surprises.

Notes

1   For the political history of Britain since 1945, see Alan Sked and Chris Cook, *Post-War Britain, A Political History, 1945–1992*, London, 1993. For an interpretation

of post-war Britain, see Alan Sked, *An Intelligent Person's Guide to Post-War Britain*, London, 1997. On Britain's political parties since 1945 see, *inter alia*, Robert Garner and Richard Kelly, *British Political Parties Today* (1st ed., Manchester and New York, 1993 (2nd ed. 1998); Terry Gourvish and Richard Kelly (eds), *Britain since 1945*, Basingstoke, 1991; Dennis Kavanagh, *The Reordering of British Politics. Politics after Thatcher*, Oxford and New York, 1997; Anthony Seldon (ed.), *UK Political Parties since 1945*, London, New York, Toronto and Tokyo, 1990; and H. Kastendiek, K. Rohe and A. Volle (eds), *Länderbericht Grossbritannien, Geschichte, Politik, Wirtschaft, Gesellschaft*, Schriftenreihe Vol. 327, Bundeszentrale für politische Bildung, Bonn, 1994.

2   For a discussion of the EEC/EC/EU's evolution and Britain's relations with Europe, see Jonathan Hollowell's chapter 4 in this volume.

3   Those interested in this subject should consult *West European Politics*, 15(1), Jan. 1992 and Peter Gerlich et al. (eds), *Sozialpartnerschaft in der Krise. Leistungen und Grenzen des Neokorporatismus in Österreich*, Vienna, Cologne and Graz, 1985.

4   Correlli Barnett, *The Audit of War*, London, 1986.

5   Robert Skidelsky (ed.), *The End of the Keynesian Era*, London, 1977.

6   R. A. Butler, *The Art of the Possible*, London, 1971, p. 160.

7   Samuel Beer, *Modern British Politics*, London, 1965, p. 271.

8   Q. Hogg, *The Case for Conservatism*, London, 1947, p. 294.

9   *Labour Party Annual Conference Report*, 1994.

10   For a discussion of the welfare state, see Helen Fawcett's chapter 23, and for health care see Raymond Fitzpatrick et al.'s chapter 17, both in this volume.

11   Quoted in Sked, *An Intelligent Person's Guide*, p. 120.

12   Sked, *An Intelligent Person's Guide*, p. 119.

13   Ben Pimlott, 'The Myth of Consensus', in L. Smith (ed.), *Making of Britain: Echoes of Greatness*, London, 1988.

14   Charles Webster, 'Conflict in Consensus. Explaining the British Health Service', *Twentieth Century British History* 1 (1990).

15   Cf. Paul Addison, *The Road to 1945*, 2nd ed., London, 1994.

16   Quoted in Sked and Cook, *Post-War Britain*.

17   Tony Crosland in 1975 to local authority executives.

18   Quoted in James Callaghan, *Times and Chance*, London, 1987, p. 426.

19   For a full bibliography on Thatcherism, see Kavanagh, *Reordering of British Politics*.

20   In M. Cowling (ed.), *Conservative Essays*, London, 1978.

21   A. Gamble, *The Free Economy and Strong State*, London, 1994.

22   On Scotland, see Patrick S. Hodge (ed.), *Scotland and the Union*, Edinburgh, 1994. Cf. the discussion in Sked, *An Intelligent Person's Guide*, ch. 6.

Further Reading

Callaghan, James, *Time and Chance*, London, 1987.
Campbell, John, *Edward Heath: A Biography*, London, 1993.
Coopey, R. Fielding, S. and Tiratsoo, N. (eds), *The Wilson Governments, 1964–1970*, London, 1993.
Dutton, David, *Anthony Eden: A Life and Reputation*, London, 1997.
Heath, Edward, *The Course of My Life: My Autobiography*, London, 1998.
Horne, Alistair, *Macmillan*, 2 vols, London, 1988–9.
Morgan, Kenneth, *Callaghan: A Life*, Oxford, 1997.

Ranelagh, John, *Thatcher's People: An Insider's Account of the Politics, the Power, and the Personalities*, London, 1991.

Sked, Alan, and Cook, Chris, *Post-war Britain: A Political History*, 4th ed., London, 1993.

Hennessy Peter, and Seldon Anthony, (eds), *Ruling Performance: British Governments from Attlee to Thatcher*, London, 1987.

Morgan, Kenneth, *The People's Peace: British History since 1945*, 2nd ed., Oxford, 1999.

Ramsden, John, *The Age of Churchill and Eden, 1940–1957*, London, 1995.

Chronology

1945   General election won by Labour with majority of 146 (393 seats). Sir Clement Attlee become Prime Minister.

1946   Churchill's 'Iron Curtain' speech at Westminster College, Fulton, Missouri.

1950   Schuman Plan announced. General election: Labour majority reduced to 5 (315 seats).

1951   General election won by Conservatives with majority of 17 (321 seats). Sir Winston Churchill becomes Prime Minister for second time.

1955   Churchill resigns. Sir Anthony Eden becomes Prime Minister. General election: Conservative majority of 58 (344 seats). Attlee retires and Hugh Gaitskell elected Leader of Labour Party.

1956   Suez crisis.

1957   Eden resigns. Harold Macmillan selected as new Conservative Leader and hence Prime Minister.

1958   EEC inaugurated.

1959   General election: Conservative majority of 100 (365 seats). EFTA treaty agreed.

1961   Britain applies to join EEC.

1963   French President de Gaulle vetoes Britain's application to join EEC. Gaitskell dies; Harold Wilson elected Leader of Labour Party. Macmillan is taken ill and resigns. The Queen calls on Lord Home (Sir Alec Douglas-Home) to lead Conservative government.

1964   General election results in a Labour majority of 4 (317 seats). Wilson becomes Prime Minister.

1965   Douglas-Home resigns; Edward Heath elected Leader of Conservative Party.

1966   General election results in Labour majority of 96 (363 seats).

1967   Labour government pursues UK application for membership of EC. application vetoed by President de Gaulle.

1969   Plans for legal restraints on unofficial strikes, *In Place of Strife*, dropped.

1970   Conservatives adopt Selsdon Park programme. General election results in Conservative majority of 30 (330 seats). Edward Heath becomes Prime Minister.

1972   Violence in Northern Ireland results in 'Bloody Sunday'.

1973   UK joins EC. Announcement of 3-day week from January 1974.

1974   General election (February) results in no overall majority for any party. Heath resigns; Wilson becomes Prime Minister of minority Labour government. New Labour government demands renegotiation of EC terms. General election (October) results in Labour majority of 3 (319 seats).

1975   Margaret Thatcher successfully challenges Heath for leadership of Conservative Party, replacing him as Leader. Referendum on EC membership results in more than 66 per cent voting for Britain to remain in the EC.

1976   Wilson resigns; James Callaghan elected Leader of the Labour Party and hence Prime Minister.

1977   Lib-Lab Pact.

1978–9 'Winter of discontent'.

1979   General election results in Conservative majority of 43 (339 seats). Thatcher becomes Prime Minister.

1980   Ronald Reagan elected President of the United States. Labour Party Wembley Conference changes party's constitution, diminishing role of the PLP in selecting party leader to 30 per cent, and giving constituency Labour parties 30 per cent and affiliated trade unions 40 per cent. Michael Foot elected Leader of Labour Party.

1981   Formation of the SDP by Shirley Williams, Roy Jenkins, David Owen and William Rodgers, and SDP–Liberal Alliance.

1982   Falkland Islands invasion.

1983   General election results in Conservative majority increased to 144 (397 seats). Margaret Thatcher begins second government. Neil Kinnock elected Leader of Labour Party.

1984   Agreement over UK rebate EC budget contribution.

1985–6 Westland Affair leads to the departure of Leon Brittan and Michael Heseltine from Cabinet.

1987   General election results in Conservative majority of 101 (375 seats). Thatcher begins third government.

1988   Liberals and SDP merge to form Social and Liberal Democratic Party (SLDP, popularly known as the Social and Liberal Democrats); Paddy Ashdown elected its first Leader.

1989   SLDP adopt shortened name of Liberal Democrats.

1990   John Major replaces Margaret Thatcher as Leader of Conservative Party and hence Prime Minister.

1992   General election results in Conservative majority of 21 (336 seats). Kinnock resigns; John Smith elected Leader of Labour Party.

1994   John Smith dies; Tony Blair elected Leader of Labour Party.

1995   Blair successfully leads special party conference to adopt a revised Clause IV.

1997   General election results in a Labour majority of 179 (419 seats). Tony Blair becomes Prime Minister. John Major resigns as Conservative Party Leader and William Hague elected new Leader. Scotland and Wales vote for devolution.

1999   Elections for the Scottish Parliament and Welsh Assembly. Establishment of the Scottish Parliament and Welsh Assembly (May). Ashdown retires as Leader of the Liberal Democrats; Charles Kennedy elected new Leader.

4 From Commonwealth to European Integration

Jonathan Hollowell

'Britain has lost an empire and has not yet found a role.' This caustic observation of the American former Secretary of State Dean Acheson struck a raw nerve when uttered in 1962. Britain had indeed withdrawn from a number of territories formerly under its control as metropole of the British Empire. But in these remarks, what wounded the most in Acheson's audience was the gnawing truth that Britain was, and ought to be, experiencing a crisis of confidence about its place in the world, having no real alternative with which to replace the Empire which was now a spent force, but with an intense, obsessive desire to avoid its inevitable fate as a minor power in a world of only two superpowers. This crisis of confidence had reverberations that could not be subdued, for the contrast between whence Britain had come and where it was heading appeared as stark as the decline of any previous world power. This prospect led to a corresponding psychological adjustment as effort was made to mitigate the stern realities of 'decline', and eventually prompted Britain's reluctant leaders to reassess their relationship with Britain's European neighbours and join with them in the unfolding project of the European Economic Community (EEC) and European integration; but for the period from 1945 until the 1960s, this re-evaluation was left to the future and was far from certain.

The Early Post-war Period

At the end of the Second World War, Britain's Empire and Commonwealth embraced one-quarter of the world's population and land mass. The leader of the world's largest empire had emerged from the war on the side of the victorious powers, in contrast to the continental European countries that had been occupied by Germany during the war. To British leaders in the immediate post-war era, this represented a vast difference between themselves, larger-than-life heroes, and their very mortal European neighbours. Britain's victory was a historic event that made Britons, in their own eyes, feel superior to their continental neighbours. Thus for Britain, there was a tremendous psychological gulf between itself and Europe, whereas the relationship with the United States was one of comrades-in-arms. Hence in searching for a partner in the post-war era, the logical choice was the USA. The 'special relationship'[1] complemented the status that Britain derived as leader of its empire and the wider Commonwealth, and to British leaders such as Foreign Secretary Ernest Bevin, it was crucially important that Britain continue to exercise an important world role and that it continue to have a place at the 'top table' of international diplomacy, just as it had been one of the 'big three' during the war. This meant that Britain would have a role in maintaining the peace in Europe, a continuing role in its empire/Commonwealth, an important role as subordinate partner to the USA. In 1945, to suggest that Britain should pool its national sovereignty with its European neighbours and join with those who had recently been defeated and occupied by Nazi Germany would have been unthinkable. Why, therefore, was Britain to apply for membership of the European Community three times, and be increasingly drawn into the process of European integration, in order to seek a place at the 'heart of Europe'?[2]

In dissecting Britain's shift from a close identification with its Commonwealth to an association with Europe, we do not seek to provide an exhaustive narrative of the activities and developments of the Commonwealth since 1945, but to give salient highlights of its history, especially in parallel with Britain's relations with 'Europe' or what has now become known as the European Union. The Commonwealth connection, it was increasingly realised, could never provide Britain with either monolithic diplomatic support or an economic underpinning that would increase British power and prestige in the post-war period. Participation in European integration was undertaken precisely because policy-makers saw diplomatic and commercial advantages that would enhance Britain's position. Thus the choice seemed obvious. But not until the 1960s. Even then the move to Europe did not involve an either/or choice with the Commonwealth; Britain could participate in the EEC without undue harm to her Commonwealth partners. However, at key moments during the reorientation, when policy-makers evaluated the two organisations side by side, they judged Europe the better of the two for the furtherance of British interests.[3] Wherever the choice for Europe presented a conflict with the Commonwealth, therefore, the advantages to Britain of choosing Europe outweighed all others; and this unspoken assumption lay behind much of what was taking place from the 1960s in both the Conservative and Labour parties. This chapter does not consider the Commonwealth and Britain's relationship with Europe co-equally; rather, it traces the evolution of the Commonwealth during the era of decolonisation alongside Britain's developing relationship with Europe, first as outsider and then as member of the EEC/EC/EU.[4] These two relationships were at the heart of Britain's national destiny, and the question of 'whither Britain' had presented itself even before the Second World War had ended. Britain's relationship with its empire and Commonwealth then witnessed a continual distancing of itself from its former colonies; at first, this involved a somewhat grudging resignation to the forces driving Britain and the Commonwealth apart, but later, as time went by, a lack of any resistance. Britain's relationship with its European neighbours, likewise, involved grudging concessions, this time of its national sovereignty to the EC, punctuated by moments of cooperation. Overall there was an unacknowledged shift in Britain's calculation of its national interests, one to which it took a great deal of the post-war period for Britons to be reconciled. This grudging interest in European integration was never stronger than immediately after the Second World War, but lasted through the 1950s, during which period it was political orthodoxy that membership of the EEC would be detrimental to the Commonwealth.

Policy during the Attlee Governments

Britain emerged from the Second World War as one of the victorious powers; having been the first to declare war upon Germany, Britain in 1945 was economically exhausted but politically victorious and morally self-righteous. Its political system and political culture had stood up to the challenge of fascism and few doubted the morality of British diplomacy, given the failed systems and defeated comrades across the Channel. Thus in 1945 Britain's achievements overshadowed those of all other European countries. Britain was also the nexus of a global empire embracing one-fourth of the world's population and land mass. The post-war Labour administration inherited a vast imperial network in 1945; the question of what to do with its colonies and dependencies was also inherited. The 'British Commonwealth' would be the successor to the Empire, incorporating concepts of independence, free association and interracial cooperation. As such, it would be unique in the world and was based on the 1931 Statute of Westminster which stipulated that the self-governing colonies were henceforth completely free and independent, co-equal, and under the titular headship of the British sovereign. The Commonwealth, however, was initially an organisation whose existence was expected to lend furtherance to Britain's role as a global player in the diplomatic field; it was not expected to detract from Britain's exercise of its diplomatic role, but to be supportive of Britain in the diplomatic arena. This was especially the case as the Commonwealth was overwhelmingly 'Old Commonwealth' (or white) in nature in the late 1940s and 1950s, and even after Indian independence in 1947, still predominantly an Old Commonwealth club in atmosphere, with annual meetings conducted in the Cabinet room of Number 10 Downing Street.

With a progressive view towards the developing former Empire, Labour Prime Minister Clement Attlee changed the designation 'British Commonwealth' to 'Commonwealth' from 1947/8[5] to note the changing character of the grouping; the move was in anticipation of its increasingly non-British, non-'old Commonwealth' elements, with the addition of India from 1947 and the special arrangement for India, a republic, to remain in the Commonwealth. The Commonwealth was, even in 1948, seen to be evolving from a group supporting Britain's diplomatic status, to one whose members could potentially espouse interests – and alliances – contrary to the former mother country's liking. Thus the change in the name of the organisation was declaratory of something that had already occurred rather than a move that led to any change in the character of the Commonwealth.

In recognising the changed conditions resulting from the war which were accelerating the trend towards independence in the aftermath of 1945, British policy-makers set about granting independence to a number of nations in the Empire, beginning in the Middle East and Asia. A major priority was the commitment to withdraw from the Indian subcontinent, and in this regard the government looked to the Government of India Act of 1935 and to an understanding between the British government and Indian leaders reached during the war that independence would be granted following the conflict's end. Thus Attlee dispatched Lord Mountbatten to India as Britain's last Viceroy, with instructions to fashion an agreement so that Britain might withdraw from the subcontinent in all reasonable haste. Labour proceeded apace with decolonisation, withdrawing from Transjordan in 1946, India and Pakistan in 1947 and Ceylon, Burma and Palestine in 1948. The African lands, however, would remain under British administration for perhaps decades to come, with the establishment of parliamentary institutions and the fostering of a native educated and administrative class so that Britain could leave these areas to governments capable of sustainable democratic government. The Attlee governments did not foresee a complete termination of the British Empire, first because this would have been an impossibility from a practical standpoint; many colonies, particularly those in Africa, were seen as not yet ready to assume sovereignty of their own and an attempt by the British government to grant independence to such lands would be premature, as Bevin believed the colonies were not ready for self-government and yet needed British guidance. But Labour also had no objection to a continuation of Britain's role as colonial administrator and centre of the Commonwealth, as this was seen as enhancing Britain's world role and diplomatic status. Thus Britain's world role, and the degree to which the Commonwealth could enhance it, was an important consideration, as the government desired to remain an important global power, even if it was no longer possible to remain the world's pre-eminent one. This self-image as a world power was evident in Britain's relations with countries in the developed world as well, notably in Europe.

There, the British government's foreign policy in the early post-war years had one goal above others, namely, to keep US forces in Europe as a line of defence against the Soviet threat to the West. Bevin, Foreign Secretary from 1945, took the initiative in encouraging continued American involvement in Europe, including a direct US military presence. While the post-war occupation of Germany meant a four-power occupation, with the US, USSR, Britain and France each administering their own zones from 1945, Bevin was concerned that, with the war over and Germany subdued, American forces would return to the US and the Americans revert to their pre-war policy of isolationism. To Bevin, this possibility posed a threat to the defence of Western Europe at a time when Soviet troops in Eastern Germany and Eastern Europe had not demobilised. Building on the mutual security arrangement of the Treaty of Dunkirk which he had signed with France in 1947, in 1948 Bevin signed a 50-year military pact with France and the Benelux countries (the Brussels Treaty), committing Britain to come to the aid of any party in the event of war. However, these efforts did not involve a US commitment, and to many in Western Europe this meant that they did not go far enough in terms of collective security. More broadly in terms of British efforts at containment, Britain was handicapped by a sheer lack of funds, with the Treasury informing the US administration in 1947 that British aid to Greece in combating communist infiltration would soon cease. Almost immediately, therefore, President Truman announced his policy of containment in March 1947 at a joint session of Congress. This injection of US muscle into the effort to assist 'free peoples' everywhere who were fighting communist insurgents would also come to be expressed in the Marshall Plan from 1948, by which the US established the European Recovery Program (ERP) to assist European countries in rebuilding their war-ravaged economies in order to be more able to resist communist influence from without and the rise of communist parties within Western Europe. In establishing the ERP, the US insisted that it be organised and run by representatives of European countries themselves; the US aim was to encourage Europeans to group themselves together as a unit, regain their economic strength, and therefore be better able to present a united front in the face of the USSR in what was coming to be a Cold War. US policy had therefore come to dovetail with Bevin's efforts in bolstering Western Europe, and in April 1949 NATO was established, with a direct US military presence in Europe from 1951 onwards, after the outbreak of the Korean War.

Developments towards the Unity of Europe

After 1945 advocates of European unity had begun to organise conferences to discuss plans for establishing a Europe-wide entity that would prevent a re-emergence of nationalism in individual countries as well as serve to formally link their nations together in more than an intergovernmental arrangement. Many of the advocates of European unity had served in their respective national resistance movements during the Second World War, and as the post-war period unfolded, sought to establish a European unity that would make traditional nationalistic attitudes a thing of the past, constructing in its place a European federal system, building on the common European civilisation inherited throughout Western and Central Europe. At the Zurich conference in 1946, Winston Churchill came to lend his prestige to the cause of European unity, urging the assembled delegates to form a 'United States of Europe'. In 1948, members of the International Committee of the Movement for European Unity organised a 'Congress of Europe' at The Hague. Attended by over 800 prominent European leaders, the most prominent figure invited was the president of honour, Winston Churchill. The Hague conference resulted in the formation of the European Movement later in 1948, and subsequently the establishment in 1949 of the Council of Europe, comprising most European countries. Though the Council of Europe was a consultative body, its authority was as an intergovernmental organisation for discussing human rights and issues of common concern, having no supranational institution to which all members were accountable or to which member states surrendered any area of national sovereignty. Advocates of genuine integration wanted more. If individual European countries continued as completely sovereign independent international actors, this result fell far short of the ideals of European integration to which most continental members of the European Movement subscribed. Meanwhile, the three allied sectors of Western Germany had regained sovereignty and the Federal Republic of Germany was established in 1949. France, concerned to contain its potential for war-making, proposed to link the coal and steel resources of West Germany with those of France and others under a supranational High Authority, thus taking advantage not only of the commercial benefits inherent in the plan but also of the national security this arrangement would afford.

By May 1950, Robert Schuman, French Foreign Minister, had announced a plan for the pooling of coal and steel resources of participating states. The Schuman Plan led to further meetings between representatives of the six participating countries of France, the Federal Republic of Germany, Italy, Belgium, the Netherlands and Luxembourg (these latter three known collectively as the Benelux countries), who established the European Coal and Steel Community (ECSC) – a customs union in coal and steel run by a supranational High Authority – in 1951 by the Treaty of Paris. The approach to European integration utilised in this first supranational organisation was one of functional integration, involving the gradual merging of defined sectors of national economies with those of other member states. The goal of the advocates of this functionalist approach was to achieve integration in the long term, by beginning with the integration of precise economic sectors of participating member states; it was expected that, over time, the necessities of operating an increasingly unencumbered customs union between the member states would lead to a 'spillover' effect into other sectors of the national economy and, indeed, into the larger political and social spheres. Some advocates of European integration at this time sought to launch into a full-scale merger of Western European countries into a larger unity, bypassing the functional approach and instead leaping ahead into a political union. However, by 1950 the climate of opinion in Western Europe was predominantly opposed to such grand schemes for the immediate realisation of European integration, so that the consensus of those in favour of European unity was that the functional approach should be employed. Given the practical and political barriers to the establishment of any overarching scheme aimed at achieving European federalism immediately in 1950, the functional option appeared much more realistic. It would arouse less opposition and have the immediately noticeable effect of working to the commercial advantage of the six participating states.

Together the Six, under the direction of France's Jean Monnet, had invited the British government to participate in the talks leading to the establishment of the Paris Treaty, albeit on a strictly supranationalist basis. Yet the Attlee government decided to stand aside. As socialists who had achieved a majority in Parliament for the first time, the Labour government had nationalised the 'commanding heights' of Britain's economy and prominent among the list of industries concerned were coal, iron and steel. Since the ECSC concept allowed for the common pooling of coal and steel within participating member states, the

British reaction was cool. Labour had no wish to see the management of the commanding heights of the British economy now surrendered to a supranational body. The Churchill government eventually signed an association agreement with the ECSC, but the Attlee Cabinet ruled out direct UK membership.

The Churchill Years

For those desirous of a more forthcoming policy on Europe, there had been hopes that Sir Winston Churchill's return to office would move British policy in this direction. Churchill, from 1945, had been making speeches across Europe, expressing his sentiment in favour of European cooperation and indeed, European integration. Representing himself and Britain's Conservative Party – in opposition since 1945 – Churchill attended the Zurich Conference for European unity in 1946, advocating that we 'must build a kind of United States of Europe'. However, he was clear that the pro-European sentiment he expressed was for the countries of the Continent, not for the UK, expressing the hope that 'Great Britain, the British Commonwealth of Nations, mighty America, and I trust Soviet Russia – for then indeed all would be well – must be the friends and sponsors of the new Europe.'[6] Churchill did not expect or advocate British participation in any supranational organisation that would emerge and he did not want Britain's relationship with the USA to be compromised by the UK's submergence in a European federation.[7] He continued to make speeches advocating closer European unity; however, this was as much because his party was in opposition and needed a weapon to use against the Labour government, as on account of his genuine commitment to end the historic rivalry between France and Germany through European unity. He was not in favour of direct British membership of any European supranational entity. If he was interested in pursuing close relations with any particular group, it was with the 'English-speaking peoples', notably with the Americans, together with whom he hoped for the eventual emergence of some sort of grand confraternity to ensure world peace.[8] Together with his interest in the USA, he also desired to maintain Britain's influence in the Commonwealth and presence in colonial territories still administered by Britain, stating that he had not become the King's first minister in order to preside over the dissolution of the British Empire. Churchill's interest in maintaining the continuing relationship with the USA and the Commonwealth, together with Britain's interest in Western Europe, led him to formulate the three-circles concept that Britain was situated at the centre of three interlocking circles; and that as far as Europe was concerned, Britain was in it but not of it, involved but not compromised.

The ultimate test of Churchill's beliefs regarding Britain's place in the scheme of European integration is to be found in his actual policies as Prime Minister. During his period of leadership from October 1951 to April 1955, Churchill never advocated UK entry to the ECSC and never considered that Britain should subject itself to any European authority that would merge or pool sovereignty. When Churchill re-entered office in 1951, his lack of interest in having Britain take the lead in European integration or in having Britain at least join the ECSC caused some surprise both to observers on the Continent and to advocates of European unity within the UK, given his 1946 speech in Zurich and his 1948 speech at The Hague. However, Churchill had significantly qualified these observations, and it is only in his speech made at the Albert Hall in 1947 that he specified that 'If Europe united, is to be a living force, Britain will have to play her full part as a member of the European family'.[9]

During Churchill's premiership, the Pleven Plan for a European army emerged from the French government in a proposal for a European Defence Community (EDC). This was to include army units from France, Italy, the Benelux countries and lastly – and most controversially – West Germany. The issue of German rearmament was deeply sensitive in France and other European states, as it was in Britain as well, and the very notion of German rearmament was one that would not have emerged in the early 1950s but for the onset of the Korean conflict, which caused US and some European forces to leave the European theatre to respond to communist aggression in Asia. The fear arose that, in order to contain communism in Asia, the US and its European allies would be undermanned in Europe; besides, the prospect of enhancing Western European security by achieving German rearmament had its own distinct advantages. Therefore, the idea of rearming West Germany and allowing it to take a place within the Western defence arrangements in NATO became a much more serious prospect than it ever had been before the start of the Korean War in June 1950. Yet, while plans for merging the armies of Europe into a single EDC might be viewed as emerging from idealistic theories of integration, in reality the EDC was a means of achieving German rearmament while mitigating fear on the part of France and other Western European countries at the prospect of a renewed German military presence within ten years of the Second World War. The Pleven Plan met with a cool reception in Britain, with Churchill dismissing it as a 'sludgy amalgam' and Eden declining to commit the UK to direct participation; however, Britain ultimately agreed to help partly out of concern that if British forces did not, then the repercussions in domestic French politics might bring about added instability to the already weak French Fourth Republic, leaving France more vulnerable to communist influence.

In August 1954, the French National Assembly voted against ratification of the EDC, and thus France – where the Pleven Plan originated – aborted the EDC. Anthony Eden (at this time Churchill's Foreign Secretary) then stepped in with a solution that, according to Monnet, 'saved Europe', by proposing both to bring West Germany into NATO through the WEU (the Brussels Treaty Organisation) and to station a British army and a tactical air force in West Germany for 50 years.

Policy during the Eden Government

On Churchill's retirement in April 1955, Eden's long-awaited premiership inherited from his predecessor the commitment to both the Commonwealth connection as well as to the special relationship with the US. While Anthony Eden's genius in solving the complex problem presented by German rearmament by creating another European organisation earned him plaudits throughout Western Europe, Europe's federalists – those in favour of establishing and furthering the powers of a supranational entity for European integration – were not satisfied. They desired to build on the success of the ECSC and expand the principle of free trade into a customs union between the Six and other European states, notably Britain, which might join them.

It is easy to undervalue Eden's achievement in Europe. However, during his premiership and previously as Foreign Secretary he successfully pursued policies aimed at achieving European cooperation. His efforts were aimed, though, at achieving an intergovernmental and decidedly non-supranational cooperation. In terms of his sentiment for Britain's involvement in European supranational organisations, he was 'bored'[10] and attached considerably greater significance to the larger arena of international diplomacy involving the USA and USSR. Though some Cabinet members such as Harold Macmillan advised giving serious consideration to joining the Six in discussions for a common market, Eden was adamantly opposed to giving the impression that his government would countenance Britain's membership in any resulting supranational organisation; indeed, he had stated in 1952 while Foreign Secretary, this is 'something which we know in our bones we cannot do'.[11] For Eden, European integration was an alien concept, one for which he maintained a consistent aversion and from which he steered Britain clear throughout his term of office. Thus when the six founding members of the ECSC desired to extend the scope of the ECSC and establish a common market with an extension in its supranational powers, proposing to hold a high-level conference to discuss the possibility of establishing a new supranational organisation, Eden reacted with characteristic antipathy and sent a minor official from the Board of Trade, Russell Bretherton, to the Messina Conference as an observer of the talks. The fact that the Six had sent their foreign secretaries and other senior diplomats while the UK had sent Bretherton[12] highlighted Eden's estimation of the proceedings' value, and revealed a fundamental variance between the seriousness and determination of the Six to succeed and the British government's blindness to this prospect. The nearly oblivious attitude and sheer apathy towards European schemes was near-universal among British policy-makers at this time, with few in Parliament and Whitehall willing to accept that the efforts of the Six could possibly have any significance for Britain or anyone else. The UK's ambassador to France, Gladwyn Jebb, went so far as to report to the Foreign Office that no important developments were likely to result from the Messina discussions.[13] Few were able to consider British membership in any resulting organisation as anything other than beneath British dignity. However, a minority in the Foreign Office took the view that Britain's active participation should be more forthcoming – not so that Britain could take the lead in establishing a supranational organisation (which nearly no one in the UK desired at this time), but so that Britain might steer the proceedings along paths in line with British interests.[14] But Eden's policy of non-engagement prevailed, and Bretherton was withdrawn from the Messina Conference during its initial proceedings. Eden's lack of interest in the affairs of the Six continued throughout his tenure, and his consideration of options for Western European economic arrangements were limited to allowing Harold Macmillan (Eden's Foreign Secretary from April 1955 and then Chancellor from December 1955) to sketch out alternatives to the EEC – a free-trade area plan – which would be palatable to the government and allow for British participation and membership. With Eden's demise hastened by the Suez crisis of 1956 and his recurrent illness, Harold Macmillan became Prime Minister in January 1957.

Macmillan: The Balance Sheet of Empire, Britain's Application for Membership in 'Europe', the Humiliation of the Veto

Macmillan had been an advocate of British participation in the European negotiations for the formation of the EEC, beginning in Messina, Sicily during June 1955 when he had been Foreign Secretary; it is notable that Macmillan had not advocated Britain's participation out of idealistic reasons concerning European integration, but rather that, as the Europeans were pressing ahead, it would be important to forestall any tendency in an emerging European union to act without British influence. However, on this point he had been overruled by Eden. When the Six pressed ahead without UK participation, eventually forming the European Economic Community with the Treaty of Rome in March 1957, Macmillan responded with an initiative to establish an organisation wider in membership than the Six, encompassing a Western European-wide free-trade area. His Plan G was thus an effort to create an intergovernmental organisation that would include the six original EEC members but would also extend to other European countries who wished only free trade and not a customs union or supranational dimension to their relations. Macmillan then offered this alternative to the Six, and resulting discussions between British and European officials continued until French representatives, under instructions from President de Gaulle, vetoed the concept and were withdrawn from negotiations in November 1958.[15] This has become known as de Gaulle's first veto, as it represents the General's refusal to allow the British to alter the character of the emerging community or to allow it to be diverted into directions more consistent with British interests. Britain had, after all, a considerable percentage of its overall trade with the Commonwealth, from which the UK was able to import foodstuffs cheaply (e.g. New Zealand, Australia and Canada had been supplying a considerable amount of Britain's agricultural needs, and the cost of importing agricultural goods from the Commonwealth, relative to the cost of doing so from the Six, was far less). This consideration was crucial to leading members of the Cabinet,[16] who wished to continue unrestricted importing from the Commonwealth.

By this time the Commonwealth was fast developing into a multiracial organisation with an ever-increasing membership, as Britain granted independence to successive colonies – with more scheduled for the 1960s. The British experience largely avoided the severe strains experienced by the French (Vietnam, Algeria), with the notable exceptions of the outrages committed on the instructions of British commanding officers in Kenya's Hola Camp while trying to suppress the

Mau Mau uprisings; the crisis involving Rhodesia (in fact, Southern Rhodesia, but since Northern Rhodesia had already been granted independence as Zambia, it became usual to refer to it simply as Rhodesia); the suppression of the Greek Cypriot terrorist/liberation movement, EOKA; and the problem of apartheid in South Africa until the latter was forced to withdraw from the Commonwealth in 1961. Whereas the French made deliberate efforts to retain Vietnam and Algeria, British policy-makers were careful to accede to colonial sentiment for independence in pace with opinion within African colonies.

In other respects, the Commonwealth was constantly changing, and so was its value to Britain. Macmillan's 'balance sheet of Empire' resulted in a programme for granting independence to colonies in Africa, which had hitherto been considered a suitable option for the long term rather than in the foreseeable future. Nationalism in Africa was in part an outgrowth of the Second World War, with African intellectuals assuming leadership positions within the British-administered colonies and increasingly demanding an acceleration of the timetable for complete responsible government (i.e. internal rule and complete sovereignty except in respect of external relations). In 1957, Ghana received independence and took its place in the Commonwealth – the first African colony to do so. Others followed in succession, both in Africa (Nigeria, 1960) and outside, as the membership swelled by the latter 1960s. The Macmillan government could see that the character of the Commonwealth was changing, exemplified by the altered tone evident in successive Commonwealth prime ministers' meetings.[17] As far as the Commonwealth's future value to Britain in a global diplomatic or economic sense, Macmillan could see the writing on the wall, as even its residual value was manifestly failing to add life to British prestige. In his 'Wind of Change' speech to the South African Parliament in February 1960, Macmillan pointed out that there was a wind blowing through Africa – the wind of African national consciousness, which could not and ought not be resisted. However progressive the government appeared from its statements about the winds of change, it was also aware of events which helped push it much further and much faster down the road of granting independence to its remaining colonies – notably, the example of the Algerian War which led France, under de Gaulle, to accelerate the granting of independence to France's African territories. This had a considerable impact on the British government, putting pressure on British colonial administrators, who had hitherto intended to pursue a slow, measured pace towards eventual self-government for its African possessions.

Compared to the waning asset of the Commonwealth, the EEC in its formative period was proving a success, much to the surprise of leading opinion-makers in Britain, including those in the Foreign Office. Macmillan, who as early as 1955 while Chancellor had foreseen this possibility, now believed that something had to be done to prevent Britain from becoming marginalised. In 1959 the Macmillan Government had taken the lead in establishing the European Free Trade Association (EFTA), intended as intergovernmental counter to the EEC. When EFTA came into existence in 1960, nevertheless the EEC was gaining widespread recognition as the centre of political gravity in Western Europe as its member states flourished in economic growth and enhanced political influence, all of which took the British by surprise.[18] Much as with his review of the likely future assets and liabilities of the areas still under British administration – the 'balance sheet of empire' – Macmillan undertook a review of Britain's proper relationship with the EEC. He was compelled to apply the balance-sheet approach to Britain's relations with the EEC, not liking 'the prospect of a world divided into the Russian sphere, the American sphere and a united Europe of which we were not a member'.[19]

During 1960 Macmillan appointed Sir Frank Lee as chairman of a new interdepartmental Whitehall committee whose remit was to review all aspects of the UK's relations with the EEC and to determine whether British membership would confer an overall net advantage, or disadvantage, and, if the former, to recommend that the government pursue an application for entry. With prior knowledge of Lee's pro-entry views, and having already reconstructed his Cabinet during July 1960 by appointing three ministers whose firm belief in the necessity of entry to the EEC was not in serious doubt, Macmillan launched an effort to carry the entire Cabinet and party with him in his move towards entry. By July 1961, he was ready; the Cabinet had approved Macmillan's plan for opening negotiations with the Six, and on 31 July the Prime Minister announced that the government would now seek to open negotiations with the EEC to determine if the conditions existed for UK entry. He and leading ministers were adamant that there would not only be EEC qualifications for Britain's entry, but also that Britain had various conditions that had to be met before the government would take the final decision on entry, with Macmillan taking the rhetorical stand that the government was not formally applying for membership but only opening negotiations to see if suitable conditions existed before deciding whether to make an application.[20] Macmillan also expected that the UK's membership in 'Europe' would enhance Britain's ability to play a leading role in the world – a preoccupation for Macmillan as much as it had been for Churchill.

Macmillan was successful in bringing the Conservative Party in Parliament, if not in the country at large, solidly behind him as he prepared to undertake negotiations to bring Britain into Europe. The dissidents were limited to very few voices of hesitation, which fell far short of resignation threats. Macmillan reshuffled his Cabinet in the summer of 1960, placing three ministers of reliable pro-entry opinions into key positions. Duncan Sandys was shifted from Aviation to the Ministry for Commonwealth Relations, which would undoubtedly be a sensitive ministry when the time arrived for Macmillan to announce an application for membership of the EEC. Edward Heath was made Lord Privy Seal and assistant to the Foreign Secretary, Lord Home, with special responsibility for European affairs. Christopher Soames became Minister of Agriculture, which would also be of crucial importance to Conservative Party constituents. Macmillan also made the strategic selection of placing R. A. Butler, the Home Secretary, in charge of allaying the concerns of agricultural interests. Butler himself was MP for an agricultural constituency, Saffron Walden in Cambridgeshire, and had expressed concerns to the Prime Minister before the approach to the EEC was decided. Butler having been neutralised, Macmillan's only critics willing to voice their concern in the Conservative Party were limited to those very few, notably Robin Turton and Derek Walker-Smith, who held no current positions of authority in the party. A lively public discussion then took place, in the columns of every leading newspaper, on television and radio, and conferences and public debates brought the issue to the attention of the public as it had never before. Professor William Pickles of the London School of Economics, a Labour supporter and determined critic of Britain's entry to the EEC, was among the academic voices raised against Macmillan's approach; however a broad spectrum of academics, the majority from Oxbridge, supported entry.

The Conservatives under Macmillan had shifted from being the party of empire to the party of Europe, or rather the party favouring entry into the EEC, out of a recognition of shifting patterns of trade and influence. The Commonwealth was rapidly proliferating into a third-world organisation that could by no means be counted upon to assist in Britain's exercise of international power or enhance its prestige, and its share of trade with Britain was shrinking annually while that of EEC member states was increasing. As Britain looked to the USA for its security as senior partner in the special relationship, Macmillan sought out the opinion of President Kennedy in 1961 and was strongly encouraged in his approach for membership of the EEC. What was especially influential in the mind of Macmillan was that if the EEC were to exist without the UK as a member, it would increasingly present a threat to Britain's economy and international influence; not only would the common external tariff make it more difficult for Britain to sell its products to the Six, making the economic case for entry all the more strong, but the political arguments were equally made that there was a risk that future American leaders would increasingly look to the EEC as their European partner in place of Britain – this prospect was of crucial significance to Britain's foreign policy elite and struck a deep chord at this time of national self-doubt and psychological adjustment, as Britain shed its former empire and became 'just another European country'. At the same time, to many there was also the bright prospect that if Britain entered the EEC, then its future would be as a partner in a collective European force in world politics; thus the possibility of moving from imperial power to European power presented an answer to the shrinking of Britain's empire and a wounded pride. Advocates of entry therefore urged others to view the loss of national sovereignty inherent in joining the EEC not as a loss at all, but as a pooling of Britain's sovereignty with that of the other member states, with the result of sharing that larger sovereignty with everyone. At any rate, within the Conservative Party Macmillan succeeded in subduing his critics, and the discussion he opened by his announcement of Britain's application to join the EEC sparked the first domestic debate of its scale on the question of whether Britain's destiny was to be as a European nation.

Regarding the Commonwealth, it is tempting to draw inferences from the fact that Macmillan made his 'Wind of Change' speech during the same year as he undertook Britain's first application to the EEC. This contiguity reveals a shift in thinking away from the Empire/Commonwealth connection, which he considered was likely to confer progressively fewer political economic advantages on to Britain in future, and towards a new European relationship with like-minded post-colonial powers with whom increased commercial relations bore every prospect of leading to Britain's economic recovery, as well as prospects for recovering Britain's diplomatic stature. The trend pulling Britain towards closer relations with Europe was parallel to a trend pushing Britain away from its erstwhile colonies, as the realities of the competitive global marketplace were brought to bear on the British economy. These realities were apparent to Macmillan, and in his shift in favour of UK membership in the EEC his sense of priorities can be seen by the scant regard he was to give to Commonwealth opinion in the process of consultation over Britain's application: he announced that his ministers would hold a series of consultations with the leaders of Commonwealth countries, allowing each member its due opportunity to express its views concerning the implications of Britain's proposed move, but during the course of consultations Macmillan effectively took action to neutralise the deep concerns expressed by several Commonwealth members, who feared the impact that the Common External Tariff would have upon them once the UK entered and EEC and was obliged to end the system of Commonwealth preferences which had allowed imports, notably foodstuffs, to flow into Britain. It was clear that Macmillan was deftly pursuing the application as a chief foreign policy aim, and by successfully navigating his policy through his Cabinet, the Conservative Party, Parliament, the country at large, and with his government's discussions with Britain's Commonwealth partners, he prevailed in marginalising his critics.

Meanwhile the Labour opposition, while having expressed an initial reserved approval for opening negotiations, during 1962 developed its own set of conditions that had to be met before Labour's leadership would support Britain's actual entry. Under Hugh Gaitskell's leadership, these included safeguards for Commonwealth goods, the maintenance of Britain's unqualified control over its foreign and defence policy, and safeguards for British agriculture – collectively known as the 'five conditions'. Above all, it was Labour's concern for the preservation of Britain's Commonwealth links and a reservation about transferring elements of Britain's national sovereignty to the EEC which prevented the party from backing Macmillan's move. By 1962, Hugh Gaitskell, party leader since 1955, announced at Labour's annual conference that for Britain to enter the EEC would go against the grain of 'a thousand years of history', and came out strongly against the government's continuing its application process. Gaitskell had identified Labour as the Commonwealth party, with Wilson contrasting Labour's policy with that of the Conservatives, who were turning their backs on British brethren in the Commonwealth: 'We are not entitled to sell our friends and kinsmen down the river for a problematical and marginal advantage in selling washing machines in Dusseldorf.'[21] These efforts to play the patriotic card were also meeting with some success, and at a meeting of the Commonwealth Labour parties in September 1962 an announcement was made that they did not feel that the British government was adequately safeguarding Commonwealth interests.

The government's prospect of carrying an eventual bill for EEC entry through Parliament was suddenly obviated in January 1963 when French President de Gaulle announced at a press conference that Britain was not ready to enter the Community. In effect, the whole process of negotiation therefore ceased with de Gaulle's veto. The instrument of Britain's humiliation, de Gaulle, was acting in the same interests that had motivated his 1958 refusal to allow French participation in a free-trade area that the British had contrived to embrace not only the Six but also several other Western European countries, which posed a threat to the cohesion of the EEC. His essential view was that the Community was something that could be used by France, and by Europe, to assert an independent line in international affairs, and that Britain's entry would considerably mitigate – even neutralise – this potential independence. In the Cold War context Western Europe played a clearly subordinate role to that of the USA, behind whose military power it found its protection. De Gaulle, however, had come to view the Cold War as something out of date, with a multi-polar world emerging as a political fact. To de Gaulle, it followed therefore that he ought to use French influence to encourage European independence of the USA, whereas permitting Britain to join the EEC would threaten this aim. In short, if the British were so frightened of the EEC that they felt they must enter it to ensure that British influence was not shut out, then it must be something good and must be protected from Britain's Atlanticist influence.

In vetoing British entry, de Gaulle's motive was also to maintain French political predominance among the Six as well as to secure the introduction of a Common Agricultural Policy (CAP) that France could use to protect French farmers. There was also the argument that the British were too close to the Americans and too distant from a 'European vocation' in their defence and foreign policies, with de Gaulle's veto coming just weeks after Macmillan had met with US President Kennedy in Nassau to conclude an agreement securing the nuclear Polaris missile system for Britain. This afforded de Gaulle a convenient pretext for intransigence. But his chief aim was to keep Britain out of the EEC so that France would hold its unquestioned political leadership, and could then be seen to 'lead Europe' from an isolationist or 'third-force' position in world affairs. In short, for de Gaulle, there could only be 'one cock on the dunghill'.[22] De Gaulle had already by this time pursued various efforts to bring France to the centre of Western decision-making; for example, he had requested President Eisenhower to refashion NATO and place it under a grand triumvirate of the USA, France and Britain. De Gaulle viewed Britain as already possessing a favoured relationship with the USA – both within and outside NATO – and as America's closest ally. Thus the odds had always been against de Gaulle allowing Britain to enter the EEC, which would threaten what he viewed as his own potential power base; so much so that commentators in the press cynically remarked that de Gaulle would veto Britain's application on any pretext, even if it contained a single misplaced comma.[23] As de Gaulle had noted when addressing a joint session of Parliament in April 1960, Britain had a unique history, Parliament, navy and Commonwealth, and was essentially extra-European.[24] Its non-European nature and connections meant that it had no place inside Europe, but rather viewed itself as belonging to the Anglo-Saxons. These compliments amounted to a polite rebuff to any thought of Britain turning 'European'. The odds for Britain's entry also worsened after December 1962, following the conclusion of the special deal at Nassau in the Caribbean between Macmillan and Kennedy for the US to supply Britain with Polaris nuclear missiles, an arrangement which highlighted the invidiousness of the Anglo-American special relationship. But at heart, de Gaulle held a fundamental *méfiance* towards Britain, which could not be overcome by blandishment or offers of collaboration; what de Gaulle desired was a reversal of relative French decline and a reordering of NATO into a triumvirate of the USA, France and the UK.

The nomination of Edward Heath, with his unchallengeable pro-European credentials (see below), as Britain's chief representative in the EEC negotiations, was a calculated appeal to de Gaulle in an effort to overcome any reluctance on the part of the latter concerning British entry. But Heath, pro-European that he was, could not neutralise criticism by de Gaulle that Britain was essentially an extra-European nation whose entry to the EEC would disturb the French pre-dominance that de Gaulle sought to maintain within the emerging Community. Not only did he believe that Britain differed from the rest of Europe, but he also wanted to reserve the EEC for his own use in his pursuit of French national interests, something which would be threatened if Britain were allowed to enter and, by its very presence inside the Community, present a challenge to French leadership. De Gaulle could not permit this to happen.

For a few years following de Gaulle's veto of Britain's application in January 1963 the issue of Britain entering the EEC appeared all but dead within the UK. However, there were strong pro-entry advocates in both the Conservative and Labour parties who bided their time, awaiting either the departure of de Gaulle from the scene or a renewed approach to the Six from a future British government. Among those adamantly opposed to entry, there was relief at de Gaulle's action. In Brussels, representatives of the other five EEC countries, together with the Commission, issued a joint statement declaring that Britain's entry to the Community and its adhesion to the Treaty of Rome were their agreed objective. But among both advocates and opponents of UK entry, there was a realisation that there was no immediate prospect of broaching the subject again so long as President de Gaulle remained opposed. Thus the issue receded from public controversy, and during the general election of 1964 few voices were raised in connection with the abortive application. The failure of the initiative caused no measurable harm to the Conservative Party, or gain to Labour in 1964, though Labour spokesmen made clear the party leadership's opposition to entry and its avowal of Commonwealth unity, characterising Britain's relationship with the EEC and Commonwealth as an either/or option which Labour had correctly judged during 1961–3, with its consistent pledges for continued and expanded Commonwealth ties. Thus Labour sought to compare its policy with that of the Conservative Party over Europe, contrasting Labour's pro-Commonwealth policy with the Tories' pro-EEC orientation, hoping to gain political advantage from the failure of the Conservative application at the hands of de Gaulle.

The First Wilson Governments, the Second Application, the Second Veto

It was in this spirit that Harold Wilson came to office in October 1964, seeking to expand Commonwealth links and establish a more meaningful relationship with Britain's former colonial empire as well as with the old or 'white' Commonwealth (Australia, Canada, New Zealand). His plan, which was rudimentary and vaguely defined, was for a Commonwealth economic and diplomatic bloc, with London its centre and the UK as its senior member. This call for the bolstering of the Commonwealth was heard repeatedly from the point at which Wilson assumed leadership of the Labour Party in February 1963 and beyond the 1964 general election.[25] The Labour Party maintained fraternal links with socialist parties of the Commonwealth, and thus throughout its period of opposition from 1951–64 was kept intimately informed as to opinion within the Commonwealth on a range of issues affecting decolonisation, as well as the emerging trend toward third-world non-alignment. It had looked forward to working with these Commonwealth socialist brethren from Number 10 Downing Street and constructing the type of Commonwealth it believed was still possible in 1964. Thus the last time that a British government gave serious consideration to shaping the Commonwealth to suit Britain's interests and enhance British global power as a significant cohesive trading bloc with Britain, was after Labour came to office in October 1964. In this regard, in its inability to adapt to the changing circumstances of increasing Commonwealth disunity and the increasing Europeanisation of Britain's trade patterns, the Labour Party lagged behind the Conservatives by several years.[26]

However, during 1965, the experience of office revealed to Wilson that his hopes for Commonwealth unity, though genuine, had been misplaced. The reality of the changed Commonwealth quickly came alive to Wilson as he witnessed the organisation being increasingly used as an advocacy group by the 'new Commonwealth' members (emerging states in Africa and Asia), who, in a fervour of anti-colonialism, were striving for foreign aid and a neutralist foreign policy in the Cold War. This was all the more apparent after the establishment in 1965 of the Commonwealth Secretariat and the office of Commonwealth Secretary-General, together significant landmarks in the development of the contemporary Commonwealth.[27] Henceforth, the non-aligned countries of the developing world in the 'new Commonwealth' would increasingly dominate its undertakings, and, far from bolstering Britain with diplomatic support, would not be averse to criticising the British government on a whole range of issues. Thus when the Rhodesian government of Ian Smith declared unilateral independence in 1965, the new Commonwealth lined up in opposition to Britain, which failed in its efforts to get Rhodesia to agree to the establishment of a multiracial democracy there. The stridency of Commonwealth critics, and the use of the Commonwealth as a forum for pressures to be brought to bear on Britain, such as the annual Commonwealth Prime Ministers' Meetings[28] and special conferences called to deal with the Rhodesian problem, convinced Wilson that his erstwhile expectations of the organisation's unity were well-nigh impossible to achieve. The fractionalising trend towards non-alignment[29] in the new Commonwealth was one factor tending towards the progressive disintegration of the Commonwealth as a pro-British grouping, though it remained nevertheless an organisation close to the hearts of Labour Party members and others. They valued its continuing importance as a forum for mutual understanding and goodwill between members of various races and levels of development, and esteemed it as representing the successful transformation of an imperialist organisation to one based on voluntary membership and mutual respect between members.

Britain was also under severe economic pressure at this time, with continuous balance-of-payments crises adding urgency to the Wilson government's efforts to find a solution for the UK's short- and long-term commercial survival, and to find a geo-commercial bloc in which it could secure itself and find a productive as well as meaningful world role. Ultimately the Labour Cabinet had to choose between three options: 'Go it alone', a North Atlantic Free Trade Area (NAFTA), entry into the EEC. On the latter, the government itself was divided. In Cabinet there were notable ministers strongly opposed, such as Jay – the strongest opponent – Castle and Peart; ministers mildly opposed or unenthusiastic about entry, such as Benn, Callaghan, Crossman, Crosland and Healey, who believed that whether or not an application was pursued it would in any case be nullified by another veto by de Gaulle; and George Brown, Michael Stewart, Anthony Greenwood and Wilson clearly in favour. Donglas Jay considered that the veto 'merely reasserted what should have been plain before: that Britain should develop and foster her own much wider influence in the world and not dispute fruitlessly with France the control of this particular corner of one continent'.[30] Jay wanted Britain to take the lead in constructing a 'North Atlantic Free Trade Area', 'leaving it to the EEC, and others such as Australia, New Zealand and Japan to join as and when they wished'.[31] Although a version of this NAFTA, or Atlantic trade, idea was strongly supported by US Senator Jacob Javits and other members of the US Congress as well as by state governors,[32] this option was in reality a non-starter, because the US State Department and executive branch led by the President were opposed to such ideas, preferring instead to see Britain enter the EEC and lend its influence towards liberalising trade with the rest of the world and giving a more Atlanticist orientation to defence and foreign policy in the Cold War.

The reasons for Labour opposition to entry were much as they had been during 1961–3, namely fear of the Common Market[33] as a bastion of the free market which would undermine Labour's socialist objectives; fears, too, that entry would not only mean tariffs on Commonwealth produce entering the UK but would lead, more significantly, to the downgrading of the Commonwealth, if not its very dissolution. But Wilson, Michael Stewart – Foreign Secretary from January 1965 to August 1966 – and George Brown – Deputy Prime Minister and, from August 1966, Foreign Secretary – prevailed over the opponents to entry, on Labour's left for the most part, by using the arguments that entry was compatible with socialist planning and that, once inside the EEC, Britain would be able to exert its influence on the Community decision-making in the direction of socialist policies in EEC institutions, and a greater world role for Britain and the enlarged Community. The socialist parties of the Six had eagerly advocated Labour's change of policy towards entry, hoping to see the UK within the Community as soon as possible. The Labour leadership also took stock of the Commonwealth and believed that, on the one hand, while it was a waning asset to the UK, on the other hand, once inside the EEC, Britain could exert its influence and be of greater economic assistance to the Commonwealth. In addition, in the USA the Johnson administration had been encouraging Wilson to consider entry, continuing its tradition of favouring increased Western European unity, a policy which the US had consistently supported since the 1950s under

President Eisenhower and the early 1960s under Kennedy. US policy-makers considered that British entry into the EEC would both bolster Europe's security against Soviet subversion and maintain its Atlanticist character against Gaullist influence. Thus Wilson knew that if he succeeded in bringing the UK into the EEC, he would both enhance Britain's status in the eyes of the USA and make Britain part of Europe's new centre of gravity. He would, in effect, succeed in bringing Britain greater prestige within Winston Churchill's 'three circles' at the centre of the American, European and Commonwealth relationships.

Also important to Wilson's conversion regarding entry was the UK's balance-of-payments crises and the overall economic and political decline afflicting Britain. Wilson saw national salvation coming from EEC membership – something that would at last address Britain's continuing economic crisis and political impotence. He believed that EEC membership would both enhance Britain's ability to be a world leader and give an expected boost to British commerce. In November, therefore, the Cabinet agreed that Wilson and Brown should undertake a 'probe' of the capitals of the Six to assess the climate of opinion for Britain's possible entry. It was decided that Brown should not go alone, although this diplomatic effort was clearly within his sphere of competence; it was thought that Brown, arguably the strongest advocate of entry in the Cabinet, would return with a report that minimised or dispelled any problems he encountered from the leaders of the Six in discussing a British application. Wilson therefore was to accompany Brown. The irony of this arrangement was that by this time Wilson himself had been converted to entry, anticipating that a successful application would confer several advantages: not only would it enhance Britain's economic situation, giving an expected boost to trade and subjecting inefficient British industries to the cold winds of competition, but it would also allow Labour to exert its influence within an enlarged Community on behalf of the European centre-left; the effort, whether successful or not, would also be electorally popular with domestic Euro-enthusiasts, including entry advocates in the Labour Party. Wilson, Brown and their senior civil servants were equally enthusiastic about entry because of what they imagined were the prospects for Britain, once part of this larger bloc, to wield significant global power again; and their delusions of grandeur also included a belief that the supposed superiority of British leadership would allow the UK to exercise dominant influence inside the EEC. As George Brown was to urge the West German Foreign Minister and Vice-Chancellor: 'Willy, you must get us in so we can take the lead' – an attitude that Professor John Young has characterised as 'naïve arrogance'.[34] In addition, Wilson also had his eye on the attitude of the US administration, which in its long-standing policy was known to be favourable to Britain's entry to the EEC.

Wilson returned from his tour of the capitals of the Six hopeful that the difficulties that persisted with French President de Gaulle could be successfully overcome by various means, including the offer of joint Anglo-French technological projects. In this regard, at the Guildhall in November 1967 Wilson was to announce his desire to see the establishment of a European Technological Community as the technological wing of the activities of the EEC. By again appealing to the efficacious powers of 'technology', Wilson was using the issue as a panacea to overcome the ideological differences in his party over the European issue, as he had during 1962–4 over internal ideological differences in the Labour Party. However, it is also clear that Wilson genuinely desired to see technological advances in British industry which, if it worked together with that of other EEC countries, would be able to stand up to the industrial dominance of the USA, and to this extent he was an advocate of Britain taking part in European integration.

However, having brought the bulk of the Labour Party to accept the idea of entry, no sooner did Wilson announce his government's intention to apply for membership in May 1967 than President de Gaulle announced another veto on British membership. Thus the application was stillborn. This brought about a sigh of relief from many Labour ministers, who wanted to avoid Britain's entry into the EC and who believed that de Gaulle had saved the British government from its own folly;[35] but Wilson and Brown, not accepting that their defeat should forever bar Britain from entry, decided to leave the application 'on the table' to be reactivated whenever the political conditions in France permitted. Thus the application was left 'on the table' at the end of 1967. In 1969, after de Gaulle resigned from office in France, the Labour government looked ahead to reactivating the application. But before negotiations could be opened, the Labour government fell at the 1970 general election and Edward Heath, an ardent Europhile, predictably took up the application to the EC[36] as his highest priority in international policy.

Heath and the Primacy of Europe: Britain Enters 'Europe'

Since his maiden speech in 1950 in which he advocated that the British government join the Schuman Plan talks leading to the ECSC, Heath was a known pro-European, consistent in his devotion to Britain's eventual entry to Europe and equally consistent in his wish that Britain take part in the development of an 'ever-closer union' in the EEC – an attitude termed *communautaire* on the Continent. Heath had seen the destruction wrought in Germany at close hand and claims that a desire to see post-war Germany wedded to the rest of Western Europe was his prime motivation in consistently advocating closer links between Britain and Europe.[37] After the Conservatives won the 1970 general election, everyone expected that as Prime Minister Heath would make entry his chief foreign policy aim, and soon after taking office he picked up the application from 'the table' to resume pursuing it with the EEC leaders, a policy that the Wilson government would have pursued had it not lost office.

The chief obstruction having been removed, Heath could now pursue an agreement with de Gaulle's successor, Georges Pompidou, and looked forward at last to Britain's application receiving consideration. Almost immediately after the June 1970 election, negotiations with the EC opened,[38] culminating in the crucial Heath–Pompidou summit of 1971 and the signing of the Treaty of Accession in January 1972; domestically, during 1971–2 Heath navigated the European Comunities Bill through the Commons, despite the large number of known sceptics[39] and outright opponents of entry within the Conservative Party and in the face of public opinion polls reflecting adverse judgements on Britain's entry to Europe. In the first reading of the European Comunities Bill in October 1971, Heath was to secure 356 votes in favour of the entry terms he had negotiated with the EC, against 244 opposed. This vote was secured by deciding to hold a free vote instead of enforcing the party whip, with many leading MPs on both sides of the aisle having strong opinions. Thus Heath was to benefit from the additional votes of pro-entry Labour MPs, and in the final arithmetic the Labour and Liberal MPs voting with the government outweighed the number of anti-entry Labour MPs voting with the Conservative opponents, as 69 Labour MPs voted their approval of entry, with 20 abstaining; this was against 39 Conservative MPs voting against the government, with 2 abstaining.[40] In February 1972, the Bill's second reading was secured by a close 309–301 vote (with 15 Conservative noes and 4 abstentions); but ultimately Heath was to see the European Communities Bill pass its third reading in July 1972 with 301 in favour, 284 against (16 Conservative noes and 4 abstentions, and 13 Labour abstentions). Thus Heath was a proud parent to the European Communities Act, 1972 and on 1 January 1973 the United Kingdom formally entered the EC.

Even in the absence of de Gaulle, Heath had been careful in his negotiations with the EC not to appear pro-American in sentiment or policy for fear of raising suspicions in France that Britain would be an American 'Trojan horse', thus risking the possibility of yet another veto. This policy did not prove difficult, for it reflected Heath's deeply held convictions that Britain's future should be within an increasingly federal Europe, and not as junior partner of the USA. From the outset of Heath's premiership, this change in outlook and policy was evident, and in this regard, as Henry Kissinger has noted in his description of Anglo-American relations at this time, throughout his time as Prime Minister, Heath sought to eschew contact with President Nixon, not even meeting him until after several months following the Conservative election victory. Similarly, Heath went to great lengths to distance himself from policies of revitalising the Commonwealth or harmonising Britain's overseas commercial and economic policies with those of Commonwealth countries. Heath's heart was not in the Commonwealth; rather, his view was that if the Commonwealth countries were themselves moving away from Britain and pursuing policies and alliances to their own advantage and to the exclusion of Britain – such as the ANZUS Treaty between Australia, New Zealand and the USA, which demonstrated the reality of centrifugal tendencies eroding any residual unity left in the Commonwealth as a single entity – then why should Britain stay attached to the outdated idea of maintaining close economic and political links with the Commonwealth?[41] Not that Heath needed to be reminded of the shortcomings of attempting to utilise the Commonwealth for the purpose of furtherance of British foreign or commercial policies, since during 1971 war broke out between India and Pakistan over Bangladesh. The Commonwealth by this time had a membership overwhelmingly from the developing world, and one of the strengths of the organisation was supposed to be its usefulness in conflict resolution among its members. In a body as geographically and racially diverse as the Commonwealth, with the full ideological spectrum represented among its membership, it would have been unrealistic to expect all its member countries to maintain agreement on anything except generalities such as the importance of world peace and understanding. However, when conflict does occur among members, the Commonwealth organisation can be useful as a forum for holding talks aimed at peaceful resolution. Britain should therefore cut the umbilical cord and join Europe, whatever impact this would have on the cohesion of the Commonwealth, just as individual Commwealth members were pursuing their own interests with decreasing regard for the former imperial nexus. Heath's earnest desire to secure Britain's place inside 'Europe', therefore, implied not only his aversion to the UK–US 'special relationship' but also to attaching any special status to the Commonwealth. Indeed, whenever possible Heath even eschewed meeting with American or Commonwealth leaders. In desiring to place such emphasis on Britain's position as a European power and to consciously de-emphasise its Commonwealth and American connections, Heath was to alter Winston Churchill's 'three-circles' approach to British foreign policy. He was a 'one-circle' man.

Britain formally entered the EC in January 1973, but Heath's expectations of the economy receiving a boost failed to materialise; indeed, within months of accession the world oil crisis began to unfold, with dire consequences for the country. By early 1974, Britain's industrial relations were also breaking down and Heath called a general election for February. The election failed to produce a majority for the Conservatives or Labour, and after overtures to the Liberals proved fruitless in securing an electoral agreement, Heath was forced to bow to the inexorable arithmetic in the Commons and resign, so that Harold Wilson returned to office as Prime Minister. In departing office with Britain inside the EC, however, Heath could still reflect that he had accomplished his one overriding objective in public life. However, there were strong indications that Labour had again swung back to a sceptical stance, an ominous sign for those anxious to secure Britain's position in the Community.

Labour's Re-emergent Scepticism, the Referendum

During Heath's entry negotiations, the Labour Party had voiced concern that the agreed terms and conditions of UK entry were giving away too much to the Community. Wilson stated that he could not in good conscience vote in favour of them, although several leading labour MPs pointed out that if such terms had been offered to the Labour government in 1967 or at any point before Heath became Prime Minister, they would have been accepted by the Labour Cabinet. Wilson was trying to appease his backbenches, whose predominant sentiment was that entry had not taken due account of British interests. In reality, this was only partly cynicism. The UK net contribution had been agreed by Heath, who was anxious to conclude entry negotiations without querulously prolonging them, which would have raised the possibility of further French objections to UK membership. Heath, having seen this happen at close quarters during 1962–3 as Britain's chief negotiator during Macmillan's application bid, now adopted an 'enter then negotiate' attitude, leaving problems such as Britain's net contribution to the EC budget for subsequent negotiation. However, Labour now seized upon the issue of Britain's EC net contribution, which became the gravamen on which the Labour government focused, pressing the issue of its disproportionate and unfair burden on the UK. Accordingly, during the October 1974 general election campaign Labour was committed to holding a referendum on Britain's continued membership of the EC and, should the referendum result in a Yes vote for continued membership, then the Labour government would insist on a renegotiation of Britain's terms of membership. Labour had decided there were three methods that might be used to address the shortcomings they discerned in Heath's terms of entry: renegotiation and adjustment to Britain's terms of accession; holding a referendum on Britain's membership; or withdrawal from the EC altogether. Following the election, Wilson's government began pursuing renegotiations with its European colleagues while simultaneously deliberating whether to hold a referendum on the question of membership itself. Eventually the government decided to adopt the first and second approaches, leaving the option for UK withdrawal from the EC as something for the people to decide. Thus, through the Cabinet's device of the referendum, Labour was to climb aboard this 'life-raft' and thereby avoid the rough seas that would inevitably have struck the government if it had adopted a firm policy in either the 'pro' or 'anti' direction. During this time, however, it is clear that Harold Wilson wanted Britain to remain inside the EC, and was convinced that the subject of debate should be limited to the terms of membership and not the principle of membership itself.[42] He moved his Cabinet therefore in the direction of negotiating improved terms for Britain.

In the Commons debate on EC membership during April 1975, after which the decision to hold a referendum was approved, the crucial vote on the question of Britain's continued membership in the EC saw the Labour Party voting 145 to 137 against. Though the divided party had voted in effect for Britain's withdrawal from the EC, Wilson's policy was saved because of the assistance of the 'pro' votes of Conservative and Liberal MPs, bringing the combined totals to 396 voting for continued membership to 170 against. Thus Wilson was able to press ahead with the referendum and renegotiation, rather than being compelled to withdraw the UK from the EC. However, it was clear that the Labour Party was not going to give in that easily, and later that month, at a party conference convened on the EC issue, members voted 2:1 for withdrawal; Wilson dismissed this as a minor hiccup. The Prime Minister had determined, on one hand, that renegotiation rather than withdrawal was the best strategy for him to appease as many sides as possible in the debate, and on the other that there was no credible alternative for Britain than to remain in the EC. This was the same conclusion Wilson had arrived at during 1966–7, so that Britain's membership of the EC should be seen, rather than as the most favoured policy, really as something *faute de mieux* as far as the Prime Minister, the bulk of the Labour Party, and the country at large were concerned.

During 1974–5 the national debate over EC membership made for some interesting temporary political alliances, such as during the February 1974 general election campaign when the Conservative notable Enoch Powell publicly announced that, because of Labour's sceptical attitude to membership of the

EC, he was voting Labour and urged all voters to vote Labour as well. Powell had been a leading Conservative front-bench spokesman in the 1960s, and before the 1970s had sounded quite different on the European question, especially as he realised that Britain's erstwhile international leadership of the Commonwealth was increasingly a burden rather than asset in the exercise of Britain's international influence.

However, his scepticism towards the Commonwealth did not lead to any faith in the EC, and his growing opposition to Britain's place inside it was to identify him as one of those who viewed the future of Britain's relationship with supranational Europe not as a matter of pragmatic partisan politics but as an issue of principle. As Powell had supported Heath and the Conservatives during the 1970 election, he explained his new opposition to Heath in terms of the Prime Minister's commitment to bringing Britain into the EC. His decision to place his conscience on Europe above party loyalty was to represent a growing trend in British politics. Already, by the early 1970s, Roy Jenkins had resigned from the front bench of the Labour Party in opposition to Britain's entry to the EC, and by the 1990s the alignment of British politics according to the European issue led to open discussion by prominent political figures about the possibility of establishing two new parties, one pro-EC and the other anti-EC, which would rupture traditional party politics and establish a new dichotomy. A foreshadowing of this sentiment was seen following the February 1974 election, when Powell was to make a telling observation on the impact that his opposition to Heath's pro-EC views had had on the outcome of the general election. He said: 'I put him in, and I took him out.'

The referendum on Britain and the EC finally took place on 5 June and confirmed UK membership, with approximately two-thirds of voters[43] expressing their approval. Though this resounding victory for advocates of membership seemed to put an end to this controversy once and for all, it was immediately pointed out that the Yes vote was achieved after a spending and media blitz undertaken by the EC office in London as well as by groups such as the European Movement, and that in total the 'pro' side had outspent the 'anti' campaign by an estimated 2:1 ratio – roughly the same proportion as had voted Yes in the referendum. In addition, the European Commission office in London had been able to exert influence by distributing leaflets and funding the dissemination of 'pro' literature throughout the UK during the pre-referendum campaign. All considered, the uneven proportion of spending had led to an uneven result. As Douglas Jay commented: 'It was perhaps not wholly surprising that with leaflets nationally distributed in the ratio of two to one, the vote should have been in the ratio of two to one', a view subsequently confirmed by Professor Vernon Bogdanor of Oxford University,[44] but later amplified or recanted.[45] Neither did this victory put an end to the question of withdrawal as a controversy within the Labour Party, although for the rest of the decade the issue was to lapse.

Following the June referendum, during the remainder of 1975, Callaghan successfully renegotiated Britain's contribution and achieved a more favourable overall financial settlement involved in Britain's obligations to the EC. Still, the Labour Party at large and Parliamentary Labour Party backbenchers sought to hold a referendum on the very issue of Britain's continued membership in Europe. Though the principle of membership had, on the surface, been settled, the issue of a single currency for the EC countries (the European Monetary Union, or EMU) also began to take on importance on the European agenda during 1975, under the terms of which all EC member states were to sign up to lock their currencies together in a system in which exchange rates would be allowed to fluctuate only within a given range. The idea of monetary union had been previously agreed by EC leaders, and the plan was that the exchange-rate mechanism (ERM) or 'tunnel' was to be a prelude to a subsequent merging of currencies into a single European currency. It was at this point that European leaders, under the initiative of Helmut Schmidt of West Germany and Valéry Giscard d'Estaing of France, sought to move forward the agenda for monetary integration. However, although urged on by his German and French colleagues to bring Britain on board as a party to the ERM, Callaghan – Foreign Secretary since 1974 – again made known his opposition to British participation in the scheme and ensured that the UK would remain outside its operation for the duration of his time in office.

The Callaghan Government

After Wilson announced his retirement in March 1976, James Callaghan won the Labour Party leadership, taking over from Wilson as Prime Minister. Callaghan was never more than lukewarm towards Britain's membership of the Community. This created some irony between January and June 1977, when, under Callaghan, Britain for the first time was to hold the rotating presidency of the EC. During his three years as Prime Minister, Britain experienced continued economic crisis, and the EC received partial blame for contributing to Britain's recession, especially regarding the matter of the UK's net contribution to the EC budget, which remained unresolved. There was also the aggravating circumstance that the British consumer was now paying rising prices for EC agricultural products which the UK was obliged to import in place of the relatively inexpensive foods formerly imported from Commonwealth countries.

Though Callaghan worked hard and pursued a hard-nosed negotiation with European colleagues regarding the UK net contribution, he has received scant credit for standing up for Britain's interests. At the time, however, this had bipartisan support, and after 1979 the new Conservative administration looked favourably towards continuing Labour's policy of seeking a recalculation of the UK's net contribution. Callaghan's policies towards the Commonwealth stood in continuity with Wilson's and included a realistic comprehension of the Commonwealth's limited value to British foreign policy. However, to the extent that the organisation's frequent consultations afforded British diplomats information valuable for subsequent interchange with American and European leaders, given that Britain's position at the centre of the Commonwealth and the goodwill it sought to maintain with its former empire at times allowed the Foreign Office to gather 'insider' information, the government recognised the Commonwealth's value. Callaghan himself had served in the Royal Navy during the Second

World War and later was to be shadow Colonial Minister, during which time he came to know leaders throughout the Commonwealth, cultivating especially close personal relations with individual socialist leaders. But the Commonwealth as it stood during the later 1970s had become a group whose raison d'être was simply a vaguely defined international goodwill and mutual understanding between peoples of all backgrounds, races and religions. Its guiding principle of mutual respect and equality between all members, together with the indistinctness of its goals, meant that while the Commonwealth was a forum for discussion and the possible resolution of conflict, it bore no direct relationship to Britain's vital national interests; it was increasingly just a talking shop for its members from the developing world.

During his premiership, as before, Callaghan's apathy towards Europe was apparent, even as he realised that, the referendum having produced a Yes vote, Britain had no realistic alternative to membership of the EC. Insofar as Callaghan's policy towards Europe meant that Britain would not be party to further moves involving concessions of Britain's national sovereignty, he was never convinced that the ideals of European integration were ones for which there was any necessity of British participation, and as for matters on the European agenda such as an eventual European common foreign policy or defence force, Callaghan considered that Western Europe's defence could best be maintained through NATO rather than through any exclusively European alternative. In considering international partnerships, if there was one in which Callaghan placed great confidence, he consistently preferred America, and during 1977, following the death of Anthony Crosland and the appointment of David Owen as Foreign Secretary, Callaghan's son-in-law Peter Jay was appointed as Ambassador to the United States. This move highlighted the special consideration Callaghan gave to maintaining smooth relations with the USA, as Jay, arguably second to none in his relationship with Callaghan, was also notable in his sympathies towards America, commenting on his appointment that 'Britain and the US are the two countries that I really love most in the world and I can think of nothing I would rather do than to represent one in the other.' As Prime Minister, Callaghan's policy and attitude towards Europe is best summarised by a celebrated remark he had made while Foreign Secretary, one which has been taken to epitomise his stance on Britain's involvement in the deepening of the EC, 'Non, merci beaucoup.' All things considered, as the end of Callaghan's premiership approached, the Conservative leader Margaret Thatcher appeared prepared to carry on Callaghan's fight for a more equitable UK net contribution, and there were favourable indications that her attitude towards the EC would stand a chance of improving relations with Britain's European colleagues.

Developments during the Thatcher Era

As Thatcher entered Number 10 Downing Street in May 1979, everyone expected that she would continue Callaghan's policy regarding the UK net budget contribution, though the general expectation was that she would do so with a tone of collegiality if not emollience with Britain's EC partners. Earlier in her career Thatcher had characterised herself as holding moderate pro-European views, including a favourable attitude to Britain's entry into the EC, and she had voted in favour of entry during the Heath government's debates in the Commons. It was therefore all the more surprising when the new Prime Minister expressed her adamant disapproval of the terms Britain was likely to get in any new round of negotiations when she made her position known to EC leaders, and few would have predicted the robustness and stridency – and domestic popularity – of Thatcher's insistence on 'getting Britain's money back'. From her entry to Number 10 in 1979, Thatcher continually raised with EC leaders the matter of Britain's disproportionate net contribution, soon making a name for herself for her resolution and insistence in overcoming the defiance of her negotiating partners.[46] Finally, at the Fontainebleau Summit in 1984, in a political trade-off the EC leaders agreed to a revised rate of contribution for the UK which was acceptable to Thatcher. Yet this episode created a controversy on either side of the pro/anti cleavage in British politics, as Thatcher is blamed by British Europhiles for having aroused, in their view, unnecessary anti-European-ism in Britain, while among Euro-sceptics she is remembered for having stood up for Britain and successfully negotiated a fair bargain in the face of adverse circumstances and tough-nosed European interests.

Subsequent to the agreement at Fontainebleau, Thatcher remained suspicious of the motives of those seeking the 'deepening' of European integration which would involve further surrenders of Britain's national sovereignty. However, she was also strongly interested in enhancing the free market and returning the British economy to profit-making and laissez-faire principles, rolling back the frontiers of state control. In seeking to denationalise industries, her governments sought to bring about wholesale privatisation of the British economy in those sectors which had seen nationalisation during the years of the 'post-war consensus' (since 1945). In this respect, Thatcher was amenable to seeing Britain involved in the extension of European integration even though it would mean a further cession of national sovereignty, as this would be excusable for the sake of expanding free-market principles throughout the EC as a single market. Thus when discussions involving the single market appeared on the agenda of European leaders during the mid-1980s, Thatcher, though still sceptical in outlook towards the ideals of European integration, was persuaded to assent to the Single European Act. By this Act, which was signed during 1986 and ratified in 1987, the powers that were given from the UK to the EC included those pertaining to the single market. Thatcher was critical of others in her government for their strong desire for increased monetary integration, and has repeatedly highlighted her personal distaste for moves towards a single currency and other moves towards 'deepening' the EU, being opposed to the ERM but forced to agree to Britain entering it because of the combined pressure of her Chancellor, Nigel Lawson, and her Foreign Secretary, Geoffrey Howe; there was also the knowledge that if she did not agree to Britain's participation in the new treaty then the rest of the EC would proceed without Britain. Under these circumstances, it was considered better if Britain agreed the Single European Act (SEA) and was therefore able to exert its influence on the EC from within, than to be influenced by it from without. This logic Thatcher found compelling, as did her ministers; however, the unity they enjoyed with regard to the SEA was a spurious one and did not extend to the issue of Europe's ultimate destination. Though kept under control during Thatcher's premiership, this controversy was later to re-emerge in the Conservative Party.

In her dealings with the Commonwealth, Thatcher evidently did not attach much importance to the organisation which, in her estimation, could neither act on its own as a geopolitical actor of any importance nor confer any enhancement to Britain's political clout. This policy was based on her realistic analysis of the status which the Commonwealth failed to command around the world, as well as a due appreciation of the limited goals and efforts of the body, whose periodic gatherings stood for the propagation of such ideals as goodwill and mutual understanding among all races and creeds. Something of Thatcher's consideration of the Commonwealth in the formation of British policy can be seen in her reaction to the sanctions which the Commonwealth had imposed on the racist regime in South Africa. These actions did not influence her own attitude, which was opposed to further sanctions, and at the 1985 Commonwealth summit, for example, Thatcher was willing to resist pressures from Commonwealth leaders desiring to isolate and force Britain to adopt a firmer posture towards South Africa. This epitomised her contemptuous attitude towards the organisation, which was based on her realistic appreciation of power politics and the Commonwealth's expendable status in Britain's exercise of international influence.

Like Callaghan, Thatcher had an instinctive preference for the US and its leaders and consistently valued the relationship that Britain had with the USA more highly than that with Europe – or with the Commonwealth. She had remarkable success in establishing close relations with the American President Ronald Reagan, relations which were arguably as close as they had ever been since the Second World War had brought Churchill and Roosevelt together, and relations which overshadowed Britain's other, secondary relationships.

Her decision in December 1985 to purchase helicopters from the US company, Westland, instead of choosing a rival European firm, caused a controversy and the resignation of two ministers from her government; it also exemplified the debate between those who favoured increased ties with Britain's European partners and others who preferred the foreign and defence policy emphasis on maintaining the pre-eminent Anglo-American 'special relationship'. Thatcher never left any doubt which direction her policy represented, and maintained and amplified these views in the House of Lords in her retirement. When, for example, she was asked about her view on the future of a European single currency, Lady Thatcher offered the observation, 'Why do we need it?'[47]

Thatcher's attitude represented a swing in Conservative policy away from the Heath years of favoured European ties and a definite European future for Britain. Indeed, inside the Conservative Party Thatcher came as close as was politically acceptable to a reversal of Heath's priorities on Europe and the USA. But it would be wrong to view Thatcher's policies as representing a significant change in the overall course of post-war British foreign policy; rather, it was the policies of the Heath years that represented an aberration in Britain's overseas policy, away from the consistently held closeness to the USA and the scepticism towards too close an involvement in European integration. Nevertheless, Thatcher's emphasis on the American relationship, the cornerstone of her foreign policy, did not imply that her government could ignore the European Communities, and together with EC leaders she was to participate in a number of summits which led to furthering the progress of European integration – notably, the moves set in train to bring about the single market. The Single European Act, negotiated during 1985–6, emerged from an intergovernmental conference of EC leaders in 1985, and was designed to create a single market by 1992 throughout the EC with rules to ensure equal opportunities for all states operating within that market. Thatcher recognised that the SEA would operate along lines that were congenial to British commercial interests, for though it had been initially propounded by EC leaders, British negotiators had fully participated in the negotiations and drafting of this European proposal. The commercial nature of the SEA, together with the inbuilt features for the extension of the market mechanism, was precisely the sort of project that Thatcher desired to see the EC embrace – if it had to embrace any – and it was therefore unsurprising that her government approved the necessary extension in EC competencies implied in economic union, which meant that British leaders were now agreeing that the EC should assume the set of competencies prerequisite to the operation of the single market. However, the goal of economic and monetary union (EMU) also contained the implied collateral goal of a common currency for the EC; and as a prerequisite step, the common currency (to be known first as the ECU or European Currency Unit, and then later, the euro) was to be prepared by membership of the ERM to which all member states were expected to commit themselves in advance of establishing the ECU. This presented a tension for Thatcher in that even though she had agreed to the commercial objectives of the single market, she disagreed with those who now viewed EMU and its ERM as being inextricably linked with the operation of the single market; and to this objective of her European partners, the record of Thatcher's resistance is clear. In addition, Thatcher was successful in keeping Britain out of certain other creations of the EC, for instance by resisting the implementation in Britain of the Social Charter (the Charter on the Fundamental Social Rights of Workers), which had emanated from the European Commission one month after the Report on European Economic and Monetary Union which had emerged during April 1989 under the aegis of the President of the European Commission, Jacques Delors. Once the Social Charter was adopted in December 1989 by the European Council meeting in Strasbourg, Thatcher pressed for a UK opt-out on account both of the costs anticipated in its implementation and what was deemed its socialist orientation.[48]

Critics of Thatcher's subsequent regrets about supporting the SEA point out that while in government she *had* actually legislated the Act and in 1990 agreed to Britain's entry into the ERM. However, it is also clear that during 1985–9 she had resisted pressures to support Britain joining the ERM and had eventually done so only because these pressures had become too great to bear. Her two pro-European ministers – the Chancellor, Nigel Lawson, and the Foreign Secretary, Geoffrey Howe – had confronted her with an ultimatum during

1989. Insofar as she had seen advantages for Britain in co-sponsoring further European integration, her motive had been mainly to secure the extension of the free-market principle that she held dear, as well as to make smooth the operation of the market throughout Europe, which was also expected to work to the advantage of British businesses whose range of operations was increasingly not only on a national but on a European scale. In any event, by the time that EMU was written into the Treaty on European Union in 1992, Thatcher, who had already left office during 1990, was vociferously opposing its ratification in the UK.

During her final years as Prime Minister, Thatcher gave an address to the College of Europe in Bruges, setting out her views of the EC's future as well as highlighting her sceptical approach to the ideals of 'ever-closer union' and her preference for a Europe of nation states. Stressing her conviction that the EC should strive to maintain the integrity of independent sovereign states, and that Europe would be great because Britain is Britain, and France is France, to paraphrase Charles de Gaulle's ideal of the EC as a 'Europe des patries', she highlighted her preference for intergovernmental over supranational arrangements. By voicing such a vision, Thatcher was viewed as standing in the way of increased or deepened integration, and immediately acquired an obstructionist image as a 'bad European', that designation having been in abeyance since the departure of President de Gaulle in 1969. Her speech (September 1988), however, was taken up by advocates of an intergovernmental approach to European cooperation as one of the definitive statements on the future of Europe. In its immediate aftermath, it inspired Euro-sceptics in Britain to establish the 'Bruges Group' (February 1989) as a pressure group comprising notables from a range of professions, including Norman Stone of Oxford University and Alan Sked of the London School of Economics.

While the Conservatives were in government under Margaret Thatcher during 1979–90, the Labour Party underwent radical shifts in its attitude towards Europe. During the early Thatcher years, the Labour opposition had again swung back to an 'anti' stance, as the party's activist left-wing contingent emerged into prominence and their leaders assumed important positions in the party hierarchy. As Callaghan stepped down as party leader in the year following Labour's election defeat, his successor from November 1980 was the radical Michael Foot, who lost no time in making known his opposition to Britain's continued membership in the EC, and under his leadership during 1981–3 Labour adopted a policy committed to withdrawing the UK from the EC in the event that Labour should win office at the next general election. By self-consciously characterising itself as a Euro-sceptic party, becoming in effect the anti-European alternative to the Conservative Party, Labour allowed the Conservatives to adopt a more sceptical approach to the EC while also avoiding the charge of being anti-European, therefore affording Thatcher more flexibility in her European policies than if Labour had adopted a moderate tone.

This, together with related developments in Labour's 'lurch to the left' at its Wembley Conference in January 1981, precipitated the departure of several moderates in the party, who then formed the Social Democratic Party (SDP), therefore leaving the rump of the Labour Party as an increasingly left-wing party and making Thatcher and the Conservatives appear moderates on European policy. The SDP received a tremendous swelling of public support, support which expanded further after it formed an electoral alliance with the Liberal Party. In the 1983 general election, the new SDP–Liberal Alliance, which was avowedly pro-European in its policies advocating Britain's involvement in the deepening of the EC, secured approximately 25.4 per cent of the popular vote (just 2 per cent less than the Labour Party obtained with 27.6 per cent), taking the lion's share of its support from Labour and allowing the Conservatives a victory based on 42.4 per cent of the popular vote.[49]

Following Foot's defeat by Thatcher in the 1983 general election, many in the Labour Party increasingly realised that its anti-EC position was prolonging Labour's intra-party strife and benefiting the Conservatives. With the accession of Neil Kinnock to the leadership in 1983, the commitment to withdrawal shifted to a moderate acceptance of Britain's membership, a policy shift that had been strongly advocated by Labour's new deputy leader, Roy Hattersley, an avowed Europhile of long-standing credentials and as stalwart an advocate of Britain's participation in the EC as was Heath or Jenkins.

Kinnock was also assisted in the reorientation of Labour's views towards the conclusive acceptance of UK membership in the EC, not only by pro-European leaders within Labour, but also by the unexpected input of the European Commission President Jacques Delors. Delors was a French socialist by origin, and in a move designed to help win the hearts of Labour's trade union supporters, in September 1988 he accepted an invitation to address the Trades Union Congress. His speech went far in convincing Labour followers that membership in the EC could be of benefit to a number of Labour interests in Britain, and successfully challenged the notion that the EC was a capitalist conspiracy, which hitherto had been widely held in the party. Therefore as Thatcher was herself demonstrating a sceptical approach towards the EC, Kinnock was able to provide Labour with a favourable European image and successively shifted his party towards a more constructive orientation to Community matters, presenting Labour as the party more likely to effectively participate with Britain's European partners and to secure agreements advancing the interests of the average Briton. Thus to avoid continued strife within the Labour Party, and in recognition of the ideological compatibility that the EC shared with Labour, Kinnock convinced the party leadership to adopt a moderate manifesto in which Britain's continued membership of the EC was to be assured under any future Labour government. However, despite Kinnock's efforts at mending Labour's European policy, including the acceptance of UK membership and the more favourable attitude that Labour had come to espouse since 1983, Labour in the general election of 1987 was able to improve its share of the vote to only 31.7 per cent, which was greater than the alliance's 23.2 per cent, but still behind the Conservatives' 43.4 per cent. In terms of seats in the House of Commons, the number of Labour MPs increased from 209 to 229, that of the Alliance decreased from 23 to 22, with the Conservatives reduced from 397 to 376 but still holding a clear majority.[50] In 1992, John Smith succeeded Kinnock as Labour leader, and maintained the party's commitment to continued EC membership, and though Labour distinguished its EC policies from those of the

Conservatives, for example in its desire for UK adherence to the Social Charter, its differences were in the main those of nuance. Still, for the Labour Party, the commitment to Britain's future inside the EC was clearly secure.

The Major Governments: 'At the Heart of Europe'

John Major succeeded Thatcher as Prime Minister in November 1990. It was expected that his European policies would resemble those of Thatcher, since he was known to be her favoured successor, and indeed, with her imprimatur, he initially pleased many Euro-sceptics, both in his efforts to preserve the remaining sovereignty of the EC's nation-states and in negotiating its next treaty in a fashion ostensibly aimed at advancing its intergovernmental character and impeding as much as possible the encroachment of supranationalism. Major's pronouncements on his vision of Britain's relationship with the EC, however, emphasised a Britain fully participating with its European colleagues in the construction of Europe, and on a visit to Germany he even stated his desire to see Britain 'at the heart of Europe'. While such a rhetorical flourish was designed to appeal to both pro-EC and sceptical sentiment at home, as well as to his EC partners abroad, appearing as all things to all men presented difficulties for Major's aims involving the EC when his government's policies were fought over in Cabinet. This, throughout the duration of his government, experienced an ever-widening rift between Europhile and Euro-sceptic ministers.

During his government, some important developments in European integration occurred, notably the negotiation of the Maastricht Treaty (or Treaty on European Union, TEU) during 1991–2. In negotiating the TEU in Britain, Major secured an opt-out from the Social Chapter, succeeded in maintaining continued passport controls, and eventually claimed that the final version of the agreement represented a net victory for British interests. Major nevertheless anticipated a difficult passage for Maastricht in the House of Commons, and therefore announced that the vote was to be taken as an issue of confidence, knowing that otherwise he risked the failure of the treaty. His gambit worked, and the sizeable contingent of Conservative Euro-sceptic MPs known to be opposed to the TEU, facing the prospect of precipitating another general election, voted in favour of ratification, thereby ensuring that the Commons majority would be achieved. Having achieved a favourable vote in the Commons, however narrow the margin, and with it, UK ratification of the Treaty on European Union, given the ratification of the treaty by other member states, the formation of the European Union could go ahead on 1 November 1993.

In its operation, the Treaty on European Union did not disestablish the EC but created a new, overarching structure, the European Union, which had three pillars within it: first was the old EC, which continued as before; the second was a new area of European cooperation agreed at Maastricht in the field of Common Foreign and Security Policy (CFSP), which was the be undertaken by all EC members but did not operate as part of the EC and its supranational organisation, but simply through intergovernmental cooperation; the third was another new area of intergovernmental cooperation in the fields of Justice and

Home Affairs (JHA). This tripartite structure became a new organisation, the European Union, whose founding Treaty also stipulated that with effect from 1 November 1993 all citizens of the EC countries would, in addition, automatically become citizens of the European Union. This latter privilege offered only rhetorical extension of rights; in real terms it signified little other than a statement of hope that Europeans were making an advance towards genuine political federation, but offered nothing in the way of bringing this about.

Apart from Major's successes, he failed to maintain the equilibrium of his Cabinet, whose Euro-sceptic and Europhile wings were increasingly outspoken in their criticism of his policies, with the Prime Minister trying desperately to appease both sides simultaneously and succeeding in mollifying few. Indeed, for much of his time in office Major is remembered for his straddling an Asquith-style middle course of 'wait and see' between these opposing forces as centrifugal tensions nearly led to his downfall. By June 1995, his Euro-sceptic critics in the Conservative Party presented such a challenge to his leadership, that Major decided to reaffirm his authority in the party by taking the unorthodox step of resigning as Conservative Party leader and standing for re-election so as to put his critics, whom at one point he dubbed 'the bastards', to the test. In this leadership election, John Redwood, former Secretary of State for Wales, emerged as Major's Euro-sceptic challenger, while the main Conservative Euro-sceptic and potentially Major's most serious opponent, Defence Secretary Michael Portillo, declined to oppose Major and openly announced his continued support for the Prime Minister. Major could, however, count on the continuing loyalty of his pro-European colleagues, led by the Chancellor of the Exchequer, Kenneth Clarke, and Deputy Prime Minister Michael Heseltine. At the eventual leadership election, Major succeeded in winning a majority of votes, defeating Redwood and the Euro-sceptic wing; for the remainder of the government any talk of a direct leadership challenge to Major ended.

Given the near-constant criticism from within his own party, Major failed to maintain harmonious relations with his European colleagues during the greater part of his premiership. One episode highlighting this tension related to Britain's position inside the ERM, which sterling had entered in October 1990. By September 1992, the pound had been subject to severe pressures, which was exposing the economy to considerable strain. Ultimately the Chancellor, Norman Lamont, and Major were forced to withdraw sterling from the ERM as speculation on the pound pushed it down to an exchange rate of £1 to DM 2.25. The events leading to Wednesday, 16 September 1992, a date which was at once labelled 'Black Wednesday', brought Major and Lamont to air their grievances against the German government for maintaining high interest rates and for breaking its promise to notify them in advance of any moves involving rate-shifts, which in September German leaders failed to do. Hence any mutual understanding collapsed in recrimination, which left a sour note with German leaders for the remainder of the Major government. The ERM crisis cast doubt on the viability of the EC schedule for achieving EMU, and, in Britain, on the objective of EMU in principle; this scepticism in turn spread across the EC and threatened the ratification of the Maastricht Treaty in countries where it had not yet been put to the vote.[51]

In addition to Black Wednesday, Major's diplomatic shortcomings with his European partners were accentuated following the rise to prominence of a crisis involving health risks caused by beef infected with a new disease known as BSE (Bovine Spongiform Encephalopathy), or 'mad cow disease', news of which persuaded the European Commission to impose an export ban on British beef. The Major government's handling of the beef crisis was open to severe criticism both at home and in Europe. Showing remarkably poor statesmanship, Major played a nationalistic tone and obstructed and at times filibustered EU business meetings – even on issues dear to the British government – and promised to continue obstructing EU business until the veto on Britain's beef had been lifted. This continuing brash display of a manifest lack of diplomatic finesse towards Britain's European colleagues, taken together with the incompetence with which the Conservatives had handled the beef crisis in domestic politics, failing in their duty of care to safeguard public health and disregarding warning signs by health experts, contributed to the feeling in Britain that the Major government was losing touch with the people.

In addition to Major's poor handling of his European diplomacy and of his party, the Conservatives found themselves further weakened by the rising threat from Euro-sceptics not to vote Conservative during the forthcoming election but to cast their votes elsewhere. This threat worsened in advance of the 1997 general election, when Euro-sceptic opinion in Britain allowed for the emergence of two separate political parties, the Referendum Party, established by the financier and MEP Sir James Goldsmith, desiring another referendum on Britain's membership of the EU, and the United Kingdom Independence Party of Alan Sked. Sked's party distinguished itself by openly advocating the UK's withdrawal from the EU and its constituent organisations, arguing that Britain was sufficiently advanced and capable of standing on its own in a competitive global marketplace in which British commercial interests were likely to continue in indefinite prosperity. In calling for withdrawal, Sked touched a deep chord in the national psyche. As Britons had undergone decolonisation of their empire, many felt at a loss for what their new role should be. During the 1960s and 1970s, a sense of malaise had permeated British society, in which the economic sluggishness of the 'British disease' was combined with poor morale and a tortured self-searching rootlessness. For many, there was an obvious solution to this identity crisis and economic recession: joining 'Europe' and finding a destiny with their European neighbours, the other post-imperial powers across the Channel. The prevailing orthodoxy which stated that there was no credible alternative to remaining in the EU, however, was increasingly challenged by prominent Euro-sceptics. This was so especially after the 1980s witnessed the UK's victory in the Falklands War, the success of Thatcher's relationship with US President Ronald Reagan which increasingly placed the international spotlight on Britain, and the prominence afforded Britain because of the widespread change in ideology in the former Soviet Union, which was adapting itself to a market economy and taking up Thatcher-inspired privatisation policies.[52] By the 1990s, supporters of withdrawal from the EU and 'going it alone' had cause to challenge the former pessimistic indictment of contemporary Britain. Alan Sked, for example, pointed out that Britain has the fifth largest economy in the world, £1.7 trillion invested around the globe (70% of it outside the EU), the most advanced nuclear weapons and the most professional armed forces in Europe. She has a stable political system and the English language. Behind her is perhaps the most successful history of any country in the world. She sits on the Security Council of the UN and is a member of the G7 Group, the IMF, the World Bank and NATO.[53]

Britain was still a robust nation-state that commanded global influence and a measure of diplomatic authority well out of proportion to its population of under 60 million in a world of 5 billion. This surely was not a country in need of its bus pass on a journey to a European regional destination.

The ultimate result of the Conservatives' mishaps was to make John Major's European policy a shambles. His government had engendered a loss of faith among many at home, bad will in Europe, and the consequent arousal of hopeful expectations among European leaders that a more positive approach would be forthcoming from the opposition Labour Party in the event that it won the upcoming election. With the Conservatives presiding over a number of crises and scandals by no means limited to its failures in European policy, it was no surprise that the they failed to win the 1997 general election, and on 1 May Labour's Tony Blair took office as Prime Minister.

The Blair Period

Following the May election, Blair made signals that his policy towards the EU would be constructive rather than continuing the tense relationship that European endured under Major. Furthering this positive image on European affairs, in his first year after the election Blair made a celebrated speech to the National Assembly in Paris, stating that

> Britain's future lies in being full partners in Europe. . . . I want to work with you to achieve this. The first vote I cast was in favour of Britain entering the Common Market. As I watch my children grow up now, I want them to live in a Europe in which they feel as at home in the glory of Paris, the beauty of Rome, the majesty of Vienna as they do in their own London. . . .

In policy questions, the Blair government has been at the forefront of pioneer thinking on the creation of a European army and has undertaken collaborative defence projects with the French and other EU governments. However, the main question which immediately arose during 1997, and which has sustained public interest, has involved the question of Britain's participation in the EU plans for establishing a common currency – the euro. In 1997 there had been hopes that Blair's seeming enthusiasm for Europe would lead his government to participating with the rest of the EU in the creation of the euro; however it soon became clear that Labour was not to join the eurozone at its inception, but would consider doing so at some future point. In 1998, the EU established a European Central Bank, successor to the European Monetary Institute, which was to be the leading decision-making body in economic policy for the EU, and the 11 member states whose governments had decided to take part in the single currency then took further steps for the eventual unveiling of the euro. However in Britain, with the Conservative Party – under its new leader William Hague from 1997 – repeating its position of keeping the pound and apparently excluding all possibility of ever adopting the euro, polls suggested that this sceptical policy was consistent with public caution on economic and monetary union, especially when Britain was experiencing lower rates of unemployment and inflation than those prevailing throughout the rest of the EU. The moderate success of this Conservative Euro-sceptic policy regarding the pound in turn has had some impact on the formation of Labour's policy, causing Blair to take a more cautious line on joining the euro, so that since 1997 he has consistently deferred questions of whether he will allow Britain to give up the pound and adopt the euro, stating that a referendum will be required before he will take any decision, at some point beyond the general election 2002. In evaluating whether joining the euro would be right for the British economy, Blair has referred time and again to the terms of entry into the euro and the related economic conditions prevailing at such time as Britain joined. In Blair's tactical handling of the delicate decision on the euro, 'the terms' have been claimed as the real test of Britain's participation in this dimension of European integration, which is a reversion to Harold Wilson's preferred device to avoid crucial decisions on Europe that, if taken, would threaten party cohesion and subject Labour to electoral dangers; it is also reminiscent of Wilson's caution concerning Labour's decision to apply for membership of the EEC in the 1960s in not moving too far in advance of public opinion; however, Blair and his Chancellor, Gordon Brown, have also demonstrated a desire to shape public opinion in favour of joining the single currency, and there is a general expectation that more leadership on the euro will come after 2002.

In other respects, Blair acted quickly to put Britain in the mainstream of opinion in the EU, for instance by immediately adopting into UK law the European Convention on Human Rights as well as the Social Chapter of the Maastricht Treaty. However, in the emerging issues of consensus on the agenda in the EU, the UK has nevertheless had to remain at the margins, rather than the heart, of European decision-making. The Labour government took the helm of the European Council presidency during its term of rotation in January–June 1998, and though it now had the opportunity for putting forward its agenda for Europe, Blair and Brown found themselves in the awkward position of bearing the responsibility for presiding over Council meetings in which the crucial decisions for the euro had to be taken. Also during Britain's Council presidency, Blair took the opportunity to highlight his vision of enlargement which would lead to a EU particularly embracing the Eastern Europe applicants and spreading 'Europe' from the Atlantic to the former USSR. Beneath the rhetorical statements about strides in integration and Euro-enthusiast ideals, the realities of Labour's vision revealed a preference for the EU to evolve into an intergovernmental organisation primarily emphasising the centrality of markets and commerce as the subject of its activities. A Union that is enlarged may be more difficult to centralise and thus more difficult to undertake the degree of supra-national action throughout its member states that is the objective of many EU governments outside the UK. Thus, with the Blair government's policy, one may notice something of the long British relationship with the EU since the days of the ECSC, in which the thrust of continental Europe's efforts has been in the direction of supranational 'integration', whereas the tenor of the British governments' involvement has been to favour the process of intergovernmental 'co-operation'.

Although this has always been the case with Britain's relationship to Europe in the post-war era, regardless of whether the Conservative or Labour Party has led its efforts, nevertheless it is also the case that the totality of Britain's involvement in the EU, its acceptance of all that is implied in the *acquis communautaire*, its embracing the European Convention on Human Rights, and its current active discussion on defence links with other EU governments, places Britain arguably more at the heart of Europe than it has ever been in the post-war era – certainly closer than it had ever been under Major.

However, in terms of public policies actualised between the Blair government and Europe, the content of substantive policies over style and spin, one must exercise caution in forming conclusions as to the actual accomplishments of the Blair government, since, in the manner of Harold Wilson in 1975, he has left one of the crucial decisions – on Britain's giving up the pound and adopting the euro – risking the character of his government's European credentials on a future referendum. It would be premature to say that Blair has to any great extent departed from the traditional main characteristics in the British approach to 'Europe', and after three years of New Labour's new closeness in the centre of EU bargaining, it is clear that the 'child of Europe' is more cautious and tentative than most expected in 1997, at times even to the extent of being compared favourably with Margaret Thatcher.[54]

The Commonwealth versus European Relationship

For over three decades, no British politician has seriously discussed ideas of Commonwealth unity as an implement in the exercise of British diplomatic influence.[55] In general domestic discourse the Commonwealth's salience in Britain is not what it once was. Even though the British monarch is styled 'Head of the Commonwealth', this designation is devoid of meaning and the annual meetings of the Commonwealth heads of government tend to hold no interest for the British public. Among even the educated population today, few can point to Commonwealth Day on the calendar, and still fewer celebrate it;[56] today, schoolchildren's maps no longer include the pink-painted lands of Britain's imperial possessions; and Britons are much more familiar with neighbouring European countries and are likely to have travelled there at some point in their lives. In contrast to the declining profile of the Commonwealth, the EU has risen tremendously in degree of media coverage and in the general interest taken in the events and debates concerning European integration since Britain entered the EEC in 1973, as witnessed by the coverage of EU news as domestic news – a signal change from the years in which such news would have captured lines merely on the inside pages. Widespread discussion is sparked by a change in president of the European Commission, and whereas the Commission President is known to most educated Britons, few people in Britain can name the Commonwealth Secretary-General. Public consciousness regarding the relative importance of the Commonwealth and Europe to Britain has also changed since 1945. This epitomises the change in consciousness and relative importance to Britain of the Commonwealth and of Europe, even though name recognition does not necessarily mean that Britons in general, or the British political system in particular, have more in common with their European counterparts than do Europeans among themselves. Moreover, prominence and name recognition do not necessarily imply desirability of taking part in the integration of Europe, as the proportion of Britons voicing their contentment with the UK's membership of the EU usually leaves room for doubt whether much has changed since the 1960s.[57]

Britain's Contemporary Relationship and Attitude towards European Integration

Despite the awkwardness of Britain's relations with its European partners, and despite the stridency that the rhetoric directed towards Europe has at times assumed, Britain's leaders nevertheless have realised that the UK's essential commercial and political interests are at stake in Europe and, as forward-thinking policy-makers realised in the mid-1950s, British leaders can be part of the EC/EU's bargaining process only if the UK is a full member of the organisation. If Britain were to remain outside, it would still be affected by choices taken by others in Brussels, but could not directly shape the policies and European Council decisions. The post-war contraction in British power eventually led to the stark realisation that Britain could not afford to 'go it alone' in economic or diplomatic terms, and that, given its geography as an island off the coast of Western Europe with its concentration of powerful industrial countries, the apparent logical choice for Britain was to avail itself of the opportunity to enter into league with the Six and help create a more powerful entity that would, it was hoped, safeguard Britain's interests and offer an opportunity for once again possessing economic and diplomatic weight. Advocates for entry were aware that joining the EEC would involve an inevitable loss of sovereignty in the areas of law and economic management, which would successively spill over into other areas of sovereignty. However, Britain would also be able to partake of that larger sovereignty of the collective whole that was to be pooled by all member states; in which the whole was to be greater than the sum of its parts. Thus at the close of the century, British leaders could on the one hand congratulate themselves at exercising influence in the European forum and thereby minimising the course of undesirable policies and 'steering' European policies into directions favourable to Britain's interests; and on the other, wring their hands at having been forced with great reluctance to enter the EC, an organisation whose rules and structures had already been designed, which made deep inroads into the UK's sovereignty, and which carried with it the ominous prospect of further integration or 'deepening' which would further erode national decision-making powers as additional areas of competency were transferred to Brussels or subjected to qualified majority voting at meetings of the European Council. These tensions have been at work on British leaders since the UK's accession to the EC in 1973, and as the new century opens they present greater opportunities either for Britain's meaningful involvement in 'ever-closer union' or, alternatively, for subjecting British involvement in European integration to greater strains than ever before as successive areas of participation such as the common currency (the euro), the European army, a common foreign policy, and other priorities emerge on the European agenda.

For Britain's leaders since 1945 the central foreign relations question, which has concerned the Commonwealth as well as Europe, has been: How do we best maximise Britain's international influence? After the war, it was obvious that the Empire could assist in Britain's diplomatic mission and contribute to the image of Britain as a continuing world power, but increasingly the material resources and residual prestige that the Empire conferred on to Britain were minor in the game of international power politics. Thus if the former colonies were no longer to be the enhancement of Britain's global stature, where should British leaders turn? As the post-war period unfolded and the Empire evolved into the Commonwealth while simultaneously the Western European countries established the ECSC and then EEC, the success of which came as a surprise to leaders of both parties in the UK, the choice became increasingly inescapable and joining 'Europe' the only recognised alternative. It was also realised that membership in 'Europe' could be achieved while maintaining membership in the Commonwealth and thus continuing to derive benefits from maintaining the frequency and intimacy of contacts with its leaders.

Having eventually made this cost-benefit analysis between membership and standing aside, British leaders felt compelled to enter the European Community, though they did not desire to embrace the objective of achieving 'ever closer union' that has been the cherished objective among others across the Channel; but Britain's relationship with its European neighbours has never been more than in its own pragmatic self-interest. Whether or not Britain would have found its self-interest better served as member state of the ECSC in the early 1950s, or the EEC in the latter 1950s, in assessing the likely importance of the European supranational entities British policy-makers were often far from the mark. They made clear errors of judgement in deciding to refuse to involve themselves with their European neighbours, as for example when, on the eve of the Messina talks, the Foreign Office's Gladwyn Jebb's advice was that 'Nothing of much importance is expected to occur at Messina' and that Britain's participation in the discussions would be ill-advised. British governments repeated mis-estimations of the Six's determination and ability to succeed in establishing supranational organisations, in their failed attempts at preventing this by proposing counter-organisations such as through Plan G and subsequently the European Free Trade Association (EFTA), and in their misunderstanding of the nature of French objections to Britain's intentions, have been described as a 'piece of incompetence on the part of the British Foreign Office'[58] – a conclusion that applies also to the leadership of both main political parties.

Since the process of European integration began, the predicament common to all British governments faced with the prospect that its European neighbours will proceed with their combined efforts towards forming a federal Europe, pressing ahead even without Britain, has been that British leaders have been faced with no real choice other than participation; the alternative has been non-membership of the EEC/EC/EU and a future that many perceive as marginalisation in European and global affairs. This was learned in the 1950s as the six original members of the ECSC and EEC decided that their goal in securing the supranational character of their organisations was more important than making the modifications necessary to secure British involvement, and since that time the response from British policy-makers has been, in effect, a reluctant admission that Britain must take part in the European entity, if only to have any influence in it – and if Britain is use membership to maintain its influence abroad.

This predicament has also meant that once Britain became a member of the EC, British leaders were obliged to make compromises inherent in membership and involving Britain's cherished national sovereignty. Britain has been faced with having to accept advances in the EU's supranational control over member states in various areas, such as by majority voting in place of unanimity in the European Council, in exchange for some added voice in deciding what these areas will be. The irony and tension has centred on the stark realisation that in order to have influence on the shape and direction of the EEC/EC/EU, Britain has had to be a party to it, and this grudging realisation was first made when in the early 1960s British leaders found that they had first of all to join the EEC. But most British leaders dislike this very supranationalism which is the absolute requirement of membership (by the Treaty of Rome and the objective of 'ever-closer union'). However, in taking part in the process of European integration, as negotiations unfold at successive intergovernmental conferences and European summits, Britain has been able to use its voice in advocating that greater emphasis be given to an intergovernmental and commercial character for the EU, which has stood in contrast to the definitive supranational, federalist ethos that in most cases other member states have desired to see realised. In this regard, Britain's leaders have acted consistent with the wisdom of their civil servants who, in the 1950s and 1960s, preferred the advice that 'You must be in it to influence it' – to exercise Britain's influence in the continuing evolution of the shape and policies of the EC, if possible steering them in directions favourable to Britain's interests. To this advice was added the cynical realisation that, once application was made and entry accomplished, if the European Commission or EC leaders desired to press ahead with the development of plans for such undesirable developments as a common defence policy or common foreign policy that was to run contrary to the UK's Atlanticist orientation, Britain would also be able to use its position as a leading member state to attempt to stifle the project. In this sense, applying the ability they have for obstructing undesired federalist moves, this awareness has constituted an unspoken though scarcely concealed agenda of British leaders to the effect that 'You must be in it to sabotage it.'[59] Or so they thought. The reality of the constraints upon a member state in contemplating singlehandedly to obstruct advances in integration has been duly recognised in Britain in the years following accession, and as majority voting becomes the norm for additional areas of decisions in the EU process, Britain's ability to stand against the agreement of its partners is wearing thin. But more important than any formal mechanisms whose effect is to constrict Britain's options in accepting additional federalist strides, are the current discussions of a possible 'two-tier' or 'two-speed' Europe in which a Britain that opted out of the continuing deepening in areas of further integration would be left behind the rest of the EU as it proceeds and forms a centre of Europe's gravity and political influence. The 'two-tier Europe' concept threatens to return Britain to its position outside the 'inner circle' of European policy formation, and as the current prospects for the euro, common foreign and defence policy, and other features of a 'first-tier' Europe are discussed and agreed by near-unanimity at future summits, Britain will find it increasingly difficult to resist taking further part in the federalist programme. This tension has been at the heart of the British relationship to the process of European integration since its beginnings in the 1950s and a hallmark of Britain's half-hearted, 'awkward partner' experience since accession to the EC in 1973.

Prospects for the Future

Today, Britain's membership of the EU, which is moving in the direction of increased integration, especially in the fields of economic as well as foreign and security policy, is presenting increasingly narrowed options for Britain's government. The traditional British penchant for desiring to benefit from both the 'special relationship' with the USA and from membership of the EU is being challenged. When members of the EU are contemplating proceeding with a common army, or a common foreign policy, the degree to which Britain may continue to side with its 'closest ally' is being successively reduced, and the result is that ultimately British policy-makers will have to do what they have resisted doing throughout the period of their involvement with their European colleagues: i.e. choose between one and the other partnerships. It is better to steer the process of European integration so that they do not have to make such a stark choice unpalatable to many in the UK. Being the crossroads as it were of the Atlantic, European and Commonwealth relationships confers on to Britain something of a unique diplomatic go-between status that has been of use to the Foreign and Commonwealth Office partly because of the insider nature of Britain's dealing with leaders at Commonwealth meetings, the use of which is at times helpful to British diplomats in subsequent dealings with European colleagues. This value has been of use notably in Britain's diplomatic relations with the USA, by which Britain serves to relay high-level information. The ultimate result of this utilisation of its membership with Europe, the Commonwealth, and from its relationship with the USA, has been, as former Foreign Secretary Douglas Hurd has put it, to enable Britain to 'punch above its weight'. In this regard, since 1997 Tony Blair has added his perspective that Britain serves as 'a bridge' for America in Europe, interpreting US policy for Europeans and European sentiment for American leaders, appropriating for

Britain the status of linchpin at the intersection of Britain's EU and US relationships reminiscent of Winston Churchill's 'three-circles' approach. Indeed, British leaders working for the enhancement of Britain's diplomatic influence have found the synergy operating by means of Britain's relationship with the USA, the Commonwealth and the EU has conferred on Britain more aggregate influence than the sum of its parts. For these ends, many in the Establishment have viewed it as an obviously advantageous policy, despite its costs, including the diminution of Britain's sovereignty. But for the future, the question will be whether this policy can withstand the increased strains placed upon it by Britain's commitments to an increasingly integrated European Union – that is, whether Britain will finally be presented with a clear and exclusive choice among relationships for its destiny.

Notes

1   The phrase 'special relationship' has come to refer almost exclusively to the defence and intelligence links between the US and UK on a formal and informal basis, and not to some larger all-encompassing reciprocal relationship which some in Britain imagine to exist.
2   John Major's cry during a visit to Bonn during the March 1991 'charm offensive'.
3   Official studies were undertaken from 1960 evaluating the importance to Britain of the Commonwealth vis-à-vis Europe, with one noteworthy study in 1966–7 concluding that the Commonwealth would continue to wane in its diplomatic and economic importance to Britain, and coming out in favour of enhancing Britain's commercial and diplomatic strength by membership of the EEC.
4   The European Economic Community (EEC), from 1957, had its institutions merged with those of the ECSC and EURATOM during 1967 to emerge as the European Communities (EC), alternatively known as the European Community. On 1 November 1994, the European Union (EU) was established, having three separate sub-units or pillars, bringing together the supranational EC together with two intergovernmental pillars – common foreign and security policy (CFSP) and justice and home affairs (JHA) – under a single structure. The EC still exists as a distinct entity, but from November 1994, when referring to the European Commission, European law, etc., for simplicity's sake we may refer to these as bodies of the European Union.
5   The designation 'Commonwealth' in place of 'British Commonwealth' had been used in the House of Commons from 1947, and unofficially, in government parlance from that point forward, both were often used interchangeably. In addition, the terms 'Dominion' and 'Dominion government' were superseded by 'Commonwealth member'. 'British' was dropped from 'British Commonwealth' as the organisation became known as the 'Commonwealth of Nations' in the 1948 communiqué of the annual Commonwealth Prime Ministers' Meeting. Foreign Office circular 7, 28 January 1949, DO 35/2255; proposed in CR (48)2, 21 May 1948, CAB 134/118. Also see *Hansard*, 1948–9 for references to the evolution in terminology.
6   David Cannadine (ed.), *The Speeches of Winston Churchill*, Harmondsworth, 1989, pp. 309–14.
7   John W. Young, 'Churchill's "No" to Europe: The Rejection of European Union by Churchill's Post-War Government 1951–1952', *Historical Journal* 28 (4), 1985: 923–37.

8   For instance, in Churchill's speech at The Hague, 9 May 1946, he not only referred to a United States of Europe but also to the closeness of the British and Americans, stating that 'It is evident of course that the affairs of Great Britain and the British Commonwealth and Empire, are becoming ever more closely interwoven with those of the United States, and that an underlying unity of thought and conviction increasingly pervades the English-Speaking world' that combined to form 'a vast and benevolent synthesis'.

9   However, Churchill's son-in-law, Duncan Sandys, a great Euro-enthusiast, not long before Churchill was due to leave Hyde Park Gate to deliver his speech, asked if he could see the text and thereupon allegedly made insertions, in which he committed Churchill to not only supporting a united Europe from without but to expressing the belief that Britain herself should form part of that wider unity. I am thankful to Winston Churchill II, for giving me his considered opinions on his grandfather's views regarding Britain's relationship with Europe and the USA and for his facilitating my access to his grandfather's papers, including the original text of the Albert Hall speech of 14 May 1947, in the Churchill Archive Centre, Cambridge.

10 David Carlton, *Anthony Eden: A Biography*, London, 1981, p. 172.

11 Eden is quoted from a speech he gave at Columbia University. Quoted in Denise Folliot (ed.), *Documents on International Affairs, 1952*, London, 1955, pp. 141–6.

12 Bretherton was given the remit of attending as an observer only and not entering into any agreement on behalf of HM Government. He had no plenipotentiary authority.

13 Simon Burgess and Geoffrey Edwards, 'The Six plus One: British Policy-making and the Question of European Economic Integration, 1955', *International Affairs*, 1988: 401.

14 Ibid., pp. 393–413.

15 Charles de Gaulle had reassumed the leadership of France during 1958, and was hostile to the idea of Britain's wresting control of European leadership, wishing to reserve the EEC as his intended forum for the expansion of French national prestige and influence.

16 For example, R. A. Butler, Home Secretary during 1957–62, First Secretary of State in 1962–3, and Foreign Secretary in 1963–4, whose East Anglia constituency of Saffron Walden contained politically important agricultural interests who were fearful that the importation of EEC agricultural products would be detrimental to their position.

17 W. David McIntyre, 'Britain and the Creation of the Commonwealth Secretariat', *Journal of Imperial and Commonwealth History* 28 (1), January 2000: 135–58.

18 In common parlance, from its inception the EEC was also known in Britain as the Common Market or Community. The EEC merged with the ECSC and Euratom to become the European Community in July 1967; the EC formally continues a discrete existence as the first pillar of the European Union from 1 November 1993, though EU is often incorrectly used as another name for the EC.

19 Harold Macmillan, *Riding the Storm, 1956–1959*, London, 1971, p. 74.

20 Although the application was announced as an effort 'in order to initiate negotiations to see if satisfactory arrangements can be made to meet the special interests of the United Kingdom, of the Commonwealth and of the European Free Trade Association', from which 'the ultimate decision whether or not to join must depend on the result of the negotiations', nevertheless it was clear that this meant that in principle the decision for entry had been taken and that in reality all that stood in the way of the UK's accession was the unanimous approval of the six member states of the EEC, as required by Article 237 of the Treaty of Rome. *Hansard*, House of

Commons, 31 July 1961; see also 1–3 August 1961 for the debate on the application.

21   Wilson speaking in the House of Commons, 3 August 1961.

22   As de Gaulle said to Macmillan, '*Mon cher. C'est tres simple. Maintenant, avec les six, il y a cinq poules et un coq. Si vous joignez... il y aura deux coqs. Alors – ce n'est pas aussi agréable.*' From Harold Macmillan, *At the End of the Day*, London, 1973, p. 365.

23   However, optimists were equally convinced that de Gaulle could be prevailed upon to permit British entry. In this regard Edward Heath, chief UK negotiator, was reluctant to accept the growing hints and diplomatic cables suggesting the likelihood of a veto, and following de Gaulle's statement in January 1963 was reluctant even to accept the veto as final. See Piers Ludlow, *Dealing with Britain: The Six and the First UK Application to the EEC*, Cambridge, 1997.

24   The text of de Gaulle's speech given on 7 April 1960, in Jean Lacouture, *De Gaulle: The Ruler, 1945–1970*, trans. Alan Sheridan, London, 1991, p. 352.

25   He had even levelled at the Conservatives the charge of having attempted to betray their Commonwealth brethren by pursuing the 1961–3 application to the EEC.

26   Peter Catterall, 'The Labour Party and Overseas Policy, 1955–64', in Wolfram Kaiser and Gillian Staerck, *British Foreign Policy, 1955–1964: Contracting Options*, Basingstoke, 2000, pp. 89–109.

27   McIntyre, 'Britain and the Creation of the Commonwealth Secretariat', p. 135.

28   From 1965, these were termed heads of government meetings.

29   E.g. this non-aligned trend was shown by the movement's international conferences beginning in Bandung (1955), and continuing at meetings such as in Belgrade (1961) and Cairo (1964).

30   Douglas Jay, *After the Common Market: A Better Alternative for Britain*, Harmondsworth, 1968, p. 11.

31   Ibid., p. 111.

32   E.g. see *The Times*, 21 February 1967. The letter was signed by 10 Senators, 29 Congressmen, 5 Governors, 29 university presidents, and other notables in favour of a direct economic association having formal links between the USA and the UK.

33   The EEC was often referred to as the 'Common Market' during this period, indicating something of the prevalent understanding that it was essentially commercial in orientation, as opposed to an unfolding political union; later it was alternatively known as the 'Community'.

34   Willy Brandt, *People and Politics: The Years 1960–1975*, London, 1978, pp. 162–3. John Young, *Britain and European Unity, 1945–1992*, London, 1993, p. 101. See also Joe Haines, *The Politics of Power*, London, 1977, pp. 71–3.

35   For one, Denis Healey, though seeing no advantage to entry and wishing to avoid another application, thought that there was no reason for opposing Wilson's efforts at bringing Britain into the EC because de Gaulle would in any event veto it and save British opponents the trouble of having to resist Wilson and Brown.

36   According to the merger treaty, the EEC, EURATOM and ECSC accepted common institutions from 1967 and henceforth in common parlance these were referred to as a single entity, the European Community or European Communities.

37   Edward Heath, *The Course of My Life: The Autobiography of Edward Heath*, London, 1998.

38   These had been planned to take place under the Labour government, which lost office before negotiations were due to begin.

39   The term 'Euro-sceptic' did not come into currency until the 1980s; however the sentiment in Britain certainly existed throughout the post-war period.

40 David Butler and Gareth Butler (eds), *British Political Facts, 1900–1994*, London, 1994, p. 184.
41 For Heath's views on the Commonwealth and Europe, see Heath, *The Course of My Life*, pp. 207–10, 476–7, 726.
42 E.g. see tape-recorded interview of Brian Harrison with Lord Stewart of Fulham, the Fawcett Library, London Guildhall University, 1978.
43 The precise result was a 64.5 per cent Yes for the UK as a whole, according to Butler and Butler, *British Political Facts*, p. 220.
44 Douglas Jay, *Change and Fortune: A Political Record*, London, 1980, p. 488. Andrew Roberts, in an editorial in *The Times*, 28 January 1997, refers to remarks made by Vernon Bogdanor at a Witness Seminar of the Institute of Contemporary British History: Roger Broad and Tim Geiger (eds), 'The 1975 British Referendum on Europe', *Contemporary British History* 10(3), Autumn 1996: 82–105.
45 Vernon Bogdanor responds to Roberts in an editorial in *The Times*, 30 January 1997.
46 The sobriquet 'Iron Lady', which had been used by Mikhail Gorbachev in describing Thatcher, was now to find resonance from within Western Europe as well.
47 To which she added, 'It already exists. It's called the dollar.'
48 The 'Social Charter', known as the European Community Charter on the Fundamental Social Rights of Workers, which was adopted by the European Council at Strasbourg in 1989, is not to be confused with the Maastricht Treaty's 'Social Chapter', formally known as the Agreement on Social Policy, which gave the 1989 Social Charter legal basis. At the inception of the Social Charter and subsequent Social Chapter, the UK was party to neither: Thatcher's government refused to sign the Social Charter in 1989, the only EC member state to withhold its agreement to the Charter; and Major's government objected to the Social Chapter in 1991–2, So the Social Chapter was removed from the main text of the TEU and instead signed as an accompanying protocol to the Treaty, with Britain again isolated in securing an opt-out.
49 However, owing to the vagaries of the UK's single-member constituency plurality voting system, which tends to over-reward parties possessing geographical concentrations in support and underrepresents parties whose support is spread throughout the country, the 1983 general election resulted in a noticeably disportionate outcome in the number of MPs elected to the House of Commons, with the Conservatives capturing 397 seats, compared with 209 for Labour, and merely 23 for the combined SDP–Liberal Alliance.
50 Figures from Butler and Butler, *British Political Facts*, p. 219.
51 In France a referendum on 20 September – four days after Black Wednesday – resulted in a narrow Yes vote of 51.05 per cent, and already a Danish referendum on Maastricht in June 1992 had resulted in a narrow No vote (50.7 per cent to 49.3 per cent), although this was to be overturned in May 1993 when in a second referendum Danish voters approved Maastricht by a 56.8 per cent majority.
52 E.g. in the economic restructuring taking place in the Russian Republic, Russian President Boris Yeltsin was to find key advisers from the Centre for Economic Performance of the London School of Economics.
53 Alan Sked, *An Intelligent Person's Guide to Post-War Britain*, London, 1997, p. 177.
54 E.g. 'Blair admits Thatcher "not all wrong" on EU', Philip Webster, *The Times*, 23 February 2000.
55 As the Indian prime minister was to point out to his visitors, British Prime Minister Tony Blair and his Foreign Secretary Robin Cook, after the latter had volunteered

advice on ending the conflict in Kashmir during the summer of 1997, Britain should remember that it was now a 'third-rate power'. This recent episode has been but the resonance of sentiment having a lifespan extending over three decades throughout the Commonwealth.

56   It is not so much celebrated as observed, annually on the second Monday in March.
57   E.g. in a European Commission survey of opinion throughout the 15 countries of the European Union, on the question of whether membership in the EU was a 'Good thing' or 'Bad thing', data for respondents in the UK ranked it the lowest among the 15, at 31 per cent. European Commission, *Eurobaromètre*, 51, 1999, p. 25. In a similar European Union-wide poll conducted in 1999 in which respondents were asked 'How European are you?', with the four possible responses being: 'By your country alone?', 'First by your country, second as European?', 'First as European, second by your country?', and 'As European only?', the country whose respondents ranked highest in identifying themselves 'By your country alone' was Britain, at over 62 per cent. European Commission, *Eurobaromètre*, March 1999, published in *The Economist*, 12 June 1999.
58   Brian Lapping, *The Labour Government, 1964–70*, Harmondsworth, 1970, p. 106.
59   The French since de Gaulle, with a cynical yet due appreciation of British motives, recognised the tactics employed as '*j'embrasse mon rival, mais c'est pour l'étouffer*' ('I embrace my rival, but only to choke him', from Corneille), which was in part the justification for vetoing Britain's membership applications in 1963 and 1967.

Further Reading

Books

Brivati, Brian, *Hugh Gaitskell*, London, 1996.
Callaghan, James, *Time and Chance*, London, 1987.
Charlton, Michael, *The Price of Victory*, London, 1983.
Darwin, John, *Britain and Decolonisation: The Retreat from Empire in the Post-War World*, London, 1988.
Darwin, John, *The End of the British Empire: The Historical Debate*, Oxford, 1991.
George, Stephen, *Britain and European Integration since 1945*, Oxford, 1991.
George, Stephen, *An Awkward Partner: Britain in the European Community*, 3rd ed., Oxford, 1998.
Gowland, David, and Turner, Arthur, *Reluctant Europeans: Britain and European Integration, 1945–1998*, Harlow, 2000.
Greenwood, Sean, *Britain and European Cooperation since 1945*, Oxford, 1992.
Heath, Edward, *The Course of My Life: My Autobiography*, London, 1998.
Kitchen, Martin, *The British Empire and Commonwealth: A Short History*, London, 1996.
Macmillan, Harold, *At the End of the Day, 1961–1963*, London, 1973.
Major, John, *John Major: The Autobiography*, London, 1999.
Marshall, Peter, *The Cambridge Illustrated History of the British Empire*, Cambridge, 1996.
Sked, Alan, and Cook, Chris, *Post-War Britain: A Political History*, 4th ed., London, 1993.
Thatcher, Margaret, *The Downing Street Years*, London, 1993.
Wilson, Harold, *The Labour Government, 1964–70: A Personal Record*, Harmondsworth, 1971.

Young, John, *Britain and European Unity, 1945–1999*, 2nd ed., London, 2000.
Young, John, 'Churchill's "No" to Europe, 1951–2', *Historical Journal* 28 (1985): 923–37.

Journals

Contemporary British History (formerly *Contemporary Record*)
Journal of Common Market Studies
Journal of Imperial and Commonwealth History

Chronology

1945   End of Second World War (May, in Europe). General election results in Labour government under Clement Attlee (July).

1946   Zurich Conference on the future of European cooperation attended by Winston Churchill, who makes reference to a 'United States of Europe'. Cripps mission to India.

1947   India gains independence (Aug.). Indian partition into India and Pakistan.

1948   Brussels Treaty signed between Britain, France, and the Benelux countries, committing Britain to the defence of Western Europe (Mar.). British Commonwealth designated as the 'Commonwealth', dropping the prefix 'British'. International Committee of the Movement for European Unity holds a Congress at the Hague attended by Winston Churchill (May). Berlin Blockade begun by USSR (June). Belgium, Luxembourg and the Netherlands (the Benelux countries) form a customs union. European Movement established (Oct.). Burma gains independence and leaves Commonwealth. Ceylon achieves full independence within Commonwealth. British Citizenship Act grants British passports to all Commonwealth citizens. State of Israel established after UK's precipitate withdrawal from Palestine. South African government adopts policy of apartheid, racial separateness.

1949   Council of Europe established as intergovernmental organisation. Republic of Ireland proclaimed in Dublin; Ireland withdraws from Commonwealth.

1949   NATO established, linking the USA to defence of Western Europe (Apr.).

1950   Robert Schuman, French Foreign Minister, announces plan for pooling of coal and steel between France and Germany and open to any other Western European countries wishing to join; the Schuman Plan called for the supra-national control of these industries by a 'High Authority' (May). Korean War begins (June). Pleven Plan put forward by René Pleven (October) for creation of a European army, the EDC, on a supranational basis – an effort really aimed at containing the remilitarisation of Germany.

1951   Treaty of Paris signed between France, West Germany, Italy, Belgium, the Netherlands and Luxembourg, establishing the ECSC.

1952   ECSC formally comes into existence (July). Proclamation of state of emergency in Kenya in response to Mau Mau rebellion.

1953   Proposals for the EDC obtain cautious endorsement from Britain; all member countries agree to proceed with its establishment except France, whose National Assembly votes against ratification.

1954   Western European Union (WEU) formed with the six ECSC countries plus the UK (Oct.). EDC Treaty rejected in vote in French National Assembly and hence plans for EDC aborted (Aug.). UK enters an association agreement with ECSC (Dec.).

1955   Messina Conference and Spaak Report discuss proposals for extension of ECSC countries into general common market (June).

1956   Harold Macmillan, Chancellor of the Exchequer, announces UK willingness to establish European Free Trade Area comprising not only the ECSC six but the UK and several other western European countries as well. Suez crisis. Sudan gains independence outside Commonwealth.

1957   Treaty of Rome signed by the ECSC six for establishment of the EEC (Mar.). The Gold Coast gains independence, the first of Britain's African colonies to do so, and Ghana joins the Commonwealth. Malayan federation established.

1958   EEC formally comes into existence; French President de Gaulle vetos Britain's plan for the establishment of a western European-wide free trade area (Nov.). West Indies federation established.

1959   With the Treaty of Stockholm, the UK with Austria, Denmark, Ireland, Portugal, Sweden and Switzerland (together known as 'the Seven') establish the European Free Trade Association (EFTA), an intergovernmental organisation dedicated to the removal of tariff barriers between all participants.

1960   EFTA comes into existence. Nigeria gains independence. Cyprus gains independence as republic, under Archbishop Makarios, within Commonwealth. Macmillan makes his 'Wind of Change' speech in Cape Town.

1961   Prime Minister Harold Macmillan announces his government's decision to open negotiations to determine whether conditions exist for joining EEC; this launches Britain's first application for membership of EEC; the UK's application is joined by Ireland and Denmark. South Africa votes in referendum to become republic, leaves Commonwealth. Sierra Leone, Tanganyika, Zanzibar gain independence.

1962   Labour Party Leader Hugh Gaitskell comes out in opposition to the government's application, announcing at the annual party conference that British entry would run counter to 'a thousand years of history' (Oct.). Uganda, Trinidad and Tobago gain independence within Commonwealth. Commonwealth Immigrants Act passed to control immigration from the new Commonwealth Countries.

1963   French President de Gaulle announces that Britain is not ready to join EEC, vetoing the British application, to the humiliation of Macmillan and the UK (Jan.). Kenya achieves independence within the Commonwealth. Association Convention between EEC and 17 African States and Madagascar signed in Yaoundé (Yaoundé Convention). Malaysian federation established.

1964   Harold Wilson leads Labour Party to victory in general election, on a platform of furthering Britain's commitment to the Commonwealth vis-à-vis the EEC. Zanzibar merges with Tanganyika to become Tanzania, a republic within the Commonwealth. Zambia gains independence, under President Kenneth Kaunda, within the Commonwealth. Ian Smith becomes Prime Minister of Rhodesia. Nyasaland becomes the independent country of Malawi. Malta gains independence within the Commonwealth.

1965   War between two Commonwealth members, India and Pakistan, leads to mediation by the USSR. Rhodesian government declares Universal Declaration of Independence (UDI), with Britain unable to prevent the breakaway nation to submit to black majority rule or to return to British administration. Commonwealth Secretariat established in London, and first Commonwealth Secretary-General, Arnold Smith of Canada, appointed. War breaks out between India and Pakistan over Kashmir. The Gambia and Singapore become independent countries. India-Pakistan War.

1966   Labour manifesto says that the government is ready to enter the Community, provided essential conditions are met – principally among them, the safeguarding of Commonwealth interests. Wilson Cabinet decides to undertake exploratory mission to the capitals of the six member-states of the EEC to determine the climate of opinion for a renewed British application. British Guina gains independence as Guyana within the Commonwealth. Barbados, Botswana and Lesotho gain independence within the Commonwealth.

1967   Wilson and Brown undertake 'probe' of entry, visiting capitals of the Six. Cabinet announces its intention of applying for membership of the EEC, leading to the UK's second application; this is joined by Ireland, Denmark and Norway. President de Gaulle announces a veto (the second veto), and the application is denied but not withdrawn as the Wilson government declare that it is to be 'left on the table'. Merger of EEC, ECSC and EURATOM into the EC with common institutions. Civil war in Nigeria (Biafran War, 1967–70).

1968   Mauritius, Nauru and Swaziland gain independence within the Commonwealth. Wilson government imposes further limitations on new Commonwealth immigration.

1969   President de Gaulle resigns; Georges Pompidou becomes President of France, opening the way for Britain's entry negotiations.

1970   Edward Heath leads the Conservative Party to victory in a general election, and continues his Labour predecessor's application for EC membership. Negotiations open in Luxembourg (30 June). Fiji, Tonga and Western Samoa gain independence.

1971   War breaks out between India and Pakistan as India comes to the aid of East Pakistan.

1972   Heath successfully negotiates Britain's third application to the EC, signs Treaty of Accession, and passes the EC Act leading to British membership. Norway rejects EC membership in referendum. East Pakistan becomes Bangladesh and joins the Commonwealth; Pakistan leaves Commonwealth.

1973   Britain formally becomes a member of the EC, along with Ireland and Denmark (1 January). The Bahamas gains independence.

1974   Wilson again becomes Prime Minister (February), pledging to have entry terms renegotiated. Grenada gains independence.

1975   Referendum on results in two-thirds majority in favour of UK remaining in the EC. Papua New Guinea gains independence.

1976   The Seychelles gain independence.

1978   Dominica and the Solomon Island gain independence.

1979   Margaret Thatcher leads the Conservative Party to victory in general election (May). St Lucia, St Vincent and the Grenadines gain independence. Lancaster House talks lead to a settlement to the Rhodesian conflict with elections.

1980   Thatcher begins campaign for a rebate on UK net contribution to EC budget. Rhodesian elections lead to the establishment of Zimbabwe with a government under Robert Mugabe.

1981   Labour Party under Michael Foot adopts manifesto commitment to a withdrawal policy for UK from EC. Departure of numerous Labour MPs to the newly established SDP; many SDP members claim the issue of Europe is a deciding factor in their departure from Labour. Antigua and Belize gain independence.

1982   Falklands War.

1983   Labour platform modifies its anti-EC membership stance under Neil Kinnock and Roy Hattersley.

1984   At EC Fontainebleau summit, Thatcher secures rebate on UK net contribution to EC budget.

1986   Single European Act signed by Thatcher government.

1988   Delors speech to TUC conference results in more favourable attitude of Labour Party towards EC.

1988   In a speech at Bruges, Thatcher emphasises the intergovernmental aspects of the Community, highlighting her vision of the continued importance of the integrity of the individual member states.

1989   Pakistan rejoins Commonwealth. Bruges Group established.

1990   John Major becomes Prime Minister (Nov.), announces that his vision of Britain's future is at the 'heart of Europe'.

1992   The European Communities Act is passed by Parliament, ratifying the Maastrict Treaty. ERM crisis, 'Black Wednesday' (16 Sept.).

1993   The EU formally comes into existence (1 Nov.), and citizens of the member states are now automatically concurrent citizens of the EU.

1994   Norway rejects EU membership in a referendum, does not enter EU in 1995.

1995   Austria, Finland and Sweden enter the EU. Standing against continued criticism of his European policies, John Major resigns as Leader of the Conservative Party and announces that he is standing in the forthcoming leadership election; he is re-elected.

1996   Britain withholds cooperation from EU meetings, adopting an obstructionist position, withholding approval for key votes in Council of Ministers in response to the imposition of an EU ban on the export of British beef.

1997   General election (1 May) contested by two Euro-sceptic parties: the Referendum Party of Sir James Goldsmith and the United Kingdom Independence Party of Dr Alan Sked. European summit at Amsterdam and Amsterdam Treaty. William Hague elected Leader of Conservative Party, adopts anti-European tone, says party disapproves of UK joining a single currency for the life of two Parliaments, calls for referendum before UK accession to a single currency. Blair says UK not to join Eurozone for lifetime of current Parliament.

1998   Blair's speech to French National Assembly (March) wins praise across France and Europe.

1999   European Single Currency, the euro, comes into existence for inter-bank transfers – paper currency to circulate from January 2002. Blair and French leaders discuss the possible formation of a European defence corps. Blair says that the UK is valuable to both Europe and to the USA, as the bridge between Europe and America.

2000   Britain's continuing agenda for EU includes enlargement to embrace Eastern European applicant countries.

5 Scotland: Cultural Base and Economic Catalysts

James Mitchell

Introduction

Until the 1960s, the dominant view was that Britain was a coherent, even uniform nation. There were divisions, but these were based on class – 'all else is embellishment and detail', as Pulzer famously stated (1967, p. 98). Scotland was different, but the differences amounted to little more than variations on the same theme. Indeed, it was generally assumed that the differences were declining and that the processes of modernisation – industrialisation, urbanisation, secularisation and modern communications – were leading ineluctably to a more unified and culturally uniform state. The rise of nationalism in Scotland from the 1960s onwards challenged these notions, and by the 1990s the prospect of an independent Scotland was no longer fantastic. The dominant view, which had suggested that regional and local identities would be subsumed within the larger identity of the State, had been wrong for two main reasons. First, it had underestimated the strength of local and regional identities, and second, it had misunderstood the consequences of the various, often contradictory, forces which were lumped together under the heading of 'modernisation'. The history of post-1945 Scotland is one in which there has been a remarkable degree of continuity in the levels of support for Scottish cultural identity, but equally remarkable has been the extent of change in the political and economic context in which that identity has existed.

In this chapter, we will look at the extent of these continuities or renewals in Scottish identity and Scottish institutions. This incorporates a discussion of the economic and other changes in the context in which Scots lived their lives during the half-century since 1945. The relationship between cultural identity and the context in which it existed has been noted by scholars of nationalism and regionalism. Rokkan and Urwin maintained that 'Together, cultural base and economic catalyst provide a base for [nationalist] mobilization' (1983,

p. 139). The cultural base in the case of Scotland was underpinned by public institutions and official recognition of Scottish distinctiveness. It was not only culture in the narrow sense of literature and the arts, important as they have been in the maintenance of Scottish identity, but also in the values and norms of the society as well as in the form of its public organisations. The economic catalysts consisted of a range of different forces. It would be wrong to suggest that the changes which ultimately led to the establishment of the first Scottish Parliament in almost 300 years were part of some unremitting force. A coincidence of events, context and underlying Scottish national identity eventually led to the establishment of the Parliament.

The orthodox modernist view which proved unfounded had some force at times. There were periods, particularly in the 1950s, when it looked as if Scottish assimilation into Britain, or perhaps more accurately England, looked likely. When the Treaty of Rome was signed in 1957 promising 'ever-closer union' in Europe, it seemed that 'ever-closer union' would be more likely within Britain than across the continent of Europe. Forty years later, the tables have been turned and a disintegrating Britain within a more integrated Europe now seems more likely. However, the course of post-war Scottish history suggests that care should be taken against reading too much into trends which appear evident at any particular time.

Scotland at the End of War: Proud to Be British

War is generally seen as a great force for reconciling differences within a state, at least so long as the state in question is victorious. Wars can act as a 'centralizing force in the life of the community and a provider of myths and memories for future generations' (Smith, 1991, p. 27). The sense of common purpose generated by fighting together against a common enemy during the Second World War was carried over into peacetime, at least for many Scots, through changes in public policy which started to take shape during the war. William Beveridge had written of 'national unity' as the great moral achievement of the war (1943, p. 109). Scots had long shown a willingness to go overseas in the name of Britain, whether to fight for it or make money from it. This was evident at the end of the war. A poll in 1948 found that over 60 per cent of Scots believed that emigration was not simply caused by poor economic conditions in Scotland (*Scots Review*, 1948). Britain gave Scots a gateway to the world. War and the Empire had been important in the early twentieth century and before in forging that sense of Britain's position in the world and Scots pride in being British. Together they created an idea of 'Great' Britain for many Scots. For most Scots in 1945, recent history gave them good reason to feel proud to be British.

The late 1940s also witnessed a political phenomenon which appeared to contradict that sense of Britishness in Scotland. A movement demanding a Scottish Parliament was launched which attracted the support of a wide body of people (Mitchell, 1996, pp. 87–97). However, a sense of Britishness was entirely consistent with the sense of Scottishness which lay behind the demand for home rule. The same survey quoted above offers one of the very few insights into what Scottish people were thinking at that time (*Scots Review*, 1948). There was a strong sense that domestic affairs should be controlled in Scotland. Almost three-quarters agreed with this, a result similar to a poll conducted by the *Scottish Daily Express* in July. Most Scots agreed that this view had arisen because of 'dissatisfaction with laws which do not take account of local Scottish conditions' and that English interests dominated in the Westminster Parliament. There was, it appeared, a general sense of grievance against London rule though a desire to remain part of the United Kingdom.

This was manifested in debates on nationalisation and opportunistically seized upon by the Scottish Unionist Party (as the Conservatives in Scotland were officially called between 1912 and 1965). The nation in nation-alisation was clearly not thought to be Scotland. Winston Churchill, in one of his speeches in Scotland, warned that nationalisation affected not only Scotland's prosperity but the 'independence which Scotland has exercised in many fields. No sharper challenge could be given to Scottish national sentiment than is now launched by the Socialism of Whitehall' (*Scotsman*, 21 May 1949). In their effort to embarrass the Labour government, the Scottish Tories did what all opposition parties have done over the post-war period. They played the Scottish card to the point of using the language of Scottish nationalism while stopping short of advocating a Scottish Parliament. 'Scottish Control of Scottish Affairs' was the title of proposals published in 1949 which amounted to some modest administrative reforms. But the Tory flirtation with Scottish nationalism was both insubstantial and unrequited. The Scottish National Party (SNP), founded over a decade before, distrusted the Tories though the Scottish Liberals, supporters of home rule, had effectively been taken over by the Tories. What was more, the Scottish Tories had other suitors. At the same time that they were playing the Scottish card, proposals were emerging to merge the Scottish Unionist Party with the Conservatives in England. Motivated by the perceived need to modernise, the idea of a merger was, however, rejected for fear that it would prove unpopular (*Glasgow Herald*, 19 October 1948).

Labour's old home rule policy, which had been a central plank in Keir Hardie's platform when Labour was first created, was discarded by the Attlee government, though a sentimental attachment to the policy remained. The 1947 Scottish Labour Conference passed a resolution urging a 'full examination of the whole question of the future Government of Scotland' in light of the 'very comprehensive social and economic measures enacted by the Government' (PRO CAB 129/22), but there was a move away from the 'model election address' of 1945 which had explicitly committed the party to home rule. In a memorandum to his Cabinet colleagues, Arthur Woodburn, Labour's Scottish Secretary, warned against assuming that the existence of the familiar pattern of two party politics in Scotland meant that Scotland was the same or that Scottish nationalism had no support. Certain issues were fuelling grievances which had nationalist undercurrents. It was his view that nationalisation had been portrayed as 'taking administration from Scotland to London'. The future of Prestwick Airport had taken on symbolic importance, as Woodburn recognised when he commented that there was a feeling that 'Scottish enterprise in civil aviation was contemptuously suppressed' (CAB 129/22). Two years later, he observed that Prestwick had 'all along been made a symbol of nationalist agitation' (CAB 129/37). The poll in 1948 showed that 88 per cent of Scots favoured retaining Prestwick, suggesting that the issue had tapped into public opinion. This would not be the last time that a Scottish industry took on symbolic national significance.

Overall, the picture at the end of the war was of Unionist Scotland, but one in which undercurrents of nationalism existed, fuelled by grievances about London's inability to take account of Scottish distinctiveness. This was manifested in a non-party movement for home rule which claimed the support of around two million Scots who had signed a grandly named 'Scottish Covenant' in favour of home rule. In a further memorandum to the Cabinet in 1949, Woodburn noted the nature of the demand for home rule:

> These campaigns obtain their success because interest in the subject in Scotland is always present, widespread and sincere. It is accordingly essential that every support should be given to the great body of reasonable opinion in Scotland which does not support drastic changes but which is liable to be shaken by any action which can be represented as imposing on Scotland decisions in the making of which she appears to have had no real voice, or as being designed primarily to meet conditions south of the Border. I hope my colleagues will keep this danger in mind and be vigilant when they are dealing with matters affecting Scotland. I think it is also true to say that there have been occasions on which decisions concerning Scotland, which could not be questioned on merits, have been announced in a way which made it possible to misrepresent them. (CAB 129/37)

Scots were unambiguously British but equally unambiguously Scottish. To many in government in London, Scots appeared extremely sensitive and ungrateful. The welfare state was in the process of construction and it would benefit countless Scots. War had been won against a common enemy and a new threat requiring unity had emerged with the onslaught of the Cold War. But as Lord Salisbury had said at the establishment of the Scottish Office in 1885, measures were required to address the 'wounded dignities of the Scotch' (Hanham, 1965, p. 230). This continued to be the case. Scots were proud to be British, but this was not the same as denying a Scottish national identity.

The Ascendancy of Britain

Two articles appeared in the *Glasgow Herald* in July 1959 concluding that Scottish nationalism was in decline (8–9 July 1959). These proved mistaken, though few at the time appreciated this. There was little direct evidence of support for nationalism but undercurrents were evident, and conditions were being created for the reassertion of demands for a Scottish Parliament. The cultural base and economic catalyst which Rokkan and Urwin saw as conditions for nationalist mobilisation had been gaining strength. Far from diminishing the Scottish cultural base, modern communications helped maintain, if not fostered, a distinct Scottish national identity. Television was to become the main medium through which people gained political news after 1959. This was very British in orientation but there was a Scottish dimension to broadcasting. The first BBC broadcast in Scotland was made in 1952 and in 1955 Scottish Television went on air. Modern communications need not lead to assimilation. Scotland's cultural base was maintained through a healthy Scottish press and developing Scottish broadcasting output. Perhaps more significant was the development of the Scottish Office. Its responsibilities continued to grow and Scots looked to it for solutions to social and economic problems. Identification with Scotland as a political entity was, in effect, given official blessing.

In 1951, the Conservatives had returned to power and the Festival of Britain was held. This was the start of a long period of Conservative and very British rule. It began with an episode which symbolised the nature of Scotland's position in the Union. Over the previous Christmas, a group of Glasgow University students broke into Westminster Abbey and removed the Stone of Destiny from the coronation throne. Press reports and the reaction of officials in Scotland and England highlight different attitudes to what had happened. In Scotland, it was seen as a student prank and at times even official Scotland seemed to see humour in 'the pinch', especially following the reaction of senior members of the English establishment. But in London, it was seen as sacrilege – quite literally in some cases – by some senior members of the Establishment. The matter even reached the Cabinet. After the retrieval of the Stone, the Attlee Cabinet discussed the possibility of returning the Stone to Scotland as a symbolic act showing willingness to acknowledge Scottish national identity within the United Kingdom. In the event it was decided to postpone making a decision to avoid the appearance of a 'concession to the recent act of vandalism' (CM 34 (51)). Hector McNeil, then Scottish Secretary, had prepared a paper considering various options. Within a year, Labour were out of office and the Conservatives decided that the Stone should be replaced in the coronation chair in Westminster Abbey (Cabinet Conclusions 15 (52) 2). This episode serves to emphasise the point that even at a time of intense Britishness there was a strong Scottish cultural base.

King George VI's death in February 1952 had necessitated some kind of decision on the Stone but the coronation of the new monarch provoked a new reaction in Scotland. While there is little evidence that republicanism had much support in Scotland, many Scots were annoyed when the new monarch was crowned Elizabeth II. The new Queen was the first Elizabeth to rule in Scotland. EIIR suggested lack of sensitivity, that Britain was merely the continuity of England in another form. Pillar boxes embossed with EIIR were blown up by a few fringe nationalists and a legal challenge to the title was brought forward by John MacCormick, a leading figure in the home rule movement with the support of Ian Hamilton, who had led the group that retrieved the Stone of Destiny (Hamilton, 1991). The case was significant in legal history less for its result – MacCormick was defeated – than because of the judgement made by Lord President Cooper, Scotland's most senior judge. Cooper ruled against MacCormick but in his judgement he raised questions about parliamentary sovereignty:

The principle of the unlimited Sovereignty of Parliament is a distinctively English principle which has no counterpart in Scottish Constitutional law. It derives its origins from Coke and Blackstone, and was widely popularised during the eighteenth century by Bagehot and Dicey, the latter having stated the doctrine in its classic form in his Constitutional Law. Considering that the Union legislation extinguished the Parliaments of Scotland and England, and replaced them by a new Parliament, I have difficulty in seeing why it should have been supposed that the new Parliament of Great Britain must inherit all the peculiar characteristics of the English Parliament but none of the Scottish Parliament, as if all that happened in 1707 was that Scottish representatives were admitted to the Parliament of England. That is not what was done. (Quoted in MacCormick, 1955, p. 216)

The question of Westminster's authority had been raised at a fairly theoretical level in the case, but less than forty years later this became a matter of practical politics.

The State which had most meaning for many Scots in the 1950s was neither the British state nor a putative Scottish state but the welfare state. It provided them with education, a health service and welfare services as never before. Crucially, the national in the National Health Service (NHS) was not Scottish but British. The home rule agitation which had marked the late 1940s all but disappeared in the 1950s. There was never any prospect of the Tories advocating home rule in the 1950s. The Labour Party in Scotland edged away from its old commitment to a Scottish Parliament. In January 1957 its Scottish Executive came out against home rule on 'compelling economic grounds' and Labour rejected home rule at the following year's annual Scottish Conference on the grounds that 'Scotland's problems can best be solved on a UK scale'. It was generally thought that the welfare state and economic intervention required a strong central state. An unstated and largely uncommented-upon part of the post-war consensus was support for the territorial arrangements of government.

High Expectations

The second part of Rokkan and Urwin's equation explaining nationalist mobilisation – an economic catalyst – was also emerging. One of the consequences of nationalisation was that key decisions on the future of the nationalised industries became highly politicised. Market considerations were often overridden by political considerations. In 1958, the Cabinet had to make a decision on the siting of a new steel strip mill. Initially, four places were identified as possible sites: Grangemouth in Scotland, Kidwelly and Newport in Wales and Immingham in England. The Cabinet's Economic Policy Committee had narrowed down the sites to Newport and Grangemouth without entirely ruling out Kidwelly. There were three aspects of the final decision which were notable: the importance of social and political considerations; the acceptance of a need to take account of national sentiment; and pressure for compromise.

Inevitably, the Scottish Secretary, with the aid of research completed by the Scottish Council (Development and Industry) – a semi-official body comprising representatives of public and private sectors, business and trade unions – made the case for Grangemouth. Prime Minister Harold Macmillan told the Cabinet in May that the matter was finely balanced and that the decision was primarily a matter of 'broad national policy' involving 'not merely economic factors but also social and political issues', 'including sensitive questions of Scottish and Welsh sentiment'. In addition, there was policy favouring the distribution of industry (Cabinet Conclusions (58) 44 (6)). High and rising levels of unemployment around Grangemouth as a result of the government's own action in closing service establishments and the decline of the shale oil industry were thought to favour Grangemouth. The case for Newport was made fairly consistently on economic grounds.

By the autumn a new claimant had emerged. Ravenscraig in Lanarkshire came into the frame and the Ministry of Power proposed that one-third of new capacity should be located at the private firm Colville's Ravenscraig operation and the other two-thirds at Newport. It proved a classic example of post-war policy-making by consensus taking account of a variety of interests and reaching a messy compromise. Its reverberations were to be felt throughout the next 30 years. The issue of steel illustrated two features of politics in the second half of the twentieth century. First, the people looked to government for jobs and economic security. Second, there was a territorial dimension to public policy: there was an expectation that special consideration should made of the impact a policy had on Scotland.

Unemployment began to rise in the 1950s, and while the problem was far less severe than the slump in the 1930s there was one crucial difference. There were greater expectations in the 1950s that government should act to alleviate, if not prevent, such problems. In 1958, a special Cabinet committee was set up to review measures the government might take to deal with the problem and a special meeting was held to discuss the situation in Scotland in December. Unemployment in Scotland was twice the British level and the rate was increasing (see table 5.1).

Senior officials in the Scottish Unionist Party were stating that their objective was to bring unemployment figures down to the British average within a decade, and voices across the political spectrum in Scotland were demanding government action. Resistance to any further special measures for Scotland did not remove demands nor expectations that government should do something. What was clearly emerging was a sense of Scotland as a distinct political and economic entity that required distinct and special policies. That would prove a small step from demanding a Scottish Parliament.

Table 5.1   Unemployment, Scotland and Great Britain, 1955–1958

1955	1956	1957	1958
Scotland			
48,700	50,800	56,400	94,800
(2.2%)	(2.3%)	(2.6%)	(4.4%)
Great Britain			
225,900	264,600	316,500	536,000
(1.0%)	(1.2%)	(1.5%)	(2.4%)

Source: CAB 134/1734.

The Era of Planning

The Scottish Office depended heavily for advice on the Scottish Council (Development and Industry) – a body described as 'Scotland's industrial Parliament' (Moore and Booth, 1989, p. 30). In 1961, an enquiry into the Scottish economy under its auspices proposed that the industrial and economic functions of the Home and Health Departments in the Scottish Office should be brought together in one department and argued for regional economic planning. The next year, the Scottish Office was reorganised, a Scottish Development Department established and the following year a White Paper, *Central Scotland: a Programme for Development and Growth*, was published.

The election of Labour in 1964 gave even more prominence to planning and state intervention. Institutional machinery was set up in these optimistic early days to plan for Scottish economic growth. The optimism gave way to grave concerns after the British economy hit difficulties in the late 1960s. Neither Scotland nor Britain could be isolated from international developments. Processes now described as 'globalisation' were of some significance. Inward investment and the Cold War had Scottish dimensions. Plans to expand production by the major motor manufacturers in response to growing demand for cars offered an opportunity for government to encourage expansions in areas suffering economic difficulties. Substantial financial support for relocation was made available and major factories were opened in the 1960s at Linwood in Renfrewshire and Bathgate in West Lothian. Despite these major injections, Scotland continued to suffer as traditional industries declined. Coal reached its peak in employment terms in 1952 and the numbers working declined after that.

There was even a Scottish dimension to the rise of the Campaign for Nuclear Disarmament (CND). In November 1960, two years after the formation of CND, Prime Minister Harold Macmillan announced that a Polaris missile base would be established at the Holy Loch in Scotland. The Government had been under pressure from the United States to reach a decision on a site for a US base. The Americans had identified the Holy Loch as ideal for their purposes, though it was situated at the mouth of the Clyde, near to Scotland's main population centre. This was agreed after some discussion. The degree to which Scottish sensitivities were taken into account in Cabinet discussion was evident in references to 'Lock' rather than 'Loch' in a Cabinet memorandum from the Defence Minister in June 1960. Four years later, Harold Wilson confirmed that the Holy Loch would be retained as a Polaris missile base. A sense that Scotland was being used as a dumping ground was beginning to emerge.

The Rise of the SNP

The SNP had won a by-election in Motherwell in the closing days of the war but lost the seat in 1945 and the party had failed to win over 0.5 per cent of the vote in elections in the 1950s. The new conditions emerging in the 1960s changed all of that. An early sign of trouble came in a by-election in West

Lothian in 1962. Tam Dalyell, an old Etonian baronet and former Cambridge University Conservative chairman standing for Labour, was pitted against Billy Wolfe, a rising star in the SNP. The result was to be a precursor of things to come. Dalyell held the seat for Labour but the SNP ran an effective campaign, winning 23 per cent of the vote by focusing less on Scottish cultural traditions and more on the economic distress caused by the decline of the local shale oil industry. In 1955, the Scottish Unionists had become the only party in Scotland's history to win a majority of votes (50.1 per cent). Seven years later in West Lothian the Tories lost their deposit, the first in 42 years in Scotland. In 1967, Winnie Ewing won the Hamilton by-election in a spectacular victory. From then onwards, the SNP would have a continuous presence in the House of Commons. It attracted new waves of members, including many from the Labour Party disillusioned with their old party.

The Tories were first to react to political developments in Scotland. In 1965, the party changed its name and reorganised itself. In 1912, the 'Conservative' label had been abandoned in Scotland and the party was styled the Scottish Unionist Party (SUP). The union in Unionist was not, however, a reference to the Anglo-Scottish Union but the British union with Ireland. At the height of debates on Irish home rule, the Scottish Tories were nailing their colours firmly to the Ulster Unionist mast. Scotland had deep historic links with Northern Ireland and many Scots had family there. Presbyterianism was shared by the majority in both places. Anti-Irish Catholic sentiment had been prevalent in parts of Scotland, especially in times of economic crisis. By calling themselves

Table 5.2 British General Elections, Scotland, 1945–1997

	Labour % (seats)	SNP % (seats)	Conservative % (seats)	Liberal/Alliance/ Liberal Democrat % (seats)	Others % (seats)
2001	43.9 (55)	20.1 (5)	15.6 (1)	16.4 (0)	4.0 (1*)
1945	47.6 (37)	1.2 (0)	41.1 (27)	5.0 (0)	3.3 (4)
1950	46.2 (37)	0.4 (0)	44.8 (32)	6.6 (2)	1.6 (0)
1951	47.9 (35)	0.3 (0)	48.6 (35)	2.7 (1)	0.5 (0)
1955	46.7 (34)	0.5 (0)	50.1 (36)	1.9 (1)	0.8 (0)
1959	46.7 (38)	0.5 (0)	47.2 (31)	4.1 (1)	1.2 (1)
1964	48.7 (43)	2.4 (0)	40.6 (24)	7.6 (4)	0.7 (0)
1966	49.9 (46)	5.0 (0)	37.7 (20)	6.8 (5)	0.6 (0)
1970	44.5 (44)	11.4 (1)	38.0 (23)	5.5 (3)	0.6 (0)
1974 (Feb.)	36.6 (40)	21.9 (7)	32.9 (21)	8.0 (3)	0.6 (0)
1974 (Oct.)	36.3 (41)	30.4 (11)	24.7 (16)	8.3 (3)	0.3 (0)
1979	41.5 (44)	17.3 (2)	31.4 (22)	9.0 (3)	0.8 (0)
1983	35.1 (41)	11.7 (2)	28.4 (21)	24.5 (8)	0.3 (0)
1987	42.4 (50)	14.0 (3)	24.0 (10)	19.2 (9)	0.3 (0)
1992	39.0 (49)	21.5 (3)	25.7 (11)	13.1 (9)	0.8 (0)
1997	45.6 (56)	22.1 (6)	17.5 (0)	13.0 (10)	1.9 (0)
2001	43.9 (55)	20.1 (5)	15.6 (1)	16.4 (0)	4.0 (1*)

*In 2001 the Speaker was returned from a Scottish constituency. Michael Martin had previously been a Labour MP.

the Scottish Unionist Party, the Tories had managed to cut out a significant place for themselves in twentieth-century Scotland. It appealed successfully to working-class Protestants, and the party allowed candidates to stand in elections as Liberal Unionists to wipe up residual support for the old Liberal Party, which had dominated nineteenth-century Scotland.

However, over the post-war period anti-Irish Catholic sentiment was in decline. In this respect at least, the predictions of modernisation theory proved accurate. The Irish immigrant community was integrated into Scottish society, though without losing its own sense of identity. Northern Ireland had receded in importance and even when 'The Troubles' exploded on to the British political agenda in the late 1960s, latent sectarian tensions in west-central Scotland failed to ignite. Conservative leader Ted Heath's view had been that the Scottish Conservatives needed to modernise to compete in Scotland. The party could no longer afford to have different names in different parts of Britain. In order to take advantage of modern communications, especially television, it was thought necessary to send the same message out to each part of Britain, and that would require the same name. From 1965, the party was officially restyled the Scottish Conservative and Unionist Party. One interpretation suggests that the party suffered as a consequence by losing its Scottish distinctiveness and throwing away a plank in its appeal to its core Protestant supporters (Seawright, 1999). At the same time, Heath reacted to the rise of Scottish nationalism in a quite different way. Assimilationist assumptions may have been behind the move towards changes in the name and structure of the party, but belief in the need for enhanced distinctiveness explains his grandiosely entitled 'Declaration of Perth' in 1968 in which the Conservative leader promised to deliver a (very) limited measure of Scottish home rule. However, Heath made no effort to implement his promise. Labour's reaction, on the other hand, was to oppose home rule fiercely. In time, the positions of these parties was reversed. Ewing lost Hamilton at the 1970 general election and though the SNP won the remote Western Isles, its first ever win in a general election, it was generally assumed that the Nationalist advance had been colourful but brief. The two elections in 1974 soon put paid to that interpretation. The SNP advanced in each election, winning seven seats in February and eleven with 30 per cent of the vote in October. Between the elections, Labour's London leadership demanded that the Scottish party should revisit the issue of Scottish devolution. Fearing a Nationalist advance, Harold Wilson used the trade union block vote to overturn Labour's anti-devolution policy at a special conference in Glasgow in August. Just as Heath had imposed devolution on a reluctant Conservative Party, so now Wilson was doing the same in his party. Scottish Labour accepted the policy reluctantly. John Smith, later leader of the Labour Party, was amongst Scottish Labour figures who spoke against devolution at that conference. Smith's position on devolution probably reflected the position of the party across Scotland. He had opposed devolution on the grounds that he felt it would diminish Scotland's influence in London and believed that reacting to the electoral threat posed by the Nationalists was not reason enough to change policy radically. He accepted the policy out of loyalty to his party and led the ill-fated Labour government's plans for Scottish devolution through the Commons in the late 1970s. In time, Smith and Scottish Labour embraced devolution to the point of regarding it as one of the party's central, defining principles.

Labour divisions on devolution in the late 1970s were papered over in Parliament with a commitment to hold a referendum. In addition, a backbench amendment to Labour's devolution legislation demanded that 40 per cent of the eligible electorate, not just those who voted, had to vote in favour before the measure could be passed into law. A slim majority voted in favour of devolution in the referendum held on 1 March 1979, but the 40 per cent hurdle was not overcome. The anti-devolutionists had outmanoeuvred supporters of a Scottish Parliament. The Conservatives were returned at the subsequent general election with Mrs Thatcher as Prime Minister. Thatcher had inherited Heath's commitment to devolution on becoming leader in 1975 at a time when the SNP appeared to be in the ascendancy. However, her policies and style dictated against supporting devolution. A strong centre would be required to pursue the radical overhaul she and her supporters deemed necessary to save Britain from terminal decline. Officially, the Conservative position during the referendum had been to oppose the measure on offer but favour devolution in principle. In reality, the Tories under Thatcher were moving against devolution.

The Thatcher Years and the Return of Home Rule

The Thatcher years began well for the Scottish Conservatives. They recovered in the 1979 election and devolution was removed from the political agenda. However, a combination of factors led to the return of devolution to the political fore and the demise of the Scottish Tories. Some commentators maintained that while the referendum suggested the demise of political nationalism, there had been an 'explosion of cultural activity in Scotland in the Seventies and Eighties' and that in effect this amounted to 'a declaration of cultural independence' (Kerevan, 1991, p. 27). There was a new vibrancy in the Scottish arts, theatre and literature evident in paintings by young artists from the Glasgow School of Art as well as pop culture, with Scottish bands proudly singing in the Scottish vernacular rather than the usual synthetic American accent. In essence, the Scottish cultural base remained healthy. Economic catalysts pushing the demand for home rule to the fore emerged in the form of rising unemployment and the closures of various businesses.

So long as people expected government to deliver jobs and prosperity, governments would suffer in recessions. The Conservative objective was to convince people that employment was no longer a responsibility of government. Thatcherite policies were designed to break the link between government responsibility in traditional post-war consensual welfare politics. In Scotland, however, the link was strong and Scots refused to accept that government could or should abnegate responsibility. This was most evident in the case of the Scottish steel industry. After the decision to extend Ravenscraig in the late 1950s, it had been decided to build a steel strip mill at nearby Gartcosh in 1961. A threat to Ravenscraig and Gartcosh emerged but George Younger, the Scottish Secretary, threatened to resign from the Thatcher government if

Ravenscraig was closed. A campaign uniting parties, businesses and trade unions as well as other groups such as the churches, arguing against closure, was successful in 1982. Three years later, a decision was made to close Gartcosh, which provoked a backlash against the government. Ravenscraig was finally closed after a long campaign in its defence in 1992. Once more, steel took on symbolic importance in Scottish politics.

Being Scottish started to have a wider meaning, incorporating political and economic dimensions. Until the 1980s, Scottishness was not associated with any particular ideological position on the traditional left–right spectrum. Public opinion research showed that under Thatcher, those who saw themselves as Scottish tended also to support a Scottish Parliament and had left-of-centre, interventionist views (Mitchell and Bennie, 1996). The issue which brought this most forcefully to the fore was the poll tax. The poll tax was a regressive form of local taxation introduced into Scotland a year ahead of England. It was widely seen as out of step with Scottish political values, and many Scots regarded it as evidence that they were guinea pigs on which new policies would be tested. Thatcher's contempt for a distinct Scottish dimension was all too evident. In a passage criticising the Scottish Office in her memoirs, she confirmed what many Scots had long suspected: 'The pride of the Scottish Office – whose very structure added a layer of bureaucracy, standing in the way of the reforms which were paying such dividends in England – was that public expenditure per head in Scotland was far higher than in England' (Thatcher, 1993, p. 67).

Both distinct public institutions which contributed to Scotland's cultural base and Scottish political and social values were perceived by a growing body of Scots to be under attack. It was hardly surprising that Scots increasingly turned to home rule. The lengthy period in power of the Conservatives, while all the time losing ground in Scotland, seemed only to underline the need for constitutional change. Home rule became the logical way of protecting Scottish public institutions and defending collectivist or corporatist policies.

Scottish support for a radical alternative was manifested in a number of ways. The SNP won a spectacular by-election victory in Glasgow Govan in 1988 with its refined objective of independence within the Europe on a platform of backing non-payment of the poll tax. The following year, Labour, Liberal Democrats, trade unions, local authorities and others established the Constitutional Convention which set out to agree a scheme of home rule within Britain. Polls suggested that support for independence was rising. The Convention scheme was in most respects similar to the ill-fated devolution proposals in the 1970s, but an alternative voting system was agreed which would make it very unlikely for any party to have an overall majority in a Scottish Parliament. Another change from the 1970s, something Labour had come to back from early in the 1980s, was support for modest tax powers.

Participants in the Convention signed a document rejecting notions of parliamentary sovereignty and asserting the sovereignty of the Scottish people. Lord Cooper's judgement in the EIIR case finally had real political meaning. The 1992 election proved a disappointment for the parties advocating some measure of home rule. The SNP's increase in its share of the vote was impressive but this did not translate into seats and the Tories, now under John Major, whose personal poll ratings in Scotland were a great improvement on his predecessor's, won an additional Scottish seat with a marginal increase in its share of the vote. As in 1979, the Tories assumed that the issue had been removed from the political agenda. In fact, the 1992 election proved to be a blip in the long-term decline of the Conservatives.

Establishing the Scottish Parliament

Shortly after the 1992 election, John Smith was elected leader of the Labour Party. He had become associated with devolution as Devolution Minister in the last Labour government in the 1970s, and made clear his determination to complete the 'unfinished business' of establishing a Scottish Parliament. He frequently referred to devolution as the 'settled will of the Scottish people', but died from a heart attack in May 1994 and never lived to finish the business himself. Tony Blair, the new leader, proved to be far less enthusiastic about devolution, though few in the party appreciated his coolness towards the issue when he was elected. Blair's ambition led him to abandoning any policy which might stand in the way of electoral progress and one aspect of the devolution was deemed potentially damaging to Labour's prospect of victory. 'New Labour' was intent on dispelling its image as a 'tax and spend' party and Labour's policy of devolution with tax-raising powers became a focus of Conservative attacks. Blair decided to confront the attacks with a decision to hold a referendum with two questions, in which Scots would be asked whether they wanted a Scottish Parliament and whether they wanted it to have tax-varying powers. Despite Labour agreeing its policy with the Liberal Democrats in the Constitutional Convention, the decision on the referendum was made unilaterally. As a referendum had been proposed in the 1970s as a means of blocking

Table 5.3   Results of the 1979 and 1997 referendums on Scottish devolution

	% of votes cast	% of electorate	% of adjusted electorate*
1979 referendum			
Support a Scottish Parliament			
Yes	51.6	–	32.5
No	48.4	–	30.5
1997 referendum			
Q1: Support a Scottish Parliament			
Yes	74.3	44.7	45.7
No	25.7	15.5	15.8
Q2: Support tax-varying powers			
Yes	63.5	38.1	38.9
No	36.5	21.9	22.4

* Figures were adjusted to take account of estimated number of deaths since compilation of register and number of people double-registered, etc.

devolution, many home rulers feared that this was a similar ploy from someone with little understanding of Scottish politics. His frequent praise of Margaret Thatcher was noted with increasing alarm in Scotland. The Tories under Major attempted to reposition themselves to be seen as sympathetic to Scottish national identity. The Stone of Destiny was even returned to Scotland – this time officially – to be housed in Edinburgh Castle, but Scots remained suspicious that the new Scottish-friendly Conservative Party was offering too little, too late.

The 1997 general election in Scotland was a remarkably British affair. The Tories lost all of their Scottish seats, though still polled more popular votes than the Liberal Democrats. A referendum was announced for the autumn and Labour, SNP and Liberal Democrats joined forces to campaign for a double Yes vote – Yes to a Scottish Parliament and Yes to tax-varying powers (generally assumed to mean tax-raising). The result was an emphatic endorsement of devolution and a convincing majority for tax powers. There was no 40 per cent rule, but even had there been enough electors voted for the Parliament to overcome the hurdle which had blocked devolution in 1979 (Denver et al., 2000).

Conclusion

In May 1999, the first elections to a democratically elected Scottish Parliament were held under the new voting system. Labour became the largest party, but without an overall majority, and a deal was made with the Liberal Democrats to govern in coalition. The SNP failed to perform as well as polls had earlier suggested, but they became Scotland's second party. In its 70-year history only 18 SNP members had ever been elected to the House of Commons. Twice that number were elected in the first elections to the Scottish Parliament. More ominous for the other parties were the polls showing support for independence at just under 40 per cent, an all-time high during an election period. Winnie Ewing, victor in Hamilton in 1967, opened the Parliament as its oldest member. Devolution had clearly not killed off the SNP as Labour politicians had predicted. The creation of the Parliament itself meant that the cultural and political base on which any future nationalist mobilisation might occur had been strengthened as never before.

Table 5.4 Results of the first elections to the Scottish Parliament, May 1999

	Constituency % vote (seats)	Regional list % vote (seats)	Seats
Labour	38.8 (53)	34.0 (3)	56
SNP	28.7 (7)	27.6 (28)	35
Conservative	15.6 (0)	15.5 (18)	18
Liberal Democrat	14.2 (12)	12.6 (5)	17
Others	2.8 (1)	10.3 (2)	3

References and Further Reading

Books

Beveridge, William. (1943) *Pillars of Security and other War-Time Essays and Addresses*. London.

Denver, David, Mitchell, James, Pattie, C. and Bochel, H. (2000) *Scotland Decides: The Devolution Issue and the 1997 Referendum*. London.

Devine, Tom. (2000) *The Scottish Nation, 1700–2000*. London.

Devine, Tom and Finlay, Richard (eds) (1996) *Scotland in the Twentieth Century*. Edinburgh.

Hamilton, Ian (1991) *The Taking of the Stone of Destiny*. Moffat.

Hanham, H. J. (1965) 'The Creation of the Scottish Office, 1881–87'. *Juridical Review*: 205–44.

Kerevan, George. (1991) 'Labourism Revisited'. *Chapman 35–36*: 25–31.

Levitt, Ian. (1992) *The Scottish Office: Depression and Reconstruction, 1919–1959*. Edinburgh.

MacCormick, John. (1955) *The Flag in the Wind*. London.

Mitchell, James. (1996) *Strategies for Self-Government*. Edinburgh.

Mitchell, James and Bennie, Lynn. (1996) 'Thatcherism and the Scottish Question'. *British Elections and Parties Yearbook 1995*: 90–104. London.

Mitchell, James and Leicester, Graham. (1999) *Scotland, Britain, and Europe: Diplomacy and Devolution*. Edinburgh.

Moore, Chris and Booth, Simon. (1989) *Managing Competition: Meso-Corporatism, Pluralism, and the Negotiated Order in Scotland*. Oxford.

Pulzer, Peter. (1967) *Political Representation and Elections in Britain*. London.

Rokkan, Stein and Urwin, Derek. (1983) *Economy Territory Identity: Politics of West European Peripheries*. London.

Scots Review. (1948) *Scottish Survey* 9(8), December: 130–1.

Seawright, David. (1999) *An Important Matter of Principle: The Decline of the Scottish Conservative and Unionist Party*. Aldershot.

Smith, A. (1991) *National Identity*. London.

Thatcher, Margaret (1993) *The Downing Street Years*. London.

Public Records Office Papers

CAB 129/22. (1947) Cabinet Paper from Arthur Woodburn, Secretary of State for Scotland on *Scottish Demands for Home Rule or Devolution*. 6 December.

CAB 129/37. (1949) Cabinet Paper from Arthur Woodburn, Secretary of State for Scotland on *Scottish Affairs*. 12 December.

CAB 134/1734 ED(58)28. (1958) *Memorandum by John Maclay, Secretary of State for Scotland, on Unemployment in Scotland*. 18 December.

CM 34 (51) 3. (1951) Cabinet decisions. 10 May.

Cabinet Conclusions 15 (52) 2. (1952) 11 February.

Cabinet Conclusions (58) 44 (6). (1958) 21 May.

Chronology

1945   Dr Robert McIntyre wins Motherwell by-election for SNP (Apr.).
1946   Scottish Council (Development and Industry) formed (Jan.).

1948	Government issues White Paper on Scottish Affairs (Cmd. 7308) proposing changes in parliamentary procedures and enquiry into Anglo-Scottish financial relations (Jan.).
1949	Launch of Scottish Covenant which eventually collected around 2.5 million signatures favouring home rule (Oct.).
1949	Scottish Unionists issue 'Scottish Control of Scottish Affairs', manifesto advocating increased administrative devolution (Nov.).
1950	Removal of Stone of Destiny from Westminster Abbey (Dec.).
1952	Royal Titles case (challenge to title of Queen Elizabeth as II) begins (Feb.). First BBC TV broadcast in Scotland (Mar.).
1953	Coronation of Queen Elizabeth – broadcast on television and seen to symbolise national unity (June).
1954	Publication of report of the Royal Commission on Scottish Affairs (chaired by Lord Balfour) recommending transfer of electricity, food, animal health, roads and bridges to Scottish Office (Cmd. 9212) (July).
1955	Scottish TV begins broadcasting.
1957	Scottish Council of the Labour Party Executive comes out against home rule on 'compelling economic grounds' (Jan.).
1960	Scottish unemployment over 100,000 (Feb.).
1960	Prime Minister Harold Macmillan announces that a Polaris missile base will be set up at the Holy Loch, Scotland (Nov.).
1961	Publication of Toothill Enquiry into Scottish economy calls for concentration on growth points and establishment of Scottish Office Development Department (Nov.).
1962	West Lothian by-election in which Billy Wolfe wins 23.3 per cent for the SNP (June).
1964	Labour Prime Minister Harold Wilson announces that Polaris missile base at Holy Loch to be retained (Dec.).
1965	Scotland treated as one unit in 'National Plan' for Scotland (Dec.).
1967	Hamilton by-election; Winnie Ewing wins seat for SNP from Labour (Nov.).
1967–68	Both BBC Scotland and Scottish TV start transmitting political programmes.
1968	Edward Heath makes 'Declaration of Perth' at Scottish Conservative Party Conference and announces establishment of committee under Sir Alec Douglas-Home (May.).
1969	Harold Wilson appoints a Royal Commission under Crowther (Apr.).
1972	Scottish Economic Planning Department set up inside the Scottish Office (Oct.).
1973	Publication of Report of Royal Commission on the Constitution (chaired by Lord Kilbrandon, following the death of Crowther) supports devolution (Oct.).
1973	Glasgow Govan by-election. Margo MacDonald wins seat for SNP with 41.9 per cent of vote but in Edinburgh North, Billy Wolfe, party leader, wins only 18.9 per cent (Nov.).
1974	Special Labour Party in Scotland Conference in Glasgow accepts devolution (Aug.).
1975	Margaret Thatcher's first visit to Scotland as Conservative leader during which she asserted her support for a Scottish Assembly (Feb.). Launch of Scottish Development Agency (July).
1976	Establishment of anti-devolution group 'Scotland is British' by industrialists (Nov.). Scotland and Wales Bill (devolution measures) given second reading by 292 votes to 247 after government concedes referendums once the Bill is enacted (Dec.).

1977   Scottish Conservatives reverse policy and oppose directly elected Scottish Assembly.

1978   'Cunningham amendment' successfully moved in Commons stating that 'if it appears to the Secretary of State that less than 40 per cent of the persons entitled to vote in the referendum have voted "Yes"...he shall lay before Parliament the draft of an Order in Council for the repeal of this Act' (Jan.). Launch of pro-devolution 'Yes for Scotland' campaign chaired by Lord Kilbrandon (Jan.). Royal Assent given to Scotland Bill (July).

1979   Lord Home argues for a No vote on the grounds that the Conservatives would produce a more powerful Assembly (Feb.). Referendum on Scottish devolution with slim majority in favour but insufficient to overcome 40 per cent rule (Mar.).

1982   Scottish Grand Committee meets in Royal High School, Edinburgh as part of Conservative alternative to devolution.

1988   Introduction of poll tax in Scotland (Apr.). Launch of 'A Claim of Right for Scotland' by group established by Campaign for a Scottish Assembly proposing a Constitutional Convention (July). Glasgow Govan by-election; Jim Sillars wins the seat for the SNP (Nov.).

1990   Scottish Council of the Labour Party votes to support alternative to first-past-the-post voting system in elections to Scottish Parliament (1990).

1992   Announcement of closure of Ravenscraig steel mill (Jan.).

1993   Government publish *Scotland in the Union: A Partnership for Good* (Cm. 2225) advocating cosmetic changes in government of Scotland (Mar.).

1994   Death of John Smith, Labour leader (May).

1995   Roseanna Cunningham wins Perth and Kinross by-election for SNP (May).

1996   Prime Minister John Major announces that the Stone of Destiny will be returned to Scotland from Westminster Abbey after 700 years (July).

1997   Labour wins general election and the Scottish Conservatives lose all their seats (May). New government's programme announced in Queen's Speech, including a commitment to hold referenda on devolution in Scotland and Wales (May). Government issue White Paper, 'Scotland's Parliament' (Cm. 3658), setting out its proposals for a Scottish Parliament (July). Referendum in Scotland with 60 per cent turnout – 74.3 per cent vote for a Scottish Parliament and 63.5 per cent for tax-varying powers (Sept.).

1999   First election to Scottish Parliament (May). This was held under a PR system resulting in the following number of seats: Labour 56, SNP 35, Conservative 18, Liberal Democrats 17, Scottish Socialist Party 1, Green 1, Independent 1.

6 Wales Since 1945

Kenneth O. Morgan

For the people of Wales, more perhaps than any other part of Britain, the coming of peace in 1945 brought a mood of renewal. Memories of the depression years, of unemployment, hunger marches and the means test would be set aside in the quest for a better world. This emerged strongly in the general election that July, where the swing to Labour was even stronger than anticipated. Labour ended up with 25 of the 35 Welsh seats; these included seven gains, amongst them all three Cardiff constituencies, where the Labour candidates returned were a notable trio, Hilary Marquand, George Thomas and James Callaghan, in the future to serve as Minister of Health, Speaker of the House and Prime Minister, respectively. Labour gained 58.5 per cent of the Welsh votes, compared with 48.0 per cent for Britain as a whole. Labour's triumph was by no means confined to the industrial valleys of the south, but also included rural Caernarfonshire, with strong votes elsewhere in north Wales. The Liberals clung on to seven rural seats, including the University of Wales; Lloyd George's daughter, Megan, retained Anglesey and his son, Gwilym (shortly to move to the Conservatives), just held Pembrokeshire. The Tories ended up with just four seats, one of them Lloyd George's old citadel of Caernarfon Boroughs, which had changed during the wartime years. The eight Plaid Cymru candidates almost all lost their deposits: nationalism was no obvious vote-winner in post-war Britain.

After this cataclysm, Labour's dominance over Welsh political culture was overwhelming. In the Cabinet, the left-wing, socialist former miner Aneurin Bevan became Minister of Health and was to launch the National Health Service (NHS) in 1948. James Griffiths, another ex-miner, passed the National Insurance Act of 1946, and was later to enter the Cabinet as Colonial Secretary. Other Welshmen prominent in the government included Ness Edwards and Lord (George) Hall at the Admiralty, while in Transport House Morgan Phillips, as party General Secretary, was the supreme apparatchik. Throughout Welsh public life, a new generation of (generally senior and almost invariably male) Labour leaders dominated much of political and industrial life. Llew Heycock, a former engine driver from Port Talbot, became a remarkable boss of local government, especially as leader of Glamorgan County Council, but with much influence also in the BBC and the University. Huw T. Edwards of the Transport and General Workers' Union dominated various public bodies, ending up as Chairman of the Advisory Council for Wales in 1949.

Despite groups of left-wing critics in the valleys, spearheaded by Aneurin Bevan himself when he resigned from the government over the charges to be imposed on the NHS in 1951, the mood in the Welsh Labour Party, with its close links of solidarity with the unions, was broadly supportive of the government. Public ownership was hailed, especially the symbolic triumph of national-isation of the mines on 1 January 1947. Full employment and an active regional industrial policy under the Board of Trade largely ended the spectre of mass unemployment, which had made south Wales the very prototype of a 'depressed area' in the 1930s and an abiding social point of reference for novelists like A. J. Cronin and film-makers like Paul Rotha. The welfare state, especially Bevan's health service and the massive rebuilding programme in the state education system (important for a nation in which English-style 'public schools' were almost unknown) was widely popular, and widely used. Thus it was that in the two general elections of 1950 and 1951, after which Attlee's Labour govern-ment fell from power, Wales remained almost as impregnably Labour as ever. In 1950 it won 27 of the 36 Welsh seats, and a similar number in 1951 when its share of the poll, at 60 per cent, was higher even than in 1945. There were losses to the Conservatives in relatively anglicised Conway in the north and Barry in the far south, but gains from the Liberals in Merioneth and Anglesey (where Lady Megan Lloyd George fell to Cledwyn Hughes) showed continuing Labour advance in the rural areas of the north-west. Throughout the years of Conservative government in 1951–64, Labour's political hegemony in Wales was not seriously challenged. Conversely, the Liberals, survivors of the noncon-formist, rural radicalism of the pre-1914 years, seemed in almost irreversible decline. By 1966 the great party of Lloyd George, almost totally dominant in Wales for more than a half a century, found its parliamentary strength reduced to Montgomeryshire alone.

The years of Labour rule after 1945 meant a transformation of the local economy and of the structure and tone of Welsh society. The economy re-covered much of the momentum last seen before 1914. It was based largely on the manufacturing sector but this time on a far broader base than before. The coal and steel industries greatly revived. The National Coal Board embarked on a massive programme of reinvestment in many south Wales pits, including £4,500 million. in a new project at Nantgarw; the collieries of Maerdy, the 'little Moscow' of yore, were reconstructed. Investment in the steel industry continued apace from Ebbw Vale in Gwent to Shotton in Deeside. Its most striking landmark was the immense Abbey Works, with its 80-inch strip mill, built at Port Talbot and coming into production in 1951. Twelve years later, another steel giant came into being in south-east Wales, the RTB/Spencer works at Llanwern near Newport. But perhaps more heartening for the longer term were newer industries to provide much-needed diversification, such as in the trading estates at Treforest (near Pontypridd), Fforestfach (near Swansea),

Merthyr, Bridgend and Marchwiel (near Wrexham in the north-east), the rubber factory at Brynmawr, the nylon plant at Pontypridd and the Hoover factory at Merthyr. A portent for the future was the growth of oil-refining in the south-west, notably the BP refinery at Milford Haven. The economic base of Wales remained less secure than in most parts of England; in rural areas, the level of economic activity was relatively poor. But, with the post-war export boom and a policy of regional development to locate industries in outlying parts of Britain, Wales faced the hazards of the post-war economy in good heart. When a partial renewal of unemployment threatened at the end of the 1950s, a new response was the expansion of motor-car production into south Wales for the first time, from Rover in Cardiff to Ford in Swansea.

Industrial revival meant social change on a massive scale. The most obvious, as in other areas of Britain, was a growing affluence. Public housing, notoriously inadequate in industrial Wales, was much expanded. Celebrated old communities such as Merthyr's 'China' or Cardiff's multicultural Bute Town and Tiger Bay were largely obliterated. Owner-occupation, traditionally low in much of Wales, grew rapidly in the 1950s; it was expanded considerably after 1967 in Cardiff and other towns with the enfranchisement of leasehold property dating from the Bute and other estates in the past. Life transformed for ordinary people, as mobility from car ownership and secularisation in all its aspects eroded the traditional components of the 'Welsh way of life'. This had historically been associated with the nonconformist chapels, and with the sober and sombre 'Welsh Sunday'. In the mining valleys in the 1950s and 1960s, while the chapels addressed dwindling congregations of the faithful, working-class clubs and pubs were throbbing with life (the radical political culture of the 1930s in miners' institutes or the Workers' Educational Association (WEA) equally seemed to dissolve). Mass sport claimed its devotees, including the revival of Welsh rugby, which saw 'Triple Crowns' won in 1950 and 1952. By contrast, the chapels (other than a somewhat inflated role in the programmes of the Welsh BBC) were no longer central to Welsh life. Defeats over opening cinemas in Cardiff and Swansea were public and painful. Far worse were the local polls in 1961 over the Sunday closure of public houses, following the Conservative government's Licensing Act. The result was a stark picture of the cultural and linguistic division of Wales. The seven counties or county boroughs in east and south Wales, from Flintshire down to Monmouthshire, voted solidly to become 'dry', whereas the eight authorities in mainly Welsh-speaking western Wales from Anglesey down to Carmarthenshire retained the Welsh Sunday. But they were to be steadily eroded in years to come; the next poll showed the dry counties reduced to only four. Eventually there were none. An historic symbol of Welsh identity, dating from the high noon of nonconformity back in 1881, was being obliterated, a victim of a secular and permissive consumer-driven society.

Welsh society, therefore, showed considerable change in the 20 years after 1945. Many felt that the old, warm, communal values of back-to-back Welsh village society, rural and industrial, were being crushed in an age of technological and cultural upheaval. But one unchanging feature remained the dominance of the Labour Party. It was hardly eroded in the years of Tory rule in the

1950s; its trade-union base remained strong, while Labour continued to progress in many rural areas (Cardiganshire, for instance) for the first time. The Conservatives still appeared as a largely anglicised upper-class minority, out of tune with Welsh sentiment. When Labour returned to office in 1964 under Harold Wilson, Wales was a major part of its recovery, with 28 out of 36 Welsh seats falling to Labour; its reward was the creation of a Secretaryship of State for Wales with the veteran James Griffiths its first occupant. In the general election of March 1966, Labour reached a new high water mark, surpassed only by the Liberals back in 1906. Now Labour claimed 32 Welsh seats to the Conservatives' 3 and the Liberals' one. Rural seats like Conwy and Cardiganshire were won for the first time, while Cardiff North and Monmouth in the south-east showed a new Labour strength amongst middle-class house-owning voters, skilled workers and middle managers. The historic pattern of political life since the end of the First World War, a Labour ascendancy succeeding an equally dominant Liberal one, seemed fully confirmed. In fact, though, the political culture was about to be spectacularly transformed.

The dominant question confronting the Welsh people after the war, as it had been for many centuries past, was the definition and protection of their identity. What precisely did it mean to be Welsh and to proclaim the eternal truth of 'Welsh values'? In an age of unionism and centralism after 1945 it seemed harder than ever to answer these questions. The most distinctive feature of that identity, of course, was the Welsh language. There remained distinguished writers and poets in Welsh after 1945, including for the first time significant Welsh novelists such as T. Rowland Hughes, chronicler of the Caernarfonshire quarrying communities, and a remarkable woman writer, Kate Roberts. Welsh poetry also remained vigorously alive, even as older giants still dominated the scene. The major figure, without doubt, was the veteran dramatist Saunders Lewis, for all the acute controversy posed by his intensely anti-English nationalism and his apparent sympathy for fascism before and perhaps during the Second World War. The national *eisteddfod* remained a major cultural event, its competitions for 'crown' and 'chair' now given a far wider audience through television. The 'all-Welsh' rule adopted by the eisteddfod in 1951 reinforced its intensely national, perhaps nationalist, character.

But the dominant feature of the Welsh-language scene for many commentators after the war was that it seemed to be in steady, perhaps irremediable decline. The language censuses showed the proportion of the population speaking Welsh falling from 28 per cent in 1951 to 25 per cent in 1961 and to 20.8 per cent in 1971. The fall amongst young people was especially alarming, while it was also noted that Welsh speakers were concentrated in areas of north and west Wales with the highest unemployment. While Welsh had become a compulsory subject at least for younger schoolchildren by 1960, the demand for Welsh-language instruction grew. In the 1960s, over 40 Welsh-language primary schools were launched, while from 1962, starting with Rhydfelen School near Pontypridd, Welsh-language comprehensive secondary schools began to develop. But enthusiasts for the language, and advocates of cultural diversity in general, called for far more, including a more extensive range of secondary

Welsh-language schools and a more positive attitude from the four Welsh university colleges of Aberystwyth, Bangor, Cardiff and Swansea (shortly to be joined by Lampeter and the School of Medicine), whose expansion of numbers inevitably meant cosmopolitanism and anglicisation. Welsh-language publications had a small readership, with only two newspapers, the *Faner* and the *Cymro* surviving, both heavily dependent on public subsidies. The BBC was much criticised for relegating Welsh programmes to late-night vigils on television; this led to BBC Wales coming into being in 1963 and a local television channel, Harlech TV, soon afterwards, but the criticism from Welsh-language patriots went on.

The course of cultural life was also not obviously helpful to the language. While the great Welsh male-voice choirs slowly diminished as heavy industry was eroded, newer developments in culture affirmed the international rather than the local. There was no Welsh film industry; novelties such as the Welsh National Opera obviously featured European classics rather than specifically Welsh music; there were some fine Welsh visual artists such as Ceri Richards or later, Kyffin Williams, but hardly a Welsh school of art. Idealistic new institutions such as the International Eisteddfod started at Llangollen in 1947 aimed to build cultural bridges between Wales and the world. Most Welsh culture was expressed, inevitably, in English and its Welshness was often in doubt. The so-called 'Anglo-Welsh' writers included passionate patriots such as Glyn Jones. But the most famous of them all, Dylan Thomas, was ambiguous about his heritage. *Under Milk Wood* was seen by some of his countrymen (mistakenly perhaps) as a satire rather than a celebration of Welsh social life. One English-speaking poet, however, did emerge to proclaim his poetry in a fiercely Welsh idiom. This was the Anglican priest R. S. Thomas, who launched in the 1940s a series of intense pastoral creations lamenting the incursions of alien elements into traditional Welsh indigenous (and rural) culture. Nevertheless, the literary world of the 'Anglo-Welsh' reflected an uncertain relationship at best with the culture and identity of Wales.

These manifold dissatisfactions with the failure to uphold the native culture, and the decline of the chapels and other institutions historically linked with it, in time were to take active political form. Nationalism in a political sense had always been weaker in Wales than in Scotland. In the years after 1945, the government at Westminster almost brushed it aside. Attlee's Labour government down to 1945 refused to create a Welsh Secretary of State or even give Wales any recognition within the framework of the nationalised industries. The nominated Council of Wales, a purely advisory body which lingered on from 1949 to 1966 almost unseen, was the best that Whitehall and Westminster could provide. Surprisingly, the Conservatives went somewhat further. Churchill in 1951 created a Minister for Welsh Affairs, linked with the Home Office in the first instance under the unmistakably Scottish David Maxwell Fyfe. But any Welsh goodwill was largely squandered after 1957 when the then Minister, Henry Brooke, sanctioned the drowning of a beautiful and historic valley, Tryweryn, in Merioneth, to provide water supplies for the English city of Liverpool which could then sell its water at a profit on the open market. This provoked a huge outcry throughout Wales, not only from nationalists. It stung political nationalism awake. After the war, Welsh nationalism had been in feeble condition. Plaid Cymru remained a small, ill-organised movement led mainly by intellectuals with little working-class support. It contested a growing number of Welsh seats with no success; in 1959, for instance, it put up 20 candidates, but only 4 saved their deposits and none came anywhere near victory. The broader-based Parliament for Wales campaign, headed by Lady Megan Lloyd George and a small number of Welsh-speaking Labour MPs, never made much headway either. However, the mood of protest in Britain generally in the early 1960s-years of CND and anti-Vietnam campaigning, and of political militancy amongst the country's youth – had its impact on Wales also. It took the form of a heightened nationalism, the implications of which had become ever clearer as the century reached its close.

It began with a remarkable radio broadcast, *Tynged yr Iaith* ('The Fate of the Language') by the veteran *littérateur* Saunders Lewis, in 1962, in which he called for direct action to save the language. There followed the creation of the Welsh Language Society to pursue these policies and a campaign, mainly by students and other young people, of civil disobedience. There were demonstrations against government offices, post offices and the like for failing to print Welsh-language forms and much defacing of all-English road signs (e.g. 'Newtown') and climbing up of television masts in rural Wales. By the late 1960s, there were angry protests against government ministers, notably George Thomas, the unyielding Cardiff-based Secretary of State for Wales from 1968 to 1970. The Welsh youth movement, *Urdd Gobaith Cymru*, found itself in part taken over by language zealots, as was the National Eisteddfod. When the government responded with the plan to have Charles invested as Prince of Wales at Caernarfon Castle in 1969 and as a preliminary he was sent to study Welsh language and culture at Aberystwyth for a term, nationalist derision knew no bounds. A satirical pop song, 'Carlo', viciously lampooned the unfortunate prince. Wales, happily bicultural for so long, now seemed divided over language issues in a way previously associated with Belgium or Quebec. There was a darker side, too; if not the Irish Republican Army (IRA), Wales had its minority of bombers and the burning of second homes owned by English people in rural areas.

Eventually Plaid Cymru became the beneficiaries. Still apparently a weak fringe movement as late as the general election of March 1966, that July it managed a political breakthrough. In a by-election in Carmarthen following the death of Lady Megan Lloyd George, Gwynfor Evans, its dignified president, won the first parliamentary seat for Plaid Cymru. This owed much to the background of cultural protest in the preceding years, but also perhaps something to the growing rundown of coal and other heavy industries in Wales in the 1960s (Carmarthen had a coal-mining area and was not purely rural at all). One appalling reminder of past industrial dereliction came at this time with the tragedy of the death of 116 schoolchildren drowned in the coal slurry of a collapsed coal tip at Aberfan. There followed remarkably high votes for Plaid Cymru in by-elections in Rhondda West in 1967 and Caerphilly in 1968. In the latter, there was a 40 per cent swing to Plaid and Labour's majority fell from over 20,000 to 1,800. Labour seemed vulnerable in its industrial heartland as never before. One response was its decision to invest Charles as Prince of Wales and this played its part in stabilising Unionist sentiment. On the other hand, the Wilson government had to do something and in 1968 set up the Crowther (later Kilbrandon) Commission to examine the British constitution, including the prospects of Welsh and Scottish devolution. Plaid Cymru's fortunes thereafter seemed to slump and Gwynfor Evans was very narrowly defeated in 1970. The Conservative government under Edward Heath renewed the Welsh Secretaryship of State, under a Welshman Peter Thomas who, curiously, sat for the distinctly English London constituency of Hendon South.

But the Kilbrandon Commission ensured that Welsh and Scottish issues would continue to haunt the public scene in the 1970s. There was a background of growing industrial conflict including national miners' strikes in 1972 and 1974 that were solid in Wales, a growing rundown of mining and other heavy industry, and a growing concentration of industrial activity in the south-east, close to the M4. To this the Labour governments of the 1970s responded with a revival of the old regional development policies. A Welsh Development Agency and a Development Board for Rural Wales were set up in 1976 but the Welsh economy continued to struggle. With this background, the case for prosperity through centralisation seemed less strong. In 1973 Kilbrandon, in a confusing range of reports, called for an elected Welsh Assembly, with a Parliament for Scotland. The Labour Party was deeply divided on the issue, but it was politically impossible to ignore Kilbrandon now. In 1976, James Callaghan, a Welsh member now Prime Minister, introduced a joint Devolution Bill. It made very slow progress in the Commons, resistance from many English members being matched by opposition from a small group of Labour dissidents headed by the youthful Neil Kinnock. In time, the Bill lapsed and was followed by separate measures being introduced for Wales and for Scotland. An 80-strong Welsh elected assembly would administer the £850 million block grant; a derelict coal exchange building in Cardiff's dockland was earmarked as its site. The Bill made slow progress in the Commons despite the Liberal–Labour pact. It became law in July 1978, but at the cost of conceding a referendum in which over half the total electorate had to vote in favour for the Assembly to be set up.

On 1 March 1979, St David's Day, the referendum duly took place. It proved to be a disaster for the government and for devolution. It followed a long phase of unpopularity for the Callaghan government, and the industrial troubles of the 'winter of discontent' with piles of litter on the streets during the referendum campaign. The Labour Party in much of Wales was lukewarm and perhaps actually hostile. In the referendum poll, only 11.8 per cent of voters (243,048) voted for devolution, and 46.5 per cent (956,330) voted against. Even Welsh-speaking Gwynedd showed a large hostile majority. For the first time in history, the Welsh people had been offered a prospect of home rule, however limited; they had rejected it almost with contempt. Shortly, the Callaghan government fell after a Commons vote, and a Conservative government under Margaret Thatcher took office with Nicholas Edwards as Secretary of State for Wales. Labour had fought the 1979 election in poor condition, with internal conflict between Left and Right, a background of corruption in local authorities such as

Swansea, and signs of organisational collapse in north and mid-Wales (there was even a Conservative gain in Anglesey). A long phase of Welsh history seemed to have come to its close.

The regime of Margaret Thatcher had a shock effect on so leftish a country as Wales. It appeared to inaugurate a period of British unionism and uninhibited market-led free enterprise. Yet in the end the Thatcher era had consequences very different from what either the Prime Minister or her opponents had visualised, or perhaps intended, in Wales. Nor did it seem at first so obviously at variance with the political instincts of the Welsh. The general election of 1983, in which Labour was poorly led and in apparently acute ideological turmoil, saw the Conservatives win no less than 14 seats in Wales, their best result since 1895. Labour won 21 but its share of the Welsh vote fell sharply to only 37.5 per cent It looked perhaps destined to follow the same path of decay and decline as had the Liberals after 1918. In fact, however, under a youthful Welsh leader, Neil Kinnock, the party was to remain the dominant force in the principality, notably in local government.

The Thatcher period saw a phase of marked decline for Welsh manufacturing industry with much related social conflict. The steel industry in the early 1980s followed the earlier closure of the ageing plants at Ebbw Vale and East Moors in Cardiff with that of Shotton in Deeside and severe cutbacks in productive capacity and employment at the giant works at Port Talbot and Llanwern. The coal industry went through an even more traumatic experience. There had been a remorseless programme of pit closures for 20 years past. The final crisis came in the year-long strike called by the National Union of Mineworkers, led by the far-left Arthur Scargill, in 1984–5. The Welsh miners remained solid but were enthusiastic about neither the strike nor Scargill himself, and with reason. When the strike ended in the predictable defeat of the miners by a well-armed government which had other energy supplies at its disposal, the result was the effective end of coal mining in Wales after 300 years. The north Wales coalfield disappeared after the closure of Bersham in Wrexham. In the south, a total of 28 pits in south Wales on the eve of the strike in March 1984 was promptly reduced to 16 and then to just one, Tower Colliery. It too survived into the 1990s, only after a period of closure had been followed by a co-operative buy-out by the men. A mine like 'Big Pit' at Blaenavon became a heritage museum. The miners' strike was the climax of a fierce period of industrial disputes. It was paralleled in some of the public services, and in stoppages by schoolteachers angry at low pay and government dictation. One consequence, it was believed, was a long-term decline in Welsh rugby, which had long relied on the assistance of teachers taking squads of boys to practise out of hours or at weekends. The Welsh rugby team, which had known the glories of Triple Crowns and Grand Slams in the 1970s with heroes like Barry John and Gareth Edwards, slumped in its fortunes from now on.

The failures of its rugby team coincided with a wider mood of bitterness in the Thatcher era. Wales was a poorer, disadvantaged part of Britain. The mining valleys, once vibrant, were centres of dereliction and a drug culture, as were many housing estates. Old icons were under fire, notably of its educational standards secondary schools, on which Wales had long prided itself. The University of Wales experienced closures and controversy, with Cardiff University College lurching into near-bankruptcy in 1987 and being bailed out only after mass redundancies. Rugby, the schools, the Welsh language, music and other forms of culture were said to be in long-term decline, while the vibrant political culture of Lloyd George or Nye Bevan appeared emasculated.

And yet the Thatcher years also saw revival in some unexpected directions. In the economy, if manufacturing and older industries were in retreat, there was a programme of inward investment, both into car manufacture (for instance in the Ford plant at Bridgend, which opened in 1980) and in newer high-tech companies, especially in south-east Wales. Especially in the Valleys Initiative programme of Peter Walker, Secretary of State from 1987, investment from the Far East, Japan and Korea above all mounted rapidly while there were also new links with European industry, as in the 'Motor Scheme' with Catalonia, Rhônes-Alpes, Lombardy and (especially) Baden-Württemberg. The Welsh Office, indeed, albeit under a series of Englishmen, Walker, David Hunt, John Redwood and William Hague down to 1997, proved to be something of a motor of Keynesian growth in the Welsh economy; during the Tory years, its English occupants went native with some effect. Much was done, too, to assist Welsh culture and institutions. The Welsh Schools movement grew rapidly, and by the 1990s a series of successful and sometimes prestigious Welsh-language secondary schools were beginning to turn the long tide of decline for the native culture. The 1991 language census showed that over 500,000 still spoke Welsh, with an actual increase amongst children and in traditionally Anglicised border areas. The eisteddfod modernised, with new departures into the visual and plastic arts. The university, for all its controversies, continued to expand, until it numbered over 40,000 students by the mid-1990s, and could claim to be, after London, the second largest university in Britain. Its colleges played a major part in generating employment and economic activity in small towns like Bangor, Aberystwyth and Lampeter. Perhaps the most evocative and controversial advance of the Thatcher years was the creation of a Welsh-language television channel, *Sianel Pedwar* (Channel Four) in 1982, a proposal that had appeared in the Tories' election manifesto but had then been disavowed. Its viewing figures were not large – perhaps 100,000 at the very most – but its programmes were lively and its shrewd marketing policies gave it a reasonable basis of finance. In addition to discussions on current affairs and academic themes such as Welsh history, and much rugby, it also featured a long-running and highly successful soap opera, *Pobl y Cwm*, which was temporarily exported (with English subtitles) to English television. Since it featured much sex, crimes, and high and low misdemeanours, it showed how Welsh popular culture had advanced from the chapel-bound straitjacket of 1945. Signs of vitality in popular art and design, and in a Welsh-language film industry, again showed how Welsh awareness was unexpectedly reinforced in the Thatcher years.

The years of Conservative rule under Thatcher and then John Major down to 1997, years apparently of unionist centralisation and authoritarian style, actually served to foster the national identity. The Welsh Office itself, an agent of Whitehall rule, in fact assisted Welsh awareness in many senses, not least by emphasising the territoriality of Wales and by using the badge of Welshness in a huge array of public bodies. Conversely, another feature of the Thatcher period, the growth of mass quangos of non-elected, appointed public bodies, often reflecting sharp Tory political partisanship, also helped to give national awareness new life. While Plaid Cymru began to show new vitality away from its three constituencies of Anglesey, Caernarfon and Merioneth in the north-west (to which Ceredigion was to be added in 1992), Labour was able to use the quangos as a a an argument for the kind of Welsh devolution so spectacularly rejected in 1979. The prospect of elected local authorities being capped while unrepresentative figures like the wives of defeated Tory candidates were appointed from London made a formidable case for democratic accountability. There was another factor in these years, too – Europe. Wales, like Scotland, was generally strongly favourable to membership of the EU, and Europhobia far less marked than in southern England. Apart from assistance to agriculture (until the 1990s), public provision through the European Social Fund and important links through the Welsh university colleges (worth over £20 million in research contracts in 1994–5), there was also the idea of a 'Europe of Nations' in which Wales might join other regions and small peoples in taking a new role. The idea that there might be a yardstick found in Brussels, not London, thus helped to foster the growing national identity of Wales in these years of Tory rule. The national awareness within Scotland, and the clear advance of Ireland within the EU, took these processes further. Devolution was not much of a theme in Wales in the 1992 general election, when Labour won 27 seats and 49.5 per cent of the vote, against the Conservatives' 6, Plaid Cymru's 4 and the Liberals' one. But it was still back on the agenda as it had not been for 20 years.

In the earlier 1990s, Wales had seemed in partly dormant condition. Like its chapels, choirs and coal mines, its political and social culture seemed in decline under apparently endless Conservative rule. By the time of the 1997 general election, however, a clear renaissance was visible, which extended far beyond the narrow confines of party politics. Some of it owed its origins to Scotland and perhaps to Ireland, north as well as south. The rapid progress of all-party moves towards devolution or a Scottish Parliament with tax powers had its impact on Wales, too. Even if Wales could not show a Constitutional Convention on the Scottish model, it could hardly be left out of a wider process of democratic accountability and devolution, especially with the possibility of Northern Ireland having some kind of local Assembly of its own after the Downing Street accord of 1994. The Europeanisation of British economic and political life, Tory Euro-scepticism notwithstanding, was another force encouraging devolution. Without doubt, a powerful factor was the emergence of Tony Blair as Labour leader in 1994, a strong advocate of revised democratic structures and constitutional reform for London, Scotland, Northern Ireland, and by implication Wales, too.

Here, political nationalism was more modest, but there were other, perhaps more important manifestations of national identity. In many aspects of intellectual life and culture, a new pride in nationhood spilled over into other spheres.

Artists and writers were refuting the assumption of the Marxist historian, Gwyn A. Williams, in his *When was Wales* (1985) that Welshness was almost artificial and dependent on antithesis to England. Welsh film-makers were active as never before, the television industry creative in both languages, while there was also for the first time a Welsh pop culture of world renown. Young people now saw Welsh cultural identity as exciting and modernistic, not the dull echo of a dead, chapel-bound world. Several Welsh pop groups achieved fame – the Manic Street Preachers, Super Furry Animals, the Stereophonics and the remarkable Catatonia, one of whose songs included the memorable phrase 'I wake up every morning and thank the Lord I'm Welsh'. When they appeared at the muddy Glastonbury festival, a mass audience waved red dragons. Welshness, it was claimed, was 'cool', evoking national pride without being aggressively national-istic. Indeed these various Welsh bands were anxious to proclaim their inter-nationalism of outlook.

In 1997 Welsh history was to be transformed. In the general election that May, Labour won 34 of the 40 Welsh seats, to the Plaid's 4 and the Liberals' 2. The Conservatives scored zero, as in Scotland. As promised in Labour's mani-festo, there followed a referendum in Wales on devolution, on 18 September 1997, a week later than that in Scotland. Wales was being offered an elected Assembly with 60 members, a limited executive devolution with no power of primary legislation, whereas Scotland was being a given a strong Parliament with tax-raising powers. The Welsh referendum campaign was a low-key affair. This may have been in part because of the restricted powers of the apparently lacklustre assembly that was being promised. It certainly reflected apathy if not hostility in Labour ranks, despite the evangelistic campaign of the new Secre-tary of State for Wales, Ron Davies. The death of Princess Diana also inter-rupted the campaign at a key moment. Even so, the initiative appeared to be with the 'Yes' campaign, designed by Ron Davies and Peter Hain as an inclusive movement, which saw Labour working closely with the Liberal Democrats and Dafydd Wigley, the president of Plaid Cymru. The 'No' campaign was a thing of shreds and patches, to some degree financed from abroad by the aged Julian Hodge in Guernsey, though it did afford a forum for genuine fears of devolu-tion. But outcome was the narrowest of victories for the 'Yes' campaign, by 50.3 per cent to 49.7 per cent, a 6,000-odd majority on a low poll of 50.3 per cent. It could hardly be claimed as a ringing endorsement of the idea of devolu-tion.

On the other hand, it was not surprising that Wales, with a low awareness of national identity in its institutional life and civil society, compared with Scot-land, should find it hard to make a psychological breakthrough. The outcome, narrow though it was, marked a considerable swing of opinion since 1979. Further, devolution was now supported not only by the Welsh-speaking north and west, but also by the city of Swansea and almost all the uplands valley constituencies of south Wales, ravaged as they were by youth unemployment, broken families and communal decay and thereby less than enchanted with the benefits of London rule. It was noticeable in 1997 that Welsh devolution was not only put forward positively by a fresh government with a huge majority, but that Welsh business, so sceptical in 1979, now accepted the importance of devolution for the economy, not least in relation to Europe. This time, the vested interests were in favour of change. Thus for the first time in history the Welsh had accepted a prospect of self-government, however narrow the result. Anyway, as George Brown once said, one was enough.

Thereafter, the process of devolution and electing a Welsh assembly went ahead. Labour's campaign was derailed quite unexpectedly in October 1998 when Ron Davies had to resign as Secretary of State following an apparent sex scandal. It had been anticipated that he would take his position as First Secretary in the new Welsh Assembly, leading a presumed Labour majority. In fact, the Labour Party underwent a damaging internal row over the succession. The narrow victory of Alun Michael, the new Secretary of State, over Rhodri Morgan, with much alleged pressure from Millbank on the Welsh electoral college, did not encourage party confidence. By contrast, Plaid Cymru seemed buoyed up and confident as never before. When the Assembly elections took place on 6 May 1999, the outcome was something of a shock. The elections had a partial element of proportional representation, with 20 members out of 60 elected through a 'topping-up' redistribution of votes, and this made an overall majority harder to achieve. Even so it was a surprise that Labour failed to get one. It won 28 seats only out of 60, 27 on the direct ballot. Plaid Cymru surprised themselves by gaining 17, including winning Labour strongholds in the south, Llanelli, Rhondda and Islwyn, in the 'first-past-the-post' contest, and doing well in most parts of Wales. The Conservatives ended up with 9 seats and the Liberal Democrats 6, both mainly beneficiaries of second-choice 'topping up'.

The results were a disappointment for Labour, but perhaps beneficial for Wales as a whole. Commentators cited factors that harmed Labour's cause – the low poll of 45 per cent with many Labour voters staying at home, the divisive Michael – Morgan leadership contest, the unpopularity or even corruption amongst some Labour local authorities in the valleys; it would be fair to mention the positive impact of Plaid Cymru's campaign as well and their greater success in firing up their voters in a Wales-only election contest. The Welsh language was no longer the divisive issue as it had been in 1979. However, the fact that Labour, under Alun Michael as First Secretary, chose to act as a minority government, with much use of the committee system, meant that there had to be close collaboration between the parties: 'inclusive politics' became the fashionable phrase. Plaid Cymru, which had disavowed any immediate aim of Welsh independence during the campaign, would benefit from some involvement in government for the first time (Dafydd Elis-Thomas, one of its members, became presiding officer), but there would be room for the Liberal Democrats and Conservatives, too. To some degree, the election returns also reflected a wider diversity of groups in Welsh public life, with some young members and 24 out of the 60 new members being women (4 of whom appeared in Labour's 8-strong Cabinet). The new Assembly, therefore, began its work amidst public rejoicing when the Queen opened the temporary Assembly building in Crickhowell House in Cardiff's old dockland on 26 May. The real test, however, would be its effectiveness and assertiveness in the years that lay ahead.

The first two years of the new Assembly, in fact, were beset with problems. Alun Michael's heading a minority administration made for political difficulties.

After much argument over obtaining Objective One funding from Europe, Michael lost a vote of confidence in February 2000 and was succeeded as First Minister by Rhodri Morgan. There was also a background of repeated economic difficulties – crises in electronics and fuel, heavy winter floods, a serious outbreak of foot and mouth disease amongst cattle in the spring of 2001, and the loss of over 3,000 steelworkers' jobs in the Corus plants at Llanwern and Shotton. Opinion polls spoke of public apathy towards an Assembly, whose legislative powers were so very limited and whose strategic plan for the Welsh economy was widely criticised. A rare achievement was the Welsh Children's Commissioner, the first piece of primary legislation Wales had to go through. A financial wrangle with the architect of the proposed Assembly building, Norman Foster, did not add to the new body's dignity. However, a breakthrough came with the creation of a coalition government between Labour and the Liberal Democrats in October 2001 which gave the administration a stable majority and a programme for government. After that, the Assembly struck a more assured and constructive note. There were new strategies for health and education, and measures to promote industrial entrepreneurship and rural recovery. The Assembly's government was reinforced by the June 2001 general election which confirmed the huge Labour majority; in Wales, Labour held 34 seats, Plaid Cymru 4 and the Liberal Democrats 2, with the Conservatives again failing to win a single seat. Labour regained Anglesey from Plaid Cymru but lost Carmarthen to them. Rhodri Morgan and his ministers now gained in confidence and proposed policies such as restoring student grants and abolishing prescription charges, whereby Wales would clearly diverge from England. The partnership between the Assembly and Westminster seemed to be going smoothly, the concordats between civil servants trouble-free, and problems such as the farming crisis effectively handled. Public opinion in Wales, if hardly ecstatic, now appeared firmly supportive of devolution, even amongst Conservatives. It was now an accepted feature of government, without generating support for independence. How far this would survive demands for further legislative powers when the Assembly completed the review of its powers in 2004 remained to be seen.

The creation, against all the odds, of a Welsh Assembly in 1999 offers an appropriate perspective on Welsh history since the Second World War. Despite massive economic change and the erosion of traditional community life, despite huge forces of Anglicisation and of globalisation that bore down on a tiny national minority, the sense of Wales and Welshness stubbornly retained its presence within the fabric of the British Isles. In some ways it was even finding new forms of expression – witness the growing role of women in a traditionally male-run society, perhaps first fully evident during the miners' strike of 1984–5 with its 'women's support groups', and newly expressed in the Assembly elections in 1999. The novelty of Welsh popular youth culture in a mass consumer age was also striking. At the same time, older forms retained their importance – the all-Welsh national *eisteddfod*, the centrality of a national university traditionally created by 'the pence of the poor', the new rugby stadium rising alongside the Taff in Cardiff to house the World Cup matches in 1999. Wales had more than survived; it had found forms of renewal unimaginable in Attlee's

Britain after 1945. Perhaps most of all, its revived identity was not an echo of a dying society, but embodied in a cult of the new. It was a part of an ongoing process of constitutional reform, modernisation, and of local accountability evident throughout Europe, a reaction against the traditional centralised form of the nation-state, and a search for new forms of communal expression in a postmodernist world. Wales at the millennium remained a vivid democracy, with an ethos and class structure distinct from England. Despite the occasional derision of London-based critics, it was no longer the elusive 'geographical expression' of the nineteenth century, nor the primitive survival of Matthew Arnold's *Celtic twilight* or George Borrow's *Wild Wales*. Still less was it the crushed victim of a capitalism in crisis of Marxist critics. It stood proudly as a bridge between the ancient past and the prophetic future, as *Cymru Fydd*, the Wales and perhaps the Britain that was to be.

Further Reading

Bogdanor, Vernon, *Devolution in the United Kingdom*, Oxford, 2001.
Davies, Janet, *The Welsh Language*, Cardiff, 1993.
Davies, John, *A History of Wales*, London, 1993.
George, K. D., and Mainwaring, L., *The Welsh Economy*, Cardiff, 1988.
Griffiths, Dylan, *Thatcherism and Territorial Politics*, Aldershot, 1996.
Griffiths, James, *Pages from Memory*, London, 1969.
Harvie, Christopher, *Europe and the Welsh Nation*, Aberystwyth, 1995.
Institute of Welsh Affairs, *Making the Assembly Work*, Cardiff, 1997.
Jones, Gareth Elwyn, *Modern Wales: A Concise History*, 2nd ed. Cambridge, 1994.
Jones, J. Graham, 'The Liberal Party and Wales after 1945', *The Welsh History Review*, 16(3), June 1993: 326–55.
Keating, Michael, and Elcock, H. (eds), *Remaking the Union*, London, 1998.
Morgan, Kenneth O., *Modern Wales: Politics, Places and People*, Cardiff, 1995.
Morgan, Kenneth O., *Rebirth of a Nation: Wales 1880–1980*, Oxford, 1981.
Morgan, Prys, *The University of Wales, 1939–1993*, Cardiff, 1997.
Osmond, John (ed.), *The National Question Again*, Llandysul, 1985.
Philip, Alan Butt, *The Welsh Question: Nationalism in Welsh Politics, 1945–70*, Cardiff, 1975.
Price, Emyr, *Lord Cledwyn of Penrhos*, Bangor, 1990.
Smith, Dai, *Wales! Wales?*, London, 1984.
Smith, Dai, and Williams, Gareth, *Fields of Praise*, Cardiff, 1981.
Stephens, Meic, *The Arts in Wales, 1950–1975*, Cardiff, 1979.
Taylor, Bridget, and Thomson, Katarina (eds), *Scotland and Wales: Nations Again?*, Cardiff, 1999.
Thomas, M. Wynn, *Internal Differences: Literature in Twentieth-Century Wales*, Cardiff, 1992.
Williams, Gwyn A., *When Was Wales?*, London, 1985.

Chronology

1945   General election: Labour wins 25 seats Wales, Liberals 7, Conservatives 4.
1946   Welsh National Opera founded.

1947	Nationalisation of the mines (1 Jan.). Steel Company of Wales established. International Eisteddfod at Llangollen launched.
1949	Council of Wales established.
1951	General election: Conservative government but Labour wins 27 seats. All-Welsh rule adopted at National Eisteddfod.
1953	Broadcasting Council for Wales established.
1954	Dylan Thomas's *Under Milk Wood* broadcast.
1955	Cardiff becomes capital of Wales.
1956	First bilingual secondary school established, Ysgol Glan Clwyd (Flintshire).
1957	Bill passed to drown Tryweryn Valley to provide water for Liverpool.
1960	*Welsh History Review* published. Welsh Sunday Closing polls. Death of Aneurin Bevan.
1962	Saunders Lewis BBC lecture on 'The Fate of the Language'.
1963	Hughes–Parry Committee on the status of the Welsh language.
1964	Labour government: James Griffiths becomes first Secretary of State for Wales.
1966	General election: Labour wins 32 out of 37 Welsh seats. Gwynfor Evans elected for Carmarthen as Plaid Cymru MP (14 July). Aberfan tragedy (21 Oct.): 116 children killed.
1967	Welsh Language Act. Welsh Arts Council established.
1968	George Thomas succeeds Cledwyn Hughes as Secretary of State for Wales.
1970	General election: Peter Thomas becomes Conservative Secretary of State.
1971	Ysgolion Meithrin (Welsh nursery schools) movement launched. Welsh rugby team win the 'Grand Slam' (and again in 1976 and 1978).
1973	Kilbrandon Report on the Constitution published. Reorganisation of Welsh local government.
1974	Two general elections won by Labour: 3 Plaid Cymru MPs returned.
1976	Welsh Development Agency created.
1978	Welsh Devolution Bill passed.
1979	Devolution rejected in referendum by nearly four to one (1 Mar.).
1982	*Sianel Pedwar* (Welsh television channel) established.
1984–5	Miners' strike: subsequently all Welsh pits, bar one, close.
1986	Cardiff Bay Development Corporation created.
1987	Peter Walker becomes Conservative Secretary of State.
1990	University of Wales linked with European universities in Motor Scheme.
1992	Conservatives win general election: Labour wins 27 Welsh seats to Tories' 7. John Redwood becomes Secretary of State.
1993	Centenary of University of Wales (30 Nov.).
1994	Welsh-language film, *Hedd Wyn*, nominated for an Oscar.
1995	William Hague replaces John Redwood as Tory Secretary of State.
1997	General election: in Wales, Labour wins 34 seats, Plaid Cymru 4, Liberal Democrats 2, Conservatives 0. Devolution carried by 50.3 per cent majority in referendum (18 Sept.).
1998	Ron Davies resigns as Welsh Secretary of State after sex scandal. Welsh-speaking pop group *Catatonia* top the charts.
1999	Welsh Assembly elections (6 May). Alun Michael becomes First Minister. Paul Murphy becomes Secretary of State.
2000	Rhodri Morgan becomes First Minister. Coalition government of Labour and Liberal Democrats (Oct.).
2001	Corus steel plant job losses. General election (June): in Wales, Labour wins 34 seats, Plaid Cymru 4, Liberal Democrats 2, Conservatives 0.

7 Northern Ireland Since 1945

Henry Patterson

At the end of the Second World War the Northern Ireland state, comprising six of Ireland's thirty-two counties and containing the vast majority of its Protestant population, had existed for less than a quarter of a century. The deep political division between the Protestant and Unionist majority which made up two-thirds of the state's population and the Catholic and Nationalist minority had deep historical roots in the resistance of Ireland's Protestant population to the rise of Catholic nationalism in the nineteenth century.

The Government of Ireland Act of 1920 provided the constitutional basis for the Northern Ireland state. It had been designed to accommodate the conflicting demands of nationalism and unionism by providing for two Irish Parliaments which would exercise a range of devolved powers while ultimate sovereignty remained with the Westminster Parliament. The dominant political force in nationalist Ireland, Sinn Fein, backed by the Irish Republican Army (IRA), rejected the Act and eventually extracted a much more substantial degree of independence from Britain in the Anglo-Irish Treaty of 1921.

Unionists had not desired to have their own regional structure of government, protesting that they wished to continue to be an integral part of the United Kingdom. However, while they grudgingly accepted the new institutions they soon came to appreciate the political advantages to be had from the control of a range of economic, social and security powers. The Northern Ireland Parliament, situated from 1932 in a new and grand building at Stormont in the eastern suburbs of Belfast, had a wide range of 'transferred' powers relating exclusively to Northern Ireland including finance, agriculture, commerce, education and internal security. A range of 'excepted' powers including the Crown, the making of peace and war, defence and foreign policy and 'reserved' powers including income tax, surtax and customs and excise duties remained with the Parliament of the United Kingdom, which in Section 75 of the Government of Ireland Act asserted its sovereignty.

However, this legal sovereignty was accompanied by clear evidence that British politicians had no desire to be drawn back into Irish affairs by getting involved in too close a scrutiny over how the Northern Ireland government exercised its powers. A ruling by the Speaker in 1923 that matters which had been devolved to Northern Ireland could not be raised in the House of Commons insulated Westminster from the this last vestige of the Irish Question. This provided the Northern Ireland government with considerable scope to develop a regime that prioritised the maintenance of protestant unity against an external and domestic nationalist threat.

Sir James Craig, Prime Minister between 1921 and his death in 1940, declared in Parliament in 1934 that the Northern Ireland regime was 'a Protestant parliament for a Protestant people'. Leading Unionist politicians like Basil Brooke, who became Prime Minister in 1943, depicted Catholics as 'disloyal' and openly proclaimed that Protestants should not employ them.[1] Catholics were discriminated against within the Northern Ireland civil service, although it needs to be said that neither the Nationalist Party nor the Catholic Church encouraged Catholics to apply.[2] The police force, the Royal Ulster Constabulary (RUC), had a Catholic representation of 17 per cent in the 1930s, a decline on the figure at the time of the state's formation and a reflection of the deepening distance between the Catholic community and the state.[3] Even more corrosive of Catholic relations with the security forces was the existence of a large force of part-time special constables, the 'B' Specials, who were totally protestant in composition. The Civil Authorities (Special Powers) Act of 1922, which was introduced to counter a major IRA threat to the state, was maintained long after that threat had been much reduced. It gave the Minister of Home Affairs draconian powers including flogging for some arms offences, arrest without warrant and prohibition of inquests. Nationalists complained that it was used solely against individuals and groups from their community.

Party Politics

Elections for the Northern Ireland Parliament had originally been held under proportional representation (PR), but losses to the Northern Ireland Labour Party (NILP) and dissident Independent Unionists led Craig to abolish PR, and from 1929 parliamentary elections had been held using a simple majority system. This contributed to an overwhelming Unionist Party domination of parliamentary representation. In a House of Commons of 52 seats the party had never fewer than 32 seats between 1921 and 1945, its share of the poll varying between 43 and 66 per cent.[4] It constructed an effective political machine across the region. The party structure had strong links with the Protestant Orange Order, an organisation which had a large membership drawn from all classes of the Protestant community and which exerted significant influence on government policy, particularly in the areas of education, employment and security.

In contrast the main opposition force, the Nationalist Party, did not attempt to develop electoral organisation, concentrating on those constituencies where there was a Catholic majority or a closely balanced Protestant/Catholic population ratio. Apart from Belfast, where Catholics constituted a quarter of the population concentrated in the west of the city, these tended to be in the western and southern periphery of the region where two of the six counties, Fermanagh and Tyrone, had actual Catholic majorities. A conservative and clericalist party, its main policy was anti-partitionism, but the difficulties in realising this objective meant that the party had a strong tendency to abstentionism from Stormont, where the Unionists made little attempt to treat them as anything else than as disloyal obstructionists. The number of Nationalist MPs elected ranged from a high of 12 in the 1921 and 1925 elections to 8 in 1938. The Nationalist share of the vote ranged from a high of 32 per cent to a low of just under 5 per cent.[5] Unlike the Unionists, the Nationalists had to face a significant competing force in the form of the more uncompromising nationalism of Sinn Fein and the IRA. Although Sinn Fein was barred by electoral law from contesting Stormont elections it did periodically put up candidates for the Westminster Parliament, to which Northern Ireland returned 12 MPs. The IRA maintained a clandestine existence and periodically launched violent but ineffective challenges to the state.

The only political party that tried to recruit across the religious divide was the NILP, but its appeal was largely confined to Belfast and even here it faced an uphill struggle. The party was ambiguous on the constitutional issue until 1949 when its annual conference adopted a clearly pro-Union stance. Between 1921 and 1945 the maximum number of seats it won in a general election was three and its share of the vote never exceeded 8 per cent.[6] The centrality of the national question and the strong correlation between religious persuasion and voting behaviour produced an electoral system where there were large numbers of uncontested seats. Unionists kept out of constituencies with clear Nationalist majorities and vice versa. In the last election before the war, 6 of the 8 successful Nationalist candidates were returned unopposed, as were 14 of the 39 Unionists.

The 1945 elections showed the continuing centrality of traditional allegiances, despite the fact that the war years had seen a shift to the left which manifested itself in a high poll of 18 per cent for the NILP candidates.[7] This change was concentrated in Belfast where the bulk of the party's candidates stood. The city, with a population of 450,000 and its large Protestant working class, had always played a central role in Unionist politics. Thus although the NILP won only two seats in 1945, the fear of working-class defections to the party was one of the main reasons why the post-war Unionist government, against much hostile comment in the party, ensured that Northern Ireland was included fully in the developing British welfare state.

Outside Belfast the picture was one of the persistence of traditional voting patterns with the Unionist Party winning 33 seats overall and the Nationalist Party 10. These patterns maintained themselves, apart from an upsurge of support for the NILP in the late 1950s, down to the eve of the 'Troubles'. In the Stormont election of 1965 the Unionist Party gained 36 seats to the Nationalists' 9, and despite Labour being in power in London the NILP lost 2 of its 4 seats.[8]

The Economy

At the time of partition the north was the only part of Ireland to have experienced significant industrialisation: in 1926 one-third of the employed population was involved in industry compared to 13 per cent in the Irish Free State.[9] However, the north's traditional staple industries of shipbuilding, engineering and linen had suffered severe problems in the inter-war years. Together with a decline in the workforce in the large agricultural sector, this had contributed to high levels of unemployment and to Northern Ireland's position as the poorest region of the United Kingdom.

The war had provided a new lease of life for industries like shipbuilding and linen but the government was well aware that the post-war world was likely to see the old problems of the staple industries re-emerge. Brooke's government was able to deal with such problems because of a radical shift in London's attitude to the financial relationship with Northern Ireland which the war had produced.

Under the Government of Ireland Act the Northern Ireland government had very limited taxation powers as all the core taxing powers, including income tax, were reserved for Westminster. Originally it had been envisaged that Northern Ireland would pay for its own services through its limited tax powers and its share of the total UK tax revenue. It was also supposed to make an annual Imperial Contribution to the cost of reserved services like the armed forces and foreign policy.

The depressed economic conditions of the inter-war period forced a revision of these provisions to allow the Imperial Contribution to lapse in difficult years and to allow the Treasury to provide a subvention. The Treasury had resisted the arguments of Craig for 'parity': that as citizens of the UK who paid the same rates of taxation as the rest of the country they should enjoy the same standard of services and benefits. He also argued for 'leeway': that because Northern Ireland was a poor region with lower standards of public provision, the Treasury should provide extra resources to narrow the gap. These arguments were finally conceded during the war, in part because of the triumph of Keynesianism associated with the massive increases in public expenditure. Another key factor was the strengthening of Belfast's bargaining position due to the strategic importance of access to Northern Ireland's ports and airfields during the war, when Irish neutrality denied such facilities in the rest of the island.

In a series of agreements with the Treasury from 1946 the extension of the welfare state to the region was financially underwritten and the Ministry of Finance was allowed to divert revenue from the Imperial Contribution to a special fund for industrial development and other projects. Both the welfare state and the new resources for industrial development did much to assist the government when, after a brief post-war boom, the problems of the staple industries returned.

Belfast's massive Harland and Wolff shipbuilding complex, which provided more than a tenth of Northern Ireland's manufacturing jobs and about a fifth of those in Belfast in 1950, faced an increasingly competitive international market. Redundancies reduced a workforce of 20,000 in 1950 to 9,000 by 1964. The linen industry had to modernise and rationalise production in the face of intense competition from artificial fibres and its workforce shrank radically. Agriculture, which still employed a sixth of the workforce in 1950, experienced an intensification of the process of amalgamation of holdings and mechanisation which resulted in a decline of a third in its labour force during the 1950s.[10]

Throughout the decade unemployment averaged 7.4 per cent. Although far removed from the figures of the 1930s, it was four times the national average and worse than any of the employment black spots in the rest of the UK.[11] The government's response was to encourage a diversification of the industrial base through the attraction of investment from outside the region. The Industries Development Act (1945) provided a range of incentives to attract new firms to Northern Ireland including investment grants, tax concessions and government-built factories at low rents. By 1963 the Ministry of Commerce, which was responsible for the government's industrial development strategy, had assisted in the creation of 50,000 jobs since 1945, the majority in plants set up as branches of British and foreign multinationals including Michelin, Goodyear, Du Pont and ICI.[12]

The process of attracting external investment accelerated in the 1960s as the government of Terence O'Neill (1963–9) persuaded Westminster to provide extra resources for improving and modernising the infrastructure of the region with new motorways, a new university at Coleraine and a controversial and ill-fated project for a new city to be called Craigavon. Between 1958 and 1973 employment in foreign-owned companies increased more than fivefold, the largest employment growth in foreign enterprises of any UK region. Northern Ireland's manufacturing production grew much faster than manufacturing in the UK as a whole.[13] However, this growth was dependent on the newly attracted firms, with little evidence that the local manufacturing sector had been able to improve its competitive position. The optimism of the 1960s would soon vanish as the end of the post-war boom in the world economy and the onset of political crisis and violence revealed the fragility of a development strategy so dependent on inward investment.

Another important contributor to job creation and improved living standards in the post-war period was the expansion of the public sector associated with the welfare state, and the Treasury's acceptance of the 'parity' and 'leeway' arguments. Between 1946 and 1963 government expenditure increased nearly sevenfold.[14] The health service was developed along similar lines to the National Health Service in the rest of the United Kingdom. Free secondary education from 1948 allowed the number of pupils in secondary schools to increase from 19,861 in 1945 to more than 104,000 in 1964.[15] There was a substantial improvement in Northern Ireland's dilapidated housing stock.[16] Average disposable income per head more than doubled in the quarter-century after 1945.[17] Some liberal Unionists hoped that economic growth and improved living standards would dissolve traditional conflicts and stabilise the political system, but instead the 1960s would see the crisis and collapse of the Unionist state.

The Challenge of Civil Rights

Sir Basil Brooke, created Viscount Brookeborough in 1952, dominated Unionist politics for the two decades of his premiership from 1943 to 1963. Down to the end of the 1950s the Unionist position appeared a strong one. The welfare state seemed, even to many Nationalists, to be a powerful argument against unity, with an Irish state experiencing major economic problems and with much inferior public services and lower rates of unemployment benefit, family allowances and old-age pensions. The Atlee government, influenced by resentment over Irish neutrality and appreciation of the strategic value of Northern Ireland during the war, had strengthened the Unionist position in the Ireland Act of 1949 which said that Northern Ireland could not cease to be part of the United Kingdom except with the consent of the Northern Ireland Parliament.

Nationalist politics also appeared to be in some disarray. The Nationalist Party had retreated from Belfast where its place was taken by a number of anti-partitionist Labour parties. It was increasingly criticised by younger Nationalists for its sole emphasis on partition, its lack of a social and economic programme and its refusal to play a more positive role in Northern Ireland politics. The violent Nationalist tradition embodied in the IRA also appeared to be in terminal decline. The organisation had launched an assault on Northern Ireland in 1956 in which six members of the RUC and eleven IRA members were to lose their lives. It was called off in 1962, largely because of the lack of support it had elicited from Nationalists in Northern Ireland.

By the end of the 1950s a number of liberal Unionists were arguing that the time was ripe for the government and party to reach out to 'reasonable' members of the Catholic and Nationalist community. Eamon de Valera, the patriarchal leader of traditional Irish nationalism, had left the political stage in the south and his successor, Seán Lemass, appeared to want to move away from the sterile irredentist politics of the past.[18] The British government favoured a rapprochement between Belfast and Dublin in areas such as cooperation on trade and tourism. However, Lord Brookeborough had no inclination to face the inner-party turmoil that any attempt to improve relations with Dublin would involve.

Although many Catholics in Northern Ireland had benefited from the welfare state and the post-war improvement in living standards, the Catholic community suffered from a long-standing pattern of economic inequality and from a more recent history of politically inspired discrimination, particularly at the local government level. Industrialisation in the region in the nineteenth century had developed on the basis of Protestant-owned capital and skilled labour, and when Catholics had been integrated into the workforce it had been largely as unskilled labour. In the shipbuilding and engineering sector, tight protestant control of the trade unions, and the tendency of labour to be recruited informally through family and neighbourhood links in a society where there was a high degree of housing segregation, meant extremely low representation of Catholics.[19]

Overall the pattern was one where Catholics were under-represented in managerial positions, amongst the skilled working class and in the most secure and well-paid occupations. They were over-represented amongst the unskilled and were crowded into sectors like building and transport, where jobs tended to be lower-paid and more insecure.[20] During the period of Unionist rule of Northern Ireland from 1921 to 1972, while there was a sharp increase in the proportion of Catholics in professional and managerial occupations there was a substantial rise in Catholic proportion of the unskilled working class.[21] Figures for improvements in average living standards in the region tended to hide this crucially important deterioration in the position of working-class Catholics under Stormont rule.

The most politically telling statistic of difference between the two communities was the fact that at the end of the most economically successful decade of Unionist rule in the 1960s, Catholic males were twice as likely to be unemployed as Protestants.[22] The unemployment problem was most severe in a number of predominantly Catholic towns in the west of the region. In the mid-1950s when Newtownards, a largely Protestant town near Belfast, had a male unemployment rate of 5.4 per cent, Londonderry had a rate of 17.3 per cent, Newry had 16.4 per cent, Armagh had 16 per cent and Strabane 23 per cent.[23]

The Ministry of Commerce experienced major problems in interesting incoming firms in the peripheral parts of the region. Many of these firms were attracted to the Greater Belfast area with its large pool of trained labour and its ease of access to ports. However, some Ulster Unionists in border areas were suspicious of new industry in case it gave jobs to Catholics. Brookeborough, by prioritising party unity at all costs, had allowed the grievances of Catholics in places like Londonderry to fester unattended to, and they were to provide the combustible material that would ignite in 1968.

The core complaints related more to the abuse of power at local government level than to the Stormont government itself.[24] In the early years of the state with a significant number of Nationalist-controlled local authorities refusing to recognise the Northern Ireland government, the Unionist response had been drastic and crude. PR was abolished and the boundaries were redrawn to ensure that even where Unionists found themselves in a minority they could still manage to hold on to power. Despite the abolition of the ratepayers' franchise for local government elections in the rest of the United Kingdom it was maintained in Northern Ireland, thus disenfranchising a sizeable sector of the working class but bearing down disproportionately on the Catholic community.

The city of Londonderry was the most graphic example of the gerrymandered system. By concentrating the bulk of the Catholic electorate in one ward while spreading the protestant vote over two wards, the result was that in 1966, 20,102 Catholics returned 8 councillors while 10,274 Protestants returned 12.[25] In areas like this Unionist-controlled councils refused to house Catholics outside areas where there already was a Catholic majority and in a small number of authorities almost no new houses were built for Catholics. There was also clear evidence of discrimination in the allocation of council jobs. Again, most of the complaints were against a relatively small number of Unionist-controlled councils in the west of Northern Ireland.

As long as the Nationalist Party had linked the question of discrimination to the overall objective of abolishing partition Unionists had been able to dismiss the issue as part of a disingenuous campaign to overthrow the state. However, the return of Harold Wilson's Labour government in 1964 opened up a new phase in Nationalist politics in Northern Ireland. The Campaign for Social Justice, set up by two Catholic doctors in Dungannon in 1964, had geared its activity to highlighting the fact that in one part of the United Kingdom a sizeable minority of the population did not have the same rights to jobs, houses and voting that existed in the rest of the country.

Terence O'Neill had been very successful in persuading successive British governments to provide extra resources to allow him to modernise the region. O'Neill had set out to provide a public image for Northern Ireland that was radically different from that bequeathed him by Brookeborough. In the early period of his premiership his major concern was to win back support lost to the NILP because of the high level of redundancies in the shipbuilding and engineering industries in Belfast. It was the employment issue and his predecessor's lack of energy and imagination in responding to it that had produced NILP gains and forced Brookeborough's retirement. O'Neill's response was to adopt the fashionable notion of 'planning' and use it as a more effective instrument for extracting extra resources from the Treasury.

But such assistance came with a price tag of also being seen to improve relations with the Catholic community. The arrival of television had begun to provide graphic and embarrassing evidence of the continuing injustices and sectarian animosities of this corner of the United Kingdom. O'Neill was well aware of the bitter resistance that any substantive reform programme would generate in the party. His decision to set up a new Ministry of Development in 1965 was bitterly unpopular for encroaching on the powers of local authorities. Already inner-party pressures had contributed to the decision, much resented by Catholics, to site a new university in the predominantly protestant town of Coleraine rather than Londonderry.

His response to these conflicting pressures was to combine a commitment to more rapid economic growth and modernisation with a number of important symbolic gestures to the Catholic community – most importantly his meeting with the Irish Prime Minister, Seán Lemass, at Stormont in January 1965, the first meeting between the leaders of the two states for more than half a century. Although this was welcomed by the Nationalist Party, which for the first time accepted the role of official Opposition at Stormont, more radical voices of dissatisfaction with his failure to address the concrete issues of discrimination and inequality at either the local government or Stormont levels began to appear within the Catholic community.

The Nationalist Party had not contested elections in Belfast since the war. Catholics in Belfast had voted for a variety of labour parties, including the NILP and the Irish Labour Party. In the Westminster general election in March 1966, Gerry Fitt of the Republican Labour Party won the West Belfast seat. Fitt was the first Nationalist MP returned to Westminster who emphasised that his major concern was not partition but the fact that his constituents lacked the full civil rights enjoyed by citizens in the rest of the United Kingdom. He directly challenged the 1923 Speaker's Ruling and with the support of the backbench group of Labour MPs, the Campaign for Democracy in Ulster, put pressure on Wilson for action.[26]

Wilson and his Home Secretary, Roy Jenkins, whose department was responsible for relations with the Northern Ireland government, initially put their hopes in O'Neill's reforming intentions. However, expectations of change had been raised in the Catholic community by a commitment from Wilson to deal with the discrimination issue given before the 1964 election. The lack of movement had encouraged the formation of the Northern Ireland Civil Rights Association (NICRA) in January 1967 and, modelling itself on the tactics of the civil rights movement in the United States, it launched a campaign of marches to highlight the discrimination issue.

Marches in Northern Ireland were traditionally associated with the marking-out of sectarian territory and had been a frequent source of violent conflict between Nationalists and Unionists. The RUC were expected to ensure that nationalist marches were restricted to areas where there was a clear Catholic majority. NICRA refused to recognise traditional sectarian geography on the basis that their demands were for equality reforms within the United Kingdom, not a united Ireland. However, the fact that the bulk of the support for the campaign came from the Catholic community and the important role in NICRA played by Republicans stimulated many protestants to see the campaign as a Republican conspiracy.

The Protestant fundamentalist preacher, Ian Paisley, who had emerged as a bitter critic of O'Neill, was able to expand his support significantly by organising counter-demonstrations to the NICRA marches. At the centre of government there was a major division between O'Neill and his supporters who felt reforms had to be introduced to deflate opposition on the streets and respond to increasing concern in London and those, represented by Bill Craig, Minister of Home Affairs, and Brian Faulkner, Minister of Commerce, who opposed any significant concession to pressure.

When on 5 October 1968, the RUC brutally dispersed a civil rights march in Londonderry, the shocking television pictures of police using batons on marchers meant that the moment of truth for O'Neill's government had arrived. Wilson demanded serious reforms and threatened to look at Westminster's financial support for the province.[27] A reform package was agreed which did not assuage NICRA pressure as it did not deal with their central demand of one-man-one-vote in local government elections. Deepening divisions in the party and government in a context of increasingly bitter and violent confrontations between Protestants and Catholics on the streets led to O'Neill's resignation, after a failed attempt to mobilise moderate support in the general election of February 1969.

His successor, James Chichester Clark, did little more than preside ineffectually over a squabbling government and party. One-man-one-vote was conceded and NICRA called off its marches, but deep sectarian animosities had been ignited and displayed themselves with a ferocity unprecedented since the 1930s during the summer of 1969. Sectarian violence in Londonderry provoked by the Protestant Apprentice Boys' annual demonstration spread to Belfast, where it resulted in 48 hours of fierce communal conflict in which sections of the security forces became involved. Five Catholics and two Protestants died and whole streets were burnt out.[28]

The August 1969 violence was the beginning of the end of the Stormont regime. British troops had to be dispatched to support a weakened and demoralised RUC. Wilson demanded a new supervisory role and two senior civil servants were sent to oversee the Unionist Cabinet and a Commission to look into policing was established. Despite this new level of involvement neither Wilson nor his Conservative successor, Edward Heath, wanted to take over direct responsibility for Northern Ireland. Direct rule was delayed until the last moment with the result that a deeply alienated Catholic community saw British troops, originally welcomed as saviours from protestant mobs and the RUC, as defenders of a Unionist regime determined to roll back any reforms that had been gained.

The violence of August 1969 led directly to a rebirth of physical-force Republicanism in the form of the Provisional IRA (the 'Provos'). The Provos split from the existing republican leadership which they saw as too interested in socialism and not enough in the defence of Catholic areas.[29] They were soon in control of hundreds of angry young working-class Catholics who they turned into a force to go on the offensive for the traditional objective of ending British rule in Ireland. A campaign of bombings that shattered the centres of Belfast and other towns in 1970 and 1971 led the to the disastrous decision by the last Unionist Prime Minister, Brian Faulkner, to introduce internment without trial in August 1971. Violence spiralled in response, as did recruitment to the Provos, and after British paratroopers killed 13 civil rights protesters during violent confrontations in Londonderry in January 1972, Heath prorogued Stormont on 24 March.

Direct Rule

Direct rule meant the replacement of Unionist Party rule by government through a Secretary of State for Northern Ireland who was a member of the British Cabinet. The senior Conservative politician, William Whitelaw, was the first Secretary of State. Assisted by a number of junior ministers, all from mainland constituencies, the Secretary of State had the support of a new ministry, the Northern Ireland Office (NIO), staffed in part by Whitehall civil servants. The NIO took over the law-and-order functions of the now defunct Ministry of Home Affairs. It was also responsible for advising the Secretary of State on the overall political situation.

Direct rule was seen as a temporary measure until a restructured devolved government could be restored. Whitelaw's objective was to encourage the emergence of a cross-community coalition of 'moderate' Unionists and Nationalists. By 1972 the political fragmentation of the Unionist community was clear. Brian Faulkner was willing to attempt to lead the Ulster Unionist Party towards participation in new structures of government, but he was assailed from the right.

Ian Paisley's Democratic Unionist Party, founded in 1971, was an increasingly significant force with its strident warnings of British and Ulster Unionist 'sell-outs' to Irish nationalism. A section of the Unionist Party shared his analysis and distrusted Faulkner. Some supported Bill Craig's Ulster Vanguard movement when it seceded from the party to support the idea of an independent Ulster and link up with the fast-growing protestant paramilitary organisations, the Ulster Defence Association (UDA) and the Ulster Volunteer Force (UVF). In the elections for a new Northern Ireland Assembly in 1973 five separate Unionist parties put up candidates. The supporters of Faulkner won 26.5 per cent of the vote and were outpolled by Unionist opponents of any compromise who obtained 35.4 per cent.[30]

Within the Catholic community the Nationalist Party had been displaced by a new formation, the Social Democratic and Labour Party (SDLP), whose leadership was an amalgam of former labourists like Gerry Fitt and civil rights activists like John Hume.[31] In the Assembly elections the SDLP won 22 per cent of the poll. Its main rival in the Catholic community was Sinn Fein, the political wing of the Provos, which opposed participation in the election. At this time the IRA believed that it could bomb and shoot its way to a united Ireland. Only when the bankruptcy of this strategy became obvious did Sinn Fein emerge as a serious political competitor for Catholic votes.

A power-sharing government was agreed at the end of 1973. It included the SDLP, Faulkner Unionists and the Alliance Party, founded in 1970 by liberal Unionists disillusioned by the failure of reformist ideas within the Unionist Party and drawing its support largely from sections of the protestant and Catholic middle class in the Greater Belfast area. However the SDLP, supported by the Irish government, insisted that any new settlement include an 'Irish Dimension' in the form of a Council of Ireland, which would have representatives from the Dublin and Belfast governments and provide for the harmonisation of economic and social policies on the island.

At a conference at Sunningdale in Berkshire in December 1973 Faulkner was persuaded by Heath to agree to a Council of Ireland and took office in the power-sharing executive in January 1974. Faulkner was assailed by Paisley and other Unionist critics for agreeing to a north–south institution which a member of the SDLP – had described as a device for 'trundling' Northern Ireland into a united Ireland. He lost the support of his party and in the Westminster election of February 1974, Unionists opposed to the Sunningdale Agreement won 11 of Northern Ireland's 12 seats. The executive's almost total loss of legitimacy in the Unionist community contributed to the success of the Ulster Workers' Council strike in May 1974. Exploiting Unionist hostility to the Council of Ireland and using a mixture of paramilitary coercion and protestant trade unionists' stranglehold on the province's electricity supply industry, it forced the collapse of the executive.[32]

Although the British government remained committed to the search for a power-sharing deal, after the strike there was a tendency to use direct rule as an engine of economic and social improvement to soften the edges of communal conflict. The need to expand public expenditure in the region was in part a response to its relative poverty compared to the rest of the United Kingdom and also because of the effective collapse of its manufacturing sector after 1973, a product of deteriorating international economic conditions which, amongst other blows, destroyed the recently arrived artificial fibres industry. High levels of violence and political instability deterred new investment.

Deindustrialisation, combined with the region's distinctive demography, intensified the unemployment problem while at the same time maintaining the tendency for it to bear most heavily on the Catholic community. Male unemployment was 10.3 per cent in 1971 and had risen to 24 per cent by 1983–4. However, the figures for Catholic males were 17.3 per cent and 35 per cent while those for Protestant males were 6.6 per cent and 15 per cent.[33] Fair employment legislation was introduced in 1976 and made much stronger in 1989.

However, discrimination was only a part, and a diminishing one, of the causes of higher Catholic levels of unemployment. Northern Ireland had a significantly higher birth rate than the UK average.[34] The two communities had developed distinct demographic profiles. In 1981 the natural rate of increase among Protestants was around 3 per 1,000 while for Catholics it was 13 per 1,000.[35] Between 1971 and 1991 the Catholic population of working age increased by 61 per cent compared with 22 per cent for Protestants.[36] Thus, given that more Catholics were entering the labour market, they had a higher probability of not finding a job, considering the low rates of employment growth.

Under direct rule a greatly expanded public sector helped to compensate for the decline in manufacturing employment and also to create the basis for a substantial expansion in the size of the Catholic middle class. By the end of the 1980s over 40 per cent of the workforce was directly employed in the public sector while another substantial group was employed in firms that were heavily dependent on state subsidies or public contracts. Successive Secretaries of State were able to insulate the province from Treasury scrutiny by arguing that public expenditure acted as a fire-damper on violence. By the end of the 1980s public expenditure amounted to 65 per cent of regional GDP.[37]

This level of public expenditure was only made possible by the increasing size of the annual subvention from the Treasury. While in the 1960s this came to about 5–10 per cent of total expenditure, by the end of the 1980s it was a third. It rose from £313 million in 1973/4 to £3.5 billion in 1994/5.[38] If the Irish Republic had to take over responsibility for funding the subvention in the 1990s it would have meant a yearly transfer to Northern Ireland of a tenth of its GDP, which was clearly an impossibility.[39] By posing an insuperable obstacle to Irish reunification it encouraged the Irish government and the Catholic middle class in the north to look for a more modest and realistic 'solution'. It also exploded the important Republican myth that the British presence in Northern Ireland was an imperialist one.

The Peace Process

Direct rule was not an acceptable long-term form of governing Northern Ireland as far as the two main parties at Westminster were concerned. It brought the Irish question back into mainstream politics and the struggle to contain and deal with terrorism was a periodic source of embarrassment in both the United States and Europe. By the beginning of the 1980s, a reorganised IRA had settled down for what it termed the 'long war' aimed at sapping British will to remain in Northern Ireland.

Levels of violence had declined dramatically from a high of 10,628 shootings, 1,382 explosions and 467 deaths in 1972 to 237 shootings, 148 explosions and 54 deaths in 1985.[40] Nevertheless there was no sign that the security forces could do more than contain the violence. The number of British troops involved had shrunk significantly from 17,000 in 1972 to 10,500 in 1982 as a result of a policy of 'Ulsterisation', where the main burden of fighting the IRA fell on the RUC and the Ulster Defence Regiment (UDR), a locally recruited regiment of the British army.[41]

The deaths in 1981 of ten IRA prisoners, on hunger strike to be treated as political prisoners, provided the impetus for Sinn Fein to launch itself into electoral politics. James Prior, Northern Ireland Secretary in Mrs Thatcher's government, had initiated a scheme for 'rolling devolution', and in elections for a Northern Ireland Assembly in October 1982 Sinn Fein polled 10.1 per cent compared to the SDLP's 18.8 per cent. In the Westminster election of 1983 the gap between the two parties narrowed and the leader of Sinn Fein, Gerry Adams, won West Belfast although he refused to take his seat in the 'imperialist' Parliament.

Fear that the moderates would be displaced by the apologists of violence, combined with Mrs Thatcher's belief that the IRA could only be defeated through enhanced security cooperation with the Irish government, led to the Anglo-Irish Agreement of November 1985. This was an unprecedented consti-tutional innovation in that it provided the Irish state with an institutionalised role in the government of part of the United Kingdom, through an Intergovern-mental Conference backed up by a secretariat of British and Irish civil servants based in Belfast.[42] Aimed at dealing with Catholic alienation from the state, it produced a wave of protestant disaffection which shocked and surprised Thatcher.

The Agreement produced important shifts in both Unionist and Nationalist politics. The Democratic Unionist Party (DUP) had been the ascendant force in Unionist politics in the 1970s and early 1980s. Now it appeared that its brand of strident immobilism had encouraged the British government to turn its back on the frustrating search for an internal settlement and launch such a radical initiative involving Dublin. Although Paisley's larger-than-life personality would see him continue to outvote rather pedestrian Ulster Unionist Party candidates in the European elections, the DUP as a party receded as a challenge to the Unionist Party after 1985. Within mainstream Unionism the traumatic effect of the Agreement did encourage the emergence of a more proactive Unionism that realised that the best means of defending the Union was a deal with moderate Nationalism. However, this rather late conversion to realism was soon faced with a radical shift in strategy by Sinn Fein and the IRA.

Gerry Adams and the other leaders of the Republican movement saw the Agreement as a clear sign that the British government could be pushed to 'persuade' Unionists that their future lay in a united Ireland. Although part of the process would continue to be IRA bombs in the centres of British towns and cities, Adams also wanted to construct a 'pan-Nationalist front' with the Irish government and the SDLP which would, with the support of Irish America, pressurise the British for a change of policy. However, in secret talks with representatives of the Irish government in 1988, it was made clear to Adams that the prerequisite for an alliance was an IRA ceasefire. In talks with John Hume, the leader of the SDLP, in 1988, the same message was conveyed.[43]

Although Adams and other leaders of Sinn Fein had by now concluded that the 'armed struggle' was never going to force a British withdrawal, they faced strong resistance to a ceasefire from their more fundamentalist comrades in the IRA. Informed by the intelligence services of a Republican interest in negotiations, the Northern Ireland Secretary, Peter Brooke, declared in November 1990 that 'The British Government has no selfish, strategic or economic interest in Northern Ireland.'[44] John Hume subsequently approached Gerry Adams with the idea that they prepare a joint statement for the British and Irish governments which would recognise the 'Irish people's' right to self-determination and commit Britain to 'persuading' the Unionists in favour of a united Ireland.

The Joint Declaration signed by John Major and the Irish Prime Minister, Albert Reynolds, in December 1993 was a disappointment to Hume and Adams. While recognising the right to self-determination it stipulated that it would be exercised in twin referendums in the Irish Republic and Northern Ireland. This amounted to a 'Unionist veto' from a Republican point of view. There was also no mention of the British government adopting the role of 'persuaders' for Irish unity.

That despite this the IRA announced a 'complete cessation' of its military activities on 31 August 1994 reflected fear of political isolation and the hope that the new political structures that would arise out of negotiations would be clearly 'transitional' to a united Ireland. The Joint Framework Documents published in February 1995 set out the British and Irish governments' proposals for a settlement and contained provision for 'dynamic' north–south institutions as an essential part of any settlement. However, the British government and the Ulster Unionists demanded that the IRA begin the process of decommissioning its weapons before Sinn Fein could enter into the negotiation process. An attempted compromise through the report of an independent Commission headed by George Mitchell, former Leader of the US Senate, which suggested a process of decommissioning in parallel with negotiations, was unacceptable to the IRA which ended its ceasefire with a massive bomb at Canary Wharf in London in February 1996.

Although Republicans claimed that the first ceasefire was destroyed because John Major's government was dependent on Unionist support at Westminster, the return of Tony Blair with a massive majority did not alter the fundamental nature of the problem of brokering a deal which would include mainstream Unionists and a party with an organic link to a terrorist organisation. Blair was prepared to fudge the issue of decommissioning to obtain a second ceasefire in July 1997. The new leader of the Ulster Unionist Party, David Trimble, realising the danger of appearing to be the major obstacle to progress, participated in negotiations which included Sinn Fein and culminated in the Good Friday Agreement of 1998.

Although this accord, which was in essence a reincarnation of the Sunning-dale Agreement, was ratified by a massive majority in a referendum in the south and substantial majority in Northern Ireland, it won the support of only a narrow majority of Unionists. Trimble's brand of proactive Unionism risked getting too far ahead of his grass roots. For a substantial section of Unionists peace was being brought at the price of the appeasement of violent nationalism. As hundreds of IRA, UVF and UDA prisoners were released as part of the deal and Gerry Adams claimed seats in the proposed new government despite the fact that the IRA insisted that none of its weapons would be handed over, it was not clear that the deeply divided people of Northern Ireland could sustain such an unprecedented attempt to accommodate political extremes in one government.

The deputy leader of the SDLP, Seamus Mallon, described the Good Friday Agreement as 'Sunningdale for slow learners'. Sinn Fein was accepting a set of institutional arrangements which were very similar to those which, almost a quarter of a century before, the IRA had denounced as a cosmetic refurbishment of British rule. It was true that the Agreement provided Sinn Fein with a guaranteed place in the government of Northern Ireland, but until recently Republicans had rejected the very idea of a Northern Ireland assembly. Republican hopes for a powerful, free-standing set of North-South institutions which could be seen as 'transitional' to a united Ireland were also disappointed. The North-South Ministerial Council was limited in powers and accountable to the Dáil, the Irish Parliament, and the Assembly. Republicans were also annoyed with the Irish government's commitment to remove the irredentist claims made on Northern Ireland in Articles 2 and 3 of the Irish constitution.

David Trimble claimed that the Agreement 'copper-fastened partition'[45] But many in the Unionist community focused not on the institutional and constitutional arguments but on more emotionally charged issues: the early release of prisoners, the prospect of 'terrorists' in government and above all on the continuing failure of Republican and loyalist paramilitaries to begin the process of decommissioning their weapons. The result was seen in the elections for a new Northern Ireland Assembly held in June 1998. Sinn Fein achieved its highest ever vote in Northern Ireland: 17.6 per cent, while the SDLP won 22 per cent. The Ulster Unionist Party had its worst-ever result, coming second to the SDLP with 21.3 per cent of the vote, to the DUP's 18 per cent. The DUP's opposition to the Agreement – for 'appeasing' terrorism and putting 'Sinn Fein/IRA' in government – was shared by a number of smaller Unionist parties which won seats in the Assembly. Although pro-Agreement parties won 73 per cent of the vote and 80 out of the Assembly's 108 seats, there was no disguising the precarious position of pro-Agreement Unionists, who held 30 seats to the 28 held by anti-Agreement Unionists.

Unionist resistance to forming a government with Sinn Fein ministers in the absence of IRA action on weapons meant that the formation of an inclusive Northern Ireland executive was delayed until the end of 1999. By this time pro-Agreement Unionism had been further undermined by the publication of the

Patten Report on policing in September 1999. The international commission on policing headed by the ex-Tory minister and last Governor of Hong Kong, Chris Patten, had been part of the Agreement. The Report, which proposed wide-ranging changes in the structure and symbolism of the RUC, was angrily received by Unionists.

IRA failure to deliver produced a suspension of the institutions in February 2000 as Trimble threatened to resign. Trimble's strategy appeared to work, for on 6 May the IRA made a statement committing the organisation to put its arms 'completely and verifiably beyond use' in a manner that would be acceptable to the Independent International Commission on Decommissioning headed by the Canadian general, John de Chastelain. For many Republicans the futility of a return to armed struggle had been made terribly clear when the so-called Real IRA, a group of disgruntled ex-Provos, exploded a car-bomb in the centre of Omagh, County Tyrone, killing 28 people on 15 August 1998.

The return of the devolved institutions took place on 27 May 2000 after Trimble was able to obtain the support of 53 per cent of the delegates to the Ulster Unionist Council (UUC) for going back into government with Sinn Fein. His margin of support had narrowed substantially from the 72 per cent of the UUC who had voted in favour of the Good Friday Agreement in April 1998. But although the IRA allowed two of its arms dumps to be independently inspected, an unprecedented development in the history of Irish republicanism, the organisation was slow to follow up with more action. Anti-Agreement Unionists claimed the inspections had been no more than a publicity stunt and support for Trimble's strategy weakened even further.

In the Westminster general election in 2001 the DUP and Sinn Fein increased their votes and seats: the UUP gained 26.8 per cent and 6 seats; the DUP, 22.5 per cent and five seats; Sinn Fein, 21.7 per cent and 4 seats, emerging as the largest Nationalist party to the SDLP with 21.0 per cent and 3 seats. Trimble's party had lost 3 seats while the DUP gained 2. The future of pro-Agreement Unionism looked bleak but it was helped by the unintended effect of the 11 September terrorist attacks. This put irresistible pressure on Republicans to disassociate themselves from 'international terrorism', and in their aftermath the IRA began the process of decommissioning. At the time of writing (March 2002), with over a year to the next Assembly elections, it is clear that while Northern Ireland has put the 'war' behind it, its new inclusive political institutions are balanced precariously on deep reservoirs of communal antagonism and distrust.

Notes

1   Brian Barton, *Brookeborough: The Making of a Prime Minister*, Belfast, 1988, pp. 79–89.
2   Paul Bew, Peter Gibbon and Henry Patterson, *Northern Ireland 1921–1996*, London, 1996, pp. 56–9.
3   David Fitzpatrick, *The Two Irelands 1912–1939*, Oxford and New York, 1998, p. 161.

4   Sydney Elliott, *Northern Ireland Parliamentary Election Results 1921–1972*, Chichester, 1973, pp. 96, 115.

5   Ibid., pp. 96, 117.

6   Ibid., p. 116.

7   Terry Cradden, *Trade Unionism, Socialism and Partition*, Belfast, 1993, p. 46.

8   Elliott, *Northern Ireland*, p. 96.

9   Cormac Ó Gráda, *A Rocky Road: The Irish Economy Since the 1920s*, Manchester, 1997, p. 108.

10   Bew, Gibbon and Patterson, *Northern Ireland*, pp. 115–18.

11   Ibid., p. 118

12   Ibid., p. 133.

13   Paul Teague, 'Multinational Companies in the Northern Ireland Economy', in Paul Teague (ed.), *Beyond the Rhetoric: Politics, the Economy and Social Policy in Northern Ireland*, London, 1987, p. 164.

14   Liam O'Dowd, Bill Rolston and Mike Tomlinson, *Northern Ireland: Between Civil Rights and Civil War*, London, 1980, p. 17.

15   *The Ulster Year Book: The Official Handbook of Northern Ireland 1947*, Belfast, 1947, p. 76 and *The Ulster Year Book 1963–64*, Belfast, 1964, p. 150.

16   *The Ulster Year Book 1963–64*, p. 213.

17   Thomas Wilson, *Ulster: Conflict and Consent*, Oxford, 1989, p. 151.

18   Henry Patterson, 'Seán Lemass and the Ulster Question, 1959–1965', *Journal of Contemporary History* 34 (1), 1999: 145–7.

19   See the detailed analysis in A. C. Hepburn, *A Past Apart: Studies in the History of Catholic Belfast 1850–1950*, Belfast, 1996.

20   E. A. Aunger, 'Religion and Occupational Class in Northern Ireland', *Economic and Social Review* 7, 1975: 1–17.

21   Bew, Gibbon and Patterson, *Northern Ireland*, pp. 149–50.

22   Paul Bew, Henry Patterson and Paul Teague, *Between War and Peace: The Political Future of Northern Ireland*, London, 1997, pp. 120–40.

23   Memorandum by Minister of Commerce on Advance Factories for Cabinet Employment Committee, 28 March 1956, Public Record of Northern Ireland, CAB 4A/38/25.

24   John Whyte, 'How Much Discrimination Was There under the Unionist Regime 1921–68?', in Tom Gallagher and James O'Connell (eds), *Contemporary Irish Studies*, Manchester, 1988, p. 31.

25   The Campaign for Social Justice, *Northern Ireland: The Plain Truth*, Dungannon, 1969, p. 21.

26   Bob Purdie, *Politics in the Streets: The Origins of the Civil Rights Movement in Northern Ireland*, Belfast, 1990, p. 63.

27   Paul Bew and Henry Patterson, *The British State and the Ulster Crisis From Wilson to Thatcher*, London, 1985, pp. 15–18.

28   Patrick Bishop and Eamonn Mallie, *The Provisional IRA*, London, 1988, p. 117.

29   Henry Patterson, *The Politics of Illusion: A Political History of the IRA*, London, 1997, pp. 121–34.

30   Richard Rose, *Northern Ireland: A Time Of Choice*, London, 1976, p. 30.

31   Ian McAllister, *The Northern Ireland Social Democratic and Labour Party: Political Opposition in a Divided Society*, London, 1977.

32   Gordon Gillespie, 'The Sunningdale Agreement: Lost Opportunity or an Agreement Too Far?', *Irish Political Studies*, 13 (1998): 100–14.

33   Bob Rowthorn and Naomi Wayne, *Northern Ireland: The Political Economy of Conflict*, Cambridge, 1988, p. 111.

34   17.7 live births per 1,000 of the population compared with a UK average of 13.3: Michael Connolly and Sean Loughlin, 'Policy-making in Northern Ireland', in M. Connolly and S. Loughlin (eds), *Public Policy in Northern Ireland: Adoption or Adaptation?*, Belfast, 1990, p. 8.
35   Rowthorn and Wayne, *Northern Ireland*, p. 208.
36   Bew, Patterson and Teague, *Between War and Peace*, p. 134.
37   See the discussion of subvention in ibid., pp. 87–90.
38   Ibid., p. 90.
39   Jonathan Haughton, 'The Dynamics of Economic Change', in William Crotty and David E. Schmitt, *Ireland and the Politics of Change*, London, 1998, p. 30.
40   Kevin Boyle and Tom Hadden, *Northern Ireland the Choice*, London, 1994, pp. 70–1.
41   Ibid., p. 86.
42   Paul Dixon, *Northern Ireland: The Politics of War and Peace*, Basingstoke and New York, 2001, pp. 190–207.
43   Eamonn Mallie and David McKittrick, *The Fight for Peace: The Secret Story Behind the Irish Peace Process*, London, 1996, p. 89.
44   Henry Patterson, *The Politics of Illusion*, p. 226.
45   David Trimble, *To Raise up a New Northern Ireland: Articles and Speeches 1998– 2000*, Belfast, 2001, p. 11.

Further Reading

There are a number of general surveys of Northern Ireland which are useful for the period: James Loughlin, *The Ulster Question since 1945* (London, 1998); Sabine Wichert, *Northern Ireland since 1945*, 2nd ed. (London, 1999) and Paul Bew, Peter Gibbon and Henry Patterson, *Northern Ireland 1921–2001* (London, 2002). Paul Arthur and Keith Jeffery, *Northern Ireland since 1968*, 2nd ed. (London, 1996) covers the 'Troubles' in outline and can be complemented with Paul Bew and Gordon Gillespie's *Northern Ireland: A Chronology 1968–1998* (Dublin, 1999).

Nationalist politics can be followed in Brendan Lynn, *Holding the Ground: The Nationalist Party in Northern Ireland 1945–72* (Aldershot, 1997); Ian McAllister, *The Northern Ireland Social Democratic and Labour Party* (London, 1977) and Gerry Murray, *John Hume and the SDLP* (Dublin, 1998).

There is no up-to-date history of the Ulster Unionist Party; for the period up to 1973 see John Harbinson, *The Ulster Unionist Party 1882–1973* (Belfast, 1973). Arthur Aughey's *Under Siege: Ulster Unionism and the Anglo-Irish Agreement* (London, 1989) deals with more recent dilemmas. Also useful is Richard English and Graham Walker (eds), *Unionism in Modern Ireland* (Dublin, 1996). The phenomenon of Paisleyism is dealt with in Steve Bruce, *God Save Ulster! The Religion and Politics of Paisleyism* (Oxford, 1986).

There are numerous histories of the IRA. The most relevant are Patrick Bishop and Eamonn Mallie, *The Provisional IRA* (London, 1987); Henry Patterson, *The Politics of Illusion: A Political History of the IRA* (London, 1997) and M. L. R. Smith, *Fighting for Ireland? The Military Strategy of the Irish Republican Movement* (London, 1995). For Protestant paramilitarism there is much sensationalist and lurid journalism but few serious analyses. The best are Sarah Nelson, *Ulster's Uncertain Defenders* (Belfast, 1984) and Steve Bruce, *The Red Hand: Protestant Paramilitarism in Northern Ireland* (Oxford, 1992).

The economic and social history of the region is undeveloped, but see relevant chapters in Paul Teague (ed.), *Beyond the Rhetoric: Politics, the Economy and Social Policy in Northern Ireland* (London, 1987) and Paul Bew and Henry Patterson, *Between War and Peace: The Political Future of Northern Ireland* (London, 1997). Much useful empirical material combined with rather tendentious analysis can be found in Bob Rowthorn and Naomi Wayne, *Northern Ireland: The Political Economy of Conflict* (Cambridge, 1988).

British government policy towards Northern Ireland is dealt with in Peter Catterall and Sean McDougall (eds), *The Northern Ireland Question in British Politics* (London, 1996) and Michael Cunningham, *British Government Policy in Northern Ireland 1969–2000* (Manchester, 2001).

The peace process is covered in Eamonn Mallie and David McKittrick, *Endgame in Ireland* (London, 2001); Michael Cox, Adrian Guelke and Fiona Stephen, *A Farewell to Arms? From 'Long War' to 'Long Peace' in Northern Ireland* (Manchester, 2000) and Paul Dixon, *Northern Ireland: The Politics of War and Peace* (Basingstoke and New York, 2001).

Chronology

1947   Education Act (Northern Ireland) revolutionises access to secondary and further education.

1949   Ireland Act declares that Northern Ireland will not cease to be part of the UK without the consent of the Parliament of Northern Ireland.

1956   IRA launches 'Operation Harvest' against Northern Ireland state.

1959   Eamon de Valera retires and is replaced as Irish prime minister by Seán Lemass.

1962   IRA calls off its terrorism campaign.

1963   Lord Brookeborough resigns and Terence O'Neill becomes Prime Minister.

1964   Campaign for Social Justice established.

1965   Seán Lemass comes to Stormont for historic meeting with O'Neill.

1967   NICRA founded.

1968   RUC use force to disperse civil rights march in Londonderry (5 Oct.).

1969   O'Neill resigns and is replaced by James Chichester Clark (Apr.). Rioting in Londonderry and Belfast leads to the arrival of British troops (Aug.).

1970   IRA splits and Provisional Sinn Fein and IRA formed (Jan.). Ian Paisley wins Stormont seat (Apr.). Paisley wins North Antrim in Westminster election (June). SDLP founded (Aug.).

1971   Chichester Clark resigns as Prime Minister and is replaced by Brian Faulkner (Mar.)/Hundreds of IRA suspects interned (9 Aug.).

1972   Thirteen unarmed men shot dead by troops in Londonderry (30 Jan.). Stormont prorogued (24 Mar.).

1973   Elections for Northern Ireland Assembly (June). Sunningdale Conference agrees power-sharing and a council of Ireland (Dec.).

1974   New power-sharing executive takes office (1 Jan.). Anti-power-sharing Unionists win 11 of 12 Westminster seats (Feb.). Ulster Workers' Council Strike starts (14 May). Executive collapses (28 May).

1979   Paisley tops the poll in first elections to European Parliament with 30 per cent of total vote. IRA murder Lord Mountbatten in Sligo (27 Aug.). IRA bombs kill 18 soldiers at Narrow Water, Co. Down. (27 Aug.).

1981   Bobby Sands and nine other IRA prisoners die on hunger strike for political status.

1983   Gerry Adams wins West Belfast seat in general election.
1985   Margaret Thatcher and Irish Prime Minister sign Anglo-Irish Agreement.
1988   Adams has talks with John Hume of the SDLP.
1990   Peter Brooke, Northern Ireland Secretary, declares Britain has 'no selfish, strategic or economic interest' in Northern Ireland.
1993   Downing Street Declaration issued by John Major and the Irish Prime Minister, Albert Reynolds (15 Dec.).
1994   IRA announces a 'complete cessation of military operations' (31 Aug.).
1995   Joint Framework Documents published (22 Feb.).
1996   Report of Mitchell Commission on decommissioning of terrorist weapons. IRA ends ceasefire with bombing of Canary Wharf in London (9 Feb.). In elections for a new Northern Ireland forum Sinn Fein gets 15.5 per cent; the SDLP 21.4 per cent; the Ulster Unionist Party 24.2 per cent and the DUP, 18.8 per cent.
1997   IRA announces new ceasefire (July).
1998   All-party talks culminate in the Good Friday Agreement.
       Agreement is put to referendums in May in the Irish Republic where it is approved by 94.4 per cent, and Northern Ireland where it gets the support of 71 per cent.
       Elections for a new N. Ireland Assembly (June). Ulster Unionists get 21.3 per cent; DUP 18.1 per cent; SDLP 22.0 and Sinn Fein 17.6 per cent. Real IRA bomb in Omagh kills 28 people (15 Aug.).
1999   Publication of Patten Report on Policing (Sept.). Formation of Northern Ireland's first power-sharing government since 1974 (Dec.).
2000   IRA commits itself to 'put weapons beyond use' (May).
2001   Westminster elections: Sinn Fein emerges as largest nationalist party: Sinn Fein gets 21.7 per cent and 4 seats; SDLP 21 per cent and 3 seats; Ulster Unionists 26.8 per cent and 6 seats and DUP 22.5 per cent and 5 seats.
       IRA begins to decommission its weapons (Oct.).

8 The Currents of Political Thought

Roger Eatwell

Introduction

One of Britain's great post-war philosophers, Sir Isaiah Berlin, has written of the important distinction between 'negative' and 'positive' freedom. The former is concerned with the absence of external restraint, whereas the latter is concerned more with the ability to achieve something – very different concepts which lie at the heart of much political debate. At times in the pages that follow, it will be necessary to consider such abstract principles and major thinkers. However, this chapter is primarily concerned with political ideologies rather than academic philosophy. 'Ideology' is an elusive term, but it is understood here to refer to collective bodies of political thought, which encompass an important policy-oriented dimension (although it can have a utopian side too).[1] In particular, this chapter looks at the thought which has helped to shape the domestic policies and rhetoric of the largest British political parties.

Berlin is a quintessentially British liberal thinker, but he was born in Eastern Europe. This fact highlights an important second opening perspective. Several other major post-war 'British' thinkers, such as the economist Friedrich Hayek, were similarly émigrés – some of whom had fled from oppression. Moreover, with the growth of globalised communications and a more integrated world economy, it has become increasingly problematic since 1945 to speak of a uniquely British form of thought. Although British social democratic thinking, so pervasive in the immediate post-war years, was clearly influenced by diverse European traditions, its roots were in many ways parochial. The propagation of New Right thought after the 1960s, on the other hand, was more a transatlantic than a specifically British phenomenon (and was hardly influenced by European thinking).

The ascendancy of the New Right during the 1970s and 1980s points to a third opening caveat: namely, the dangers of simple periodisations of change. Although most commentators accept that there was an extensive consensus in Britain for a generation or more after the Second World War, the argument is open to notable objections. This is especially true if the focus is placed on new political thought rather than continuities in policy. There were notable differences within the social democratic camp about the extent of state ownership and other crucial issues. Moreover, Hayek published his seminal defence of the free market and attack on the growth of the state, *The Road to Serfdom*, in 1944; the pioneer British laissez-faire think-tank, the Institute for Economic Affairs (IEA), was set up in 1955 and provided the inspiration for many later bodies. There are similar problems with the common claim that the New Right came to provide the intellectual basis of a new consensus. From the outset there were notable divisions within New Right ranks, especially between its more individualist and collectivist strands. While at the very time that its laissez-faire wing was first gaining notable influence, some British socialists sought a break from consensus in the opposite direction.

Nevertheless, there is much to be said when writing an introductory survey for using the metaphor of major currents. This chapter, therefore, follows a threefold basic division. The first section examines the flood tide of the postwar social democratic 'consensus'. The second considers its New Right-wing ebb. A shorter final section maps some of the eddies of thought which lie behind the quest to find a 'Third Way' – a term which has recently aroused much controversy.[2]

The Social Democratic Consensus

The 1945–51 Labour governments, led by Clement Attlee, were the first majority Labour administrations in Britain. Historians have shown that the initial detailed planning of some of Labour's legislation took place during the wartime Coalition government, and reflected a variety of interests and motives. However, the broad programme set out in Labour's 1945 manifesto, *Let Us Face the Future*, reveals much about the ideas and influences which helped shape the specifically British variant of social democracy.[3]

The early Labour Party was characterised by ethos more than systematic ideology, an 'us versus them' creed of 'labourist' solidarity. Doctrinally, it owed more to Methodism than Marx and continental socialism, exhibiting a millenarian, although essentially tolerant, religious streak which helped mollify its class-consciousness. It owed even more to liberal values – which had strong links with Protestantism. Particularly important was the turn-of-the-twentieth-century 'New Liberalism', which accepted state action if it helped make individuals more autonomous, more truly free (the 'enabling' state rather than the 'nanny' state, which encouraged dependency). Two other notable influences on the early Labour Party were the trade unions and the Fabian Society. The latter, especially its key theorists Beatrice and Sidney Webb, helped to set out the core strategy of the party through its technocratic belief in 'the inevitability of gradualness'. In other words, socialism could be demonstrated to be more efficient than capitalism, and could come about in stages within 'advanced' states like Britain. The unions tended to pursue more specific goals, including legal protection and the nationalisation of industry (often their 'own', usually in the belief that this would improve wages and conditions). Their more general ethos strongly underpinned the labourist collectivist ethic.

After the schismatic collapse of the 1929–31 minority Labour government, there was widespread agreement with R. H. Tawney, a historian and leading academic member of the party, that existing programmes were too sweeping and lacked a sense of priorities. In one sentence they would propose to nationalise several industries (without offering any clear idea what this meant), followed by the abolition of fox-hunting in the next. But there was considerable disagreement about what should form the basis of a Labour short-term programme. Left-wing academics, such as G. D. H. Cole and Harold Laski, argued forcefully that it was vital to gain control of the 'commanding heights' of the economy, including the banking system. In order to do so, a Labour government would need effectively to suspend normal parliamentary working for a time. The more moderate wing of the party rejected such views, focusing on developing a managerial–state corporation model of nationalisation, linked to specific policies of welfare reform. By the late 1930s, a rising generation of Labour academics, such as the economist Hugh Gaitskell, believed that they had found in Keynesianism the intellectual prop which would underpin their gradualist, piecemeal views.

In *The General Theory of Employment, Interest and Money* (1936), John Maynard Keynes developed systematically his earlier arguments that governments, by regulating demand through tax and other measures, could solve the curse of unemployment.[4] The book immediately had a major impact on 'middle opinion', spanning the main parties. During the Second World War, the most famous plan for welfare reform – the 1942 Beveridge Report – was directed by a Liberal. The fact that both William Beveridge and Keynes were supporters of the Liberal Party underlines the dangers of overstating the specifically socialist side of the post-1930s consensus. Nevertheless, there were clearly Labour aspects to the 1945–51 legislative record. The plan for a totally free National Health Service covering all citizens, introduced by the left-wing Health Minister Nye Bevan in 1948, went well beyond Beveridge. Liberals, and especially Conservatives, opposed most of Labour's nationalisation plans. Moreover, Labour's strong, organised working-class base encouraged corporatist links between government, union leadership and management. Indeed, this corporatist-statist side to Labour involved a very un-Keynesian tampering with the supply side (namely, a 'micro' economic focus on production rather than a 'macro' focus on economy-wide counter-cyclical demand management).

After Labour's defeat in the 1951 general election, a major ideological split developed within the party. One divisive issue was whether Britain should unilaterally give up its nuclear arms (and weaken or sever links with the USA). But the main ideological split occurred over what came to be known as 'revisionism' – namely, whether Clause IV of the party's 1918 Constitution, which committed Labour to state ownership, should be removed or substantially modified. One major motive of the revisionists was the belief – which intensified after Labour lost three general elections in a row from 1951–9 (each with an increased Conservative majority) – that nationalisation was a vote-loser. But there was a more theoretical side too.

The key ideological work in the 'revisionist' debate, which clearly inspired many on the moderate wing of the Labour Party for years to come, was C. A. R. Crosland's *The Future of Socialism* (1956). Crosland, an economist by training, argued that socialism was too rooted in the pre-Keynesian era, during which socialists of all hues saw capitalism as inevitably inefficient and wasteful of human and other resources because of the trade cycle. Crosland claimed that Keynesian macro-demand-management techniques now made mass unemployment a chimera of the past. He further argued that socialism had an outmoded view of the ownership of capital. Industrial robber-barons exploiting labour had become – like dinosaurs – extinct. Crosland claimed that the twentieth-century reality was an increasing divorce of ownership and control, with new management more socially aware and responsible.[5]

There was also a political side to Crosland's sweeping thesis. He argued that socialism in the past had paid too little attention to the issue of checks and balances (so central to American liberal thinking). Soviet communism and fascism had shown the dangers of excessive state control or ownership. The key task, therefore, was to achieve a mixed-market, private-state accommodation, in which each side exerted a check on the other. Crosland boldly asserted that the post-1945 Labour governments had created basically the correct state–private balance. The predominantly private market ensured economic dynamism, but government and other democratic forces such as trade unions ultimately held the reins of political and social power.

Yet Crosland did not believe that Britain had already become a social democratic utopia. He held that there was still much work to do in order to achieve the ultimate goal – namely, the achievement of a high level of equality. However, he separated this end from traditional socialist means, in particular the pursuit of nationalisation outside specific areas where this could be shown to be beneficial (for instance, where there were market failures, or natural monopolies, such as water supply). Crosland believed that a dynamic free market would, through taxation, provide high levels of income which governments could spend to pursue the goal of equality. He tended to see this programme more in terms of promoting rights than in terms of directly ensuring high levels of income equality. Whilst there was to be a generous welfare state, it did not seek to provide similar benefits to those in work; nor was taxation to be too punitive on the rich. Rather, the state sought to provide institutional 'fixes'. The policies which were to become most associated with this form of reasoning centred on education. In particular, there was to be a move towards comprehensive rather than selective schooling at the age of 11 (which had led to a grammar – secondary modern split in the state system), and provision for a vast increase in access to higher education.

Although the revisionists failed in their quest for Labour constitutional reform, their ideas unquestionably influenced policy in key areas. Moreover, their philosophical foundations were reinforced during the 1970s by the publication of John Rawls's *A Theory of Justice* (1971) – an American work which exerted a considerable influence on British thinkers and some politicians. At the core of Rawls's arguments was the question of what kind of society individuals would choose to be reborn in if they knew nothing of their likely position and chances in that society. The answer suggested was that most would opt for a society which gives everyone the greatest amount of freedom compatible with that of others, and with inequalities tolerable only as far as they benefit the least well-off. The overall thrust of the argument clearly reinforced the moderate redistribution at the heart of revisionism.

However, during the 1970s, the death knell sounded for the Croslandite economic strategy. Low economic growth and rising unemployment were accompanied by relatively high inflation ('stagflation'). Government macroeconomic policy seemed incapable of controlling these events, whilst recession meant falling real tax revenues and pressure on welfare expenditure. In 1975, inflation peaked at over 20 per cent. During the following year, the minority Labour government was forced to accept a package of deflationary measures outlined by the International Monetary Fund (IMF). Evidence that the 1964–70 and 1974–9 Labour governments had failed to achieve a significant redistribution of income or wealth added to the funeral pyre of the social-democratic consensus (critics even claimed that Britain had become more unequal under these Labour administrations).

Against this 1970s background, a reinvigorated Labour left emerged. The best-known representative of this position was the aspiring party leader Tony Benn, who had successfully in the early 1960s fought a campaign to give up his inherited peerage. At this time, Benn had appeared more on the technocratic wing of the party, but his writings in the 1970s and 1980s, for instance, *Arguments for Socialism* (1979), exhibited a blend of more traditional statist and moral socialist arguments. Key policies characteristic of the Labour left by the turn of the 1980s were the nationalisation of profitable industries, the need to control the capitalist media, the reform of a 'conservative' civil service, and unilateral nuclear disarmament. Another key concern was withdrawal from the European Communities (EC), which Britain joined in 1973 amid hopes of economic regeneration. The Left argued that trade liberalisation, fostered by the USA and bodies such as the EC, promoted the power of multinational corporations – undemocratic organisations which undermined national sovereignty and threatened the gains in wages and welfare which the working class had made during the twentieth century. The Left advocated the creation of a 'command' (highly statist) economy which would limit imports and target state investment. A section of the Left also advocated the introduction of some form of industrial democracy, arguing that Croslandite social democracy was a form of condescending middle-class do-goodism which rejected the workers' ability to run their own affairs.

However, this left-wing wave was short-lived. Labour suffered a major breakaway at the turn of the 1980s, which took many of its more moderate members into the new Social Democratic Party (SDP). Its humiliating performance in the 1983 general election was the final nail in the Left's coffin in terms of influence within the party's higher echelons. Nevertheless, the Left remained stronger among the rank and file, and a handful of academic critics continued to plough their left-wing furrows.

In terms of political thought, a more original challenge to Crosland's technocratic and limited vision of social democracy came from the so-called New Left.

This mainly grew out of a small group of ex-Communists disillusioned by the traumas of 1956 – the year in which the Soviet leader, Nikita Krushchev, denounced the former Stalinist terror, and in which the Soviet government brutally suppressed the Hungarian liberalisation process. Earlier defectors from communism had often become mainstream Labour supporters; some even metamorphosed as Liberals or Conservatives (it was often among these ranks that CIA-funded cultural organisations and journals, such as *Encounter*, recruited in an attempt to stem the tide of what it saw as left-wing intellectual hegemony in Europe). The goal of New Left apostates, such as the historian E. P. Thompson, was more to identify and proselytise alternative strands in Marxism. One key source was Marx's early writings. In these, the key concept was the 'alienation' of 'man' by a capitalism which treated him simply as another means of production. This version of Marxism seemed to offer a more flexible tool than the pretensions of 'scientific socialism', based on rigid laws of history, and the belief that the political 'superstructure' was determined by the socio-economic 'base' (namely, class relations). It also meshed with an arguably even more important key source for the New Left – the early Italian Marxist theorist Antonio Gramsci. His emphasis on the power of capitalist 'hegemony' (namely the ability through institutions such as education and the media to make ideological views seem common sense) encouraged a growing interest in topics such as 'discourse'. However, Gramsciism's impact was more in academic circles than on Labour policy – although within the party it did reinforce fears about the power of a 'capitalist' media.

The New Left was not simply a form of Marxism, as its main journal, the *New Left Review* (1960–) shows. Its intellectual pedigree was eclectic, turning to other socialist traditions for inspiration, including guild socialism (which reinforced a concern with workplace democracy) and anarchism (which produced a strand suspicious of the state and more concerned with individual activism). The latter often meshed with ecological ideas, which began to gather force in the 1960s and 1970s. The ecology movement's primary motivation was often specific issues, such as nuclear power-station building, but behind it lay a wider ideology, hostile to both capitalism and statist forms of socialism. It sought a more decentralised, communal world, more in keeping with nature – an idea encapsulated in the evocative book title, *Small Is Beautiful* (1973), written by German-born but British resident E. F. Schumacher. An important figure in disseminating Green ideas was Jonathan Porritt, one-time director of Friends of the Earth (though Porritt was relatively pragmatic and more concerned with policy than with developing radical ecological political theory). However, it is important to stress that some Green thought which emerged at this time was perfectly consistent with conservatism, often celebrating England as a green and pleasant land. It is therefore useful to distinguish between a more general rise of a reformist 'environmentalism', which is consistent with other forms of thought, and a radical 'ecologism'. Although there was a growth of the former type of thought in the Labour Party during the 1970s and 1980s, the party's main concerns at this time remained centred on largely traditional views of socio-economic organisation and structure.

Another source of criticism of Labour which initially had little effect in terms of affecting mainstream thought within the party came from the peripheral nationalists – with both the Welsh and Scottish nationalist parties gaining electorally after the late 1960s. Labour had long supported the strong central state, which it saw as necessary to achieve redistribution from rich to poorer areas. Certainly British public expenditure favoured such areas, but this did not compensate for the ravages of structural economic decline in activities such as steel or coal mining. Some nationalists, like Ned Thomas in *The Welsh Extremist* (1971), portrayed their creed as a reflection of the failure of technocratic English socialism to deliver either economic prosperity or the rebuilding of communities (a very different line from the right-wing politics of Plaid Cymru founder-member, Saunders Lewis). The nationalist cause was further helped intellectually by British membership of the EC. Small nations could point to a vital role in a new 'Europe of the regions', in which the big decisions needed to be moved up to a higher level of government (for instance, controlling multinational corporations), but where other decisions needed to be moved closer to the people (there were clear signs of a general decline in political participation after the 1960s). Indeed, by the late 1970s, a growing group on the left, best epitomised by the academic Tom Nairn in works such as *The Break-up of Britain* (1977), had become critical of the party's historic defence of the 'British' unitary state.

Like the ecologists and nationalists, the growing feminist movement was also divided. Socialist feminists believe that the oppression of women stems essentially from capitalism. The views of radical feminists are typified by the best-selling book, *The Female Eunuch* (1971), written by the Australian-born but British resident, Germaine Greer. This view holds that men themselves are the problem: women suffer a particular type of patriarchal domination, which cannot be reduced to class issues. Liberal feminists believe that discrimination can be rectified by legal means. It has been the liberal strand which has had more influence in the Labour Party, helping to lay the intellectual seeds of new equal opportunities legislation from the 1970s onwards. The more immediate relative success of this wing of feminism compared to the nationalists before the late 1990s, and the ecologists, stemmed from the fact that there had always been a strand within social democracy which advocated women's rights. Liberal feminism was thus not so much a new challenge to classic social democracy, as a rediscovery by a new generation (of mainly middle-class women) of a cause which had often been neglected in a party characterised by a strong male, work-oriented ethos.

The New Right Challenge

After the return of a Conservative government in 1979, debates about social democracy were largely eclipsed by analyses of a new force. The extent to which 'Thatcherism' was ideologically driven by the 'New Right' rather than electoral expediency and wider socio-economic factors remains strongly contested.[6] For some, Thatcherism was largely a continuation of the practice of Conservative 'statecraft', which had characterised the party since its foundations. On this account, the Conservatives were motivated by a pragmatic interplay between the party's individualist and collectivist wings, with one or the other coming into the ascendancy largely depending on the needs of the hour. Thus in the early nineteenth century, the Conservative Party (known as the Tories before the 1840s) was the primary home for the landed interests and the Church of England. After the 1870s, the Conservatives sought to appeal to the working class, especially through social imperialism. And by the 1920s the Conservatives had become the main party of 'opportunity' and business (whilst still retaining the support of about one-third of the working class).[7] By the 1960s, the Conservatives had accepted the loss of empire and become the main party supporting entry into the European Communities – although there were notable critics of this policy, including MP Enoch Powell, who in works such as *The Common Market: The Case Against* (1971) defended the sovereignty of Parliament and criticised the bureaucracy of 'Europe'.

In the post-1945 era, some academic Conservatives, most notably the philosopher Michael Oakeshott, set out in a sophisticated form a defence of pragmatism and suspicion of philosophies which were based on abstract principles and utopian blueprints. In works such as *Rationalism in Politics* (1962), Oakeshott pointed to the wisdom which could reside in convention and tradition. In policy terms, he pointed to the need to prevent excessive state growth. For him, politics was not the quest for some more perfect – yet alone utopian – destination, but rather the defence of civil association and a body of relatively fixed laws and institutions. He elaborated, in an academic form, a common Conservative suspicion of 'grand theory' and a priori plans to make a better world ('nation' would perhaps be a better term in the context of historic Conservative thought).

Nevertheless, there can be no doubt that many key figures around Thatcher, such as fellow-MP Keith Joseph, were influenced by the growth of New Right publications which had a radical ideological basis. These often emanated initially from think-tanks such as the IEA and a variety of similar groups, like the Adam Smith Institute, which has been cited as a key inspiration for the notorious 'poll tax' of the late 1980s'.[8] Indeed, think-tanks have in some ways usurped the role traditionally held by 'intellectuals' – although the New Right had some notable advocates in universities, especially in economics departments. Several prominent economic journalists, such as Samuel Brittan, further spread the word. Whilst Thatcher was not a sophisticated political thinker, key tenets of the New Right appealed because they accorded with her homespun, hard-working, small-business philosophy. A sweeping New Right world-view also reinforced Thatcher's firm sense of self-belief: 'There is no alternative' was the key early 'sermon'. Indeed, there is an important sense in which early Thatcherism, like a notable strand within early British social democracy, was a form of secular religion.

The term 'New Right' is in a sense a misnomer, as the basic doctrines advocated by many on its economic wing were hardly new. In particular, the celebration of free markets and minimal government ('laissez-faire') echoed mainstream nineteenth-century British thinking. However, there are important ways in which the 'New Right' deserved its label. First, it reflected a renewed confidence, a belief that the future did not belong to the Left. The 1930s had been the great age of 'fellow-travelling', of people who – whilst not joining the Communist Party – admired the Soviet 'experiment' with its Five-year Plans and apparent full employment at a time when the West was racked by depression. In the late 1950s, it was the USSR which put the first man in space, seeming to underline its economic power and technological advances. Yet by the 1980s, it was clear to all but the most blind that Soviet communism had failed economically and had led to brutal dictatorship rather than liberation. During the 1960s to the 1980s, the economic and social problems that afflicted Labour and other social democratic governments, including the once much-vaunted Scandinavian model, gave further solace to the Right.

A second important sense in which the New Right was original concerns its analysis of these failures. It was not simply a reworking of old theories.[9] Arguably the most important figure behind the intellectual rise of the New Right was Friedrich August von Hayek. Hayek is typically seen as the great prophet of laissez-faire, a man who endured an arduous journey through the post-1945 social democratic desert before settling in the promised land (he left Britain for the USA at the turn of the 1950s).[10] Yet Hayek was never a laissez-faire supporter in the sense that he espoused the classic model of perfect competition, which posits rationality in a competitive market of many buyers and sellers, and in which (reasonable) profits are a reward for the efficient allocation of resources. Hayek developed what can be termed the 'epistemological defence' of the free market. His empirical starting point was the failure of state planning (both communist and social democratic). He held that a market was a remarkably sophisticated transmitter of knowledge about prices, taste, and so on. Planning produced inefficiency. No matter how publicly spirited or well trained, state planners could never acquire the rich knowledge which markets transmitted. In particular, they would lack the sense of hunch or intuition which was so crucial to much entrepreneurial activity – talents which could not be codified in any economics text. Hayek accepted that some companies could achieve a monopolistic market position. Markets could fail to supply needed goods. Profit could owe more to luck than virtue. But government intervention was almost invariably worse.

Hayek's writings also encompassed an analysis of the welfare state. Whereas the most extreme laissez-faire advocates rejected all state provision, Hayek was willing to accept some form of safety net as long as it was defended on pragmatic grounds. What he objected to was the use of terms such as 'justice' to legitimise redistribution, and especially the claim that market outcomes were unfair. Hayek believed that it was the pursuit of social justice which most differentiated the welfare state from the liberal state, which was his goal. He held that as market outcomes were not intended, they were not an issue of fairness and morality. Terms like 'justice' or 'need' were manipulated by social democratic elites (a 'New Class', to adopt a term later popularised by others within the New Right) to legitimise further public expenditure, typically on unresponsive, monopolistic state provision of services. In turn, this growth of the state removed a sense of individual responsibility, and in some cases the desire to work (creating what others within the New Right were to term a 'dependency culture'). Moreover, the concepts of justice and need were intimately connected with a belief in rights, for instance, the right to a 'decent' standard of living. Such open-ended, subjective rights (in comparison with defending basic rights such as free speech) threatened to undermine the legitimate authority of the state, as demands for ever-greater 'rights' failed to be fulfilled.

Hayek's arguments were not simply about economic efficiency and welfare. He held that freedom was indivisible, that it was impossible to have a truly democratic political system without a high degree of freedom in the market. To adopt Berlin's terminology, Hayek held that 'negative freedom' was the crucial form. Government intervention in the economy would lead to mounting bureaucracy and – worse – a form of growing authoritarianism. Keynes tried to reassure Hayek that planning would not necessarily lead to inefficiency and loss of freedom if those in charge had the right moral views. Hayek rejected this argument not simply on economic grounds, but also because he believed that it involved a form of social democratic elitism – encapsulated in the post-1945 Labour aphorism: 'The man from the Ministry knows best'.

Whilst he was undoubtedly a great early prophet of the anti-state revolution, it is important not to overemphasise Hayek's role. There were a variety of strands within the New Right which did not owe any significant debt to Hayek. By the late 1970s, 'monetarism' had become arguably the key economic buzzword. The doctrine was associated most with the American economist Milton Friedman. He held that inflation rather than full employment was the key variable, and saw excessive money supply, typically caused by high government expenditure, as the main cause of rising prices. By the 1980s, most Western governments were exerting some form of control over money supply (in Britain's case, an approach hastened by IMF conditions after the 1975–6 economic crisis). Friedman's linked idea of a 'natural rate' of unemployment, which government spending could not remove, also came to replace the post-war British target of seeing around 3 per cent unemployed as the desirable rate. As unemployment rose to well over 10 per cent during the 1980s, with a notably higher rate in some regions, such ideas were helpful in defusing charges that Thatcherism was uncaring. Whilst the Thatcher governments were never monetarist in a strict sense of the word, they did broadly conform to the wider Friedmanite agenda of what became known as 'supply-side' economics. This focused on the need to ensure that the free market operated with the maximum efficiency and minimum distortion. Among the policy conclusions which flowed from this was the need for government to curb inflation, excessive state interference with business (unless monopolistic), excessive taxation and excessive trade union power.

Some government policies were also influenced by a group of 'public-choice' (or 'Virginia School') theorists which grew up after the 1960s. Such thinkers adapted the academic economists' core conception of maximisation to the political sphere. For instance, they hypothesised that bureaucrats, far from being honourable public servants in pursuit of the collective good, were in fact a self-interested elite, seeking to maximise departmental budgets, and so on. Such analyses almost certainly reinforced Thatcher's unwillingness to negotiate with powerful groups, such as doctors. Public-choice theory of parties also pointed to the dangers of at least one party seeking to maximise its support by promising an unsustainable increase in state munificence, often under the guise of moral terms such as 'compassion' or 'equality'. Charity', according to this New Right view, involved giving away one's own money – not other people's, or the state's.

Most New Right thought was clearly linked to economic liberalism, but there was a strand within the New Right which was suspicious, even hostile, to aspects of liberalism. This strand is best epitomised in Britain by the academic philosopher, Roger Scruton, for instance in his book *The Meaning of Conservatism* (1980). Scruton was (and remains) self-avowedly a Conservative rather than a Liberal. Whereas he saw liberalism as based on abstract reasoning and individualism, Scruton celebrated the importance of tradition above rationality, of collective happiness above rights. He saw laissez-faire economics as corrosive of both authority and communities. For Scruton, the key institutions that held society together were the family and the church. He also held that there was a need to preserve a strong belief in the nation – a strand in his thought which pointed to the alleged dangers of immigration and multiculturalism. For others within the authoritarian wing of the New Right, the preservation of a traditionally conceived nation became the main concern. This was often linked to what has become known to its critics as the 'new racism'. Instead of dealing in racial hierarchies, this portrayed a world of different communities, each needing a separate existence in order to retain its identity and vitality. New racism deployed the language of democracy and naturalness in an attempt to defuse charges of extremism ('it's only natural that the majority of people in Bradford do not want . . .', etc.). Critics countered by arguing that apparently acceptable principles were being used to legitimise a discredited politics of exclusion and even hatred.

Scruton's concern with tradition set him apart from the technocratic economic side of the New Right, though not entirely from Hayek. Whilst Hayek wrote a famous essay in his book *The Constitution of Liberty* (1960) entitled 'Why I am not a conservative', his rejection of conservatism owed much to his belief that it was opportunistic, that it lacked a core philosophy which could fend off the challenges of the Left. Hayek in some ways sought a Third Way between liberalism and conservatism. Certainly his defence of the market was not based on the decontextualised rationalist assumptions of academic 'neoclassical' economics. Rather, he stressed the importance of tradition and strong social structures in helping society to overcome the inequalities and other problems associated with market economics. However, Hayek distinguished between tradition in the sense of tolerant communal bonds and norms, and a more authoritarian traditionalism which advocated policies such as harsh punishments and which demonised the outsider as a means of reinforcing in-group social allegiance.

A much-quoted Thatcher aphorism opined that 'there is no such thing as society', but by the turn of the 1990s some New Right laissez-faire advocates were beginning to have doubts about the corrosive effects of individualism. Did not effective markets rely on strong pre-existing social bonds and trust? Was not the cult of the individual, epitomised in the 1980s by the hedonistic 'yuppy' driving his/her new Porsche 911 around a landscape of inner-city deprivation, destroying the very fabric of society? Among the Conservative leadership, the former academic John Redwood showed clear signs of being influenced by this trend in thought when he developed ideas such as 'popular capitalism', characterised by a broad share-base and sense of social concern.

An even more notable convert who came to espouse this type of view was the academic, John Gray, who was to make the intellectual journey from Thatcherite to New Labour supporter. In *Endgames* (1997), one of his many commentaries on contemporary political thought, Gray argued that in future conservatism would seek to repair the damage done by the New Right through a mixture of 'techno-utopianism', such as stressing the rise of new virtual communities, and a more crude kind of fundamentalism. The former is implausible: the Internet is no substitute for the imagined, but not imaginary, communities of religion, nation, etc. The latter raises the possibility of a reaffirmation of the collectivist strand in the Conservative tradition in the form of a new nationalism – perhaps an English nationalism, linked to the New Right economic language of self-interest.

Towards a 'Third Way'?

After the election of a 'New' Labour government in 1997, cartoonists frequently depicted Tony Blair in Thatcher-like drag – a man whose 'Third Way' rhetoric concealed a conservative bent. Other critics have stressed that Labour has been more concerned to manipulate media coverage or to garner votes than to set out a new ideological vision. Certainly at times it is hard to see the concrete policy outcomes of proclaimed new initiatives, such as the renunciation of old Labour suspicions of the European Union, though after winning a second term of office in 2001, Blair sought to prepare the way to win a euro referendum. Nevertheless, during the 1980s and especially the 1990s a new body of thought, often embryonic rather than fully-formed, began to emerge, which differed notably from both the New Right and old British social democracy.

The New Right, especially the 'Hayekian Revelation', undoubtedly had a major effect on many who had seen themselves as socialist. Some became apostates, turning to the creed of the free-market. But the main lesson drawn by most who had seen themselves as left of centre was the importance of market mechanisms rather than market values. Unlike Hayek, many held that capitalism could not be exonerated from its social consequences by claiming that market outcomes were unintended: people who are guilty of manslaughter do not intend to kill, but they are held in some way to blame.

One response to the rising laissez-faire tide was the idea of 'market socialism'. This sought to promote cooperatives as the main form of productive organisation, using state banks and other means to help their formation. Cooperatives would buy and trade within broad market frameworks which set prices, etc., but their inherently egalitarian and participatory nature was seen as likely to produce a very different type of society to a capitalist one. Market socialists realised that their vision was in many ways utopian, but they argued that socialists needed to return to such inspiring forms of arguments. For far too long, socialists had been concerned with technocratic issues that often failed to work, let alone fire the imagination. However, although market socialism attracted a brief flurry of academic interest, during the 1990s it largely sank without trace. In an era of globalisation, its emphasis on relatively small-scale, consensual economic organisation appeared too divorced from stark market reality.

By the early 1990s, 'stakeholding' had become the buzzword for those who sought a new form of economic organisation. Although the term had its origins in management theory, it became popularly associated with Will Hutton, a journalist and best-selling author of *The State We Are In* (1995). Hutton, like some academics, remained committed to a form of neo-Keynesianism, a reflection of the dangers of overstating the New Right's impact on economic thinking. This new Keynesianism was more cautious about the limits of government economic power. As a result, it is often linked to a form of Europeanism, arguing that the nation-state was too small to buck globalisation. Neo-Keynesianism also tended to be more conscious of the distinction between the enabling and the nanny state, seeking to encourage both individual and corporate enterprise.

Hutton accepted the academic argument that Britain had been characterised by a form of 'gentlemanly capitalism', which favoured the short-run financial interests of the City rather than long-run interests of productive entreprise. The British class system had further, according to this account, failed to build the kind of trust ('social capital') which was so important to economic dynamism. Stakeholding theorists sought to redress this situation by arguing that business needed to become more inclusive, incorporating itself in a dense web of interlocking interests, including suppliers, workers and consumers. Hutton linked this to an argument for reform in political institutions, such as the introduction of a proportional representation electoral system. This would effectively lead to coalition government, with greater stress on consensual rather than 'adversary politics', and providing a more stable environment for business success.

Discussions of stakeholding had a wider resonance than those about market socialism, but by the late 1990s the term was visibly fading from the political horizon. It had always been a somewhat vague concept. More damagingly, it seemed to derive broad inspiration from the West German 'social market economy', which sought to integrate business, worker and consumer concerns within a broad consensus based on economic prosperity. However, by the late 1990s the German economy had begun to show notable signs of serious malaise – whereas in Britain key indicators, like growth and employment, were relatively healthy. The much-vaunted post-1945 German model appeared to be in danger of following its Swedish social democratic cousin into the dustbin of history. Certainly there seemed to be danger in consensus when it became ossified and resistant to change.

Against a background of increasing social inequalities which accompanied post-1970s changes in Britain, there was a revival of political thinking which sought to reforge the community. 'Citizenship' increasingly became one of the key words in this new strand in thought. For some, like the think-tank, Charter 88, this was linked to a liberal-institutionalist approach. Britain needed constitutional reform, such as a new Bill of Rights, to underline that people were no longer – as British passports had historically proclaimed-merely 'subjects'. Supporters of the European Union sought to broaden the conception of citizenship to Europe, reflecting a desire for symbolic devices to help forge a greater European dimension to identities (the citizenship afforded by the 1992 Maastricht Treaty afforded precious little by way of new rights). Scottish and Welsh nationalists, together with English regionalists, argued for a new tier of institutions at these levels – often linking the argument to the claim that active citizenship was best promoted at the 'local' level.

Another of the new key terms reflecting this sense of loss of community was 'social inclusion' – although it also pointed to fears about growing socio-economic inequalities. 'Inclusion' most typically referred to making the poor, ethnic minorities and others feel more a part of society. As such, it was often linked to new proposals for welfare, albeit ones which sought to empower individuals rather than strengthen the nanny state. But inclusion could also mean encouraging the growing band of the relatively well-off not to drop out of social institutions such as state education and medicine. Such was the flexibility of the term, it could even be used to justify workfare: making people work was a vital entrée to mainstream society.

A major school of 'communitarian' thinkers grew up in Britain and the United States after the 1980s, who argued that the world is not made up of atomised individuals. It is peopled by social beings, rooted in families and wider communities. The communitarians held that individual autonomy presupposes a strong public culture in which choice and responsibility go together. To ask, as the followers of Rawls did, hypothetical questions about individual social rebirth misses the crucial point that moral truths are communal rather than individual or universal. According to the American sociologist Amitai Etzioni, in works such as *The Spirit of Community* (1993), the crucial task was to rebuild communities rather than engage in abstract philosophical reasoning. Communitarians advocated the need for people to take responsibility for themselves, and to accept duties towards their families and their local communities. They put great premium on good parenting, which involves actively discouraging parents from splitting up. The education system too was seen as crucial, including the vital role of instilling a sense of civic duty. In spite of the self-publicising claims of some leading communitarians, much of this was hardly new thought. Indeed, feminists especially have argued that it involved a dangerous right-wing form of paternalist and authoritarian social thinking.

A more left-wing contribution to thought can be discerned in the works of Anthony Giddens, a leading British sociologist who has specifically written about *The Third Way* (1998). Giddens argues that the late twentieth century was a period of revolutionary change. He charts the decline of the old certainties of Left and Right – the loss of faith in the Enlightenment 'modernist' project (encapsulated in both liberalism and socialism), which held that the world could be fashioned in a better, universal fashion. Against this background, Giddens seeks to chart the way for a 'reflexive' discovery of a new sense of belonging and purpose – a more cautious and pluralistic rediscovery of faith in the ability to make a better world.

Whilst some advocates of the Third Way hold that social democracy is a spent force, Giddens seeks more its renewal. He sees four main points as central to this process. First, Giddens does not accept that globalisation necessarily means a single form of redneck individualist capitalism. Relatively 'egalitarian' (a term he often prefers to the more fashionable but slippery 'inclusion') communities can survive if they guarantee investors social peace and high productivity. Secondly, Giddens argues that there is a need for new thinking about the relationship between state, markets and individuals. Accepting the need to pursue social justice does not necessarily involve state monopolistic provision of benefits and services to ensure this. Thirdly, he holds that there is a need to democratise democracy – at the local, regional, national and international level. And finally, Giddens holds that there is a greater need to face environmental dangers – again reinforcing both the radical and international nature of his agenda.

Giddens points to a series of important issues currently being debated by political thinkers. For instance, what exactly does democracy mean in the context of the European Union's transnational 'multi-level governance'? Can democracy be transposed from the national to the 'cosmopolitan'-international level? However, Giddens's work is often little more than a pot-pourri of bullet points and neologisms. In part this may be explained by his close connection with New Labour policy-making and the quest for soundbites rather than deep thought. Certainly many of Giddens's points have been developed more cogently by the German sociologist Ulrich Beck – who is arguably a more important European influence on serious Third Way thinking – or by the British academic David Held.[11]

Nevertheless, there remain a variety of problems with key aspects of all current Third Way thinking. In particular, the quest for a new sense of community is a double-edged one. The largely middle-class, intellectual advocates of the Third Way seek a new community of inclusion which provides a greater sense of belonging for the poor, ethnic minorities and others (usually within a European framework, although the more utopian works are truly internationalist). The task is unquestionably an important one. But it raises major philosophical problems, for instance over the extent to which the liberal state can legitimately interfere with the lives of non-liberal groups (e.g. Muslims seeking to repress females), and more generally it poses the issue of whether there are limits to 'communal' multiculturalism.

Moreover, in recent years there have been others in society – especially less skilled white males – who feel excluded or threatened by changes such as the loss of job security engendered by globalisation, or their declining status in a world characterised by technological deskilling and growing feminism. This leaves a potential for an anti-Establishment populist rather than a social-democratic Third Way. This would seek to base its identity more on the 'Other', a demonised group of outsiders, especially immigrants. Fellow-Europeans too are clearly beyond the pale for many *Sun* (and other tabloid) readers, but such a populist Third Way would, most plausibly, in an era of globalisation, encompass the idea of 'Fortress Europe' – offering a high level of welfare chauvinism for those (ethnically privileged) who live within its walls.

One of the most academically discussed British political theory works of the 1990s was David Miller's *On Nationality* (1995). Miller, a philosopher with left-wing roots, who had made a notable contribution to the market socialism debate, turned to the defence of nationalism as a kind of meta-ideology which was vital to a whole series of desirable goals – such as redistribution from rich to poor (a process aided by collective identity). Miller was emphatic that he was defending a tolerant form of pluralistic identity. However, his interpretation marks a notable move away from the tendency – especially strong after the horrors of Nazism – to see all forms of nationalist political thought as essentially a mobilising myth lacking a serious intellectual basis. Liberal Welsh and Scottish nationalist theorists, such as Neil MacCormick, produced similar arguments to Miller, seeking to defuse the charge of insular parochialism by linking such nationalism to the wider cause of European Union.

At the turn of the 1990s, a former American State Department official, Francis Fukuyama, published a book entitled *The End of History and the Last Man* (1992), which proclaimed the end of ideology. For Fukuyama, liberalism and democratic capitalism had come to provide the basis of a universal world order. A decade later, it seems clear that whilst a limited new consensus has emerged in some areas of economic policy, many other issues remain unresolved – not least about cultural and national identity. Even in the economic sphere, there remain arguments about the extent to which globalisation constrains the 'nation-state', or regional political groupings like the European Union, from pursuing their own policies and defying a 'McDonaldisation' of the world economy.

Indeed, a crucial issue raised by this chapter generally concerns the power of individuals and ideas ('agency') compared to socio-economic forces ('structure'). This complex question about causality is beyond the scope of an introductory survey. But what can be said by way of conclusion is that political thought since 1945 has helped to define the British political agenda, and especially to legitimise or rule out certain policies. Ultimately, political studies have to explain individual behaviour, something which 'structuralist' approaches alone cannot achieve. Individuals may not always be fully aware of the currents of political thought: but such ideas are crucial to both elite and mass political behaviour.

Notes

1   For an introduction to the concept of ideology, and the main contemporary ideologies, see R. Eatwell and A.W. Wright (eds), *Contemporary Political Ideologies*, Pinter, 2nd ed., London, 1999.

2   It is worth noting that the term 'Third Way' has historically been used in very different contexts, including by fascist intellectuals in the 1920s (neither right nor left), 1950s leaders of non-aligned countries (neither East nor West), etc.

3   On the Labour ideological tradition see A. W. Wright (ed.), *British Socialist Thought from the 1880s to the 1960s*, Longman, London, 1983. See also W. H. Greenleaf, *The British Political Tradition. Volume Two: the Ideological Heritage*, Routledge, London, 1973.

4   For an introduction to the seminal ideas of Keynes, and his wider impact, see R. Skidelsky, *Keynes*, Oxford University Press, Oxford, 1996.

5   For a favourable view of Crosland see D. Leonard (ed.), *Crosland and New Labour*, Macmillan, Basingstoke, 1999.

6   See D. Kavanagh, *Thatcherism and British Politics*, 2nd ed., Oxford University Press, Oxford, 1990, and A. Gamble, *The Free Economy and the Strong State*, 2nd ed., Macmillan, Basingstoke, 1994.

7   On the Conservative ideological tradition see F. O'Gorman (ed.), *British Conservatism: Conservative Thought from Burke to Thatcher*, Longman, London, 1986. See also Greenleaf, *British Political Tradition*.

8   A. Denham and M. Garnett, *British Think-Tanks and the Climate of Opinion*, University College Press, London, 1998.

9   For a sympathetic overview of New Right theorists see D. Green, *The New Right*, Wheatsheaf, Brighton, 1988. For a more critical view of its core economic policies see G. Thompson, *The Political Economy of the New Right*, Pinter, London, 1990.

10 On Hayek see C. Kukathas, *Hayek and Modern Liberalism*, Clarendon Press, Oxford, 1990.

11 See also A. Giddens (ed.), *The Global Third Way Debate*, Polity, Cambridge, 2001.

Further Reading

As well as the more specialised works referred to in the text and notes for this chapter, the following general works should be useful.

A basic survey, stretching well back before 1945, which will help the A-level student or first-year undergraduate, is Ian Adams, *Ideology and Politics in Britain Today* (Manchester University Press, Manchester, 1998). A more advanced survey is Rodney Barker, *Political Ideas in Modern Britain* (2nd ed., Routledge, London, 1998). D. Marquand and A. Seldon (eds), *Ideas that Shaped Post-War Britain* (Fontana, London, 1996) is the most lively guide to specifically post-1945 influences, although its contributors sometimes lapse into advocacy rather than textlike balance. David Marsh et al., *Post-war British Politics in Perspective* (Blackwell, Oxford, 1999), is mainly about interpretations of policy change, but is worth noting as it included discussion of the post-war consensus thesis and the often-neglected issue of the relative importance of individuals and political thought in the policy process.

Chronology

For the sake of brevity this chronology does not list significant changes in party platforms (such as the 1970 Conservative Selsdon Programme, which broke with the post-war 'social democratic consensus'); nor major events – often international in scope – which influenced thought (such as the economic crisis of the mid-1970s).

1945   K. Popper, *The Open Society and Its Enemies*. Key harbinger of anti-collectivist and historicist thought.

1955   Creation of the Institute of Economic Affairs (IEA), pioneer laissez-faire think-tank.

1956   C. A. R. Crosland, *The Future of Socialism*. Key intellectual source for those within the Labour Party who sought to revise Clause IV of the party's Constitution (committing the party to state ownership).

1958   Sir Isaiah Berlin, 'Two Concepts of Liberty'. Seminal statement of liberal philosophy.

1960   Launch of *New Left Review*, bringing together ex-Communists and radical socialists.
       F. A. Hayek, *The Constitution of Liberty*. Together with his *The Road to Serfdom* (1944), a highly influential critique of the 'big' state.

1962   M. Oakeshott, *Rationalism in Politics*. Key statement of pragmatic, traditionalist conservatism.

1971   G. Greer, *The Female Eunuch*. Best-selling radical academic feminist tract.
       E. Powell, *The Common Market: The Case Against*. The most articulate of the Conservative MP Euro-sceptics (and fervent prophet of the free market).
       J. Rawls, *A Theory of Justice*. Seminal (American) academic work which influenced centre-left thinking.
       N. Thomas, *The Welsh Extremist*. A socialist example of the new wave of nationalist thinking.

1973   E. F. Schumacher, *Small Is Beautiful*. Early example of the rise of ecological thought.

1977   T. Nairn, *The Break-up of Britain*. Left-wing academic critic of the British unitary state.

1979   A. Benn, *Arguments for Socialism?* Key turn of the 1980s statement of Labour left views.

1980   R. Scruton, *The Meaning of Conservatism*. Notable academic restatement of traditionalist conservatism.

1993   A. Etzioni, *The Spirit of Community*. Influential (American) communitarian theorist.

1995   W. Hutton, *The State We're In*. Best-selling journalistic compilation of 1990s centre-left thinking.
       D. Miller, *On Nationality*. Academically much-discussed defence of liberal nationalism.

1997   J. Gray, *Endgames: Questions in Late Modern Political Thought*. Important thinker travels from New Right to New Labour.

1998   A. Giddens, *The Third Way*. Key, albeit lightweight, guide to recent centre-left thought from prolific sociological theorist.

9 The Civil Service

Keith Dowding

The civil service is the non-military administration of the central state. It has performed a central role in the governance of Britain since 1945 and long before. In terms of production, the state machinery provides management of the economy, including maintaining the peace internally and externally. In terms of consumption, the state provides for redistribution within the economy through social insurance, health, education and welfare. Part of the public administration of the state is undertaken directly through central state machinery; in other areas the central machinery oversees provision made by other actors. Government uses instruments to take in information to decide what is necessary ('detectors') and other tools to implement their policies ('effectors') (Hood, 1983).

According to Christopher Hood, government uses four basic resources: nodality – its position in the centre of the information and political network; treasure – the money raised to pay for its activities; authority – its legal and official power; and organisation – the arrangement of personnel manning its administration, of which the civil service is a major component. Since 1945 all aspects of these resources have changed somewhat. Whilst the legal and official power of the British government has expanded as further functions have been drawn to it, some legal authority and official powers have shifted to the European Union (and to a much lesser extent, other international bodies). The Treasury has been a major preoccupation in the post-war period as British governments have tried to contain public expenditure even as the scope of the state increased. As part of that strategy, governments have continually questioned the role and organisation of government and examined the staffing and efficiency of the civil service. The way in which the civil service is organised is one concern, the quality and technical capacity of its servants another. Until the mid-1980s most of the changes may be viewed as fiddling at the edges. More recently, however, the civil service has undergone a radical overhaul, partly as a result of new ideas, which may be seen as combining an ideological movement in the views of the political elite and a global shift reflecting broader changes in informational and managerial technology.

At the end of the Second World War there were some 1.1 million civil servants in Britain. They were vital in the British war effort, leading Hennessy (1989, p. 88) to describe this effort as *'the* high point of achievement in the history of the British Civil Service'. If true, then this chapter would be a history of decline. But this would be to misunderstand the nature of the wartime administrative structure and what politicians and civil servants have been trying to achieve in the civil service since then. It is certainly true that the British administrative war machine was formidable. The war effort was directed at getting results – what in modern parlance is called effectiveness. It was not about achieving results efficiently: that is, providing those results at lowest cost. No one could claim that the British war effort was efficient. Even during the war its efficiency was questioned by the press and by Parliament, but these criticisms were directed more at ensuring the best results were achieved, and less at whether those results could be achieved at lower cost. The exigencies of total war do not allow us to worry too much whether the best means were used for some result. All that matters is that the right result is achieved. The post-war history of the civil service can be seen as the attempt to achieve efficiency, to curtail costs, to review management, and all at a time of ever-increasing regulation of society.

Attlee's government swiftly cut the number of civil servants by 33 per cent to 740,000 by 1951. This was not as easy to achieve as might be thought. Whilst many war-related activities were being wound down, Attlee's government was introducing a raft of policies for the new welfare state it was in the process of creating. This involved a new administrative machinery or 'clerical factories', such as National Insurance offices in Newcastle. This period saw a geographical shift of the civil service from London to the provinces; by the end of the 1950s less than a third of non-industrial civil servants worked in London. The Attlee government abolished the marriage bar, allowing married women to work in the civil service, and the civil service introduced equal pay for women in 1955 (in non-industrial grades), 15 years before the Equal Pay Act tried to enforce some occupational equity. But the post-war reconstruction saw few changes in the administrative structure beyond the changing departmental architecture and a restructuring of the technical and scientific classes. There were many who argued for a radical overhaul of the civil service, but Attlee and his ministers seemed content with the organisation they had inherited. Sir Edward Bridges, Secretary to the Cabinet (1938–46) and Permanent Secretary to the Treasury and Head of the Civil Service (1945–56), was very conservative and intent on keeping the service much as it had been pre-war. He argued that the civil service had little to learn from business, and an internal review conducted between October 1946 and July 1947 produced no suggestions for anything other than tweaking.

There were two main problems with the senior civil service at this time. First there was a lack of expertise. It was not that there was no one with experience – there were plenty – but they were not trained in the types of jobs that were required. During the war years many experts had been drafted into the civil service. These so-called irregulars went back to their civilian jobs after the war. For example, in 1944 the Treasury had economists of the calibre of John Maynard Keynes, Hubert Henderson and Dennis Robertson, whilst Lionel Robbins was in the Economic Section of the Cabinet Office. By 1947 the Treasury had no one with economic training on its staff! Whilst the technical and scientific staffs were reorganised at this time, the service already saw such staff, as indeed did British industry, as secondary to their generalist administrators. It was clear that in peacetime the 'irregular army' of professional, scientific and technical advisers would not remain in permanent civil service positions, but the opportunity was clearly lost by the conservative, self-interested, elitist and self-confident senior civil service to introduce a set of expert policy advisers to guide government based on something approaching expert knowledge. It is difficult to judge what this amateur upper-class arrogance cost Britain over the next 40 years, but it certainly did not help.

Little changed with the incoming Conservative administration of Churchill in 1951, despite manifesto promises to simplify the administrative machinery, cut costs and bring about a more efficient bureaucracy. It did set up a Royal Commission on the Civil Service (which produced the Priestley Report), but its scope of inquiry was limited to pay and conditions. These issues seemed important in the 1950s when full employment meant that civil service job security, pay and pension schemes did not look as attractive as during the high unemployment of the inter-war period. Many of the report's recommendations were in fact implemented over the next few years, including the most important recommendation that civil service pay should be comparable with remuneration in the private sector. The aim of the Priestley Report was to take civil service pay out of political controversy, but it did not address the key question of whether governments would always be prepared to match civil service pay to that of comparable work in the private sector.

The Conservative government was determined to cut civil service numbers. This proved more difficult than the incoming government had anticipated, but nevertheless the non-industrial civil service was reduced by 39,000, from 425,000 to 386,000. The industrial civil service, however, peaked in this period at 347,000. In 1956 Prime Minister Anthony Eden announced that he had asked his Chancellor, Harold Macmillan, to review the civil service and to cut further. The Suez crisis intervened, and whilst small cuts were made there were no serious inroads into civil service numbers. If the Second World War had been a high point in the history of the British civil service, the Suez crisis was a low point. Many senior civil servants were appalled at the actions of the government and felt excluded from decision-making circles. The mindset of the senior civil service may have been fixed at this time. Many senior elites among the 'mandarinate' came to see their job as managing the decline of Britain as a major world power.

The incoming 1964 Labour government of Harold Wilson advocated reforms throughout society, placing emphasis on technocratic solutions. This included the belief that the civil service needed to be reformed to take on more of a planning role and become more managerial. In fact, the emphasis on management perhaps emerged prior to Wilson's taking power and can be seen both in the setting up of the National Economic Development Council (NEDC) under Macmillan in 1961 and also in that year, the Plowden Report. It recommended

Table 9.1 Civil servant numbers in the UK, 1797–1998

Year	Number
1797	16,267
1815	24,598
1832	21,305
1861	31,947
1881	50,859
1901	116,413
1911	172,352
1914	280,900
1922	317,721
1939	347,000
1944	1,164,000
1950	746,000
1960	643,000
1970	701,000
1979	732,000
1988	436,232
1991	413,664
1995	400,754
1998	359,103

Source: G. Drewry and T. Butcher, *The Civil Service Today*, Oxford, 1988 p. 48. Civil Service Statistics 1988, 1991, 1995, 1998.

new procedures for planning and managing public spending. The general feeling at the end of the 1950s was that the civil service suffered from short-termism and a lack of coordination across departments. Indeed, this criticism has been echoed throughout the post-war period. During the 1960s the public expenditure survey (PESC) was developed which placed emphasis on planning over five-year periods, the so-called medium term. Other changes at this time included the creation of larger departments, notably the Ministry of Defence with 111,000 staff. Wilson's 1964–70 governments also saw the creation of the Department of Economic Affairs, the Ministry of Overseas Development, the Ministry of Technology and the Welsh Office, as well as a Ministry of Land and Natural Resources. Most of Wilson's machinery of government changes were due to the need to give departments to his increasingly fractious ministers. But the most important thing that happened to the civil service in the 1960s was something that did not happen to it: the recommendations in the Fulton Report of 1968.

Wilson set in train the Fulton Inquiry in 1966 whose brief was to 'examine the structure, recruitment and management, including training, of the Home Civil Service'. The Fulton Report notoriously castigated the civil service as 'amateur', fomenting controversy which diverted attention from its 158 recommendations, many of which were uncontroversial. Essentially Fulton believed in a large civil service, with large departments headed by mandarins with managerial skills and the advice of experts. He wanted to encourage the entry of more specialists such as economists and scientists into the service, recommending that preference be given to applicants with 'relevant' degrees, and suggested that specialists should be given more encouragement to make it to the top of the hierarchy. He proposed more and better training, and a Civil Service College to train administrators in management. He recommended widening graduate entry to correct the Oxbridge imbalance. Fulton wanted to see greater mobility between the private sector and the civil service. He also noted the complex grading systems in different departments which made it difficult to transfer from one to another. There were 47 general classes across the service and over 1,400 departmental classes. Fulton recommended a uniform grading structure covering all civil servants.

Many of these recommendations were never fully implemented. Favouring relevant degrees was rejected. The Civil Service College was set up, but rather than being a centre of excellence with high-grade research scholars teaching high-level analysis, it became a centre for short courses staffed by non-researchers, while training was still dominated by individual departments. In many ways 'on-the-job' training is best done in departments, but what has been missing from the senior civil service through the post-war period has been personnel with research degrees. In comparison with the senior bureaucracy in North America, Australasia, and most of Western Europe, the top levels of the civil service are short of Ph.D.s and thus lacking in understanding of the nature of research and evidence. Whilst some rationalisation of grading systems occurred and there has been greater mobility between the private sector and the civil service, nothing like a unified grading structure ever came into being. Whilst the percentage of Oxbridge entrants did decline during the 1970s, Oxbridge still dominates (with around 50 per cent in the top ranks of the 'open structure'). Other recommendations, such as hiving off certain departmental functions and making management more accountable, had little impact at the time. All in all, the Fulton Report was perceived to be a failure. It was overlong, poorly written and, since its execution was left in the hands of those whom it criticised, implemented patchily and without conviction (Kellner and Crowther-Hunt, 1980, Chapters 4 and 5).

The Civil Service Department (CSD) was created in November 1968 from the pay and management side of the Treasury (which opposed this split and regained the role in 1981). The CSD's failure to implement Fulton more fully was due to its limited powers being able only to advise departments on efficiency issues. Splitting the employment and capital expenditure responsibilities from more general public expenditure issues at the Treasury did not aid efficiency. Departments would fight one battle over policy with the Treasury and then fight the CSD for the instruments to carry them out. In practice the same issues were discussed over and again. The CSD had some success with 'management by objective' – a fashionable management tool of the 1960s – and some privatising of agencies occurred, but in retrospect these were just tinkerings. Heath amalgamated some departments to create super-departments to enable greater strategic thinking across issue-areas, but these were perceived to be a failure. Like Wilson's, Heath's carving up of responsibilities across departments depended upon the Prime Minister's need to satisfy the demands of powerful Cabinet colleagues.

Later commentators have been less critical of the Fulton Report (Fry, 1993). It provided the starting point for most discussions of the ills of the civil service until the advent of a Prime Minister, Margaret Thatcher, who believed in action rather than talk, and began to introduce change without much discussion. By the 1980s and 1990s, moreover, the junior civil servants of the 1960s and 1970s, who had tended to support Fulton, were now senior mandarins much more willing to oversee reform.

The major effect of Heath's government on the civil service was long-term: the entry of Britain into the Common Market in 1973. This gave the mandarinate a new focus post-empire, and gradually changed the career structure and pecking order of departments as the Foreign and Commonwealth Office (FCO), in charge of relations with the Common Market as it progressed towards the European Union, became involved with policies outside its traditional domain.

The European Community (EC) has had a major effect upon the running of the British civil service. Its own bureaucracy was always small: numbers have never gone much over 12,000, distributed amongst 23 Directorates-General (DG) or 'departments'. There are also various other units, such as the Euratom Supply Agency, the Legal Service, and the 'Spokesman's Group' (or Press Office) which helps service the DGs and other aspects of Community business. The majority of the British national 'Eurocrats' have come from Whitehall, though some have entered the service from outside government altogether. These Eurocrats work closely with civil servants from the member states and serve as the main focus of pressure-group activity and outside professional advice.

Entry into Europe made a greater difference to some departments than others. With the great importance, or rather cost, of the Common Agricultural Policy, the Ministry of Agriculture greatly increased its workload and became more powerful. Whilst Britain, by and large, has lost autonomy over agricultural policy, being forced, often reluctantly, into policies against its instincts, the Ministry of Agriculture has become more autonomous. Other departments whose workload has increased considerably include the departments of Trade and Industry, Environment and the Treasury.

In the mid-1980s the Treasury introduced new controls to stem the enthusiasm of other departments for EC spending. These controls, called EUROPES (pronounced 'Euro Pez'), involved a trade-off for a department of its overall budget, given any EC spending on programmes under its control. EUROPES means that the first consideration of any British department is to try to keep the costs of EC programmes down, thereby doing the Treasury's job in Europe for them. Secondly, it has decreased Whitehall enthusiasm for the EC, given that civil servants' own pet schemes may have to be casualties of the Commissioners' pet schemes. Thirdly, it means that sometimes, no department wishes to be the 'lead' department on issues that do not obviously come under its own sphere of influence.

Because no special 'Department of European Affairs' was created, no champion of Europe nor target of discontent could be set up, and the coordination of European affairs has been carried out through the normal interdepartmental channels, using the services of the Cabinet Office. In this way the collective responsibility of government for EC affairs has been assured. The European Secretariat within the Cabinet Office provides the main civil service back-up for Cabinet committees on matters pertaining to the European Union. It is more than a body merely reviewing initiatives emanating from the Commission and other parts of Whitehall. It convenes meetings where it believes coordination is necessary. It tries to ensure departments are aware of the implications of their negotiations and of decisions being taken in other parts of the civil service. Three bureaucratic aspects of this central coordination role are important: (1) the United Kingdom has a policy on all EC matters, (2) these policies remain consistent with the broader objectives of the government, and (3) these policies are implemented in practice. The second of these bureaucratic objectives hints at the important political aspect of the European Secretariat's role: ensuring the Prime Minister remains the key actor. Without the European Secretariat at the centre, the FCO would have powers well beyond those of any other department, with the exception of the Treasury, and the Foreign Secretary would be the most important job apart from the Prime Minister.

The Office of the United Kingdom's Permanent Representative to the European Communities (known as UKRep) provides the representation for Britain on the Committee of Permanent Representatives (COREPER, which services the Council of Ministers) and the European Council. British representation on Council working groups may come from Whitehall but will always have assistance and advice from UKRep and usually representatives as well, even if they are junior to the Whitehall officials. Generally speaking, UKRep also provides the negotiators for these working groups, for they tend to have the specialised knowledge required for detailed EC negotiations. UKRep keeps in constant contact with Whitehall through the FCO EC Departments.

The second major function of UKRep is to ensure that it always maintains contact with the Commission, the Presidency, and other Permanent Representations within the Community. By keeping in constant contact with the Commission, UKRep tries to influence its policies and ideas. In this way UKRep operates much as a pressure group upon the Commission. It tries to discover what proposals the Commission is likely to take up, and to influence its ideas in ways advantageous to Britain. It tries to ensure that where Britain has potentially breached EC law some form of accommodation can be reached without recourse to the European Court. Similarly the Commission will try to discover what policies are likely to emanate from Britain. Part of UKRep's role is to inform the Commission about the policy proposals of the British government. UKRep has the major job of trying to discover what is happening in the other nations' Offices of Permanent Representatives to strengthen the bargaining position of Britain. It tries to build alliances with the other Representatives against the Commission.

Thirdly, UKRep provides advice to civil servants back in Whitehall and thereby to government ministers. Policy is officially formulated and coordinated in Whitehall but UKRep can influence decisions through its expertise on matters pertaining to Europe. It will be aware of what is and is not possible within Community regulations and have a good idea of what is likely to be non-negotiable with other member nations. Officials from UKRep regularly attend meetings in Whitehall, as many Whitehall officials regularly attend meetings in Brussels.

Fourthly, UKRep is the centre of a network of pressure groups trying to influence both British and EC policy. The relationship between these groups and the civil service is often close and each side uses the other to its own advantage. Lobbying in Britain is rather different from other EC nations, since Britain is a far more centralised state in which the bureaucracy is the key actor. Brussels has a more complex institutional structure and thus for lobbyists poses strategic problems similar to those faced in other EC nations. This causes some difficulties for British pressure groups used to the simpler symbiotic relationship which exists in Britain. As a result UKRep has become the European key for many British pressure groups – a source of both information and hope. UKRep has special facilities for helping British firms make the best of opportunities under EC programmes. This strengthens the hand of British civil servants and allows them to play the 'British interests' card in much the manner they please, sometimes advising British pressure groups on tactics.

Europe has provided both an opportunity and a threat to the civil service. It offers the opportunity for individual civil servants and Whitehall departments to use the authority and power of the EC to expand their own sphere of influence. Dealing with Brussels is time-consuming and complex and broadens the policy network in which civil servants operate. It is difficult for politicians, both ministers and other parliamentarians, to oversee this work, though the opportunity for autonomous action should not be overstated. The tradition of the British civil service is for bureaucrats to work within the political constraints and policy decisions made at the highest levels. Civil servants from Britain tend to consult with their political masters far more often than their counterparts from other EC nations. Nevertheless the EC has provided a big opportunity for departments to alter the map of influence in Whitehall.

During the 1970s there were changes in the grading structures of the civil service, but the principal targets of the would-be reformers remained largely unscathed. The three grades of 'administrative class' and equivalent specialist grades of the civil service were renamed the 'open structure', with a unified grading system for the 700–800 officials. An administrative group of around 200,000 people was created in January 1971 and in September of that year a 'science group' was formed. Further restructuring of the grading system went on throughout the 1970s but these changes did not create a unified service-wide structure. Whilst the top of the Whitehall structure was open in principle to the best people from any category, in practice it was far from open. When Labour returned to government in 1974 it showed little interest in further unifying the grades, and it was some surprise when Thatcher's government unified the grades down a further two levels in 1984 and 1986. But this move was soon swamped by the radical, almost revolutionary changes in the structure of the civil service which started from 1988 under the name 'Next Steps'.

One view of the civil service since 1945 is that nothing much happened until 1988 when a revolution started. But revolutions do not arrive without a history, and the tinkerings and experiences of politicians and bureaucrats prior to 1988 were important for the success of the changes initiated under Thatcher's government.

The truly radical administrative reforms of the Thatcher government did not start until 1988, after she had won her third term of office. This in itself is not without significance. Many premiers, including Wilson and Heath, had considered civil service reform important, but their attention was diverted to other issues before the reforms got under way. Had Thatcher not lasted as long as she had (and it should not be forgotten that pre-Falklands she was perceived as weak), much the same might have happened in the 1980s. The reform programme that was started built up enough momentum to continue not only under her Conservative successor, John Major, but also under Labour's Tony Blair. The precursor of those changes includes not only the Fulton Report of 1968 and its popular interpretation (Kellner and Crowther-Hunt, 1980), but just as importantly a public attitude towards the civil service which had formed over the years from popular films such as *Carlton-Browne of the FO*, books such as C. P. Snow's *The Corridors of Power*, the TV series *Yes Minister* and *Yes Prime Minister*, the popular critiques of civil service waste by Chapman (Chapman, 1978; 1982), and memoirs of Labour ministers such as Crossman, Benn and Castle. These drew a picture of the civil service as old-fashioned, inefficient and self-serving rather than benefiting their political masters or the public. In fact this view fitted perfectly Margaret Thatcher's own outlook, deriving from her time as a junior minister (Hennessy, 1989, pp. 592, 630).

Thatcher could not move as fast as she would have liked. In some ways, her views on the senior civil service were altered by the effective manner in which the Falklands War was organised, but her first move was to set up under Sir Derek (now Lord) Rayner a small unit of around six civil servants based in her Private Office. The Rayner scrutinies started a process which led to the creation of the Financial Management Unit (FMU), later the Joint Management Unit (JMU), the Financial Management Initiative (FMI) and, finally, the programme of budgetary devolution and agency creation usually referred to as the Next Steps initiative, after the title of the report written under the tutelage of Rayner's successor Sir Robin (now Lord) Ibbs (Jenkins, Caine and Jackson, 1988).

The Rayner scrutinies involved small teams sent to examine a department for three months, come up with suggestions for savings, and ensure that these were implemented within 12 months. In the first 6 years a total of 26 reviews were completed, identifying annual savings of around £600 million, with a further £67 million in one-off savings. Many of the savings were trivial in themselves, but together mounted considerably. By the end of the Rayner scrutinies in 1986 over £950 million of savings were identified against only £5 million of costs. However, many critics have argued that the identified savings were often not carried out and overall savings of 6 per cent are relatively small. Nevertheless, these scrutinies were stopping the type of waste that Chapman identified. But they did not make the types of savings nor cut the size of the state in the manner the government required. How successful they really were depends upon one's views of the true scale of 'waste' in the civil service at that time.

The success of the Rayner scrutinies in different departments depended largely upon the enthusiasm of the Permanent Secretary or the Minister. One of the most enthusiastic ministers was Michael Heseltine at the Department of the Environment (DoE). Following a Rayner scrutiny, the DoE introduced a managerial system known as the Management Information System for Ministers (MINIS). MINIS was supposed to let ministers know what was happening and who was responsible for it. Related to this was the Financial Management Initiative (FMI), which was the natural continuation of the Rayner scrutinies. Its aim was to produce a system which gave managers at all levels greater responsibility and control. Each manager should have a clear idea of his or her objectives which would be developed under specific priorities. All did so, but the objectives are often exceedingly vague. Departments found it much easier to establish objectives for administrative costs – which make up on average 13 per cent of total costs – than for the bulk of their programme costs.

The FMU – which later became the JMU – was set up by the Management and Personnel Office (MPO) and the Treasury in 1982 to help all 21 departments examine all aspects of their work and develop programmes to improve financial management. Departments followed the lead of the DoE and set up management systems. Twenty-one departments did so, producing sixteen different management systems somewhat mitigating their purpose. In 1988, under the supervision of Sir Robin Ibbs, the efficiency unit produced a document, *Improving Management in Government: The Next Steps* (Jenkins, Caine and Jackson, 1988). It took the idea of new management in the civil service further than FMI and sketched out the idea of creating agencies to implement government policies. The major thrust of *Next Steps* was the break-up of the unified civil service. The uniformity of pay structure and grading, and the nature of civil servants were changed and a two-tier civil service created with a policy-making core and a policy-implementing periphery. The latter are hived off into agencies. The core is designed to provide a policy-making service for ministers and to manage the department, which then contracts out policy implementation to agencies employing their own staff. Largely to allay the fears of staff, it was at first claimed that agency staff would remain as civil servants. However, as *Next Steps* gathered pace, some agencies were effectively moved to the private sector, some remained within the civil service, and others an uncertain status, much like the proliferating quasi-public agencies which provided government services within the remit of health and welfare within the former province of local government.

The agencies can hire and fire their own staff, allowing for more flexible pay rates and work conditions. Thus agencies can pay wages at the local rate where their offices are situated, and can pay higher salaries and have bonus schemes for senior management to match the spiralling salaries of the private sector. Each agency signs a 'framework agreement' which states the services they are to provide and the financial issues governing their relationship with their 'parent' department. At first the Treasury feared the control given to employment conditions, but it has since realised that the term 'flexible pay rates' has generally meant lower wages for junior staff with high remuneration for chief executives and senior management, bringing overall savings.

Sir Robin Butler claimed the agency process would create a civil service 'unified but not uniform' – a typical piece of 'mandarinese' nonsense. During the 1990s the term 'civil servant' has conveyed a widening variety of contracts, pay scales, negotiating rights, pension schemes, job structures and prospects. Previously, the civil service was unified by at least a salary structure and common negotiating and pension rights, embodying the notion of the state as the ideal employer.

However today there is not much to the idea of a unified civil service other than the fact that it is the agent of the government, paid for by the government, doing what the government wants it to do. There are other non-governmental agencies which carry out tasks for the government. In the case of agriculture, for example, much of the policing and care of standards is carried out by the National Farmers' Union (NFU) rather than civil servants, but that does not make the NFU part of the public sector. Charities carry out functions for people who have no choice and do not pay; like governments, they fill in where market failure occurs. Some charities receive government money for services they provide, having been drawn into that provision as government has cut public expenditure. But that does not unite them to the public sector. Indeed, whilst once figures for civil service personnel (together with local government employees) may have given some reckoning to the overall size of the state, such figures are now meaningless in this regard. Many workers are now employed in the private sector, but carrying out public-sector functions through a contracting-out process, and whose remuneration depends upon money raised through the tax system. The only unifying feature of the agency system is that they are accountable through the Minister to Parliament. Even this is a clouded issue, as chief executives appear before parliamentary committees. Table 9.2 shows the growth of agencies both in terms of numbers and their staffing. There were 120 separate agencies by the end of 1998 (see table 9.2). Whilst most of the agency chief executives come from a civil service background, few conform to the 'generalist' origin of most permanent secretaries, and over a quarter have been appointed from outside the civil service.

Peter Kemp was appointed the *Next Steps* project manager the day the Ibbs Report was published, reporting directly to the Prime Minister. He was a genuine enthusiast for the *Next Steps* programme and deserves recognition for its success. *Next Steps*, whilst initially viewed with suspicion by senior civil servants and some ministers, soon appealed to them. The top and middle-rank officials quickly realised that it had the potential to remove responsibilities for operational details from them, freeing them to concentrate on strategic policy. Indeed, despite the radical nature of the change, there were relatively few critics, with the Commons Treasury and Civil Service Committee and Opposition generally approving. The only doubts expressed were over the line of accountability from administrative functions through ministers to Parliament.

Ibbs was replaced by Angus Fraser just after the *Next Steps* Report suggested that the agency programme was not compatible with a unified civil service. The Fraser Report of 1991 suggested that core departments needed to reconsider their traditional roles and delegate more financial and managerial responsibility. After the 1992 election the Next Steps Project Office and Efficiency Unit was brought into the new Office of Public Service and Science, still within the Cabinet Office. Kemp was forced to resign, probably because ministers wanted to

Table 9.2   Staff numbers in executive agencies, UK, 1991–1998

	1 April 1991	1 April 1995	1 April 1998
Non-industrial	166,677	251,060	256,963
Industrial	10,727	15,588	20,518
All staff	**177,404**	**266,648**	**177,481**
Executive agencies	**48**	**105**	**115**

Source: Civil Service statistics, 1991, 1995, 1998.

start a programme of privatisation that Kemp had repeatedly denied would occur. The White Paper *Competing for Quality* published in 1991 advocated 'market testing' and 'contracting out'. Departments had market tested 30 per cent of their work between 1992 and 1994, covering £2 billion of activity. In many ways this was a new direction from Next Steps. Chief executives of agencies had signed contracts with core departments to deliver services according to some specifications, but had been left free to manage those contracts as they saw fit. Now they were being required to see if the private sector could do their work more cheaply. Sometimes agencies were given the option of submitting in-house but only if they left the service in the event of their winning the contract.

Between 1991 and 1996 the pay and grading aspects of the civil service below senior levels was delegated to departments and agencies, further weakening the unified civil service. The senior civil service has written contracts and individually determined pay. A further change has occurred in core departments, with a move away from traditional cash accounting systems to Resource Accounting and Budgeting. Following the lead of the New Zealand civil service, this introduces accrual accounting techniques which integrate capital and current spending in a more 'businesslike' manner.

Paradoxically, one of the areas in which contracting out has been most rife is that in which Hood's concept of 'nodality' – being at the centre of an information network – is important. In some ways, the public administration of a state can be seen as the gathering and using of information (Dowding, 2000). The new managerial changes within the civil service at the end of the twentieth century may be typified, and in part created, by the radical changes in methods of information technology, and at the end of the century the private sector has been most adept at developing and using this technology. When the Attlee government created the welfare state in 1945, it set in train the requirement for ever-increasing amounts of information-gathering about the British people. At the same time Alan Turing, himself an important 'irregular' in British intelligence in the wartime years, was laying out the principles for the binary computer which was to revolutionise state capacity for holding and using information. Today the Police National Computer, Criminal Records, Vehicle Licensing, Social Security, MI5 and the Inland Revenue Computer are the major systems holding data about Britons. But at the beginning of the twenty-first century that expertise about information-holding is moving from directly paid agents of the state to private companies. Whereas in the 1950s the civil service was at the forefront of information technology use and expertise, today it is contracting out much of its capacity to multinational companies. It may have the central use of this information, but the nodal point of collection may no longer reside in Britain, let alone in Whitehall.

In the late 1950s the British government was one of the most experienced computer users outside the university sector. In 1959 the Department of Health and Social Security (DHSS, now DSS) developed huge computer systems to deal with different welfare benefits. By the end of the 1970s this system was outdated. In 1977 they planned a complete revamp under an 'Operational Strategy' for a three-tier system combining some of the advantages of centralisation together with decentralisation. The Operational Strategy had three aims: a better service to the public with fewer errors, efficiency in reducing staff numbers, and providing a more satisfying job for staff. But the planning and implementation of this strategy was flawed from the start. Despite the opportunities provided by new-generation computer systems, the mindset of planners remained resolutely sectional. Even within the DHSS different systems were used for income support and pensions – meaning that operators had to log off one system to use another when dealing with the same person. When the Benefits Agency was launched in April 1991 it too developed a new computer strategy, but the expected time and money savings did not accrue; the administration of the Social Fund cost a staggering 60 per cent of the amount paid out in benefits.

Fewer problems occurred in the other major departmental computer user, the Inland Revenue. From the 1970s the Inland Revenue largely used in-house staff for information technology (IT) but supplemented them with consultants or contract staff. Its links became so close that in the late 1980s the National Audit Office reported that the Revenue was dependent upon consultancy firms. Following the 1991 *Competing for Quality* White Paper the Revenue contracted out more and more work, outsourcing its entire IT operations to Electronic Data Systems (EDS). It is now entirely dependent upon that firm.

Today, much of the British state's major information-gathering is contracted out, with over 50 per cent to EDS, the largest information-processing company in the world with a global turnover of $8500 million, employing over 4,000 staff in Britain. EDS has contracts for Drivers, Vehicles and Operators Information Technology (DVOIT), the Inland Revenue, the DSS, the Home Office and the Ministry of Defence (MoD). Any new computer or information systems desired by the British government will undoubtedly require the advice and co-operation of EDS: witness the Inland Revenue's introduction of self-assessment in 1995. Helen Margetts concludes that the major players in IT in the new century are not likely to be governments (Margetts, 1999).

The outsourcing of this information-gathering and expertise may have unheralded effects upon some of the traditional tenets of British public administration and politics. Parliamentary oversight of the Executive is one of the central planks in the uncodified British Constitution. Individual ministerial responsibility to Parliament has been at the forefront of accountability in British government. Accountability to Parliament has never operated as straightforwardly as is sometime fondly imagined (Dowding, 1995, Chapter 8; Dowding and Kang,

1998), but the changing form of the administrative structure of the central state does have important repercussions. Outside Parliament, professional investigators (the National Audit Office and the Parliamentary Commissioner for Administration) and the system of select committees oversee various domains of policy.

As we enter the twenty-first century with ever-larger numbers of political appointees at the highest levels, with new public management techniques, new technology, contracting out, privatising, and the subsequent loss of state expertise, the civil service may play a less important role. In many ways the civil service is returning to the organisational form it held in the nineteenth century where patronage was rife, and one's political views were important to one's position, many different types of contract and remuneration existed, and wage levels were often tied to output. In that century also many private concerns carried out state roles. That system was reformed, slowly, following the famous Northcote–Trevelyan Report of 1854 which discovered inefficiency and corruption throughout the civil service system. The radical reforms of the late twentieth century were designed to increase efficiency, though there is no evidence that major efficiency gains (as opposed to cost reductions) have occurred, and corruption in state functions is undoubtedly growing. The twenty-first century may well see a new Northcote–Trevelyan and return to the traditions of the British civil service. Alternatively, the growth of the European state may see British civil service traditions replaced by European ones and the continuation of the complex governance system that has evolved. Either way, at the beginning of the twenty-first century we have a very different public administration of the central state than we had 50 years earlier.

References and Further Reading

Chapman, L. (1978) *Your Disobedient Servant*. London.

Chapman, L. (1982) *Waste Away*. London.

Dowding, K. (1995) *The Civil Service*. London and New York.

Dowding, K. (2000) 'Civil Service'. In P. B. Clarke and Joe Foweraker (eds), *Encylopedia of Democratic Thought*. London.

Dowding, K. and Kang, W.-T. (1998) 'Ministerial Resignations 1945–97'. *Public Administration* 76: 411–29.

Fry, G. (1993) *Reforming the Civil Service: The Fulton Committee on the British Home Civil Service 1966–68*. Edinburgh.

Hennessy, P. (1989) *Whitehall*. London.

Hodges, A. (1985) *Alan Turing: The Enigma of Intelligence*. London, 1985.

Hood, C. (1983) *The Tools of Government*. London.

Jenkins, K., Caines, K. and Jackson, A. (1988) *Improving Management in Government: The Next Steps: Report to the Minister*. London.

Kellner, P. and Crowther-Hunt, L. (1980) *Civil Servants: An Inquiry into Britain's Ruling Class*. London.

Margetts, H. (1999) *Information Technology in Government: Britain and America*. London.

Chronology

1945   Election of Attlee government.
1946   Marriage bar for women abolished.
1951   Election of Churchill government.
1955   Priestley Report.
1955   Equal pay for women in civil service (non-industrial grades).
1956   Eden asks Macmillan (Chancellor) to review civil service numbers.
1957   Suez crisis.
1961   Plowden Report. NEDC set up.
1964   Opposition given access to civil servants prior to general election.
1964   Election of Wilson government.
1964   MoD first 'giant department': 111,000 staff.
1964   Beginning of post-war 'irregulars' (Wilson).
1968   Fulton Report.
1968   CSD created (Nov.).
1970   Election of Heath government.
1970   Equal Pay Act.
1970   Heath sets up 'super departments' DoE, Department of Trade and Industry.
1971   PAR set up.
1973   Civil service strike.
1973   UK joins EC.
1974   Election of Wilson's second administration.
1979   Civil service strikes (under Labour).
1979   Election of Thatcher government.
1979   Public Administration Reform (PAR) abolished.
1979   'Rayner scrutinies' started.
1980   MINIS started at DoE.
1981   Civil Service Department abolished (Nov.).
1982   FMI launched.
1983   CPRS abolished.
1984   Extension of unified grading.
1986   Extension of unified grading.
1988   *Next Steps* Report published.
1992   Civil Service Management Functions Act.
1991   Citizens Charter.
1991   *Competing for Quality* Report.
1993   Oughton Report.
1996   New 'Senior Civil Service'.
1997   Election of Blair government.

10 Local Government

Nirmala Rao

Local government has been perhaps the greatest constitutional casualty of the post-war era in Britain. As the war in Europe ended, local authorities were gearing up for a great expansion in their role as partners of the central ministries in the reconstruction drive. While some municipal services were lost to nationalisation, these losses were outweighed by the gains made. New responsibilities in town planning, housing development and education were followed by massive growth in personal social services. In the next quarter-century, this portfolio of local services was developed and extended with continuous central encouragement, to create what, with hindsight, seems the golden age of local government. It was not to last. By the mid-1970s it was clear that the central government was determined to rein in local government expenditure, and bear down upon local authorities' discretion. The bubble of continuous expansion had burst. Thereafter, central control was progressively tightened, culminating in a wave of legislation to restrict local autonomy and relegate local authorities to the periphery of power.

This chapter will trace the growth, development and expansion of local government since 1945. Its focus is not upon the local authorities themselves, but upon the high politics of local government. The central theme is the shifting balance of power between central and local government, and its implications for the role and status of local authorities. Three key issues are chosen to illuminate the changing landscape of sub-national government. Structure and management, finance and functions: each in turn tells its own story of hopes, achievements, disappointments and ultimate reconciliation. But this is not a finished story. For some, the election of the Blair government holds out the prospect of a revitalised local democracy in which local authorities will once again become key players in national political life. Any assessment of their prospects of success can only be made in the light of the overall post-war record.

The Politics of Structure

The nineteenth century laid down the basic structure of local government which survived, with minor amendment, to the 1970s. England and Wales were governed by a system of county, urban and rural districts and (within some rural districts) parish councils. The larger and more important towns and cities, including the fast-growing towns of the industrial revolution, had been granted the status of 'county boroughs' in 1889, and were all-purpose authorities independent of their surrounding counties. Urban expansion, however, undermined the apparent stability of this structure. The growing towns encroached upon the smaller authorities on their periphery, leading to conflict between the county and county borough councils. The more important non-county boroughs sought, and many obtained, promotion to county borough status, further weakening their counties. The Local Government Act, 1926 provided for the promotion to county borough status by means of private act procedure, whereby the individual local authority could promote a Bill in Parliament. However, governments were reluctant to see the number of county boroughs increase further. Meanwhile, these unresolved tensions threatened to tear apart the nineteenth-century settlement.

The wartime reconstruction period, which lasted from 1941 to 1945, provided a foundation for the post-war debates and legislative developments that sought to secure a modern structure of local government, solve the problems left by the Victorian legacy, and put in place a new settlement. The Coalition government set itself the task of wholesale reorganisation to better equip local government for its post-war tasks. An extended, and secret, inquiry was set up under Sir William Jowitt, the Solicitor-General, to review 'the main peacetime problems of local government in England and Wales, in so far as they arise from the existing arrangement of local government areas'. He initially favoured a drastic simplification of the structure but later embarked upon a round of discussions with the local authority associations, leading him to conclude that any change to boundaries should follow an extended and careful case-by-case examination of the need for adjustment. The overriding consideration was to secure the cooperation of the local authorities themselves, who were naturally suspicious that the wartime emergency pattern of regional commissioners might be continued into the post-war world. Their fears had to be allayed, and a consensus forged, if any action were to be feasible. By 1943, support was growing for a Royal Commission to undertake a thorough review of local government structure, but these calls were readily dismissed as an inappropriate diversion of effort during the period of the emergency. Modernisation would have to await the peace.

One of the last acts of the coalition was to publish a White Paper, *Local Government in England and Wales in the Period of Reconstruction*, dismissing wholesale reform, and establishing a Local Government Boundary Commission under Sir Malcolm Trustram Eve to bring about necessary adjustments. The Commission dug its own grave by going far beyond what was expected of it and proposing radical change in the basic structure. Minister of Health Aneurin

Bevan accused it of exceeding its powers and making recommendations without hearing evidence. He blocked its proposals and prevailed upon Attlee to stand it down; in 1949 the defunct Commission was abolished. The underlying problem was that Labour ministers were lukewarm about the Commission model, seeing it as an unwelcome inheritance of the Coalition years. Bevan presented his own proposals to the Cabinet, based on a streamlined system of around 300 'unitary' – or all-purpose – councils with populations ranging from 50,000 to more than a million. The plan had no chance of agreement, and in 1951 Labour left office with hopes of local government reform dashed.

The tensions remained, and the Conservative government faced a wave of potential demands for county borough promotion. As Minister of Housing and Local Government, Harold Macmillan foresaw that reform was possible only by consensus, though the prospects of achieving it seemed remote. It was left to his successor, Duncan Sandys, to seek that consensus through long and patient negotiations with the warring local authority associations. This he achieved in what became known as the *concordat*. In July 1956 Sandys was ready to publish the first of three White Papers, on the structure of local government, reflecting the agreements reached between central and local government. The subsequent Local Government Act, 1958 established a new Local Government Commission under the chairmanship of Sir Henry Hancock to investigate boundary problems, receive representations from local authorities and report to the Minister with recommendations for action, where appropriate. The Commission was also given the power to propose radical change in the five conurbations – excluding London – designated as Special Review Areas. In undertaking its reviews, the Commission was required to 'have in mind...the interests of effective and convenient local government'. In spite of its careful construction, and the prolonged discussions to arrive at mutually acceptable solutions, the 1958 Commission achieved little. Its standing was gravely damaged by ministers rejecting its proposals, while the fate of its plans for the Manchester and Merseyside conurbations demonstrated the difficulty inherent in any attempt at wholesale reform of local government structure. The Commission's work went into abeyance and, like its predecessor, it was to be wound up, in this case by the incoming Wilson government.

The question of Greater London was so complex, and its politics so volatile, that a separate Royal Commission of inquiry was set up in parallel with the Hancock Commission in 1957. Chaired by Sir Edwin Herbert, the Royal Commission took three years of intensive investigation to conclude that a new metropolitan authority, the Council for Greater London, should be established to cover an area of some 8.5 million population. More than a hundred local authorities would be merged to form 52 strong metropolitan boroughs. The Macmillan government reduced this number further to 32, giving them responsibility for the entire education service, with the exception of Inner London, where a special joint education authority (ILEA) was formed. Against ferocious opposition inside and outside Parliament, the government forced through its Bill to bring about the first radical reorganisation of local government since 1888. Perhaps most significant was that the traditional local authority veto on change had been broken. Consensus was no longer a requirement for change.

The 1964–70 Wilson governments, which inherited and implemented the London reorganisation, also marked the beginning of a new era in local government reform. Although civil servants were convinced that the Local Government Commission was the most appropriate vehicle for achieving change, Minister of Housing and Local Government Richard Crossman was determined otherwise. He found the constitutional framework of local government 'obsolete' and looked for new solutions to be applied to the whole country in the shortest possible space of time. For this purpose a new Royal Commission on Local Government in England was established in May 1966 under the chairmanship of Sir John Maud, soon to become Lord Redcliffe-Maud. Three years later the Commission proposed a drastic reduction in the number of authorities, with a single-tier system of 'unitary' authorities for England (outside London), and a powerful two-tier structure for a limited number of metropolitan areas. If implemented, it would be a thorough redrawing of the map.

The Labour government welcomed the proposals in a 1970 White Paper, but lost the ensuing general election before it was able to progress with them. Conservatives looked for something very different from local government reform. Peter Walker rejected the Commission's proposals, dismissed his civil servants' advice, and wrote his own White Paper. His new structure, established in the Local Government Act, 1972, was based on a uniform two-tier system of counties and districts for non-metropolitan England, preserving as much as possible of the then-existing system, but merging many small authorities and abolishing county boroughs. In the larger conurbations, seven Greates London Council (GLC)-type metropolitan county councils, together with 36 boroughs, were established. Overall, nearly 1,000 smaller authorities were reduced to fewer than 300.

Meanwhile, Wales had been treated separately, with its own Local Government Commission established under the 1958 Act. Although the Welsh Commission made a number of proposals for rationalising Welsh local government, Labour's newly-established Welsh Office undertook its own process of consultation in 1964, producing a new framework based, as in England, on a sharp reduction in the number of authorities, and on the demotion of county boroughs to district status. These changes, too, were incorporated in the 1972 Act.

The desire to create a stable local government structure which would meet the needs of the late twentieth century had driven successive governments down the road of imposed change. However, if the weakness of the *concordat* had been that insistence on consensus ruled out radical change, the weakness of the imposed system was that it reflected no widespread commitment to change. Within few years, the provincial ex-county boroughs were lobbying hard to regain their status under a scheme for 'organic change'. 'We are a great city,' complained one, 'and we'll always be so and, whatever the local government institutions, it is imperative that we should be able to talk to the county on equal terms. . . . If you can't do that, you might as well have parish council status.' In January 1979, the Labour government published a White Paper favouring the promotion of former county boroughs – it had Bristol, Norwich, Leicester Nottingham, among others, in mind – while leaving many details still unresolved. Two months later the government fell.

Margaret Thatcher's own approach to local government reform paid scant attention to structure other than wanting to remove the metropolitan authorities, which, together with the GLC, were abolished in 1986. Like Mrs Thatcher, many Conservatives had come to favour the unitary system as providing clearer accountability, relating local government structure more closely to local communities, increasing public interest in local affairs, and making for more responsible and representative local government:

> People can identify one authority which secures services in their area. Having a single tier should reduce bureaucracy and improve the coordination of services, increasing quality and reducing costs.... Such a structure is also important for proper financial accountability on the part of local authorities to local tax-payers: people must know who's responsible for setting a budget and achieving value for money in services in their area and how the size of their local tax bills relates to what is spent on local public services. (*Department of the Environment, Local Government Review: The Structure of Local Government in England: A Consultation Paper*, London, DoE, 1991)

The Major government established a new Local Government Commission, initially under the chairmanship of Sir John Banham, to simplify the structure outside the metropolitan areas with a pattern of unitary authorities. Unlike all previous reforms of the system, this was intended to be flexible and responsive, providing a structure 'which best matches the particular circumstances of each area'. The Commission worked across England with a phased review in five tranches, tackling such obvious anomalies as the Isle of Wight and the artificial counties of Humberside, Avon and Cleveland first, before moving on to local hearings elsewhere. The Commission was enjoined to take into account local loyalties and opinions before making recommendations to the Secretary of State. Yet the Major government's aspiration to introduce a pattern of unitary authorities across England could hardly be realised under such a locally responsive process. The end result was modest, with just 46 unitaries created by 1998, when the review was completed. Nevertheless, the unitary principle was uniformly applied to Wales – without the impediment of a Commission – in the reorganisation of 1996.

One expected outcome of creating larger authorities was that they would prove more attractive to a particular class of potential councillor: able, educated and with the management skills required to run large organisations with expanding programmes. A corollary of structural change was, then, the recasting of the internal decision-making system of local authorities along business lines to provide further inducements to the 'best men'. The problem of attracting men of 'calibre' persisted throughout the post-war period and, for many commentators, the root of the problem lay in the traditional committee system of local government.

The ways in which decisions are made in local authorities also originated in the nineteenth century. The council has always been the ultimate authority, with much of its work carried out in committees established for separate services (social services, housing, planning), or for overall corporate purposes such as finance or policy. Many committees spawn subcommittees to deal with more detailed issues, leading to a complex – and at times cumbersome – decision process. Powers may also be delegated to officers, but not to councillors. It has long been argued that such a system is slow, ineffective and inefficient, leading to delays, bureaucracy, and a plethora of time-wasting meetings.

By the 1960s, the growth in local government functions and the scale of its expenditure made traditional structures of decision hard to defend. The local authority associations themselves acknowledged the defects, and in 1964 pressed central government to set up an inquiry. Two committees, under Sir John Maud and Sir George Mallaby, were to deal with councillors and officers, respectively. Of these, the Maud Committee produced far-reaching proposals aimed at modernising local authority decision-making. The traditional system of decision-making committees was to be swept away, and replaced by a two-tier system of a small 'management board' of between five and nine members, responsible for the overall direction of policy, and a web of essentially advisory committees with no decision-making powers, with which the remaining council-lors would occupy themselves.

Maud's recommendations found little favour in local government, and were criticised as being too radical a departure. Few councillors would be satisfied with such a system, for the majority would be left with little incentive to remain in office with so little access to power. Significantly, neither the Redcliffe–Maud Commission, nor the group set up in 1972 under Laurence Bains to advise on management structures for the new authorities, adopted the recommendations. Instead, they urged a general streamlining of effort and a clearer focusing of responsibility. The traditional system was, then to continue with little revision: councillors sitting on a large number of committees, meeting frequently for lengthy debate and deliberation.

By the 1980s, the realities of power in local government had moved on. The spread of political parties, the conflicts between and within them, and the rise of the full-time political councillor, less inclined to accept officer advice, created a new and more assertive climate. Officers were seen less as impartial expert advisers, with some local authorities setting out to appoint officers sympathetic to their politics. The potential for abuse of power gave rise to concern: the age of 'the new corruption' had arrived. Many Conservatives were worried about Labour using its power base in local government for party ends. Prime Minister Margaret Thatcher in particular was determined to rein in the left-wing coun-cils, and a committee of inquiry was set up in 1985 under David Widdicombe, QC. It reported the following year with a host of recommendations to limit questionable political practices, notably restricting council officers above a cer-tain modest level from any form of political activity, and requiring committee seats to be allocated in proportion to party strength. The Local Government and Housing Act, 1989 carried many of these recommendations into law.

John Major's administration took a less confrontational line, launching a new review aimed at improving management with streamlined, responsive, decisive local authorities. In his March 1991 consultation paper on the internal manage-ment of local authorities, Michael Heseltine set out options for change, to include a Cabinet-style system reminiscent of Maud's management board, an executive mayor, directly or indirectly elected or, where appropriate, the continuation of the traditional committee system. Little interest was excited by these suggestions, although a handful of councils experimented with House of Commons-style select or scrutiny committees. The Blair government elected in May 1997 took these same proposals forward more positively in the guise of its 'democratic renewal' programme. Legislation was introduced to remove the barriers to the more radical changes proposed, allowing elections for executive mayors; a number of local authorities moved speedily to adopt such arrangements. By early 2002, a number of referendums had taken place in authorities as varied as Berwick-upon-Tweed, Gloucester, Cheltenham, Sedgefield, Middlesborough, North Tyneside, Hartlepool, Lewisham, Doncaster and Watford. Turnout ranged from 10 per cent to 36 per cent, with the sole exception of Berwick-upon-Tweed, which polled on general election day with a turnout of 64 per cent. Only in six of these authorities did proposals for a directly elected mayor command sufficient electoral support, and they will hold their mayoral elections in May 2002.

Paying for Local Government

Finance proved to be the most awkward problem of local government. The immediate post-war period was one of cooperation between local authorities and central departments in the pursuit of the agreed objectives of physical reconstruction and social welfare. As local authority expenditure grew, it became impossible to finance new services from local resources. Central government aid became increasingly important, and brought with it financial and, ultimately, political dependence upon the centre. By the mid-1970s, the relationship was no longer one of partnership, but rather one in which local authorities were seen as the agents of central government. Given the failure to find any new source of local revenue, this change of status was inescapable.

Local government expenditure was financed from three sources: local property taxes (rates), central government grants, and borrowing. As their proportions shifted in the early post-war years, astute commentators recognised their possible implications for local government. The post-war Labour government had two main objectives in local finance: to promote service development, and to shift resources from richer to poorer areas. Specific, or percentage, grants were targeted on the development of particular services, and their use increased with the expansionist policies of the welfare state. Their second objective was attained through the system of block grant. This was distributed on the basis of a formula which took into account the characteristics of the local area rather than the expenditure of the local authority, a principle which was confirmed in the Local Government Act, 1948 as the Exchequer Equalisation Grant (EEG). The period of the Attlee governments marked the high tide of specific grants, but because such grants tended to encourage expenditure, the Conservatives would eventually move to restrict them.

Accordingly, the return of the Conservatives in 1951 heralded a period of concern about expenditure growth and the concomitant financial dependence of local government: 'from the constitutional point of view', declared 'Rab' Butler, 'the fundamental issue is how far a Conservative government should try to make local government more democratic and self-reliant, and how far they should allow local authorities to become increasingly mere agents for the execution of social and educational policy nationally conceived and directed' (CAB 129/84, 'Local Government Finance: Memorandum by the Lord Privy Seal', 14 December 1956, para. 24).

Butler's colleagues were more pragmatic, their predominant concern being to find ways of further developing the services for which they had assumed responsibility. As Britain's post-war economic crisis deepened, it seemed that local autonomy was a luxury the country could not afford. Henry Brooke's Local Government Act, 1958 recast exchequer support, scrapping a host of percentage grants and substituting for them a general grant. He justified the change to the local authorities as a means of liberating them from central control, but the reality was very different. The annual grant settlement, focused on a single figure, became a convenient means of regulating local authority expenditure in the Treasury interest. In 1961, Chancellor of the Exchequer Selwyn Lloyd warned of expenditure growing faster than resources, and with such momentum that the government was becoming committed beyond any politically acceptable horizon. Locally-planned expenditure growth had become the mid-term nightmare.

When Labour took office in 1964, they inherited the Conservatives' crisis, and added to it commitments of their own. The Local Government Act, 1966 aimed to increase domestic ratepayer support through the new rate-support grant (RSG). In this version of the block grant, a new subsidy element (equivalent to a 5p rate) increased year-on-year, easing the political problems of high-taxing councils, but progressively shifting the balance of responsibility from local government to central. The underlying problem of local finance was exacerbated, rather than solved, by this device. The Redcliffe–Maud Commission insisted that financial reforms were a prerequisite of any fundamental reform of the local government system, but there were no concrete proposals. Meanwhile, rate increases in the early 1970s which flowed in part from local government reorganisation prompted a search for a new financial regime. In 1975, the Layfield Committee was set up to inquire into the whole basis of local government finance, but the Committee's penetrating analyses of the need for a new system – a local income tax was favoured – failed to convince the Labour ministers.

Throughout the post-war period, governments of both parties had struggled to restrict the growth of local expenditure. Mrs Thatcher's administrations made repeated attacks on this problem, initially through a revised block grant system, introduced by the Local Government, Planning and Land Act, 1980. Based on a complex statistical exercise, it produced a single 'grant-related expenditure' (GRE) figure for each authority, the intention of which was to equalise the rate poundage charged to ratepayers across the country. These expenditure figures in effect were targets, as higher levels of expenditure would incur severe financial penalties. Intended to hold down local rate increases, the system proved ineffective, leading to the Rates Act, 1984, which instead enabled ministers to bear down upon rate levels in individual authorities through the 'selective limitation' or rate-capping.

The Conservatives, meanwhile, had pledged themselves to abolish the rating system. A series of White and Green Papers reviewed the options, but there was little support for any of them. Margaret Thatcher, however, was determined to 'abolish the unfair domestic rating system and replace rates with a fairer community charge'. Her election victory of 1987 made it possible for her to translate this commitment into action, despite the scepticism of many Cabinet members. A flat rate per capita charge, to which the negative term 'poll tax' soon came to be attached, was intended to encourage financial responsibility on the part of voters, through a clearer link between consuming services and paying for them. Only a minority of individuals paid rates personally and directly; the poll tax would be all but universal, and would create a culture of awareness about the financial consequences of electoral decisions.

That the logic of the new system was clear was undisputed, but the semantics of a 'charge', as distinct from a tax, provoked hostility. The practicalities of implementation, the costs and complexities of collection and follow-up were formidable. The decision to implement it in a single 'big bang' rather than in stages had the effect of maximising the political opposition. The introduction of the community charge, first in Scotland, in the Local Government Finance Act, 1988, provoked a political upheaval and violent civil disorder, while self-defeating attempts to soften its impact in the shires produced a costly system of compensation. With Margaret Thatcher's replacement by John Major in 1990, the community charge was immediately abandoned in favour of a hybrid system, the council tax. This new tax, introduced in the local Government Finance Act, 1992, combined an element of property valuation with a personal charge based on an assumed two-person household. The controversies were immediately stilled. However, the effect was to shift the balance of financial responsibility still further towards the central government and, by the late 1990s, no more than one-fifth of total local expenditure was met by locally-raised taxes. Towards the end of their first term, the Blair government elected in 1997, published a green paper *Modernising Local Government Finance* putting forward proposals for a reform of local government finance. The aims were to provide for greater flexibility in local authority borrowing and promote new opportunities for businesses to invest in local communities. The new financial regime was intended to ensure predictability and stability in local finance, balancing funding for local government's delivery of national priorities and targets with financial freedom and responsibility for local authorities. In so far as it sought to sustain fairness, accountability and transparency in decision-making, the Blair government was rolling forward the broad financial regime brought about by the poll tax.

Providing Local Services

The underlying theme in the history of local government services since 1945 is the progressive collapse of the post-war consensus, leading to the repeated intervention of central government in pursuit of their own, increasingly divergent, values. Although local authorities lost certain services under the Attlee government, even the Conservatives scarcely opposed the transfer of, for example, gas and electricity to nationalised boards, and local authority hospitals to the new National Health Service (NHS). Arguably, the gains outweighed the losses; indeed, even the nationalised fire service was handed back to local government at the end of the wartime emergency. The range of services provided by the 1950s were accepted across the board as representing the proper scope of what local government could, and should, do. That acceptance came under strain during the years of financial crisis after 1960, and by the end of the period had dissolved, to be replaced by bitter division on the role of local government. It was a conflict in which the central government view was bound to prevail, at the expense of local preferences.

Throughout the first half of the century, local authorities had gained responsibility for an expanding range of services. The housing drive to provide 'homes for heroes' at the end of the first World War converged with programmes to eradicate slums and reduce overcrowding. Local authorities had taken the lead role in providing elementary, secondary and technical education. By the end of the war, the larger of the local authorities were strong, professionally and politically, enough to take on the burden of additional responsibilities in building the new Jerusalem. One important new role was in providing what came to be the personal social services, of which the Children Act, 1948 provided a foundation with both new legal responsibilities and a professional cadre that would, after 1970, take the lead in the new social services departments. Another was the Town and Country Planning Act, 1947, which enabled them to regulate development in accordance with master plans, whose preparation required the growth of another new profession. Developments of these sorts, combined with the expansion of existing services, both with the strong political and financial support of ministers, heralded local government's all-too-brief golden age. Housing and education were two key areas in which this changing relationship between central and local government are best exemplified.

The wartime coalition government's White Paper set out the aspiration of a separate home for each family, which, given the depletion of the housing stock by the Blitz, would require three-quarters of a million new homes. A range of financial incentives and new subsidies were offered to encourage local councils to build. Under Labour, Bevan's particular contribution was to push for quality, and not just crude quantity of housing, in terms of building standards, space and equipment. 'While we shall be judged for a year or two by the number of houses we build,' he told Labour Party Conference, 'we shall be judged in ten years, time by the type of houses we build.' However, the immediacy of the rehousing need made temporary hosusing – the famous 'prefabs' – a priority, and the main housing construction programme fell behind its targets. Whereas the coalition proposed 100,000 houses in the first year of peace, and 200,000 in the second, completions turned out at 55,400 in 1946, rising sharply to 139,690 in 1947 and to 227,616 in 1948. These were massive achievements in the context of the post-war shortages.

Not only did both political parties nationally endorse the housing drive, they competed electorally in terms of their ability to deliver it. But after 1951, the

Churchill government aimed at achieving its target of 300,000 houses by a combination of municipal and private provision. This target was surpassed when 319,000 houses were built in 1953, rising to 348,000 the following year. By 1957, 2.5 million new houses and flats had been built, three-quarters of them by local authorities. The balance was to change as the Conservatives advanced the socially and politically congenial idea of a 'property-owning democracy' by restricting the local authority role and stimulating the private sector.

Thereafter, the parties diverged in the role they ascribed to local authorities in housing. Despite divisions of opinion within the party, Labour edged towards a policy of municipalisation, in which the entire private rented sector would be taken into council ownership. Conservatives, for their part, feared the political consequences of the growth of a passive, Labour-voting council tenant class. As Housing Minister, Macmillan's grand design was to inflate the private sector and reduce expenditure on local authority subsidies for housing. Keeping public expenditure under control was a continuing concern, but by the 1960s, the problem of housing subsidies had also acquired a political dimension. Labour-controlled councils tended to use the subsidy to keep down municipal rents, a policy that was electorally popular in proportion to the size of the municipal stock in any locality. Conservative governments juggled the subsidies in an attempt to restrict this practice, but not until 1971 did they attack it directly through the 'fair rents' scheme that effectively removed local authorities' rights to fix their own rents.

The Heath government's White Paper *A Fair Deal for Housing* signalled the final end of bipartisanship in local authority housing. The Conservatives' new approach was to subsidise people according to their means, rather than the physical structure in which they were housed. Market-level rents would be tempered by a scheme of rent rebates, 'fair rents' were expected to eliminate deficits on their hosusing revenue accounts – into which rents were paid – bringing local authorities under greater scrutiny than ever before. Nothing in the previous history of central–local relations was as polarising as fair rents. Nationally, the Housing Finance Act, 1972 pushed the Labour Party into a corner, inflaming local passions and restricting future Labour governments' abilities to tame local authority housing. The Clay Cross affair, in which the council of that name, by refusing to raise rents, chose to defy central government, and the commissioner it appointed to supplant them, symbolised the new, conflictual politics of housing.

By the time Labour repealed the Housing Finance Act in 1975, they no longer had a distinctive policy agenda for housing. The party's electoral base was changing as Britain edged towards the reality of a property-owning democracy. Labour could not expect to be elected on the votes of its own limited constituency of the publicly housed and employed, but in coming to terms with social change, they had lost the initiative in housing policy. There was little opportunity for the Wilson and Callaghan administrations to revive the local authority role before Labour fell from power, and Margaret Thatcher, local government's most trenchant critic, entered Downing Street.

In the first few years of her governments, Mrs Thatcher pursued traditional Conservative policies towards housing, albeit more vigorously than her predecessors. Home ownership grew steadily, while new local authority building was severely restricted. Not until her third term did the introduction of the Housing Act, 1988 bring about a radical transformation in the role of local authorities. Enhancing choice and diversity through encouraging the transfer of whole estates to housing associations or the independent sector (voluntary transfers), by passing housing management responsibilities to the tenant associations (tenants' choice), and inviting the private sector to take over, renovate and manage run-down inner-city housing estates (housing action trusts) were the distinctively new initiatives. Alongside these schemes, tenants were given for the first time the right to buy their homes, while steps were taken to reverse the long-term decline of the private rented sector, and promote the independent housing association sector.

Local government began a post-war period under the aegis of the consensus inherited from the wartime coalition. This consensus was, if anything, stronger in education than in housing, where Butler's Education Act, 1944 provided a stable framework. That Act, though, was itself a milestone in centralisation. It established a strong central ministry and restructured local education authorities (LEAs), on whom new duties were laid, to be performed under the oversight of the Minister. The basis of post-war secondary schooling was a tripartite division into grammar, 'modern' and technical schools, with children selected for them on the basis of their ability.

In practice, the issue of selection had never achieved consensus, its justification being hotly contested within the Labour Party during the war years. Gradually, the more critical view came to predominate, driving the party towards favouring the concept of the common or comprehensive school, and the abolition of selection. In time, this came to provide the principal battleground for central–local relations in the field of education. Dissatisfaction with the consequences of selection, and the failure to achieve 'parity of esteem' between grammar and secondary modern schools, led a number of local authorities to experiment with the comprehensive model for some of their schools. While 'tripartism' was the widely-endorsed concept in the immediate post-war period, by 1960 the critics were portraying it as 'separatism'.

Somewhat surprisingly, the newly elected Labour government in 1964 chose to promote comprehensive schools by requiring local authorities to submit plans to end selection. Legislation was ruled out, and a rather toothless policy of exhortation by circular, beginning with circular 10/65, was pursued. Legislation was introduced, but failed to pass through Parliament before the 1970 general election. The attempt to impose a particular policy on local authorities had galvanised the Conservatives into the defence of the grammar school and of the prerogatives of LEAs. Margaret Thatcher became Education Secretary, and immediately revoked circular 10/65. Her policy was one of 'variety and choice', leaving school systems to the LEAs to determine, rather than having the central Ministry plan them.

Paradoxically, Mrs Thatcher's insistence on considering each submission on a school-by-school basis did nothing to stem the tide. Indeed, by early 1975 there were more than 2,500 comprehensive schools in England, catering for 68 per cent of the secondary school population. The number of grammar schools had fallen by more than half, from 1,285 to 566 in the course of 10 years since circular 10/65. Labour had by this point returned to power, reintroducing their Education Bill, and making comprehensives mandatory. Although the return of the Conservatives in 1979 saw the immediate repeal of Labour Education Act, the move to comprehensives was already all but complete. Local autonomy, meanwhile, had been the casualty.

With the battle over comprehensives effectively over, educational thinking entered a new phase, characterised by public expenditure constraints, demographic changes, and the gathering controversy over teaching methods and educational standards. The educational critique of the 'Black Papers' encapsulated wider concerns about low standards of discipline and poor academic performance. Industry demanded that education become more responsive to the needs of employers. Before leaving office, James Callaghan launched the new debate in a well-publicised speech at Ruskin College in October 1978, in which he called for a centralised curriculum, closer involvement of parents and industry, and the monitoring of performance through national standards, testing, and inspection.

The incoming Conservative government was able to capitalise upon this groundwork. Their 1980 Education Act was their first step towards enhancing parental power. At least two parents were to be included on the governing bodies of schools, while their representation and power was further increased by the 1986 Act. The 1980 Act also strengthened the influence of central government over the school curriculum by abolishing the teacher-dominated Schools Council, and establishing the centrally-controlled Secondary Examinations Council and the School Curriculum Development Committee. A flood of initiatives followed, including Sir Keith Joseph's White Paper, *Better Schools*, which set out a new vision for education. It was not until Kenneth Baker replaced Joseph in 1986 that anything was done to reverse the post-war settlement: 'No one had yet grasped the nettle of major legislative overhaul', he argued. 'While Keith Joseph had planted many of the seeds...I realised that the scale of the problem could only be tackled by a coherent national programme.'

The Education Reform Act, 1988 (ERA) was the most far-reaching legislation since the Butler Act of 1944. It restored to central government powers over the curriculum which it had surrendered to LEAs through a core National Curriculum, testing and assessment procedures. It gave parents greater autonomy by allowing them more choice in the schools their children attended, by eliminating catchment areas, and giving them the right, by majority vote, to take their school out of LEA control to be directly grant-aided by central government. The Act also contained a new form of financial delegation, Local Management of Schools, whereby head teachers and governors were given the freedom to manage their own budgets and to determine the use of resources to meet needs and priorities as they saw them. The overall effect of the ERA was, then, to tip the balance of power in favour of schools, their governing bodies and parents, and away from the LEAs, which were no longer to enjoy the full range of powers and responsibilities conferred upon them by the 1944 Act.

The period from 1979 to Margaret Thatcher's departure in 1990 marked a wholesale shift to centralised power, not only in housing and education, but across the range of locally-provided services. The Major government continued, and in some respects pressed further, this new trend. Increments in ministerial prerogatives and the loss of financial autonomy severely constrained the local authorities. In a number of significant areas, their local leadership role was eclipsed by the rise of special-purpose, centrally-appointed bodies – quangos – with responsibilities ranging from urban regeneration to employment and training. The long-standing Conservative desire to eliminate the monopoly position of local authorities as service providers, and to tame the public service unions, was to be achieved by exposing them to market disciplines through compulsory competitive tendering (CCT). To this end, a series of Acts between 1980 and 1992 required local authorities to compete with alternative providers across an expending range of services, from building maintenance to white-collar corporate services. So far-reaching were these changes that they amounted to a distinctive new role for local authorities, encapsulated in the slogan 'From providing to enabling'.

The election of the Blair government in May 1997 raised hopes that local government might emerge from its new dark age. Labour had fought centralisation for nearly two decades, and was bound to promise a restoration of local autonomy. Their long-standing hostility to compulsory competitive tendering ensured that it would not survive a change of government. The Blair government introduced in its place a 'best value' regime, under which councils were required to demonstrate effectiveness and quality, not just economy and efficiency, for a wider range of services than those covered by CCT. Competitive tendering would no longer be compulsory, except where ministers required a council to expose services to competition on the ground that they had failed to meet required standards. This apart, the tight central control of service provision remained.

Labour's distinct approach to revitalising local government, however, lay in their programme of 'democratic renewal'. In 1998 the government published its White Paper, *Modern Local Government: In Touch With the People*, setting out a strategy for reform and modernisation of local government in England. Following the white paper, the Beacon Council scheme was set up, to disseminate best practice in service delivery across local government. Involving communities, fostering electoral turnout, and enhancing public participation in key decisions affecting local authority service provision were seen as the most promising route to revival.

On their re-election in May 2001 the Labour government pushed forward these reforms. In January 2002 the White Paper *Strong Local Leadership: Quality Public Services* set out to build on Best Value to put in place 'a comprehensive and integrated performance framework', a performance assessment regime to define the standards on which all local authorities will be expected to deliver and clear criteria against which they will be judged. The 'modernising Britain' agenda promises to restore the status of local government in community leadership in the twenty-first century. Whether or not this can be achieved independent of the return of power to local authorities remains to be seen.

Conclusion

The post-war history of British local government falls broadly into three distinct periods. The first, which lasted for 20 years from the end of the war, was one of high aspiration. 'Building Jerusalem' would not have been feasible without the full participation of local authorities as partners in that enterprise. As a result, they enjoyed a surge in funding, and accumulated new powers in order to implement national policies. Councillors and officers worked harmoniously together, and with central officials, towards widely-agreed goals of social renewal. The growth of dependence was subtle, and was not to become apparent until the consensus crumbled in the second phase, beginning with the election of the Wilson government in 1964. The central–local partnership came under strain as ministers increasingly used their powers instrumentally, with little regard for local autonomy. They readily assumed unprecedented responsibility for local government structure, finance and services. Consent was no longer a prerequisite for change. The third phase, from 1979, contrasted sharply with the supposed 'golden age' of the immediate post-war period: centralism was the new orthodoxy. The following years saw local government relegated to the margins of the Constitution as a wave of legislation brought a transformation of their role. For the first time, local authorities were seen not as a solution to Britain's problems, but as the source of many of them. Local government itself had faded into the twilight zone of politics, from which the Blair government hopes to rescue it. Meanwhile, however, it has lost the respect, trust and support that once it enjoyed. Therein lies the real contrast between 1945 and today.

Further Reading

For a full treatment of the post-war history of the subject, see K. Young and N. Rao, *Local Government since 1945*, Oxford, 1997. For more detailed accounts of particular aspects see:

Alexander, A., *The Politics of Local Government in the United Kingdom*, London, 1982.

Barker, R., *Education and Politics, 1900–1951: A Study of the Labour Party*, Oxford, 1972.

Butler, D., Adonis, A. and Travers, T., *Failure in British Government: The Politics of the Poll Tax*, Oxford, 1994.

Byrne, T., *Local Government in Britain* (7th ed.) London, Penguin, 2000.

Gibson, J., *The Politics and Economics of the Poll-tax: Mrs Thatcher's Downfall*, Warley, 1990.

Hepworth, N. P., *The Finance of Local Government*, 7th ed., London, 1984.

Lawton, D., *The Tory Mind on Education, 1979–1994*, Lewes, 1994.

Letwin, S. R., *The Anatomy of Thatcherism*, London, 1992.

Loughlin, M., *Local Government in the Modern State*, London, 1986.

Lucas, Keith B. and Richards, P. G. *A History of Local Government in the Twentieth Century*, London, 1978.

Murie, A. and Malpass, P., *Housing Policy: Theory and Practice*, London, 1987.

Rao, N., *Towards Welfare Pluralism: Public Services in a Time of Change*, Aldershot, 1996.

Rao, N., *Reviving Local Democracy: New Labour, New Politics?* Bristol, 2000.

Rhodes, R. A. W., *The National World of Local Government*, London, 1986.

Short, J. R., *Housing in Britain: The Post-war Experience*, London, 1982.

Stanyer, J., 'The Local Government Commissions', in H. V. Wiseman (ed.), *Local Government in England: 1958–69*, London, 1970, pp. 15–35.

Chronology

1945   Coalition government White Paper, *Local Government in England and Wales in the Period of Reconstruction* published. Local Government Act: Local Government Boundary Commission established.

1946   New Towns Act: excluded local authorities from development.

1947   Town and Country Planning Act: local authorities to prepare development plans and control development.

1948   Children Act: local authorities given extensive powers in child protection. National Assistance Act: Poor Law ended. Local Government Act: EEG introduced.

1949   Local Government Boundary Commission dissolved.

1956   Central–local government *concordat*. White Paper, *Areas and Status of Local Authorities in England and Wales* published.

1957   Royal Commission on Local Government in Greater London established. White Papers *Local Government: Functions of County Councils and County District Councils in England and Wales* and *Local Government Finance: England and Wales* published.

1958   Local Government Act: Local Government Commission established. Rate Deficiency Grant introduced.

1960   Report of the Royal Commission on Local Government in Greater London.

1963   London Government Act creates GLC and new London boroughs.

1964   Committee on the Management of Local Government established.

1965   DES circular 10/65 issued: LEAs to prepare comprehensive plans.

1966   Local Government Act: introduced 'domestic ratepayer relief'. Royal Commission on Local Government in England established.

1967   Local Government Commission dissolved.

1968   Seebohm report on social services recommended integrated local authority social services departments.

1969   Report of the Royal Commission on Local Government in England.

1972   Local Government Act: local government in England and Wales restructured. Housing Finance Act: 'fair rents' introduced.

1975   (Layfield) Committee on the Finance of Local Government established.

1976   Education Act: LEAs required to go comprehensive. Report of the Layfield Committee published.

1978   James Callaghan's Ruskin speech launches 'great debate' on education.

1979   Education Act: LEAs freed to maintain selective education.

1980   Local Government Planning and Land Act: introduction of CCT. Education Act: provided for parent representation on school governing bodies.

1982   Local Government Finance Act: introduced grant 'holdback', and prohibited supplementary rates.

1984   Rates Act: introduced rate-capping.

1985   Local Government Act: Greater London and Metropolitan County Councils abolished. Widdicombe Committee of Inquiry into the Conduct of Local Authority Business established.

1988   Local Government Act: CCT extended. Education Reform Act: introduced national curriculum, 'opting out', open enrolment, local management of schools. Housing Act: introduced voluntary transfers, tenants' choice and Housing Action Trusts. Local Government Finance Act: rates abolished, and community charge – or poll tax – introduced.

1989   Local Government and Housing Act: embodied recommendations of Widdicombe Committee.

1992   Local Government Act: further extension of CCT and establishment of Local Government Commission. Local Government Finance Act: poll tax abolished and council tax introduced.

1998   White Paper *Modern Local Government: In Touch With the People* published.

2000   Green Paper *Modernising Local Government* published.

2002   White Paper *Strong Local Leadership: Quality Public Services* published.

11 The Media

Michael Bromley

In 1996 the Institute of Contemporary British History organised a two-day conference, coinciding with the centenary of the first publication of the *Daily Mail* newspaper, to mark 'a century of the popular press'.[1] The association of the idea of the 'popular' with the *Daily Mail* arguably appeared less justified than it might have done two generations previously. In the intervening period, the 'popular' daily newspaper of the 1930s, of which the *Mail* was not only an example but also the prototype, had been redesignated the 'middle-market' press and had shrunk from representing nearly 72 per cent to accounting for not much more than 23.5 per cent of all national daily newspaper sales.[2] The reason for this was the rise of the tabloid newspaper and its appropriation of the epithet 'popular'.[3]

By the end of the Second World War, and for the first time, the working class was dominating the aggregate consumption of all available forms of mass media, and reformulating what constituted 'the popular' in this domain.[4] The first of three post-war Royal Commissions on the Press identified the key aspect believed to be confronting all the British media after 1945: 'social requirements which grow steadily more exacting...[and] a need for public instruction on an entirely new scale'.[5]

Viewed through the prism of a generally widening, if still circumscribed, popular presence in the structure of the so-called mass media, the history of those media in the period since 1945 conveys the primary importance of the social conditions of reception, while also accounting for, but not being determined by, technological developments.[6] The mass media passed through five distinct, if often overlapping and always interconnected, phases, each associated with specific technical means of production, but principally representing incremental shifts towards greater popularisation – pleasing 'ordinary folk'.[7]

The period 1945–55 (in which cinema and the press were prominent, with radio in a subsidiary role) can be seen as one of post-war reconstruction, when attempts were made to reconcile the high commercialism of the 1930s with the idealisation of democratic participation exemplified by the concept of 'the people's war'. The following decade (predominantly the era of television, but with cinema and radio, again, of some significance) was characterised by concerns over the maintenance of (national) social and cultural coherence in the face of a tendency to atomisation. The 1970s and early 1980s (a period of television and the press) represent a response to the 1960s; a grappling with the paradoxical juxtaposition simultaneously of individualism and societal cohesion inherent in a mounting acknowledgement of social and cultural diversity. The decade following the mid-1980s (in which there was a rising preoccupation with cross-media and forms of digitalisation) was characterised by a highly-contested confidence in 'the market', embodied in Thatcherism, to resolve complex issues of mediation and representation. Since the mid-1990s, the apparently exponential growth of public relations, 'spin', presentation and news management has given rise to, on the one hand, scepticism over the emergence of the 'public relations' state compromising the 'independence' of the media, and, on the other hand, faith in the recuperative powers of the media in digital form, especially via the Internet.

Each phase, in confirmation of the secular trend towards greater popular expression, has been accompanied, among some, by fears of cultural debasement and, among others, by the celebration of a 'long revolution'.[8]

Highbrow, Middlebrow and Lowbrow

By the late 1940s it was a common contention of (usually middle-class) observers that the difference in approach, for example, among newspapers, between 'the best . . . and the general run of the popular' was beginning to widen, and there was insufficient appeal to 'intermediate' tastes.[9] In the terminology of the period, there seemed to be distinctively highbrow and lowbrow media, but a shrinking middlebrow sector. 'The most lowbrow' newspapers were supposedly characterised by ' "stunt" make-up . . . [and] screaming headlines'; they included not only the tabloid *Daily Mirror*, but also the larger-circulation Sunday papers (notably, the *News of the World*), which were still broadsheet in size.[10]

The process of massification was viewed by many as a tendency of the middlebrow and the lowbrow to 'merge', resulting in 'a levelling effect' – downwards.[11] This was in contradistinction to efforts which were made in the United States to valorise the 'social responsibility' of the media, in which mediation was oriented along a single axis of influence, with elites filtering what was to be made publicly available to (gatekeeping for) audiences who were generally seen to be passive consumers of information.[12] To George Orwell the situation in the UK seemed to be the almost natural outcome of popularisation: 'this is a lowbrow country', he observed,[13] characterised by 'the narrow interests of the average man, the rather low level of English education, the contempt for "high-brows" '.[14] This manifested itself clearly in the media: 'One of the greatest troubles of broadcasting in this country has been that no programme is regarded as economic unless it can appeal to millions of people, and that anything in the smallest degree highbrow provokes storms of indignation from ordinary radio-users.'[15]

The 'seriousness' of the media during the war years was a chimera – at best, an interlude before a return to the normalcy of the 1930s. By the late 1940s much of the dominant pattern of later twentieth-century mass audio-visual media content was already apparent, comprising a miscellany of individual celebrity, popular music, soap opera, comedy, game shows and audience partici-pation.[16] In the press, there were recurrent anxieties over the excesses of the 1930s – 'the low-down kind of journalism which exploits the bawdy and the horrific and cares not how it gets its stories of frailty, folly, crime and the abnormal' and 'papers that wallow for their own profit in the sordid, sensa-tional and salacious'.[17] Over the next 50 years these approaches seemed to converge across the media, and to be exemplified in the late twentieth-century media preoccupation with the private lives and public personae of the Royal Family.[18]

'A Proletarian Revolution'?

Demands in the 1940s for an investigation into the press were formally couched in terms of a need to address fears of the pernicious effects of the concentration of ownership and the rise of autocratic newspaper barons; of the marginalisa-tion and even silencing of diverse opinions; of the failure to meet 'democratic needs'; of the erosion of press and journalistic independence; of the malign influence of advertisers, and of the absence of 'professional standards'.[19] This masked a more mundane resistance to the perceived corruption of 'lowbrow' culture, which was often seen as being far more virulent than the 'potential authority' of newspaper magnates,[20] and which seemed to focus unhealthily on one particular dimension of life:

> Sex...was the commonest ingredient in curiosity's daily fodder; often enriched by violence and bloodshed, with money to sweeten it, and social position to make it fragrant. It called down from posters, sparkled when night came in innumerable coloured lights, permeated cinema darkness. Loudspeakers and gramophones roared or crooned it, books and newspapers and illustrated periodicals made it their concern.... Like gold-prospectors looking in their sieves for the minutest particle of precious ore, the faintest gleam amidst dull mud, each day's happenings were painstakingly searched for their sex-deposit. Crime provided a rich yield, misery and despair were not to be neglected.... Here a woman picked up, naked, from the sea. Her nakedness deserved a mention, at any rate in the early editions. Clothed, she has been nothing.[21]

This supposed engrossment with sex symbolised for some the possible immi-nence of 'a proletarian revolution' – in taste if not in politics,[22] and raised fears about the extent to which this might subvert ideas of the close interdependence, in the interests of 'the welfare of the community as a whole', of 'the emancipa-tion of the middle class', the freedom of the press, and a 'responsible' journal-ism of 'tacit censorship'.[23] Yet the keystone in this edifice, the journalist, was of indeterminate, indifferent and often indigent status – suspiciously like 'any cheapjack whose vociferations draw pence from passers-by'. Power to shape the media was seen to lie rather in the direct association between public demand and corporate enterprise, and that, in order to ensure commercial success, the latter was prepared to accede to the former at almost any sacrifice. Journalists, for whom news, which in occupational discourse had been isolated from, while remaining closely related to, 'views', gave the press its *importance*, were regarded as the last bastion against this 'pandering'.[24] Readers, however, also wanted what they found to be *interesting*. 'People want to be pleased,' Kingsley Martin observed, 'and truth is not always pleasing.' Cost, too, was a factor, especially for working-class readers.[25] Discerning what the mass readership wanted from its newspapers at the price it was prepared to pay while protecting and promoting standards of journalism became a major concern.

Even idealists on the left, who were almost instinctively hostile to the commercialised newspaper, recognised the legitimacy of many of the novelties of the 'popular press', such as the use of banner headlines, shorter stories and more and bigger photographs, the almost relentless pursuit of scoops, and a fascination with 'human interest'. Naturally, they condemned 'stunts', the suppression and distortion of news, and the fascination with trivia and gossip, but they were equally dismissive of newspapers which were 'ponderously "judgmatic"' or committed 'the sin of dullness'.[26]

'The mass-production, mass-consumption, mass-communication, mass-advertising age marches on', Francis Williams noted, not wholly disapprovingly, in the mid-1950s.[27] Between 1937 and 1947 the sales of national daily newspapers had risen from 9.9 million copies to 15.45 million copies, and of national Sunday newspapers from 15.7 million copies to 29.3 million copies. In 1947, the two best-selling daily papers, the *Daily Express* and the *Mirror*, each sold nearly four million copies, and sales of the *News of World* had almost doubled to eight million copies. The press, Raymond Williams argued, had at last become 'fully popular'.[28] New reading publics demanded new forms of journalism, which were sensationalist, scandalous, trivialising, strident and unethical, but also educative, crusading and radical, eschewing the 'serious' content which filled most of the other papers.[29] Chiefly, this meant news.[30]

A Changing Mediascape

Whether this amounted to a transfiguration of the press remains debatable.[31] The quintessential mass circulation newspaper of the 1940s and 1950s, the *Daily Mirror*, can be seen as an example of the professionally packaged, homogenised media dispensing instantaneous gratification, which for many were exemplified by the developments in broadcasting, the cinema and recorded music which had certainly begun before 1945, and which were already beginning to have a negative impact on older establish 'popular' forms.[32] All the same, television particularly came to be seen as 'more . . . opiate than . . . stimulus . . . providing pap on tap'.[33] It was initially radio, however, which challenged the press directly, entering what many see as its 'golden age';[34] but the union of Reithian high-minded paternalism and 'popular' entertainment in the BBC was an uneasy one.[35] Television, which had been suspended for the duration, resumed broadcasting in 1946, but only as a metropolitan novelty for the relatively well-off, even though its programming has been dismissed as 'dull, dreary and unimaginative'.[36] Nevertheless, there was widespread acceptance that television had 'come to stay'.[37] Soon the debate focused on whether the future of radio and television should lie exclusively in the hands of the BBC, and was coincidentally subsumed within the wider argument over 'quality' and 'standards'. The Beveridge Committee denounced the idea of competition in broadcasting as degrading, and accepted the view that advertising was 'objectionable': Reith himself equated it to smallpox, the bubonic plague and the Black Death.[38] On the other hand, in a minority report, the Conservative politician Selwyn Lloyd argued in favour of commercially financed 'freedom of choice', which would meet what he believed was the inclination of the majority of the public to opt for television which entertained rather than provided 'compulsory uplift', but which operated alongside a protected public-service BBC — the position adopted by the 1951 Tory government.[39] The introduction of Independent Television (ITV) from 1955 provoked further debates about so-called standards, culminating in the fulminations of the Pilkington Committee against what it regarded as ITV's excesses, especially in the over-zealous portrayal of violence, the lack of attention paid to minority interests and a pervasive trivialisation.[40] There is little doubt that this animosity arose out of a belief that, in order to maximise profits, the ITV companies were pandering to the lowest possible taste, shaped by North American popular culture, to secure the largest audiences they could; exercising what Lord Thomson, who owned Scottish TV, famously called 'a licence to print your own money'.[41] Pilkington forced ITV to move closer to the BBC model, while at the same time the success of Independent Television in attracting audiences aroused the Corporation to make more concessions to 'popular' taste.[42]

Although this can be fairly characterised as the institution of a 'cosy duopoly',[43] it must also be acknowledged that in the 1960s and 1970s television in particular embarked on a sustained period of innovation, experimentation and technical development, which laid many of the foundations of broadcasting for the rest of the century, including satellite and colour television transmission, and the beginnings of segmented multi-channel radio and TV and multimedia output available all hours of the day, and with better sound and picture quality.[44] Generally, though, radio was a 'becalmed' medium.[45] Film-making, although apparently thriving artistically, was also heavily constrained by straightened economic circumstances, and cinema-going collapsed: in 1975 cinemas filled fewer than a tenth of the seats sold 30 years before, and the newsreel, once an important medium, had effectively disappeared.[46] Apart from television, the medium which offered the greatest potential for marrying popularity with profitability was recorded 'pop' music.[47]

It was important, however, not to confuse profitability *with* popularity: literature, opera, drama, art and documentary all attracted growing audiences – but also needed substantial public subsidies to survive.[48] National newspapers were not always run primarily for profit, although by the 1970s this was increasingly the case.[49] As a result, a number of 'popular' newspapers, with readerships measured in the millions, were closed down because they did not generate sufficient surpluses. These included the *News Chronicle* (with a circulation of more than one million), the *Daily Herald* (1.25 million), the *Sunday Citizen* (around one million), the *Sunday Graphic, Empire News* and *Sunday Dispatch*.[50] The second Royal Commission on the Press was set up to investigate this phenomenon which appeared actually to threaten the survival of the press.[51] Newspaper reading peaked in the 1950s, thereafter declining in all its forms (national, provincial, local, daily and weekly) more or less relentlessly. Even among the papers which did survive, there was a tranche, representing a kind of 'old guard' (the *Daily* and *Sunday Mirror, Daily Express, Daily Mail, News of the World, People*) whose heydays passed in the 1950s and 1960s.[52] At more or less the same time demand for general-interest magazines, such as *Picture Post*, and even *Radio Times*, as well as women's weeklies which had flourished in the 1940s, began to tail off. More contemporary titles, such as *Cosmopolitan* (1972), and, particularly in the 1960s, 'youth' publications (*Honey, Jackie* and *19*) were introduced.[53] Although the readerships of the 'quality press', and their share of the overall national newspaper market, rose steadily, by the 1960s it was clear that 'the significant development... was the rise of the tabloid press':

> this is even more important when it is noted that there has been a steady development, in magazines, towards the same kind of journalism.... This does not even begin to look like the developing press of an educated democracy. Instead it looks like an increasingly organised market in communications, with the 'masses' formula as the dominant social principle, and with the varied functions of the press increasingly limited to finding a 'selling point'.

The process of levelling down, identified by Orwell, now seemed to be involving even those who were supposedly 'defending traditional culture, and the interests of the "highly-educated and politically-minded minority"'. The daily newspaper most widely read among the highest socio-economic groups was the *Daily Express* – 'which of all the "popular" press is nearest the tabloid style'.[54] On a broader front, the falling popularity of reading *per se* gave rise to a recurrent question: 'Was not the printed word – and even much of language at large – becoming secondary to a culture of electronic sound and vision rather less demanding of active intellectual response?'[55]

The tabloid culture was more a matter of style than either form or content: in 1962 there were still only four tabloid-sized national newspapers, and broadcasting remained heavily committed to news and current affairs.[56] The BBC's preferred format for local radio comprised daytime programming of 'news of the community and local utility information' with the evenings given over to 'a full curriculum of educational programmes'.[57] News and information were regarded as the 'bedrock' of local radio broadcasting, which began in 1967, and the airwaves were supposed to be given over to 'vigorous' journalism based on the Corporation's public service traditions in news and current affairs.[58]

The floodgates had opened by the 1970s, however, and between 1969 and 1977 the surviving 'popular' daily papers (the *Herald*, transformed into, first, the *Sun* and then *The Sun*; the *Mail* and the *Express*) adopted the tabloid format. Perhaps not surprisingly, the rate of decline of the staple of the late-nineteenth-century and early-twentieth-century newspaper reader, the staid, broadsheet provincial morning paper, accelerated in the decade after 1955. Provincial evening papers, which were far less affected by competition from the national press, fared better, especially where there was no local alternative. All the same, the net result was that by the mid-1970s the city with more than one morning and/or evening paper (which in 1945 had included Belfast, Birmingham, Bristol, Edinburgh, Glasgow, Leeds, Leicester, Liverpool, Manchester and Nottingham) was a rarity.[59] A parallel trend towards anti-competitiveness in the local weekly press was noted by the third Royal Commission in 1977. By then, this sector was already coming under siege from the freesheet, which made no pretence about providing editorial content, and relied first and foremost on raising advertising revenue on the basis of guaranteeing delivery direct to households. The impact on the traditional paid-for local papers was enormous.[60] Meanwhile, the advent of independent local radio highlighted the extent to which that medium was now expected to broadcast recorded music rather than a general mix of programming, and that its audience regarded 'news as secondary listening'.[61]

Thus, by the mid-1970s both the Royal Commission and the Committee on the Future of Broadcasting (Annan) surveyed from their different perspectives a mediascape which appeared to be changing fundamentally, and yet possibly was still not changing enough. The Annan Committee especially reflected on the effects of the 'social revolution' of the 1960s, and the incapacity of an implicitly unitary 'middle-class culture', situated more in the nineteenth than the twentieth century, to represent a more openly pluralist contemporary society. An obvious basis for at least some of the fissures which began to appear in UK society lay in publicly expressed attitudes to sex. 'Swinging London' was a media invention of the mid-1960s; in 1965 the director Kenneth Tynan was the first person to say 'fuck' on British television; in 1960 the so-called trial of *Lady Chatterley* symbolically marked the dismantling of much of the apparatus of public censorship. This process of liberalisation was closely linked to forms of democratisation, and particularly the modernising agenda of the Labour governments of Harold Wilson. On the one hand, legislation was introduced in the areas of contraception, abortion, divorce and homosexuality; while on the other, there was a popular anti-establishment and iconoclastic groundswell. Anything, it seemed, went, and communities which relied on conformity to prop up sometimes fragile social relations, such as Northern Ireland, felt themselves to be destabilised.[62]

The Annan Report proposed the expansion of broadcasting under a scheme of 'regulated diversity'. It eschewed open competition as inimical to 'excellence'. In contrast, the Royal Commission was accused of not dealing robustly enough with the issue of 'market pressures' as 'a serious *impediment* to existing diversity, and an even greater one to hopes of expanding upon that diversity' in the press.[63] Nevertheless, it has been pointed out that, while in three decades the underlying issues may have changed little, formal debate over the role and performance of the media now took into consideration the interests of, and the need for accountability to, a far wider public. This may have been more apparent with regard to broadcasting (there were often furious public 'battles' over television content), but it was hardly less true of the press.[64]

Two further trends both reflected and stimulated public concern with the media. One was the publication of accessible texts (many by the Penguin publishing house, the popularity of whose paperbacks was itself a manifestation of the tendency). From the late 1950s the work of academics such as Richard Hoggart, Raymond Williams and Marshall McLuhan appeared in paperback editions intended for general readership.[65] The second was the emergence of media studies as a field of academic endeavour. Media research was fostered primarily by the desire of those running television to learn more about their audiences, and began to be located in universities in the mid-1960s. Media teaching started, albeit tentatively, slightly earlier, with film, radio and television courses in the Drama Department at Bristol University from 1957, a British Film Institute Education Department also from the 1950s, and a Film Department at the Slade School of Art from 1960. Some media training, which had traditionally been undertaken in the workplace, moved into the academy somewhat later – notably with the establishment of both the first journalism school at the University of Wales in Cardiff and the National Film School (in 1970). Yet media studies struggled to gain recognition as 'a distinctive discipline or even a separate field of study': in 1975 it was clear that 'media studies are less readily accepted as a valid area of academic concentration'. Media elements were still chiefly taught as parts of degrees in 'proper' subjects, such as English, Education, Drama and Social Psychology. At this precise moment, however, led by the examples of the Polytechnic of Central London and the City of Birmingham Polytechnic, media and media-related degree courses began to proliferate.[66] The extent to which they continued to do so is evident from a comparison of two lists of courses published 23 years apart. In 1975 the number of offerings in British universities in the field was barely enough to fill a page in a book: in 1998, an incomplete compilation of media courses in the UK ran to more than 180 pages.[67]

In the 'real' media world, in 1978 the *Sun* formally overtook the *Daily Mirror* as the largest-selling national daily newspaper. It did so, not as the direct competitor it had originally been designed to be, but as a publication which progressively eschewed news. The *Sun* had always prioritised sex, sport and contests above news, although it had carried plenty of the latter in its earliest days. By 1977, however, it felt no longer bound by 'the old newspaper conventions'. Moreover, stung by the paper's success, other titles started to adopt aspects of what was felt in Fleet Street to be a winning formula. Most obviously, the *Mirror* began directly aping the *Sun*, to the extent of even publishing its own 'page three' pictures. In 1978, too, the *Daily Star* was launched with no pretence at being anything other than 'all tits, bums' and bingo.[68] A more general 'depoliticisation' of the popular press, in which the coverage of public affairs was displaced by an increased attention paid to sport, human interest, entertainment and 'women's articles', has been traced in this period.[69] The 'quality' press is sometimes exempted from this tendency. Interestingly, it is the work of the *Sunday Times* Insight investigative journalism team which is often cited to demonstrate the widening gap which supposedly existed between broadsheet and tabloid newspapers in the 1970s.[70] It should be remembered, however, that not only were the readers of Sunday 'quality' newspapers as eager for human interest and celebrity stories as the readers of the tabloid press, but Sunday 'quality' titles, starting with the *Sunday Times*, introduced magazine supplements from the 1960s precisely to capitalise on the demand for lifestyle-led features.[71]

If there had been a project for state-led cultural inclusiveness and the co-optation of 'the mass' (which might have been evoked in the 1940s by concepts such as 'the people's war'), then by the late 1970s popular use of the media was signalling it was more likely to fail than succeed. Media audiences seemed not to seek active participation in public affairs through traditional forms of mediated communication, but to make their 'voices' heard through channels of consumptive behaviour facilitated by the exchange of displays of affluence, the exercise of material choice, and gossip, more often than not overlaid by a conscious dissonance. Even more than the *Mirror* in the 1940s, when it condemned the rest of the press for being 'too nice altogether, too refined', and unashamedly defended its own sensationalism, the *Sun* was a form of charivari.[72] In the 1970s the way to make a raucous din in public was through the representation of sex.[73] In this important respect, it appeared, 30 years after the post-war settlement the media had changed very little from those over which so many commentators had agonised in the 1930s.[74]

Thatcher's 'Revolution'

A certain orthodoxy has shaped the immediate analyses of the impact of Thatcherism on the media, particularly during the 1980s. Broadly speaking, it is that, driven by a free-market dogma, successive Conservative governments under the prime ministership of Margaret Thatcher 'rebuilt the landscape' and caused 'earthquakes' to happen.[75] While governmental influence over broadcasting was always likely to be greater, since it was a regulated sector, the ideology of liberalisation was applied to the press as well.[76] The major manifestations of this policy are to be seen in the introduction of commercialism into the BBC, and a parallel attack on its supposed corporatist privileges; further marketisation in commercial broadcasting (both radio and television); and support for editorial 'freedoms' in the press as an articulation of the freedom of the market.

Thatcher argued that 'the free movement and expression of ideas is guaranteed far better by numbers and variety than it ever can be by charters and specific statutes'.[77] The consequences of this approach included the imposition of significant changes in the BBC, and the emergence of feelings inside the Corporation that it was under semi-permanent siege, acutely summed up in the idea of 'Birtism';[78] the withdrawal of public service obligations from ITV; the proliferation of commercial radio stations under a policy of liberalisation; the rapid and largely unregulated development of satellite television and, in a more controlled manner, cable TV; the auctioning of commercial television franchises; and the dismantling of the national newspaper publishing system which had existed almost unaltered for at least 100 years – the so-called 'end of Fleet Street'.[79]

One proponent of the 'bloodless revolution' theory of the 1980s, Peter York, later suggested the extent to which the media were complicit in the entire process: 'We are talking about a whole change of mood, of tone.' The 'frightening growth of the media' fed, and in turn fed off, a marketised vacuity which often amounted to no more than 'rabid self-promotion'. This saw 'the rise and rise of soft journalism ... features, profiles, lifestyle matters, and especially, "service features" – information about what to do and what to buy', epitomised by the *Mail on Sunday*'s *YOU* magazine (started in 1982), which was 'long on fashion, celebrity profiles, how-to hedonism and eighties' cheek', and the profileration of 'little' programmes on television. 'Make it big on colour, make it big on fun.'[80] After Rupert Murdoch, who had bought Times Newspapers in 1981, became personally involved in the organisation's interest in publishing the so-called Hitler Diaries, 'all serious journalistic standards were swept aside', according to a former editor of both *The Times* and *Sunday Times*. When the diaries proved to be fakes, threatening the papers' credibility, Murdoch shrugged it off: 'After all, we are in the entertainment business', he argued.[81]

Two particular long-term and interrelated effects have been singled out for deeper analysis. The first is the growing concentration of media ownership and control.[82] By 1992, about 92 per cent of national newspapers (by circulation) were owned by five companies, and nine businesses dominated the provincial and local press. In three cases, the same companies were major presences in both sectors. During the 1980s public anxiety with this concentration was encapsulated in the pejorative use of the phrase 'the Murdoch press', reflecting the status of Murdoch's News International, both domestically as the owner of the largest-selling daily and Sunday newspapers (respectively, the *Sun* and *News of the World*) and the controller of 34 per cent of all national press circulations; and internationally as part of the second largest media conglomeration in the world.[83] By 1999, if anything, the situation had hardened; for example, while 77 per cent of the regional press had changed ownership in three years, more than half of all titles were still controlled by the ten largest companies.[84] At the same time, the majority of new newspaper publishing ventures, assumed to be made possible by the 'Wapping revolution' which was meant to deliver a new 'Golden Age', had failed, and there was little evidence of any increase in diversity in the press.[85]

In the 1980s both television and radio services proliferated to provide multi-channel, three-platform (terrestrial, satellite and cable), advertising-led, 24-hour broadcasting, supposedly facilitated by a deregulated free-market environment in which 'customer choice' prevailed.[86] The commercialisation of broadcasting formed part of the Conservative Party's election manifesto in 1987.[87] By 1999, and despite both the 1997 Labour government's general adoption of the approach of its Conservative predecessors and the further (commercially driven) diversification of the BBC, the expanded take-up of cable, the spread of satellite TV and the introduction of digital broadcasting, the number of organisations running television had actually declined. Several ITV companies were either taken over or merged, resulting in four major owners (Carlton, Granada, United News and Media and Scottish Television). Two of these (Carlton and United) proposed a further mega-merger in November 1999, prompting speculation over the ultimate collapse of the regional broadcasting base of ITV and its replacement with a single Channel 3 operator. As with the failure of liberalisation to deliver diversity in the press, this seemed to signal the end of the Thatcherite 'dream'.[88]

A similar pattern was discernible in radio. By the end of the century, while the number of commercial radio licences had risen to nearly 250 (in only 25 years), 15 groups controlled the bulk of radio broadcasting. Of these, 5 ran at least 100 stations, including EMAP Radio (with 18 stations), Capital (15 stations), GWR Group (40 stations), Scottish (16 stations) and the Wireless Group (11 stations).[89] Sometimes this has been seen as the transformation (inevitable or not) of economic liberalism into monopolistic tendencies; of channel proliferation into fewer outlets; of greater choice into less pluralism.[90]

Yet the idea of untrammelled Thatcherism instigating untold changes in broadcasting needs to be treated with caution.[91] First of all, the Thatcherite agenda was deeply ambiguous, somewhat incongruously combining economic libertarianism with a desire for control. As a consequence, in some areas regulation was *extended* – for example, to establish both a Broadcasting Complaints Commission (1981), a project proposed by Lord Annan, and a Broadcasting Standards Council (1988). Similarly, the arguments of both the Pilkington and Annan committees were accepted in setting up the minority-interest Channel 4, 'a most unlikely proposition for support from the Thatcher government', and the Welsh language S4C in Wales in 1982. The appointments of both the 'liberal' George Howard, as chairman, and Alasdair Milne, a programme-maker who, in the Thatcherite phrase, was not 'one of us', as Director-General of the BBC, also date from this period.[92] Thatcherism in the media was characterised at least in part by a sense of paternalist continuity inherited from the apparently despised corporatist past.[93]

The height of the 'Thatcherite moment' can be traced to the relatively short period between 1984 and 1990.[94] The expansion of broadcast services began in earnest with the start of satellite TV (Sky in 1984 and BSB in 1986) and cable (1983–5), but significantly without public service participation. Direct broadcasting by satellite (DBS) started in 1989, again as a wholly commercial venture. Twenty-four-hour TV was introduced in 1987. The regulation of radio was eased, and plans for the first three commercial national channels, where the BBC enjoyed a monopoly, as well as hundreds of community stations, were unveiled in 1988: incremental radio stations were introduced the following year.[95] Such developments seemed to strain the existing regulatory framework, for which the Conservative government had little appetite anyway. Public service requirements on commercial radio were reduced, supposedly to enhance their viability, and in 1990 Sky and BSB merged to form BSkyB, which was clearly in breach of broadcasting regulations but about which the government was either unable or unwilling to do anything.[96] The press, while more or less unregulated, nevertheless both symbolically and pragmatically embodied the broader Thatcherite 'revolution' as 'public monuments to . . . entrepreneurial talents'.[97] The events at Wapping, the Prime Minister said later, had brought 'sanity' to the national newspaper sector.[98]

The vicarious attack on Fleet Street was posited as part of the assault on the corporatist past.[99] The broadcasting institution which most represented this idea – allegedly being 'over-bureaucratised, badly managed, overstaffed, and not properly exposed to the winds of competition and market forces'[100] – and on which the Thatcher government first fixed in its sights, was the BBC. While many of the developments in television and radio (as well as the press) already outlined were simply left to 'the (unanticipated) play of market forces', the BBC was specifically targeted for reform.[101] The government began to 'pack' the board of governors, and Milne was 'sacked' in January 1987.[102] His successor, Michael Checkland, set about running – and marketing – the Corporation 'like a...business'. The subsequent appointment of John Birt as deputy Director-General signalled the completion of 'stage one of a clean sweep of the BBC's leadership'.[103] Meanwhile, the Peacock Committee, briefed to explore whether the BBC should be funded at least partly by advertising, had rejected the idea but broadly supported the further marketisation of broadcasting as a whole. Attempts to privatise public services, such as the BBC, were not universally popular in the country at large.[104] All the same, the BBC was taking seriously the 1980s mantra of being 'lean and efficient'.[105]

The Broadcasting Bill of 1989 brought together many of what Conservatives saw as the 'radical' elements inherent in the promotion of a competitive market in television and radio.[106] This focus naturally led attention away from the BBC and towards the commercial sector, where it was proposed that television licences were to be bid for competitively, and a new regulator, the Independent Television Commission (ITC), would operate with a 'lighter touch', while at the same time 'standards' would be protected. This recurrent ambiguity (noted above) provided an opportunity for opponents of the proposals to effect many substantial changes in the final Broadcasting Act, 1990, which sought to preserve the existing public service dimension of commercial television and to counteract 'the perils of deregulation'.[107] This proved to be only a partial respite, however: in 1993 the television licence regulations were relaxed to permit the ownership of two ITV franchises, and within weeks Carlton and Granada had taken over Central and London Weekend (LWT), respectively.[108] The 1996 Broadcasting Act further eased media-ownership controls, accommodating 'concentrations of power' driven by 'commercial imperatives'. Moreover, the Labour opposition now favoured fewer rather than more controls on ownership.[109]

The impact of marketisation was felt elsewhere, too. In terms of simple numerical expansion, nowhere was this more so than in radio. In less than a decade of operation the Radio Authority, established as a separate entity in 1990 with a remit to increase listener choice, licensed 166 stations of all kinds, a 210 per cent increase on the number it inherited.[110] Similarly, the magazine sector expanded considerably, the number of titles rising by more than a third during the 1990s alone, and profits almost doubling over a similar period.[111] Nonetheless, it was possible to claim that the changes were even more 'dramatic' among newspapers.[112] The obvious effects were on production and distribution, resulting in greater pagination and more supplements (that is, fatter newspapers), and a growing concentration on lifestyle matters, features and personal columns.[113] Titles were consciously positioned as 'brands', similar to fast-moving consumer goods, in order to sustain and grow profits.[114] This led in turn to the subjugation of traditional journalism, traced in detail by Jeremy Tunstall.[115] Press owners like Murdoch, it was argued, were 'motivated 99 per cent by commercial considerations'.[116] Even long-held shibboleths, such as the inelasticity of newspaper cover prices, were abandoned in a price 'war' beginning in 1993 as a manifestation of 'super-competition'.[117]

The BBC, as a public broadcaster, was not immune from this 'super-competition'. Its response, as the government imposed stringency on the licence fee while others opined that the BBC's share of the broadcast audience was bound to decline as commercial channels multiplied, was to adopt a two-pronged approach: cost-saving and commercialisation.[118] This represented the BBC's attempt at the entrepreneurism favoured by Conservatives. As a result, on the one hand, 2,000 jobs were lost in one year alone; an internal market, 'Producer Choice', was introduced; management was fundamentally restructured, and overall costs were cut by half in the 1990s. In some areas programme cuts of up to 30 per cent were made in five years. Bi-media working for journalists also reduced expenditure; but the overall effect was to alienate many both inside and outside the BBC. Birt was designated Director-General elect in 1991 and took over at the beginning of 1993, and the changes were closely associated with his name.[119] The second strand of the strategy was, in the Corporation's own phrase, a matter of 'competing worldwide'. In the 1990s, the BBC established, often in partnership with a commercial broadcaster, a range of channels, including World (Service) television and the UK TV channels Horizons, Arena, Style, Play and Gold. Within the UK, it inaugurated Choice and News 24, both of which were available digitally.[120] In 1997, the BBC announced itself to be a tri-media organisation with the launch of BBC Online, which it was claimed was the most successful website outside the USA. When Birt stood down at the beginning of 2000, he remained unapologetic: he insisted that the BBC was not only more efficient, 'better managed' and a 'global force', but that it was 'at the top of its creative powers', too.[121]

'Spin' and Dumbing Down

Such assertions did not alleviate a growing public anxiety that in the BBC, and the media as a whole, the quality of content was in some kind of decline. These views were shared by leading media figures, such as Michael Grade, Jon Snow, Harold Evans and John Pilger, the anonymous listeners who complained about what they regarded as falling standards on Radio 4, and newspaper readers who abandoned the more excessive, 'red-top' tabloids in their droves.[122] Even some media owners were prepared to argue that 'deteriorating editorial standards' resulted from excessive commercialisation.[123] By the close of the century the idea of 'dumbing down' in the media had become endemic – extending even to the choice of films on television and publishing houses' attitudes to poetry.[124]

There were a number of interconnected themes to the debate, ranged around the media's increasing incursions into the private domain, a public focus on so-called 'sleaze', the belief that the media as a whole were subject to a process of tabloidisation, and the rise of public relations, in particular political 'spin'.

The national press seemed to career out of control in the late 1980s, culminating in one respect in a brief but notorious episode in which the *Daily Star* espoused what was called at the time 'bonk journalism'.[125] In another respect, two inquiries headed by David Calcutt, the institution of a new voluntary regulatory body, the Press Complaints Commission (PCC), and a measure of self-restraint in what used to be Fleet Street, brought matters to a head, too. It became possible to argue that the limits of marketisation had perhaps been reached. Even Conservative MPs called for extended regulation.[126] In the 1990s the press focus turned to political scandal (soon to be called 'sleaze'), chiefly but not exclusively concerning sex. The Royal Family also came under unprecedented scrutiny as the marriage of the Prince and Princess of Wales fell apart. One difference was that both broadsheet newspapers and broadcasting now seemed to share what had previously been a tabloid agenda.[127] This phase, too, reached a climax in the death of Diana in 1997. Market-driven journalism seemed irrepressible, however, and within weeks it was 'business as usual' in the tabloids.[128]

The exposure of the private lives of the rich, famous and powerful was not generally regarded with disfavour by the public.[129] Besides, it also made public genuine cases of malfeasance. Any process of tabloidisation involved more than a fascination with other people's sex lives, however. It included the marginalisation, even suppression, of the 'serious' by the supposedly inconsequential. In television, for most of the 1990s this forced a struggle for survival of current affairs and the preservation of traditional news. In 1992, as a by-product of marketisation, the public-service requirement on ITV was eased, and immediately the future of current affairs programmes seemed 'uncertain', while within a year there was a plan to scrap the flagship Channel 3 news bulletin, *News at Ten*.[130] By 1999 both *News at Ten* and the remaining prime-time current affairs strand, *World in Action*, had gone, victims of the replacement of 'news-facts' with 'docu-facts...as a way of tempting younger, aspirational viewers'.[131] At its inauguration in 1997, Channel 5 attempted to recast news to focus more on 'music, football, clothes and entertainment' to reflect the interests of a younger audience in order for it 'to work commercially'.[132] Similarly, commercial radio, it was argued, had been reduced to formulaic 'format' output consisting of top 40 music and 'inane' chat.[133] Commercialism seemed to be driving information into the arms of entertainment to form the new category 'infotainment'.[134]

For most of the 1980s and 1990s changes in the structure and financing of the media were inextricably linked with regular outbreaks of hostility over content between the media and politicians. These involved (in television alone) the reporting of Northern Ireland, the Falklands/Malvinas conflict and the US bombing of Libya; accusations of right-wing infiltration of the Conservative Party; and the Zircon affair.[135] For most of the 1980s and 1990s, the national press was virulently partisan in favour of the Tories, but, as we have seen, this did not prevent the outbreak of 'sleaze' stories, aimed chiefly at government ministers and supporters, from the early 1990s. As a result, the topic was a significant factor in the 1997 general election. Arguably, the media output which generated most hostility among politicians of all parties was Radio 4's morning news magazine programme, *Today*.[136] Allied to the rise of the political public relations machine, and its greater visibility, this kind of confrontation raised questions about media–politics relations and the essential independence of the former from the latter.[137] Although the use of 'spin' by politicians was ages old, it seemed to take on a new dimension in the 1980s, built around media manipulation and news management which, some believed, included bullying the media when it was thought expedient to do so.[138] This produced a suspicion that 'serious' news consisted largely of

> politicians, iron-clad by party and government machines...cruis[ing] into studios determined to utter prefabricated banalities or pieties in order to shield themselves against what they see as a circling wolf-pack of journalists ready to tear their flesh if they expose it in the kind of free-ranging discussion on which, ultimately, a sensible discussion of public affairs depends.[139]

That many of the same politicians also acted as media regulators perhaps did nothing to allay any public unease.

The 1990s witnessed the return of anxieties over the 'popular' which had been evident in the 1930s: in many ways this was the dominant recurrent theme of the last 55 years of the twentieth century.[140] BBC research conducted towards the end of the decade suggested, unsurprisingly, that 'popular' taste had changed little.[141] Public concerns, noted throughout the period since 1945, pivoted around issues of choice, independence and diversity.[142] If the idea of popular democracy had any substance, then 'the people' (a phrase which came back into favour in the late 1990s) would have to be provided with the media they wanted. The digital forms of the Internet and broadcasting held out such promises, based on seemingly unlimited channels of more individuated communication.[143] All the same, in the emerging ecology of 'communicopia', the BBC remained in 1999 the largest single media organisation in the UK and the most successful non-American presence on the World Wide Web. It is an open question whether users were drawn by the quality of the BBC's programming and content.

Notwithstanding the Labour government's general adoption of its predecessors' determination at further commercialisation of the media and even 'lighter' regulation, it retained a concern with 'quality of content'. Unlike the Thatcher governments, however, the Labour administration professed its interest to be less ambiguous. Content 'quality' seemed to be tied to the survival of the notion of 'public service': the media, the Culture Secretary argued, amounted to more than a mere market.[144]

Conclusion

In the immediate post-war period, the media – no less the press than the BBC[145] – were party to a consensus-building project founded on corporatism, inclusive of a tradition of paternalism. A persistent strain of 'popular' resistance to this paternalistic tendency was evident in a willingness to accede to the media portrayal of (often sexually explicit) topics not considered 'nice' by the dominant bourgeois culture as a means of 'turning the world upside down', and always rendered the ideal of a consensus somewhat problematical. This consensus came under further strain in the 1960s with the growth of awareness and expressions of broader cultural diversity (coincidentally also associated with forms of sexual 'liberation'). Nevertheless, concerted attempts were made incrementally to accommodate and co-opt the 'popular', as it grew in importance in relation to the media, and the idea of a consensus largely survived in broadcasting into the 1980s, notwithstanding the considerable commercialisation and expansion of both television and radio. This provided the underpinning to shared notions of 'public service' in the media. By the mid-1970s, however, this no longer extended as comprehensively to the national press, which was less independent, less diverse, and offered less choice than it had in 1945.

In the mid-1980s, Thatcherism set out to destroy any consensus (as a manifestation of corporatism) but without dismantling its broad paternalist determination, only making adjustments to reflect a narrower set of sectarian concerns. This was based first and foremost on libertarian economics, which abhored the arrangement by which the BBC and ITV raised their revenues in uncompetitive and protected markets (the so-called cosy duopoly). It had the effect, on the one hand, of undermining the concept of 'public service' while at the same time protecting aspects of it as embodied in ideas of 'standards'. The consequences of this approach could be seen in the performance of the national press, where hyper-marketisation had led to the almost total abandonment of any adherence to 'public service' ideals, exemplified in 'the lowest standards of journalism',[146] and by the end of the century there was ample evidence that multi-channel multimedia on demand contained as much potential to further narrow choice (through the transmission of increasingly homogenised content), independence (as a result of commercial, if not always political, partisanship) and diversity (by means of mergers and acquisitions which squeezed out alternatives).

The imposition of 'the market' substituted 'numbers and variety' for independence, choice and diversity. In the broad economic and social contexts of the UK (which are beyond the scope of this chapter), this may have addressed issues around the growing importance of the media to the national economy and changing beliefs in class and identity, but in retaining the paternalist turn and simultaneously dismantling 'public service' ideals, it hardly met 'popular' aspirations for everyday media performance. For example, at the end of the century, 'popular' television viewing habits betrayed a remarkable constancy: the 18 most watched programmes in 1999 were all broadcast by ITV, yet the audience for the BBC's coverage of the 'landmark' New Year was more than three times greater than that for Channel 3. Other forms of viewing, although growing, remained very much in a minority.[147] Notions of 'quality' appeared to coexist with demands for entertainment, access and charivari in the construction of the 'popular.' It is difficult to clearly identify a moment when the media in the UK were configured to meet the aspirations of 'the people'.

Notes

1   Institute of Contemporary British History, 'A Century of the Popular Press', University of London, 9–10 September 1996. The conference gave rise to the publication of a collection of essays, edited by Peter Catterall, Colin Seymour-Ure and Adrian Smith, *Northcliffe's Legacy: Aspects of the British Popular Press, 1896–1996*, London, 2000. See also *Newsletter* 21, British Library Newspaper Library, Summer 1996, p. 12.

2   Raymond Williams, 'The Growth of the Popular Press', in *The Long Revolution*, London, 1961, p. 211; Audit Bureau of Circulation figures, June 1996, reproduced in *Press Gazette*, 19 July 1996, p. 5.

3   See Michael Bromley, 'Was it the *Mirror* Wot Won It? The Development of the Tabloid Press During the Second World War', in Nick Hayes and Jeff Hill (eds), '*Millions Like Us*'? *British Culture in the Second World War*, Liverpool, 1999, pp. 93–124.

4   Michael Bromley and Howard Tumber, 'From Fleet Street to Cyberspace: The British "Popular" Press in the Late Twentieth Century', *European Journal of Communication Research* 22(3), 1997: 368–7.

5   Royal Commission on the Press (1947–9), Cmd 7700, London, June 1949, pp. 154–5, cited in Ralph Negrine (ed.), *Television and the Press since 1945*, Manchester, 1998, pp. 133–4.

6   See John B. Thompson, *The Media and Modernity: A Social Theory of the Media*, Cambridge, 1995, esp. pp. 23–31.

7   This periodisation owes something to Arthur Marwick's approach in *British Society since 1945*, 2nd ed., Harmondsworth, 1990; see pp. 12–15. The quotation is from the same source, p. 10.

8   For an indication of the post-war resilience of Leavisite critiques see Andrew Milner, *Contemporary Cultural Theory: An Introduction*, London, 1994, pp. 29–35; Raymond Williams, *The Long Revolution*, London, 1961.

9   Royal Commission on the Press (1947–9), pp. 175–7, cited in Negrine, *Television*, p. 135.

10 George Orwell, 'London Letter' to *Partisan Review*, 15 April 1941, in Sonia Orwell and Ian Angus (eds), *George Orwell. The Collected Essays, Journalism and Letters: Volume 2*, Harmondsworth, 1970, p. 127.

11 George Orwell, 'The English People', in Sonia Orwell and Ian Angus (eds), *George Orwell. The Collected Essays, Journalism and Letters: Volume 3*, Harmondsworth, 1970, p. 39.

12 Bruce A. Williams and Michael X. Delli Carpini, 'Unchained Reaction: The Collapse of Media Gatekeeping and the Lewinsky–Clinton scandal', in *Journalism: Theory, Practice and Criticism* 1(1), 2000, pp. 63–6.

13 Orwell, 'London Letter', p. 144.

14 Orwell, 'The English People', p. 52.

15 George Orwell, 'London Letter', to *Partisan Review*, Summer 1946 in Sonia Orwell and Ian Angus (eds), *George Orwell. The Collected Essays, Journalism and Letters: Volume 4*, Harmondsworth, 1970, p. 225.

16 Jeremy Tunstall, *The Media in Britain*, London, 1983, pp. 111–16; Siân Nicholas, 'The People's Radio: The BBC and its Audience, 1939–1945', in Hayes and Hill, '*Millions Like Us*', pp. 62–92.

17 F. J. Mansfield, *Gentlemen, the Press!*, London, 1943, pp. 523–35.

18 See Michael Bromley, 'The Media', in P. Catterall et al. (eds), *Britain in 1997*, London, 2000.
19 Tom O'Malley, 'Labour and the 1947–9 Royal Commission on the Press', in M. Bromley and T. O'Malley (eds), *A Journalism Reader*, London, 1997, pp. 131–6.
20 Malcolm Muggeridge, *The Thirties: 1930–1940 in Great Britain*, London, 1940, pp. 16–19, 80–1.
21 Ibid., p. 168.
22 Ibid., p. 270ff.
23 Henry Wickham Steed, *The Press*, Harmondsworth, 1938, pp. 10–11.
24 Ibid., p. 12–50.
25 Kingsley Martin, *The Press the Public Wants*, London, 1947, pp. 62–7.
26 Wickham Steed, *The Press*, pp. 10–11.
27 Francis Williams, *Dangerous Estate: The Anatomy of Newspapers*, 1957; London, 1959, p. 179.
28 Williams, 'The Growth', p. 209; Williams, *Dangerous Estate*, p. 184.
29 Williams, *Dangerous Estate*, pp. 194–7.
30 Bromley, 'Mirror', p. 101.
31 Stephen Koss, *The Rise and Fall of the Political Press in Britain*, London, 1990, p. 1052.
32 See Bromley, 'Mirror'; Michael D. Bidiss, *The Age of the Masses: Ideas and Society in Europe since 1870*, Harmondsworth, 1977, p. 336; Simon Frith, 'The Making of the British Record Industry, 1920–64', in J. Curran, A. Smith and P. Wingate (eds), *Impacts and Influences: Essays on Media Power in the Twentieth Century*, London, 1987.
33 Bidiss, *The Age of the Masses*, p. 335.
34 Andrew Crisell, *An Introductory History of British Broadcasting*, London, 1997, p. 68.
35 Kevin Williams, *'Get Me a Murder a Day!' A History of Mass Communication in Britain*, London, 1998, pp. 144–50.
36 Ibid., p. 152; Barrie MacDonald, *Broadcasting in the United Kingdom: A Guide to Information Sources*, 2nd ed., London, 1993, pp. 8–9.
37 *Report of the Television Committee, 1943*, London, 1945, cited in MacDonald, *Broadcasting*, pp. 7–8.
38 MacDonald, *Broadcasting*, p. 9; K. Williams, *'Get Me a Murder a Day!'*, p. 155; J. Reith, *House of Lords Debates*, 22 May 1952, col. 1297, cited in Negrine, *Television*, p. 20.
39 Selwyn Lloyd, Minority Report submitted to the Committee on Broadcasting 1949, Cmd 8116, London, 1951, cited in Negrine, *Television*, pp. 18–19.
40 Labour Party Research Department, *Twelve Wasted Years*, London, 1963, pp. 274–5.
41 Crisell, *Introductory History*, p. 102.
42 Williams, *'Get Me a Murder a Day!'*, pp. 164–8.
43 Ibid., p. 167.
44 See MacDonald, *Broadcasting*, pp. 14–19; Crisell, *Introductory History*, pp. 117–24, 133–4, 188.
45 Colin Seymour-Ure, *The British Press and Broadcasting since 1945*, 2nd ed., Oxford, 1996, pp. 73–4.
46 K. Williams, *'Get Me a Murder a Day!'*, pp. 203–7; See Seymour-Ure, *British Press*, p. 170; Tony Aldgate, 'The Newsreels, Public Order and the Projection of Britain', in Curran, Smith and Wingate, *Impacts and Influences*, pp. 145–56.
47 Crisell, *Introductory History*, pp. 136–8.

48   Bidiss, *Age of the Masses*, pp. 335–6; Anthony Sampson, *Anatomy of Britain Today*, London, 1965, pp. 623–4.
49   Graham Murdock and Peter Golding, 'The Structure, Ownership and Control of the Press, 1914–76', in G. Boyce, J. Curran and P. Wingate (eds), *Newspaper History: From the 17th Century to the Present Day*, London, 1978, pp. 141–3.
50   K. Williams, '*Get Me a Murder a Day!*', pp. 215–16.
51   Negrine, *Television*, p. 137.
52   See Seymour-Ure, *The British Press*, pp. 17, 28–31. The *Mail* enjoyed something of a relative revival in the 1990s, and by September 1998 had overtaken the *Mirror* as the second best-selling daily newspaper: see Steve Peak and Paul Fisher (eds), *The Media Guide 2000*, London, 1999, p. 29.
53   Michael Bromley, *The Press in Twentieth Century Britain*, Huddersfield Pamphlets in History and Politics HP1, Huddersfield, 1995, pp. 19–20, 23.
54   R. Williams, '*The Growth*', pp. 211–13.
55   Bidiss, *The Age of the Masses*, pp. 330–1.
56   See Crisell, *Introductory History*, p. 113, 143.
57   Frank Gillard, 'Radio Station in Every City', *Yorkshire Post*, 11 December 1963, reprinted in *The BBC and Local Broadcasting*, London, 1964, p. 11.
58   Michael Barton, *BBC Radio in the Community*, London, 1976, p. 6.
59   See Seymour-Ure, *The British Press*, pp. 32, 49–58.
60   K. Williams, '*Get Me a Murder a Day!*', pp. 219–20.
61   Crisell, *Introductory History*, p. 187.
62   John Sutherland, 'Crashing through the gentility barrier', *Guardian 2*, 18 October 1999, p. 5; Anthony Sampson, *Anatomy*, pp. 668ff.; Michael Bromley, 'Sex, Sunday Papers and the "Swinging Sixties": Cultural Consensus in Northern Ireland before the Troubles', in Y. Alexander and A. O'Day (eds), *The Irish Terrorism Experience*, Aldershot, 1991, pp. 57–79.
63   *Report of the Committee on the Future of Broadcasting*, CMND 6753, London, 1977, cited in Negrine, *Television*, pp. 30–2; Minority Report in Royal Commission on the Press, *Final Report*, Cmnd 6810, London, 1977, cited in ibid., pp. 150–1 (emphasis added).
64   Tom O'Malley, 'Demanding Accountability: The Press, the Royal Commissions and the Pressure for Reform, 1945–77', in H. Stephenson and M. Bromley (eds), *Sex, Lies and Democracy: The Press and the Public*, London, 1998, esp. pp. 88–94; Crisell, *Introductory History*, pp. 176–7; K. Williams, '*Get Me a Murder a Day!*', p. 169.
65   See editions of Hoggart's *The Uses of Literacy*, 1958; Williams's *Communications*, 1962, *The Long Revolution*, 1965 and *Culture and Society, 1780–1950*, 1966; and McLuhan's *The Medium is the Message*, 1967, as well as *Discrimination and Popular Culture*, 1964, edited by Denys Thompson, Vance Packard's *The Hidden Persuaders*, 1963 and E. S. Turner's *The Shocking History of Advertising*, 1965. Other paperback imprints also published a variety of media-related trade titles; for example, *The Effects of Television*, 1970, ed. J. D. Halloran, Roy Braddon's biography *Roy Thomson of Fleet*, 1968, Martin D. Carter's *An Introduction to Mass Communications*, 1971 and Francis Williams's *Dangerous Estate*, 1959. (Place of publication all London.)
66   May Katzen, *Mass Communication: Teaching and Studies at Universities*, Paris, 1975, pp. 145–54; Crisell, *Introductory History*, p. 177.
67   Lavinia Orton (ed.), *Media Courses UK 1999*, London, 1998.
68   Matthew Engel, *Tickle the Public: One Hundred Years of the Popular Press*, London, 1996, pp. 253–68; K. Williams, '*Get Me a Murder a Day!*', pp. 220–5.

69 James Curran and Jean Seaton, *Power Without Responsibility: The Press and Broadcasting in Britain*, 5th ed., London, 1997, pp. 95–7.

70 K. Williams, '*Get Me a Murder a Day*!', pp. 249–50.

71 Curran and Seaton, *Power*, p. 97.

72 See Bromley and Tumber, 'From Fleet Street', pp. 372–5.

73 Larry Lamb, *Sunrise: The Remarkable Rise and Rise of the Best-Selling Soaraway 'Sun'*, London, 1989, p. 129.

74 Curran and Seaton, *Power*, p. 96.

75 Steve Peak (ed.), *The Media Guide 1994*, London, 1993, p. 76.

76 Hugh Stephenson, 'Tickle the Public: Consumerism Rules', in Stephenson and Bromley, *Sex, Lies and Democracy*, p. 22.

77 Address to the Press Association, June 1988, cited in Alastair Hetherington, 'The Mass Media', in Dennis Kavanagh and Anthony Seldon (eds), *The Thatcher Effect: A Decade of Change*, Oxford, 1989, p. 291.

78 After John Birt, who was appointed Deputy Director-General of the BBC in 1987 and Director-General in 1992. See below.

79 See Linda Melvern, *The End of the Street*, London, 1986.

80 Peter York and Charles Jennings, *Peter York's Eighties*, London, 1995, pp. 45–9, 160–3.

81 Harold Evans, *Good Times, Bad Times*, London, 1994, pp. 464–5.

82 For the former Heritage Secretary David Mellor's comments on this in 1994, see John Eldridge, Jenny Kitzinger and Kevin Williams, *The Mass Media and Power in Modern Britain*, Oxford, 1997, p. 41.

83 Steve Peak (ed.), *Media Guide 1993*, London, 1992, p. 13; Peak, *Media Guide 1994*, p. 19.

84 Peak and Fisher, *Media Guide 2000*, pp. 36–7.

85 Andreas Whittam Smith, 'A New "Golden Age" ?', *British Journalism Review* 1(1), 1989, pp. 19–21; Brian McNair, *News and Journalism in the UK*, 2nd ed., London, 1996, pp. 135–57.

86 MacDonald, *Broadcasting*, pp. 21–6.

87 Ibid., pp. 27–8.

88 Mathew Horsman, 'Tomorrow's World', *Media Guardian*, 29 November 1999, pp. 2–3.

89 Peak and Fisher, *Media Guide 2000*, pp. 235–6; The Radio Authority Online *www.radioauthority.org.uk*: accessed 24 February 2000.

90 John Pilger, *Distant Voices*, rev. ed., London, 1994, p. 7; Anthony Bevins, 'The Crippling of the Scribes', *British Journalism Review* 1(2), 1990: 13–17.

91 See Peter Goodwin, *Television under the Tories: Broadcasting Policy, 1979–1997*, London, 1998.

92 Chris Horrie and Steve Clarke, *Fuzzy Monsters: Fear and Loathing at the BBC*, London, 1994, pp. 10–11, 16.

93 Peter Riddell, *The Thatcher Era and its Legacy*, Oxford, 1991, p. 180; MacDonald, *Broadcasting*, pp. 19, 23, 28; Anthony Weymouth, 'The Media in Britain', in A. Weymouth and B. Lamizet (eds), *Markets and Myths: Forces for Change in the European Media*, London, 1996, p. 66.

94 See Riddell, *The Thatcher Era*, pp. 4–5; Goodwin, *Television*, pp. 163–4.

95 MacDonald, *Broadcasting*, pp. 23–31.

96 Ibid., p. 32; Crisell, *Introductory History*, pp. 216, 223.

97 Simon Jenkins, *The Market for Glory: Fleet Street Ownership in the 20th Century*, London, 1986, p. 217.

98   Michael Bromley, 'From Conciliation to Confrontation: Industrial Relations, Government and the Fourth Estate, 1896–1986', in A. O'Day (ed.), *Government and Institutions in the Post-1832 United Kingdom*, Lampeter, 1995, pp. 357–85; 'Introduction' to Stephenson and Bromley, *Sex, Lies and Democracy*, p. 5.
99   Andrew Neil, the editor of the *Sunday Times*, cited in Bromley, 'From Conciliation', p. 357.
100 Eldridge et al, *The Mass Media*, p. 55.
101 Goodwin, *Television*, p. 163.
102 Horrie and Clarke, *Fuzzy Monsters*, pp. 60–1, 65–70; Hetherington, 'The Mass Media', p. 301.
103 Horrie and Clarke, *Fuzzy Monsters*, pp. 80–5, 95.
104 Weymouth, 'The Media', p. 63; Eric Jacobs and Robert Worcester, *We British: Britain under the MORIscope*, London, 1990, p. 17ff.
105 Horrie and Clarke, *Fuzzy Monsters*, p. 158; Crisell, *Introductory History*, p. 229.
106 MacDonald, *Broadcasting*, p. 31.
107 Goodwin, *Television*, pp. 93–108, 118.
108 *Ibid.*, p. 120.
109 Steve Peak and Paul Fisher (eds), *The Media Guide 1997*, London, 1996, pp. 10–13; Goodwin, *Television*, pp. 152–3.
110 Meg Carter, *Independent Radio: The First 25 Years*, London, 1998, p. 12.
111 Weymouth, 'The Media', p. 52; McNair, *News*, p. 159; Peak and Fisher, *Media Guide 2000*, p. 87.
112 Hetherington, 'The Mass Media', p. 290.
113 Els De Bens and Helge Østbye, 'The European Newspaper Market', in D. McQuail and K. Siune (eds), *Media Policy: Convergence, Concentration and Commerce*, London, 1998, pp. 7–22; Julian Petley, 'Faces for Spaces', in Bromley and O'Malley, *A Journalism Reader*, pp. 251–72.
114 McNair, *News*, pp. 147–8, 155.
115 Jeremy Tunstall, *Newspaper Power: The New National Press in Britain*, Oxford, 1996.
116 David Linton, cited in Eldridge et al., *The Mass Media*, p. 41.
117 Negrine, *Television*, pp. 160–1; 'super-competition' is Tunstall's word (*Newspaper Power*).
118 Goodwin, *Television*, pp. 125–38.
119 Peak and Fisher, *Media Guide 1997*, pp. 146–7; Eldridge, et al., *The Mass Media*, pp. 56–9; Ian Hargreaves, '"I wasn't born to be content"', *Media Guardian*, 17 January 2000, pp. 2–3.
120 Peak and Fisher, *Media Guide 2000*, pp. 179, 198.
121 Interview with Sir John Birt, *Today* Programme, BBC Radio 4, 26 January 2000.
122 Michael Bromley, 'The Media', in P. Catterall et al. (eds), *Britain in 1998: A Review of the Year*, London, 1999, p. 65; and 'The "Tabloiding" of Britain: "Quality" Newspapers in the 1990s', in Stephenson and Bromley, *Sex, Lies and Democracy*, p. 26.
123 The magazine publisher Felix Dennis made this complaint in 1999; see Peak and Fisher, *Media Guide 2000*, p. 86.
124 The most comprehensive treatment to date of this topic is to be found in Bob Franklin, *Newszak and News Media*, London, 1997.
125 Engel, *Tickle the Public*, pp. 286–90.
126 *Ibid.*, pp. 294–95; Curran and Seaton, *Power*, p. 330.
127 Michael Bromley, '"Tabloiding" of Britain', pp. 32–4.

128   McNair, *News*, pp. 172–7; Michael Bromley and Hugh Stephenson, 'Digging Journalists out of Holes', *British Journalism Review* 9(1), 1998: 59–66.

129   Robert M. Worcester, 'Demographics and Values: What the British Public Reads and What it Thinks About its Newspapers', in Stephenson and Bromley, *Sex, Lies and Democracy*, p. 46.

130   Steve Peak (ed.), *Media Guide 1993*, London, 1992, p. 82; Peak, *Media Guide 1994*, p. 82.

131   Peak and Fisher, *Media Guide 2000*, p. 182.

132   Tim Gardam, 'Television News You Can Use', *New Statesman*, 14 November 1997, pp. 16–17.

133   Such criticisms go back two decades: see Local Radio Workshop, *Nothing Local about It: London's Local Radio*, London, 1983 ed.

134   Bob Franklin, *Packaging Politics: Political Communication in Britain's Media Democracy*, London, 1994, pp. 4–5.

135   McNair, *News*, pp. 71–5; Horrie and Clarke, *Fuzzy Monsters*, pp. 94–5.

136   Horrie and Clarke, *Fuzzy Monsters*, p. 10; Bromley, 'The Media', pp. 82–94.

137   Franklin, *Packaging Politics, p. 3.*

138   K. Williams, '*Get Me a Murder a Day!*', pp. 253–54.

139   John Lloyd, 'What's On After the News?', *New Statesman*, 28 November 1997, p. 28.

140   Stephen Hayward, 'New Labour, New Britain. Campaign Politics and the Ethics of spin', in D. Berry (ed.), *Ethics and Media Culture: Practices and Representations*, Oxford, 2000, pp. 169–70.

141   Cited in Lloyd, 'What's On', pp. 26–7.

142   T. O'Malley, 'Demanding Accountability: The Press, the Royal Commissions and the Pressure for Reform, 1945–77', in Stephenson and Bromley, *Sex, Lies and Democracy*, p. 92.

143   See Crisell, *Introductory History*, pp. 249–61.

144   Chris Smith, 'Pennies from Heaven: Public Broadcasting in the Digital Age', speech to the Royal Television Society biennial convention, Cambridge, 18 September 1997, reproduced in Chris Smith, *Creative Britain*, London, 1998, pp. 91–102.

145   Paul Addison, *The Road to 1945: British Politics and the Second World War*, London, 1994 ed., pp. 151–3.

146   Hetherington, 'The Mass Media', p. 294.

147   Will Woodward, 'ITV wins Christmas Day peak-time ratings war', *Guardian*, 27 December 1999, p. 3; Matt Wells, 'BBC wins Big Ben rating battle', Guardian, 3 January 2000, p. 3; Vikram Dodd, 'BBC programmes fail to make TV top 10', *Guardian*, 12 February 2000, p. 5.

Further Reading

The contemporary media have not been particularly well served by history. On the other hand, as Martin Carter noted nearly 30 years ago, journalists, broadcasters and others with direct experience of the media have produced (and continue to produce) a large volume of more or less historical work in the area – some of it is decidedly better than the rest.[1] Unfortunately, while the recollections and ramblings of journalists and broadcasters may contain unwitting testimony and useful primary evidence, they are more often than not so self-serving and unreliable as to require careful decoding.[2] On the other hand, there are some colourful, often amusing, analyses by journalists, including a number written with various co-authors by Chris Horrie:

Fuzzy Monsters: Fear and Loathing at the BBC (London, 1994) and *Stick it Up Your Punter! The Rise and Fall of the 'Sun'* (London, 1999) edn, are two of the better known.

Only a small number of books survey the media predominantly over the period since 1945: they include Colin Seymour-Ure's self-explanatory *The British Press and Broadcasting Since 1945* (2nd ed., Oxford, 1996); Jeremy Tunstall's snapshot *The Media in Britain* (London, 1983; now out of print); the four volumes of *Independent Television in Britain*; Ralph Negrine's collection of historical documents, *Television and the Press Since 1945* (Manchester, 1998); the fourth and fifth volumes of Asa Briggs's *The History of Broadcasting in the United Kingdom* (London, 1995 ed.); and Michael Leapman's *Treacherous Estate* (London, 1992). Jeremy Tunstall's contribution to the literature also includes *Newspaper Power* (London, 1993) and *Television Producers* (London, 1996).

The standard text, James Curran and Jean Seaton's *Power Without Responsibility: The Press and Broadcasting in Britain* (5th ed., London, 1997) has a decidedly historical slant, despite being ostensibly 'about the press, broadcasting and *politics*'.[3] It covers a time period far longer than the second half of the twentieth century, however. So do Kevin Williams's '*Get Me a Murder a Day!' A History of Mass Communication in Britain* (London, 1998), Matthew Engel's *Tickle the Public: One Hundred Years of the Popular Press* (London, 1996), and Andrew Crisell's *An Introductory History of British Broadcasting* (London, 1997). Nevertheless, each has useful chapters on the last 50 years which benefit from being set within a broader historical context.

Brian McNair's *News and Journalism in the UK* (2nd ed., London, 1996) is essentially contemporary, although it has a historical dimension. Tom O'Malley's *Closedown: The BBC and Government Broadcasting Policy, 1979–92* (London, 1994), and Peter Goodwin's *Television under the Tories: Broadcasting Policy, 1979–1997* (London, 1998) focus on specific and important topics.

Arthur Marwick's *British Society since 1945* (3rd ed., Harmondsworth, 1996) deals with the media and provides a useful contextual introduction. Peter Catterall and James Obelkevich (eds.), *Understanding Post-war British Society* (London, 1994) has informative contributions, and *Contemporary Britain: An Annual Review* (London, 1999), continued as *Britain in 1997* (London, 2000) and *Britain in 1998: A Review of the Year* (London, 1999), edited by Peter Catterall, cover most of the 1990s.

1   Martin D. Carter, *An Introduction to Mass Communications*, London, 1971, p. 7. For contrasting examples of media history written by journalists see Engel, *Tickle the Public: One Hundred Years of the Popular Press* (London, 1966) and Huw Richard's *The Bloody Circus: The 'Daily Herald' and the Left*, London, 1997.

2   See Sally Bailey and Granville Williams, 'Memoirs Are Made of This: Journalists' Memoirs in the United Kingdom, 1945–95', in M. Bromley and T. O'Malley (eds), *A Journalism Reader*, London, 1997, pp. 351–77.

3   Jean Seaton, 'Introduction' to Curran and Seaton, *Power Without Responsibility: The Press and Broadcasting in Britain*, 5th ed., London, 1997, p. 1.

Chronology

1945   Television Committee (Hankey) concludes 'television has come to stay'. Ownership of the *Financial Times* changes.

1946   BBC TV resumes service (7 June). BBC Radio Third Programme begins broadcasting.

1947–9   First Royal Commission on the Press.
1950   European Broadcasting Union established with UK as founder member. BBC transmits first UK election broadcast.
1951   Broadcasting Committee (Beveridge) rejects commercialisation and competition, both of which are supported in Selwyn Lloyd's minority report.
1953   General Council of the Press established.
          Televising the coronation of Queen Elizabeth II increases TV ownership, and more than seven million copies of the coronation day issue of the *Daily Mirror* are sold. Roy Thomson acquires *The Scotsman*.
1954   Television Act sets up ITV.
1955   ITV transmission begins in London with Associated-Rediffusion and Associated Television, as well as Independent Television News (ITN). The *News Chronicle* absorbs the *Daily Dispatch*.
1957   *Picture Post* ceases publication.
          The *Financial Times* becomes part of the Pearson Group.
1958   End of newsprint rationing.
1959   The *Manchester Guardian* becomes the *Guardian*. Thomson acquires the *Sunday Times*.
1960   The *News Chronicle*, *Sunday Graphic*, *Empire News* and *The Star* cease publication.
1961   The *Sunday Telegraph* launched.
          The Mirror Group acquires the *Daily Herald*.
1961–2   Second Royal Commission on the Press.
1962   The Committee on Broadcasting (Pilkington) report is highly critical of ITV. First transatlantic satellite television exchange takes place between the USA and 16 European countries. *Reynolds News* merges into the *Sunday Citizen*.
1963   International Publishing Corporation (IPC) formed.
1964   BBC 2 begins transmission (20 Apr.). The 'pirate' radio station, Radio Caroline, transmits from ship moored off the Essex coast. The *Daily Herald* is replaced by the *Sun*. The General Council of the Press becomes the Press Council. *The Guardian* moves from Manchester to London.
1965   Government ban on advertising cigarettes on television comes into force.
1966   Thomson buys *The Times*, which carries news on its front page for the first time.
1967   BBC 2 inaugurates regular colour broadcasting. The *Sunday Citizen* ceases publication. Responding to the radio 'pirates', BBC starts Radio 1 and renames its other services Radios 2, 3 and 4. Radio Leicester becomes first local radio station on 8 November.
1968   Yorkshire gets its own ITV franchise.
1969   BBC 1 and ITV start broadcasting in colour.
          Rupert Murdoch acquires the *Sun* and *News of the World*.
1970   Reed International formed from Reed Group and IPC.
1971   Open University transmissions begin (10 Jan.). The *Daily Mail* becomes a tabloid.
1972   Television Advisory Committee (Cockburn) recommends fourth TV channel.
1973   The first Independent Local Radio (ILR) stations (LBC and Capital in London and Clyde in Glasgow) go on air. Teletext unveiled by the Independent Broadcasting Authority.
1974   Committee on Broadcasting Coverage (Crawford) recommends that the fourth channel in Wales should be a distinct service prioritising Welsh-language programming.

1974–77   Third Royal Commission on the Press.

1975   Reed International creates Mirror Group as a subsidiary.

1976   The *Evening Post* (Nottingham) is first UK newspaper to introduce direct inputting by journalists.

1977   Committee on the Future of Broadcasting (Annan) reports. Trafalgar House acquires the *Daily Express* and *Sunday Express*.

1978   First regular sound broadcasting of Parliament begins (3 Apr.). The *Daily Star* is the first new national daily newspaper for 75 years.

1979   First international edition of the *Financial Times* is published in Frankfurt.

1980   The (London) *Evening News* ceases publication.

1981   Broadcasting Complaints Commission begins work.
          Joint BBC–ITV television ratings system, BARB, starts operating. Murdoch acquires *The Times* and *Sunday Times*. Experimental pay-TV launched. More than 750 million viewers in 74 countries watch the broadcasts of the wedding of the Prince of Wales and Lady Diana Spencer.

1982   Channel 4 begins broadcasting (2 Nov.). The separate Sianel Pedwar Cymru (S4C) opened the previous day. *The Mail on Sunday* is launched as the first national newspaper to use photocomposition.

1983   Breakfast TV begins. BBC launches its programme *Breakfast Time* (17 Jan.), prior to start-up of the ITV service operated by TV-am (1 Feb.). Industrial dispute at the Messenger group owned by Eddy Shah.

1984   Sky, first satellite television service, begins (16 Jan.). First 'broadband' cable system starts in Swindon. Mirror Group sold to Robert Maxwell. Reuters, the news agency, floated as a public company.

1985   Experimental televising of the House of Lords starts (23 Jan.). New Cable Authority begins granting franchises. United Newspaper acquire the *Daily Express*, *Sunday Express*, and *Daily Star*. Conrad Black secures control of the *Daily Express* and *Sunday Telegraph*.

1986   Murdoch moves his Fleet Street newspapers to Wapping. Committee on Financing the BBC (Peacock) recommends deregulation of television but not wholesale commercialisation of the BBC. Eddy Shah launches *Today*, first colour national newspaper. *The Independent* and *Sunday Sport* begin publication. Marmaduke Hussey appointed Chairman of the BBC.

1987   24-hour TV broadcasting begins. The *London Daily News* and *News on Sunday* are new but short-lived national newspapers.

1987–9   Most of the national press leaves Fleet Street.

1988   MPs vote to permit experimental televising of House of Commons. *Scotland on Sunday* and *Sunday Life* (Belfast) launched by Thomson. The *Daily Mirror* becomes first colour mass-circulation tabloid national newspaper. Broadcasting Standards Council begins work. 'Broadcasting ban' (restricting the reporting of proscribed organisations associated with Northern Ireland) implemented.

1989   First 'incremental' independent radio stations go on air (Sunset Radio in Manchester, Sunrise Radio in London and WNK and London Greek Radio). Sky Television begins direct broadcasting by satellite (DBS). Televising of Commons proceedings starts. *Wales on Sunday* launched by Thomson. The *Sunday Correspondent* begins publication.

1990   British Satellite Broadcasting (BSB) begins transmitting, initially by cable then by DBS. BSB and Sky merge only eight months later to form BSkyB. Incremental music stations (Jazz FM, Melody and Kiss FM) go on air. BBC launches Radio 5 (27 Aug.). Broadcasting Act sets up Independent Television

Commission (ITC) and Radio Authority (RA) and gives statutory status to Broadcasting Standards Council. Authorises privatisation of IBA's transmission system and introduces competitive tendering for ITV franchises. *The Independent on Sunday* launched, and *The European* started by Maxwell. First Calcutt Report on privacy is strongly critical of the press.

1991 ITV franchises are awarded through competitive tendering. Twelve franchisees retain their licences: Carlton replaces Thames in London and GMTV takes over from TV-am. Programmes listings publication monopoly of *Radio Times* and *TV Times* ends. Classic FM, first national commercial radio station, goes on air. Press Council replaced by Press Complaints Commission (PCC). *Daily Sport* begins publication. Robert Maxwell dies. John Birt appointed Director-General designate of the BBC. BBC and Thames Television launch the cable and satellite channel UK Gold.

1992 *Yorkshire on Sunday* launched by Westminster Press. *Sunday Times* serialises book *Diana: Her True Story*, and the *Daily Mirror* publishes pictures of Duchess of York sunbathing topless with a man. Obligation on ITV to broadcast minimum of peak-time current affairs programming ceases. Radio Join Audience Research Company (RAJAR) established. Channel 4 starts *The Big Breakfast*.

1993 Second Calcutt Report into press self-regulation. Guardian Media Group acquires *The Observer*. Cover prices of the *Sun* and *The Times* are cut, initiating a national newspaper 'price war'. Channel 4 TV becomes a public body. By law both BBC ITV are required to commission 25 per cent of programming from indepent producers. BskyB changes from mainly free-to-air to largely subscription service. Relaxation of the controls on mergers and takeovers within ITV leads to Carlton bidding for Central Television and Granada for London Weekend.

1994 Mirror Group Newspapers leaves Fleet Street and acquires control of *The Independent* and *Independent on Sunday*. PCC appoints a privacy commissioner. Anglia TV taken over by the group owning Meridian. New censorship controls on videos introduced. BBC Radio 5 is relaunched as Five Live. First five regional independent radio stations go on air.

1995 Three major regional and local newspaper companies, Thomson, Reed and Emap, sell out. Conservative Government announces a relaxation of cross-media ownership regulations. *Today*, owned since 1987 by Murdoch, ceases publication.

1996 BskyB agrees to pay £670 million for the broadcasting rights for the next four years to Premier League football. Pearson sells its regional and local newspaper group, Westminster Press. Net book agreement, fixing the price of books, effectively abandoned by publishers.

1997 Channel 5 goes on air (30 Mar.). Broadcasting Standards Commission replaces Broadcasting Standards Council and Broadcasting Complaints Commission. British Digital Broadcasting wins licence for the first digital TV service. The company controlling Anglia and Meridian television takes over HTV. Yorkshire-Tyne Tees bought by Granada. A record 31.5 million people watch TV broadcast of the funeral of Diana, Princess of Wales. Elton John's *Candle in the Wind 1997* is biggest selling record of all time. Chris Evans buys Virgin Radio. BBC launches News Online.

1998 Digital television services begin. Reed Elsevier sells IPC. United News and Media sells its local newspapers. Vacancies for BBC governors advertised for first time. Murdoch attempts to take over Manchester United FC. New arrangements introduced for fewer party political and election broadcasts. ITV scraps *News at Ten*. *The European* ceases publication.

1999   Culture Secretary Chris Smith suggests that analogue TV will be switched off by 2010. Trinity, largest publisher of regional newspapers, merges with the Mirror Group. The Davies Report recommends supplementary licence fee be imposed on those receiving digital television services.

Part II
Society

12 Social Trends, Structures, Values and Behaviour

Arthur Marwick

The social trends I am concerned with in this chapter are those relating to population, births, marriages and deaths. Britain is often said to be the most class-ridden and class-conscious of all the developed countries: that question is addressed in the second of my topics where I consider class structure and class attitudes, the implications of these, and how far class has changed since 1945. By social values I means such things as religious belief, and how far people subscribe to collectivism and 'secular anglicanism' (broadly meaning consensus and tolerance). This leads on to the major issues of permissiveness and sexual behaviour, 'consumerism' and leisure activities. Finally, I take up the topic of crime. We should not think of social trends as proceeding ineluctably and in one direction: social trends are much affected by economic circumstances and, in particular, global developments, by events and accidents, and by the actions of politicians. The first part of our period was much influenced by the Second World War and its aftermath, by shortages and austerity, and then by economic recovery. In the arena of values and behaviour, striking, and in many ways unique, changes took place during the period I refer to as 'the long sixties' (*c*.1958 to *c*.1974). The abandonment at government level, if not among the people at large, of social democratic Keynesian and consensual values after 1979 had profound effects in some areas, though none in others.

Population and Vital Statistics

The population of the United Kingdom has grown steadily since the pre-war years (see table 12.1).[1] Rates of change vary from decade to decade, and in different parts of the country. Growth rates are highest in Northern Ireland (where population rose by 17 per cent between 1961 and 1997), while in Scotland the population was actually 1 per cent lower in 1997 than 1961, although it was slightly higher than in 1991. The English population increased by 13 per cent over the same period and the Welsh by 11 per cent (table 12.2). The

Table 12.1 Population change in the UK, 1921–1997 (000s)

			Average annual change			
	Population at start of period	Live births	Deaths	Net natural change	Net migration and other	Overall change
1921–31	44,027	824	555	268	−67	201
1931–51	46,038	785	598	188	25	213
1951–61	50,287	839	593	246	6	252
1961–71	52,807	963	639	324	−12	312
1971–81	55,928	736	666	69	−27	42
1981–91	56,352	757	655	103	43	146
1991–97	57,808	754	640	113	87	200

Table 12.2 Population of the UK by countries, 1931–1997 (000s)

	1931	1951	1961	1971	1981	1991	1997
England	37,359,045	41,159,213	43,561	46,412	46,821	48,208	49,284
Wales	2,593	2,599	2,635	2,740	2,813	2,891	2,927
Scotland	4,843	5,096	5,184	5,236	5,180	5,107	5,123
Northern Ireland	1,243	1,371	1,427	1,540	1,538	1,601	1,675
United Kingdom	46,038	50,225	52,807	55,928	56,352	57,808	59,009

fundamental and continuing reason for rise in population was that of older people living longer. Traditionally, Britain had always lost population through people going to live overseas, particularly in the Commonwealth countries and the United States. Although immigration from the West Indies and the Indian subcontinent increased sharply in the later 1950s and early 1960s, outward migration was still greater than inner in both the 1960s and the 1970s (as table 12.1 shows). More recently, through immigration from Europe, the white Commonwealth and the United States, as much as from the West Indies and the Indian subcontinent, which was now being strictly controlled, the balance has reversed.

The United Kingdom, in common with other Western countries – most notably France, which had been particularly severely affected by a declining birth rate in the inter-war years – had a 'baby boom' during, and in greater degree, immediately after, the war. It does seem to be a truism that amid the excitements and horrors of war sexual activity increases. It is not hard to understand that with men going out to face dangerous and terrifying conditions on land, sea and in the air, couples should want to make the most of every precious moment and, perhaps, ensure that there would be a child for the father to be remembered by. Illegitimate births, naturally, increased, as well as legitimate ones. And while many women enjoyed their wartime activities, or at least felt proud to be doing their bit for their country and their menfolk, many also expressed a wish at the end of the war to get on and build homes and families.

That men returning from the war should seek the solace of domesticity is not in any way surprising.

The baby boom of the 1940s gave rise to there being a large number of young people within the population of the 1960s; the 1960s, a time of general buoyancy, in turn, had a 'baby boom' of its own, meaning that there were again large number of young people in the 1980s. But in the 1970s, a disturbed period of economic crisis, and the doubling of world oil prices in 1973, the birth rate was the lowest of the century. Another very important point is brought out by table 12.3. For centuries, women had been disadvantaged in the search for a sexual partner. Although more male children are always born, their survival rates are lower than those of females, this being particularly true, of course, in times of war. But just as medical improvements were keeping older people alive, so too were they keeping male children alive.

Women are tougher than men so that in the older age groups, and in the total population, they continue to outnumber men. But the critical age groups to look at are those for the 15–29, and to a lesser degree 30–44, age groups in table 12.3, and the 16–24 and 25–34 age groups in table 12.4. There is still a slight scarcity of young men in 1951, but already by 1961 the balance is, for the

Table 12.3   Population of the UK by age and gender, 1931–1981 (000s)

	1931	1951	1961	1971	1981
Males: all ages	22,060	24,118	24,118	25,481	26,952
0–4	1,784	2,215	2,162	2,312	1,717
5–14	3,859	3,566	4,159	4,561	4,159
15–29	5,804	5,073	5,159	5,195	6,294
30–44	4,495	5,461	5,225	4,909	5,401
45–64	4,647	5,554	6,397	6,452	6,003
65–74	1,099	1,561	1,602	1,976	2,210
75+	372	687	776	828	1,019
Females: all ages	23,978	26,107	27,228	28,562	28,286
0–4	1,747	2,111	2,051	2,194	1,632
5–14	3,784	3,433	3,964	4,321	3,946
15–29	6,049	5,255	5,100	5,764	6,115
30–44	5,222	5,663	5,300	4,850	5,359
45–64	5,229	6,425	7,003	6,931	6,293
65–74	1,361	2,128	2,369	2,737	2,839
75+	586	1,091	1,442	1,765	2,102

Table 12.4   Age and gender structure of the UK population, 1991 and 1995 (%)

		Under 16	16–39	40–64	65–79	80 and over
1991	**Males**	21.4	36.7	29.0	10.6	2.3
	Females	19.3	34.0	28.2	13.3	5.2
1995	**Males**	22	29	27	10	8
	Females	20	26	26	10	9

first time ever, shifting in favour of women. There were to be many reasons for the growing self-confidence among women and the rise of the new wave of feminism: this demographic change may possibly have been one of them. While we can see what was happening among young people, the strongest fact of all to emerge is that Britain has an ageing population – a higher proportion of old people, as well as the increasing numbers of young ones staying on in higher education, was being supported by a shrinking working population. In 1961, around 12 per cent of the population were aged 65 and over and 4 per cent were aged 75 and over. In 1997 these figures had increased respectively to 16 per cent and 7 per cent.

Relating to that much pontificated-over institution, marriage, there is one steady trend from the end of the previous century: the number of households grew at a much faster rate than the population, while the size of households got smaller. The trend to smaller families begins with the better-off classes, then, as higher living standards spread to the working class, particularly after the Second World War, family limitation becomes more general, particularly with the spread of effective contraception. The contraceptive pill became available in 1961, but it is important to be aware that even by 1968 only 2 million women out of about 15 million of childbearing age were on the pill, which only went into widespread use in the 1970s.

There have been scares over, and fluctuations in, the use of the pill since then, but the overall figures have not changed drastically. We may note only 14 per cent of married women not using some form of contraception, and that the pill was most used by the younger married women, while being quite widely used by unmarried women in the 20–24 age group. Almost half of all women in this age group were using some form of contraception, while this was true of about a quarter in the 16–19 age group. With the exceptions just noted, younger women who started on the pill tended to stay with it. The Aids scare beginning in the 1980s brought an increased use of condoms, particularly among the unmarried, with women often being the purchasers.

In 1911 average household size had been 4.5 persons: this had fallen to 3.2 in 1951, 2.9 in 1971, 2.7 in 1981, 2.5 in 1991 and 2.4 in 1998. The long-term trend to smaller households apart, the history of the family in our period went through two distinctively different, though overlapping, phases. In the first phase, up to 1970–1 there was a 'marriage boom'. In the 30 years up to the middle or late 1960s the proportion of the whole population who were married rose from 43 to 51 per cent, while the proportion of single persons in the population over 15 years of age fell from nearly a third to under a quarter. This was mainly due to an increase in marriage rates among men and women in their late teens and early twenties. In 1931 only 25 per cent of young women be-tween the ages of 20 and 24 were married; by the early 1960s this figure was 60 per cent. After the 'marriage boom' peaked at 402,000 marriages in 1951, the figures dropped slightly to 387,000 in 1961, then began their sharp rise to the all-time high of 447,000 in 1970. Already, as the number of marriages reached its peak, the cultural revolution of the 1960s was spreading general acceptance of the notion that marriage was not necessarily for life, and that there was nothing untoward in having several sexual partnerships. In pre-war years

Table 12.5 Use of contraceptives by women in Great Britain by age and marital status, 1976 (%)

	Sheath/ condom	Pill	Cap	Intra-uterine device	Female sterilisation	Male sterilisation	Withdrawal	Other methods	None
Married									
Age groups									
16–19	15	62	0	8	0	1	2	1	13
20–24	12	67	–	7	2	2	2	2	8
25–29	17	46	2	10	4	7	5	2	10
30–34	21	29	2	9	11	13	5	2	9
35–39	23	18	3	9	15	13	8	3	10
40–44	24	13	4	5	13	10	10	5	18
45–49	31	8	4	1	9	2	14	5	31
All age groups	22	28	2	7	9	9	8	3	14
Single									
Age groups									
16–19	5	20	–	0	0	0	1	–	74
20–24	3	43	0	1	0	0	1	–	52
25–29	9	26	2	2	0	0	1	3	57
30–34	4	17	2	2	0	0	0	6	70
35–39	3	11	0	3	0	0	3	0	80
40–44	2	4	2	0	0	0	0	0	91
45–49	3	0	0	0	0	0	6	0	91
All age groups	4	26	–	1	0	0	1	1	67

divorce had been practically out of the question for the vast majority, partly because of social pressures, more because of expense. The introduction of Legal Aid in 1948 made some difference, the Divorce Law Reform Act of 1969 (effective from 1971), making divorce possible upon the irredeemable breakdown of a marriage, much more. It is important to note that divorced people frequently went on to marry again: in 1961 remarriages amounted to only 14 per cent of all marriages; by 1981 the figure had gone up to 34 per cent. Meantime there had been a very sharp fall in the total number of marriages since 1970: a drop of 24 per cent to 340,000 in 1991, with, however – no trends being inevitable – a slight rise to 347,000 in 1992. The figure for 1994 is 338,000, and for 1996, 185,000, a drop by half since 1970. Over the same period the number of divorces more than doubled, with remarriages remaining fairly constant at one-third of all marriages. But there is another blip to note: from 1993 to 1996 the number of divorces declined slightly. Overall, the figures, in thousands, are as follows: 1961, 27; 1971, 79.2; 1981, 155.6; 1991, 171.1; 1993, 180; 1996, 171. Blip or not, Britain by a clear margin had the highest divorce rate in the European Union.

What did rise notably was the number of people formally recorded as 'cohabiting', that is, living together in apparently fairly stable relationships, 'partners' rather than 'husbands and wives'. The proportion of all non-married women aged 18 to 49 who were cohabiting in Britain doubled from 1981, to 25 per cent in 1997. All of these trends continued, and, if anything, accelerated during the years of the Thatcher governments. In the new circumstances, one no longer talked about 'illegitimate births', but simply 'births outside marriage'. Here, certainly, the rise was 'particularly steep in the 1980s',[2] so that in 1997 the proportion of such births was four times that in 1974. The United Kingdom headed another European league table in having the highest number of births per thousand women aged 15 to 19. At the same time there was a marked increase since 1991 in the number of women over 35 conceiving.

The proportion of families headed by a lone parent, under 8 per cent in 1971, was 23 per cent in 1994, with just 2 per cent of that total being men. The overarching trend throughout our period, compared with before the war, was that of more people finding more sexual partners, even if only temporarily, a trend which began to accelerate in the 1960s, and perhaps again, in certain aspects, in the 1980s. Yet a distinctive feature of the second phase was the growth in the number of people, often relatively young, living alone. In 1961, only 4 per cent of people under pensionable age lived in single-person households: the figure was 6 per cent in 1971, 8 per cent in 1981, 11 per cent in 1991, and 14 per cent in 1998.

Class

Distinctions of class probably interpenetrate the rest of British life more extensively than elsewhere, but it would be quite wrong to think that such distinctions do not exist in other countries. Up to the late 1970s, under the influence of the war, deliberate government policy, and a general public ethos of consensus (even if not always privately subscribed-to), the trend was towards higher status and better conditions for the working class, within an unchanging class structure, and towards greater opportunities for mobility out of the working class. A broad trend throughout, a result of economic and industrial change, was a steady shrinkage in the size of this class. The shrinkage became more marked after 1979, when the forces and ideology of market economics led to some shaking of traditional class shibboleths, though also to the emergence of an underclass of the dispossessed and unfortunate. After conducting a meticulous social survey between 1948 and 1951 in the Oxfordshire town of Banbury, Professor Margaret Stacey concluded that 'it was impossible to ignore the existence of upper-class people'. Furthermore, 'insofar as this class sets the standards and aspirations of traditional social class attitudes...it is important out of all proportion to its size. Finally, members of the traditional upper class...were all educated at one of the major public schools.' At the other end of the scale, Professor Stacey found, 'the majority of the working class have received only an elementary education while a much higher proportion of the middle class received a secondary education'. But, in keeping with the variegated character I have mentioned, a common educational background was not a specific middle-class characteristic: the middle classes recruited from all sections of society.[3]

Regularly throughout the 1960s, interviews and opinion polls showed that well over 90 per cent of the population recognised the existence of social classes. When a representative sample were asked, without prompting, to allocate themselves to a social class, 67 per cent said they were 'working-class' and 29 per cent said they were 'middle-class'. Of the remainder, one per cent said 'upper-working-class', one per cent said 'lower-middle-class', and one per cent said 'upper-class'; this left only one per cent unable to allocate themselves to any of the traditional classes, including one 'twenty-five-stone eccentric' who said he belonged to the 'sporting class'.[4] On the whole, members of the upper class do not participate in such polls. I would reckon these figures, in respect to occupations, incomes and social behaviour, to be broadly right, but would allow 3 per cent or so for the upper class.

Also in the 1960s, the sociologists J. H. Goldthorpe, John Lockwood, Bechofer and Platt carried out a famous survey of 'the affluent worker' in Luton, covering assembly-line workers at Vauxhall Motors, machine operators and craftsmen servicing machines at Skefco's Ball Bearing Company, and process workers and craftsmen engaged on process maintenance at Laporte Chemicals. This did suggest some fragmentation of traditional working-class images and some blurring of class lines. Fourteen per cent claimed for themselves definite 'middle-class' status, while 8 per cent took the view that they could be described equally well as 'working'-class or 'middle'-class. Yet 67 per cent had no difficulty in allocating themselves to the 'working class'. The Luton workers stressed the unpleasantness of their work, giving the high pay as its only advantage, but expressed no very strong feelings against separate canteens: 'I don't like the idea of the boss breathing down my neck at mealtimes', said one. All three of the Luton firms encouraged promotion upwards from the shop floor, but the mass of the labour force continued to think of themselves as being merely waged workers.[5] To be working-class in the 1960s, then, despite the occasional instance of rapid upward mobility, meant a 'life sentence' of hard manual work where, by an implicit irony, the attainment of middle-class living standards was only possible through expending, on overtime, even more excessive amounts of energy in a traditionally working-class way.

The critical developments in the Thatcher era were an acceleration in the breaking-up of the rigid frontiers of the working class, and more abrupt openings to positions of power and influence for people who had not taken the trouble to absorb the traditional upper-class lifestyle. The much talked-of 'yuppie', though overpublicised, did have corporeal existence. In this era of buying and selling (in information services, shares, land for development) there were large incomes and commissions to be earned in finance, accountancy, law and in agencies and consultancies of all kinds, as well as in commerce. That, combined with vigorous propaganda on behalf of the notion that success was far more important than social origins, was the basis for the yuppie phenomenon.

We are fortunate in having the carefully presented results of a well-conceived survey carried through in the period 1 March to 3 July 1984 (published in 1988 as *Social Class in Britain Today*, by Gordon Marshall, Howard Newby, David Rose and Carolyn Vogler). The authors came up with figures of 58 per cent working-class and 42 per cent middle-class, once again ignoring the upper class. They demonstrated a very high sense of class awareness in this reduced working class, though little class- consciousness in the Marxist sense.[6]

Thatcherite policies entailed a general Americanisation of British society. But if some of the cultural badges of class were worn off, the more fundamental divisiveness of sharp economic inequality was intensified. What was happening at the bottom was documented in the Joseph Rowntree Foundation Report on *Income and Wealth* published in February 1995. Between 1979 and 1992 the bottom 10 per cent grew steadily worse off, while the next 10 to 20 per cent derived no benefits from economic growth. The number of people with incomes less than half of the national average trebled. And many of the traditional features of class did remain. On 12 December 1993 the *Observer* presented interviews with individuals said to be representative of 'the working class' (a 44-year-old production-line worker at the Ford plant in Dagenham, East London), the 'middle class' (a young mother of two who worked as a gardener and in her husband's computer consultancy), 'the upper middle class' (the director of an exclusive merchant bank) and 'the upper class' (the eleventh duke of Devonshire). It is quite clear that the merchant banker is, by any sensible criteria, upper- class, and from the attitude of ineffable superiority which comes through, it is clear that he really thinks so himself, while considering it bad taste to actually say so. The middle-class woman is from the Irish working class, but has clearly married upwards. The car-worker tells it as it is, 'In our plant there really is a class society, you've got the management canteen and car park, workers' canteen and car park, and we all know our place.' The 73-year-old duke would almost be an irrelevance, save that, as I have said, the aristocrats provide the core for the upper class. His vantage point is so far above society that he thinks Margaret Thatcher 'working-class', a sentiment which would have infuriated that upwardly mobile lower-middle-class lady.

Speaking in December 1998, Prime Minister Tony Blair declared: 'slowly but surely, the old Establishment is being replaced by a new, larger, more merito-cratic middle class'. In that same month the old official classification of people into classes I–V, which dated from 1911, was replaced by a more complex system, broadly suggesting that almost everyone was now middle-class. With manufacturing contributing only 20 per cent of GDP, the traditional working class had shrunk still further. But a recognisably three-class society still existed, with the regrettable addition of an underclass.

Social Values: Collectivism, Religion, Secular Anglicanism

The general election of 1945 was no people's rising on behalf of the Establish-ment of a socialist society, and detailed analysis of opinion polls has brought out that the public were certainly not deeply collectivist by conviction.[7] All subsequent evidence from voting behaviour suggests that a majority of the elect-orate preferred moderate, consensual policies, and certainly had no liking for the policies of the extreme Left. Thatcher never had anything like a majority in the electorate, and while, obviously, the extreme collectivist policies of Labour in the 1980s found little support, attitude surveys suggest that despite Thatch-er's radical market economics and denial of the very existence of society, sub-stantial sections of the public remained attached to moderate collectivist or communal policies.[8] Attitude surveys balancing taxation against welfare are slightly suspect in that when it comes to elections people don't always put their votes where their mouths are. However, table 12.6 is striking in that it shows a steadily growing collectivist sentiment – and, after all, Labour did win the 1997 election.

In religious belief and practice the steady trend, from well before our period and right through it, has been a decline, save for Northern Ireland, and the ethnic and American evangelical religions. At the beginning of the 1950s 26 per cent of men and 18 per cent of women declared that they had no religious affiliation at all. The figures for regular churchgoing were 11 per cent of women and 7 per cent of men; 45 per cent of the population were intermittent

Table 12.6 Survey on higher welfare spending versus lower taxes in the UK, 1983–1993 (% of respondents)

	1983	1986	1990	1993
If the government had to choose it should ...				
Reduce taxes and spend less on health, education and social benefits	9	5	3	4
Keep taxes and spending at the same levels as now	54	44	37	29
Increase taxes and spend more on health, education and social benefits	32	46	54	63

churchgoers, that is to say they went to church once or twice a year, while 40 per cent of the population did not attend church at all. However, 93 per cent did expect to attend church for weddings or funerals and 50 per cent of all parents still sent their children to Sunday school. Continuing decline in the main Christian churches, and growth in the minority ones, can be seen in Table 12.7; but note some apparent recoveries in the 1990s.

If mainland Britain was distinguished by the absence of religious conflict, it was also distinguished by the fact that its police forces were unarmed. Generally, that did reflect a unified society, where civil disturbances were rare, and civic loyalty high. Perhaps the British were deferential, but it was what one might call a bounded deference: deference to the social structure and to the established ways of doing things, rather than to agents of the state. Geoffrey Gorer's survey in January 1951 found that 73 per cent of the men and 74 per cent of the women in his sample thought highly of the police; though 18 per cent were prepared to voice critical opinions, this was over individual police activities, not of the police as an institution.[9] The 1960s cultural revolution was time of challenge to, and questioning of, all authorities, a trend which accelerated in the Thatcher period when divisions between a centralising and authoritarian government and a population becoming ever more libertarian with their attitudes became wider and wider. With Labour having successively failed to replace the Conservatives, there was not a great deal of trust for politicians in any party. In a poll in December 1993, 43 per cent said they found no party trustworthy, with 14 per cent giving that label to the Conservatives, 23 per cent to Labour, and 19 per cent to the Liberal Democrats. Only 14 per cent thought the government told the truth, with 77 per cent disagreeing. A poll[10] showing

Table 12.7   Church membership in the UK, 1970–1995 (000s)

	1970	1980	1990	1995
Traditional Christian				
Roman Catholic	2,714	2,457	2,201	1,915
Anglican	2,994	2,179	1,728	1,785
Presbyterian	1,666	1,438	1,214	1,100
Other three churches	646	516	601	648
Methodist	642	521	452	401
Baptist	269	240	231	223
Orthodox	191	203	266	289
Non-traditional				
Mormons	85	114	160	171
Jehovah's Witnesses	62	85	117	131
Others	138	154	182	220
Non-Christian				
Muslim	130	306	495	580
Sikh	100	150	250	350
Hindu	80	120	140	155
Jewish	120	111	101	94
Others	21	53	87	116

which professions were most and least trusted, (in percentages) showed how far police officers and other figures of authority had fallen.

I draw my phrase 'secular anglicanism' from the broad tolerance shown by the Anglican church from the eighteenth century onwards towards dissenting congregations.[11] This characteristic was clearly put under some strain in the 1980s and 1990s, but when Britain's urban riots of that era are compared with similar events abroad, and the loss of life generally incurred there, and when one moves back to the 1960s and considers the way in which the country adapted to, and absorbed the various counter-cultural protest movements, then this characteristic does seem something of a constant theme throughout our entire period. Of course, along with it there went a certain complacency, a reluctance to learn lessons from abroad, and up until the 1960s, anyway, an insularity, 'a poverty of aspiration', as Labour leader Ernest Bevin put it, and the prudishness on which many foreign commentators remarked. Just over half the men and nearly two-thirds of the women interviewed by Gorer in 1951 expressed disapproval of sex before marriage: 43 per cent of his total sample admitted to having had a sexual relationship before or outside marriage, while 47 per cent gave an emphatic denial. With regard to the statements that sex was 'very important' in marriage, and that 'women really enjoy the physical side of sex just as much as men', 65 per cent of the men agreed as against 51 per cent of women.[12]

Openness, Permissiveness, Frankness

The heart of the cultural revolution lay in the transformation in human relationships, between parents and children, between men and women. Not least of the new freedoms was the freedom to be honest, to speak frankly, to be free of the old conventions and circumlocutions. Before the 1960s, what were widely referred to as 'dirty books' had to be imported surreptitiously from France. Most notorious was D. H. Lawrence's novel of the 1920s, *Lady Chatterley's Lover*. In 1955 a shopkeeper in a lower- class part of London was sentenced to

Table 12.8 Results of poll showing respect in UK for various professions, 1993

	Most	Least
Doctors	81	4
Nurses	79	2
Teachers	49	6
Police officers	41	17
Judges	27	21
Civil servants	20	15
Estate agents	6	45
Politicians	5	59
Journalists	3	57
Car salespeople	3	62

six months in prison for having this book in stock. In was in the latter half of 1959 that ultra-respectable paperback publishers Penguin Books decided to mark the thirtieth anniversary (falling on the following year) of Lawrence's death, and the twenty-fifth of Penguin's birth, with eight Lawrence titles, including an unexpurgated *Lady Chatterley's Lover*. Of this, 200,000 copies were printed, but held back while a dozen copies were sent to the Director of Public Prosecutions. Thus it came to pass that that the most celebrated and illuminating trial of this critical time of change was held at the Old Bailey during five days in November 1960. The jury (five of whom had difficulty in just reading the oath) acquitted *Lady Chatterley* of obscenity: printing hundreds of thousands of new copies (two million were sold within the year), Penguin added a blurb referring triumphantly to the trial: 'it was not just a legal tussle, but a conflict of generation and class'.

Changes in sexual attitudes and behaviour affected large sections of society, but were most striking among young people. Even among the more restrained and conformist, there tended to be an admiration for the more daring. The first really systematic survey ever of *The Sexual Behaviour Of Young People* – the title of the book by Michael Schofield, research director of the Central Council for Health Education and organiser of the survey, published in 1965, concluded that while some teenagers (mostly boys) certainly were sexually active, any idea of teenagers being generally promiscuous was quite incorrect. Government statistics did show that in 1960, 31 per cent of girls who married in their teens were already pregnant.

Guides to etiquette are valuable sources: important changes can be tracked, as between the 1956 and 1969 editions of the popular publication *Lady Behave*, written by Anne Edwards and Drusilla Beyfus. The rather hesitant 1956 section on 'The New Frankness in Speech' was replaced in 1969 by the direct 'Frankness in Speech':

> One of the significant changes in manners over the past few years has been the liberalisation of attitudes towards what can be said in mixed company. Candour, frankness and honesty in conversation have become admired attributes...Particularly this relates to the old inadmissibles, intimate sexual experiences, detailed descriptions of violence and every kind of physical expression and emotion.

Evidence of marriages becoming more equal, and of the changing position of children within the family, is strong. In one survey, 62 per cent of middle-class wives felt that they gave their children much greater freedom than their mothers had given them, whilst 69 per cent of working-class mothers felt they were bringing up their children differently from the way in which they had been brought up, which in 80 per cent of cases meant 'less restriction and more understanding'. Permissive attitudes continued to advance throughout the 1970s and throughout the Thatcher period. Given the proposition 'a single mother can bring up her child as well as a married couple', respondents to a National Opinion Poll (NOP) in 1987 agreed to the extent of 30 per cent, while 51 per cent disagreed, but when the same proposition was posed in December 1993, 48 per cent now agreed, with 41 per cent disagreeing.[13]

The most massive sex survey ever undertaken in Britain, eventually published as Kaye Wellings et al., *Sexual Behaviour in Britain: The National Survey of Sexual Attitudes and Lifestyles* (1994), demonstrated that by this stage British attitudes towards sex where characterised by pragmatism, common sense, tolerance, and a certain respect for traditional monogamous ideals. Three recent trends were identified: 'A progressive reduction . . . in the age at which first intercourse occurs, an increase in the proportion of young women who have had sexual intercourse before the age of sexual consent [16] and a convergence in the behaviour of men and women.' There was no doubt that a 'sizeable minority of young people are now sexually active before the age of sixteen'; in the 16–19 age group, 18.7 per cent of females had had sexual intercourse before the age of sixteen, and 27.6 per cent of males; both change and convergence are demonstrated by the statistics that of women in the age group 55–59 only 1 per cent had had sex before sixteen, while the figure for men was 5.8 per cent. The view which emerges, the report concluded: 'is one of the British as a nation strongly committed to the idea of the heterosexual monogamous union, but of considerable relaxation in attitudes towards teenage sexuality and, in particular, sex before marriage. . . . Acceptance of pre-marital sex is now nearly universal, as indeed is its practice.'

Mod Cons and Leisure Activities

As the war ended, there was a great and immediate resurgence of the leisure activities characteristic of the inter-war years. Blackpool, Scarborough and the Isle of Man boomed. Cinema attendances reached a peak in 1946 (when one-third of the population were going once a week, 13 per cent twice a week) and remained high; football enjoyed a golden age of large crowds. A few things remain central to 'the British way of life'; others underwent enormous change once the period of post-war austerity had come to an end. Here is an encapsulation of Britain before the tidal wave, taken from *Britain 1956: An Official Handbook, written in 1955*:

> One traditional social rendezvous, the public house, has maintained and even increased its popularity, although there has been a marked decrease in drunkenness and in consumption of alcohol per head since the nineteenth century. The public house now attracts a very wide circle of casual customers (both men and women) as well as many 'regulars', who meet for a drink and a chat, and perhaps to play some traditional public house game such as darts. A new, and in some ways rival, feature of urban life, especially in London, is the coffee bar. A characteristic of many of these coffee bars, which stay open until late at night and are becoming increasingly popular as a rendezvous for young people, is their modern *décor*. On the other hand many people, especially the married and the elderly, spend much of their leisure time at home – reading, listening to the radio, viewing television or pursuing hobbies. The most widespread hobbies are practical, for example, knitting and needlework for women and gardening for men. The standard of town and country gardens is high. (p. 18)

Shortly there came both a great widening in leisure activities, and also the arrival in force of the new domestic consumer products ('mod cons'). But the theme of the pub and consumption of alcohol is a good one to follow through: it is both central to British life, and, in all its striking modulations, central to the explosive social change during our period. In 1997/8 visiting a pub was still the most frequent leisure activity away from home for all those aged between 16 and 44, and, for those over that age, second only to going out for a meal in a restaurant. In 1955 the hours during which a pub could remain open for business were very strictly controlled. The Scottish Act of 1976 made it possible for pubs in Scotland to stay open all day; the English Act of 1988 permitted pubs both to stay open all day and to stay open late. Overall, alcohol consumption remained lower than had historically been the case with a slight decline in male consumption and, from the 1970s, a rise in female consumption. Attention began to be focused on alcohol abuse (with, in particular, stricter drink-driving laws) as well as on tobacco abuse. Two world wars, coupled by free distribution by the tobacco companies, had spread the cigarette-smoking habit, first to men, then to women. The concerted attack on smoking, establishment of no-smoking areas, etc., intensified through the 1970s and 1980s. In 1955 the big breweries were just beginning their assault on the palates and stomachs of beer-drinkers, introducing mass-produced, gasified and sterilised 'keg' beers. Consumer protest, in the form of the Campaign For Real Ale (CAMRA), got under way in the 1970s, while Thatcherite legislation in the 1980s forced the breweries to divest themselves of many of the pubs they controlled. Pubs began to specialise in one or more of a variety of traditionally-brewed 'real ales', bottled lagers from all over the world, and drinkable wines. Italian coffee machines entered the pubs, and many coffee bars and cafes metamorphosed into brasseries. Alcohol, as distinct from alcohol abuse, was no longer a special evil subject to strict segregation.

The great expansion in the availability of consumer goods began in the later 1950s and moved towards maximum impact during the cultural revolution. Table 12.9 shows the limits which still existed at the beginning of the 1970s, and how the spread of ever-new consumer products continued in the 1980s and

Table 12.9   British households with consumer durables, 1972–1996 (%)

	1972	1981	1991–2	1995–6
Colour television	(93)	74	95	97
Black-and-white television only		23	4	2
Telephone	42	75	88	93
Washing machine	66	78	87	90
Deep freezer	–	49	83	89
Video recorder	–	68	77	79
Microwave	–	–	55	70
Compact disc player	–	–	27	52
Tumble dryer	–	23	48	50
Home computer	–	–	21	25
Dishwasher	–	4	14	19

1990s. In table 12.9, blank figures in columns do not mean that nobody possessed these goods, but simply that they were still so relatively unusual that the statisticians had not got round to recording them. The diffusion of consumer durables was the biggest single influence on home-based leisure activities. It is too soon to say that the much-heralded swing to entirely home-centred leisure has yet come about. Compared with the 1940s and 1950s the opportunities for *all* kinds of leisure activity have greatly increased. Because there are so many alternatives, the days of massive cinema audiences are over: but, with the appearance of the first multiplex cinemas in the 1970s, cinema attendances began a modest, but steady, recovery from 1978; average first-division football attendances stood at 31,352 in 1971, while by the 1990s (much more expensive) premier league games were drawing average attendances of around 22,000. With regard to the total population, opportunities for, and participation in, leisure and entertainment were almost certainly considerably greater at the end of our period than at the beginning of it, as table 12.10 suggests.

With regard to home leisure activities, the British by the 1990s were the greatest users in Europe of home videos, home computers and the Internet. They were also the greatest practitioners of do-it-yourself home improvements (DIY). From the mid-1990s, with the establishment of the National Lottery, they were joining the rest of the world in one of humankind's most loved activities.

Crime

With the growth in practically everything else, there has been a considerable growth in crime. A slow but steady rise began in the 1950s, accelerated in the mid-1970s, then rose very sharply in the later 1980s and early 1990s; thereafter, with economic recovery in the mid-1990s, there has been a slight decline, crime, however, remaining the biggest cause of anxiety of the British people, as shown in opinion polls. Note that statistics for recorded crime as shown in table 12.11, greatly underestimate the amount of crime committed. The blanks occur because of the crimes listed being recorded under different headings. As can be seen, the most disturbing feature is the ever-continuing rise in offences against the person (violence, robbery, and sexual offences). What the statistics do not

Table 12.10 Number of people in Great Britain attending cultural events, 1986–1997 (%)

	1986–7	1991–2	1996–7
Cinema	31	44	54
Plays	23	23	24
Art galleries/exhibitions	21	21	22
Classical music	12	12	12
Ballet	6	6	7
Opera	5	6	7
Contemporary dance	4	3	4

Table 12.11 Notifiable offences recorded by the police in the UK, 1981, 1991 and 1997 (000s)

	England & Wales			Scotland			Northern Ireland		
	1981	1991	1997	1981	1991	1997	1981	1991	1997
Theft and handling stolen goods,	1,603	2,761	2,165	201	284	188	25	32	30
of which; theft of vehicles	333	582	407	33	44	29	5	8	9
of which; theft from vehicles	380	913	710	–	–	52	7	7	5
Burglary	718	1,219	1,015	96	116	55	20	17	14
Criminal damage	387	821	877	62	90	81	5	2	5
Violence against the person	100	190	251	8	16	15	3	4	5
Fraud and forgery	107	175	134	21	26	21	3	5	4
Robbery	20	45	63	4	6	4	3	2	2
Sexual offences,	19	29	33	2	3	4	–	1	1
of which; rape	1	4	7	–	1	1	–	–	–
of which; drug trafficking	–	11	23	2	3	8	–	–	–
Other notifiable offences	9	23	37	12	28	43	3	1	1
All notifiable offences	2,964	5,276	4,598	408	573	421	62	64	62

reveal is growing public concern over child molesters and the long-hidden history of institutional child-abuse, now at last being fully revealed.[14]

Drug-taking and drug-trafficking have become such a massive problem that not only have the Labour government, in imitation of the United States, set up a special 'Drugs Tsar', but the 1999 issue of *Social Trends* began with a special essay on the problem. Addiction, and the need to finance it, lies behind much of the rise in crime. The use of dirty syringes has become an important element in the spread of Aids. Up until the 1960s, drug use was well controlled in Britain, with registered addicts being able to obtain the drugs they needed on prescription. But, with all the nonsense during the cultural revolution of the mind-expanding qualities of drugs, the situation ran out of control. The big expansion in drug consumption among young people took place in the 1980s and 1990s. There may have been some levelling-off in the mid-1990s as the fashion for ecstasy or raves declined, and the new alcopops became all the rage. The evidence is that apart from the marginalised groups of addicts, drug- taking does tail off as people grow older. Furthermore; 'Most people who have tried drugs do just that – try them and stop.' Still:

> throughout the United Kingdom drug use among schoolchildren increases with age as they come into contact with other young people and lifestyles in which drugs are commonplace. Around one in twelve 12-year-olds, one in three 14-year-olds, and two in five 16-year-olds will have tried drugs, and one in five 16 year olds will have done so within the last month.[15]

Drug seizures by both police and customs officials have gone up, quite remarkably in some years, during the 1980s and 1990s, but this is seen much less as a victory for law and order than as a symptom of the growing size of the problem. And Britain, indeed, occupies yet another place at the top of a European league table: largest consumer of drugs.

British society in 1945 was safe, worthy, overly self-satisfied, insular, and rather dull. British society in 1999, disfigured by inequality and great pools of deprivation, and not without smugness and complacency, yet open to cosmopolitan influences, offered far greater opportunities for a full and exciting life, but was beset by social problems and dangers scarcely known in 1945.

Notes

1 My statistics are taken from the relevant government publications, notably *Annual Abstract of Statistics* and (from 1970) *Social Trends* (both London).

2 Office for National Statistics, *Social Trends 29*, London, 1999: 50.

3 Margaret Stacey et al., *Tradition and Change: A Study of Banbury*, London, 1960.

4 Arthur Marwick, *Class: Image and Reality in Britain, France and the United States since 1935*, 2nd ed., London, 1990.

5 J. H. Golthorpe, John Lockwood, F. Bechofer and J. Platt, *The Affluent Worker*, 3 vols, Cambridge, 1968–9.

6 Gordon Marshall, Howard Newby, David Rose and Carolyn Vogler, *Social Class in Modern Britain*, London, 1988.

7   Steven Fielding, Peter Thompson and Nick Tiratsoo, *'England Arise!': The Labour Party and Popular Politics in 1940s Britain*, Manchester and New York, 1995.
8   Social and Community Planning Research, *British Social Attitudes Reports 5–13*, place, 1988–97. Table 12.6 is taken from *Report II*, 1995.
9   Geoffrey Gorer, *Experiencing English Character*, New York, 1955.
10 NOP polls reported in the *Independent*, 13 December 1993.
11 Arthur Marwick, *British Society since 1945*, 3rd ed., London, 1996.
12 Gorer, *English Character*.
13 NOP polls reported in the *Independent*, 13 December 1993.
14 Department of Health, *The Government's Response to the Children's Safeguards Review*, London, November 1988, and *Report of the Committee of Inquiry into the Personality Disorder Unit, Ashworth Special Hospital*, 2 vols, London, 1999.
15 *Social Trends 29*, 1999: 17.

Further Reading

Abercrombie, Nicholas et al., *Contemporary British Society*, Cambridge, 1988.

Cannadine, David, *Class in Britain*, New Haven and London, 1988.

Davis, John, *Youth and the Condition of Britain: Images of Adolescent Conflict*, London and Atlantic Highlands, NJ, 1990.

Garfield, Simon, *The End Of Innocence: Britain in the Time of AIDS*, London and Boston, 1994.

Gorer, Geoffrey, *Exploring English Character*, New York, 1955.

Gorer, Geoffrey, *Sex and Marriage in England Today*, London, 1971.

Halsey, A. H., *Change in British Society*, Oxford and New York, 1995.

Halsey A. H., *Trends in British Society since 1900*, London and New York, 1972.

Halsey, A. H., Heath, A. F. and Ridge, J. M., *Origins and Destinations: Family, Class and Education in Modern Britain*, Oxford, 1980.

Marshall, G., Newby, H., Rose, D. and Vogler, C., *Social Class in Britain Today*, London, 1988.

Marwick, Arthur, *British Society since 1945*, 3rd ed., London, 1996.

Marwick, Arthur, *Class: Image and Reality in Britain, France and the United States since 1935*, 2nd ed., London, 1990.

Marwick, Arthur, *The Sixties: Cultural Revolution in Britain, France and the United States, c.1958 – c.1974*, Oxford, 1998.

Morris, Terence, *Crime and Criminal Justice since 1945*, Oxford and New York, 1989.

Neville, Richard, *Hippie Hippie Shake: the Dreams, the Trips, the Trials, The Love-ins, the Screw Ups . . . The Sixties*, Port Melbourne, 1995.

Office of National Statistics, *Social Trends 1*, London, 1970.

Office of National Statistics, *Social Trends 10*, London, 1980.

Office of National Statistics, *Social Trends 29*, London, 1999.

Parsons, Bill, *Youth in Britain since 1945*, London, 1997.

Parsons, Gerald (ed.), *The Growth of Religious Diversity: Britain from 1945*, vol. 1 *Traditions*, vol. 2 *Issues*, London, 1994.

Paxman, Jeremy, *Friends in High Places: Who Runs Britain?*, London and New York, 1991.

Scott, John, *The Upper Classes: Poverty and Privilege in Britain*, London, 1982.

Wellings, Kaye et al., *Sexual Behaviour in Britain: The National Survey of Social Attitudes and Lifestyles*, London, 1994.

Chronology

1945   Labour general election victory with 47.8 per cent of vote (Conservatives, 39.8 per cent).
1947   Over one million births mark height of first baby boom.
1948   Cinema attendances reach their peak.
1949   Legal Aid and Advice Act.
1954   R. A. Butler, Conservative Chancellor for the Exchequer, suggests that standard of living could be doubled in 25 years.
1960   *Lady Chatterley* trial.
1961   Census shows men now a majority in marriageable age group.
1961   Contraceptive pill available in Britain.
1961   75 per cent of families have TV.
1964   Over one million births mark peak of second baby boom.
1967   Abortion Reform Act.
1967   Sexual Offences Act (homosexual law reform).
1967   National Health Services (Family Planning) Act.
1968   Family Reform Act.
1968   Representation of the People Act.
1969   Divorce Reform Act.
1970   Equal Pay Act.
1970   Number of marriages reaches peak.
1971   91 per cent of families have TV.
1976   Licensing Act (Scotland).
1979   General election victory for Conservatives under Margaret Thatcher, with 43.9 per cent of vote.
1980   Matrimonial Property Act.
1987   Third successive victory for Margaret Thatcher with 42.3 per cent of vote.
1988   Licensing Act (England and Wales).
1992   Fourth successive Conservative general election victory (under John Major) with 43 per cent of the vote.
1993   National Opinion Poll demonstrates steady growth of permissiveness and opposition to Thatcherism.
1994   *Sexual Behaviour in Britain* published.
1995   Joseph Rowntree Foundation Report, *Income and Wealth*, demonstrates growth of poverty and inequality.
1997   Labour general election victory with 44 per cent of vote.
1998   'Drugs Tsar' appointed.

13 Women and Social Change, 1945–1995

Jane Lewis

The most dramatic social trends in the post-war period are also ones that have had a particularly strong impact on women: the rise in the female labour market participation rate, the rise in the divorce rate, the rise in the extramarital birth rate, and the increase in cohabitation. Gender relations in respect of paid work have shifted, with it becoming increasingly the norm for all adult women, whether single, married or mothers, to be employed. Men's employment rates have fallen slightly. Family change has been more dramatic still. It is tempting, but premature, to say that the twentieth century saw the rise and fall of marriage. Certainly in the 1960s marriage was never younger or more popular. Yet at the end of the century, the rate of first marriage fell, almost one-third of children were born outside marriage and there was a dramatic rise in lone motherhood. This chapter will look at changes in women's participation in paid work and at the nature of family change in more detail, before considering the possibility of a causal relationship: have we witnessed a real increase in female autonomy, both sexual and economic?

The chapter suggests that there has been real change since the war, but that it is also important to consider the continuities, especially in respect of unpaid work. There are, of course, many other areas of change that are not covered by this chapter, for example, in terms of the political participation of women, which have been considerably slower. There are also important issues such as domestic violence, which have been rediscovered as social problems in the post-war period, and issues such as artificial reproduction, which are entirely new. However, the focus on those aspects of women's lives which also represent the most striking social trends for society as a whole is justified not least because of the way in which they have disturbed the assumptions of policy-makers. The whole of the post-war social settlement was built on the twin assumptions of full male employment and stable families. Neither of these has survived the course.

Women's Paid Work

Prior to the Second World War, women tended to work until marriage. The overall labour market participation rate for women remained remarkably constant, at around 29 per cent for the first three decades of the century, always remembering the vagaries of census categories and the continuing failure to record the casual part-time work performed by married women. During both the First and Second World Wars there was an enormous increase in women's paid employment, but by 1921 the female participation rate was 2 per cent lower than before the outbreak of war. Still, between 1923 and 1939, the number of insured – that is, regularly employed, full-time – women workers increased more rapidly than that of men. The retreat of women from paid work after the Second World War was also dramatic. By 1951, women's economic activity rate was almost exactly the same as that for 1931.

Table 13.1 shows a major shift in the labour market experience of women marrying after the Second World War, with the emergence of the 'bimodal work pattern', whereby women left the labour market on the birth of a first child and re-entered it when the child/children were older. Viola Klein and Alva Myrdal argued strongly for married women's right to work in their book, *Women's Two Roles*, published in 1956. They were the first to suggest, with extreme caution, that there might be a case for women 'having it all', albeit sequentially, becoming first workers, then wives and mothers and finally re-entering the labour market to become workers again. Unlike some other feminist proponents of women's employment, Myrdal and Klein preferred the bimodal pattern of employment to part-time work, which they felt might still prove damaging to children's welfare. Their idea that women should not have to make a straight choice between paid work on the one hand and marriage and motherhood on the other, was nevertheless potentially radical in the light of first, the strong conviction on the part of so many post-war psychologists (especially Bowlby, 1951) and sociologists (especially Parsons and Bales, 1955) as to the functional superiority and psychological necessity of the male breadwinner family model, and second, the continuing concern about the quality of family life and the level of the birth rate. The 1951 Census provided the first hint of the emergence of a bimodal pattern: after a sharp drop in the economic activity rate for 24–34-year-olds, there was a slight increase for married women in older age groups. By 1961 the bimodal pattern had emerged clearly, with a first peak of economic activity for women aged 20–24, and a second for those aged 35–50. By 1981, older wives were actually *more* likely to be working than younger ones (table 13.1).

The bimodal pattern has proved long-lived in Britain, but it is only part of the story. The percentage of married women in the labour market rose steadily from 26 per cent in 1951, to 35 per cent in 1961, 47 per cent in 1971, 55 per cent in 1981 and 59 per cent in 1991. Married women's labour market 'attachment' also increased. The economic activity rate of women with dependent children was 24 per cent in 1961, 39 per cent in 1971 and 65 per cent by the mid-1990s. Half the women who had a first baby between 1970 and 1979

Table 13.1 Age-specific participation rates, females, by marital status, England and Wales, 1911–1991

Year	>15	14–15	16–17	18–20	21–24	25–34	35–44	45–54	55–64	65–74	75+
Single women											
1911	677[b]	480	707	756[c]	777[d]	740	661	589	462	260	94
1921	683[b]	448	710	789[c]	805[d]	763	682	604	490	271	86
1931	719[c]	509	759	830	841	805	728	645	510	254	88
1951	730	NA	NA	NA	912	869	812	750	501	249	45
1961	696	NA	NA	NA	896[d]	893	851	817	576	154	38
1981	608	NA	394	754[c]	820[d]	855	817	853	454	NA	NA
1991	637	NA	416	693	776	800	788	732	353	NA	NA
Married women											
1911	103[b]	NA	NA	137[c]	129[d]	106	106	105	88	57	23
1921	91[b]	NA	NA	150[c]	132[d]	99	93	88	76	49	20
1931	104[b]	NA	NA	196	193	138	105	88	66	33	12
1951	225	NA	NA	NA	377	252	267	246	221	33	10
1961	301	NA	NA	NA	428[d]	302	373	362	208	42	7
1981	470	NA	307	472[c]	546[d]	484	638	642	374	NA	NA
1991	530	NA	433	517	632	623	724	703	378	NA	NA
Widowed and divorced women											
1911	301[b]	NA	NA	500[c]	592[d]	664	623	470	321	170	58
1921	261[b]	NA	NA	445[c]	504[d]	468	458	411	294	147	44
1931	216[b]	NA	NA	490	599	556	457	360	256	113	35
1951	212	NA	NA	NA	669	679	643	548	480	76	17

Year											
1961	228	NA	NA	NA	625[d]	687	719	668	383	93	17
1981	230	NA	NA	484[c]	545[d]	623	712	701	272	NA	NA
1991	258	NA	475	437	506	599	727	722	355	NA	NA

[a] Number per 1000 in each category in the labour force

[b] >14 years

[c] 18 + 19 years

[d] 20–24 years

NA = not available.

Figures for 1991 and 1981 are the number of women who are economically active which includes the unemployed who are seeking work or waiting to start a job.

Both 1991 + 1981 figures are for Great Britain.

Sources: Derived from 1931 Census, *General Report*, Table LXVII (HMSO, 1950), p. 163; 1951 Census, *Occupational Tables*, Tables 2 to 5 (HMSO, 1956); 1961 Census, *Economic Activity Tables*, Table 4B (HMSO, 1984), 1991 Census, *Economic Activity Tables*, vol. 1, Table 1 'Economic position' (HMSO, 1994).

returned to work within four years, compared to almost ten years for women having a first child between 1950 and 1954. The proportion with babies under one year who are working has almost tripled since 1981 to 60 per cent in 1997. However, as table 13.2 shows, the vast majority of women joining the labour force in Britain since the war have worked part-time, the percentage rising from 11 in 1951 to 44 in 1991. The number of women employed full-time in 1951 was almost as great as in 1991, something that must be remembered whenever it is suggested that the increase in women's labour market participation rate in the post-war period constitutes a 'revolution' (Hakim, 1996). Table 13.3 shows that while the labour market participation rate of British women has been relatively high, exceeded only by the Scandinavian countries in the 1990s, the increase in British married women's employment rate since 1945 has been accounted for almost entirely by part-time work. Nevertheless, it is important to note that by the end of the century, the gap between women's and men's employment rates had closed considerably (table 13.3).

In fact, the increase in married women's post-war employment has been largely in the service of the welfare state, often in low-paid, low-status jobs in hospitals and schools. Some (e.g. Kolberg, 1991) have argued that such employment represents a genuine widening of opportunities. However, Scandinavian feminists observing a similar rise in welfare state-related employment in their countries suggested that it amounted to little more than a form of 'public patriarchy' (for example, Siim, 1987). In other words, women were doing in the public sphere the same sort of 'caring' jobs as they had always done at home. It is also the case that more casual forms of employment in the form of 'home-work', for example, making ballpoint pens and tailoring, has not disappeared. Such work was investigated by Parliament at length at the turn of the century and again in 1980 (HC 39, 1981), when witnesses found it just as difficult as their late-nineteenth-century counterparts to estimate the numbers of women involved. There has, however, been a substantial change in attitudes on the part of women, men and policy-makers regarding the desirability of married women's employment. Post-war economists found the increase in married women's paid work particularly puzzling, because during a period of full male employment and rising real wages, adults were expected to opt to increase their leisure time. From women's point of view, the immediate post-war decades were

Table 13.2   **Trends in women's full-time and part-time work, Great Britain, 1951–1991**

	Total in employment (000s)	Full-time employment (000s)	Part-time employment (000s)	% part-time
1951	6,826	6,041	784	11
1961	7,590	5,698	1,892	25
1971	8,701	5,413	3,288	38
1981	9,146	5,602	3,543	39
1991	11,072	6,230	4,842	44

Source: Hakim, 1996, p. 64, T.3.3.

Table 13.3 Selected labour-force statistics in Denmark, France, the UK and Germany (FDR), 1960, 1979 and 1990

Country	Labour-force participation				Part-time employment[a] as a proportion of			
	1960		1990		1979		1990	
	Male	Female	Male	Female	Male	Female	Male	Female
Denmark	99.5	43.5	89.6	78.4	5.2	46.3	9.0	41.5
France	94.6	46.6	75.2	56.6	2.4	16.9	3.5	23.8
UK	99.1	46.1	86.4	65.1	1.9	39.0	5.0	43.8
Germany (FDR)	94.4	49.2	80.7	56.6	1.5	27.6	2.1	30.6

[a]Based on country definitions of part-time work.

Sources: OECD (1992) Economic Outlook Historical Statistics, Paris: OECD, OECD (1991) Economic Outlook, Table 2.9.

the first in modern history to offer the possibility of pursuing a variety of activities voluntarily rather than out of pure necessity. Nevertheless, constraint as well as choice played a major part in determining their behaviour.

Attitudes towards married women's work changed substantially during the period. In a 1943 wartime survey of women's work, 58 per cent of the women questioned did not believe in women working after marriage. By 1965, 89 per cent approved if there were no children, but this figure dropped to 39 per cent if the woman had school-age children. The 1980 national sample survey of women's employment found that only 11 per cent of women felt that married women should stay at home if they had children at school, but 60 per cent continued to feel that women with pre-school children should be at home. Shirley Dex (1988) has pointed out that not all changes in attitudes on the subject have been progressive: while in the 1965 national survey of women's work only 22 per cent of respondents felt that working women took jobs away from men, in the 1980 national sample survey of women's employment, which came after the more economically insecure 1970s, 51 per cent agreed that women should stay at home in periods of high unemployment.

Women's motives for working have become more complex and, in the recent past, have varied considerably according to age, marital status, socio-economic class and ethnicity. The 1980 survey showed that 28 per cent of women working part-time gave 'working for essentials' as their main reason for work, while 46 per cent reported that they would be able to 'get by' without working (Martin and Roberts, 1984). Yet money was not the aspect of a job rated as most important by the majority of women; 'work you like doing' was rated more highly, which lends some support to the conclusion of post-war American studies that married women's own goals have become a more important factor in motivating them to work than the size of their husbands' incomes (Roberts, 1985; Morris, 1990). While there is no large national sample survey evidence to draw on after 1980, it is likely that in the more uncertain labour market of the 1990s, women may have worked as much out of necessity as choice. Black women have always been more likely to be in full-time employment and to make a major contribution to the family economy, not least because of the low labour market status of black men. Catherine Hakim (1996) has argued that in the late twentieth century there were effectively two female labour markets in Britain: one comprising career women, who behave very similarly to men, and the other of women who are more marginally attached to the labour market. Hakim's argument is controversial because she maintains that this division arises from women's own choices. However, the lack of affordable, high-quality day care for children is certainly a constraint for many women who might want to participate in the labour market.

The prescriptions of policy-makers have also changed. In the wake of the Second World War, politicians and professionals stressed the importance of rebuilding the family and the importance of motherhood, a view echoed in the circulars of the Ministries of Health and Education, which ruled that the children of working mothers were not to be given priority for day care or nursery education. Indeed, 50 per cent of wartime nurseries were closed by 1955 (Riley, 1983). But at the same time, the Ministry of Labour faced the prospect of labour market shortage and appealed 'to women who are in the position to do so to enter industry' (Cmd. 7046, 1947). What emerged from the wartime experience was, as Penny Summerfield (1984) has convincingly argued, the conviction on the part of some policy-makers that it was possible for women to combine a limited amount of paid work with marriage and motherhood without their home responsibilities being seriously undermined. Full-time work for women with dependent children was not encouraged, but both government and employers saw the extension of part-time work as a means of ensuring that women would be able to fulfil their responsibility as wives and mothers while also engaging in paid employment. The *Report of the Royal Commission on Population* published in 1949 (Cmd 7695) anticipated the increasing demand for women's labour and welcomed the idea of women doing two jobs.

Since the war, the government has maintained an officially 'neutral' stance on the issue of married women's paid work, meaning that it has treated it as a private decision. This in turn has meant that families, but in practice women, have been left to reconcile the claims of paid work and the unpaid work of caring for children and adult dependants as best they can with minimal support from the state. Joshi and Davies (1992) have shown that the opportunity costs of having and caring for children – the 'family penalty' – are twice as high for women in Britain as in France, where the primary aim of the post-war social security system has been to compensate parents for the costs of children and where women's claims as both mothers and workers have been recognised, resulting in extensive childcare provision. Within the European Union, France was one of only three countries in the late 1980s where more than 50 per cent of women with children under the age of five were in employment (Lewis, 1992).

Family Change

There have in fact been two major sets of family change during the post-war period. First there was the widespread separation of sex and marriage. Sexual activity among the young increased dramatically during the 1960s, and the increasing use of the contraceptive pill from the beginning of the 1970s strengthened this trend. However, when a baby was conceived in the 1960s, the majority of women married, whereas in the 1970s, the majority either got married or aborted. The latter option was made possible by the legalisation of abortion following the 1967 Abortion Act. (The end of the 1960s was marked by the passing of 'permissive legislation' in respect of divorce and homosexuality, as well as abortion.) In addition, during the 1960s divorce rates, although increasing, remained at a low level. Thus, for the most part, marriage and parenthood, if not sex and marriage, remained firmly linked.

The second major shift has been more recent and is arguably more radical, involving as it has the separation of marriage and parenthood. The proportion of births outside marriage increased from 5 per cent in 1960 to 28 per cent in 1990, while the divorce rate increased more than sixfold over the same period; from 2 per 1,000 to 13 per 1,000 of the married population.

Sex outside marriage was hardly a new phenomenon in the post-war period. However, there is evidence to suggest that more single teenagers began to have sex in the late 1950s and 1960s, before the pill became widely available (e.g. Black and Sykes, 1971). Between the mid-1960s and the mid-1970s large sample surveys showed a marked increase in unmarried teenagers with sexual experience, especially at younger ages. In addition, the gap between girls and boys narrowed to some extent (Schofield, 1968; Farrell, 1978).

The increase in sexual activity outside marriage resulted in a sharp rise in both the extramarital and marital birth rates during the 1960s (table 13.4). This contrasts with the war years, when the extramarital birth rate rose much more sharply than the marital rate because so many marriages were thwarted by wartime disruption and, to a lesser extent, death. The pattern for the 1960s also differs from that of the period since the mid-1980s, when the extramarital birth rate rose dramatically and the marital birth rate fell as a consequence of the movement away from marriage.

The 1960s were therefore different. Increased sexual activity resulted in an increased pregnancy rate, but there was still a tendency to marry. A majority of births to women under 20 were conceived outside marriage in the 1960s, but the majority of premaritally conceived births took place inside marriage. In 1969, 54 per cent of extramarital conceptions were legitimised by marriage, 32 per cent resulted in 'illegitimate'[1] births and 14 per cent were aborted. In fact, small-scale studies of illegitimacy carried out during the late 1950s and 1960s showed that between 35 and 40 per cent of illegitimate births were to separated, divorced and widowed women (Kiernan, Land and Lewis, 1998).

It is perhaps therefore not so surprising that there was seemingly little panic about what amounted to a significant increase in the separation of sex from marriage. The fact that a majority of premarital conceptions were legitimised

Table 13.4   Marital and extramarital births per 1,000 women aged 15–44, 1940–1995

	Marital birth rate per 1,000 married women	Extramarital birth rate per 1,000 single, divorced, and widowed women
1940	98.8	5.9
1945	103.9	16.1
1950	108.6	10.2
1955	103.7	10.3
1960	120.8	14.7
1965	126.9	21.2
1970	113.5	21.5
1975	85.5	17.4
1980	92.2	19.6
1985	87.8	26.7
1990	86.7	38.9
1995	82.7	39.6

Sources: Office of Population Censuses and Surveys (OPCS), *Birth Statistics: Historical Series 1837–1983*, Table 3.2b and c, Series FM1 No. 13 (London: HMSO, 1987); OPCS, *Birth Statistics: Historical Series 1837–1983*, Table 3.1, Series FM1 No. 22 (London: HMSO, 1995).

and that divorce rates were low (table 13.5) resulted in a series of optimistic statements about family stability. Considerable concern was expressed at the beginning of the 1960s about teenage sexual behaviour in relation to the increasing incidence of venereal disease (e.g. Eppel and Eppel, 1966), but not about family change. Ronald Fletcher's 1966 study of marriage and the family in Britain concluded that although there was real change, there was no sign of moral decay; and Geoffrey Gorer's study of sex and marriage published in 1971 concluded that England still appeared very chaste – 26 per cent of married men and 63 per cent of married women in his sample were virgins at marriage. Gorer had carried out a similar survey in 1950 and found that the main change over the 20-year period was the increase in the proportion of those who thought that sexual experience had a good effect on the person's character (Gorer, 1971).

Possibly in part because of the confidence expressed in family stability during these early post-war decades, attitudes towards sexual morality, particularly on the part of the policy-making elite, changed considerably during the 1960s. The church was particularly important for shifting away from its belief in the necessity for an externally imposed moral code, towards the idea that the only true basis for sexual morality was the emotional sincerity of the individuals concerned (Kiernan, Land and Lewis, 1998). It was this rethinking of the whole basis for sexual morality that helped to pave the way for divorce reform. If, as the Bishop of Woolwich argued most influentially, nothing could be labelled as wrong – not divorce, nor premarital sex, unless love were lacking (Robinson, 1963) then it became impossible to oppose divorce in cases where the parties claimed that they did not love each other any more. Thus partial no-fault divorce law reform became possible in 1969. Couples were able to get a divorce by proving marital breakdown, for reasons of fault on the part of one of the parties (most commonly adultery and cruelty), or on grounds of long-term separation. Some doctors and birth-control campaigners went much further than the church and argued in favour of a more liberal approach to sexual behaviour, based on the new-found availability of birth control. G. M. Carstairs, a professor of psychological medicine, gave the Reith Lectures on BBC Radio in 1962 and spoke of the way in which young people were rapidly

Table 13.5   Divorce rate per 1,000 married population, 1950–1993

1950	2.8
1960	2.0
1965	3.1
1970	4.7
1975	9.6
1980	12.0
1985	13.4
1990	13.0
1993	13.9

Source: OPCS, *Marriage and Divorce Statistics 1837–1993*, Historical Series, FM2, NO. 16, Table 5.2 (London: HMSO, 1995); OPCS, *Marriage and Divorce Statistics 1837–1983*, Table 2.1, FM2, NO. 21 (London: HMSO, 1995).

society into one 'in which sexual experience, with precautions against conception, is being accepted as a sensible preliminary to marriage, making marriage itself more mutually considerate and satisfying' (Carstairs, 1962, p. 51).

Since the beginning of the 1970s, there have been marked changes in marriage patterns, with declines in the marriage rate and older marriage; a dramatic rise in the divorce rate, which plateaued from the 1980s (table 13.5); and the emergence of widespread cohabitation. The rise in extramarital childbearing evident during the 1960s levelled off for a time during the 1970s as a consequence of the 'contraceptive revolution' in the form of the birth control pill for women and the availability of legal abortion. Increasingly, young unmarried women who found themselves pregnant opted for an abortion or an illegitimate child rather than a 'shotgun marriage'. From the late 1970s the proportion of births outside marriage began to increase, slowly at first and then rapidly throughout the 1980s, with signs of stabilisation in the early 1990s at about one in three of all births (Table 13.4).

Declining marriage and increased childbearing have been inextricably linked to the growth of cohabitation. Cohabitation was apparently common in the early part of the twentieth century, when divorce was rare (Gillis, 1986), and was probably at its nadir in the 1950s and 1960s, when marriage was almost universal (Kiernan and Estaugh, 1993). Living together as a prelude to marriage began in the 1970s. In the 1990s, typically 70 per cent of never-married women who married had cohabited with their husbands, compared with 58 per cent of those marrying between 1985 and 1988, 33 per cent marrying between 1975 and 1979 and 6 per cent marrying between 1965 and 1969. The proportion of spinsters who were cohabiting more than trebled between 1979 and 1993, from 7.5 per cent to 24 per cent. Additionally, in 1993, 25 per cent of divorced women were in cohabiting union. Cohabitations have tended to be shortlived and childless, but during the 1980s children were increasingly being born within these relationships.

Increases in divorce, cohabitation and childbearing outside marriage have all contributed to the separation of marriage and parenthood. Lone parenthood is the result of this development. Between 1970 and 1990, the percentage of lone-mother families more than doubled (table 13.6). As table 13.7 indicates, the UK

Table 13.6   Distribution of the different types of lone-mother families with dependent children, 1971–1991

	Percentage* of all families with dependent children			
	1971	1981	1986	1991
Single lone mothers	1.2	2.3	3.2	6.4
Separated lone mothers	2.5	2.3	2.6	3.6
Divorced lone mothers	1.9	4.4	5.6	6.3
Widowed lone mothers	1.9	1.7	1.1	1.2
All lone mothers	7.5	10.7	12.5	17.5

*Estimates are based on three-year averages, apart from 1991.
Source: John Haskey, 'Trends in the Numbers of One-Parent Families in Great Britain', *Population Trends*, 71 (Spring 1993).

Table 13.7   Family change in Denmark, France, the UK and Germany (FDR), 1960–1990s

	Proportion of live extra-marital births, per 100 live births		Crude divorce rate, divorces per 1,000 average population		Lone-parent families with at least one child of less than 15 years of age as a percentage of all families with dependent children	
	1960	1995*	1970	1994	1980/1	1990/1
Denmark	7.8	46.9 (94)	1.9	2.6	18.1	20.8
France	6.1	34.9 (93)	0.8	3.0	8.3	10.7
UK	5.2	33.6	1.1	1.9	13.7	16.0
Germany (FDR)	6.1	12.4	1.3	2.2	9.8	15.4

*Unless otherwise specified
Sources: 1970–95: Council of Europe, 1996: 1960 United Nations 1965, Council of Europe 1996, Eurostat 1994.

is in fact the divorce capital of Europe, has one of the largest extramarital birth rates and one of the highest percentages of lone-parent families.[2] The Scandinavian countries have larger extramarital birth rates and rates of lone motherhood, but also have higher rates of cohabitation and less young motherhood.

The late-twentieth-century debate about marriage, non-marriage and parenthood was very different from that of the 1960s and 1970s, when growing numbers of lone-mother families (formed mainly as a result of rising divorce rates) resulted in increasing concern about the poverty of all lone mothers. Social investigators emphasised the common material needs of all one-parent families, and the historical divisions between the widowed, the divorced and the unmarried mother, whereby the first of these groups was considered the most 'deserving', were consciously blurred in the debate. There was little outright condemnation of lone parenthood in the 1970s. The 1974 *Finer Committee Report on One Parent Families* recognised that in a liberal democratic society, government could not seek directly to control marital and reproductive behaviour and conceded that, as a result, the task of supporting lone-mother families would inevitably fall on the state: 'The fact has to be faced that in a democratic society, which cannot legislate (even if it could enforce) different rules of familial and sexual behaviour depending on the ability to pay for the consequences, the community has to bear much of the cost of broken homes and unmarried motherhood' (Cmd. 5629, 1974, para. 4.224).

However, the 1980s saw a marked increase in anxiety about the separation of marriage and parenthood. The optimism of both the new moralists and the sexual reformers of the 1960s seemed to have been mistaken. Easier divorce had resulted in more divorce, not less, and access to improved methods of birth control had made cohabiting relationships more possible. From the mid-1980s these relationships increasingly turned into couples with children, which have in turn have been shown to be less stable than marriages and more economically disadvantaged. Thus, cohabiting women with children may go on to swell the numbers of lone mothers drawing state benefits.

Some twenty years after the publication of the Finer Report, the government announced its intention of introducing a measure to cut the rate of divorce. In fact, the 1996 Family Law Act focused mainly on extending the waiting period for a divorce and on making mediation between the parties mandatory. It has been difficult for governments to act to change behaviour in respect of marriage, divorce and parenthood. The very nature of the relationship between law and behaviour is a matter of considerable debate, and most late-twentieth-century politicians acknowledge the difficulty of trying to put the clock back. Instead, policy-makers at the end of the century have focused on the social implications of the increasing separation of marriage and parenthood, in terms mainly of the effects on children (for the latest summary of the evidence, see Rodgers and Pryor, 1998), and on the extent of 'welfare dependency' among lone-mother families and the cost to the public purse.[3] In respect of the first of these, the proportion of children experiencing the break-up of their parent's marriage was 10 per cent or less among those born prior to the mid-1960s. For children born during the early part of the 1970s this figure rose to 23 per cent.

In respect of the second of these concerns, public policy shifted dramatically in its treatment of lone-mother families at the end of the century in Britain and the United States, but much less so in other continental European countries, where social welfare programmes pay less attention to the category of lone mothers and more to the needs of all mothers and children (Lewis, 1992, 1997). While post-war policy had treated lone mothers as primarily mothers, and did not require them to register for employment, in the 1990s government acted first to cut the benefits paid to lone mothers, and second to encourage more of them into the labour market. Such a policy was not dissimilar to that pursued by the nineteenth-century poor-law authorities, which worked on the principle that women with children and without men to support them had to become breadwinners in their turn. The British government also tried to elicit more financial support from the only other source of income for lone-mother families besides the state and the labour market: the absent father. The Child Support Act was passed in 1991, but due mainly to faults in implementing the policy the legislation has been singularly unsuccessful.

There are continuities in the story of post-war family change; for example, it has been the increased availability and reliability of contraception for women that has made extramarital sexual relationships of all kinds more possible, and these in turn laid the foundations for the separation of marriage from parenthood. However, there was a clear break between behaviour in and before the 1960s on the one hand, and post-1980 on the other. Above all, the story is about what has happened to marriage. It is too simplistic to say that we have seen the 'rise and fall' of marriage in the twentieth century; remarriage is still extremely popular (62 per 1,000 divorced men and 49 per 1,000 divorced women remarried in 1991). But the whole 'marriage system' has undergone profound change, with the result that large numbers of women and children live together either with an adult male cohabitant or alone.

Have Women Become More Autonomous and 'Individualised'?

Lone mothers have become increasingly visible in post-war society. This has been due in large part to the increase in their numbers, but it is also due to changes in where lone mothers are to be found. Until relatively recently, they were 'hidden away'. Since the 1970s, a majority of never-married mothers have joined the dramatically increased numbers of divorced women living autonomously in the community. Until the last quarter of the twentieth century, the majority of unmarried mothers found refuge with kin. A century ago, the options facing those whose kin rejected them comprised infanticide, abandonment, informal adoption or the workhouse. Even in the immediate post-war decades, relatively few were able to gain access to affordable housing. To live independently, women with children and without men must have an alternative source of income. In the view of most academic social scientists, it is the growth in women's employment that has provided lone mothers with income and that explains the growth in their numbers (Garfinkel and McLanahan, 1986; Ellwood and Bane, 1985).

However, women with children are often in low-paid, low-status jobs, and are usually in part-time employment because they must combine paid work with the unpaid work of caring. Only a minority of mothers, married or solo, can combine the unpaid work of caring for a child with sufficiently remunerative employment to provide the wherewithal for independent living. Women who divorce or have a child outside marriage seemingly choose to make themselves worse off. It is difficult to explain such behaviour; certainly no single variable can do so. The nature of the choices and constraints faced by women who become lone mothers by whichever route are complicated. In the first place, it is significant that men's capacity to act as breadwinners has been conspicuously eroded. William Julius Wilson (1987) was among the first to suggest that we should pay more attention to the deteriorating economic position of black men in the United States in order to explain the high incidence of black unmarried motherhood in that country. In this country, too, the proportion of income contributed to married-couple families by men has fallen sharply (Harkness, Machin and Waldfogel, 1996). In Ann Phoenix's (1991) qualitative study of young unmarried mothers, the vast majority of the fathers were unemployed. There were certainly few economic reasons for these young women to marry the fathers of their children. The economic prospects of young unmarried mothers, who are disproportionately lacking in education and skills, are also poor.

Indeed, from the mid-1980s, many commentators charged that the cause of lone motherhood had more to do with the availability of welfare benefits, including priority of access to social housing, than with women's increased employment (see especially Murray, 1984). In fact, social provision by the post-war welfare state has been Janus-faced. On the one hand, it has endeavoured to promote the traditional two-parent family. Thus the 'cohabitation rule' which is applied to those drawing benefits assumes that if a woman cohabits with a man he will be supporting her. But on the other hand, the existence of benefits and social housing in the post-war period have enabled lone mothers to live autonomous lives, albeit at or around the subsistence minimum. The majority of academic commentators have agreed that welfare provision may have facilitated, but has not caused, family change.

In the case of women seeking divorce, Hilary Graham (1987) showed that those who had suffered violent treatment in their marriages were also likely to have been mistreated economically. Divorced and living on state benefits, these women reported that they were nevertheless better off. The point is that decision-making about marriage, divorce and motherhood, and about mothers entering the labour market, have been about more than economic rationality (*pace* the analysis of neoclassical economists such as Becker, 1981). Women make choices about becoming lone mothers in widely differing circumstances which may, in the case of many divorcing women, involve prioritising identity and emotional well-being over material well-being. Recent academic work has shown more appreciation of the importance of cultural variables. Thus Karen Oppenheim Mason and An-Magritt Jensen (1995) have suggested that the meaning that is attached by the majority to marriage may well have changed. If at the end of the century it has become important to maximise income, then it may be high-earning women who will be more likely to marry and less likely to divorce – the reverse of what has traditionally been assumed to happen. In addition, women's increased labour market participation may lead them to prioritise sexual satisfaction and emotional companionship over their husbands' capacity to provide economically. Unmarried motherhood has also been interpreted by some commentators in terms of women's pursuit of sexual autonomy, which, at the extreme, threatens to make men redundant (Dench, 1994). More generally, sociologists (see especially Giddens, 1992; Beck and Beck Gernscheim, 1995) have suggested that the recent past is marked by the increasing individualisation of men and women, who enter relationships for what can be derived by each person from them in terms of material, but more usually emotional, exchange.

However, it is difficult to see the changes affecting women in terms of labour market participation and family change purely in terms of increasing autonomy and individualisation, not least because it is still women who do the bulk of the unpaid work of caring in society, work that is based on a commitment to 'connection' (Gilligan, 1982) rather than individualism. It has often been charged that the development of modern welfare states has meant that the state has usurped the role of 'the family' in caring for the old and the young (e.g. Parsons and Bales, 1955). However there is little evidence for this view. In Britain, the percentage of elderly people in institutions has been remarkably similar throughout the twentieth century, notwithstanding greater longevity (Anderson, 1983), and while schools and clinics have taken on many responsibilities in respect of children, the family has found new tasks, especially in regard to fostering the emotional development of children (Smith, 1988). Research in the 1980s showed that care in and by families usually meant care by women (most importantly, Finch and Groves, 1983). The 1980 survey of women and employment found that 13 per cent of all women had caring responsibilities for sick or elderly dependants, and more than 20 per cent of women aged 40 or more had such responsibilities (Martin and Roberts, 1984). Between 1971 and 1981 alone, the number of people over 75 – the age group commonly agreed to be in need of most care – increased by 20 per cent, and will probably rise by a further 30 per cent by early in the new millennium. High rates of divorce and remarriage have meant that a significant number of women faced 'collapsed caring cycles', meaning that they face caring for young children and an elderly parent at the same time.

Women's obligation to care has been both internalised and prescribed. Any simple notion that women's increased participation in the public sphere results in a diminution of their caring work is misplaced. Women's decision to care for children and adult dependants is made within a framework of widely held assumptions that caring is women's work and that, in the end, caring should take precedence over other types of work, although in the late 1990s this was being questioned in respect of lone mothers who are being asked to do both. In his research on nineteenth-century Lancashire, Anderson (1971) uncovered strong elements of calculation in respect of the decision to care, in terms of whether the old person could make a contribution to the household; but as Hareven (1982) has pointed out, this does not account for reciprocal relationships between the generations that do not operate on the basis of current exchange but rather over an extended period of time. Nor does it address the gendered nature of unpaid care work. Longitudinal data in Gershuny Godwin and Jones (1994) show an increase in men's participation in household work over the period 1975–87, especially if their partners were in full-time employment, but from a very low base. There is evidence to suggest that women have internalised the injunction to care (Graham, 1983), but government policy which has from the early 1980s made more explicit assumptions that women will care for the increasing numbers of elderly people in need of it (Cmnd. 8173, 1981) also enforces a kind of 'compulsory altruism' (Land and Rose, 1985).

There is little doubt but that women's own aspirations have changed significantly in the post-war period. A majority of early-twentieth-century women faced with hard household labour and frequent pregnancy gave their support to the idea of a male-breadwinner model whereby men went out to work and women took responsibility for unpaid household work. A good husband was one who provided and a lucky wife was one who did not have to add paid labour to her burdens. Women's desire to care for young and old seems not to have changed, but in the context of technological change that has made housework easier, contraception more effective and pregnancy and childbirth much safer, they have added ambitions in respect of paid employment. At the same time, better employment prospects and better social entitlements to state benefits have facilitated family change. The unequal gendered division of labour in the post-war period, whereby women do an increasing proportion of paid work while retaining responsibility for the great bulk of unpaid work, has meant that state provision in respect of services for elderly people and childcare have become more important to them. It is continuity in the form of women's unpaid work as well as the change in respect of employment behaviour and family formation that makes the balancing act performed by most adult women a difficult one.

Notes

1   The term 'illegitimate' was replaced by 'extramarital birth' when the status of illegitimacy was abolished by the 1987 Family Reform Act.
2   'Lone-parent families' is something of a misnomer. Over 90 per cent of these families are in fact lone-mother families.
3   The work of Charles Murray (1984), using American data, was most influential in this regard, on both sides of the Atlantic.

References and Further Reading

Anderson, M. (1971) *Family Structure in Nineteenth Century Lancashire*. Cambridge.
Anderson, M. (1983) 'What is New about the Modern Family: A Historical Perspective'. In British Society for Population Studies, *The Family*, pp. 1–16. London.
Beck, U. and Beck-Gernscheim, E. (1995) *The Normal Chaos of Love*. Cambridge.
Becker, G. (1981) *A Treatise on the Family*. Cambridge, MA.
Black, S. and Sykes, M. (1971) 'Promiscuity and Oral Contraception: The Relationship Examined'. *Social Science and Medicine* 5: 637–43.
Bowlby, J. (1951) *Maternal Care and Maternal Health*. Geneva.

Carstairs, G. M. (1962) *This Island Now*. London: Hogarth Press.

Cmd. 7046 (1947) *Economic Survey for 1947*.

Cmd. 7695 (1949) *Report of the Royal Commission on Population*.

Cmd. 5629 (1974) *Report of the Committee on One-Parent Families*.

Cmnd. 8173 (1981) *Growing Older*.

Dench, G. (1994) *The Frog, the Prince and the Problem of Men*. London.

Dex, S. (1988) *Women's Attitudes towards Work*. London.

Ellwood, D. and Bane, M. J. (1985) 'The Impact of AFDC on Family Structure and Living Arrangements'. In R. G. Ehrenberg (ed.), *Research in Labour Economics*, VII: 137–207. Greenwich, CT.

Eppel, E. M. and Eppel, M. (1966) *Adolescents and Morality*. London.

Farrell, C. (1978) *My Mother Said: The Way Young People Learned about Sex and Birth Control*. London.

Finch, J. and Groves, D. (eds) (1983) *A Labour of Love: Women, Work and Caring*. London.

Fletcher, R. (1966) *The Family and Marriage in Britain*. Harmondsworth.

Garfinkel, I. and McLanahan, S. S. (1986) *Single Mothers and their Children: A New American Dilemma*. Washington, DC.

Gershuny, J., Godwin, M. and Jones, S. (1994) 'The Domestic Labour Revolution: A Process of Lagged Adaptation?' In M. Anderson, F. Bechhofer and J. Gershuny (eds), *The Social and Political Economy of the Household*, pp. 151–97. Oxford.

Giddens, A. (1992) *The Transformation of Intimacy: Sexuality, Love and Eroticism in Modern Societies*. Cambridge.

Gilligan, C. (1982) *In a Different Voice. Psychological Theory and Women's Development*. Cambridge, MA.

Gillis, J. (1986) *For Better, For Worse: British Marriages, 1600 to the Present*. Oxford.

Gorer, G. (1971) *Sex and Marriage in England Today*. London.

Graham, H. (1983) 'Caring: a Labour of Love'. In J. Finch and D. Groves (eds), *A Labour of Love*, pp. 13–30. London.

Graham, H. (1987) 'Being Poor: Perceptions and Coping Strategies for Lone Mothers'. In J. Brannen and G. Wilson (eds), *Give and Take in Families*, pp. 56–74. London.

Hakim, C. (1996) *Key Issues in Women's Work*. London.

Hareven, T. (1982) *Family Time and Industrial Time*. Cambridge.

Harkness, S., Machin, S. and Waldfogel, J. (1996) 'Women's Pay and Family Incomes in Britain, 1979–1991'. In J. Hills (ed.), *New Inequalities: The Changing Distribution of Income and Wealth in the UK*, pp. 158–80. Cambridge.

HC 39 (1981) *Report of the Employment Committee of the House of Commons on Home Working*.

Joshi, H. and Davies, H. (1992) 'Daycare in Europe and Mothers' Foregone Earnings'. *International Labour Review* 132: 561–79.

Kiernan, K. and Estaugh, V. (1993) *Cohabitation. Extra-marital Childbearing and Social Policy*. London.

Kiernan, K., Land, H. and Lewis, J. (1998) *Lone Mothers in Twentieth Century Britain*. Oxford.

Kolberg, J. E. (1991) 'The Gender Dimension of the Welfare State'. *International Journal of Sociology* 21(2): 119–48.

Land, H. and Rose, H. (1985) 'Compulsory Altruism for Women or an Altruistic Society for All?' In P. Bean, J. Ferris and D. Whynes (eds), *In Defence of Welfare*, pp. 74–96. London.

Lewis, J. (1992) 'Gender and the Development of Welfare Regimes'. *Journal of European Social Policy* 2(3): 159–73.

Lewis, J. (1997) 'Gender and Welfare Regimes: Further Thoughts'. *Social Politics* 4(2): 160–77.

Martin, J. and Roberts, C. (1984) *Women and Employment. A Lifetime Perspective.* London.

Mason, K. O. and Jensen, A-M. (eds) (1995) *Gender and Family Change in Industrialized Countries.* Oxford.

Morris, L. (1990) *The Workings of the Household.* Cambridge.

Murray, C. (1984) *Losing Ground. American Social Policy, 1950–1980.* New York.

Myrdal, A. and Klein, V. (1956) *Women's Two Roles.* London.

Parsons, T. and Bales, R. F. (1955) *Family Socialization and Interaction Process.* Glencoe, IL.

Phoenix, A. (1991) *Young Mothers.* Cambridge.

Riley, D. (1983) *War in the Nursery: Theories of the Child and the Mother.* London.

Roberts, C. (1985) 'Research on Women in the Labour Market: The Context and Scope of the Women and Employment Survey'. In B. Roberts, R. Finnegan and D. Gallie (eds), *New Approaches to Economic Life*, pp. 232–98. Manchester.

Robinson, J. A. T. (1963) *Honest to God.* London.

Rodgers, B. and Pryor, J. (1998) *Divorce and Separation: the Outcomes for Children.* York.

Schofield, M. (1968) *The Sexual Behaviour of Young People.* Harmondsworth.

Siim, B. (1987) 'The Scandinavian Welfare States – Towards Sexual Equality or a New Kind of Male Domination?' *Acta Sociologica* 30 (3/4): 255–70.

Smith, D. (1988) *The Everyday World as Problematic. A Feminist Sociology.* Milton Keynes.

Summerfield, P. (1984) *Women Workers in the Second World War: Production and Patriarchy in Conflict.* London.

Wilson, W. J. (1987) *The Truly Disadvantaged.* Chicago.

Chronology

1945   Family Allowances Act.
1948   NHS established; free health care for women.
1949   Report of Royal Commission on Population.
1956   Publication of Klein and Myrdal's *Women's Two Roles*.
1962   The pill introduced in Britain.
1967   Abortion Act.
1969   Divorce Act.
1971   Publication of Gorer's *Sex and Marriage in England Today*.
1970   Equal Pay Act.
1974   Finer Committee Report on One Parent Families.
1975   Sex Discrimination Act: Equal Opportunities Commission established.
1979   Margaret Thatcher becomes first woman Prime Minister.
1987   41 women MPs, a record number, elected to House of Commons
1991   Child Support Act establishes Child Support Agency.
1992   58 women MPs elected to House of Commons. Anglican Church allows ordination of women.
1996   Family Law Act.
1997   121 women MPs elected to House of Commons.

14 Cultural Change

Jim McGuigan

Frank Launder and Sidney Gilliat's film of 1943, *Millions Like Us*, reaches its climax at a lunchtime concert in a munitions factory in the north of England, which is put on by ENSA (the temporary wartime organisation, Entertainments National Service Association). Character actors join 'real people' in the massive factory canteen as the camera pans around at the conclusion to this fictionalised account of the campaign on the Home Front during the Second World War. Celia, the young widow from London, whose newly-wed Scottish husband has just died in an RAF raid over Germany, is cheered up by the music. Prompted sensitively by her university-educated companion on the production line, working-class Celia, who is played by a very middle-class actress, Patricia Roc, finds herself actually singing along with everyone else: 'Can't get away to marry you today. My wife won't let me!' This may now be judged a cloyingly senti-mental piece of propaganda, yet nonetheless, I still find it moving. It is the most moving moment I know in British cinema. Brief amelioration of personal loss is subsumed in a collective project, 'the people's war',[1] albeit rather easily, I would readily concede, via a silly song.

Everyone in Britain, not just the armed forces, was expected to join in the battle with fascism. The Blitz had already wreaked havoc early on in the war and destroyed many people's homes. Sheltering from aerial bombardment in the London Underground became associated with a shared sense of pride in holding out bravely against adversity, which is supposed to be a peculiarly British trait, but of course is not. The fortitude of civilians in the capital city itself echoed the Dunkirk spirit, whereby defeat was turned into a kind of victory. The Battle of Britain demonstrated the capacity to fight back. However, in 1943, the Luft-waffe was still a great and damaging threat, especially where armaments were manufactured. In the desperate circumstances of the time, people from different social backgrounds, it was generally agreed, needed to overcome old barriers and 'pull together' in the effort to stay alive and win the war. Class relations are explored very finely in the black-and-white, semi-documentary *Millions Like Us*, yet there is not a person of dark hue in sight despite the fact that many

West Indians, for instance, amongst others from the British Empire, fought and worked for Britain during the war. This is the well-meaning representation of an all-white, plucky little nation – albeit head of the largest empire in the world – standing up to Hitler. Whilst earnestly evoking everyday heroism and morale boosting on the Home Front, the film also optimistically envisages the prospect of an egalitarian settlement in British society after the war.

In 1981, the BBC first televised the filmed drama, *Country*, about the ruling-class response to Labour's general election victory in 1945, written by Trevor Griffiths, produced by Ann Scott and directed by Richard Eyre, with a glittering cast including James Fox, Wendy Hiller and Leo McKern. This was a late addition to the tradition of single plays on television that reflected critically upon 'the state of the nation'. *Country* needs to be seen in the context of that tradition. Extremely important was the commercial company, ABC's *Armchair Theatre* in the 1950s, scheduled on Sunday evenings following the hugely popular variety show, *Sunday Night at the London Palladium*, thus inheriting a very large audience for serious dramas that were often on themes of class and culture but hardly ever on race. One rare exception, however, was Ted Willis's *Hot Summer Night* (1959), in which a white trade unionist and his wife are thrown into crisis by their daughter's wish to marry a black immigrant. In the 1960s the BBC picked up the baton for socially engaged drama, most notably with the *Wednesday Play*. A key figure in this was the producer, Sidney Newman, a Canadian who had worked with the documentary film-maker, John Grierson. Newman launched *Armchair Theatre* on commercial television and then moved to the BBC in the early 1960s, where he oversaw the introduction of the *Wednesday Play* in addition to undertaking his general responsibilities for organising drama production. There was a shift in the 1960s from the kind of studio dramas that had been transmitted live in the 1950s to recorded studio drama and, eventually, location shooting that was facilitated by the advent of 16mm film. The most famous *Wednesday Play* was *Cathy Come Home* (1966), written by Jeremy Sandford, directed by Ken Loach and produced by Tony Garnett. Both Garnett and Loach were still active and indeed extremely successful in television and film at the turn of the millennium. *Cathy Come Home* represented the dire conditions of the homeless in a society that had supposedly rid itself of poverty. It was a cause célèbre for a number of reasons: formally, in the way it mixed documentary technique, sociological evidence and realist fiction; and socially, since it brought the issue of homelessness to widespread public attention and led to the setting up of the housing charity, Shelter. *Cathy Come Home* was viewed by over 20 million people.

Country is also, in part, about homelessness. Appropriating the framework of the 1930s West End play *Dear Octopus* by Dodie Smith, it is set at the Carlion (Corleone) country house in Kent in July 1945 where the various branches of the family have gathered for their annual dynastic celebration. It is a drama of succession. Old man Carlion, Sir Frederick, is dying. His eldest son was killed in the war. Sir Frederick wants his younger son, Philip, a 35-year old homosexual and non-combatant, to succeed him as head of the family brewing firm. Other members of the family are not so sure. 'The Socialists' have just won the general election, to the consternation of the family, with the exception of the left-wing daughter Ginnie, who is visiting for the first time in years in order to do a piece of photojournalism on her family for the magazine, *Picture Post*. Ginnie confirms her class betrayal by denouncing the company of gentlemen at the dinner table, warning them that 'the people' are going to expropriate their wealth and run them out of the country.

In fact, 'the people' are already seen to be encroaching upon the Carlions' property. Seasonal hop-pickers on the Carlion estate have occupied the barn since there is nowhere else under shelter for them to sleep. One of the displaced horses wanders into the house. Sir Frederick is incensed: he takes his shotgun to the hop-pickers. Philip intervenes, seizing the gun from his father but also succeeding, without violence, in emptying the barn of the hop-pickers. This is a key moment in the legitimation of Philip's succession. He has also found a wife at short notice in a middle-class and, it is hinted, lesbian employee of the household. Another crucial move is Philip's presentation of recarbonated beer, 'weasel piss', the fountain of post-war profits, to the assembled company of gentlemen, the leading shareholders in the brewery.

Country ends with a bonfire at which estate workers drink beer supplied by the Carlions: 'Roll out the barrel. We've got the blues on the run', they sing. Philip and his father look on. The old man asks, 'Is it a funeral?' Philip replies, 'They've not yet noticed the grave is empty.' Philip is by no means complacent. Echoing his socialist sister, he has warned the company of gentlemen: 'Before the year's out we may all be living in the West Indies on such capital as we have been able to muster from the expropriation of our possessions that the socialists have been elected to effect. The ship's sinking, gentlemen. That's water around your ankles.'

The newly elected government had a programme for nationalising industries like railways and coal mining, but not for brewing. Financial compensation for the 'expropriated' shareholders was, in any case, generous. The 1945 Labour government posed something of a challenge to entrenched wealth and power. However, its greatest achievement, in effect, was to establish the welfare state and the National Health Service, which did not, of course, bring about the final expropriation of the rich. On the 1979 election of Margaret Thatcher, who promised to turn back the tide of post-war social democracy, which she partly succeeded in doing, Trevor Griffiths conceived of a project that he provisionally entitled *Tory Stories*, a six-part television drama that would trace the trajectory of the Conservative ruling class at conjunctural moments from 1945 to the present. In the end, however, this turned out to be just one expensively made television film, *Country*, dramatising Tory Britain's response to Labour Britain on the occasion of the latter's greatest victory, the general election of 1945.[2] Labour Britain gave Tory Britain a fright, but post-war consumerism and the 'property-owning democracy' would eventually win out against the socialist republic that was hoped for by George Orwell early in the war.[3]

This political story, to be sure, is not peculiar to Britain. British cultural history since the Second World War, as elsewhere, is heavily marked, however, and in specifically national ways, by ideological struggles and accommodations between Left and Right. That may no longer be the case at the turn of the millennium, according to currently conventional wisdom. Anthony Giddens,

Britain's leading sociologist, argues that the polarities and conflicts of Left and Right have become much less relevant than they were in the very recent past for understanding the cultural, economic and social challenges now faced by Britain and similar countries. The New Labour politics of 'the Third Way' presents itself as a consensual principle that supersedes the divisiveness of the Thatcherite 1980s, but does not return to the same kind of social-democratic consensus that had managed to survive periods of Conservative government until it broke up in the 1970s.[4] Whether or not Giddens and New Labour are right about the present condition and the way forward, it is demonstrably the case, nevertheless, that the clash between Left and Right was at the heart of post-war culture in Britain.

Throughout most of the post-war period, culture in Britain, it should be remembered, was highly politicised; and, particularly so by a 'New Left' that broke with Stalinism and sustained a critical relationship to Labourism.[5] Selective examples of such cultural phenomena are the 1950s 'angry young men' in literature, drama and cinema; the 1960s 'underground' in music and lifestyle; the 'political theatre' of the 1970s; and 1980s feminist, lesbian and gay movements impacting upon the arts and media. The question was posed of how post-imperial Britain might become an egalitarian society with a popular, participatory culture.[6] The early New Left believed that it was possible to socialise the economy and democratise the state. Emancipatory social movements, the labour movement, and middle-class movements like the Campaign for Nuclear Disarmament (CND) around 1960, through to Greenham Common women protesting against cruise missiles in the 1980s, and many such movements in between and since, like the more recent road protesters, were deemed to be in the vanguard of social change. While the New Left, in its original form and various reincarnations, relied a great deal upon the spaces opened up by state intervention, especially in the cultural field, and the comparative freedom of semi-autonomous public bodies like the Arts Council, the BBC and the universities, the rhetoric was typically anti-statist from the late 1950s to the 1990s.

From the Right, Thatcherism used the state against the Left, whilst also speaking anti-state rhetoric, and sought to return to 'Victorian values' and nineteenth-century market economics – a programme of 'regressive modernisation'.[7] The 'welfare state model' of culture, which had been subsidising successive waves of left-wing and avant-garde arts workers as well as maintaining the traditional arts organisations, was considered a burden upon 'the taxpayer'. It was severely curtailed but not actually destroyed during the Thatcherite 1980s. Publicly subsidised culture was required to function more like private business and the Great British 'heritage', invoking nostalgia for the past glories of an 'old country', was promoted at home and abroad. When the Thatcherite project eventually faltered and collapsed, its New Labour successor posed the old cultural question of national renewal yet again but in a different way, in which signs are more important than substance, by suggesting that Britain might be 'rebranded' as, say, 'a young country'.[8]

Another immensely consequential structural division and set of political negotiations have shaped the contours of post-war culture and society in Britain in such a way that cuts across the Left/Right divide to some extent and raises a

further question. Cultural identity in Britain has been caught between the coun-
tervailing forces of the so-called 'special relationship' with the USA on the one
hand, and membership of Europe on the other. From joining the Common
Market in the 1970s to qualified participation in the European Union during
the 1990s, which was exemplified by the Conservatives' refusal to sign the
Social Chapter of the Maastricht Treaty, the British government and public
opinion in general have never been quite sure that the future lay with Europe.
On the terrain of everyday life, the pleasures of American mass-mediated culture have far outweighed identification with the abstraction of 'Europe'; and
not only in Britain. Even when Labour signed up to the Social Chapter in 1997,
it was hard to be sure that the question concerning Britain's – and especially
England's – semi-detached relationship to continental Europe had been finally
answered. The question was asked periodically from the 1950s onwards: was
Britain to be a European social democracy where, amongst other things, the
good of state intervention in the cultural field is taken for granted, or was it to
be the fifty-first state of the USA, a free-market society in which 'consumer
demand' is the more or less exclusive determinant of what will be supplied,
including cultural products? This has been a governmental issue in the broadest
sense. Nowadays, the question tends to be reframed by 'globalisation', on the
assumption that no nation-state, with the possible exception of the USA itself, is
in command of its own fate economically or culturally. Belief in the possibility
of a social-democratic culture in one country or in fortress Europe, for that
matter, is difficult to sustain in the age of the American-dominated global
market, satellite communications, the Internet, Hollywood synergy, endless television, hip hop and Nike trainers. Still, Britain hangs between Europe and the
USA.

   Millions Like Us illustrates the condition of Britain towards the end of the
war. *Country* reflects upon the Tory response to the socialist threat as the war
ended. What, then, does a more recent British film, such as *Imagine What We
Can Do for Tomorrow*, represent? It was shown several times on television in
January 1999. It is one minute long. That is because it is an advertisement,
though quite what is being advertised is not instantly evident since there is no
mention, except for its obscure logo, of the New Millennium Experience to be
opened on 1 January 2000 with hugely overestimated visitor numbers projected
for the year of 12 million. *Imagine What We Can Do for Tomorrow* was made
at the cost of £2 million by the Saatchi brothers' advertising agency. They ran
the Conservatives' election campaign in 1979 with the slogan, 'Labour Isn't
Working', to great acclaim in the advertising, marketing and public relations
businesses. The slickness and ironic wit of British advertising have been admired overseas and agencies based in Britain operate extensively in other
markets, particularly the USA. The Saatchis were one of the great success
stories of the Thatcherite 1980s. After business problems in the early 1990s,
however, they re-emerged in the late 1990s to project New Labour Britain at
home and abroad. One of the brothers, Charles, is a famous art collector who,
through his buying policy, was instrumental in creating the phenomenon of
Young British Art, such as the work of Damien Hirst of shark-in-the-tank
fame. At its height, 'Young British Art' was represented to much public

comment and controversy by the Royal Academy's *Sensation* exhibition in 1997. In this and other respects, the relations between art and advertising have become blurred.

Imagine What We Can Do for Tomorrow is an arty ad. The visuals are all of Easter Island at speed, from sunrise to sunset, with the shadows cast by the famously lugubrious figures shortening and lengthening rapidly; and clouds flying about and billowing. Jeremy Irons's portentous voice-over asks the viewer to 'Imagine that the last one thousand years took place in just one day.' He then reels off a series of names and events, from Edward the Confessor building Westminster Abbey in the morning to John Logie Baird inventing television in time for the evening's viewing. Eight names are mentioned, six of them British and two non-British (Michelangelo and Mother Teresa). Important events at the end of the day include landing a man on the moon, the fall of the Berlin Wall and the abolition of apartheid in South Africa, none of them 'British'. There is a curious mixing of national and international elements in *Imagine What We Can Do for Tomorrow*, implying none too subtly that Britain has been at the heart of world civilisation over the past thousand years and is in a position, some-how, to lead the way into the next millennium. There is, however, no image of present-day Britain and no sign of the people. The first television advertisement for the New Millennium Experience signifies an empty Britishness, vague nos-talgia for past greatness and a would-be global role in the future: Britain, once again and farcically, as world leader.

The absence of contemporary Britishness, whatever that might be, from the Saatchis' Millennium Dome advertisement is not accidental since, quite apart from the 'global' pretensions of the project, 'Britain' is now difficult to repre-sent. It is necessary to ask whether or not there is a distinctively British culture and identity at all, that is, one distinguishable from the Englishness that has dominated the British Isles. There are distinctive and evidently self-confident national identities on the Celtic fringe: Scottishness, Welshness and, more com-plicatedly, Irishness of North and South.[9] The conflation of Britishness with Englishness is abhorrent to subordinate nations in a multinational state. In the case of Scottish nationalism, in particular, there has been the possibility since the 1970s, revived with devolution at the end of the century, that the United Kingdom might eventually break up. An important feature of contemporary Britishness remains, however, England's complex set of interactions with the traditionally subordinate nations, once characterised by imperial imposition but now, much more typically, featuring the confident presence and voice of periph-eral cultures, not only on the margins but also at the centre: for instance, the hybrid music of the London-Irish band, the Pogues, in the 1980s; and, later, Scottish bands and film-making, *Trainspotting* and all that, in the 1990s. Not everything passes through London. Edinburgh, most prominently, is internation-ally famous as a major cultural centre with its heritage finery, summer festival and New Year's Eve party on Princes Street. Responding to deindustrialisation and as part of urban regeneration strategy, other cities have asserted their cul-tural distinctions, such as Glasgow, Cardiff, Birmingham, Leeds, Manchester and Sheffield. These are meeting places and crossroads, not just provincial pockets of arts, media and architecture.

Quite apart from the dynamics of cultural mixing and crossover, the Scots, the Welsh and the Irish seem to know who they are wherever they are – but do the English? The apparent vacuity of contemporary Britishness derives, in part, from the hollowing-out of Englishness. While it is no longer credible to simply represent Britain as England, the fact of the matter is that 'the English' themselves do not have as strong a sense of identity as the Scots, the Welsh and the Irish. This is possibly why Englishness has sometimes been expressed hysterically: for instance, in spectacular outbreaks of soccer hooliganism at international competitions abroad, such as the European Championship in Germany in 1988, the 1998 World Cup in France and, most recently, at Euro 2000, thus finally destroying England's chance of staging the 2006 World Cup. Football fans have appropriated 'traditional' English symbols – the bulldog, the red-cross-on-white-background of St George's flag, and so forth – to articulate a xenophobic Englishness, as much as anything in order to try and conjure up a sense of identity for themselves. Occasional violent outbursts of this kind can also be read as desperate attempts to recapture the spirit of 'the people's war'. That was undoubtedly so for Margaret Thatcher's ludicrously inflated Falklands War of 1982. Flag-waving and belligerence towards foreigners represent the dark side of an uncertain Englishness/Britishness.

On the brighter side, however, England/Britain is extremely cosmopolitan due to a number of factors, including its maritime history, its comparatively libertarian political traditions, its cultural, scientific and technological achievements and, indeed, the legacy of the British Empire. The problem for Britishness (and, also, for Englishness) is not the rediscovery of an essential identity, a checklist of attributes that need to be distilled and protected, T. S. Eliot's 'all the characteristic activities and interests of a people'[10] or John Major's cricket and warm beer. There is little doubt that interesting excavations can be made of 'traditional' English/British culture: for instance, an historical anthropology of orderly queueing. Much more important than this, though, is coming to terms with the contemporary reality of hybrid identities in process and emergent multiculturalism, responding to, say, Linton Kwesi Johnson's accusation of the 1970s that 'Inglan is a bitch', from the point of view of the black Caribbean diaspora.

In 1998, the fiftieth anniversary of the docking at Tilbury of the *Empire Windrush* from Jamaica was marked and celebrated in several publications and on BBC television. The arrival of the *Windrush* in 1948 was the legendary and not quite accurate beginning of post-war West Indian migration to Britain, bringing people with British passports to better material conditions of life at the heart of the Empire and actively recruited because of a labour shortage. Mike and Trevor Phillips subtitled their book on the subject *The Irresistible Rise of Multi-Racial Britain*.[11] The New Commonwealth immigrants who settled in Britain have stories to tell of disappointed expectations, racial prejudice and discrimination, stoicism and struggle. Their children and grandchildren negotiate hybrid identities, usually in relation to 'Britishness' rather than 'Englishness': Black British, Asian British, etc. Typically, and quite rightly, they may routinely fail the Conservative politician Norman Tebbit's loyalty test by supporting the West Indies, India or Pakistan against England at cricket.

That Britain has not achieved the status of a genuinely harmonious multicultural or multi-communal society is frequently demonstrated and commented upon, such as in the alienation felt by many Muslims around the Rushdie affair in 1989, when it became clear that in a comparatively irreligious and secular country only anti-Christian blasphemy counted. More recently, the failure of the Metropolitan Police to put together a satisfactory case against the young white men suspected of murdering the black teenager, Stephen Lawrence, reopened questions of institutional racism. However, at the risk of being misunderstood as complacent, rather like the reputation of the BBC and British public service broadcasting generally, as perhaps the 'least bad' in the world, it has to be said, Britain has one of the 'least bad' records for racial antagonism and conflict in comparative terms. Moreover, in spite of enduring forms of discrimination and prejudice, black and Asian Britons have had an enormous impact on 'the culture', for instance, in music, cuisine and sport, to an extent that would have been unimaginable back in the 1950s when the major flow of Commonwealth immigration occurred. The appeal of black popular music is especially pronounced in Britain, though it is, of course, an international rather than peculiarly national phenomenon. Mixing black and Asian music in bangra, for instance, and the interaction of subcultural styles amongst ethnic minorities and in relation to majority ethnicity are developments of great significance. White Britain routinely appropriates cultural elements from Black Britain in, most manifestly, youth styles and musical tastes. For another example, the curry house is, arguably, one of the major sites of intercultural exchange in British towns and cities. In a country that is undistinguished internationally for its cuisine, other cuisines associated with substantial minorities, such as Hong Kong Chinese, become, in effect, part of the national culture. Furthermore, the most popular sandwich filling is said to be chicken tikka masala. The postcolonial impact is not confined to everyday popular and youth culture, music, cuisine and in the success of sporting heroes like Linford Christie. In 'elite' culture, the literary exchange in English between Britain and its former colonies is particularly notable, including the Booker Prize-winning works of Salman Rushdie (*Midnight's Children*, 1981) and Arundhati Roy (*The God of Small Things*, 1997).

At its best, 'Britain' serves as a site of international cultural exchange and cosmopolitanism. And there are many diverse and hybrid kinds of Britishness itself. Recognition of difference, cultural diversity, sharing and mixing: these are the signs of an emergent multicultural Britain. Yet fleeting moments of symbolic unity still occur that evoke a sense of national belongingness amongst very large numbers of a heterogeneous people, such as the funeral of Diana, Princess of Wales, the parallel and virtual monarch, in 1997. There have been several such moments since 1945. One of the earliest and prototypical of these postwar moments of apparent public unity and British nationhood was the televised coronation of the actual Queen, Elizabeth II, in 1953.

The spectacle of the coronation, in fact, inaugurated mass-popular television in Britain. Early television was a luxury commodity. In the late 1930s there were only a few thousand viewers in and around London. Television sets were very expensive pieces of furniture and technology, costing the same as a small motor car. Even when television started up again in 1946 (transmission was suspended from 1939), it remained a minority medium under conditions of post-war austerity. By the early 1950s, however, a network of transmission facilities was being built across the country. Cheaper wooden and Bakelite sets became available, making the medium a more affordable commodity. Many people actually bought their first television set to watch the coronation and those with no set crowded into the homes of those who did have one.

Popular memory of a sense of British nationhood since the 1950s is very much associated with televisual mediation – and hence its very construction – of major events, such as the funeral of Winston Churchill in 1965, England's World Cup victory in 1966 and innumerable other sporting events, the Iranian Embassy siege and the wedding of Charles and Diana in 1981. Such televisual moments are not exclusively national. The launch of Telstar in 1962, for instance, later enabled the Beatles to sing 'All You Need Is Love' around the world. Television is also its own memory bank. The television commentator's remark about the crowd invading the pitch towards the end of the 1966 World Cup final, as Geoff Hurst was just about to slam in the fourth goal for England, 'They think it's all over', became the title of a television quiz show in the late 1990s. The archive of a rich and complex televisual culture is constantly being raided to remind us of, in the title of a 1960s television programme, 'all our yesterdays'.

The 1953 coronation is not only significant for inaugurating popular television in Britain. As the sociologists Michael Young and Edward Shils argued at the time, it was a ritual articulation of Britishness. According to them, the very idea of Britain is sustained by the institution of monarchy.[12] Extending the argument, it might be suggested that the crisis of the British monarchy in the 1990s, beset by scandal and disaster, corresponds to a currently unstable and shifting sense of Britishness. The coronation underlined the resilience not just of the idea of Britain in general but, quite specifically, of Conservative Britain in particular. Labour lost office in 1951 within weeks of the termination of the Festival of Britain, its own 'tonic to the nation'.[13] Although popular with the general public, the Festival was not, however, a televisual event like the coronation. The Festival's concrete legacy was the South Bank complex of high art venues, the Festival Hall and later additions, such as the National Theatre, controversial monuments to architectural modernism. The coronation was more memorable than the Festival because it was such a notable television event, thereby providing Conservative Britain with yet another symbolic edge over Labour Britain. During the next 11 years, the Conservatives presided over the first post-war consumer boom and the spectacular growth of mass, commercial culture, 'the affluent society'. At their third successive general election victory in 1959, the Tories were able to tell the Great British public that they had 'never had it so good'.

The sale of television sets shot up further after the coronation. Business interests associated with the Conservative party soon lobbied Churchill's government to introduce commercial television alongside the staid public monopoly of the BBC. The new commercial network, Independent Television (ITV), drew upon tried and tested popular formats from American commercial television, such as game shows. ITV's populism contrasted sharply with the BBC's high-mindedness. Moreover, loss of audience to ITV began to call the legitimacy of the BBC into question. Since all television viewers were required to pay the licence fee for funding the BBC whereas ITV was 'free', thanks to advertising, the BBC was obliged to address everyone. Since the late 1940s this had been treated as a matter of 'brow' with the three radio channels, the Light Programme (low), the Home Service (middle) and the Third Programme (high).

With only one television channel, until the introduction of the higher-brow BBC2 by a Labour government in 1965, BBC TV had to find a new formulaic mix towards the end of the 1950s. In effect, the Corporation responded very successfully to populist competition from ITV, creating the nostalgic 'golden age' of British television. The BBC succeeded in making both 'popular' programming, like extensive sports coverage (for instance, *Grandstand*), and 'serious' programming, such as innovative documentaries on the arts (for instance, *Monitor*). Under Hugh Carlton Greene's regime at the BBC in the 1960s there was scope for young broadcasters to experiment with form in drama and to criticise 'the Establishment' in satire shows. However, pushing at the limits occasionally resulted in overt censorship: series were discontinued (such as *That Was the Week that Was*) and programmes not shown (such as *The War Game*) in order to avoid governmental displeasure. Less controversially, on the populist end of the spectrum, for instance, the situation comedy, a broadcast form originally developed in the USA, became a BBC speciality tradition from *Hancock's Half-Hour* in the late 1950s to *Absolutely Fabulous* in the mid-1990s.

The ITV network was required to observe public service principles and not just appeal to 'the lowest common denominator'. With their regional monopolies of advertising revenue, ITV company franchises were, in a famous remark, 'a licence to print money'. When the 1964 Labour government, led by Harold Wilson, capped ITV profits, money was poured back into programming. BBC revenue was also rising year by year with the spread of television-set ownership and the introduction of colour in the late 1960s.[14] The money was there, then, to make 'good' programmes at every level: quantity was routinely turned into quality. Granada, which held the northern franchise, for instance, made the hard-hitting current affairs programme *World in Action*. ABC, in the South, sought to match Granada with *This Week*.

Much of the cultural debate from the late 1950s, echoing similar debates in the USA and elsewhere in Europe, was about the alleged meretriciousness of 'mass culture'. In Britain there was an emphasis on the need for state intervention and governmental control, though at 'arm's length', so as to ensure the production and circulation of 'good culture', creating conditions for 'serious' modern culture to flourish as well as preserving 'traditional' high culture and 'authentic' folk cultures. A key voice articulating such concern was Richard Hoggart, whose *The Uses of Literacy*, published in 1957, framed many of the arguments.[15] An offshoot of Hoggart's portrayal of the authentic culture of working-class community under attack from 'Americanised' mass culture, ironically, was Granada's long-running soap opera set 'up north', *Coronation Street*, launched in 1960. The BBC's *EastEnders*, set 'down south' in London and launched in 1985, introduced a more multicultural and somewhat gloomier version of a similar sense of communal life whilst also smuggling in public service messages about health care and so on.

The popularity of representations of community in urban settings may be a compensation for the actual lack of neighbourliness that is associated with the long retreat into the home. The trend towards increasingly home-based leisure consumption since the Second World War is an international rather than purely national phenomenon. However, it is especially pronounced in home-owning and home-loving Britain. Products like the videocassette recorder, the on-line personal computer, music centres and recording decks, when they have come on to the British market, have tended to sell more quickly to a greater proportion of the population than in comparable European countries.

British cinema attendance peaked in 1946 (1.63 billion recorded admissions) and attendance at Football League matches peaked at 41.2 million in the 1948–9 season.[16] The long-term decline of cinema attendance was arrested in the 1990s with the advent of multiplex cinemas, but cinemagoing still remains a tiny fraction of the 1940s level (137.3 million in 1997). Films are now mostly seen in the home, via terrestrial, satellite and cable channels or on video. There are various transmission and payment systems in the developing multi-channel environment. And the new high-tech wonders of digital and wide-screen TV bring the qualities of cinematic image and sound into the domestic space of the home, for those who can afford it.

For many working-class football fans, standing on cold, wet and dangerous terraces has given way to watching games on television either at home or in the pub. All-seater stadia in the Premiership and rocketing entrance charges, season tickets and merchandising have made going to a match very expensive. The 'people's game' has become, in effect, a predominantly middle-class spectator sport at the grounds of the top clubs. Furthermore, the capture of live coverage of Premiership matches in the 1990s by Rupert Murdoch's BSkyB had an enormous impact on football. At the end of the decade, Murdoch was even seeking to buy up the mega-club, Manchester United, unsuccessfully, however, as it turned out. Massive capital accumulation, commodification of everything, squeezing more money out of the customer: these forces accelerated everywhere towards the end of the twentieth century, not only in British entertainment and screen culture. While such developments are usually seen as unstoppable, it is understandable that some older people express anger and a justifiable sense of loss since Britain was rather well-served with media and culture under more predominantly public service arrangements.

Let us turn the clock back just one more time. The 1960s is rightly remembered as an extraordinary decade both culturally and politically, although it probably started some time in the 1950s and ended some time in the 1970s. Civil rights movements, student revolts and countercultures of resistance were citadel-shaking in the USA and parts of continental Europe. They were less significant in Britain. The most spectacular British contribution was not in oppositional politics but, instead, 'Swinging Sixties' style and popular culture: in fashion with, for instance, the 'invention' of the miniskirt; the transatlantic success of rock groups led by the Beatles and the Rolling Stones, playing the Americans successfully at their own game; the succession of spectacular youth subcultures (Teds, Mods, Rockers, Skinheads, etc.). These styles were to become elements in a pick'n'mix, postmodern, recycling and finely differentiated youth culture around the world, heralded particularly by Punk from the late 1970s.[17]

The cultural and political Right in Britain labelled the 1960s 'permissive' and promised to turn the clock back at the earliest possible opportunity. That was not feasible at the beginning of the 1970s as progressive and oppositional forces grew in strength up to the point of bringing down a Conservative government in 1974. In the 1980s, however, punishment would be meted out to the cultural remnants of the 1960s, as it was to the miners, 'the enemy within', for the defiance they showed in the 1970s. However, the clock can never really be turned back. Abolition or obliteration of institutionalised practices and routines do not result in the return to a preceding condition unsullied by subsequent history. Much more typically, the recycling of past styles, forms and their attendant sensibilities in a changed context is a salient characteristic of latter-day culture in Britain. In fact, for some, the Thatcherite 1980s was a kind of rerun of the 1960s in which everything was up for grabs again, although this time in a less restrained capitalist economy where money-making and conspicuous consumption ruled the roost over considerations of social justice.

Conservative rhetoric since the troubled 1970s associated the public sector generally and subsidised culture, in particular, with the Left, conveniently forgetting that cultural agencies of the state had usually been either set up or shaped decisively by past Conservative governments, such as the BBC in the 1920s. The Arts Council owed its permanent incorporation at the end of the war to the efforts of a card-carrying Liberal, the economist John Maynard Keynes. It was run in a very conservative and metropolitan elitist way in the 1950s. During the six years of Wilson's Labour governments of the 1960s, however, the Arts Council's annual grant-in-aid trebled: the Regional Arts Associations were established and regional theatres and cultural facilities were built around the country. Left-wing and avant-garde cultural practices received subsidy but most of the money still went to major national organisations like the Royal Opera House in Covent Garden, the National Theatre and the Royal Shakespeare Company. The Arts Council was hardly a left-wing plot. Thatcher did not abolish it; nor did she the BBC.[18] The Peacock Committee was formed to work out a rationale for abolishing the licence fee and turn the BBC into an advertising-funded broadcaster. Sir Alan Peacock did not in the end, however, recommend advertising on any BBC channel, mainly because of protests from the ITV companies, fearful of loss of revenue. The Peacock Report of 1986 did, nevertheless, formulate the crucial argument for applying the all-important principle of consumer sovereignty, customer choice, right across the broadcasting landscape; and, in addition, it suggested that the BBC's role should be reduced to that of an Arts Council of the air, solely confined to serious documentaries and uncommercial high culture.[19] The BBC managed to avoid such a dismal fate and it remains both a 'popular' and 'serious' broadcaster in spite of the traumatic restructuring it has gone through, new managerialism and accommodation to market ideology.

Technological developments, in any case, meant that a closed and highly regulated system of national broadcasting on the public service model would probably cease to command the field. Still, many in broadcasting were shocked by the speed and enthusiasm with which Conservative governments tried to shift the whole system from public to market regulation. Added to that was the foundation of Channel 4 in 1982 by a Conservative government, yet implementing aspects of left-wing campaigning against 'consensus' broadcasting from the 1970s. It prefigured a new industrial model, facilitating the growth of an independent production sector to supply programmes to 'the channel' (and, subsequently, to BBC, ITV and other distributors as well). 'Independence' broke with the restrictive practices of the BBC and ITV duopoly. Channel 4 was much trumpeted, at its inception, as innovative and different. And, eventually, BBC2 was to copy some of its formats and style. The independent production sector in broadcasting was instrumental, most importantly, in facilitating the dismantlement of 'Fordism' in the industry, bringing about a looser network structure of production, including much greater insecurity and casualisation amongst broadcast workers, similarly to wider developments in a 'post-Fordist' economy and society.

The shift from an exclusive system of public service broadcasting to a diverse 'screen culture', much of it driven by capitalist imperatives that are not peculiarly national, and reconfigurations of cultural consumption in public and private spaces are illustrations of change in British culture and society since the war. The rise of multiculturalism and the fracturing of Britishness are also of immense consequence. These are significant but differently motivated strands in a complex history of culture and governmentality; and they are not the only ones. No single strand, moreover, is reducible to any other. It is impossible to tell the whole story. In fact, there are many stories that are told of cultural change in Britain over the period under consideration.[20]

Yet I would suggest an underlying dialectic is discernible, one of long-term decline and periodic renewal, a succession of 'modernisations' that are more or less successful. Such a dialectic makes sense of the cycles of hope and disappointment in the post-war period. British power, wealth and cultural influence have been in steady decline for a century.[21] It remains debatable, however, to what extent Britain's permanently reduced status in the world has been absorbed into popular consciousness and public culture. Periodic renewal or, at least, attempts to arrest decline tend to be associated with key moments of governmental change and regeneration promises: Labour's victory in the 1945 election; the Conservatives' return to power in the 1950s; Wilson's Labourist 1960s; and, of course, the Thatcherite counter-revolution from 1979. It is perhaps too soon to tell just how significant culturally will be the New Labour government that came to power in the landslide election of May 1997.

Labour was also tempted by a project that had been initiated by the outgoing Conservative government, completion of the Millennium Dome next to the prime meridian on a southern peninsula of the Thames at Greenwich, to be funded mainly by the National Lottery, perhaps the emblematic institution of the 1990s, and supported overweeningly by corporate sponsorship. This was to be a business expression of public culture, recalling the Great Exhibition of 1851, as the Tories had intended, more than the Festival of 1951. Under the direction of Peter Mandelson, the exposition was reconceived as an 'experience' to be enjoyed as much as a trip to Disney World. The gigantic tent, designed by the Richard Rogers Partnership, was supposed to be instantly recognisable when its image circulated around the globe. Like similar projects historically, the creation of the New Millennium Experience met with widespread scepticism and derision at home. It was a gamble that was, with hindsight, bound to fail. It proved to be a monumental act of hubris and symbol of the vacuum at the heart of New Labour. Was Britain merely simulating past greatness yet again by marking time in the Millennium Dome?

Notes

In writing this essay on culture in post-war Britain I have taken advice from a great many people, friends and colleagues. They expressed interesting and diverse opinions about what really happened. I have not heeded all the advice and I have difficulty remembering exactly who suggested what. I am grateful to everyone who chipped in, whether I agreed with them or not, but would like to thank Graham Murdock especially for checking my original plan.

1 See A. Calder, *The People's War – Britain 1939–1945*, London, 1971 [1969]; and S. Fielding, P. Thompson and N. Tiratsoo, *'England Arise' – The Labour Party and Popular Politics in 1940s Britain*, London, 1995.
2 As a script editor at the BBC in 1979, I did background research for three of the plays, including *Country*. The second was to be set around the bank rate leak of 1957 and the third around the Profumo scandal of 1963. On the work of Trevor Griffiths, see M. Poole and J. Wyver, *Powerplays – Trevor Griffiths in Television*, London, 1984.
3 G. Orwell, *The Lion and the Unicorn – Socialism and the English Genius*, London, 1982 [1941].
4 See A. Giddens, *Beyond Left and Right – The Future of Radical Politics*, Cambridge, 1994; and his *The Third Way – The Renewal of Social Democracy*, Cambridge, 1998.
5 M. Kenny, *The First New Left – British Intellectuals After Stalin*, London, 1995.
6 The work of cultural and political theorist Raymond Williams was a vital inspiration for New Left politics, especially his *The Long Revolution*, London, 1965 [1961]. Also, see his *Towards 2000*, London, 1985 [1983].
7 S. Hall, *The Hard Road to Renewal*, London, 1988.
8 M. Leonard, *Britain^{TM} – Renewing our Identity*, London, 1997. Also see Tony Blair's *New Britain – My Vision for a Young Country*, London, 1996.
9 In *The Atlantic Celts – Ancient People or Modern Invention?*, London, 1999, Simon James contests the ancient unity of the Celtic fringe, which does not, however, affect the argument in this chapter. In modern times, a certain Celtic identity, shared by Irish, Scots and Welsh, has to an extent been constructed unitarily simply by its otherness from England.
10 T. S. Eliot, *Notes Towards the Definition of Culture*, London, 1962 [1948], p. 31.
11 M. Phillips and T. Phillips, *Windrush – The Irresistible Rise of Multi-Racial Britain*, London, 1998. Also see O. Wiambu (ed.), *Empire Windrush – Fifty Years of Writing About Black Britain*, London, 1998; and 'Windrush Echoes', *Soundings* 10, autumn 1998.

12 E. Shils and M. Young, 'The Meaning of the Coronation', *Sociological Review* 1(2), 1953.

13 M. Banham and B. Hillier (eds), *A Tonic to the Nation – The Festival of Britain 1951*, London, 1976.

14 S. Hood and T. Tabary-Peterssen, *On Television*, 4th ed., London, 1997.

15 R. Hoggart, *The Uses of Literacy*, London, 1958 [1957]. Also, see his *The Way We Live Now*, London, 1995.

16 Figures cited by D. Philips and A. Tomlinson, 'Homeward Bound – Leisure, Popular Culture and Consumer Capitalism', in D. Strinati and S. Wagg (eds), *Come On Down? Popular Media Culture in Post-War Britain*, London, 1992.

17 D. Hebdige, *Subculture – The Meaning of Style*, London, 1979.

18 The Conservatives did, however, abolish a whole tier of regional government, including the Labour stronghold of the Greater London Council which, amongst other things, had encouraged radical cultural politics and, for instance, the development of black political and ethnic minority arts. See G. Mulgan and K. Worpole, *Saturday Night or Sunday Morning? From Arts to Industry – New Forms of Cultural Policy*, London, 1986; and K. Owusu, *The Struggle for Black Arts in Britain*, London, 1986.

19 *Report of the Committee on Financing the BBC* (The Peacock Report), Cmnd 9824, London, 1996.

20 A short chapter like this one can only skim the surface of cultural change in Britain since the war, whilst making a limited selection of salient points. For further and in-depth reading, I would recommend D. Hebdige, 'Digging for Britain – An Excavation in Seven Parts', in Strinati and Wagg, *Come On Down?*; R. Hewison, *Culture and Consensus – England, Art and Politics Since 1940*, London, 1995; A. Sinfield, *Literature Politics and Culture in Post-war Britain*, 2nd ed., London, 1997, M. Storry and P. Childs (eds), *British Cultural Identities*, London, 1997.

21 A. Gamble, *Britain in Decline – Economic Policy, Political Strategy and the British State*, 4th ed., London, 1994.

Further Reading

Alibhai-Brown, Yasmin, *Who Do We Think We Are? – Imagining the New Britain*, London, 2000.

McGuigan, Jim, 'National Government and the Cultural Public Sphere', *Media International Australia incorporating Culture and Policy* 87, May 1998: 68–83.

McGuigan, Jim, 'British Identity and "the People's Princess"', *Sociological Review* 48(1), February 2000: 1–8.

Parekh, Bhikhu, *The Future of Multi-ethnic Britain – The Parekh Report*, London, 2000.

Storry, Mike and Childs, Peter (eds), *British Cultural Identities*, London, 1997.

Westwood, Sally, 'Re-Branding Britain – Sociology, Futures and Futurology', *Sociology* 34(1), 2000: 185–202.

Chronology

This is not meant to be treated as an exhaustive chronology of cultural change in Britain since the Second World War. It merely indicates a selection of key moments that relate to the argument of the chapter.

1943   *Millions Like Us* – war on the Home Front.
1945   Labour's landslide victory and first overall majority in a general election.
1946   Permanent incorporation by Royal Charter of the Arts Council of Great Brit-
          ain, successor to the temporary wartime Council for the Encouragement of
          Music and the Arts. British cinema attendance peaks at 1.63 billion.
1948   Arrival of the *SS Windrush* at Tilbury from Jamaica.
1948–9   Attendance at Football League grounds peaks at 41.2 million.
1951   Festival of Britain. Labour's fall from power.
1953   Coronation of Queen Elizabeth II. Inauguration of popular TV in Britain.
1955   Launch of ITV (commercial TV).
1956   'Angry young men' movement in literature, theatre and film. Suez invasion,
          signifying Britain's nostalgia for lost imperial power. Soviet invasion of Hun-
          gary, a key factor in the formation of the 'New Left'.
1957   Publication of Richard Hoggart's *The Uses of Literacy*, which sets agenda for
          debates concerning 'mass' and 'popular' culture, working-class culture and
          consumerism.
1958   Campaign for Nuclear Disarmament (CND) formed.
1959   Conservative Prime Minister Harold Macmillan tells the electorate, 'You've
          never had it so good.'
1964–70   Labour governments led by Harold Wilson, coinciding with 'Swinging Sixties'
          (fashion, beat music, design, sexual freedom, etc.). 'Underground' (counter-
          culture, heavy rock, student rebellion, etc.). Expansion of public-sector cul-
          ture (trebling of the Arts Council grant-in-aid, network of Regional Arts
          Associations, increased revenue for the BBC, etc.).
1965   Winston Churchill's televised funeral.
1966   World Cup victory of England over West Germany at Wembley. *Cathy Come
          Home* – homelessness and poverty in 'the affluent society'.
1968   Protest against Vietnam War (Grosvenor Square), etc., but student and revolu-
          tionary politics less pronounced in Britain than in France, Germany and USA.
1972   Britain joins European Economic Community.
1974   Fall of Edward Heath's Conservative government following miners' strike and
          three-day week. Key moment in development of the '68 generation's impact
          on arts and media, including political theatre, cultural feminism, gay liber-
          ation, etc.
1976   Punk – ironic commentary on post-war succession of youth subcultural styles
          by picking and mixing from them. Key moment in general sense of cultural
          decay and political dereliction.
1979   Margaret Thatcher's first of three successive general election victories, leading
          to 'regressive modernisation' of the 1980s.
1981   *Country* – reflecting upon Tory Britain's post-war response to Labour Britain.
1980s   Thatcherism's undermining of 'welfare-state' culture and marketisation in the
          public sector, requiring its organisations, including those in the arts and
          media, to act like private businesses. Right-wing 'money culture' and left-wing
          'radical culture' still representing sharply alternative principles but the Left
          becomes increasingly attracted to populist and consumerist values promoted
          by the Thatcherite 'revolution'.
1982   Falklands/Malvinas War, conjuring up popular images from British imperial
          past and its naval supremacy. The launch of Channel 4 at this time is also
          especially significant. It was to be more diverse and experimental in program-
          ming than mainstream channels, thus realising, to an extent, the aims of left-
          liberal broadcasting campaigns of the 1970s. Channel 4 also represented,

however, a model of 'independent' production, in effect, outsourcing, that was instrumental in breaking down union power within broadcasting and bringing about greater casualisation and insecurity in television and related creative industries generally.

1986   Peacock Report on financing the BBC, while recommending continued prohibition against advertising on the BBC, argues for the development of a comparatively unregulated multi-channel environment based on consumer choice and in which public service broadcasting would become marginalised.

1989   Ayatollah Khomeini issues his *fatwa* against Salman Rushdie for blasphemy against the prophet Muhammad in *The Satanic Verses*. The book is burnt in Bradford.

1990s   The legacy of Thatcherism throughout the institutions of British society, including public and private cultural institutions, is consolidated under John Major's Conservative premiership from 1991 to 1997.

1997   The election of New Labour in May signals a change of mood and renewed sense of 'British' identity that is promoted heavily by Tony Blair's government: 'Young Britain', 'Cool Britannia', 'Third Way', etc. New Labour also becomes connected by symbolic association and by deliberate governmental action to the emotional populism of Diana, Princess of Wales's funeral in September. In addition, the Millennium Dome, originally sanctioned by outgoing Conservatives, appropriated by New Labour as means of imagining future and representing Labour's 'New Britain' to world at large. British cinema attendance is 137.3 million.

1999   *What We Can Do For Tomorrow* – television advertisement (Jan.).

2000   New Millennium Experience opens at Greenwich on the South Bank of the Thames in London (1 Jan.).

15 Education Since 1945

Anthony Heath

The second half of the twentieth century in Britain saw a number of striking changes in British education. First, Britain moved from a structure of selective schools and what has been called a 'sponsored' system of educational and social mobility to a largely comprehensive structure and an associated 'contest' system of mobility (Turner, 1960). Secondly, the last 50 years witnessed a dramatic increase in the length of pupils' school careers and in the proportions taking the major public examinations, such as the General Certificate of Education at Ordinary and Advanced level (GCE O and A level). This was followed by major expansions in higher education and a gradual shift from elite to mass-participation higher education. These reforms were accompanied by some changes in the extent to which the British educational system was stratified by class and gender, the gender inequalities in particular being largely eliminated.

From Sponsored to Contest Mobility

The 1944 Education Act provides a natural starting point for the history of British education in the second half of the twentieth century. The key features of the Act were that it provided for free secondary education for all pupils. Before the war, a proportion of pupils had been educated in 'all-age' elementary schools; the 1944 Act replaced this by a formal transfer for all pupils at the age of 11 from primary to secondary schools. Fees in these secondary schools (or at least in the aided/maintained sector) were also abolished; previously, some places at secondary schools had been awarded on the basis of a competitive scholarship examination while others had been open to fee-payers (the proportions varying from one local authority to another). The 1944 Act was not, however, quite as radical as its subsequent reputation implied. It rounded off a process that was already well advanced: by 1938 the majority of pupils admitted to secondary schools had paid no fees.

The post-war period was also characterised by the tripartite system of grammar schools, technical schools and secondary modern schools. This was not actually a provision of the 1944 Education Act itself, but emerged from various government reports such as those of Spens and Norwood. Nor was the tripartite system really all that new. It was largely a systematisation of arrangements that had been widespread before the war. It continued as the dominant arrangement for schooling in Britain up until 1965 (and rather longer in many places) when the Labour government began its programme of comprehensive reorganisation.

The grammar schools of this tripartite system had an academic curriculum and provided a preparation for university, the professions and white-collar work. Pupils were expected to stay on until the completion of their secondary education at the age of 18, although in practice many pupils, particularly from working-class backgrounds, left grammar school much earlier at the minimum school-leaving age (which had been raised to 15 in 1947).

Technical schools offered a more vocational education and were geared to the needs of skilled work in industry. They were relatively few in number and, indeed, many local authorities had no technical schools at all. In this respect the tripartite system was something of a misnomer: around two-fifths of local authorities operated binary systems of grammar and secondary modern schools during the 1950s.

Finally, secondary modern schools catered for the bulk of the age group. They were the successors to the pre-war elementary schools and offered a basic education, their pupils leaving at the minimum school-leaving age and entering relatively low-level jobs in the working class.

Selection for these three types of schools took place at the age of 11 through the 'eleven-plus' examination, and so the three types of school were essentially stratified by academic ability. Reformers at the time perhaps naively called for parity of esteem between the three types of school. They anticipated that selection would be meritocratic and would avoid the unfairness of the pre-war system, that had allowed affluent parents to buy fee-paying places for less able children while more able children of less affluent parents were excluded. In practice, however, it soon became evident that the three types of school continued to be stratified by social class as well as by academic ability. It was not a pure meritocracy, and parents and children had no illusions about parity of esteem.

These arrangements have been described as a 'sponsored' system of educational mobility: children were selected by the educational authorities at a relatively early stage in their school career, and their subsequent educational and occupational prospects were heavily influenced by the decisions made at the age of 11. Able children from the working class (together with their able peers from the middle classes) were effectively sponsored at the age of 11 for upward educational and occupational mobility. This can be contrasted with a 'contest' system of mobility. In a contest system, of which the paradigm example was the USA, all children were allowed to remain in the educational competition for as long as they wished. By and large, decisions how long to continue in education were taken by the children and their families, rather than by the educational authorities, and the crucial decisions were delayed to a much later stage of the educational career. From 1965 onwards Britain gradually began to move away from the sponsored system towards an American-style contest system, although progress was slow and incomplete.

The Labour Party and the trade unions had long campaigned against selection at the age of 11 as unfair and socially divisive, and when Labour won the 1964 general election after 13 years of Conservative government it took its opportunity to introduce reform. Circular 10/65 from the Department of Education asked local authorities to introduce plans for reorganising secondary education along comprehensive lines, and a gradual process of reform was then begun. The process of comprehensivisation continued over many years and was resisted but not reversed by the following Conservative government under Edward Heath (when Margaret Thatcher was Secretary of State for Education). In most education authorities the eleven-plus examination was eventually abolished and pupils attended mixed-ability neighbourhood comprehensive schools. In practice, there were few purpose-built comprehensive schools and most children simply continued to attend the same school as they had done before, albeit with a different name.

The complications, however, are legion. First of all, in a number of places, particularly rural areas of Scotland and Wales, some comprehensive schools had been established long before the main programme of reform in 1965 (for further discussion see Gray et al McPherson and Raffe, 1983). Second, not all local authorities went fully comprehensive. At the time of writing, two authorities still retain a selective system while several other authorities retain a few elite, and highly selective, grammar schools with the majority of pupils attending neighbourhood comprehensive schools. Moreover, Northern Ireland has retained a selective system of secondary schooling throughout the whole period. (For a discussion of education in Northern Ireland see Breen et al Heath and Whelan, 1999.)

Third, voluntary-aided church schools continued into the comprehensive era. These schools did have some scope for selecting pupils (although ostensibly not on the basis of ability) and were often believed to be more desirable on educational as well as on religious criteria. There was thus a persisting element of selection within the state sector.

Fourth, in the 1980s Margaret Thatcher's Conservative governments introduced various reforms that sought to unpick some aspects of Labour's comprehensive system. Most notably, schools were allowed to opt out of local authority control and measures to introduce competition between schools were introduced. These measures were seen by some critics as an attempt to reintroduce selection by the back door.

Finally, private fee-paying schools continued throughout the period. Britain has a long history of fee-paying schools, some of which confusingly began life as local grammar schools. They include a number of prestigious boarding schools, some academically selective day schools, and some less selective schools which, in the days of the tripartite system, had catered for middle-class children who had failed the eleven-plus examination (Halsey, Heath and Ridge, 1980). The private schools were not immune from political reform; some of them (the direct grant schools) received a grant from the government in return for providing places, on the basis of selective examinations, to children from state primary schools. This grant was abolished by Harold Wilson's Labour government in 1976. An alternative scheme of 'assisted places' was introduced by Margaret Thatcher's Conservative government, and this in turn was abolished by Tony Blair's Labour government. These changes will have had some effects at the margins, but the bulk of the private schools continued throughout our period more or less unchanged.

Tables 15.1a and 15.1b show the changing distributions of pupils at the different types of school over time. The data are drawn from the 1991 British Household Panel Study (BHPS), a representative cross-section of the adult population of Great Britain. (We use the BHPS partly because the official government data tend to be patchy, with constantly changing definitions and formats, and partly because the official data never report the social class origins of pupils – a topic to which we turn in a later section. For a detailed summary of trends using official data see Smith, 2000.)

Table 15.1a   Type of school attended by men, by birth cohort, Great Britain, 1930–1969 (column %)

School type	Birth cohort			
	1930–9	1940–9	1950–9	1960–9
Private	5	4	5	6
Grammar	22	21	18	7
Technical	7	4	2	1
Elementary/Secondary modern	60	58	41	20
Comprehensive	7	12	35	66
All	100	100	100	100
N	563	806	889	918

Table 15.1b   Type of school attended by women, by birth cohort, Great Britain, 1930–1969 (column %)

School type	Birth cohort			
	1930–9	1940–9	1950–9	1960–9
Private	8	7	5	4
Grammar	21	24	19	9
Technical	2	4	2	1
Elementary/Secondary modern	63	55	44	21
Comprehensive	5	9	31	65
All	10	10	100	100
N	0	0	908	1069
	57	89		
	7	8		

Source: BHPS, 1991.

In order to look at the trends over time, we distinguish respondents according to their period of birth. Thus the first birth cohort covers respondents born between 1930 and 1939, who were thus educated during the early stages of the post-war period under the tripartite system. The second birth cohort, born between 1940 and 1949 and entering their secondary schools between 1951 and 1960, would have been educated for the main part of their school careers in the tripartite system. The third birth cohort, who were born between 1950 and 1959 and thus were entering secondary schools between 1961 and 1970, would have included many children who experienced the early stages of the comprehensive system, while the final birth cohort would have been educated during the more established period of comprehensive schooling.

As we can see, the private sector continued throughout the period with around 5 per cent of pupils. Grammar schools expanded slowly during the first part of the post-war period, covering just over 20 per cent of pupils in the heyday of the tripartite system, before gradually declining once more as comprehensive reorganisation increased in pace. However, even by the end of our period, 7 per cent of our youngest birth cohort reported that they had been educated in grammar schools.

Comprehensive schooling shows the expected rapid rise in the last two birth cohorts, displacing elementary and secondary modern schools as the dominant type of school. Even in our youngest cohort, however, there were still an appreciable number of pupils attending secondary modern schools. Official figures indicate that in England in 1990/1 86 per cent of pupils in the public sector were at comprehensive schools, only 3.5 per cent at secondary modern schools and 3.8 per cent at grammar schools (Smith, 2000). The discrepancy between the BHPS data and the official data may be because many of the new comprehensive schools were simply renamed secondary modern or grammar schools, and were housed in the same buildings with the same staff as before. Some respondents may therefore simply have reported their school's original status.

Not unrelated to these changes in the school system have been changes in the examination system. Unsurprisingly, the examination system of Britain is also complicated. Scotland has its own distinctive system, which has more in common with continental systems such as the French baccalauréat than it has with the English system. During the tripartite era of the immediate post-war period England, Wales and Northern Ireland had two main examinations – the General Certificate of Education at Ordinary level (GCE O level), usually taken at the age of 16, and the GCE Advanced level (GCE A level), taken at the age of 18. These examinations were introduced in 1947 to replace the pre-war School Certificate and Higher School Certificate, which dated from 1917. But, like School Certificate, the GCE O and A levels were largely geared to the educational needs of pupils at grammar schools, many of whom would be preparing for university entrance. Two passes at A level became the standard minimum requirement for university entrance.

Pupils at secondary modern schools were not initially expected to take any formal school-leaving certificates, and most of them left school before the age at which it was normal to sit GCE O level. The conventional official wisdom in the 1950s was opposed to external examinations for pupils at secondary modern schools, but under pressure from teachers and parents moves were made to introduce a new examination, the Certificate of Secondary Education (CSE). The Crowther Report of 1958 suggested that external examinations below the level of the GCE might serve a useful purpose for the 'examinable minority' in secondary modern schools. This idea was developed in the Beloe Report of 1960 and was eventually introduced in 1963. Pupils sat this new examination at the same age as their contemporaries sat GCE O level, but the standards were set at a lower level and the examinations were geared to a lower level of ability than the GCE. (A pass at the top grade 1 of CSE was usually taken to be equivalent to a pass at grade C at GCE O level.)

This examination system, which had been geared to the differing needs of pupils at grammar and secondary modern schools, persisted well into the period of comprehensive reorganisation. But eventually, in 1988, the two examinations were merged to form a new examination called the General Certificate of Secondary Education (GCSE), which effectively combined the CSE and GCE O level into a single system.

Alongside these institutional changes, the post-war period saw the introduction of so-called progressive teaching methods. These aimed to be more child-centred and encouraged the child to discover things for herself; they reduced the emphasis on traditional 'blackboard and chalk' methods and gave more prominence to group and project work. They were particularly popular among teachers in primary schools, and were given official blessing in the Plowden Report on primary education of 1967 which claimed that '"Finding out" has proved to be better for children than "being told"' (p. 460). While the development of progressive methods predated comprehensive reorganisation, the ending of selection and the eleven-plus examination gave primary schools greater flexibility and opportunities for innovation.

Like comprehensive reorganisation, however, progressive methods became a source of political controversy and ideological dispute. They were blamed by the political Right for declining educational standards, particularly declining standards in traditional virtues such as accurate spelling. A notable counter-attack was provided by the 'Black Papers', the first of which was published in 1968. In the Black Papers the emerging educational orthodoxies were challenged, with notable critiques of egalitarianism and of discovery methods. However, it was not until Margaret Thatcher's Conservative government in the 1980s that a major reversal was attempted. The 1988 Education Act introduced a compulsory national curriculum together with a system of testing all school children at the ages of seven and eleven.

Expansion

Britain, like other European countries, saw a dramatic rise in the length of pupils' school careers, and in the proportions with formal educational credentials, during the second half of the twentieth century. This was the consequence both of autonomous social and economic processes and of institutional reforms. The demand for education was rising-partly, one suspects, because of the nature of changes in the job market, with demand for unskilled labour declining but opportunities for qualified manpower increasing. This autonomous process was given additional impetus by the raising of the school-leaving age from 15 to 16 in 1973/4. It also meant that the great majority of pupils now remained in school until the age at which it was usual to sit public examinations such as GCE O level and CSE.

Tables 15.2a and 15.2b show how the length of the school career changed across our four birth cohorts. In the oldest cohort, two-thirds or more of boys and girls left school at the age of 15 or below. By the time of the youngest cohort, the modal leaving-age had become 16, and the proportions staying on until 17 and 18 had more or less doubled.

In turn, the increasing numbers of well-qualified school-leavers put pressure on higher education institutions and the last third of the century saw a transformation of higher education. Halsey (2000) divides the post-war growth of higher education into three main phases:

Restricted growth, 1945–63
The binary phase, 1964–92
Mass tertiary education, 1992–

Table 15.2a Age at leaving school of men, by birth cohort, Great Britain, 1930–1969 (column %)

School-leaving age	Birth cohort			
	1930–9	1940–9	1950–9	1960–9
18 and over	8	12	19	20
17	6	8	11	11
16	17	22	40	59
15 or below	69	58	30	10
All	100	100	100	100
N	592	840	925	951

Table 15.2b Age at leaving school of women, by birth cohort, Great Britain, 1930–1969 (column %)

School-leaving age	Birth cohort			
	1930–9	1940–9	1950–9	1960–9
18 and over	7	12	16	18
17	7	10	11	13
16	18	25	41	60
15 or below	68	54	33	9
All	100	100	100	100
N	644	941	950	1109

Source: BHPS, 1991.

In the period from 1945 up to 1963, higher education was dominated by the universities, which took around 3–4 per cent of the age group, the proportion increasing only slowly over the period. There were also many students at teacher training colleges (usually on two-year courses) and a smaller proportion pursuing higher education in other institutions. As with the tripartite system of secondary education, this was largely a continuation of arrangements that had been current before the war. Overall, the proportion of the age group in higher education grew from around 5 per cent at the beginning of the post-war period to 8 per cent by 1962.

The Robbins Report (1963), which recommended a major expansion of higher education, is usually seen as the turning point. However, as so often with educational reforms, the report to some degree reflected changes that were already under way: the new University of Sussex had already been founded in 1959 (receiving its Royal Charter in 1961) and was proving to be very popular with students. The binary system -a division between the 44 autonomous universities and a public sector led by 30 polytechnics — also largely reflected pre-existing divisions in higher education.

Expansion of student numbers continued throughout the binary phase. Halsey reports that in 1962 the number of full-time students had been 216,000 (Halsey, 2000, p. 234). By 1989, including home and overseas students, part-timers in universities, the Open University, the polytechnics and other colleges offering advanced courses, the number had grown to 1,095,000 students. Halsey also argues that higher education gradually changed in character over this period: 'The stereotyped view of higher education as a three-year residential system of high-quality learning for young men has been overturned. The definition moved gradually, and continues to move, towards an American concept of higher education' (p. 234).

In many ways, then, the changing nature of higher education parallels the move towards comprehensive schools and an American system of contest mobility at the secondary level. Halsey's final phase of mass tertiary education is the natural development of this process, with the formal division, if not the differences in standing, between universities and polytechnics being abolished by the Conservative government in 1992. However, this is still not a mass system of higher education in the American sense: in Britain the Age Participation Index (the number of home initial entrants to full-time higher education as a proportion of the 18–19-year-old population) was projected to increase to 32.1 in 2000, still a minority of the age group and well short of American figures.

The increase in the length of the school career, and the expansion of higher education, means that there was a major transformation in the qualifications of the British population. Tables 15.3a and 15.3b show the highest academic qualifications of our four birth cohorts. Note that in the case of O level there have been changes over time in the precise nature of these qualifications, and we cannot claim that we are strictly comparing like with like. In particular, at the beginning of our period there would have been some respondents with the pre-war qualification of School Certificate while at the end of our period there would have been a few with GCSE. We have also included the growing number of people with grade 1 passes at CSE, as this was generally regarded as the equivalent of an O-level pass.

In our earliest cohort, born before the war, three-fifths of the men and an even larger proportion of the women reported that they had none of these formal school or university qualifications. By the time of our youngest birth cohort, however, the proportion of unqualified respondents had been reduced to around one in seven. Contrary to the conventional wisdom of the 1950s, the great majority of pupils proved to be 'examinable'.

The biggest absolute increases were in the acquisition of the intermediate qualifications of O and A level, where women made rather larger gains than men. There were substantial increases in all the other categories, too, particularly in the last two birth cohorts at CSE. At the higher levels of qualification, the rate of increase seems to have slowed somewhat in the youngest birth cohorts, but this may be in part because of life-cycle effects: it takes time to acquire degrees and many members of our younger cohorts may still be on course to obtain them in the future. (We should note that the BHPS asks

Table 15.3a Highest qualification obtained by men, by birth cohort, Great Britain, 1930–1969 (column %)

Highest qualification	Birth cohort			
	1930–9	1940–9	1950–9	1960–9
Degree	6.6	10.2	14.2	13.7
Post-A level	5.0	7.3	6.1	7.9
A level, etc.	8.7	16.5	26.1	22.1
O level, etc.	18.8	23.3	22.6	28.5
CSE	0.2	0.2	5.2	12.1
None	60.7	42.4	25.7	15.7
All	100.0	100.0	100.0	100.0
N	575.0	806.0	879.0	904.0

Table 15.3b Highest qualification obtained by women, by birth cohort, Great Britain, 1930–1969 (column %)

Highest qualification	Birth cohort			
	1930–9	1940–9	1950–9	1960–9
Degree	3.0	6.8	9.9	10.8
Post-A level	5.0	5.9	5.9	4.1
A level, etc.	5.7	8.0	10.6	19.3
O level, etc.	17.8	28.9	31.6	36.6
CSE	0.5	0.7	7.3	14.4
None	68.1	49.6	35.5	14.8
All	100.0	100.0	100.0	100.0
N	636.0	935.0	946.0	1086.0

Source: BHPS, 1991.

respondents for the names of the qualifications that they have at the time of interview, and so in some cases the qualifications may have been obtained after leaving school.)

Some questions can be raised about this apparent increase in educational attainment. Specifically, there has been concern that standards have been falling as a result of 'grade inflation' and that it is now easier to achieve, say, a pass at A level than it used to be. Do the increasing numbers obtaining A level mean that pupils are doing better or that examiners are doing worse? This is probably an unanswerable question. (Goldstein and Heath, 2000 provide a thorough review of the notion of 'standards' in education.)

However, the debate over standards has tended to confuse two very different concepts – change in the measuring instrument, in this case the examination procedures, and change in the performance of the pupils. The issue of the maintenance of standards in the sense of the comparability of the measuring instrument over time is certainly a worrying one for the kind of investigation we have carried out in this chapter. Our analysis assumes some degree of comparability between the pre-war School Certificate, the post-war O level, a grade 1 CSE and the combined GCSE. Since these examinations were catering for rather different groups, and more importantly numbers, of pupils it would be surprising if they were of exactly comparable standard (assuming that we could know when exact comparability had been achieved). Our yardstick, then, has almost certainly not remained constant over time. The most likely possibility is that the yardstick has to some degree became debased over time, and that a modern-day GCSE is of a somewhat lower standard than a pre-war School Certificate.

Possible debasement of the yardstick suggests that the increase in qualifications shown in tables 15.3a and 15.3b may be somewhat misleading as a guide to students' changing levels of attainment. On the other hand, it is certainly true that a much larger proportion of young people now have some paper qualifications, even if the precise meaning of those qualifications is unclear.

Class, Gender and Ethnic Inequalities

Throughout the twentieth century, the British educational system was stratified by social class. One of the hopes of the reformers who supported the 1944 Education Act was that the abolition of fees in public-sector grammar schools would reduce class inequalities in access. But research on the tripartite system soon showed that pupils' chances of gaining a place at grammar school did not depend solely on their intellectual ability but was also influenced by their social origins, the type of primary school they attended, and the area of the country in which they lived (Floud, Halsey and Martin, 1956). Similarly, one of the hopes of the supporters of comprehensive reform had been that reform might reduce the class inequalities in educational attainment that had been so stubbornly resistant to the reforms of the 1944 Act. There were also hopes that expansion both at secondary and tertiary level might reduce class inequalities.

To explore questions about class differences in British education we distinguish three broad groupings:

> *the salariat*, consisting of relatively secure and advantaged positions in the professions and management;
> *the intermediate classes*, consisting of routine white-collar workers, the petty bourgeoisie, foremen and technicians;
> *the working class*, consisting of rank-and-file manual workers in industry, services and agriculture.

As is conventional, we use father's class as the indicator of social background. However, if data on father's class are not available, we use mother's social class instead.

To explore this question using the BHPS data we begin by focusing on the percentages from each social class background who obtained an O level pass (or a higher qualification). Tables 15.4a and 15.4b show the percentages in each birth cohort as a whole obtaining a pass at O level or better.

As might be expected, much higher proportions of respondents from salariat origins than from working-class origins obtained a pass at O level or above, and this remained true throughout the period. As we would also expect from the earlier tables, all three social classes showed substantial increases over time in the proportions obtaining these qualifications. However, our data suggest that the growth was more notable among pupils from working-class origins –

Table 15.4a Men obtaining O level or above, by class origin and birth cohort, Great Britain, 1930–1969 (cell %)

Social class origins	Birth cohort			
	1930–9	1940–9	1950–9	1960–9
Salariat	76	87	83	90
Intermediate	44	64	76	70
Working	29	47	60	64
All	41	60	71	74

Table 15.4b Women obtaining O level or above, by class origin and birth cohort, Great Britain, 1930–1969 (cell %)

Social class origins	Birth cohort			
	1930–9	1940–9	1950–9	1960–9
Salariat	57	79	77	89
Intermediate	34	53	60	73
Working	24	36	43	61
All	31	51	57	73

Source: BHPS, 1991.

up from 29 per cent to 64 per cent in the case of men -than it was among respondents from salariat backgrounds – up from a much higher initial level of 56 per cent but then stabilizing at around 90 per cent.

The upshot of this is that there has indeed been some narrowing of class differentials at O level as the working class began to catch up while the salariat approached saturation levels. The difference between the classes in absolute terms thus tended to decline. The absolute gap between men from the salariat and working class fell from 47 percentage points in the oldest birth cohort to 26 points in the youngest.

The reduction in absolute class inequalities was not so dramatic in the case of women. This is partly because, as we saw earlier, women started from a lower initial baseline than men, and table 15.4b shows that this held true even for women from salariat origins. Thus in our earliest birth cohort only 57 per cent of women from salariat origins, compared with 76 per cent of men, achieved intermediate qualifications or above. The absolute gap between women from salariat and working-class backgrounds was thus much smaller initially than was the gap between men; in the oldest birth cohort the absolute gap was 33 points, and by the time of the youngest birth cohort it had fallen only slightly to 28 points.

However, the absolute differences between the classes will depend to a considerable extent on what can be thought of as 'floor' and 'ceiling' effects. In particular, as expansion proceeds, there must come a point at which the absolute gap declines. For example, if the growth in the percentage of working-class pupils acquiring intermediate qualifications continues until 80 per cent or more of them are successful, the absolute gap from the salariat must inevitably fall below 20 points (since the salariat percentage cannot rise above 100). For this reason, sociologists of education have used alternative measures of class inequality, notably odds ratios, which take account of these floor and ceiling effects. These alternative measures suggest that the reduction in class inequalities has been relatively modest (Shavit and Blossfeld, 1992).

One possibility is that, as more and more children acquire O levels and intermediate qualifications, so the focus of competition shifts upwards. A closing of the gaps at O level might then in part reflect the devalued nature of O levels in the labour market. In tables 15.5a and 15.5b, therefore, we show the trends in class inequalities at degree level.

Table 15.5a   Men obtaining degrees, by class origin and birth cohort, Great Britain, 1930–1969 (cell %)

Social class origins	Birth cohort			
	1930–9	1940–9	1950–9	1960–9
Salariat	27	25	33	31
Intermediate	7	12	11	10
Working	3	5	8	5
All	7	11	15	15

Table 15.5b Women obtaining degrees, by class origin and birth cohort, Great Britain, 1930–1969 (cell %)

Social class origins	Birth cohort			
	1930–9	1940–9	1950–9	1960–9
Salariat	17	20	26	22
Intermediate	1	5	7	10
Working	1	3	3	5
All	3	7	10	12

Source: BHPS, 1991.

As we can see, at university level the salariat is still a long way short of saturation, with only a third of men and rather fewer women obtaining degrees even in our youngest birth cohort. We can also see that the absolute gaps between the classes changed very little over the post-war period: among men, the absolute gap between those from salariat and working-class origins was 24 points in the oldest birth cohort, but 26 points in the youngest cohort. Similarly, among women the gap was 16 points in the oldest cohort and 17 in the youngest. (In the case of degrees, floor effects are rather more important than ceiling effects, and if we use odds ratios to take account of these floor effects, we do find some modest narrowing of the class inequalities.)

Still, it is quite clear that, despite half a century of reform, British education remains highly stratified by social class. Educational expansion appears to have led to some reduction in the absolute differences between the classes at O level, but if there has been some devaluation of these credentials, the real consequences of these equalisations may be rather limited. At higher levels, where the full effects of the recent expansion are not yet visible, no reduction in absolute inequalities is yet apparent.

Class differences in educational attainment also remain a great deal larger than gender inequalities. In table 15.6 we summarize the gender inequalities at O level and degree level. As we can see, the overall differences between men and women have tended to be rather small-8 points at O level and 4 at degree level in our oldest birth cohort. Moreover, at O level the gap had largely disappeared by the time of our youngest birth cohort (and more recent data suggests that women may now have overtaken men at this level).

While major gender differences in subject choice persist, the reduction in the gender inequalities in attainment is one of the more striking education changes in the second half of the century. However, the change was probably due to autonomous processes rather than to deliberate policies of reform. Similar reductions have also been observed in many other European societies in this period. However, it should be noted that the post-war period also saw a gradual shift from single-sex to co-educational schools. Comprehensive schools in particular tended to be co-educational, unlike the single-sex grammar and secondary modern schools that they replaced. It is certainly conceivable that co-education may have played a part in the reduction of gender inequalities.

Table 15.6 Men and women obtaining O level or above, by birth cohort, Great Britain, 1930–1969 (cell %)

	Birth cohort			
	1930–9	1940–9	1950–9	1960–9
% men obtaining O level or above	39	57	69	72
% women obtaining O level or above	31	50	57	71
% men obtaining a degree	7	10	14	14
% women obtaining a degree	3	7	10	11

Source: derived from tables 4a, 4b, 5a and 5b.

Alongside class and gender inequalities, ethnic inequalities have sources of concern in the most recent period. The growth of a multicultural society has been one of the notable features of post-war Britain, and issues of ethnic differences in educational attainment became major concerns in Britain as evidence of 'underachievement' by some ethnic minority children in British schools became apparent in the 1970s. The Swann Report of 1985 was indicative of this official concern and focused on the role of racial prejudice and discrimination within the educational system.

The 'first generation' of migrants from the Caribbean, East Africa and the Indian subcontinent had largely completed their education before migration. Their patterns of education reflected those pertaining in their countries of origin (together with the selective factors that lead some people to migrate and others to remain). It is therefore the experience of the second generation, born and brought up in Britain, that is of greatest interest and has been of greatest concern.

With the exception of the Irish (who unfortunately cannot be identified in our surveys), the second-generation ethnic minorities were born relatively late in the century and we cannot as yet study trends over time. However, we can study the educational qualifications of ethnic minority members of our youngest birth cohort born between 1960 and 1969, and these are shown in tables 15.7a and 15.7b. (For these tables we use the Labour Force Survey, LFS, rather than the BHPS as the BHPS is not sufficiently large to give reliable estimates of ethnic minority education. The LFS unfortunately does not include class origins, however.)

Table 15.7a Educational qualifications of ethnic minority men born in Britain, 1960–1969 (row %)

Ethnic origins	O level or above	Degree
British-born white	73.9	14.9
British-born black Caribbean	65.4	7.6
British-born Indian	82.5	31.6
British-born Pakistani	67.3	19.6

Table 15.7b Educational qualifications of ethnic minority women born in Britain, 1960–1969 (row %)

British-born white	70.7	11.7
British-born Black Caribbean	76.7	8.2
British-born Indian	73.1	24.5
British-born Pakistani	69.6	11.0

Source: cumulated Labour Force Survey, 1991–7.

The data show some substantial differences between the various ethnic minorities. They also show some somewhat different patterns for men and women. The second-generation Indians, both men and women, actually surpass the British-born whites, both at O level (or its equivalent) and degree level. The black Caribbean and Pakistani women have rather similar levels of achievement to the British-born white women, while the black Caribbean and Pakistani men lag somewhat behind the British-born white men, at least at O level.

Whether these ethnic inequalities are as large as the social class inequalities is a moot point. In absolute terms, the gap between the most and least successful minority (Indians and black Caribbean, respectively) at O level is 17 points and at degree level is 24 points among men, although among women the gaps are substantially smaller. These compare with gaps of 26 points (both at O level and degree level) between the salariat and the working class among members of the same birth cohort. On the other hand, the gaps between the least successful ethnic minority (the black Caribbean) and the white British are substantially smaller than the class differences.

It should be noted, moreover, that part of the ethnic inequalities can probably be explained by differences between the ethnic groups in their social class profiles and by their geographical concentration in inner-city areas with poor educational provision. Stratification by class is unlikely to be the whole story but it nonetheless continues to be an important part of it.

Conclusions

The second half of the twentieth century saw major changes in British education. Most notably, there was a huge expansion in the proportions of the school population who stayed on at school or continued into higher education and who obtained formal educational qualifications. These changes, however, were common to most European societies and probably reflected autonomous social processes.

Unlike most other countries, however, British education was also highly politicised during the post-war period. The primary focus of this political conflict was over the abolition of selective grammar schools and the establishment of neighbourhood comprehensive schools. There were additional political disputes over the private sector, especially over the place of direct grant schools and assisted places. Related to these overtly political disputes were ideological disputes over educational standards and over progressive teaching methods. These disputes were accompanied by a huge volume of government reports, legislation and institutional changes.

The actual success of these government interventions in raising educational standards or reducing class, gender or ethnic inequalities is wholly unclear. There has been remarkably little official evaluation of these reforms and academic research has not reached any consensus either. However, it does appear that rather similar patterns of rising levels of qualification, declining gender inequalities but persisting class inequalities have occurred in other European societies that have not been subject to so much political intervention. It is likely, therefore, that the British reforms have had at best marginal impact.

References and Further Reading

Breen R., Heath, A. F. and Whelan, C. W. (1999) 'Educational Inequality in Ireland North and South.' In Heath, Breen and Whelan (eds), *Ireland North and South: Perspectives from Social Science*, Proceedings of the British Academy, Vol. 98: 187–213. Oxford: Clarendon Press.

Cox, C. B. and A. E. Dyson (1969) *Fight for Education: A Black Paper*. London: Critical Quarterly Society. (Reprinted in Cox and Dyson, *The Black Papers on Education*. London: Davis-Poynter, 1971.)

Floud, J. E., Halsey, A. H. and Martin, F. M. (1956) *Social Class and Educational Opportunity*. London: Heinemann.

Goldstein, H. and Heath, A. (eds) (2000) *Educational Standards*. Proceedings of the British Academy 102. Oxford: Oxford University Press.

Gray, J., McPherson, A. and Raffe, D. (1983) *Reconstructions of Secondary Education*. London: Routledge and Kegan Paul.

Halsey, A. H. (2000) 'Further and Higher Education.' In A. H. Halsey with J. Webb (eds), *Twentieth-Century British Social Trends*. Basingstoke: Macmillan (now Palgrave Macmillan).

Halsey, A. F., Heath A. F. and Ridge, J. M. (1980) *Origins and Destinations: Family, Class and Education in Modern Britain*. Oxford: Clarendon Press.

Heath, A. (ed.) (1984) 'Comprehensive and Selective Schools.' Special issue of *Oxford Review of Education* 10 (1).

Leschinsky, A. and K. U. Mayer (eds) (1999) *The Comprehensive School Experiment Revisited: Evidence from Western Europe*. Frankfurt am Main: Peter Lang.

McPherson, A. and Willms, D. (1987) 'Equalisation and Improvement: Some Effects of Comprehensive Reorganisation in Scotland.' *Sociology* 21: 509–39.

Shavit, Y. and Blossfeld, H.-P. (eds) (1992) *Persistent Inequality: Changing Educational Attainment in Thirteen Countries*. Boulder, CO: Westview Press.

Smith, G. A. N. (2000) 'Schools.' In A. H. Halsey with J. Webb, (eds), *Twentieth-Century British Social Trends*. Basingstoke Macmillan (now Palgrave Macmillan).

Turner, R. H. (1960) 'Sponsored and Contest Mobility and the School System.' *American Sociological Review* 25.

Walford, Geoffrey (ed.) (1991) *Private Schooling: Tradition, Change and Diversity*. London: Paul Chapman.

Walford, Geoffrey (ed.) (1997) 'Choice, Diversity and Equity in Secondary Schooling.' Special issue of *Oxford Review of Education*, 23(1).

Chronology

1938   Spens Report on Secondary Education.

1943   Norwood Report on the School Curriculum.

1944   Education Act establishes free secondary education for all pupils in schools which are publicly provided.

1946   Parliament revises terms of reference of University Grants Committee, which greatly increases public funding of universities.

1947   Raising of minimum school-leaving age to 15. Establishment of GCE O and A and Scholarship level in place of school certificate.

1959   Crowther Report on Education from 15 to 18.

1960   Beloe Report on secondary school examinations other than the GCE recommends establishment of CSE.

1961   Sussex, first of new universities, receives its Royal Charter.

1963   Robbins Report on Higher Education.

1965   In circular 10/65 Department of Education asks all local authorities to submit plans for reorganising secondary education on comprehensive lines.

1967   Plowden Report on Children and their Primary Schools.

1970   Conservative government suspends policy of universal comprehensivisation.

1972   Raising of minimum school-leaving age to 16.

1976   Direct grant schools phased out. 119 of 170 direct grant schools become independent.

1976   Education Act requires local education authorities to submit comprehensivisation proposals.

1980   Education Act establishes Assisted Places Scheme to provide financial support for some students (from less well-off families) in independent education and includes other measures to increase parental choice between state schools.

1985   Swann Report on the Education of Children from Ethnic Minority groups.

1988   Education Reform Act introduces National Curriculum to be followed by all pupils from the ages of 5 to 16. Schools given the right to 'opt out' of local authority control. Funding of higher education transferred from local authorities to a Polytechnics and Colleges Funding Council. University Grants Committee replaced by a Universities Funding Council.

1988   GCE O level and CSE combine to form the General Certificate of Secondary Education (GCSE).

1992   End of binary system. Further and Higher Education Act 1992 sets up Higher Education Funding Councils for England and Wales, replacing Universities Funding Council and the Polytechnics and Colleges Funding Council.

1997   Abolition of Assisted Places.

16 Race Relations

Shamit Saggar

Introduction

Social and political historians are familiar with the claim that the twentieth-century history of the United States has been defined by the great division of race. Equally, many commentators would instinctively deny the credibility of any similar characterisation of British society. It is difficult to argue that Britain has been a country that has been locked into turmoil and self-examination on matters of race to the same degree witnessed on the other side of the Atlantic. It has, nevertheless, been a society whose ethnic, cultural and group identity has undergone considerable change, especially in the period after 1945. The prime force behind this transformation was the influx of sizeable numbers of non-white immigrants, chiefly from former colonial sources, and the longer-term impact that has resulted from their settlement in Britain. The picture of post-war race relations in Britain is therefore one that, on one hand, has been linked with substantial political controversy and, on the other, has generally been accommodated into the aggregation and articulation functions of the party political system. If it is reasonable to say that Britain has avoided the rise of a US-style, fundamental racial fault line, it is essential to describe this process and also to define the key hallmarks of the British race relations experience.

In this chapter we are concerned with mapping post-war race relations and the role played by political institutions in managing the large-scale changes brought about through immigration. For the most part this is a story of the rise and fall of immigration as a mass political issue. However, the seeming simplicity of this picture is disturbed by two questions. First, we are concerned to know how far immigration has been seen as a purely – or even largely – economic question. Indeed, there is an important debate, chiefly linked to the late 1950s and early 1960s, in which the economic framework for the management of immigration is increasingly displaced by a social and cultural framework that is predicated on what became known as 'the absorptive capacity' of Britain. This question, in other words, attempts to throw light on the paradigm adopted by the political process in response to the challenges created by post-war immigration. Second, there is a large question about the role and perform-ance of political institutions themselves. It is striking that immigration could rise and fall in salience so significantly within a relatively short period. Has this been the result of a set of unique political traditions and customs, as some have suggested?[1] Or is it more probable that many of the deeper conflicts associated with immigration have been pushed to the margins of mainstream politics?[2]

This chapter comprises three main sections that flesh out these questions. First, we begin with an overview of the politics of immigration during the early part of the post-war era. This discussion reveals that considerable caution and policy ambiguity drove the political management of the issue more or less up to the mid-1970s. Second, we consider the origins, basis and work of Britain's integration institutions. The track record of these institutions has been an area regularly subject to evaluation, frequently involving heated argument between those who believe that radical racial equality programmes are the way forward, pitted against those who regret the involvement of the British state in such affairs altogether. The approach taken, it is suggested, has been nothing short of a liberal race relations *settlement*, featuring selective legal reform coupled with a promotional ethos. The longer-run efficacy of this approach has been the subject of an evaluative debate about the uniqueness – or otherwise – of British race relations. Third, the chapter turns to consider the role of immigrant and immigrant-originated ethnic minorities in the political process. This section puts forward a picture of growing participation, accompanied by tangible results, but in the absence of any substantial breakthroughs for the job of exercising political muscle.

Immigration as a Political Issue

In the immediate aftermath of the Second World War, Britain contained a number of noticeable pockets of non-white settlement. Black African- and Caribbean-descended communities had existed for many years in the great sea-faring cities of Liverpool, Bristol, Cardiff and Southampton.[3] London's docks had also fostered a number of such settlements. However, the scale of this more or less continuous presence did not compare with the substantial numbers in-volved in migration from the late 1940s onwards. For instance, the 1951 Gen-eral Census recorded a non-white population (derived mainly from birthplace indicators) of no more than 75,000; the next census count in 1961 revealed that this figure had swollen to around 337,000.

The new post-war migration was distinctive largely because of the colour of the immigrants themselves. The bulk of newcomers during the early to mid-1950s came from Caribbean sources, whilst those from the Indian subcontinent began to grow in number during the latter part of the decade. The figures reveal that the heaviest inflows were recorded in the years spanning the 1956 Suez crisis and the passage of the first major piece of restrictive legislation in 1962. Within this period, it is also noteworthy that the 1962 Commonwealth Immi-grants Act itself was probably responsible for a good deal of the surge. Rationally responding to the signals of likely impending controls, many would-be immigrants opted to bring forward and crystallise any plans for resettlement: the eighteen months prior to the enactment of the new Act saw a greater number of fresh migrants than for the entire previous five years.[4]

It is clear that voices of objection and concern were evident from a very early point. An early opportunity to weigh up the options for population management and labour force optimisation was contained in the findings of the 1949 Royal Commission on Population. Established during the war, its job was to examine the pros and cons of peacetime labour market options, taking into account a welter of social and cultural assumptions about inter-group relations. Its report stated plainly that any real chances for industrial recovery were contingent upon filling various actual and expected labour shortages. However, this did not mean that the Commission accepted that boosting immigration would itself be a solution to the population 'gap'. In a deeply influential extract, the report signalled that labour market and social trade-offs would remain at the heart of the immigration option:

'Immigration on a large scale into a fully established society like ours could only be welcome without reserve if the immigrants were of good human stock and were not prevented by their religion or race from intermarrying with the host population and becoming merged with it.'[5] Related worries were also expressed in the world of politics more directly. For instance, a ginger group of backbench Labour MPs wrote to their party leader and Prime Minister, Clem Attlee, in 1948 to warn that: 'An influx of coloured people domiciled here is likely to impair the harmony, strength and cohesion of our public and social life and to cause discord and unhappiness among all concerned.'[6]

The scene had been set, therefore, for a long-run tussle over the basis, legitimacy and terms of the new immigration. The mid-1950s were a period in which the issue continued to dog aspects of parliamentary life and yet, as importantly, conspicuously failed to gel into a fully coherent policy consideration for government. At grass-roots level, several anti-immigration protest groups and lobbies began to flourish, such as the Birmingham Immigrants' Control Association (BICA). In Southall in west London, the Southall Residents' Association became a vocal opponent not so much of non-white immigration, but of Whitehall's preferred policy of laissez-faire lack of involvement in trying to direct settlement away from such areas. In Parliament, the first stirrings of an hostile lobby were also detected, led by figures such as Cyril Orborne (Louth) and Norman Pannell (Kirkdale). Both were Conservative members and were successful in attracting limited support from their party backbench colleagues in several parliamentary debates between 1954 and 1958. The Orborne–Pannell campaign, however, failed to place any sort of veto upon the Conservative administrations at this time,[7] though it is fair to note that they did secure selective backing from a small number of Labour MPs. The lobby therefore represented an awkward hurdle for frontbench politicians (from both sides) at this time and care was taken not to dismiss these concerns out of hand. The decisive change occurred in August 1958 when a series of racial conflicts and episodes of racial violence took place in Nottingham in the East Midlands and in Notting Hill in west

London. Orborne's response to these events was categoric when, in a Commons debate in November 1958, he lectured his colleagues on the need to avert a coming racial divide. The racial aspects of immigration had been sidelined for too long, according to his argument, and 'it was time someone spoke out for the white man in this country', he declared.

The debate over immigration almost immediately entered a new charged phase. Katznelson, an American scholar of this era, describes the transformation as moving the issue into the political arena as a coherent matter of response for government, having previously been a pre-political, unstructured matter of loose concern. The new debate effectively hinged on two themes. First, the link was made between whatever domestic needs there might have been to limit or influence non-white settlement on one hand and the impact this might have on Commonwealth foreign policy on the other. A strong note of caution was apparent in the instinctive reaction of many politicians right across party labels, even though, oddly, the recent Suez affair had served to emphasise the real limitations of basing global policy interests on Commonwealth foundations. Consequently, it was possible to restrict discussion to the question of possible legal amendment to the 1948 Nationality Act rather than wholesale writing of fresh restrictive legislation. Second, the debate also involved some consideration of the calculus that suggested that immigration controls would, and in some eyes should, affect relations between whites and settled non-whites in Britain. The premise for this calculus held that 'excessive numbers' and 'over-concentration' in certain areas had been responsible for the racial tensions beneath the violence of August 1958. Furthermore, the debate emphasised the idea that unrealistic numbers had placed unmanageable burdens on local authority housing, education, health and social services. Additionally, many calls for restrictions included allegations about immigrant criminality. This calculus has also been referred to as the 'numbers game' by many commentators, especially in relation to immigration rows in the 1960s and 1970s. Miles and Phizacklea, for instance, describe an immigration–race relations 'dualism' as one of the products of this debate by which any and all policy moves to introduce liberal reforms to promote migrant interests were – and remained – contingent on tight legal curbs on migrant entry. This stance, they argue, was deeply insincere and likely only to escalate anti-immigrant hostility by effectively practising discrimination at the point of entry whilst attempting to tackle discrimination in society more broadly.[8]

The government's initial response to oppose fresh laws was only successful to a point. The grass-roots campaigns of BICA and others only grew larger, and by early 1961 Osborne had managed to introduce his own Private Member's Bill on the issue. His Bill had appeared despite the fact that previously in 1960 the Conservative Home Secretary, R. A. Butler, had met with a group of Tory MPs led by Osborne and Pannell and conceded some ground to them. A change of mind was being signalled by the government by late 1961. It recognised that the public mood had not been, and probably would not be, assuaged by the existing wait-and-see approach. Opinion is sharply divided on the causal factors behind this turnabout but the role of the October 1961 party conference appears to have been fairly central. The platform found itself smothered by constituency associations seeking debates on the immigration question, signalling to even the most remote elite member of the party that the issue could no longer be dodged.

The new Bill was announced by Butler shortly afterwards and, significantly, was opposed by the Labour opposition led by Hugh Gaitskell. Labour's early stance to block and, if necessary, repeal statutory controls on immigration has been the subject of considerable historical analysis and debate. Some three different schools of thought have been advanced. First, the Bill highlighted the degree to which Labour stood in sharp contrast to the Tories by declaring that the new Bill, if enacted, would result in irreparable damage to domestic race relations. Many commentators have suggested that this line of opposition was chiefly the product of Gaitskell's own personal leadership, both of the party and on the issue specifically. The force of personality is sometimes easy to overstate but in this case it is arguable that Gaitskell's approach stood in sharp contrast to his successor, Harold Wilson, whose instincts on the matter were far more pragmatic and who was also a good deal more sensitive to trade union anxieties about immigration. Second, it has been argued that the Bill was attacked by Labour because of the party's long-standing association with, and commitment to, socialist internationalism. By playing along with policy that divided labour according to nationality, it was claimed that Labour would only ally itself to nationalistic instincts that few in the party were said to share with the Conservatives. Ideological fault lines, in other words, ran through the policy and Labour was sensitive to this kind of division. Plainly this approach was mainly pursued by the ideological Left in the party but not those of the Left spurred by economic nationalist and protectionist arguments about the need to shelter domestic jobs. Third, the Bill was subjected to criticism by Labour because of the anticipated damage it would do to the Commonwealth project. In striking this posture, the Gaitskell leadership allied itself to many Conservatives who shared this worry and also united the Left and Right of the Labour Party. For this reason, Wilson's pragmatic approach after 1963, however sub-populist in tone towards domestic opinion, remained cautious in assessing the impact of controls among Commonwealth partners. One of Wilson's earliest moves in office after 1964 was to dispatch the Mountbatten mission to explore the chances to agreeing bilateral voluntary controls with major Commonwealth 'sending' countries. The initiative failed, though few in all probability expected it to achieve its aim.

The 1962 Commonwealth Immigrants Act established a new statutory regime based on essential labour market requirements as well as the objective skills of would-be immigrants. Labour's tough line against the legislation was eventually loosened, with the first signs of reconsideration shown in Wilson's maiden speech in the Commons as party leader. This may have caused some disquiet in Labour's ranks at the time but any doubts were quickly set aside in the new political climate created by the 1964 general election. Besides winning an historic victory, Labour's leadership learnt a powerful lesson in the 1964 campaign. The unexpected loss of the party's shadow Foreign Secretary, Patrick Gordon Walker, in his Smethwick constituency to a tough, anti-immigration Conservative opponent meant that few, if any, in the new administration were not convinced that Labour was electorally vulnerable on this issue. More than that, the episode sent a signal to the new government that it needed to take seriously grass-roots hostility, especially amongst its working-class constituency fearful of perhaps greater immigrant access to employment, housing and other opportunities. Commentators such as J. Rex have characterised the 1964–8 Labour government as basically short-term and expedient in its approach to immigration.[9] This stance, he has argued, meant that a gradual policy of appeasement was the product of a failure of government to chart a principled path towards immigration. For that reason, the party's readiness to first adopt the provisions of the 1962 Act once in office and then preside over a dramatic curtailment in Commonwealth citizenship rights in 1965 and again in 1968 are policies that have attracted widespread criticism. Indeed, the real criticism of Labour's strategy lay in the way in which it served to undermine its own position by escalating anti-immigration sentiment to ever-higher levels. Z. Layton-Henry has remarked that:

> The [1968] Act was the logical outcome of the policy of appeasement that the Labour government had adopted to achieve the bipartisan consensus with the Conservatives and to reduce the electoral salience of the issue. The political consequences, however, were more damaging for the Labour government. They had shown that they were so afraid of the electoral consequences of appearing weaker than the Conservatives on the issue of immigration controls that both in 1965 and 1968 they had introduced tougher measures than even the Conservatives, if they had been in government, would probably have introduced. The supporters of immigration control now knew...that they could dictate the political agenda.[10]

The Liberal Race Relations Settlement

Notwithstanding this indictment of Labour's shortsightedness, it cannot be forgotten that this administration was also the architect of post-war Britain's integration infrastructure. Labour was originally elected in October 1964 with a clear pledge to introduce a new law to outlaw racial discrimination. The scope and details of this statutory promise remained unclear at first, though it was widely accepted that the new government would look first at the series of failed Private Member's Bills that had been introduced for the same purpose in the 1950s. The eventual result was the first Race Relations Act, passed in 1965, which contained three key elements. First, the statute was only really achievable on the back of an inter-party consensus with the Tory front bench. The need to keep on board the Opposition exercised the Home Office and this meant that its original idea of bringing in a tough system of criminal sanctions gave way to a 'softly, softly' system based on voluntary conciliation. Second, the Act was widely criticised for exempting the housing and employment markets, areas that many moderate observers felt were fairly crucial to the job of tackling discrimination where it mattered most. The opt-out was at least partly the consequence of bitter trade union opposition and lobbying against the draft Bill. This weakness, as many saw it, was eventually remedied by the 1968 Race Relations Act. Third, the law established a new race relations public watchdog, the Race Relations Board. This body had two prime tasks: to police the anti-discrimination clauses of the 1965 law and to act as chief promoter of the new spirit of tolerance and racial integration. It should not be forgotten that aspects of this approach to law and public policy had their roots in US experience in civil rights during the 1950s and early 1960s. Indeed, the new government's initial feasibility study of anti-discrimination laws was in fact conducted by an ad hoc committee of the Society of Labour Lawyers, whose main focal point was the 1964 US Voting Rights Act.

Labour's purpose was to go further than bringing in new modest laws and aimed additionally to build, however gradually, a fresh integration strategy. The key to understanding the limitations of the 1965 Act, then, is to recognise that it was meant to serve as a staging post. Indeed, in spring 1965 the government published its White Paper, *Immigration from the Commonwealth*, spelling out the themes and goals of future public policy. Its most important measure was to expand the role of the Commonwealth Immigrants Advisory Council (first established in 1962), by giving it the task of thinking through and coordinating the longer-run integration challenge. However, this document also contained much to reinforce the 'dualism' of controls that traded off against integration measures. In a telling extract, it called for a balance whereby 'immigrants do not outrun Britain's capacity to absorb them'.[11] In the first instance this meant a new 1965 immigration law that cut back annual work vouchers from 20,000 to just 8,000, and an ending altogether of voucher entitlement for those without jobs or specific skills.

Between 1965 and 1967 the core of the liberal hour was mapped out and established. The spirit of reform was more clearly signalled with the installation of Roy Jenkins as Home Secretary in late 1965. His purpose was twofold: to champion the liberal thinking on philosophy and strategy that his supporters believed to be long overdue; and to navigate a legislative path for a second Act. He quickly commissioned an in-depth study on the nature and extent of racial discrimination from Political and Economic Planning, an independent research body. Thereafter he signalled that any draft Bill would need to wait for a consolidation of Labour's parliamentary majority, a dramatic increase that resulted from the 1966 re-election victory. Additionally, he commissioned the so-called 1967 Street Report to return to the question of the US legal framework, further underlying the sense of transatlantic commonness in race relations policy at this time (and, arguably, beyond). The liberal-hour policy framework that lay at the heart of the exercise was crystallised in a 1966 speech given by Jenkins in which he set himself the task of outlining a vision that would, he hoped, outlast the actions of his or indeed any specific administration. He proposed an integrated multiracial society characterised by equal opportunity, in which 'Integration was not seen as a flattening process of assimilation but rather as equal opportunity, accompanied by cultural diversity in an atmosphere of mutual tolerance.'[12] There is little doubt that this grand plan had much to commend it and generated considerable success in the short run. Press leaders throughout the middle part of 1966 were regularly punctuated by a willing acceptance that the role of government in this field was, despite the rude shock of Smethwick, to lead public and policy opinion. The liberal hour, it was sensed, had truly arrived and was to be embodied in the new second Race Relations Act of 1968. This assessment was essentially flawed and bore little resemblance to the longer-run picture.

The reason for this abrupt disturbance was the return of the immigration question. By late 1967 the Kenyan Asian nationality crisis had begun to stimulate the rate of arrivals of British nationals in the UK and it was clear that a strong element hostile to further immigration could not be contained. With Jenkins's departure from the Home Office in November, it was apparent that progressive voices had been sidelined. A new Immigration Bill was introduced and passed in record time in February 1968, effectively curbing entry rights but, more significantly, refocusing attention on the seemingly diminished capacity of government to deliver its own objective of tightened, reliable controls on immigration. The Commonwealth Immigration Bill was secured whilst the new Race Relations Act was enacted, thus further emphasising the conditionality of the former upon the latter. However, the sense of panic could not be mistaken. Across the country in 1968 there was a sudden and substantial upsurge in anti-immigration public sentiment, some of it loose and sporadic, some proactively engineered and given political leadership. By April the simmering row could no longer be left on the back burner and was ignited by the intervention, without notice to even parliamentary colleagues, of Enoch Powell. Though immediately sacked from the shadow Cabinet, Powell ensured that both front-bench teams were placed on the back foot on the issue. His complaint was essentially two-fold. First, he publicly denied that any worthwhile grass-roots support or legitimacy for non-white immigration had existed in British society. This claim was amended and repeated on various occasions by Powellites in the two decades following the 1968 'rivers of blood' speech and effectively placed Powell at the head of the generally disorganised anti-immigration lobby. Second, and arguably more importantly, Powell castigated the political parties and their leaders for 'selling out' and conspiring against the popular will. He complained that the chapter of post-war non-white immigration had taken place without legitimacy and merely on the basis of an elite cross-party tacit consensus. Never mind that Powell had himself promoted Caribbean immigration whilst holding office as Health Minister in the 1950s, his belief was that the political process had ceased to be sufficiently issue-responsive.

The impact of the intervention was to escalate dramatically the sense of racial tension. The 1968 backdrop was also one in which US racial politics had dived into crisis and violence. The philosopher-practitioners of the liberal-hour settlement were put on the defensive, unable to rebut effectively Powell's twin charges and powerless to recapture the moral or political high ground. Populist politics now took priority. The immediate victors from this new mood, ironically, were the Conservatives, despite their move to distance themselves from Powell. In the June 1970 general election, Powell's legacy continued to deliver support for the party on the immigration issue. In their landmark study of electoral choice, Butler and Stokes have described the Tories' relationship with the immigration question as a quintessential illustration of issue voting in action. Indeed, two separate psephological assessments have concluded that the net 'Powell effect' delivered an important boost to Tory fortunes in 1970.[13]

Notwithstanding the huge setbacks of the late 1960s, it is important to note that very little of this in fact led to a new Conservative agenda to further restrict immigration, let alone immigrant rights. Indeed, the Tories' own 1971 Immigration Act succeeded in quelling the debate only temporarily and by 1972 the party, now in office, led a new official policy to admit a second wave of East African British Asians (from Uganda). The potency of the issue only rose further and by 1974 the far-right National Front Party had secured a record share of the popular vote. On regulating the rights enjoyed by the newcomers, a confirmed line of pragmatism remained in place. The Conservatives, having agreed to support the 1968 Race Relations Act, decided to leave basic integration-oriented legislation alone. Moreover, after 1974 when back in opposition, the party agreed to back, albeit with reluctance and some internal dissent, the new Labour administration's plan to enact a third race relations statute. The 1976 Act had been in gestation in Labour circles for many years and during 1974–6 had been the subject of considerable intra-party controversy. The final legislative product amounted to a major extension of the provision of law and came into jurisdiction in July 1977 at the height of domestic racial turmoil. Whatever view is taken of its genesis, it would be impossible to sustain any claim that it was in any way policy-linked to voter preferences or to the articulation and aggregation roles of mass democratic parties. The Act contained three core reforms. First, it introduced the doctrine of indirect discrimination and attempted for the first time to make employers and others accountable for the non-intentional consequences of their actions or inactions. Second, it placed a statutory duty on local government to promote good race relations, a requirement that many Labour local authorities interpreted broadly through their pioneering and radical racial equality measures in the 1980s. Finally, the Act gave fresh powers to a new Commission for Racial Equality (CRE) to pursue investigations, issue non-discrimination notices and also begin to innovate in promoting its integration and equality agenda.

Though new fresh legislative changes have appeared for over twenty years, the 1976 Act has presented a strong platform for race relations. Debate in the 1990s raised the possibility of using more radical measures to deliver equality of substantive outcome and not merely of participative opportunity. It is likely that little will emerge from this debate by way of legislative reform of the same order as earlier Acts. What is rather more clear is that the CRE and the 1976 Act have survived and in some senses prospered. The odds against this were very great in the late 1970s, chiefly as a result of a Tory policy to reconsider, often in principle, not only immigration policy but also many aspects of integration policy. The populist ticket, adopted in 1976 by the Tories under Margaret Thatcher, had given way, once more, to the triumph of pragmatism by the early 1980s. The most important reason for this was that the Tories' own promise to curb immigration and consolidate nationality laws was realised in the 1981 British Nationality Act. With immigration no longer seen as 'out of control' Conservative populist strategists had effectively shot their own fox. By 1983, one commentator reported that, against most expectations, the immigration question had fallen off the political agenda.[14] The possibility of resurrecting the immigration rows of the 1960s and 1970s was severely diminished as a consequence.

Ethnic Minority Political Participation

In placing so much attention on the political management of race relations, integration policy and the immigration issue, it is all too easy to overlook the part played by Britain's ethnic minorities in shaping the character and content of politics and public policy. Opinion is sharply divided in academic circles as to the degree of political muscle that has been wielded by immigrants and ethnic minorities.[15] On the question of influence over public policy there is even less consensus, not least because of doubts about the capacity of minorities to act together politically under a common political label. One thing is clear: the liberal reforms of the 1960s and mid-1970s can be attributed to many inputs within and beyond the major parties, but it is extremely unlikely that ethnic minority electoral – or other – leverage played an important part. That kind of calculus, relying as it does on the force of liberal opinion among the white community, is arguably less compelling at the start of the twenty-first century. For one thing, local politics have revealed the quite considerable numbers of ethnic minorities – especially Asians – that are now involved in, or could be mobilised into, the formal arena of political participation. Additionally, the leverage question is perhaps no longer solely dependent on minority group numbers, and attitudinal evidence suggests that it is likely that white–ethnic minority alliances exist on many public policy issues involving race and ethnicity.[16] The support for laws against racial hatred, to say nothing of their enforcement, is a powerful case in point.

Ethnic minority mainstream political participation has been characterised by four central features. First, and most centrally of all, it is wise to note that postwar British history has lacked any significant debate over the political rights of immigrants, a debate that has been fairly common across other European countries of immigration. The main reason for this has been the colonial and former colonial sources of the migration that took place, whereby virtually all New Commonwealth immigrants entered the United Kingdom enjoying full political rights. In some cases subsequent registration of British nationality delayed this process, but no more. The upshot has been that party politicians have been ever-more conscious of immigrants and their offspring as political participants. Question marks may have remained about the extent of their participation, to say nothing of their partisan loyalty (see below), but it has been clear that party politics in Britain could not afford to be silent on the matter.

The first real efforts to woo minority voters came on stream after 1974, following pioneering quantification of minority electoral participation. This revealed the second core feature, namely the striking Labour bias that has driven the vast bulk of minority voter participation over 25 years. Table 16.1 tells the story.

The data shows a very clear picture of Labour loyalty. Significantly, this allegiance remained unaffected by Labour's long wilderness between 1979 and 1997 and arguably enabled the party to hang on to some of its previous strongholds in the rout of 1983. There have been various schools of thought advanced to account for Labour's strong record. One of these has argued that high

Table 16.1 Party support among ethnic minorities, UK general elections: 1974, 1979, 1983, 1987, 1992, and 1997 (%)

	1974[a]	1979	1983[b]	1987	1992[b]	1997
Labour	81	86	83	72	81	85
Conservative	9	8	7	18	10	11
Other party	10	6	10	10	9	4

[a]October 1974 general election.
[b]Recalculated average of Asian and Afro-Caribbean support levels.
Sources: Adapted from Community Relations Commission, *Participation of Ethnic Minorities in the General Election of October 1974*, CRC, 1975; Commission for Racial Equality, *Votes and Policies*, CRE, 1980; Commission for Racial Equality, *Ethnic Minorities and the 1983 General Election*, CRE, 1984; Harris Research Centre, 'Political attitudes among ethnic minorities', unpublished data set JN98746 (Harris, 1987); A. Ali and G. Percival, *Race and Representation: Ethnic Minorities and the 1992 Elections*, CRE, 1993; S. Saggar and A. Heath, 'Race: Towards a Multicultural Electorate?', in P. Norris and G. Evans (eds), *Critical Elections*, Sage, 1999.

Labour voting appears quite remarkable, but in fact masks the socio-demographic reality that these minority communities have been over-represented among working-class voters. The argument is correct in pointing to the imbalance in class composition across ethnic groups, but recent research has revealed that a discernible 'class effect' was at work distinguishing black and Asian working-class voting choice from middle-class partisanship.[17] A second approach has been essentially historic in claiming that the Labour Party's long association with decolonisation generally – and the move to quit India in 1947 especially – resulted in a particularly close affinity between minorities and Labour. Of course there is only limited scope for this influence to impact on younger generations of ethnic minorities and it is curious that relative youth, if anything, is linked with a slight hardening of support for Labour. A third per-spective is basically rational choice in orientation and examines the group–party bond in issue-voting terms. This stresses the idea that Labour has triumphed among this group of voters because it has been seen as the 'ethnic minority-friendly' party. In other words, calculations of issue-voting have brought minor-ities to Labour's ranks and kept them there with the evidence of fulfilled – or at least not broken – promises. In some respects this perspective contains grains of truth, since only the Labour Party can, after all, claim authorship over three successive race relations laws. On the other hand, there is some reason to doubt that minorities hold universally more progressive – and thus more supportive – positions than their white counterparts on questions such as the role of law in race relations.[18] Additionally, on the immigration issue it seems that large parts of the evidence do not fit the model: to be sure, it was a Labour administration that rushed to bolt the door to Kenyan Asian refugees in 1968 whilst the Tories chose, in contrast, to go out on a limb and welcome the Ugandan influx in 1972.

Behind formal participation in the electoral arena, the British Asian and black communities of course boast thriving participation in non-electoral and community-based forms of politics. This forms a third central element of minority politics and derives importance from its complementary – and occasionally substitutive – role in relation to the formal democratic process. The early period of immigration following the end of the war tended to be characterised by the establishment of numerous local self-help organisations designed to support and develop minority self-confidence in the political system. Many of these initiatives were also linked to developing service provision for these communities, involving both private- and public-sector input. Others had a more direct interest in forging links with political institutions such as political parties. Others still were founded as effective overseas branches of political parties and movements based on home-country political affiliations. In Southall, in outer west London, as well as in several Midlands towns, the 1950s and 1960s witnessed the birth of local branches of the Indian Workers' Association (IWA).[19] Many of these local IWA groups were instrumental in organising political involvement in local parties at this time, thereby providing a powerful recruitment body for parties interested in the potential voting impact of these new voters. Similar developments also took place in the Caribbean-origin immigrant population at this time, several of which were coordinated by the work of the West Indian Standing Conference.

However, the real importance of ethnic minority community politics derives from its role in defending immigrants and their offspring from hostile action. For instance, in June 1976, in response to a far-right demonstration on the streets of Southall, a new protest body emerged to lead the counter-response. Known as the Southall Youth Movement, this group served not only to tackle the far-right local presence but also acted as a powerful catalyst in reducing the paternalistic influence of the local IWA. Later in April 1979, an ugly police – community 'riot' broke out on the streets of Southall that further reinforced the strong influence of voluntary, self-help groups and weakened, at least in the short run, the command of mainstream parties. The establishment at national level of the Anti-Nazi League in 1976 was also spearheaded by the participation of ethnic minorities, especially from among the young, acting outside the boundaries of party-based involvement. During the 1980s, the spectacle of riots in places such as Brixton, St Paul's (Bristol), Toxteth (Liverpool) and Tottenham all revealed the centrality of informal group politics in these communities and the seeming sidelining of political parties in matters at local level. The 1993 election of a far-right local government councillor in Millwall in London's East End was yet another illustration of this pattern. Whilst mainstream parties eventually profited from the local campaign to unseat the extremist through the ballot box, it was clear that much of this effort was driven by non-party activists. Finally, few observers in the 1990s can have missed the leadership role provided by community-based groups during the Stephen Lawrence murder inquiry.[20]

A fourth aspect of ethnic minority political participation relates to an aspect of the figures in table 16.1 above, namely the chequered and rather disappointing record of Labour's rivals in attracting support. The Conservative record here stands out. As long ago as 1976 the Conservatives first recognised the potential folly of overlooking the need to appeal to minority voters. Dedicated units were established in Conservative Central Office to promote the party's message to Asian and black voters and also to coordinate the party's limited efforts on this front. Several Anglo-Asian and Anglo-West Indian Conservative Societies were subsequently launched at local level, though few among the latter category were sustainable beyond an initial wave of enthusiasm. Later, in 1986, when intra-ethnic rivalry began to impact on some of these bodies, the party's Central Office stepped in and abolished them by creating a new umbrella organisation known as the Conservative One Nation Forum. This was more centrally controlled than its various predecessors and was able to achieve a much higher profile for the growing number of initiatives taken by the party. Whereas many black and Asian activists in the party had complained about the 1983 poster campaign, featuring the 'Labour says he's black; we say he's British' theme, by the 1987 and 1992 elections there was no dissent surrounding the party's extensive campaigning in black and Asian areas.

The continuous thorn in the side of One Nation race-liberals in the party was the recurring tendency for Little Englander sceptics to give voice to their criticisms of the multicultural society the party in office had presided over. The 1994 study by P. Whiteley J. Richardson and P. Seyd of grass roots Tory attitudes highlighted the basic problem: with a minority membership of less than one per cent, and with a large slice of members continuing to hanker after the 'repatriation option', the party's leaders remained highly circumscribed in their ability to sell the liberal integrationist message even to their own supporters.[21] This normally latent difficulty exploded in 1991–2 in Cheltenham. In selecting a black barrister, John Taylor, the party appeared to provoke a rebellion amongst its uncompromising doubters and the subsequent row and election defeat reinforced this worrying impression. Taylor's disaster oddly served to overshadow the breakthrough of another non-white Tory, Nirj Deva, who successfully captured a Tory marginal in 1992. In the election campaign of 1997 the party returned to previous themes of stressing the alleged cultural bond between putative Tory and Asian values. The personal dimension of John Major's association and familiarity with ethnic diversity was another clear foundation of this strategy. It appears that the efforts made yielded few worthwhile results, for not only did Deva suffer defeat but minority Tory victories of any kind failed to be recorded at all. However, a closer examination of the voting data suggests that some advancement of the cause did result. For one thing, the Tory share of the overall black and Asian vote, although modest, held up by the standards of previous elections. Meanwhile, the party's share of the numerically large Asian Indian electorate touched 18 per cent in 1997, a performance that must carry importance because of the generally abysmal backdrop of a poor election result more generally.[22] Additionally, this vote share exceeded half that secured by the party across the electorate as a whole and is also between five and seven times the rate of Tory support recorded among black Caribbean and black African voters. These data may not signal a clear Tory breakthrough but they do nevertheless remind us that there are differential campaigns and results among various components of the ethnic minority electorate.

Closing Remarks

This chapter has looked at the broad-brush changes that have resulted in British society as a result of mass immigration in the post-war period. Census data from 1991, now considerably out of date, shows that those of black African or Caribbean descent constitute a little under one million residents, with South Asians totalling around 1.5 million. Added together with other non-white minorities, such as Chinese and south-east Asians, Britain's total ethnic minority population stands clearly in excess of one in twenty of the population. Estimates put forward in the mid-1990s suggested that additional growth between 1991 and 2001 (the last General Census) might be as much as a further fifth. These kinds of demographic projects are already being reflected in large-scale social surveys as well as the official Labour Force Survey.

The discussion has shown the extent of change in three important respects relating to the control of immigration and its issue salience, the public policy infrastructure, and the nature of ethnic minority political participation. In tying these changes together, it is possible to highlight three general concluding thoughts. First, although immigration has waned substantially as a mass political issue, it is open to debate just how far it has been removed from the basic rules of engagement covering party competition in Britain. In the long run-up to the 1997 general election, Labour's shadow Home Secretary, Jack Straw, declared that 'we should not allow so much as a cigarette card to come between the Labour Party and the Tory government over immigration'.[23] His aim, to neutralise Labour's historic weak flank, was unmistakable and it is probable that he was successful in a fairly immediate sense. However, beneath this lies the problem of unintentionally feeding public sentiment that is not only hostile to immigration, however modest and feasible to absorb, but continues to see many of the social issues raised by immigration as deeply problematic and exacerbating, possibly with a racial twist, the politics of distribution. 'Mainly because I am an MP for a constituency in the West Midlands, where racialism is a powerful force, I [am] on the side of the Home Secretary', wrote Dick Crossman in the late 1960s.[24] These remarks, arguably, remain as pertinent over 30 years on and for reasons that are not so dissimilar.

Second, in assessing the longer-term influence of the liberal settlement it is worth making the point that race relations in Britain have often been about the defence and consolidation of a unique policy framework. So often the arguments and debates over race and ethnicity in the post-war period have revealed underlying tensions over the legitimacy of the state in this field. With liberals committed to establishing a central guiding role for government, largely in place by the end of the 1960s, it has not always been clear which strategic direction such a framework ought to be committed to by way of policy content itself. This vacuum has been conveniently filled by the radical lobby which has argued that there is little point in bringing about reforms in the policy infrastructure unless this can be linked to, and serve the purpose of, achieving greater inter-racial equality. Such an approach has been characterised as focusing on policy outcomes, along the lines of the fixation with the politics of 'who-gets-what' widely seen in US racial politics. For this reason, radical-led developments have tended to be highly limited and most visible in rhetorical terms alone. Neo-conservative critics, meanwhile, have not only questioned the wisdom of the liberal settlement's original scope, but have also argued that an emphasis upon educational and promotional means may prove to be counter-productive. How far this criticism accurately reads the public mood, and the degree to which it is an argument bogged in outdated assumptions about the basis of racial exclusion, is a moot point, however.

Finally, as we have seen, high levels of formal and non-formal political participation by ethnic minorities have characterised post-war Britain. Starting from a low base, electoral involvement has certainly grown tremendously and there are few mainstream politicians based in urban areas who can any longer overlook the potential of black and Asian voters to command political influence. Equally, involvement in community-based politics has also acted to stimulate the mainstream policy process at different times, be it in relation to urban stress questions in the 1980s or the threat posed by extremist political forces in the 1970s. Underlying these different areas of political participation, one central question has remained: namely, how far does the evidence suggest signs of political integration amongst ethnic minorities? For instance, the exceptional Labour bias referred to earlier on can be interpreted in highly circumstantial terms, that is, the result of the labour market and related profile of the groups in question. However, having allowed for these structural differences, if levels of Labour partisanship or even levels of registration and turnout cannot be explained in circumstantial terms, it is likely that some more fundamental process of racial differentiation are at play. If race then serves to divide, or at least distinguish, political behaviour, the conclusion we must draw is that political integration remains a long way off, at least in respect to some minority communities rather than others.

Notes

1 For instance, M. Banton, 'The Beginning and the End of the Racial Issue in British Politics', *Policy and Politics* 15 (1987): 39–47.

2 See A. Messina, *Race and Party Competition in Britain*, Oxford, 1989.

3 A full discussion of the non-white presence in the pre-war period, especially in the port settlements, can be found in C. Holmes, *John Bull's Island: Immigration and British Society 1871–1971*, Basingstoke, 1988, esp. pp. 20–55.

4 J. Walvin, *Passage to Britain*, Harmondsworth, 1984, p. 111.

5 *Report of the Royal Commission on Population*, Cmnd 7695, London, 1949, p. 124.

6 Quoted in R. Carter et al., 'The 1951–55 Conservative Government and the Racialisation and Black Immigration', *Policy Papers in Ethnic Relations*, No. 11, University of Warwick, 1987, p. 2.

7 R. Hanson citation – cf. Butler refusing to meet with them.

8 R. Miles and A. Phizacklea, *White Man's Country*, 2nd ed., London, 1989.

9 J. Rex, 'The Race Relations Catastrophe', in T. Burgess (ed.), *Matters of Principle: Labour's Last Chance*, Harmondsworth, 1968.

10 Z. Layton-Henry, *The Politics of Immigration*, Oxford, 1992, p. 79.

11 *Immigration from the Commonwealth*, Cmnd 2739, London, 1965, p. 2.

12 R. Jenkins, transcript of speech to the National Committee for Commonwealth Immigrants, London, 23 May 1966.

13 W. Miller, 'What Was the Profit in Following the Crowd? Aspects of Conservative and Labour Strategy since 1970', *British Journal of Political Science* 10, Part I (1980): 15–38; D. Studlar, 'Policy Voting in Britain: The Coloured Immigration Issue in the 1964, 1966 and 1970 General Elections', *American Political Science Review* 72, 1(1978): 46–72.

14 I. Crewe, 'How Labour was trounced all round', *Guardian*, 14 June 1983.

15 See for instance the perspectives put forward by O. Messina, S. Saggar and O. Le Lohe in S. Saggar (ed.), *Race and British Electoral Politics*, London, 1988.

16 See for instance some of the evidence put forward in Y. Alibhai-Brown, *True Colours: Public Attitudes to Multiculturalism and the Role of Government*, London, 1999.

17 S. Saggar and A. Heath, 'Race: Towards a Multicultural Electorate?', in P. Norris and G. Evans (eds), *Critical Elections: Understanding the 1997 British General Election in Long-term Perspective*, London, 1999.

18 S. Saggar, 'The Transformation of the "Race" Issue and Black Political Participation', *New Community* 20 (1993): 27–41.

19 A. Josphedes, 'Principles, Strategies and Anti-racist Campaigns: The Case of the Indian Workers' Associations', in H. Gouldbourne (ed.), *Black Politics in Britain*, Aldershot, 1990.

20 Cf. H. Gouldbourne, *Race Relations in Britain Since 1945*, Basingstoke, 1998, pp. 149–51.

21 P. Whiteley, J. Richardson and P. Seyd, *True Blues: The Politics of Conservative Party Membership*, Oxford, 1994.

22 S. Saggar, 'A Late, Though Not Lost, Opportunity: British Ethnic Minority Electors and the Conservative Party', *Political Quarterly* 69 (1998): 148–59.

23 Quoted in A. Lansley, 'Race Issue Leaves Straw Blowing in the Wind', the *Observer*, 10 December 1995.

24 R. Crossman, *Diaries of a Cabinet Minister*, vol. 2, London, 1977, p. 679.

Further Reading

Books

Geddes, A., *The Politics of Immigration and Race*, Manchester, 1995. Brief introduction.

Saggar, S., *Race and Politics in Britain*, Hemel Hempstead, 1992. Full textbook account of several main themes, though some chapters now fairly dated.

Saggar, S. (ed.), *Race and British Electoral Politics*, London, 1998. Collection of specialist essays on electoral themes, including some material on 1997 election.

Skellington, R. and Morris, P., *'Race' in Britain Today*, London, 1992. Very helpful background source of information, though increasingly dated.

Journals

British Journal of Political Science
British Journal of Sociology
Critical Social Policy
Ethnic and Racial Studies

Immigrants and Minorities
International Migration Review
New Community
Patterns of Prejudice
Policy and Politics
Race and Class
Race and Immigration, renamed in 1993 as *The Runnymede Bulletin*, monthly news
   bulletin published by the Runnymede Trust

Chronology

1947   Indian and Pakistan gain independence.
1948   Nationality Act.
1948   *SS Windrush* arrives at Tilbury Docks.
1949   Report of Royal Commission on Population.
1953   Fenner Brockway MP introduces first Bill to outlaw racial discrimination.
1953   Immigration worries first expressed at Cabinet.
1956   Suez crisis.
1958   'Race riots' in Notting Hill and Nottingham.
1960   Harold Macmillan's 'Wind of Change' speech.
1962   Commonwealth Immigrants Act. Establishment of Commonwealth Immigrants
        Advisory Council (CIAC); first three reports on aspects on integration strategy
        published 1963–4.
1963   Harold Wilson succeeds Hugh Gaitskell as party leader and makes Commons
        speech in which he declares that 'we [Labour] no longer contest the need for
        [immigration] controls'.
1964   Defeat of Patrick Gordon-Walker in Smethwick.
1965   White Paper, *Immigration from the Commonwealth*, published.
1965   First Race Relations Act (exempting housing and employment markets); Mark
        Bonham-Carter, former Liberal MP, installed as first chairman of the new Race
        Relations Board.
1965   Race riots in Watts, Los Angeles.
1967   Collapse of CARD, Campaign Against Racial Discrimination.
1966   Roy Jenkins, Home Secretary, gives speech to National Committee for Common-
        wealth Immigrants outlining definition of liberal race relations strategy and ob-
        jectives for public policy.
1967   Beginning of Kenyan Asian crisis.
1968   Commonwealth Immigrants Act.
1968   Enoch Powell's 'rivers of blood' speech followed by Powell's immediate sacking
        from the Tory front bench.
1968   Second Race Relations Act; creates new Community Relations Commission
        alongside pre-existing Race Relations Board.
1970   Surprise Conservative victory in 1970 general election partially linked to immi-
        gration issue.
1971   Immigration Act.
1972   Ugandan Asian crisis.
1976   Malawi Asian crisis.
1976   Third Race Relations Act, containing new principle of 'indirect discrimination'
        and legal provision to combat it.

1976   Anglo-Asian and Anglo-West Indian Conservative Societies established.
1978   Margaret Thatcher's 'swamping' remarks create substantial rise in saliency for the immigration issue and are also linked to surge in poll support for the Conservatives.
1979   Anti-National Front demonstration in Southall, resulting in the death of protester Blair Peach at the hands of the Metropolitan Police's Special Patrol Group.
1980   Riots in St Paul's, Bristol.
1981   British Nationality Act, fulfilling Tories' 1979 manifesto pledge.
1981   Riots in Brixton, Toxteth and elsewhere.
1981   Publication of Scarman Report on urban riots; concludes that insensitive policing played part in stimulating violence and that official programmes to encourage employment prospects had been inadequate to the task; Michael Heseltine, Environment Secretary, sets up new task force to forge business-led response to urban blight in Merseyside and elsewhere.
1981   Labour victory in Greater London Council elections brings in new era of radical race equality measures.
1985   Brixton and Tottenham riots (latter leads to one police fatality).
1986   Labour left-wing victories in local elections in London.
1986   Ray Honeyford affair fuels the neo-Conservative critique of British multicultural policy.
1986   Conservative One Nation Forum supersedes Anglo-Asian and Anglo-West Indian Conservative Societies.
1987   Four ethnic minority MPs elected (all Labour), marking first such representation since the 1920s.
1989   Publication of Salman Rushdie's *The Satanic Verses*.
1990   First ethnic minority shadow ministerial appointment (Paul Boateng at HM Treasury).
1991   Ashok Kumar becomes first ethnic minority by-election winner (Langbaurgh) but loses in 1992 general election (re-elected 1997).
1991   Treaty of European Union (Maastricht) establishes two intergovernmental 'pillars' of responsibility for the European Commission, one of which covers justice and home affairs (including immigration policy).
1992   John Taylor, Conservative candidate in Cheltenham, loses safe seat.
1992   Six ethnic minority MPs elected, including first Conservative since 1900 (Nirj Deva in Brentford and Isleworth – subsequently defeated 1997).
1993   Winston Churchill MP makes speech criticising Conservative immigration policy and black British identity.
1993   British National Party local council by-election victory for Derek Beacon in Millwall, Tower Hamlets (defeated in May 1994 local elections).
1993   Asylum Act (previously scuppered by the timing of the 1992 election).
1995   *The Times* outlines possibility of 'race card' behind Tory immigration and asylum policies. Tony Blair attempts to stage debate over Asylum Bill in special *ad hoc* House of Commons committee; he fails but is seen to be trying to tackle his party's perceived weakness on the immigration issue.
1996   Fresh legislation to cope with shortcomings of 1993 Asylum Act.
1997   Launch of fresh Conservative high-profile campaign to woo ethnic minority supporters in general election. William Hague makes an appearance at the August Bank Holiday Notting Hill carnival; criticised by Conservative opponents of his modernisation project; widely applauded by younger generation of Tory supporters and activists sharing his liberal instincts towards ethnic diversity.

1997   Nicholas Budgen MP (Conservative) makes only high-profile anti-immigration speech in 1997 general election campaign; heavily marginalised by Central Office and party leadership.

1997   Record number of main party ethnic minority parliamentary candidates (44); 9 successfully elected (all Labour); defeat of only Tory incumbent (Deva); minority MPs elected in Bethnal Green and Bow (Oona King) and in Bradford West (Marsha Singh) suffer heavy loss of vote share through local pro-Conservative swings. First ethnic minority ministerial appointment (Boateng as Minister of State at Health Department; moved to Home Office in 1998). New Conservative Party Leader, William Hague, launches party modernisation project (includes clear objective to raise ethnic minority participation in party affairs and candidate selection). Lord Tebbit makes speech at party conference attacking multiculturalism as a recipe for another Yugoslav-style disaster. Tony Blair makes speech to party conference emphasising racial inclusion and opportunities for ethnic minorities.

1998   Commission for Racial Equality (CRE) widely criticised for its high-profile and provocative advertising campaign on racial stereotypes and injustice; campaign appear to mark a new attempt to give visibility to the CRE's promotion role.

1999   Publication of the MacPherson Report into the murder of Stephen Lawrence in 1993; report cements a new government initiative to tackle racial violence and harassment; strategy receives broad cross-party support. Mohammed Sarwar (Labour), the first elected Muslim MP, is cleared of charges of corruption and electoral misconduct.

17 Health and Health Care

Ray Fitzpatrick, Rebecca Surender and Tarani Chandola

Health care is one area in which Britain since 1945 has experienced a quite distinctive arrangement compared with other Western industrialised societies. In 1948 a single health service funded from general taxation was established with aspirations to provide comprehensive and universally available health care facilities. By comparison, most European countries have developed similarly extensive health care systems but have relied mainly on social insurance to fund health care, and the United States has to date largely confined public funding of health care to two groups, the elderly and the poor. This chapter examines the reasons for the emergence of a unique form of health service and considers the many pressures and changes it has faced. Also assessed are trends in the health of British society over this period.

Health Services Prior to the NHS

To understand why a single, publicly funded health service was established so soon after the Second World War, it is essential to examine the state of health care facilities prior to and during the war. Following the 1911 National Insurance Act, that section of the working population below the level at which income tax was levied (approximately 40 per cent of the working population in 1939) for the first time received free health care from a general practitioner (GP). The new scheme did not cover their hospital care, nor the health care needs of their family. National Insurance was funded by individuals' own contributions, together with contributions from the employer and from the state. Two main forms of hospital existed: the voluntary hospital and the local authority or municipal hospital. Earlier in the century the voluntary hospitals had been financed by private charitable donations. By the Second World War they were reliant on fees from more affluent patients and contributions from pre-paid insurance schemes which some middle-class individuals joined. These sources of income were insufficient and hospitals generally struggled to finance adequate services. Municipal hospitals evolved out of Poor Law hospitals and were even less adequately funded from local authority sources.

By the end of the Second World War, therefore, the main concerns focused on the fact that over half of the population were not covered by National Insurance and so had quite inadequate access even to the basic care provided by a GP, and ability to afford hospital care was worse. Major reports had drawn attention to the low overall standard of health in Britain and the severe problems of ill health experienced by low-income families (Political and Economic Planning, 1937). In the same way inquiries concluded that the number of hospital beds was insufficient for the population of Britain and drew attention to shortages of hospital facilities overall and the uneven nature of provision across the country.

It was increasingly recognised that hospitals in particular were desperately short of funds and the system of voluntary and municipal hospitals unsustainable. Because of the high levels of civilian as well as military casualties expected from the war, special steps were taken by setting up an Emergency Medical Service to run hospitals. The experience contributed considerably to the recognition of potential advantages of a national health service. The wartime Coalition government in 1944 published a White Paper on plans for a national health service based on two key principles; that it be comprehensive in covering all health needs and that it be free at the time of use.

The Founding of the National Health Service (NHS)

In 1946 a National Health Services Bill was passed, to be followed two years later by the establishment of a National Health Service. Negotiations over the form this service should take, between government and interested parties, particularly the medical profession and local government, were difficult and protracted. The issues behind these disputes are important because they explain many of the enduring features and problems of the NHS since 1948. In particular the medical profession was afraid of being taken over by local government, which they expected to challenge their autonomy in health care. They were successful in this respect and the new health service was to be organised via Regional Hospital Boards, largely independent of both central and local government. GPs particularly wished to avoid any form of civil servant status, to protect autonomy. Their view prevailed and they were left with independent contractor status, paid by the NHS but with few external controls on professional conduct. Hospital consultants also successfully retained their right to private practice, and to work part-time in the NHS if desired and private beds were retained within NHS hospitals. The medical profession was given a key role in decision-making at every level of the new service.

In return for these and other concessions the medical profession accepted the establishment of the NHS, which provided free general practice as well as hospital care to all citizens. Local government emerged as a 'loser' from negotiations as, by contrast with health care systems such as Sweden's, the NHS was not to evolve under their control. They did, however, retain control of community and public health services such as home nursing, school health, maternity and child health services.

The compromise required because of disputes between the government and the medical profession resulted in an NHS that was essentially split into three sectors, with very weak integration and communication across sectors. The sector that has been most important in terms of share of expenditure, status and public visibility has been that of hospital medicine. In a second and contrasting sector were the general practitioners, contracting their services with local Executive Councils. For much of the rest of the twentieth century GPs remained somewhat isolated from the rest of the health service. Whilst scientific breakthroughs and professional developments focused on hospital medicine and added considerably to its status and reputation, increasingly general practice became something of a 'backwater', lacking the premises, facilities, income and career structure as well as prestige enjoyed by their hospital counterparts. Separate again was the third sector of local authority health services such as school and maternity services. So the NHS began life fragmented between these three sectors, therefore tending to be poorly coordinated and planned.

Politics of Technocratic Change

The period from the inception of the NHS until the mid-1970s has been seen as a period of the 'politics of technocratic change' (Klein, 1995). The description aptly describes a period in which there was widespread consensus about the NHS as a central institution of the welfare state, and disputes only focused on the technical means of improving the service. One major concern from the inception of the NHS was a profound fear of costs escalating out of control, now that services were free at the time of use. It was thought that health services would be confronted by infinite demands with very finite resources. As early as 1953 the Minister of Health ordered an inquiry into the costs of the NHS. In 1956, the resulting Guillebaud Committee reported that it could find no evidence of profligacy or inappropriate use of services and, indeed, concluded that there was evidence of a decline in health care as a proportion of national wealth (Ministry of Health, 1956). They recommended that there be a substantial increase in health care expenditure. For most of the first 15 years of the NHS, expenditure was tightly controlled and few new hospitals built. However by 1962, the government announced a Hospital Plan to build a large number of new hospitals ensuring a modern district general hospital for every quarter of a million members of the population. This brief period of expansion in the early 1960s was again followed by long periods in which NHS expenditure only modestly grew. It is quite striking how perpetual have been concerns about unsustainable costs of the NHS whilst in reality Britain has, for all of the period covered by this book, remained behind almost all other Western European and North American countries in the percentage of national wealth that has been devoted to health care expenditure. Thus, in the early 1990s, while France, Germany and Holland spent 8–9 per cent of their GDP on health, the UK was spending 7 per cent (Schieber, Poullier and Greenwald, 1994).

Calls for Reform

The period of the late 1950s and 1960s was also one of growing recognition of how little governments of all political persuasions could influence the direction and quality of the NHS. As has been argued above, the settlement between government and the medical profession in establishing the NHS had left doctors with very high levels of professional autonomy and substantial influence over policy- and decision-making. One illustration of the frustration experienced by governments may be found in the field of mental illness. Successive ministers for health had deplored the poor standards of care for the mentally ill and mentally handicapped. Repeated requests for reform failed to produce results. Minister of Health Richard Crossman resorted to using public exposure of scandal to provoke change; he insisted on the full publication of reports of inhuman conditions in mental hospitals to induce reforms such as the introduction of a Hospital Advisory Service, essentially to act as an inspectorate of mental hospitals.

The limited power of government to influence the direction of the NHS was demonstrated throughout the 1950s through to the early 1970s. Marked differences in clinical practice and the quality of services across the country were frequently reported but seemed resistant to change. The failures of GPs, local authority health and social services and hospital doctors to collaborate and coordinate care seemed equally beyond change. Increasingly, the health needs of many groups such as the elderly and chronically sick and disabled required services that cut across the rather rigid boundaries of the tripartite NHS. Areas of the country were repeatedly identified as being under-provided with health care facilities. The introduction of financial incentives in 1966 went a small way to overcome this problem in general practice; a designated area allowance was created to increase the incomes of doctors prepared to work in under-doctored areas.

Managerial Reorganisation

Finally a National Health Service Reorganisation Act was passed in 1973 to come into effect the following year. Overall the purpose was to address the many problems of the NHS by reorganisation. First it was intended to unify the three branches of the health service; general practice, local authority and hospital services. This was to be achieved by unifying them under area health authorities, in turn accountable to regional health authorities. The objective was only partially achieved because the administrative system for GPs (now named Family Practitioner Committees) again successfully resisted incorporation. Secondly, health care facilities were to be better coordinated with those provided by local government, by making their geographical boundaries for the first time the same and by setting up joint consultative committees. Thus care for groups such as the chronically sick, disabled and mentally ill, typically requiring combined efforts of hospital, primary care and social services, would be better coordinated. Thirdly, the whole system was to be better managed. The roles and duties of administrators and professionals in the health service were to be more clearly delineated; doctors were to be drawn more closely into management decisions and processes. Lines of accountability upwards were specified and the concept of 'consensus management' devised, whereby decisions at local level required agreement of key parties such as representatives of general practice, hospital doctors, nurses, managers and finance.

In short the 1974 reorganisation, the first major administrative reorganisation of the NHS since its inception, was a radical attempt to introduce managerial methods to the NHS to make the system more effective, efficient and responsive. It was generally agreed not to have worked (Brown, 1979). Decisions now took longer to emerge; layers of bureaucracy had been added and a very complex planning system still failed to get right the need to balance central government's wishes to implement change and the need to respect local freedom to get on with the provision of health care. Above all, reorganisation did nothing to address the disadvantages of medical professionals' lack of accountability. This reform is seen by many observers as a watershed in the history of the NHS, because up to this point there remained a consensus about the value and ends of the NHS and dispute only about the means of achieving them.

Redistribution of Resources

A hostile economic climate (a result of the oil crisis and socio-demographic pressures on public expenditure) prevailed for most of the period of the 1974–79 Labour government. Nevertheless the administration made the first sustained attempt to address the problems of health inequalities. Two policy priorities dominated this period: the reallocation of funds to relatively deprived regions, and a reallocation of expenditure to the so-called 'Cinderella' services for the mentally ill, the mentally handicapped and the elderly. A Resource Allocation Working Party (RAWP) was established to examine ways of distributing health care resources according to need. The result was a formula which measured need using a proxy index of mortality (needy areas were those with high standardised death rates). The RAWP recommendations were successful and resulted in a redistribution of expenditure from London and the South-East to the Midlands and North. The attempt to achieve improvements for the 'Cinderella' groups were, however, less successful. Despite Green Papers on 'Better Services' for the mentally ill and mentally handicapped, no new money or earmarked funds were forthcoming, and a gap between national policy and local action was evident. A final inequality to be recognised during this period was that of inequalities in health between social classes. In 1997 a Working Party was established under the chairmanship of Sir Douglas Black to investigate the evidence on social class differences in health and use of health services, and to make proposals for changes in policy. They did not produce their findings (Black, 1980) until after a new Conservative government had taken office. Unsympathetic to the philosophy and policy priorities of the previous administration, the new government rejected the proposals made by the Working Party, in particular their call for additional expenditure to improve the impact of services.

The 1980s: Restructuring the Old NHS

In contrast to the concern with variations in the quality of health care services and health status of different groups, the 1980s were marked by persistent controversy about the level of NHS funding. Despite increased pressure (and an ideological predisposition) to reduce public expenditure, the first two Conservative administrations were unable to decrease NHS spending in real terms. The focus changed therefore from an attempt to cut costs to a concern for greater efficiency; in essence the attempt to 'squeeze more out of the system'. In 1982 Area Health Authorities were abolished and annual reviews of the performance of Regional and District Health Authorities instituted. Performance indicators for Regions and Districts were constructed (with particular stress on measures of their activity and unit costs) in order to assist managers in identifying areas where improvements might be achievable. Between 1980 and 1985, a study of NHS information requirements was also carried out and resulted in a major revision of the system for collecting statistics about performance.

In 1983, a review was commissioned of the management of the NHS, headed by Sir Roy Griffiths, who diagnosed a state of 'institutionalised stagnation' in the NHS; 'if Florence Nightingale were carrying her lamp through the corridors of the NHS, she would almost certainly be searching for the people in charge' ('Griffiths Report', 1983). Griffiths recommended that the existing system of consensus management be replaced by a more businesslike system of regional and district unit 'general managers'. This shift in structure was intended to create the conditions for a more entrepreneurial culture and flexible decision-making, and as part of this effort managers were hired from outside on short-term contracts, and their pay became related to performance.

Also in 1983, District Health Authorities were obliged to introduce competitive tendering for cleaning, laundry and catering in their hospital and community health services. The importance of the contracting-out of these ancillary services lay less with the financial gains that were achieved and more with the establishment of the principle that the responsibility of Health Authorities was to 'steer' (purchase and regulate services) but not necessarily 'row' (provide and manage services themselves). The process also enhanced managers' skills as buyers.

Finally, in 1987, the government published a White Paper on Family Practitioner Services *Promoting Better Health* Department of Health, 1987). The proposals were primarily designed to encourage GPs to be more responsive to their patients, and resulted in a new contract being 'imposed' on GPs in 1990. The contract introduced the themes of consumerism and 'better value for money' and marked the transformation of a relationship based on trust to one based on contract. The government took the view that professional ethics had been an inadequate control on the delivery of primary care, and the responsibilities and duties of GPs were for the first time externally defined and made explicit.

In retrospect, it could be argued that these changes all formed part of an overall strategy which was necessary in creating the preconditions for an eventual shift from a tightly planned administered system to a competition-driven system. Private-sector mechanisms were slowly replacing the traditional command-and-control budgeting and reporting process. These strategic changes created the philosophy and structures which eventually enabled the government to implement its plans for its later, more radical experiment.

The Rise of the Market in Health Care

The continual need to reduce public spending, the pro-market orientation of the government and new information on variation and 'slack' in the system, merged at the end of the 1980s and resulted in the most fundamental reform of the NHS since its creation. The package of reforms were first articulated in the 1989 White Paper, *Working for Patients* (Department of Health, 1989), subsequently translated into legislation in the National Health Service and Community Care Act of 1990, and finally implemented in 1991.

Despite suspicion that the proposed reforms were the 'thin end of the wedge' of privatisation, the changes which were implemented in 1991 did not alter the financial underpinnings of the NHS. Rather, they attempted to retain the advantages of the NHS – universal coverage and relative cost control while overcoming its perceived failings – low consumer choice and supply-side inefficiencies. The government preserved free access to health care and kept the tax-based financing, but aimed to use competition between providers of services to improve the efficiency and quality of those services. Essentially this was to be achieved through the creation of an internal market and the separation of health care purchasing from the provision of services. Producers of hospital and specialist services would now compete with each other for the custom of purchasers of health services: District Health Authorities and GP Fundholders ('opted-out' GPs who could volunteer to manage and control a share of their patients' budget). The relationship between providers and purchasers would be formalised through NHS contracts.

With the division of purchasers and providers, and the creation of an internal health market, the NHS embarked on a new trajectory in which established power structures, systems and values were challenged. Notions of bureaucracy, professionalism and paternalism were replaced with those of markets, consumerism and user rights. The previous post-war preoccupation with service coordination and universal care now took second place to concerns about efficiency and choice. Until the late 1980s the NHS had been essentially a command-and-control bureaucracy; hospitals were owned and operated by the state, and health care staff were government employees. GPs, although nominally self-employed, contracted almost exclusively with the state for the provision of their services. The system had many merits. Since doctors were not paid on a fee-for-service basis there was little incentive to over-treat patients. The system was also what economists call 'macro-efficient', absorbing a relatively small proportion of GNP compared to other countries, while providing a service that was not notably inferior in quality or outcome. In other respects, however, the system was less satisfactory. It was generally considered to be 'micro-inefficient' (Enthoven, 1985). The combination of clinical freedom and the absence of costing mechanisms led to resources being used in a manner that bore little relationship to their cost-effectiveness, and wide variations in the performance and costs of medical practice. Moreover, the familiar complaint that the monopoly power of the NHS made it unresponsive to consumers was shared by those on the policy left and right.

The government took the view that centralised controls and the managerialism of the 1980s had been insufficient forces for change, especially at the clinical level. The route to increased cost-effectiveness and quality lay in influencing medical behaviour, and this was to be achieved through the introduction of market mechanisms and competition. Once 'money followed the patient', providers would have a systematic financial incentive to cut costs, improve quality and be more responsive to what consumers wanted. Purchasers, in turn, since they would still be cash-limited, would have an incentive to bargain for improved value for money on behalf of patients. It was argued that GP fundholders were better placed to understand patient needs and preferences than remote health authorities, and that they would lead the way in negotiating improvements in services.

1997: The New NHS?

In December 1997 the new Labour government announced its plans for the NHS: the White Paper, *The New NHS: Modern, Dependable* (Department of Health, 1997). It claims to offer a new model of health care for the UK, one which seeks to replace the internal market with a system of 'integrated care', founded on partnership rather than competition. The model is not a return, however, to the 1970s command-and-control system, which 'focused on the needs of organisations rather than the needs of patients'. Instead the latest reforms set out a 'Third Way', which keeps the separation between planning and provision; expands the central role of primary care, and retains decentralised responsibility for operational management.

There is much debate currently about whether Labour's 'Third Way' truly represents a break with the previous model, or actually is a continuation of it in another guise. Certainly there is much that is similar in the two systems, and many have commented that the fully developed model looks much like an extension of total purchasing (Le Grand, Mays and Mulligan, 1998). Many structures and processes, though called by different names, bear the hallmarks of the 1989 package. NHS Trusts are to remain, as is the separation of purchasers and providers and the contracts between them (though they are now to be longer-term and called 'agreements'). The continued emphasis on waiting lists and performance indicators could also be interpreted as a continuing response to consumerism. Most notably, the strong emphasis on a primary care-led NHS remains the cornerstone of current health care policy. Although GP fundholding is to be abolished, groups of GP practices (primary care groups) covering geographical communities of up to 100,000 will be responsible for purchasing hospital, community and primary care services for their populations. It seems that despite the claims and counter-claims about the merits of the internal market, there exists, for now at least, a degree of consensus about the value of many of the principles and features of the 1991 reforms.

Trends in Mortality

The period since 1945 has been one of steady increases in life expectancy in Britain, although it is not clear to what extent the NHS can be credited with such improvements compared to other social changes described earlier in the chapter. Trends in mortality and life expectancy in Britain since 1945 have largely been continuations of earlier patterns. Both adult and infant mortality rates have been decreasing since the start of the century, while life expectancy has been increasing (figure 17.1). From 1950 to 1995, overall life expectancy at birth increased by 7.9 years for women and 7.7 years for men. The improvements in life expectancy for younger age groups began earlier in the century, while life expectancy at older ages (65 and over) increased rapidly only in the latter half. Increases in life expectancy at older ages is noticeable after 1945 in women and after 1970 in men.

Women have benefited more than males from the reductions in mortality and increases in life expectancy. The difference between the sexes in life expectancy has increased since the start of the century, more so after 1945, and is particularly marked at older ages (figure 17.1).

Causes of Death

Death rates from most infectious diseases such as tuberculosis, typhus, cholera and smallpox declined substantially in the twentieth century (Charlton and Murphy, 1997b). In 1911, infectious diseases accounted for around 25 per cent

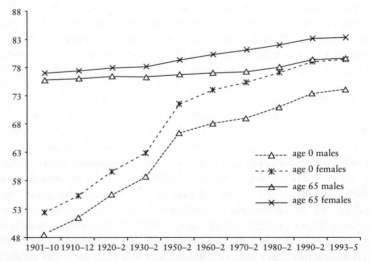

Figure 17.1 Life expectancy at age 0 and 65 by sex, England and Wales, 1901–1995
Source: ONS, 1997a.

of all deaths. This fell to 3.6 per cent by 1951 and to under 1 per cent by 1994. Deaths from tuberculosis remained a major cause of death until the introduction of specific chemotherapies in the 1950s. Mortality from childhood infections declined rapidly after immunisation programmes were introduced from 1940 onwards. However, towards the end of the twentieth century, some infectious diseases re-emerged partly as a result of greater international travel (malaria and cholera), changing lifestyles (sexually transmitted diseases) and resistance to antibiotics (drug-resistant tuberculosis).

Cardiovascular diseases accounted for 48 per cent of all deaths in 1951 and 41 per cent in 1997 (ONS, 1998). They had been increasing in Britain since the 1920s but peaked in the 1970s and subsequently fell. While trends in heart disease for men and women are similar, men are more likely to have heart disease compared to women. Strokes account for fewer deaths (10 per cent of all deaths in 1997) but they have a major impact on sufferers through disability. The incidence of stroke is strongly related to high blood pressure. There has been a decline in stroke mortality this century, increasingly so since the 1970s.

Deaths from cancers have risen from 16 per cent of all deaths in 1951 to 25 per cent in 1996 (ONS, 1998). Lung cancer increased markedly over the twentieth century and only began to decline in the 1970s. Breast cancer has continued to increase; Britain has one of the highest rates in the Western world. Rates of other cancers such as skin, testicular and cervical cancers have been increasing since the 1960s. Furthermore, mortality from cancers at older ages (over 70 in men and over 50 in women) has been rising since 1970. However, cancer mortality for men and women in younger age groups (under 70 in men and 50 in women) has fallen over the last 20 years.

Death rates from diabetes fell in the twentieth century, especially for younger age groups after 1945 when better insulin treatments were developed. Deaths from diseases of the digestive system also reduced considerably over the century although there has been some increase in deaths from cirrhosis of the liver among younger age groups in recent years. Deaths from all accidents have been declining since the 1930s. Deaths from road traffic accidents have been decreasing since the 1960s, despite the growth of motor traffic primarily attributable to successful accident prevention measures.

Morbidity

Data on morbidity (or sickness) can provide a complementary indication of trends in health. While there is no significant pattern in asthma deaths (except in the 1960s, when deaths increased due to a particular treatment used), hospital records reveal that asthma in the population has probably increased over the past 20–30 years (Marks and Burney, 1997). 'Arthritis and rheumatism' are the most frequent self-reported long standing condition in Britain and yet account for less than one per cent of all deaths (ONS, 1998). With an increasingly elderly population, the prevalence of musculoskeletal diseases has been increasing without a corresponding increase in the mortality rates. In contrast to the declining rates of mortality from accidents, there appears to be an increase in morbidity from accidents during the last 20 years.

While life expectancy has been increasing, trends in healthy life expectancy do not show an equivalent increase (Bone et al., 1996). Healthy life expectancy is calculated as the expectation of life free from illness and disability. Furthermore, disability in the population may be increasing. The percentage of the population with a self-reported long standing illness has increased from 21 per cent in 1972 to 31 per cent in 1995 (ONS, 1997a). The percentage of patients consulting their GPs has increased from 66 per cent in 1970–1 to 78 per cent in 1991–2 (Department of Health, 1998). The rates of new cases presenting at accident and emergency services have also increased.

The prevalence of mental health problems in the population is hard to ascertain because of problems of definition and measurement. General practice consultation rates indicate an increase in major psychiatric illness (Grundy, 1997). However, this increase may be an artefact of changes in health policies.

While rates of mortality have decreased markedly since 1945, evidence from morbidity data do not show a similar trend. The ageing of the population with continuously increasing life expectancy could also mean an increase in the number of years spent with disabling, chronic degenerative diseases. For example, the ageing of the population has led to an increase in chronic neurological diseases such as Parkinson's and Alzheimer's.

Inequalities in Health

Although mortality rates improved markedly in the twentieth century, inequalities in mortality between social classes increased since 1949. Poorer mortality rates for lower social classes have been observed for most causes of death and at nearly all age groups. Improvements in mortality for those in the higher social classes were greater for most of the second half of this century than for individuals in the lower classes (figure 17.2).

Other social patterns in the distribution of health have also been observed. Unemployment is an important risk factor for ill health and premature mortality. Mortality from cardiovascular diseases is high among South Asian men and other ethnic groups. A 'North–South' divide in mortality has been observed, with regions north of the Midlands and Wales having higher mortality rates than more southern regions (Britton, 1990). Furthermore, the relative position of the northern region may have worsened since 1959. These inequalities have persisted despite attempts to change the distribution of health services described earlier in the chapter.

Explanations for Health Trends

An important debate concerns the extent to which improvements in health in Britain have been due to the increased access to health services arising from the establishment of the NHS, as opposed to more general social and economic

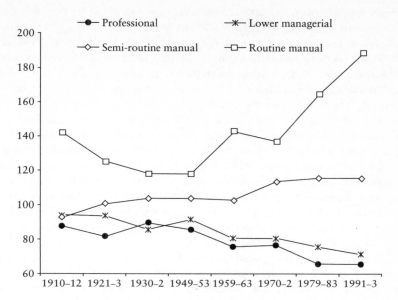

Figure 17.2   Standardised mortality ratios for selected Registrar General's social classes, males aged 20–64, England and Wales, 1910–1993
Sources: McPherson and Coleman, 1988; Drever and Bunting, 1997.

changes, particularly improved standards of living. McKeown (1979) argued that improvements in nutrition and diet explain most of the decline in mortality rates in the nineteenth and twentieth centuries. The steady increase in calorie intake improved resistance to a wide range of infectious diseases. The rationing of food during the Second World War may paradoxically have improved the nutritional diet of the British population and possibly resulted in greater equality in access to an adequate diet. Diet plays an important role in cardiovascular disease, particularly because of the role of high saturated fats in the narrowing of arteries. Trends in the consumption of fats closely coincide with the rise and fall of heart disease in the twentieth century. Furthermore, the consumption of fruit and vegetables is associated with lower risks of heart disease. Fresh fruit consumption increased in Britain by nearly 60 per cent between 1950 and 1994.

Despite overall improvements in diet, in recent years there has been growing concern about poor dietary behaviour in Britain. The over-consumption of food, combined with decreasing levels of physical activity, have resulted in an increase in obesity in the population from the 1980s. Obesity is a risk factor for a number of diseases such as hypertension, diabetes and osteoarthritis.

Smoking was one of the most important influences on health in Britain in the twentieth century. Smoking directly causes lung cancer and deaths from chronic obstructive lung disease and is also associated with other cancers and cardiovascular disease. The use of tobacco products increased rapidly in the Second World War and continued to increase until the 1970s when it began to fall (Doll, Darby and Whitley, 1997). Trends in lung cancer mortality can, for the most part, be explained adequately by trends in the consumption of cigarettes and the type of cigarette smoked. Over 50 per cent of men aged 16 and over were cigarette smokers in 1970; this declined to 18 per cent in 1994 (OPCS, 1996). Trends among women show a similar pattern of decline in cigarette smoking since the 1970s, although with lower levels of consumption. While cigarette smoking has decreased in recent years, social class differences in cigarette smoking have been increasing since 1974 (ibid., 1996).

Overcrowding and lack of sanitation have been linked to the spread of infectious diseases such as tuberculosis prior to in the nineteenth and early twentieth centuries. Much of the new housing that was built for low-income groups was provided by local authorities. However, much of this form of housing has since been neglected and fallen into disrepair. The effects of damp, inadequate heating and overcrowding can lead to ill health through respiratory disorders, heart disease, accidental injury and emotional problems (Hunt, 1997). Furthermore, the adverse effects of poor housing in childhood can continue into adulthood.

It is clearly possible to chronicle a wide range of social, economic and life-style changes that may have influenced health, regardless of the influence of health care. However, the last 50 years have seen dramatic changes in health care, with repeated scientific breakthroughs feeding through into treatments. Medical advances must also have played a role in the improvements in health (Charlton, Fraser and Murphy, 1997). The development and wide-scale use of antibiotics since 1945 have decreased the death rates from infectious diseases. Immunisation programmes for childhood diseases such as diphtheria, whooping cough, poliomyelitis, tetanus, measles and mumps have been accompanied by sharp reductions in death rates. Other medical advances since 1945 include improved slower-acting insulin for diabetes, beta blockers for reducing high blood pressure, medical technology such as ultrasound, CAT scanners and fibre-optic surgery, cardiac bypass and joint-replacement surgeries, organ transplants (especially of kidneys) and chemotherapy for cancers. Nevertheless, scholars have become more cautious in attributing improvements in health to the growth of health services, primarily because many treatments provided are still of unproved effectiveness (Cochrane, 1972).

Conclusion

Life expectancy has continued to improve since the Second World War. It remains unclear how much the NHS is responsible for improving health. Increasingly, at the beginning of the twenty-first century, important decisions are faced about how many of the constantly appearing scientific products of medical science can be provided by public funds. More than at any stage of its history, the value and effectiveness of services in the NHS are scrutinised. Nevertheless, because access to a wide range of modern health care facilities has been provided via public funding of the NHS for so long, the NHS has remained a strikingly popular institution in public opinion, despite its many upheavals.

References and Further Reading

Black, Sir Douglas (Chairman) (1980) 'Inequalities in Health.' London: Department of Health and Social Security.

Bone, M., Bebbington, A, Jagger, C., Morgan, K. and Nicholas, G. (1996) *Health Expectancy and Its Uses*. London.

Britton, M. (1990) *Mortality and Geography*. London.

Brown, R. (1979) *Reorganising the National Health Service*. Oxford.

Charlton, J. and Murphy, M. (eds) (1997a) *The Health of Adult Britain 1841–1994*, 2 vols, London.

Charlton, J., Fraser, P. and Murphy, P. (1997b) 'Medical Advances and Iatrogenesis.' In J. Charlton and P. Murphy (eds), *The Health of Adult Britain 1941–1994, Vol. 1*, pp. 217–29. London.

Charlton, J. and Murphy, M. (1997) 'Trends in Causes of Mortality: 1841–1994 – An Overview.' In J. Charlton and P. Murphy (eds), *The Health of Adult Britain 1941– 1994, Vol. 1*, pp. 30–57. London.

Cochrane, A. L. (1972) *Effectiveness and Efficiency*. London: National Provincial Hospital Trust.

Department of Health. (1987) *Promoting Better Health*. London.

Department of Health. (1989) *Working for Patients*. London.

Department of Health. (1997) *The New NHS: Modern, Dependable. London.*

Department of Health. (1998) *Health and Personal Social Services Statistics for England 1998*. London.

DHSS (Department of Health and Social Services). (1980) 'Black Report: Inequalities in Health, Report of a Research Working Group.' London.

Doll, R., Darby, S. and Whitley, E. (1997) 'Trends in Mortality from Smoking-related Diseases.' In J. Charlton and P. Murphy (eds), *The Health of Adult Britain 1841– 1994, Vol. 1*, pp. 128–55. London.

Drever, F. and Bunting, J. (1997) 'Patterns and Trends in Male Mortality.' In F. Drever and M. Whitehead (eds), *Health Inequalities*. pp. 95–107. London.

Enthoven, A. (1985) *Reflections on the Management of the National Health Service*. London.

'Griffiths Report.' (1983) NHS Management Enquiry. London.

Grundy, E. (1997) 'The Health and Health Care of Older Adults in England and Wales, 1841–1994.' In J. Charlton and P. Murphy (eds), *The Health of Adult Britain 1941– 1994, Vol. 2*, pp. 182–203. London.

Ham, C. (1992) *Health Policy in Britain*. Basingstoke.

Hunt, S. (1997) 'Housing Related Disorders.' In J. Charlton and P. Murphy (eds), *The Health of Adult Britain 1841–1994, Vol. 1*, pp. 156–70. London.

Klein, R. (1995) *The New Politics of the National Health Service*. London.

Le Grand, J., Mays, N. and Mulligan, J. (1998) *Learning from the NHS Internal Market*. London.

Marks, G. and Burney, P. (1997) 'Diseases of the Respiratory System.' In J. Charlton and P. Murphy (eds), *The Health of Adult Britain 1941–1994, Vol. 2*, pp. 93–111. London.

McKeown, T. (1979) *The Role of Medicine*. Oxford.

McPherson, K. and Coleman, D. (1988) 'Health.' In A. H. Halsey (ed.), *British Social Trends since 1900*, pp. 398–461. Basingstoke.

Ministry of Health. (1956) Committee of Enquiry into the Cost of the National Health Service, 'Report'. London.

ONS (Office for National Statistics). (1997a) *Mortality Statistics General*. London.

ONS. (1997b) *Living in Britain: Results from the 1995 General Household Survey*. London.

ONS. (1998) *Mortality Statistics Causes 1997*. London.

OPCS (Office of Population and Census Studies). 1996. *Living in Britain: Results from the 1994 General Household Survey*. London.

Political and Economic Planning. (1937) *Report on the British Health Services*. London: PEP.

Schieber, G. Poullier, J. and Greenwald, L. (1994) 'Health System Performance in OECD Countries 1980–1992.' *Health Affairs* 13: 100–12.

Townsend, P., Davidson, N. and Whitehead, M. (1990) *Inequalities in Health*. London.

Chronology

1946   National Health Service Act.

1948   Establishment of National Health Service (NHS).

1956   Report of a Committee of Inquiry into the Cost of the NHS: the Guillebaud Report.

1962   Ministry of Health publishes *A Hospital Plan for England and Wales*.

1973   The National Health Service Reorganisation Act.

1976   DHSS publishes *Sharing Resources for Health in England: Report of the Resource Allocation Working Party*.

1980   Sir Douglas Black chairs committee of the Department of Health and Social Security; issues a report, *Inequalities in Health*.

1982   Area Health Authorities abolished. Annual reviews of performance of Regional and District Health Authorities instituted.

1983   Griffiths Report on NHS Management Inquiry. District Health Authorities obliged to introduce competitive tendering for ancillary services.

1987   DHSS publishes *Promoting Better Health*.

1989   Department of Health issues report, *Working for Patients*.

1990   National Health Service and Community Care Act.

1997   Department of Health issues *The New NHS: Modern, Dependable*.

18 Science and Information Technology

Jon Agar

Introduction

In 1945 the Second World War ended with the detonation of atomic bombs over the Japanese cities of Hiroshima and Nagasaki. While the production of the weapons was an engineering feat of which only the United States was capable in wartime, the Manhattan Project – as the bomb programme was named – had its origins in science. Physicists in Britain, including many who had fled Nazi Europe, played a key role: it was they who first understood the possibility of the bomb, had begun the research, and had crossed the Atlantic to continue the project to completion. The Manhattan Project symbolised the potential of what was then a new scale of research. Turning our attention to the end of the century and the Sanger Centre, outside Cambridge: here, in the 1990s, part of the human genome – the information contained in our DNA – was mapped and sequenced. The work was part of the huge international collaboration, the Human Genome Project (HGP), funded partly by governments, and partly by charities (the Sanger Centre was financed by the Medical Research Council and the Wellcome Trust). The HGP was biology-based, dependent on extensive use of electronic computers, and carried the expectation of immense commercial spin-offs. While the Manhattan Project was intensely secret, the Human Genome Project has been the subject of broad public debate, the poles of which stretch from enthusiasm, through ethical disquiet and intense criticism and distrust, and on its edges blurs into controversies surrounding 'genetic engineering' and 'cloning'.

These two cases serve to introduce several of the contextual themes which organise the following history of British science and information technology since 1945: the growth in scale and expense of research, the spread of computing, the importance of international organisation of science, the decisive role of warfare in shaping science and technology (either through the legacy of the Second World War, or the Cold War which dominated all but the last decade of the period), the new relations between public and private expenditure, a shift of emphasis from the physical to the life sciences, and, finally, a crisis of public trust in science.

The Funding, Growth and Organisation of British Science

The main feature of British science since 1945 has been growth, as the following statistics illustrate (figures in brackets refer to rough equivalents in 1996 pounds).[1] In 1925/30 approximately £6 million (£180 million) per year was spent by government and industry on research and development (R&D). By 1964/5, gross domestic expenditure on R&D had jumped to £777.4 million (£7,800 million), an increase which continued at a slower pace in later decades: in 1978 the figure stood at £3980 million (£11,900 million), and in 1996 £14,340 million. Research was organised in three settings: government establishments, industrial laboratories and the universities. Behind this growth lay a belief in a link between R&D and national economic performance, an increase in scale and expense of cutting-edge science in all three settings, and a capitalisation on Second World War achievements – a factor intensified by the Cold War. An immediate consequence was an increase in the production of qualified scientists and engineers: numbers in higher education doubled in the late 1940s, and grew again in the expansion of the sector following the Robbins Report in the mid-1960s. Although numbers were never very high (0.8 per cent of the working population in 1962), the aspirational values of scientists and technologists gave them a political profile: the modern, professional and future-oriented image of science has often been recruited by politicians, most famously by Harold Wilson, who proclaimed in 1963 that a new Britain would be 'forged in the white heat' of the 'scientific revolution'. Such rhetoric did not translate into sudden jumps in R&D expenditure. The proportion of women scientists, according to census data, increased from 8 per cent (1951) to 35 per cent (1981).

Rules of thumb which have held good for most of the decades since 1945 are that defence research has formed over a quarter of total R&D, and that R&D was mainly financed by government but performed by industry, at least up until the 1960s.[2] The big science-based industries – such as chemical combine ICI, pharmaceuticals companies (e.g. the forebears of GlaxoWellcome and SmithKline Beecham), food (Unilever), oil (British Petroleum and the Anglo-Dutch Shell), and particularly the electrical industries (GEC, EMI, Plessey) – possessed large research programmes in the post-war years, with laboratories often founded in the early decades of the century. It is a mistake to think of industrial laboratories as concentrating on 'discoveries'; instead most scientists were employed on such activities as understanding patents, improving processes, assessing quality and maintaining standards (the latter, it has officially been estimated in the United States, absorbed 6 per cent of GNP, and there is no reason to think that the British case is much different).[3] Industrial companies' investment in university science was significant, although uneven.[4] Most money for academic research came from government sources. Under the 'dual support system', both university funding bodies (the University Grants Committee in the early decades, others including the Higher Education Funding Council for England by the 1990s) and the research councils funded science. Typically, university funding supported staff, buildings and inexpensive research, while staff could apply for research council funding for more ambitious projects. The research councils date from the First World War and worked on the 'Haldane Principle' in which direct government control of science was avoided by placing decision-making in the hands of a committee of scientists, who advised on the allocation of resources. The research councils have also funded laboratories, some with little academic involvement (such as the National Physical Laboratory in Teddington, London), others forming highly productive partnerships (as will be seen in the case of the Medical Research Council (MRC) Laboratory of Molecular Biology in Cambridge). In addition, some government departments, such as the Ministry of Defence and the Ministry of Agriculture, Fisheries and Food directly control research establishments. Indeed this departmental funding of science exceeded amounts spent through the research councils.

Cold-War Science

Science shaped the Cold War, and vice versa. The emphasis on nuclear weapons, electronics and aviation made the Cold War, in the words of Sir John Carroll, Scientific Adviser to the Board of the Admiralty, 'a research and development race and not one for the provision of equipment'.[5] In Britain, work intensified at the key establishments: nuclear weapons at Aldermaston, electronics and radar at Malvern, aviation at Farnborough, chemical and biological warfare at Porton Down. Management of research establishments has been shaped since 1945 by concentration and merger. Most of the non-nuclear establishments were brought together under the Defence Research Agency in 1990, a process completed in 1995 with the creation of the Defence Evaluation and Research Agency, DERA (see table 18.1).

The real situation was much less simple: establishments merged and split, had outstations, and changed names. The west-of-London distribution of these sites contributed to the growth of an 'M4 high-technology corridor'.

Within this Cold War context other factors shaped defence research, in particular matters of dependence on allies versus strategic independence and competition for markets. The nuclear programme illustrates the latter. The decision to build a British nuclear bomb was taken in January 1947 by the Prime Minister, Clement Attlee. The weapon programme was intensely secret, with details kept from Parliament and even members of the Cabinet. Churchill, for example, claimed to be 'rather astonished' to find on his return to office in 1951 that over £100 million had been spent on atomic projects.[6] (The secrecy was somewhat misdirected since the Manhattan Project and Harwell atom spy, Klaus Fuchs, had passed bomb secrets to the Russians before his arrest in 1950.) The reason for the largesse was as much political as it was military: independent nuclear capability bought an apparent continuation of Great Power status. Tests presented crucial demonstrations of this position, the first taking place on the Monte Bello Islands, off the Australian coast, on 3 October 1952 – after the Soviet Union but

Table 18.1   Major UK defence research establishments, 1989[7]

Establishment	Main site	Main research areas	Staff
Atomic Weapons Research Establishment (AWRE)	Aldermaston	Nuclear weapons	Not known
Atomic Energy Research Establishment (AERE)	Harwell	Atomic energy	c.2,000
Radar Research Establishment (RRE, later Royal Radar Establishment), later Radar and Signals Research Establishment (RSRE)	Malvern	Electronics radar	1,586
Microbiological Research Department (later Establishment) and Chemical Defence Establishment	Porton Down	Biological and chemical warfare	560
Royal Aircraft Establishment (RAE)	Farnborough	Aviation and aerospace	5,200
Admiralty Surface Weapons Establishment (ASWE) and Admiralty Research Establishment (ARE)	Christchurch Portsdown Teddington	Naval weapons and sensors	2,931
Aeroplane and Armament Experimental Establishment	Boscombe Down	Aeroplane and armament testing	1,101
Royal Armament Research and Development Establishment (RARDE)	Fort Halstead	Army weapons, vehicles and engineering	2,262

before France. A thermonuclear hydrogen bomb, a device with roughly the ratio of destructive power to fission weapons as the latter to conventional arms, followed in May 1957, the decision having been taken by Churchill in 1954.

While the main motivation was to build up what was hoped would be a lucrative industry, the civil nuclear programme was never fully separate from the military weapon project. The Atomic Energy Authority (UKAEA), was set up as a corporation in July 1954 to manage the research and foster commercial involvement in construction. The reactor programme formally began in February 1955 and envisaged 12 stations, 8 of the Magnox design, to generate 1.5–2 gigawatts of power – a target trebled in 1957. The first civil reactor was Calder Hall in 1956, championed as a British engineering success. Consortia of British industrial firms eventually built a further 8 Magnox reactors. In 1958 the Ministry of Defence intervened and modified the designs so as to produce military plutonium. A second programme began in 1965 with the decision to favour British Advanced Gas-cooled Reactors (such as Dungeness B) over American designs and a third in 1973–4 based on the short-lived Steam Generating Heavy Water Reactor (SGHWR). The decisions to proceed with the first two programmes were remarkably uncontentious and largely unaffected by party political division or public opposition. In contrast, the 1970s policy shift was subject to intense discussion.[8] Debate focused on four areas: the possible use of Three Mile Island-type designs, proposals by British Nuclear Fuels Limited to reprocess fuel at Windscale/Sellafield, the location of nuclear waste-disposal sites, and the future of fast breeder reactors (plutonium producers, of which an experimental prototype had been built on the north Scottish coast at Doun-reay). The true reverse of the nuclear reactor programme, however, came in the late 1980s when preparation for privatisation revealed prohibitive hidden costs.

Similar issues shaped ballistic missile development and high-profile aviation projects such as Concorde in the 1960s and 1970s. While nuclear research was shaped by the fragility of US–UK relations in the late 1940s, their very strength encouraged exchange in three other areas: intelligence and espionage, chemical warfare and biological warfare. For example, the Government Communications Headquarters (GCHQ), the post-war incarnation of the code-breaking centre Bletchley Park, continued an unprecedented sharing of signals intelligence, a pact which extended to the construction of American listening stations in Brit-ain. Chemical and biological warfare represented stopgap 'weapons of mass destruction' before nuclear devices could be produced in quantity, a categorisa-tion encouraged by the initial exclusion of the Defence Research Policy Com-mittee (DRPC) from nuclear matters (and until the hydrogen bomb radically changed the meaning of the term 'mass destruction').[9] Chemical warfare went from research at Porton Down to pilot production plant stage, at Nancekuke in Cornwall, before being mothballed in 1956 when emphasis shifted to defensive, rather than offensive, capabilities. Biological warfare work on foot and mouth disease at the Virus Institute at Pirbright was supported precisely because it was banned in the United States – an odd variant of the special relationship! As an R&D war, the Cold War had to be based on predictions of future possibilities, estimates predominantly shaped by what was under way in friendly research establishments, and *not* by certain knowledge of Soviet capabilities: despite the US–UK intelligence exchange the DRPC was told in 1955 that 'direct penetra-tion of the Russian research and development programme was impossible. We had never seen a single [piece of] Russian equipment until it was in operational service or deliberately shown.'[10] This ignorance made visits by British scientists to Russia, such as radio astronomer Bernard Lovell's in 1963 or Imperial Col-lege professor Willis Jackson's in 1957, particularly sensitive. Nor, sometimes, did scientific knowledge flow between friends. News of the laser did not reach the DRPC until 1960, although the idea had been published two years earlier (the American-invented laser eventually found many applications, including bar-codes, compact disc players, and chemistry – for example, enabling Harold Kroto and others to discover a new form of carbon, C_{60}, in 1985).

The Spread of Information Technologies

Britain in 1945 depended on information technologies: radio was a mass medium, the telephone was found in every office and was complemented by a telegraph network which linked the nation's industry to its overseas markets. The consumer boom in the 1950s fuelled the spread of television: the BBC's service, suspended for the duration of the Second World War, resumed transmission in time for the coronation of Queen Elizabeth II, and was joined by the end of the decade by commercial rivals. However, the more recent 'convergence' of these communications technologies depended on developments in techniques to handle 'data', in particular digital electronic computing.

Without the Second World War the history of computing would have been radically different. Mid-twentieth-century warfare required efficient planning, the organisation of humans and materials across the globe, and made imperative the speedy translation of messages and scientific calculation. Such demands brought together three previously independent activities: data processing (of the kind found in commercial offices and government bureaucracies), mechanised calculation, and the logical processes of making and breaking secret codes. Britain excelled at the third of these – witness Bletchley Park, where Alan Turing worked – although the historian's judgement is severely hampered here: the area was, and is, shrouded in secrecy.

Turing described the logical possibilities of a computer in the 1930s, but we must turn to the United States for the reinvention and popularisation of the idea. At the University of Pennsylvania a military-funded project to speed up vital calculations needed for the operation of new guns resulted in the ENIAC, a massive calculator that filled a room and used 18,000 valves. Completed in 1946, it was too late for direct war work (although it was soon making calculations for the hydrogen bomb), but it was from the ENIAC team that the idea of a stored-program computer emerged. A race began to turn idea into reality, including teams of scientists at Cambridge and Manchester universities. A second wartime technology, radar, gave the Manchester team the edge. Professor F. C. Williams and Tom Kilburn had worked on radar at the Telecommunications Research Establishment (TRE), Malvern, and Williams brought back from TRE the crucial methods of storing and manipulating electronic data. This advantage enabled the first stored-program computer to be built at Manchester University in 1948. Cambridge followed with its EDSAC machine the following year.

Military support to the early computers was crucial. Ferranti's involvement with Manchester University was funded by the military Ministry of Supply, a major player in post-war British science and technology.[11] The Atomic Weapons Research Establishment at Aldermaston could demand the purchase of the fastest computers in the world in the 1950s, even if that meant dollar expenditure. The navy – always keen to reduce the number of sailors – enthusiastically pursued computerisation, and in 1958 trounced their opponents in Anglo-American trials by deploying the Action Data Automation (ADA) system. The Cold War, although occasionally turning 'hot' in Korea and Vietnam, centred on opposing conventional and nuclear weapons, the infrastructural component of which was a dense network of radar and communications systems. The computer made sense of this world by controlling the networks, and was shaped by it.[12] Weapons delivery systems concentrated research on miniaturisation of electronics (a trend that led to PCs): the 1950s V-bomber, which would deliver a nuclear bomb to its target, needed 1,000 valves and therefore a large unwieldy power source, its ballistic missile replacements (the failed Blue Streak, Polaris deployed in 1982, and Trident now) needed lightweight and low-power transistors or integrated circuits and computing. Radar systems, such as the early warning stations built at Fylingdales in Yorkshire in the early 1960s, or the increasingly sophisticated air traffic control network, likewise made heavy demands on electronic data processing. The comprehensive monitoring of air-space by computers was an achievement of the Cold War.

The first 'mainframe' machines were, by today's standards, massive in size but puny in power. However, a British computer manufacturing industry was quickly established in the early 1950s by electronics firms such as Ferranti (working with Kilburn's group) and, most remarkably, the teashop and cake company Lyons & Co. (which based its Lyons Electronic Office, LEO, computer on the EDSAC). Manufacturing runs grew from tens of machines in the early 1950s to hundreds by the early 1960s. Computers became smaller and more powerful, as valves were replaced by transistors, and later integrated circuits (both depended on the properties of semiconductors, materials such as germanium and silicon. The British computer industry, however, was soon suffering because of competition from American firms such as IBM, which had the benefits of both bigger markets (allowing economics of scale, and therefore cheaper machines) and generous Cold War funding. The response, encouraged particularly under Harold Wilson's industrial policy, was for firms to merge, and by 1968 nearly all British computer manufacture was undertaken by a 'national champion', International Computers Limited (ICL). This experiment was a mixed success: ICL still exists but it manufactures for niche markets and is owned by the Japanese company Fujitsu.

Until the 1970s few people in Britain would have seen a computer, yet by the 1990s they could be bought in supermarkets. The appearance of smaller and cheaper machines, and new techniques for connecting computers together, made possible the entry of computers into new settings, particularly the front office and the home. The advantages of small computers were first felt in laboratories: American minicomputers such as Digital's PDP series in the 1960s and 1970s could sit on a laboratory bench and enable direct computerised control of instruments, a 'hands-on' experience accessible to many, and a wholly different one to using mainframes (where data and program had to be sent in a 'batch' to the computer operators who would return the results sometimes days later). The first small home computers (sold as kits and made possible by mass-produced microprocessors) directly appealed to this experience of hands-on computing. Some tiny American start-up companies, such as Apple, grew rich marketing small machines, emphasising their contrast to IBM's monsters. Small British consumer electronics companies such as Sinclair and Amstrad followed in the early 1980s, leading to short-lived hopes of a revived British industry. Accompanying this hope was a recurring feature in the history of computing: a futurological fad (similar cases occurred in the late 1950s over automation and in the mid-1990s with the Internet). Newspaper articles and books with utopian titles such as *The Micro Millennium* predicted that everyday life would be revolutionised by home computers, from household budgets to Christmas card lists (in the event, most machines were either used to play games or were retired to the attic).

Of undoubted greater importance was the spread of computers through offices. Most large companies possessed a mainframe to produce sales statistics for managers or to keep accounts of stocks. Cheap mass-produced computers, particularly 'clones' of IBM's PC (Personal Computer) in the 1990s, meant that industry's 1970s aim of 'one per desk' could be realised. The skills needed for secretarial work changed from shorthand to knowledge of word-processing packages (typing, however, remained unaltered, the PC being locked in to the same keyboard as the typewriter). The same period saw the much-debated convergence of communications and computing. Crucial to this slow change was the development of digital techniques, either for transmission of data (optical cables replaced copper wire in trunk telephone lines, mobile cellphone ownership grew rapidly in the 1990s), controlling where the data moves (computers and automated telephone exchanges), or displaying data (digital TV). The geography of information remained the same, key nodes were still cities such as London or international link-stations such as Goonhilly in Cornwall, but the quantity massively increased. The effect of this intensification on political power remained unclear in the 1990s, although increased capacities of surveillance by means as diverse as closed-circuit TV in city centres and bureaucratic databases suggest the reinforcement of centralised power – an anxiety reflected in law by the Data Protection Acts of 1984, which only applied to information held on computer, and 1998.

British Science and International Collaboration

International cooperation has been of increasing importance to British science, with unexpected outcomes for the development of information technology. A relatively unimportant case was the establishment of the United Nations Educational, Scientific and Cultural Organization (UNESCO), the constitution of which was signed in London on 16 November 1945 by 37 countries and came into force with the twentieth ratification on 4 November 1946 (there were 20 founding member states). Although UNESCO members made a commitment to 'full and equal opportunities for education for all, in the unrestricted pursuit of objective truth and in the free exchange of ideas and knowledge', British involvement was patchy: it faded after geneticist Julian Huxley's brief director-generalship (1946–48) and Britain even left the organisation over budgetary arguments between 1985 and 1991.

Of much greater significance was European collaboration in high-energy physics, which grew from early UNESCO discussions. In 1945 Britain was placed in a very strong position in the physical sciences: the country had been spared the disruption of invasion, if not the devastation of bombing, and the atom bomb had advertised the importance of nuclear physics – a national strength centred initially on Liverpool, Birmingham and Cambridge universities. This position could have been turned into European leadership. However, as with coal and steel organisation, the British were sharply divided over the advantages of European cooperation. High-energy physics was, and is, an extremely expensive field, and the discoveries and prizes went to groups with the highest energy and most pricey particle accelerators. European collaboration therefore opened the possibility that the member states could compete with the United States, and plans circulated from 1949. Politicians and the Royal Society, the body representing the interests of elite scientists, reacted coolly. Many of the older generation of physicists, such as Professor James Chadwick of Liverpool University, preferred for a model a loose organisation that would build on relations with Niels Bohr at Copenhagen, rather than strike new partnerships with French or German institutions. The equivocal British were overtaken by the speed of events on the Continent, and by the time R. A. Butler was persuaded by young Harwell engineers in 1952 to commit Britain to CERN, the European Organisation for Nuclear Research,[13] it was with reluctance and after key decisions had been made. CERN, based at Geneva, built a succession of large accelerators on the French–Swiss border and quickly caught up with the United States, an achievement marked most clearly by the discovery of 'neutral currents' in 1973 and the W and Z bosons (fundamental particles predicted by theory) in 1983.

The scale of projects – such as CERN, where 3,000 people were employed in addition to teams of visiting researchers – was a key problem of post-war science (the combination of large research teams and expensive, state-funded, large-scale machinery has come to be labelled 'big science'). Britain's decision to fund parallel international (CERN) and national facilities in sub-nuclear physics (establishing the Rutherford and Daresbury laboratories, collectively NIRNS, in the 1957 and early 1960s, respectively), severely strained budgets. The policy collapsed with the commissioning of the 300 GeV Super Proton Synchrotron at CERN in the late 1970s, and the two NIRNS laboratories have searched for more practical justifications since – part of a general change in policy direction discussed later.[14] High-energy physics is not the only area where such strains were evident, merely where they appeared earliest. Financial, foreign policy and scientific factors drove similar European collaborations in the areas of nuclear research (Euratom), space research and satellites (ESRO), satellite launchers (ELDO), optical astronomy (ESO), molecular biology (EMBL), fast nuclear reactors (EFR) and fusion research (the Joint European Torus, or JET).[15] Only the latter had headquarters in Britain, but it provides a good illustration of the pressures that drove such change: a combination of threatened cuts to the national programme (inability of any European country to go it alone) and a symbol of warmer relations with France after the abdication of de Gaulle (foreign policy).

The scale of European projects presented technical problems. Computer networks based on packet-switching (where messages are broken up and travel separately and flexibly around a network) had existed since the US military ARPANET and the National Physical Laboratory's experimental network of the late 1960s. Planned primarily as a means of sharing scarce time on expensive supercomputers, the ARPANET grew through the 1970s, adding new civil users and novel functions such as email and newsgroups. Meanwhile, at CERN the headache was how to coordinate the research and administration of many international scientists and administrators. Furthermore, CERN depended on massive computing power so the resources in that area were extensive. In 1990 Tim Berners-Lee, a British second-generation computer scientist (his parents had worked at Ferranti), devised a means of reading linked documents, a concept named the World Wide Web, and 'browser' software for viewing them. Such software made it easy to use computer networks which had previously been the domain of experts, and was responsible for much of the excitement around the Internet in the 1990s.

Internationalisation of British science, partly driven by growth in the expense of science and technology, could also stem more directly from the nature of the science. The environmental sciences provide a good example. In the immediate post-war years the key bodies were national, such as the Nature Conservancy Council set up in 1949. But in the mid-1950s the Cold War need for gravitational, magnetic and electrostatic data-gathering for missile guidance, foreign policy moves to clarify Antarctic land claims, and scientific curiosity set in motion the International Geophysical Year (IGY), which ran between 1957 and 1959. The British contribution, a research base at Halley Bay in the Antarctic, included an aurora camera and a Dobson spectrometer for measuring ozone levels. In 1985 the British Antarctic Survey drew on this, and later its data was used to report a rapid decline in ozone levels (a link between chlorofluorocarbons and depletion of the ozone layer had already been proposed by American scientists). The decline was modelled by computer and then televised as the 'ozone hole', to great alarm (ozone blocks harmful ultra-violet rays). This combination of computers creating visualisable global models illustrating potential environmental catastrophes was new in the post-war period, the first example being the controversial analysis by the Club of Rome, *The Limits to Growth*, in 1972. This plea for sustainability provoked Michael Noble, Minister of State for Trade and Industry, to proclaim that 'the age of the computer model is now with us'.[16] Understanding of the world, economically and ecologically, as well as militarily and scientifically, became mediated by computer techniques.

Recombinant Science: Physics, Chemistry and Biology

There was a shift of emphasis in British research from in the post-war period from the physical to the life sciences. Put crudely, the context of the early decades (traditional industries, the Cold War and state funding) encouraged the physical sciences, whereas that of the later decades (the need for new sources of industrial creativity, the growth in relative importance of medical charities, pharmaceutical companies and biotechnology) aided the latter. However, the twist in the story is that the life sciences have been transformed through the importation of techniques, concepts and attitudes from physics and computing.

Scientists drew on Second World War techniques, contacts and materials to build new research specialities in the 1950s. Radio astronomy provides an exemplary case: physicists such as Bernard Lovell, returning to Manchester University from TRE, began with military-surplus radar equipment and, by investigating mysterious radar echoes noted during wartime, identified them by

1946 with the trails of meteors. A radically new window on astronomical phenomena had opened, one which depended not on light but radio: the techniques of physics and electrical engineering. In Britain teams at Cambridge and Manchester universities grew and specialised: Manchester on large single-dish telescopes, and Cambridge on combinations of smaller telescopes called interferometers. The giant Manchester steerable dish at Jodrell Bank, completed in 1957 and now called the Lovell Telescope, was a triumph of engineering designed by H. C. Husband. It was funded as 'a national spectacle of science', an icon of Great Power prestige.[17] Martin Ryle's team at Cambridge undertook extensive surveys of 'radio sources', and the publication of some of these results in 1961 resulted in a profound controversy between Ryle, who claimed they supported a 'big bang' universe, and the proponents of the 'steady-state' alternative. The steady-state cosmology, in which the universe had no beginning, had been proposed in 1948 by three Cambridge 'cosmologists' (the name had only recent respectability): Herman Bondi, Thomas Gold and Fred Hoyle – soon the best-known scientist in the country. Like most scientific controversies, mere data could not settle the argument which smouldered over the decades, the big bang adherents coming to outnumber the steady-statists. Discoveries of novel phenomena in the 1960s (pulsars at Cambridge, quasars and the cosmic microwave background radiation in the United States) confirmed the vigour of radio astronomy. Optical astronomy in Britain, on the other hand, lurched from crisis to crisis, with the Royal Greenwich Observatory being moved, first to Herstmonceaux Castle in Sussex, then downsized to Cambridge, and finally closed in 1998. Success, however, came with involvement in international collaborations, especially the operation of telescopes at remote sites with clear skies (La Palma in the Canaries, the summit of Mauna Kea in Hawaii, and Australia).

Radio telescopes, especially interferometers, generated masses of data, and their growth from the early 1960s depended on utilising computers. This phenomenon was experienced even earlier in molecular biology, another new speciality. Although molecular biology emerged as a highly interdisciplinary area drawing on the insights of biochemistry, genetics, physics, and the biology of viruses and bacteria, in post-war Britain it was dominated by an aggressively reductionist agenda. During the inter-war years scientists such as the Braggs (father and son) and J. D. Bernal had begun using X-rays to investigate the structure of metals and crystals, a fruitful application of new physics called X-ray crystallography. W.T Astbury at the University of Leeds had used X-ray diffraction patterns to draw conclusions about the shape of protein molecules. Interest in the structure of large molecules was also heightened by the industrialised production of penicillin during the Second World War. In Cambridge in 1953 an American with ideas drawn from studies of phages (viruses of bacteria), James Watson, and Francis Crick, a British physicist, constructed from Rosalind Franklin and others' data the 'double helix' structure of Deoxyribonucleic Acid (DNA). DNA was known in 1944 to be the 'transforming principle', the hereditary substance in bacteria. The significance of the double helix was that it enabled claims to be made as to how the genetic 'information' of all organisms was stored at the molecular level ('the genetic code') and opened questions about how it was subsequently expressed in the proteins of cells.

The reduction of biology to matters of molecular structure was the credo of the MRC Laboratory of Molecular Biology at Cambridge. Protein-nucleic acid relations were touted successfully as a new foundation for biology. Francis Crick summarised the theory in an influential lecture to the Society of Experimental Biologists in 1957, articulating the 'Central Dogma' whereby information passes unidirectionally from nucleic acids (DNA and RNA) to protein. The concentration on structure, a rich source of British Nobel prizes, was institutionalised as research programmes in the 1950s and 1960s: Dorothy Hodgkin at Oxford on vitamin B_{12}, John Kendrew and Max Perutz at the Cambridge MRC laboratory on protein structures (myoglobin and haemoglobin respectively), and David Phillips at the Royal Institution on enzymes (lysozyme). Crucially the path taken by these scientists, from X-ray diffraction picture to structure, depended on access to fast calculation: electronic computers being essential by the late 1950s. It is impossible to separate the bio-medical sciences of the late twentieth century from computing, either as data processors (e.g. molecular structure), databases (e.g. the Human Genome Project) or as controlling imaging technologies (e.g. Nuclear Magnetic Resonance, or Sir Godfrey Hounsfield's CAT scan techniques developed at EMI which revolutionised non-invasive medical imaging and diagnosis after its introduction in the early 1970s), or even as language (e.g. 'code').

Molecular biology in the 1970s and 1980s revealed that the translation from DNA to proteins and cells was highly complex. Biochemical understandings of the cell had more direct application. Indeed chemistry in general has had a more pervasive, but less high-profile, influence on everyday post-war life than molecular biology. The preponderance of industrial research relied on armies of chemists: of 17,970 scientists in industry in 1956, 12,393 were chemists.[18] Significant advances were made in drug design, for example James Black's beta blockers, which bolstered Britain's already strong position in pharmaceuticals, and in inorganic chemistry, where work such as that of Sir Geoffrey Wilkinson, another member of the wartime atomic bomb diaspora, revitalised the subject. His ferrocene, an organo-metallic molecule with a surprising 'sandwich' structure, became a profitable fuel additive.

Commercial applications of biological research were deeply significant for agriculture and medicine, but often built on existing techniques. For example, plant breeding contributed, with new chemical fertilisers and pesticides, to a post-war doubling of yield of wheat in England and Wales, before the importation of the techniques of molecular biology.[19] Likewise, biotechnology had roots that went back a century in the brewing industry and in utopian writings, such as those of Patrick Geddes.[20] Some biotechnological innovations, such as 'Mycoprotein' foods launched in 1985, stemmed from these traditions, although the fermenting technology came from the ICI chemical combine, and the idealism from the Methodist Lord Rank of bread-makers Rank Hovis Macdougall. British Petroleum also attempted a similar project – the 1960s 'overpopulation' debate had started the rash of interest in alternative foodstuffs – and the British location of such schemes can be explained by the considerable accumulation of microbial fermentation expertise at sites such as Porton Down, the biological warfare laboratory. However, the intense interest that surrounded biotechnology from the 1970s depended on the invention of simple but effective techniques of genetic manipulation, in particular recombinant DNA (using viruses to place genes in other 'transgenic' organisms where that gene will be expressed, thus allowing, for example, pesticide-resistant crops or insulin-producing bacteria) and hybridoma techniques for monoclonal antibodies, devised by George Kohler and César Milstein at the Cambridge MRC laboratory in 1975 and controversially not patented. Biotech companies sprung up first in the United States in the early 1970s. Celltech, the first British start-up, was formed in 1980 with the National Enterprise Board as the major shareholder. In common with many other biotech firms, development was slow – Celltech had yet to put a drug on the market by 1999.

Science's Discontents

While science stabilised as a profession, which it had been by the late nineteenth century, and was seen as a national state-funded project (like the National Health Service), it was largely uncriticised from the outside. (The late-nineteenth-century science versus religion conflict was an artefact of science's birth as a profession, and 1930s critiques of science, such as the Marxist Bernal's, came from within.) Yet by the late 1960s there was evidence of a crisis in public trust in science. For example, the worst nuclear accident in British history occurred at Windscale in October 1957 when an air-cooled nuclear pile had caught fire, 20,000 curies of the radioactive isotope iodine-131 had been released, and two million litres of contaminated milk from local cows had to be poured away.[21] Only a few months earlier the *New Scientist* could report that 'prospective holiday-makers on the West Coast will note with joy the increase in temperature of the Bristol Channel expected by the ... proposed [nuclear] power station at Hinkley Point, West Somerset'.[22] What is remarkable is that this sanguine attitude was largely unaffected by the 1957 fire. But the 1973 'catastrophic blowback' accident at the same site, when ruthenium-106 contaminated 35 workers, attracted for greater contemporary attention (and this was a decade before Chernobyl). We have also seen that the first two civil reactor programmes were the outcome of uncontentions, private debate, whereas the third, in the 1970s, was heated and public. Likewise, industrial, health or environmental controversies in which science has been a focus have become a recurring feature since the 1960s: thalidomide (1960–1), chloracne from the Coalite chemical accident (1968), the Torrey Canyon oil spill (1969), the Flixborough explosion (1974), bovine somatotropin (BST, 1970s), salmonella in eggs (1980s), Bovine Spongiform Encephalopathy (BSE, 1980s and 1990s), cloning (the Roslin Institute's 'Dolly' the sheep, 1997) and genetically modified foods (1970s and again in 1999).

A second area of discontent can be located in a perceived shift from science as a public good to science as a commercially-driven enterprise. This perception was encouraged by key government initiatives. First, the Rothschild Report of 1971 recommended that public-funded, applied R&D should be based on the customer-contractor principle (the separation of the commissioning of research from its delivery). Second, the major privatisation programme during Prime Minister Margaret Thatcher's administration in the 1980s, beginning with radio-isotopes factory Amersham International, radically shifted the political context of public-funded science. Both government and university laboratories were under intense pressure to justify expenditure. (The irony of Thatcher, a chemistry graduate, threatening cuts in academic science, was widely noted at the time.) Finally, William Waldegrave's 1993 White Paper, *Realising Our Potential*, incorporated in the research councils' missions the duty to meet the needs of users of research, specifically UK industry. Such initiatives provoked often fierce criticism and a sense of crisis within science, which, when combined with the threat of overall budget cuts, spawned pressure groups such as Save British Science (formed in 1986). Underpinning the policy shifts since 1971 were two largely untested assumptions: that national economic performance was directly related to R&D, and that Britain, while good at discovery, was poor at commercial application. The evidence for either assumption is sparse.

Myths and Realities of British Science and Technology

In 1959 novelist and failed chemist C. P. Snow's Rede Lecture, 'The Two Cultures and the Scientific Revolution', was published. Its simplistic dichotomy of undervalued scientists and an over-powerful arts-educated elite has framed much discussion of science in the media, but is unreliable history. British science has had a prestigious place in official images of British culture, from the Dome of Discovery centrepiece of the 1951 Festival of Britain, to its millennium counterpart. Educational reforms have favoured science and technology, from Imperial College (1953), through the doubling of higher education that followed the Robbins Report of the 1960s, to science and mathematics confirmed as 'core subjects' in the school National Curriculum. As science's budget increased in the post-war period, its relations with the media became ever-more important. British science has not had trouble getting reported, but, in common with all other institutions, it has not been able to control how it is reported and understood. One response has been the encouragement of a sympathetic popular press. The *New Scientist* was established in 1956 with the main mission to explain nuclear science 'accurately' to the public, an institutionalisation of a pre-existing symbiotic relationship between journalists and scientists. The *New Scientist* succeeded because there was an expanding marketplace for science graduates (and advertising aimed at them). Bodies with a critique of science, such as the British Society for Social Responsibility in Science (BSSRS), launched in 1969, developed equally sophisticated media strategies: public awareness of harmful aspects of bovine somatotropin – the first modern food-scare – was shaped by the BSSRS's succinct presentation of technical issues to a print media which was aiming to target new female customers.

The growing discontent with science since the 1960s was *part and parcel* of science's increasing links with the media, and not a reflection of poor media presence or presentation. Britain's elite scientific organisations drew an opposite conclusion, arguing that scientific facts were not portrayed by the media with enough clarity, nor was science's importance properly appreciated. Their institutional response, collectively named Public Understanding of Science (PUS), was launched by the Royal Society, British Association and Royal Institution in the mid-1980s and handsomely supported by research councils and the Wellcome Trust in the 1990s. PUS did not address the structural problem at the heart of post-war science's relations with the media, public and government, which the high-profile case of BSE illustrates. 'Mad cow disease', or BSE, was first identified in British cattle in 1986. Ten years later 160,000 cattle had died, and a mathematical model indicated that a further 700,000 infected cows had passed into the human food supply. In 1996 a new variant of Creutzfeldt-Jakob disease in humans (nvCJD) was confirmed, prompting speculation that it was a consequence of eating BSE-contaminated food. Cattle were slaughtered, and beef banned from export and use in school dinners. Scientific opinion in the mid-1990s diverged sharply, from Leeds microbiologist Professor Richard Lacey who predicted a massive epidemic, to other scientists who, while being more cautious, also disagreed with each other. The intense scrutiny of this episode opens a window on science–government–public relations. While it was the case that politicians and scientist-advisers fundamentally misunderstood each other (particularly as to what constituted 'low risk'), the key problem was that scientists were expected to report clear, stable facts. In reality science is a process whereby facts are only slowly made and often remain provisional.

Notes

The author would like to thank Jeff Hughes, John Pickstone, Kathryn Packer and David Edgerton for reading and criticising an earlier draft of this chapter.

1   Sources are as follows: 1925/30 and 1964/5: David Edgerton, *Science, Technology and the British Industrial 'Decline'*, Cambridge University Press, 1996, pp. 38–9, the 1925 government-funded figure excludes money spent through the universities; 1978: OECD *Science and Technology Indicators: Resources Devoted to R&D* OECD, 1984, p. 75; 1996: UK Government, Office of Science and Technology, *SET Statistics*, 3rd ed., 1998.

2   Philip Gummett, *Scientists in Whitehall*, Manchester University Press, 1980, p. 38.

3   Theodore M. Porter, *Trust in Numbers*, Princeton University Press, 1995, p. 28.

4   Michael Sanderson, *The Universities and British Industry, 1850–1970*, Routledge and Kegan Paul, 1972.

5   PRO DEFE 10/40 Minutes, DRPC, 1 March 1955. Discussed in Jon Agar and Brian Balmer, 'British Scientists and the Cold War: The Defence Research Policy Committee and Information Networks, 1947–1963', *Historical Studies in the Physical and Biological Sciences* 28 (1998): 209–52.

6   See Margaret Gowing, *Independence and Deterrence, Britain and Atomic Energy, 1945–52*, 2 vols, Macmillan, 1974, and David Vincent, *The Culture of Secrecy, Britain 1832–1998*, Cambridge University Press, 1998, pp. 194–202.

7   Adapted from Robert Bud and Philip Gummett (eds), *Cold War, Hot Science: Applied Research in the UK's Defence Research Laboratories, 1945–90*, Harwood Academic Press, 1999.

8   Roger Williams, *The Nuclear Power Decisions: British Policies, 1953–78*, Croom Helm, 1980.
9   See Agar and Balmer, 'British Scientists'.
10 PRO DEFE 10/40. Minutes, DRPC, DRP/M(55)7, 24 May 1955.
11 For the role of the Ministry of Supply see David Edgerton, 'Whatever Happened to the British Warfare State? The Ministry of Supply, 1945–1951', in H. Mercer, N. Rollings and J. Tomlinson (eds), *Labour Governments and Private Industry*, Edinburgh University Press, 1992, pp. 91–116.
12 Paul Edwards, *The Closed World: Computers and the Politics of Discourse in Cold War America*, MIT Press, 1996. Jon Agar and Jeff Hughes, 'Open Systems in a Closed World: Ground and Airborne Radar in the UK, 1945–1990', in Bud and Gummett, *Cold War, Hot Science*, pp. 219–50.
13 Now the European Laboratory for Particle Physics. See A. Hermann, J. Krige, U. Mersits and D. Pestre (eds), *History of CERN*, 2 vols, North-Holland Physics Publishing, 1987.
14 John Krige, 'The Politics of European Scientific Collaboration', in John Krige and Dominique Pestre (eds), *Science in the Twentieth Century*, Harwood Academic Press, 1997, pp. 897–918.
15 Acronyms stand for: European Space Research Organization, European Launcher Development Organization, European Southern Observatory, European Molecular Biology Organization and the European Fast Reactor programme.
16 News item reported in *Nature* 329 (1972): 361.
17 Jon Agar, *Science and Spectacle: The Work of Jodrell Bank in Post-war British Culture*, Harwood Academic Press, 1998.
18 PRO CAB 139/715. Third international survey on the demand for and supply of scientific and technical personnel.
19 Agricultural Research Council, *Agricultural Research 1931–1981*, ARC, 1981.
20 Robert Bud, *The Uses of Life: A History of Biotechnology*, Cambridge University Press, 1993.
21 Lorna Arnold, *Windscale 1957: Anatomy of a Nuclear Accident*, Macmillan, 1992, provides a detailed account of the fire and its consequences.
22 *New Scientist*, 28 February 1957, p. 44.

Further Reading

Agar, Jon, *Science and Spectacle: the Work of Jodrell Bank in Post-war British Culture*, Harwood Academic Press, 1998.

Bud, Robert and Gummett, Philip (eds), *Cold War, Hot Science: Applied Research in the UK's Defence Research Laboratories, 1945–90*, Harwood Academic Press, 1999.

Cathcart, Brian, *Test of Greatness: Britain's Struggle for the Atom Bomb*, J. Murray, 1994.

Edgerton, David, *Science, Technology and the British Industrial 'Decline', 1870–1970*, Cambridge University Press, 1996.

Edgerton, David, 'British Industrial R&D, 1900–1970', *Journal of European Economic History*, 23 (1994): 49–68.

Gowing, Margaret, *Independence and Deterrence, Britain and Atomic Energy, 1945–52*, 2 vols, Macmillan, 1974.

Horrocks, Sally M., 'Enthusiasm Constrained? British Industrial R&D and the Transition from War to Peace, 1942–51', *Business History*, 41 (1999): 42–63.

Krige, John and Pestre, Dominique (eds), *Science in the Twentieth Century*, Harwood Academic Press, 1997.

Sanderson, Michael, *The Universities and British Industry, 1850–1970*, Routledge and Kegan Paul, 1972.

Wilkie, Tom, *British Science and Politics since 1945*, Blackwell, 1991.

Williams, Roger, *The Nuclear Power Decisions: British Policies, 1953–78*, Croom Helm, 1980.

Chronology

1945   Atomic bombing of Hiroshima and Nagasaki. UNESCO constitution signed in London.

1946   Atomic Energy Act gives Ministry of Supply responsibility for nuclear programme.

1947   Clement Attlee takes decision to build British atomic bomb.

1948   First stored-program computer at Manchester University.

1952   Chancellor of the Exchequer, R. A. Butler, persuaded to commit Britain to CERN.

1953   Watson and Crick propose double-helix structure of DNA. Expansion of higher education in technology announced.

1954   Atomic Energy Act sets up UK Atomic Energy Authority.

1955   Civil nuclear programme formally started.

1956   Calder Hall nuclear power station operational. *New Scientist* first published.

1957   Jodrell Bank large steerable radio telescope completed, a few months before first Soviet satellite Sputnik. Interferon discovered by Alick Isaacs. Windscale fire. Duncan Sandys's defence White Paper confirms reliance on high technology. National Institute for Research in Nuclear Science (NIRNS) created. International Geophysical Year begins. Francis Crick articulates the Central Dogma of molecular biology.

1958   John Kendrew and Max Perutz publish three-dimensional structures of proteins.

1959   First Minister for Science appointed.

1960   Thalidomide shown to cause birth defects.

1963   Ariel I, the first British satellite, launched.

1964   Report of Committee of Enquiry into the Organisation of Civil Science (Trend Report) published.

1965   Research councils reorganised following Trend report: the Department of Scientific and Industrial Research (DSIR) wound up, and the Science Research Council (SRC), Natural Environment Research Council (NERC) and Social Science Research Council (SSRC) created. David Phillips publishes first three-dimensional structure of an enzyme; second programme of nuclear power stations decided.

1966   'Brain drain' scare.

1968   ICL formed.

1969   British Society for Social Responsibility in Science launched.

1971   Rothschild Report on *The Organisation and Management of Government R&D*. BNFL formed.

1972   White Paper *Framework for Government R&D* published in response to Rothschild.

1975   George Kohler and César Milstein's hybridoma technique for producing monoclonal antibodies.

1979   Sir Godfrey Hounsfield wins Nobel Prize for Physiology or Medicine for Computer Assisted Tomography (CAT).
1980   Spinks report on biotechnology published.
1983   European fast breeder programme begun by Britain, France, and Germany. Social Science Research Council became ESRC.
1984   Data Protection Act.
1985   British scientists report drop in Antarctic ozone levels. Mycoprotein foods launched.
1986   Save British Science launched. BSE discovered in British cattle.
1990   Defence Research Agency created. Tim Berners-Lee at CERN outlines World Wide Web.
1993   White Paper *Realising Our Potential* published.
1994   Research councils reorganised: Biotechnology and Biological Sciences Research Council (BBSRC), Engineering and Physical Sciences Research Council (EPSRC) and Particle Physics and Astronomy Research Council (PPARC). Council for the Central Laboratory of the Research Councils created. MRC, ESRC and NERC remain.
1995   Meteorological Office produces computer model of global warming; Defence Evaluation and Research Agency (DERA) formed.
1996   Confirmation of new variant CJD (n.v. CJD).
1997   Roslin Institute annnounces 'Dolly', a cloned sheep.
2001   Publication of detailed sequencing and mapping papers of the international Human Genome Project (11 Feb.). Chromosomes 1, 6, 9, 10, 13, 20, 22 and X were sequenced at the Sanger Institute (one of 16 institutions that formed the HGP Consortium).

19 Pressure Groups

Wyn Grant

The history of pressure groups in Britain since the Second World War may be divided into four main phases. These phases should be seen as ideal typical models of the relationship between groups and government rather than as precise and mutually exclusive descriptions. As will be noted below, there has been considerable continuity in the relationship between groups and government over the post-war period. Nevertheless, there have been significant changes as well and the phases model offers a means of highlighting them.

The period from 1945 to 1960 was characterised by a limited number of sectional groups enjoying a close working relationship with government. There were cause groups, a few of which enjoyed a dialogue with government, but there were far fewer of them than at the end of the century. The emphasis during the period was on executive-focused, low-profile pressure-group activity with a considerable emphasis on informal personal links among the 'Establishment'. The period from the 'Brighton Revolution' in 1960 to the Thatcher government in 1979 was characterised by the growing importance of tripartite relationships between government, the Confederation of British Industry (CBI) and Trades Union Congress (TUC). Relations were still executive-focused, but towards the end of the period, Parliament and the media started to become more important. The 1970s saw the emergence of a new generation of environmental groups which were to be important in later phases.

The 1980s saw a move away from tripartism with the CBI and the TUC become much less important. The Thatcher government expressed a general distaste for 'vested interests', although routine consultations between pressure groups and civil servants continued. However, because the established executive channels were less reliable, pressure groups started to operate in a number of arenas, including Parliament, the media and the courts. Towards the end of the decade, after the decision to create the single market and the greater use of qualified majority voting in the European Community, operating at the European level became much more important.

The 1990s saw some revival of more traditional relations between government and pressure groups. In particular, under Michael Heseltine, the Conservative government revitalised government interest in the structure of business associations. The importance of activity at the EU level continued to grow. However, what characterised this decade more than anything else was the continued growth of 'single-issue' pressure groups and their increased reliance on tactics of 'direct action'.

Patterns of Continuity

What persisted throughout the second half of the twentieth century was a belief that pressure groups were a legitimate adjunct of the machinery of government, provided that they accepted the prevailing 'rules of the game'. During the tripartite period, a limited number of pressure groups were elevated to the status of partners of government in running the economy. The groups were not up to the task and the privileges accorded to a few groups raised questions of fairness. However, once tripartism waned, the traditional practices of group consultation continued. What has proved more of a challenge to the system is the growth of single-issue pressure groups using unorthodox tactics. The general predisposition of civil servants has been to consult extensively with pressure groups. Except in a very few cases, they are under no legal obligation to do so (as is the case in relation to American trade policy), but the prevailing norms encourage consultation, as a civil servant explained in evidence to the House of Lords:

> We consult on any proposal those organisations which seem to be representative of the subject or interests under discussion. It is a subjective judgement on every occasion but we work on the basis that we would sooner over-consult rather than under-consult because you cannot from our position judge the importance on occasions of a particular proposal to a particular group of people. (Quoted in Coates, 1984, pp. 146–7)

Without reviving arguments about the extent to which the Second World War was a watershed in governing practice, it is evident that the expansion of public activity in a number of different areas drew government into relationships with a new set of interests. The formation and operation of the National Health Service, for example, was seen to require the development of a close consultative relationship with a range of organisations representing medical opinion. The war had involved the trade unions closely in the mobilisation of the labour force, and their continued cooperation was required to run a full-employment economy which also sought to restrain inflation.

However, given that Britain had at this time a strong executive, unconstrained by legislative challenge and operating in what was effectively a unitary state, why did not goverments simply go ahead and impose their policies regardless of the views of pressure groups? One reason was that, despite the proliferation of specialist groupings within the civil service, the government lacked expertise on a range of matters. Thus, when the Home Office was establishing a fire brigades division just before the war, a civil servant plaintively noted in an internal memorandum, 'there is very little experience in the Home Office to build on' (HO 45/18108/694142). Without consultation, there was a danger of devising policies that were impractical or ineffective.

The government built up its own information sources over time, in particular through the much-used device of the advisory committee, but many policies required the active cooperation, or at the least the acquiesence, of affected interests. The disruptive effects on a recovering economy of the use of the strike weapon by the trade unions led successive governments to seek to co-opt them into the management of the economy. The emphasis on maximising food production after the war was thought to require the active cooperation of the representative organisations of farmers. Consultation thus drew those consulted into the embrace of government. As Sir Norman Kipping, the long-serving director of the Federation of British Industries (FBI), put it: 'Consultation entails the probability of "involvement" on the part of the consultee. If he recommends or consents to a certain policy or course of action, he cannot then contract out of its consequences. Those who call for participation in decision-making become parties to the decisions they accept. (Kipping, 1972, p. 30)'.

There are two contrasting views about what this close relationship between interests and government meant for the British polity and economy. One view, argued by J. P. Nettl in a seminal article, was that the British consensus was a social institution which emasculated groups 'while preserving their outward shell of autonomy and independence' (Nettl, 1965, p. 22). He argued that 'the flow of influence is greater from government towards organised industry than from industry inwards' (ibid., p. 31). This perspective sees the executive manipulating groups in the 'public interest' so that groups that had the appearance of autonomy became the 'chosen instruments' (a much-used phrase in the earlier post-war period) of government policy.

An alternative argument put forward by Mancur Olson is that 'with age British society has acquired so many strong organisations and collusions that it suffers from an institutional sclerosis that slows its adaptation to changing circumstances and technologies' (Olson, 1982, p. 78). This, in Olson's view, helps to explain Britain's relatively slow rate of post-war growth. There is something in Olson's view. The Victorian or early-twentieth-century origins of Britain's system of employers' associations and trade unions left Britain with a structure of producer organisations that, in Olson's terms, was 'narrow rather than encompassing' (ibid., p. 78). In other words, they were good at defending the immediate short-term interests of their members but not at taking a longer-term view, which might have led them to consider that collusion between employers and unions to protect outdated technology and maintain traditional working practices was ultimately self-defeating (the textile and shipbuilding industries provide many examples). Nor were they capable of engaging in any dialogue about removing obstacles to economic growth, which is not surprising, as their very purpose was to maintain those obstacles in order to protect the status quo for their members. They were thus incapable of undertaking the roles of promoting research, innovation and training so successfully carried out by their German counterparts.

At least until 1960, however, government did not envisage them performing such a role. It was therefore content to enjoy a collusive relationship with producer and professional associations which tended to reinforce an equilibrium established by the post-war settlement (e.g. the 1947 Agriculture Act, or the balance between public medicine and some continued private provision embodied in the National Health Service). This process was assisted by the emergence of a leadership in the pressure groups that was capable of taking a 'wider view', i.e. able to recognise that the relationship with government was based on what Kipping termed 'a form of partnership, with some concessions on either side...establishing a mutually acceptable compromise' (Kipping, 1972, p. 30).

1945 to 1960: Sectional Groups Work Alongside 'the Establishment'

Although government (and the Bank of England) had been quite significantly involved in the reorganisation of industry in the 1930s, the Second World War and its aftermath was a watershed in government–business relations. This change was exemplified by the extensive nationalisation programme of the Attlee government. Although the extensive apparatus of wartime physical controls was eventually dismantled, the adherence to the Treasury's interpretation of Keynesianism involved government in attempts to engage in aggregate economic management, while controls remained in place to influence the regional distibution of industry.

These developments drew government into a closer relationship with the organised interests representing business. According to Kipping's account, this relationship was closer with Labour than the Conservatives, in part because the Conservatives did not wish to be identified too closely with 'big business', and in part because they placed greater reliance on informal advisers they had chosen themselves. What was important to the relationship was that the FBI 'strongly reflected [Kipping's] own personality and values' (Blank, 1973, p. 47). From the author's recollection, the FBI (later the CBI) headquarters in Tothill Street resembled an outstation of the civil service, even to the rather dreary green paint in the corridors. This was no accident, as '[Kipping] resembled much more closely the civil servants with whom he preferred to deal than either the industrialists or politicians whose interests they represented. Kipping's image of himself was always that of a "Permanent Secretary", working behind each successive FBI President in a 'National Ministry of Industry' (Blank, 1973, p. 48).

Kipping is important not just because he was influential, but also because he was emblematic of a type of 'Establishment' figure who acted as a broker between government and organised interests. He had served in the Ministry of Production during the war and then as an under-secretary in the Board of Trade. His memoirs open with a conversation at his club lunch table which is illuminating in itself as the London clubs served, in those more leisurely times, as a meeting ground for traditional social elites, civil servants, and the 'new men' from minor public-school or even provincial state-school backgrounds who had been brought in to renew and reinforce the governing elite during the war. Kipping made it clear that he preferred informal consultation, albeit re-inforced by formal methods. In one sentence he captures the operation of rela-tionships between government and pressure groups in the earlier post-war period: 'Informal consultation is the private and confidential sounding of the opinion of trusted individuals' (Kipping, 1972, p. 32). The flavour of Kipping's elite status is captured by a conversation he records in his obscure but interest-ing book, *The Suez Contractors*:

> 'Could you come over, Norman [Kipping] straight away?' [Permanent Secretary at War Office]
>
> 'Well, I suppose I could, George. What's it in aid of?'
>
> 'We need a bit of advice from someone on your side of life. We know you are all a lot of sharks, but we happen to know you, so be a good chap and come over.' (ibid., 1969, p. 13)

The relationship was, of course, not without its strains. The 'backwoodsmen' in the CBI had to be managed, but 'The progressives almost always won' (ibid., 1972, p. 48). Nationalisation was a tricky issue for the FBI. Their strategy was to ritualistically restate opposition to the goal and then to engage in detailed work on particular clauses of the bills. The FBI resolutely refused to break off relations with the government over the controversial issue of steel nationalisa-tion, Kipping maintaining that withdrawing cooperation from the government would not be in the national interest, while propaganda could be left to 'chosen instruments' such as Aims of Industry, which were very much kept at arm's length (Blank, 1973, p. 102).

The expansion of government activities also led government into closer and more intensive relationships with local authorities, the medical profession, those concerned with education, and farmers. In each case, it was generally possible to find 'responsible' leaders who were willing to engage in a continuing dia-logue with government and to discipline any 'irresponsible' elements in their ranks. The leadership of the British Medical Association (BMA) tended to be dominated by senior members of the profession with private practices, often in London, while the weathier arable farmers from southern and eastern England predominated in the National Farmers' Union (NFU).

The relationship with the farmers was a particularly close one, whether or not it can be classified as 'corporatist' (Smith, 1989). The annual price review process generally produced a relatively good deal for farmers, who acquired a new prosperity after the inter-war depression in agriculture. The government generally seemed to be supine in face of demands from the farmers, recognising that their demands were excessive, but calculating that the political costs of resisting them were too high. This is effectively illustrated by an extract from the Cabinet minutes discussing the outcome of the annual review process in 1955 which boosted producers' incomes by the substantial sum (at the time) of £28 million:

> The practice of seeking an agreed settlement with the farmers' representatives was costly to the Exchequer. This method of conducting the negotiations at the annual review had the result that the farmers were able to extract from the Government

more than they were justified in obtaining on economic grounds alone. This situation would continue until the Government showed that they were prepared, on a suitable occasion, to impose a settlement. There was, however, general agreement that this was not a suitable occasion on which to take a stand. This could be done better earlier in the lifetime of a Parliament. (Cabinet Minutes 22 (55)), p. 5)

These close relationships with a number of producer and professional groups were not generally intruded on by cause groups. However, those groups which were able to mobilise influential individuals did intrude on the consciousness of government. For example, the stance of the Howard League on Penal Reform was discussed by the Cabinet in 1955 in the context of the debate about the future of capital punishment.

The Howard League was a classic 'insider' cause organization whose influence was challenged in later decades by new and more radical groups. It enjoyed a close working relationship with the Home Office. Many of its members were middle-class professionals involved in the operation of the penal system who could thus claim to have some relevant specialist expertise. At least two-thirds of its members lived in the South-east, most of these in London itself (Ryan, 1978, p. 3); so it was well placed to network with a largely metropolitan elite. It 'traditionally functioned as a small, well-connected, London-based elite with no democratic structures' (ibid., p. 86). Its low-profile insider activities were very different from those of the high-profile mass membership groups which developed from the 1970s onwards.

Towards the end of the 1950s this largely invisible world of pressure groups began to be systematically studied by political scientists for the first time (Finer, 1958; Stewart, 1958; Eckstein, 1960). The fact that the Establishment world of often informal contacts between like-minded civil servants and pressure-group officials was at last being brought into the open signalled the beginning of a change in the relationship itself.

The Development of Tripartism

As is often the case, fundamental reappraisals of policy take place during the lifetime of a government (1972 and 1976 are other examples), rather than immediately following an election. During the late 1950s there was growing concern about Britain's poor economic performance compared with the achievements of France and Germany. In November 1960 Britain's economic establishment (industrialists, bankers, nationalised industry chiefs, civil servants) decamped to Brighton for a conference organised by the FBI on 'the next five years'. The so-called 'Brighton Revolution' produced a commitment to economic planning as a means of achieving higher and more sustainable economic growth.

There was an enthusiasm for the French model of indicative planning, which was misunderstood in Britain as it was seen as being less interventionist than in fact it was at the time (Leruez, 1975). The practical consequence of Brighton was a new enthusiasm for 'tripartite' management of the economy by government, business and the unions. This was exemplified by the formation of the National Economic Development Council with a tripartite constitution in 1962. In order to facilitate tripartite consultation, three separate buisness organisations were merged into the CBI with government encouragement in 1965. The government also tried to do something about the incoherent structure of sectoral business associations by loaning a high-flying young civil servant as secretary to the Devlin Commission on Industrial Representation, which reported in 1972, but to little effect.

The real driving force between tripartism was, however, the increasing reliance on incomes policies by both Conservative and Labour governments for much of the 1960s and 1970s. The Heath government said it would have nothing to do with such interventionist policies, but reverted to them in 1972 and introduced a highly interventionist Industry Act in the same year for good measure. By the end of the 1970s, the Queen's Speech contained references to the government's intention to cooperate in the management of economic policy with the CBI and the TUC.

An effective incomes policy depended on the cooperation of the unions and the employers, particularly the former. If groups of workers breached the norm, then the policy collapsed. Hence, the willingness of government to offer permanent legislative concessions in return for short-term pay restraint, e.g. in 1976 the Chancellor offered a package of conditional tax relief in return for TUC adherence to a pay guideline.

The problem was that neither the unions nor the employers were set up to deliver on any tripartite agreements. They could not control their own memberships. The union movement was incoherently structured in that there were often several unions in any one industry and certainly in any one plant. Local stoppages were often called by militant shop stewards who had effective control over the organisation of work on the shop floor. For its part, the CBI delivered a voluntary prices restraint initiative by its members to the Heath government in 1971–2. However, despite the influence of a group of revisionist business leaders in the organisation who constituted a 'self-appointed vanguard of business' (Boswell and Peters, 1997, p. 41), strains within the organisation grew. After 1974, realignments of business opinion became more apparent and businessmen started to speak out for more liberationist policies (ibid., p. 123). As it happened, in alliance with the predominant centrist majority in the Labour Cabinet, the CBI had a particularly influential period under the 1974–9 Labour government.

The principal deficiency of tripartite management of the economy was that it did not work. It proved impossible to turn the square of full employment policies, an attachment to free collective bargaining, unions that were simultaneously strong and weak and exogenous economic shocks into a circle of industrial peace and ecomomic prosperity. Even if it had worked, however, it is questionable whether it would have been desirable. It privileged a limited group of producer interests over other sectional interests (notably small businesses) and consumers.

While the tripartite interests were 'sitting round the table and hammering it into the ground', as satirists put it at the time, another set of developments were taking place which were to prove of long-term significance for the world of pressure groups. The early 1970s had seen an upsurge of interest in the 'environment', which may broadly be interpreted as an awareness of the interaction between different pollution problems within a complete ecosystem. The Heath government had responded to the new mood by creating a giant Department (DOE) of the Environment (DoE) in 1970, although most of its tasks were not environmental in nature.

There had been in existence for many years 'amenity' organisations such as the Council for the Preservation of Rural England and the Civic Trust which sought to conserve landscapes and townscapes. They were insider groups who often operated in terms of a particular vision of 'Englishness'. Local amenity societies were often a means of defending middle-class values and protecting property prices by opposing any developments which might 'lower the tone' of the neighbourhood.

The early 1970s saw the formation of new environmental groups which had a much broader vision, a more comprehensive agenda, and were characterised by a willingness to use unorthodox tactics such as staging stunts which attracted media attention. The two most important of these organisations were Friends of the Earth (founded in Britain in 1971) and Greenpeace (founded in the USA in 1972). Their memberships were initially small (Friends of the Earth had only 1,000 members in 1971) and did not grow rapidly until the late 1980s. However, their formation signalled the emergence of a new type of politics centred around collective consumption rather than production (Grant, 1999).

The formation of these environmental groups was paralleled by the establishment of other new cause groups which were less inclined to engage in a conventional relationship with civil servants but resorted to tactics such as leaking government documents to embarrass the government, e.g. the Child Poverty Action Group, formed in 1965. A number of underlying forces sustained the formation and development of these groups, including the radicalism of the late 1960s; disillusionment with the Labour government of 1964–70, and with political parties more generally; and the development of a more educated and questioning population with graduates in the social sciences available to staff the new groups.

The Labour government's loss of its majority during the lifetime of the Parliament elected in 1974 and its subsequent pact with the Liberals meant that pressure groups started to pay more attention to Parliament. The Liberals exerted less influence on the government than their successors in 1997 did through a joint Cabinet committee. Nevertheless, important questions were decided by votes in Parliament (Grant, 1981). Also, contacts between pressure groups and the government were dominated by those managed through routine relationships with civil servants. These contacts persisted in the next decade, even though the failed tripartite experiment was brought to an end.

The Thatcher Decade

As far as Mrs Thatcher was concerned, the tripartism of Heath's government 'proposed and almost implemented the most radical form of socialism ever contemplated by an elected British government' (Thatcher, 1993, p. 7). Mrs Thatcher's distaste for vested interests extended beyond the trade unions and tripartite forms of economic management. In a television interview in 1984, she stated, 'I can give you a checklist now of the way in which we have tackled vested interest' (*Weekend World*, p. 2/6). As well as the trade unions, the list included opticians and the Stock Exchange.

As far as the trade unions were concerned, contacts with the Prime Minister virtually came to an end after 1979. A meeting between Mrs Thatcher and the TUC General Council in June 1980 at their request could not be described as a meeting of minds, with Mrs Thatcher, by her account, delivering a lecture to the TUC on competitiveness. She records, 'I got nowhere ... it was hopeless trying to change the attitudes of most trade union leaders, who were socialist politicians first, second and third' (Thatcher, 1993, p. 100).

Ministerial contacts continued in the early years of the government through Employment Minister John Prior, but this reflected a tactical decision by Mrs Thatcher:

> There was still the feeling in the country...that Britain could not be governed without the tacit consent of the trade unions. It was to be some years before that changed. If we had signalled the wholesale reform of the unions over and against their opposition at the outset, it would have undermined confidence in the Government and perhaps even provoked a challenge we were not yet ready to face. Jim was the badge of our reasonableness. (Thatcher, 1993, p. 28)

It is therefore not surprising that an analysis by Mitchell (1987) shows that the perceived effectiveness of such contacts from the trade union standpoint fell away sharply.

Matters were not much better for the CBI. As CBI members became increasingly concerned about the fall in industrial output in 1980, in large part the result of an appreciating exchange rate, the organisation's new Director-General, Sir Terence Beckett, promised the CBI Conference a 'bare-knuckle fight' with the government. When the President and the Director-General went to Downing Street the day after the conference ended, Mrs Thatcher recalled, 'I am glad to say the knuckles were not in evidence' (Thatcher, 1993, p. 130). The delegation emerged on the pavement apparently empty-handed and declaring that Mrs Thatcher's performance had been 'magnificent'. As one industrialist who resigned from the CBI over this episode commented, 'They went in like Brighton rock and came out like Turkish delight' (Grant, 1987, p. 124).

The CBI's position as the principal representative of business interests was increasingly challenged by the Institute of Directors (IOD), which was more in tune with government thinking. 'The IOD established itself very quickly in the early 1980s as the government's most reliable supporter and a source of new ideas' (Boswell and Peters, 1997, p. 155). Until 1979 the CBI had existed entirely within a tripartite environment and its main predecessor, the FBI, had enjoyed close and informal relations with government. Suddenly, the CBI looked like an organisation that was not adjusting very well to changed political circumstances.

Mrs Thatcher's desire for radical change brought her into conflict with another organisation that had enjoyed substantial influence on decisions since the post-war settlement, the British Medical Association (BMA). Proposals for an internal market in the health service produced an outcry from them 'based squarely on a deliberate and self-interested distortion of what we were doing' (Thatcher, 1993, p. 616). In Mrs Thatcher's view, the BMA shot themselves in the foot. 'The stridency of the BMA's campaigns against our reforms was leading to a backlash among moderate doctors' (ibid., p. 617).

Throughout 1989 the government was not only in open conflict with the doctors. There was also 'conflict between Government and teachers over the concept of a core curriculum, national testing of standards, and teacher evaluation; conflict between the Government and barristers over the possibility of granting the solicitors the right to appear in higher courts; and conflict between the Government and the universities over changes in the funding mechanism for universities' (Richardson, 1990, p. 25). Quite possibly, fighting all these fronts at once, alongside the battle over the unpopular poll tax, contributed to the mood in the Conservative Party that led to Mrs Thatcher's removal from office in the following year. The challenge was, of course, launched by Michael Heseltine, who held 'long-standing corporatist and interventionist views' (Thatcher, 1993, p. 841).

One should not imagine, however, that the Thatcher governments consistently rode roughshod over opposition from any vested interest. 'Radical changes would be proposed, thus producing a sense of crisis in the policy area, to be followed by a degree of indecision by government, as the group activity (fury sometimes) developed' (Richardson, 1990, p. 26). In relation to privatisation, for example, the concerns of the managers of the privatised industries were taken note of to such an extent as to ensure that in most cases privatisation was accompanied by minimum exposure to competition.

Moreover, at the level of the middle ranks of the bureaucracy, the meetings between assistant secretaries and principals and their counterparts in the trade associations continued much as they always had. A meeting between the civil servant responsible for the widget industry and the Director-General of the British Widget Manufacturers' Association complaining about dumping from Eastern Europe might be dull and tedious, but the issues were important to those involved. As Richardson points out, traditional bargaining practices generally reasserted themselves at some stage in the decision-making process. The government might directly challenge groups, but would then go on to consult and bargain with them 'over the practicalities of policy implementation. Providing the main policy thrust remains intact, the government has been prepared to accommodate group pressures' (Richardson, 1990, p. 26). What had changed was that groups like the unions or the BMA were no longer allowed to veto particular proposals (before 1979 this had sometimes happened through a process of anticipated reactions).

With the arrival of the internal market and the greater use of qualified majority voting, pressure groups began to devote more attention to the European Community level of representation, in some cases making efforts to revitalise somewhat ineffective European federations. For some groups, the European

Community, with its notion of a 'social Europe', offered respite and succour from a Thatcherite Britain. In September 1988 the Commission's President, Jacques Delors, came to address the TUC congress, making a speech that could readily be interpreted as critical of the government's policies. What was becoming apparent was that the domestic arena was no longer the only one in which major decisions were made, and that pressure groups would have to adapt to a system of multi-level governance which was more complex and yet also offered new opportunities for exerting influence.

The 1990s: The Growth of Direct Action

John Major was Prime Minister from 1990 to 1997, but, given the extent of analysis of his government, one might suppose that it was as brief and ineffective as the Lord Protectorship of Richard Cromwell from 1658 to 1659. (For exceptions, see Kavanagh and Seldon, 1994; Bonefeld, Brown and Burnham, 1995.) Analysts have in general preferred to continue to assess the impact of Thatcherism or to ponder the true meaning of Blair's 'Third Way'. The day before yesterday is the period most quickly forgotten, but does the lack of attention paid to the Major governments reflect a view that they were a gentler and more confused form of Thatcherism, confounded by internal divisions within the Conservative Party over Europe?

The Major government did usher in a change of emphasis in the approach to relations between governments and groups:

> There were clear signs of a re-emphasis on the philosophy of consultation. The Major governments offered an olive branch to many groups which had been disadvantaged in the previous decade, such as the trade unions, the doctors, the teachers, and the local authority associations. Ministerial speeches began to emphasise the importance of these groups as partners rather than opponents. (Baggott, 1995, p. 495)

Nevertheless, difficulties continued in relations with groups such as the doctors and the teachers, if only because the policies themselves were so unpopular with the affected groups. The government was seeking to implement policies designed by its predecessor and this perpetuated the politics of confrontation (ibid., p. 498) Continuing difficulties with the teaching unions under the Labour government suggest that what may be at work here is part of a more general shift of power from producers (in this case teachers) to consumers (in this case parents, pupils and employers) rather than the product of the policy style of a particular government. Nevertheless, Baggott concludes that there are a number of examples, such as the privatisation of British Rail, the reform of the Child Support Agency, and the handling of the Justice and Public Order Bill, which showed: 'the way [the Major Government] adopted an approach to policy-making not dissimilar from its predecessor, attempting to ride roughshod over interested parties, failing to consult adequately, and grudgingly giving concessions when the forces rallied against it proved too strong' (ibid., p. 500).

With the 'corporatist' Michael Heseltine installed as Secretary of State for Trade and Industry and later as deputy Prime Minister, one of the most interesting features of the Major governments' relations with trade associations was a revived interest in the structure and effectiveness of these associations, this time under the banner of 'competitiveness'. As well as encouraging firms to look at the effectiveness of the associations to which they belonged, Heseltine also made it clear that the Department of Trade and Industry (DTI) would encourage lead associations that would coordinate the views of a particular sector. Once such an association had emerged, only its views would be referred to the minister for consideration (May, McHugh and Taylor, 1998, pp. 260–1.)

This initiative was followed through in 1996 with a DTI 'best-practice guide for the model trade association'. A quantitative benchmarking study of trade association performance was commissioned and benchmarking clubs were formed to enable trade associations to share best-practice. The DTI supported the establishment of a Trade Association Forum by the CBI to develop this work. However, the Blair government seemed less interested in revitalising trade associations and by 1999 the forum was operating on a self-funding basis.

The Blair government established its credentials as a government that accepted the Thatcherite settlement by showing a coolness towards the trade unions, particularly during the dispute over trade union recognition. Groups such as the teaching unions received little comfort from the new government. If anything, it showed a greater warmth towards big business than its predecessors. After a long period in which it was treated under the Conservatives in a way that varied between polite indifference and thinly veiled contempt, the CBI found itself regularly and extensively consulted by the new government.

The government showed that it was as susceptible as any of its predecessors to an upsurge in public protest. The scale of support for the Countryside March in London in March 1998 appeared to have wide-ranging effects on the conduct of government policy. The government made it clear that it was very cool towards the Private Member's Bill introduced by one of its own MPs to ban hunting; backed away from pledges to give ramblers the 'right to roam'; and, after an initially hardline approach to farmers who were facing one of their biggest ever falls in income, replaced the agriculture minister with a more sympathetic figure and introduced a new compensation package.

The Countryside March represented a non-violent and peaceful example of a form of direct action that was increasingly prevalent in the 1990s. There had been a long history of direct action by hunt saboteurs, but in the 1990s the practice spread, with protesters establishing themselves on the sites of planned new roads or airport extensions and digging tunnels to make it difficult to evict them. More well-established environmental groups such as Friends of the Earth found themselves outflanked by more decentralised and spontaneous organisations, such as Earth First! or Reclaim the Streets, that were prepared to contemplate forms of direct action such as sabotaging construction equipment or holding parties on busy roads.

In many ways direct action should not be seen as a traditional form of pressure-group activity. It was not intended to exert influence on decision-makers who, in many cases, were seen as beyond redemption by the protesters.

A study of direct-action politics argued that 'increasing numbers of people are coming to the conclusion that their needs will never be addressed by those in power' (Brass and Koziell, 1997, p. 7). Often the intention was to prevent an activity that was disapproved of from taking place at all, or at least to make it more expensive or difficult while raising public consciousness about the issues involved. These tactics could be very effective. A series of raids on test plots where genetically modified plants were being grown in 1998–9 destroyed the trials and made it increasingly difficult to find any farmer who would be prepared to take part.

Direct-action politics often seemed to be characterised by an emphasis on instant gratification, on politics as a kind of lifestyle linked with expressive forms of individualism. At a roads protest near Bath, people turned up at the weekend from the town 'resplendent in tribal warpaint and "Levellers" T-shirts ... [they became] part-time Dongas for the day and got value from the protest not from its eventual success or failure, but from the experiences they felt along the way' (North, 1998, p. 18).

Away from the wilder fringes of politics, it was clear that the media was playing an increasingly important role in giving salience to particular issues and boosting the campaigns associated with them. The media played a key role in promoting the 'Snowdrop' campaign which eventually successfully secured a complete ban on the private ownership of handguns. Rather more controversially, the media played a role in arousing concern about genetically modified foods in 1999. This was an issue which raised difficult questions of science and of international trade policy which it is hard to discuss in an emotively charged atmosphere.

The growth of direct action reinforced concerns about the role of single-issue pressure groups in British politics at the end of the century. The argument was advanced that such groups were simply concerned with advocating their own demands, with no concern about the impact on other groups who might be disadvantaged by having a hitherto legitimate activity banned or by the effect on the level of public expenditure. An analysis of the content of Radio 4's *Today* programme showed that 'by far the most regular demand of anyone campaigning for anything is for taxpayers' (now also lottery players') cash' (Waldegrave, 1996, p. 9).

The European Union continued to grow in significance as an arena of pressure-group activity throughout the 1990s. One consequence has been the growth of potentially more effective direct membership associations at the European level, rather than federations of federations. The creation of elected assemblies in Scotland and Wales brings a new dimension to pressure-group activities which both offers more opportunities to exert influence, but also makes the operating environment for pressure groups more complex.

At the beginning of a new century pressure groups thus find themselves operating in a more complex world of multi-level governance that contrasts sharply with the discussions between the executive and recognised groups in the immediate post-war years. Pressure-group activity is much more visible and relies on a much wider range of tactics. In a more diverse society, the range of issues being addressed is also much broader. 'The overall market for political activism has grown in terms of overall levels of participation but the parties now take a smaller share of it' (Riddell, 1996, p. 5).

The 'Establishment' world of Norman Kipping now seems to belong to another era. Even the tripartism of the 1960s and 1970s now seems remote. However, a more transparent politics conducted in the full glare of media scrutiny brings its own problems. As the political process develops more levels and becomes more complex, it is increasingly difficult for the citizen to know how to relate to it. Direct action thus becomes more attractive as a means of securing the attention of politicians among so many conflicting messages. A challenge for the new century is to develop forms of intermediary networks, perhaps making increasing use of electronic forms of communication, which allow the citizen to feel that her voice is being heard without having to resort to disruptive forms of politics.

References

Baggott, R. (1995) 'From Confrontation to Consultation: Pressure Group Relations from Thatcher to Major.' *Parliamentary Affairs* 48: 484–502.

Blank, S. (1973) *Industry and Government in Britain: The Federation of British Industries in Politics*. Farnborough.

Bonefeld, W., Brown, A. and Burnham, P. (1995) *A Major Crisis?* Aldershot.

Boswell, J. and Peters, J. (1997) *Capitalism in Contention*. Cambridge.

Brass, E. and Koziell, S. (1997) *Gathering Force*. London.

Coates, D. (1984) 'Food Law: Brussels, Whitehall and Town Hall.' In D. Lewis and H. Wallace (eds), *Policies into Practice*. London.

Eckstein, H. (1960) *Pressure Group Politics: The Case of the British Medical Association*. London.

Finer, S. E. (1958) *Anonymous Empire*. London.

Grant, W. (1981) 'The Politics of the Green Pound.' *Journal of Common Market Studies*. 19: 313–29.

Grant, W. (1987) *Business and Politics in Britain*. London.

Grant, W. (1999) *Pressure Groups and British Politics*. London.

Kavanagh, D. and Seldon, A. (eds) (1994) *The Major Effect*. London.

Kipping, Sir N. (1972) *Summing Up*. London.

Leruez, J. (1975) *Economic Planning and Politics in Britain*. Oxford.

May, T. C., McHugh, J. and Taylor, T. (1998) 'Business Representation in the UK since 1979: The Case of Trade Associations.' *Political Studies* 46: 260–75.

Mitchell, N. J. (1987) 'Changing Pressure-Group Politics: The Case of the Trades Union Congress, 1976–84.' *British Journal of Political Science* 17: 509–17.

Nettl, J. P. (1965) 'Consensus or Elite Domination: The Case of Business?' *Political Studies* 8: 22–44.

North, P. (1998) '"Save our Solsbury!": The Anatomy of an Anti-Roads Protest.' *Environmental Politics* 7: 1–25.

Olson, M. (1982) *The Rise and Decline of Nations*. New Haven.

Richardson, J. J. (1990) 'Government and Groups in Britain: Changing Styles.' Strathclyde Papers on Government and Politics, No. 69.

Riddell, P. (1996) 'Introduction: Pressure Groups, Media and Government.' In Social Market Foundation (ed.), *Pressure Group Politics in Modern Britain*. London.

Ryan, M. (1978) *The Acceptable Pressure Group: A Case Study of the Howard League for Penal Reform and Radical Alternatives to Prison*. Farnborough.

Smith, M. J. (1989) 'The Annual Review: the Emergence of a Corporatist Institution?' *Political Studies* 37: 81–96.

Stewart, J. D. (1958) *British Pressure Groups*. Oxford.

Thatcher, M. (1993) *The Downing Street Years*. London.

Waldegrave, W. (1996) 'Politicians and Pressure Groups.' In Social Market Foundation (ed.), *Pressure Group Politics in Modern Britain*. London.

Weekend World, transcript of interview with Mrs Thatcher, 15 January 1984.

Chronology

1947   Agriculture Act introduces annual price review.
1960   'Brighton Revolution'.
1962   National Economic Development Council established.
1965   CBI formed. Child Poverty Action Group formed.
1970   DoE formed.
1971   Friends of the Earth founded.
1972   Devlin Commission on Industrial Representation reports. Industry Act. Greenpeace founded (USA).
1979   Effective end of tripartism.
1986   Single European Act stimulates European Community-level activity.
1992   National Economic Development Council dissolved.
1993   Heseltine initiative on trade associations launched.
1996   DTI document on trade association benchmarking.
1999   Trade Association forum becomes self-funding.

Part III
Economy

20 Economic Policy

Stephen Broadberry

Introduction

Economic policy in Britain has changed remarkably in the period since the end of the Second World War. Whereas in 1945 the first majority Labour government believed that it was the primary responsibility of government to maintain full employment through a policy of Keynesian demand management and to intervene directly in the running of industry through nationalisation and economic planning, the Labour government elected in 1997 with an even larger parliamentary majority accepted fighting inflation as the primary macro-economic objective, explicitly rejected nationalisation, and refused to return to an interventionist industrial policy. The story of this scaling-down of expect-ations concerning what could be achieved through economic policy in both the macroeconomic and microeconomic spheres is in many ways common to all Western countries. Here, however, we focus on the details of the British case.

The bulk of this chapter will provide an historical narrative of economic policy in Britain by decade. Since policy has been shaped by ideas as well as events, however, it will be helpful to briefly review some of the key ideas before launching into the narrative.

In the aftermath of the war, policy was influenced by two strands of thinking, based on central economic planning and Keynesian demand management.[1] The mass unemployment of the 1930s had discredited the market economy in the eyes of many, and the experience of planning during the war led some socialists to propose a continuation of planning during peacetime. However, whereas there was a clear objective during the war and a willingness to accept compulsion, this was much less the case in a consumer-driven peacetime society. Hence the more influential idea was demand management, arising from the work of Keynes, who argued that in a market economy demand may not be sufficient to provide full employment. Although Keynes had envisaged using investment to stabilise demand, in practice governments found it easier to influence consumption through tax changes. Hence fiscal policy became the primary instrument of economic policy in the early post-war period.[2]

In fact, contrary to the expectations of most observers, the early post-war period was characterised not by a lack of demand, but by boom conditions and exceptionally low levels of unemployment. As persistent inflation became a problem during the 1960s, focus shifted to monetary policy, with monetarists arguing that control of inflation required control of the money supply. In fact, a fixed exchange rate acts as an anchor for monetary policy, since interest rates have to be used to defend the parity. Hence the need to control monetary growth became much more important once the pound was allowed to float in 1972. During the 1970s, governments were faced with the uncomfortable situation of rising inflation and unemployment, a combination known as stagflation. Economists began to recognise that the supply side could not be ignored, and the idea of a 'natural rate of unemployment' was introduced. In this approach, inflation was seen as a result of government attempts to hold the level of unemployment below its natural rate, with the supply side of the economy thus seen as setting clear limits to what could be achieved by demand management. The emphasis in recent macroeconomics is on the need for governments to commit credibly to achieving the limited objective of price stability.

Accompanying this downgrading of expectations concerning what the government could achieve through macroeconomic policy, there has been a shift away from interventionist microeconomic policy in recent years. Although the Attlee governments shied away from central economic planning, they did preside over a major programme of nationalisation, with a number of important industries being brought under direct state control. In addition, state intervention was common in other industries. Frustration with what was seen as an unsatisfactory growth rate led Labour governments during the 1960s and 1970s to extend nationalisation and to adopt a highly interventionist industrial policy, in an attempt to modernise British industry. Although the Conservative government elected in 1970 had aimed to rely more on market forces, it became equally interventionist when difficulties arose. It was left to the Thatcher governments to make the decisive break with interventionism during the 1980s, launching a major scheme of privatisation as well as refusing to bail out ailing firms and limiting intervention in industry more generally. The return of Labour to power in 1997 has not reversed this major policy shift. Rather, both parties now stress the role that governments can play in helping firms and individuals to compete in the marketplace. Education and training have become the new priorities, with the government seen as helping to provide the infrastructure of growth rather than 'picking winners'.

The focus on economic policy in this chapter carries with it the danger that the reader will be left with the impression that economic performance has been determined largely by economic policy. It must be emphasised, therefore, that this is not the conclusion to be drawn. On the contrary, as already noted, many would argue that one of the most important economic lessons of the second half of the twentieth century is that there are limits to what can be achieved by policy. Although at times we shall need to discuss issues such as the underlying rate of economic growth and British relative economic decline, space constraints will preclude a full discussion of these matters, which would require a very different kind of analysis.

Before beginning the narrative, it will be helpful to set out the trends in the key macroeconomic variables, which are graphed in Figures 20.1 to 20.6. In figure 20.1 we see that unemployment fluctuated gently around 2 per cent during the 1950s and 1960s before rising steadily during the 1970s and dramatically during the early 1980s to more than 10 per cent of the workforce. Although it fell during the booms of the late 1980s and early 1990s, there has been no return to the low unemployment of the early post-war period. Despite the low unemployment of the 1950s and 1960s, inflation also remained low, apart from a brief inflationary episode at the time of the Korean War. Inflation rose rapidly during the 1970s, since when it has dominated the agenda of policy-makers. Apart from a brief period around 1990, inflation has been brought back down to the early post-war level during the 1980s and 1990s.

Figure 20.2 shows the annual growth rate of GDP in constant prices. Although there has always been a cycle, it is clear that slumps became more severe after the relatively stable years of the 1950s and 1960s. The 1970s stand out as a relatively stagnant decade apart from the unusually rapid growth of 1973. Measuring the growth rate between business cycle peaks, growth averaged 3 per cent per annum between 1951 and 1973, falling back to just 1.4 per cent per annum between 1973 and 1979 and rising back to 2.4 per cent per annum during 1979–89. Growth during the 1980s and 1990s was faster than during the 1970s, but not as rapid as during the 1950s and 1960s.

The balance of payments played an important role in economic decision-making, particularly during the fixed exchange rate period of the 1950s and 1960s. The periodic current account deficits that can be seen in figure 20.3 triggered major changes in economic policy, leading in some cases to devaluation of the pound. The value of the pound against the dollar and the Deutschmark can

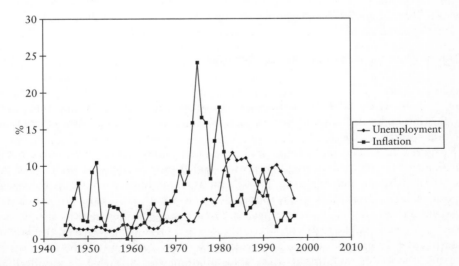

Figure 20.1 Unemployment and inflation rates, 1945–2000

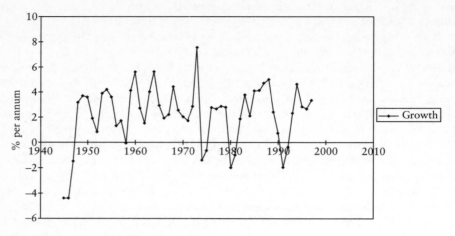

Figure 20.2 Group of GDP, 1945–2000

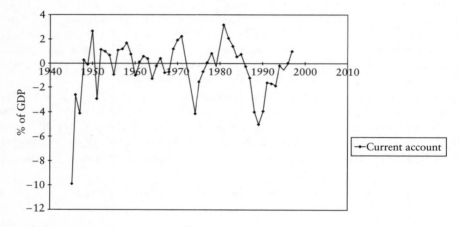

Figure 20.3 Balance of payments, 1945–2000

be seen in figure 20.4, with the general downward drift of the exchange rate reflecting higher inflation in Britain than in Germany and (to a lesser extent) the United States.

Figures 20.5 and 20.6 plot trends in the main policy instruments. Large fiscal deficits were avoided during the 1950s and 1960s as governments acted to restrain demand, but the early 1970s saw a dramatic turnaround in the fiscal position. Although this was followed by a trend reduction in the fiscal deficit during the 1980s, there was a further surge in the deficit during the early 1990s. Monetary growth and interest rates were relatively low and stable during the 1950s and 1960s. However, a dramatic surge in monetary growth during the 1970s, associated with rapid inflation, was followed by attempts to rein in monetary growth during the 1980s and 1990s.

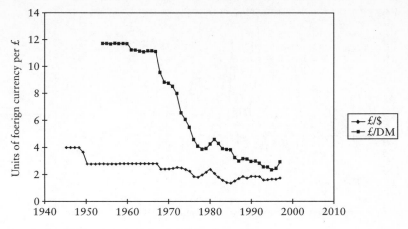

Figure 20.4   Exchange rate, 1945–2000

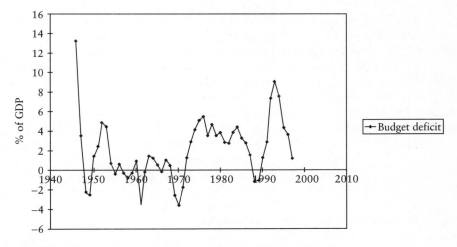

Figure 20.5   General government financial deficit, 1945–2000

1945–50: Reconstruction

At the end of the war, the government faced severe difficulties in both external and internal affairs. On the external side, the decline of exports during the mobilisation of the economy for war, the rundown of overseas assets, and the reliance on lend-lease supplies from the United States meant that at the end of the war foreign receipts were inadequate to pay for essential imports.[3] The strain on the balance of payments was worsened by the need to keep troops overseas in the tense post-war situation. Since the United States was the only feasible source of supply for Britain's needs, there was talk of a 'dollar shortage'

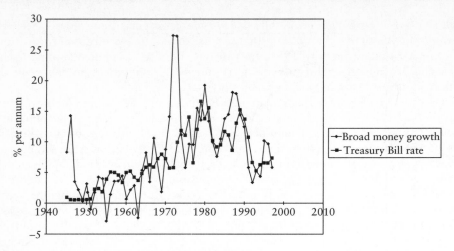

Figure 20.6   Broad money growth and the short-term interest rate, 1945–2000

and policy-makers focused on the need for a US loan. A recurring problem for post-war policy-makers was provided by the sterling balances accumulated by Commonwealth countries that were also members of the Sterling Area in lieu of payment for war supplies. Any attempt to convert these balances into dollars ran down Britain's reserves, needed to maintain the external value of the pound.

After taking office in July 1945, the Labour government sent a mission under Keynes to Washington, and after long negotiations a loan agreement was reached in December and approved by Congress in July 1946. One of the conditions attached to the loan was that Britain should make the pound convertible by mid-1947. However, when the pound was made convertible on 15 July 1947 there was a massive drain on reserves and convertibility had to be suspended on 20 August. In June, meanwhile, General Marshall had delivered a speech at Harvard University, which would result in the Marshall Plan for European recovery based on US aid. Marshall Aid helped to relieve the dollar shortage, but in 1949 the government bowed to the inevitable and devalued the pound from $4.03 to $2.80. Since most other countries also devalued against the dollar, the value of the pound changed much less against other currencies.

The internal situation also required urgent attention.[4] With more than five million in the armed forces and many others in support services, the chief priority was reconversion to a peacetime economy. In addition, it was necessary to make up for years of under-investment across all activities, and to do so whilst satisfying the consumption aspirations of a population that had endured much hardship to achieve victory. Furthermore, expectations had been raised during the war of a welfare state, as well as a commitment to full employment, and this required extra resources. Although the new Labour government inherited a vast array of controls, these were generally seen as transitional. Although some within the Labour Party were attached to the idea of central economic planning, the details remained rather vague, and the government rapidly came to see demand management as the primary policy instrument for achieving full employment. Although in some cases rationing initially became even more restrictive than during the war, as for example with the introduction of bread rationing in July 1946, the various 'bonfires of controls' announced from 1948 onwards indicated the government's commitment to the view of controls as a transitional arrangement only.

Despite the view of Keynes that investment should be varied to control the level of effective demand and hence to maintain full employment, ministers found it easier to manage demand by varying tax rates. This was because investment expenditures were viewed as long-term commitments that were difficult to alter in response to short-term needs. The techniques of demand management that were to be the main focus of economic policy for the next two decades emerged gradually from wartime practice. Forecasts of national income were made, enabling ministers to make a judgement about the level of excess demand, and tax rates were then adjusted in the annual budget. It should be emphasised that fiscal policy during this period was restrictive, with a budget surplus on current account to reduce excess demand.[5] Although there were widespread fears of a post-war slump, as had occurred after the First World War, such a slump never materialised. Despite the inflationary pressure arising from excess demand, monetary policy played a secondary role, since it was seen as having little impact on investment or economic activity more generally.[6] The main concern was to keep interest rates low, since the government was a huge net borrower, and Bank Rate was held at 2 per cent, a continuation of the 'cheap money' policy of the 1930s. Inflationary pressure was damped down by direct controls and exhortations to voluntary restraint over increases in prices, wages and dividends.

Turning briefly to microeconomic issues, a major plank of the Labour Party's strategy for industrial modernisation was nationalisation. The major nationalisations included the Bank of England and civil aviation in 1946, the coal industry and Cable and Wireless in 1947, the railways, electricity, road haulage, the buses and the ports in 1948, and gas in 1949.[7] In addition, the steel industry was nationalised in 1951, although the return of the Conservatives to power later in the same year led to denationalisation in 1953. Road haulage was also denationalised from 1953. Even where industry remained in private hands, the government often adopted a highly interventionist approach. Sometimes, this was simply a reflection of the importance of the remaining direct controls, since decisions on steel allocations, for example, had an obvious effect on the level of activity of different industries. In other cases, the government became involved in rationalisation schemes for particular industries with the setting-up of official bodies such as the Working Parties and Development Councils.[8] Furthermore, in all industries, the acceptance of protection, restrictive practices and collusion had adverse consequences for productivity performance in the long run.[9] Although a Monopolies and Restrictive Practices Commission was established in 1948, its powers were limited and it had little impact on the collusive behaviour that permeated the British economy during the early post-war period.[10]

One issue which arose in the context of industrial policy was to have much wider implications for Britain's relations with other countries. This was the

Schuman Plan of 1950, which led to the formation of the European Coal and Steel Community (ECSC).[11] Britain's decision to stay outside the ECSC was complex, but it can be seen as grounded in the historical legacy of ties to Commonwealth countries and reflecting an ambivalence towards European integration that still exists today.

The 1950s: Stop-Go

By 1950, the economy had made large steps towards the successful reconversion to a peacetime basis.[12] Production was substantially above the pre-war level, unemployment and inflation were both low, the balance of payments was showing a surplus on current account, and reserves were increasing. However, in June the Korean War broke out and imposed new strains on the economy. Stockpiling led to world shortages of commodities and rising prices, while the necessary increase in defence spending led to new strains on the civilian economy and the balance of payments.

The strain on the balance of payments was mitigated to some extent by the formation in September 1950 of the European Payments Union, which allowed surpluses and deficits between member countries to be offset against each other, requiring only the net balance with the union to be settled. However, the balance of payments problem would not go away, and shortly after the election of a new Conservative government in November 1951, the Treasury and the Bank of England came up with plans for a radical solution, code-named 'Robot'.[13] The scheme proposed to block the sterling balances, allow convertibility for externally held sterling, and let the pound float against other currencies, but was rejected by the Cabinet in favour of more traditional deflationary policy measures to deal with the balance of payments difficulties. Further external crises occurred in 1956 and 1957 before convertibility was finally achieved for sterling held by non-residents in December 1958 as part of a concerted European move.

The ambivalence towards European integration continued, with Britain remaining outside the European Economic Community (EEC) upon its inauguration in January 1958.[14] Although Britain had been involved in the original EEC negotiations, Commonwealth relations made joining a customs union, with a common external tariff, difficult.[15] Accordingly, Britain remained outside the EEC and formed instead a European Free Trade Area (EFTA) with a number of smaller European countries in November 1959.

Domestic policy under the Conservatives during the 1950s continued much as it had under Labour with a commitment to full employment to be maintained by demand management. The acceptance of Keynesian principles was eased by the fact that in a period of general excess demand it was necessary to run a budget surplus on current account rather than a deficit. The consensus between the two parties led *the Economist* to coin the term 'Butskellism' to describe this approach to policy, compounding the names of the outgoing Labour chancellor Hugh Gaitskell and the new Conservative Chancellor R. A. Butler.[16] The frequent switching between periods of deflating the economy in response to balance of payments crises and rising inflation and other periods of stimulating the economy in response to worries about inflation and slow growth led to the policy being labelled 'stop-go'.

Although much is often made of the decision by the new Conservative government to raise Bank Rate in November 1951 from 2 per cent to 2.5 per cent, monetary policy remained very much of secondary importance during the 1950s.[17] One way of understanding this is to see the economy as operating under a fixed exchange-rate regime, so that Bank Rate had to be used to defend the value of the pound.[18] Whilst this is clearly a useful way of looking at the matter, we should remember that the pound remained inconvertible until 1958, and this allowed the government a certain amount of monetary freedom. Following difficulties in exercising monetary control during the mid-1950s, the introduction of a Special Deposit scheme in July 1958 allowed the Bank of England to vary the liquidity ratio of banks and hence exercise more effective control over the money supply. In 1957 a public inquiry was also instituted into the workings of the monetary system under the chairmanship of Lord Radcliffe. The Radcliffe Report of August 1959 is a landmark in monetary economics, representing the high tide mark of Keynesian scepticism on the role of money.

The Conservatives were as reluctant as Labour to deflate the economy in response to excess demand and urged instead voluntary restraint over increases in wages, prices and dividends.[19] In 1956 the government began a campaign for moderation, but this was rejected by the Trades Union Congress (TUC) at its annual conference, and in July 1957 the government appointed a Council for Prices, Productivity and Incomes (COPPI) with the aim of providing general guidance on the size of wage awards that would be consistent with price stability. This was also unsuccessful and was wound up in 1961 when the government turned to an explicit 'pay pause'.

Industrial policy under the Conservatives also showed a high degree of continuity with Labour policy. Although, as we have seen, steel and road haulage were denationalised from 1953, the majority of industries nationalised under Labour remained in state ownership. Although competition policy was strengthened with the establishment of a Restrictive Practices Court in 1956, progress in the abandonment of restrictive agreements was slow.[20] Rather than outlawing restrictive agreements, the 1956 Act required merely that they be registered, and then be subject to a court case to decide if they were against the public interest. Progress on dismantling controls was also cautious, with food rationing being abandoned only in July 1954.

The 1960s: The Pound in Your Pocket

Economic policy during the 1960s was dominated by external issues.[21] Recurrent balance of payments crises led eventually to the devaluation of 1967, and although this was followed by a return to external balance during 1969, the respite was short-lived. For three years after the election of October 1964, Labour battled to avoid devaluation, adopting import surcharges, deflationary measures, and borrowing from the International Monetary Fund (IMF) in response to external crises in November 1964, July 1965 and July 1966 before bowing to the inevitable in November 1967, when the pound was devalued from $2.80 to $2.40. The announcement in Parliament was the occasion of Prime Minister Harold Wilson's famous enigmatic remark about devaluation not affecting the value of 'the pound in your pocket'. By 1969 the current account was back in surplus.

As trade with the Commonwealth stagnated and trade with Europe grew, two unsuccessful attempts were made to join the EEC during the 1960s.[22] The Conservatives applied to join in August 1961 and Labour applied in May 1967, but both applications were blocked by the French. The key disagreements concerned British agriculture, Commonwealth relations, and the unwillingness of EFTA partners to join the EEC.

Domestic macroeconomic policy remained dominated by budgetary policy, continuing the stop-go policies of the 1950s. However, by now, dissatisfaction with the instability of stop-go was leading to a search for ways to improve the policy framework. One change was the use of the regulator, introduced in 1961 to allow the Chancellor to vary indirect tax rates by up to 10 per cent between budgets. However, given data uncertainty, forecasting inaccuracy, delays in making and implementing decisions, and lags in the transmission process, it is now generally agreed that such attempts at 'fine-tuning' the economy amplified rather than dampened the business cycle. It is usually argued that governments lacked the freedom to pursue an independent monetary policy during the 1960s because of the fixed exchange-rate regime.[23] Again, as in the 1950s, although this is a helpful way to view the basic context of monetary policy, we should bear in mind that in practice the government was unable to hold the external value of the pound, which was devalued in 1967 to reflect the higher rate of inflation in Britain. Hence, although at any point in time the government was constrained to use Bank Rate to defend the value of the pound, over the decade as a whole the more expansionary monetary policy pursued in Britain made it impossible to avoid devaluation.

The 1960s also saw an increasing reliance on incomes policy as governments sought ways to dampen down inflationary pressures without adopting conventional deflationary policies.[24] Under the Conservatives, a pay pause introduced in July 1961 met with resistance in the public and private sectors and had had little discernible effect by April 1962, when it ended. Shortly after returning to office in October 1964, Labour persuaded employers and unions to sign a joint statement of intent on incomes policy and in March 1965 a National Board for Prices and Incomes (NBPI) was established. Despite the TUC agreeing to a 3 to 3.5 per cent norm, wages continued to rise at substantially higher rates, and in July 1966 the government introduced a six-month wage freeze. The freeze was followed by a further six months of 'severe restraint', but after this period wage settlements picked up again. The failure of incomes policy to secure a sustained moderation of wage settlements led the government to attempt the reform of industrial relations, aiming in particular to tackle the problem of unofficial strikes. However, the White Paper, *In Place of Strife*, was strongly opposed by the TUC and was abandoned by the government in July 1969 in return for a 'solemn and binding undertaking' by the TUC to curb unofficial strike activity.

Industrial policy saw a general strengthening of interventionism during the 1960s. With higher growth rates in continental European countries, British industry was seen as in need of modernisation. Although this view can be seen most obviously in the policies of the Labour governments, it was also reflected to a more limited extent in Conservative policies. It was the Conservatives, for example, who established the tripartite National Economic Development Council (NEDC) in 1961. However, it was left to Labour to draw up a fully-fledged National Plan in 1965, which envisaged an annual growth rate of 3.8 per cent.[25] Nevertheless, the decision to fight devaluation forced the government to deflate and effectively scuppered the plan, which was abandoned in the external crisis of July 1966. Although the Conservatives had strengthened competition policy by making resale price maintenance illegal in April 1964, the thrust of Labour policy during the 1960s was to encourage mergers in the hope of creating 'national champions' that would benefit from economies of scale.[26] The instrument for achieving this was the Industrial Reorganisation Corporation (IRC), which was established in January 1966. The Labour government also introduced the Monopolies and Mergers Act of 1965, which required the Board of Trade to vet large mergers and make reference to the Monopolies and Mergers Commission where competition was threatened. It is hard to see how these two policies could have been consistent without clear criteria being laid down. There was a further extension of the public sector in 1967 with the renationalisation of the steel industry.

The 1970s: Stagflation

The external situation was quite favourable when the Conservatives returned to office in June 1970, with the current account back in balance.[27] However, the weakness of the dollar led to the breakdown of the Bretton Woods system of fixed exchange rates, usually dated from the Smithsonian agreement of December 1971, and the pound was floated from June 1972. This was followed at the end of 1973 by the first oil shock, when the Organization of Petroleum-Exporting Countries (OPEC) cartel quadrupled the price of oil. This gave a boost to inflationary pressures and led to the reappearance of a large balance of payments deficit. Under Labour from March 1974 the balance of payments deficit declined, particularly once North Sea oil came on stream from June 1975, but the deficit was not eliminated until mid-1977. In the meantime a serious depreciation of the exchange rate in 1976, with the pound falling to $1.57 in October, forced the government to seek the assistance of the IMF, which imposed tough deflationary conditions. When the world economy was hit by the second oil shock at the end of 1979, with a further doubling of the price of oil, although Britain still suffered from the inflationary impact, the direct effect on the balance of payments was positive since Britain had become a net oil exporter.

International relations during the 1970s saw a decisive strengthening of ties between Britain and continental Europe.[28] Negotiations for British membership were reopened in the summer of 1970 and this time agreement was reached. The currency was decimalised in February 1971 and Britain formally joined the

EEC in January 1973. The terms were renegotiated by Labour and put to the country in a referendum in June 1975, which produced a two-thirds majority in favour of continued membership.

Domestic macroeconomic policy saw some major changes during the 1970s, leading effectively to the abandonment of the whole Keynesian system of demand management that had dominated economic thinking for the previous 30 years. The decade opened with an orthodox expansionary fiscal policy from 1971 aimed at reducing unemployment. However, whereas the 'Barber boom' which followed was accompanied by a balance of payments deficit and accelerating inflation, unemployment remained stubbornly high.[29] Economists coined the word 'stagflation' to describe the combination of high unemployment and high inflation. The idea gained ground that attempts to hold unemployment below its 'natural rate' would lead only to accelerating inflation.[30]

Increased concerns about rising inflation led to increased attention being paid to monetary policy. Monetarists argued that there was a strong link between the rate of inflation and the rate of monetary growth. Prior to 1972, the fixed exchange rate had provided a nominal anchor for the economy, because if inflation was faster at home than abroad, British goods became uncompetitive and a balance of payments problem emerged. Defence of the exchange rate then forced a restrictive monetary policy, which reduced inflation and helped to improve competitiveness and correct the deficit.[31] This all occurred without a need to focus explicitly on the rate of growth of the money supply. With the pound floating from 1971, however, the economy needed a new nominal anchor, and monetarists began to argue for an explicit targeting of the rate of growth of the money supply. During the 1950s and 1960s governments had relied on measures such as directives to banks to limit lending and hire-purchase controls to curb the growth of credit and thus the supply of money. In September 1971, however, the Conservatives introduced competition and credit control, which sought to eliminate reliance on directives.[32] However, after a dramatic surge in credit the money supply spiralled out of control and in December 1973 a new system was introduced requiring banks to lodge Supplementary Special Deposits with the Bank of England. This was labelled the 'corset'. Although there was a gradual movement towards monitoring the growth of the money supply throughout the 1970s, monetary targets were only formally adopted in 1976 as a condition of the IMF loan.[33] Targets were also adopted for the Public Sector Borrowing Requirement (PSBR), which signalled the primacy of monetary policy over fiscal policy. By 1976 the budget deficit had risen above 5 per cent and was widely seen as being in danger of spiralling out of control.

The problem with adopting deflationary monetary and fiscal policies was that they worked by increasing unemployment, at least in the short run. Hence both Conservative and Labour governments were driven to rely on incomes policy as an alternative way of reducing inflation, even despite strong misgivings in both parties.[34] Indeed, the Conservatives had been elected promising less government intervention, and this included opposition to formal incomes policy. Like the previous Labour administration, however, the Conservatives did take action to try to control union militancy, introducing an Industrial Relations Bill in December 1971. However, the unions refused to cooperate with the National Industrial Relations Court, and the bad relations between unions and government that developed at this time hampered attempts to get cooperation over incomes policy when the government changed its mind over this issue. In November 1972, as unemployment continued its upward trend, the government began to see the advantages of an incomes policy and was forced into a major U-turn. Stage 3 of the incomes policy from November 1973 included threshold payments to link wage increases to retail prices, which proved very costly when inflation accelerated as a result of the oil price shock the following month. As the miners started an overtime ban in support of a wage increase well above the incomes policy limit, the government declared a state of emergency and announced a three-day week. When the miners went on strike in February 1974, Edward Heath called a general election, which produced an indecisive result, with no party having an overall majority and the Labour Party under Harold Wilson forming an administration. With inflation rising to nearly 25 per cent in 1975, the Labour government soon felt compelled to adopt a formal incomes policy. This culminated in July 1978 with an ambitious limit for wage increases of 5 per cent, and the Labour government's last period in office was marked by a 'winter of discontent', with a series of strikes in support of higher wage claims.

In industrial policy, the 1970s began with an attempt to break away from the interventionist philosophy of the 1960s. However, the Heath government's philosophy of greater reliance on market forces was soon put to the test when in 1971 Rolls Royce and Upper Clyde Shipbuilders (UCS) became insolvent. Faced with the prospect of standing by while unemployment increased further, the government made a U-turn, nationalising Rolls Royce and bailing out UCS.[35] Under Labour, the policy of intervention was strengthened with the formation of the National Enterprise Board to take a public stake in industry and to help with the rationalisation of industries in difficulty.[36] This resulted in the nationalisation of British Leyland and Jaguar in 1974, and British Shipbuilders, Royal Dockyards and British Aerospace in 1977.[37]

The 1980s: The Thatcher Revolution

The Conservatives were elected to office in May 1979 and remained in government until 1997. With Margaret Thatcher as Prime Minister until 1990, policy during the 1980s had an unprecedented degree of continuity and coherence.[38] The key policy objectives of the Thatcher governments were to reduce inflation and to roll back the frontiers of the state. Although the Heath government had similar objectives in 1970, it rapidly backed down in the face of rising unemployment and the bankruptcy of large industrial enterprises; however, Mrs Thatcher was determined to avoid such a U-turn.

The centrepiece of the anti-inflation strategy was the Medium Term Financial Strategy (MTFS), which set declining targets for money supply growth and the PSBR. Although this is often seen as a radical break with the previous Keynesian system of demand management, it should be remembered that the previous Labour government had been forced by the IMF to adopt similar policies after the 1976 crisis. The aim had been to bring down inflation without causing a substantial rise in unemployment, and this was to be done by preannouncing the policy so as to shape expectations. In practice, unemployment rose quickly and reached 3 million in January 1982. One problem was that the government adopted a more restrictive policy than intended, because its chosen measure of the money supply was distorted by the abolition of the corset in June 1980.[39] Another important point to bear in mind is that it took time for the government to acquire credibility; only when Mrs Thatcher refused to do a U-turn in the difficult circumstances of the early 1980s did she really cement her reputation for toughness. An important way in which the monetary deflation led to higher unemployment was through its impact on the exchange rate, with sterling soaring to $2.45 in November 1980 as a result of high interest rates.

Fiscal policy was clearly subservient to monetary policy under the Conservatives, with targets being set for the PSBR in line with monetary targets. Rather than being seen as an instrument to manipulate aggregate demand, fiscal policy was increasingly seen as affecting the supply side of the economy through incentives, and priority was given to reducing income tax rates, particularly during the second half of the 1980s. After an initial reduction from 33 to 30 per cent in the 1979 budget, the standard rate had remained fixed until 1986, but it was then lowered in three steps to reach 25 per cent in the 1988 budget. The top rate of income tax fell from 83 per cent to 40 per cent. The demand effects of this fiscal change helped to fuel a boom that led not only to rapid economic growth but also to a resurgence of the inflation problem. Other factors behind this boom included a worldwide reflationary policy in response to the stock market crash of October 1987 and confusion over British monetary policy. Concern over the sharp rise of the exchange rate during the early 1980s had led some members of the government to doubt the wisdom of relying solely on money supply targets to provide the nominal anchor to the economic system, and these doubts were confirmed by subsequent exchange rate volatility. In January 1985, with the pound falling rapidly towards $1, action was taken to stabilise the exchange rate. Minimum lending rate (MLR), which had been suspended in August 1981 to allow a greater role for market forces, was reactivated for a day and fixed at 12 per cent.[40] In 1987, despite the fact that Britain remained outside the Exchange Rate Mechanism (ERM) of the European Monetary System, the Chancellor, Nigel Lawson, began to shadow the Deutschmark.[41] To keep the exchange rate stable, Lawson was forced to lower interest rates and allow a rapid growth of the money supply, and inflation rose back to nearly 10 per cent in 1990.

During the boom of the late 1980s, a substantial deficit emerged on the current account of the balance of payments. In contrast to the stop-go era of the 1950s and 1960s, however, the financial markets did not see the deficit as a serious problem and there was no exchange rate crisis. The 'Burns Doctrine', named after Sir Terence Burns, Chief Economic Adviser at the Treasury, argued that the deficit was not a problem because it was temporary, came after a long period of Britain building up a strong asset position, was due to private behaviour rather than a public-sector deficit, reflected the fact that invisible earnings and exports of services were replacing manufactured exports, and could be financed easily due to the high degree of international capital mobility.[42]

One notable absence from the government's anti-inflation strategy was incomes policy. In place of 'beer and sandwiches' at Number 10 Downing Street, the trade unions were treated to a major assault on their privileges. The most important pieces of legislation to curb union power were the 1982 Employment Act, which limited immunities to strikes on account of disputes over wages or conditions of work with members' own employers; the 1984 Trade Union Act, which required a secret ballot before industrial action; and the 1989 Employment Act, which outlawed the pre-entry closed shop. The failure of the year-long miners' strike beginning in early 1984 is usually seen as marking a significant shift in the balance of power between unions and employers, and strike activity fell markedly thereafter.[43]

Another important supply-side measure was the policy of privatisation, which represented a dramatic reversal of industrial policy. In fact, privatisation had not been mentioned in the 1979 Conservative Party manifesto, and the proceeds of sales remained relatively unimportant before the 1983 general election. However, the sale of British Telecom shares in 1984 proved very popular with investors and the policy was extended; the privatisation of British Gas in 1986 also attracted much attention among small investors. One issue which was not satisfactorily resolved at the time concerned competition, these major public utilities being privatised with a large amount of monopoly power. This affected the shape of the electricity privatisation in 1990–1, with generation being separated from distribution and opened up to competition. Other measures to introduce more competition into the economy included the abolition of exchange controls in 1979, the Competition Act of 1980, which allowed any kind of 'anti-competitive practice' to be referred to the Monopolies and Mergers Commission, and the 'Big Bang' of 1986 which ended fixed commissions in the City of London. Although productivity growth recovered during the 1980s so that Britain no longer grew more slowly than most other West European countries, the improvement was not so impressive as to enable Britain to close the gap in living standards that had opened up during the 1970s.[44]

Relations with Europe remained strained during the 1980s. Between 1979 and 1984 there was a dispute concerning Britain's contribution to the EEC budget. Since the largest item of expenditure was the Common Agricultural Policy (CAP) and British farmers received rather less under this scheme than their less efficient continental counterparts, the issue was eventually settled, with Britain receiving a rebate. During the second half of the 1980s Mrs Thatcher took a hostile position towards plans for increased political and economic integration that left Britain increasingly out of step with other EEC members.

The 1990s: Towards the New Millennium

The Conservative governments of John Major and the Labour government of Tony Blair continued with broadly Thatcherite economic policies, combining

low inflation as the primary macroeconomic objective with microeconomic policies to help individuals and firms to compete in the marketplace. John Major
replaced Margaret Thatcher as Prime Minister in November 1990, shortly after
Britain had joined the ERM. Macroeconomic policy was thus based around
maintaining the value of the pound within a band of ± 6 per cent around the
central parity of DM2.95. However, it was widely believed that this rate was
too high, and to keep the pound within the band required high interest rates,
which helped to keep the economy in recession during 1991–2. As markets
came to doubt the sustainability of the government's position, the pound came
increasingly under speculative pressure and on 16 September 1992, known as
'Black Wednesday', Britain left the ERM. Given the difficulties with money-
supply targets during the 1980s, the government needed to find a new policy
framework that provided a credible commitment to low inflation. This involved
the adoption of an explicit inflation target, the monitoring of a wide range of
monetary indicators, and the appointment of an independent panel of economic
advisers (dubbed 'wise men' by the media). The Labour government elected in
May 1997 immediately signalled its commitment to a strict anti-inflation policy
by making the Bank of England independent.

Fiscal policy also provided a serious problem for the early years of the first
Major government, as a relaxation of government spending controls combined
with falling tax revenues during the recession of the early 1990s to produce a
general government financial deficit that reached 9 per cent of GDP in 1993.[45]
However, the subsequent economic recovery and fiscal changes reduced the
deficit sharply by the late 1990s.

The Major governments also continued with Thatcherite microeconomic policies, placing greater reliance on market forces. The railway network was privatised in 1994, whilst regulators battled to inject more competition into
previously privatised industries such as telecommunications and gas. The
Labour Party, having removed its Clause IV commitment to public ownership
of the means of production while in opposition, has avoided any commitment
to renationalisation while in government. To the extent that Labour sees a more
positive role for government than do the Conservatives, it is in areas such as
education and training rather than direct intervention in industry.

Britain has continued to have strained relations with Europe during the
1990s, despite the avowed intention of both John Major and Tony Blair
to adopt a more positive approach to European policy. Although Britain was
able to embrace the idea of the Single European Market with enthusiasm,
the federalist overtones of Economic and Monetary Union (EMU) created
strong opposition in both parties. Despite these misgivings, Britain did sign the
Maastricht Treaty in 1992 – although this was only after securing an opt-out
from the social chapter. A dispute over a ban on British beef exports after
an outbreak of BSE ('mad cow disease') led to Britain withdrawing cooperation with the European Union during 1996. Most importantly, however,
Britain remained outside the single European currency when it was introduced
in 1999.

Concluding Comments

The second half of the twentieth century saw quite a change in the framework of economic policy. With hindsight, it seems clear that the early post-war policy-makers were too optimistic about what could be achieved by demand management and interventionist industrial policies. After a period of substantial disagreement, particularly during the 1970s and the 1980s, a new consensus appears to have emerged as we enter the new millennium – namely, that macro-economic policy should be aimed primarily at providing price stability and microeconomic policy should help firms and individuals to compete in the market.

Notes

1 J. C. R. Dow, *The Management of the British Economy, 1945–60*, Cambridge, Cambridge University Press, 1964, pp. 11–12.
2 Alec Cairncross, *The British Economy since 1945*, Oxford, Blackwell, 1992, p. 7.
3 Ibid., pp. 47–57.
4 Ibid., pp. 57–67.
5 Note that in some years there was still an overall government financial deficit because of a deficit on capital account.
6 Cairncross, *British Economy*, pp. 72–4.
7 Leslie Hannah, 'The Economic Consequences of the State Ownership of Industry, 1845–1990', in Roderick Floud and Donald McCloskey (eds), *The Economic History of Britain Since 1700, Second Edition, Volume 3: 1939–1992*, Cambridge, Cambridge University Press, 1994, p. 171.
8 Nick Tiratsoo and Jim Tomlinson, *Industrial Efficiency and State Intervention: Labour 1939–51*, London, Routledge, 1993, ch. 4.
9 S. N. Broadberry and N. F. R. Crafts, 'British Economic Policy and Industrial Performance in the Early Post-War Period', *Business History* 38(4), 1996: 65–91.
10 Helen Mercer, *Constructing a Competitive Order: The Hidden History of British Antitrust Policies*, Cambridge: Cambridge University Press, 1995, chs 5–6.
11 Cairncross, *British Economy*, pp. 80–5.
12 Cairncross, *British Economy*, p. 90.
13 Cairncross, *British Economy*, pp. 120–6.
14 Cairncross, *British Economy*, pp. 128–30.
15 Britain's involvement in the Messina conference discussions for the formation of the EEC was very limited. See Jonathan Hollowell's chapter 4 in this book.
16 Samuel Brittan, *Steering the Economy: The Role of the Treasury*, Harmondsworth, Penguin, 1971, pp. 187–90.
17 Cairncross, *British Economy*, pp. 95–9.
18 N. H. Dimsdale, 'British Monetary Policy Since 1945', in N. F. R. Crafts and N. W. C. Woodward (eds), *The British Economy since 1945*, Oxford, Clarendon Press, 1991, pp. 92–3.
19 Cairncross, *British Economy*, pp. 112–14.
20 Mercer, *Constructing*, chs 5–6.
21 Cairncross, *British Economy*, ch. 4.

22   John Young, *Britain and European Unity, 1945–1999*, 2nd ed., London, Macmillan, 2000, chs 3 and 4.
23   Dimsdale, 'British Monetary Policy', pp. 92–3; see also Susan Howson, 'Money and Monetary Policy in Britain, 1945–1990', in Floud and McCloskey, *Economic History of Britain since 1700*, pp. 226–9.
24   Cairncross, *British Economy*, pp. 143–6, 161–2, 193–4.
25   Cairncross, *British Economy*, pp. 154–6.
26   Cairncross, *British Economy*, pp. 171–4.
27   Cairncross, *British Economy*, p. 182.
28   Cairncross, *British Economy*, pp. 200–1.
29   Anthony Barber was Chancellor of the Exchequer in the Heath government.
30   S. N. Broadberry, 'Unemployment', in Crafts and Woodward, *British Economy since 1945*, pp. 219–21.
31   Dimsdale, 'British Monetary Policy', pp. 92–3; Howson, 'Money', pp. 226–9.
32   Dimsdale, 'British Monetary Policy', pp. 117–25.
33   Dimsdale, 'British Monetary Policy', pp. 126–9.
34   Cairncross, *British Economy*, pp. 193–200, 220–4.
35   F. T. Blackaby, 'Narrative, 1960–74', in F. T. Blackaby (ed.), *British Economic Policy, 1960–74: Demand Management*, Cambridge, Cambridge University Press, 1979, p. 57.
36   Andrew Britton, *Macroeconomic Policy in Britain, 1974–87*, Cambridge, Cambridge University Press, 1991, p. 28.
37   Hannah, 'Economic Consequences', p. 171.
38   Cairncross, *British Economy*, p. 226.
39   Christopher Allsopp, Tim Jenkinson and Derek Morris, 'The Assessment: Macroeconomic Policy in the 1980s', *Oxford Review of Economic Policy* 7(3), 1991: 72.
40   Cairncross, *British Economy*, p. 251.
41   Allsopp, Jenkinson and Morris, 'The Assessment', p. 76.
42   John Muellbauer and Anthony Murphy, 'Is the UK Balance of Payments Sustainable?', *Economic Policy* 11, 1990: 348–9.
43   Britton, *Macroeconomic Policy*, pp. 67–8.
44   Charles Bean and Nicholas Crafts, 'British Economic Growth since 1945: Relative Economic Decline . . . and Renaissance?', in Nicholas Crafts and Gianni Toniolo (eds), *Economic Growth in Europe Since 1945*, Cambridge, Cambridge University Press, 1996, pp. 133–4.
45   Nigel Pain, Garry Young and Peter Westaway, 'The State of the Public Finances', *National Institute Economic Review* 145, 1993: 29–42.

Further Reading

Introduction and overview

Alec Cairncross, *The British Economy since 1945: Economic Policy and Performance, 1945–1990*, Oxford, Blackwell, 1992.
N. F. R. Crafts and N. W. C. Woodward (eds), *The British Economy Since 1945*, Oxford, Clarendon Press, 1991.
Roderick Floud and Donald McCloskey (eds), *The Economic History of Britain Since 1700, Second Edition, Volume 3: 1939–1992*, Cambridge, Cambridge University Press, 1994.

1945–1950: reconstruction

Alec Cairncross, *Years of Recovery: British Economic Policy 1945–51*, London, Methuen, 1985.

Martin Chick, *Industrial Policy in Britain, 1945–1951: Economic Planning, Nationalisation and the Labour Governments*, Cambridge: Cambridge University Press, 1998.

J. C. R. Dow, *The Management of the British Economy 1945–60*, Cambridge, Cambridge University Press, 1965.

Nick Tiratsoo and Jim Tomlinson, *Industrial Efficiency and State Intervention: Labour 1939–51*, London, Routledge, 1993.

G. D. N. Worswick and P. H. Ady (eds), *The British Economy, 1945–1950*, Oxford, Clarendon Press, 1952.

The 1950s

Samuel Brittan, *Steering the Economy: The Role of the Treasury*, revised ed., Harmondsworth, Penguin, 1971.

G. D. N. Worswick and P. H. Ady (eds), *The British Economy in the Nineteen-Fifties*, Oxford, Clarendon Press, 1962.

The 1960s

Wilfred Beckerman (ed.), *The Labour Government's Economic Record*, London, Duckworth, 1972.

F. T. Blackaby (ed.), *British Economic Policy 1960–74*, Cambridge, Cambridge University Press, 1978.

Peter Browning, *The Treasury and Economic Policy, 1964–1985*, London, Longman, 1986.

Michael Stewart, *Politics and Economic Policy in the UK since 1964*, Oxford, Pergamon Press, 1978.

The 1970s

Michael Artis and David Cobham (eds), *Labour's Economic Policies, 1974–79*, Manchester, Manchester University Press, 1991.

F. T. Blackaby (ed.), *British Economic Policy 1960–74*, Cambridge, Cambridge University Press, 1979.

Andrew Britton, *Macroeconomic Policy in Britain 1974–87*, Cambridge, Cambridge University Press, 1991.

The 1980s

Christopher Allsopp, Tim Jenkinson and Derek Morris, 'The Assessment: Macroeconomic Policy in the 1980s', *Oxford Review of Economic Policy*, 7(3), 1991: 68–80.

Andrew Britton, *Macroeconomic Policy in Britain, 1974–87* (Cambridge: Cambridge University Press, 1991).

Chronology

1945 General election won by Labour with majority of 146 (July). US loan agreed (Dec.).

1946   Bank of England nationalised (Mar.).

1947   Coal industry nationalised (Jan.). Fuel crisis: use of electricity restricted (Feb.) General Marshall's Harvard speech on European recovery (June). Sterling made convertible (July–Aug.).

1948   Railways nationalised (Jan.). Monopolies and Restrictive Practices Act (May).

1949   Devaluation of the pound to $2.80 (Sept.).

1950   Schuman Plan for the ECSC announced (May). European Payments Union established (Sept., with retrospective effect from July).

1951   Steel industry nationalised (vesting date) (Feb.). General election won by Conservatives with majority of 17 (Oct.). Bank Rate raised to 2.5 per cent (Nov.).

1952   Cabinet sets aside 'Robot' plan for sterling convertibility (Feb.).

1953   Steel industry denationalised (Mar.).

1954   Food rationing ends (July).

1956   Restrictive Trade Practices Act (May).

1957   COPPI appointed (Aug.).

1958   EEC inaugurated (Jan.). Special Deposit scheme announced (July). Convertibility for external sterling (Dec.).

1959   Radcliffe Report (Aug.). EFTA treaty agreed (Nov.).

1961   'Pay pause' (to April 1962); first use of tax regulator. NEDC to be established (July).

1964   Resale Price Maintenance abolished (Apr.). $1 billion loan from IMF (Dec.).

1965   Monopolies and Mergers Act (Aug.). NBPI established (Mar.). National Plan announced (Sept.).

1966   IRC established (Jan.). Six-month wage freeze (July).

1967   Steel industry renationalised (Mar.). Devaluation of sterling to $2.40 (Nov.).

1969   Plans for legal restraints on unofficial strikes dropped (June).

1970   Industrial Relations Bill introduced (Dec.).

1971   Rolls Royce nationalised; decimalisation of the currency (Feb.). Competition and Credit Control introduced (Sep.). Smithsonian agreement on exchange rates (Dec.).

1972   Sterling allowed to float (June). Bank Rate becomes MLR (Oct.). Ninety-day freeze on prices, pay and dividends (Nov.).

1973   UK joins EEC (Jan.). Phase 2 of incomes policy (Apr.). Phase 3 of incomes policy (Oct.). First oil price shock (Oct.–Dec.), Announcement of 3-day week from January; introduction of Supplementary Special Deposits (the 'corset') (Dec.).

1974   Labour government; end of 3-day week and miners' strike (Mar.). UK demands renegotiation of EEC terms (Apr.). Repeal of Industrial Relations Act; abolition of Pay Board (July).

1975   British Leyland nationalised (Apr.). Aircraft and shipbuilding industries nationalised (May.). Britain's first North Sea oil extracted (June). £6 a week limit on wage increases (July). NEB established (Nov.).

1976   Pound falls to $1.57; negotiations with IMF begun for a loan (Oct.). Letter of intent submitted to IMF; target set for £M3,000 (Dec.).

1978   Government proposes 5 per cent pay increase guideline (July). Pay guideline rejected by Labour Party Conference (Oct.).

1979   Exchange control discontinued (Oct.). Second oil price shock (Oct.–Feb.).

1980   Medium Term Financial Strategy announced (Mar.). Competition Act (Apr.). 'Corset' ends (June). £ peaks against the dollar at $2.45 (Nov.).

1981   MLR suspended (Aug.).

1982   Unemployment figures pass 3 million (Jan.). Employment Act (Oct.).

1984   Miners' strike begins (Mar.). Agreement over UK rebate on contribution to EEC budget (June). Trade Union Act (July). British Telecom privatised (Nov.).

1985   £ falls to $1.11 (Jan.).
1986   'Big Bang' on London Stock Exchange (Oct.). British Gas privatised (Dec.).
1987   Chancellor describes informal targets for sterling (Apr.). Sharp fall in stock exchange prices (Oct.).
1989   Employment Act (Nov.).
1990   Privatisation of electricity distribution (Sept.). Britain enters ERM (Oct.).
1991   Privatisation of electricity generation (Feb.).
1992   Maastricht Treaty signed (Feb.). Britain leaves ERM (Sept.). Panel of economic advisers appointed (Dec.).
1993   Single European Market established.
1994   Railways privatised (Apr.).
1997   Bank of England given independence (May.).
1999   EMU: eleven countries adopt the Euro (Jan.).

21 Employment and the Labour Market

Duncan Gallie

The second half of the twentieth century was a period of radical restructuring of the British labour market. The changing structure of industry and the impact of the most pervasive technological revolution since the nineteenth century altered the nature of the jobs available and the types and levels of skill required. At the same time, there was a striking change in the composition of the workforce. The combination of new forms of work and changing social values brought about a marked increase in women's participation in the labour market, giving a new salience to issues of gender equality. Particularly in the closing decades of the century, this restructuring of work and of the workforce was accompanied by a marked decline in employee security, as a result of the reduction of trade union influence, the growth of short-term contracts and extended periods of high unemployment.

The Changing Structure of Employment

The second half of the twentieth century saw a fundamental transformation of the types of jobs available on the labour market. This process was driven by three main factors: the growing importance of service employment, the rapid spread of new technologies from the 1980s and, finally, the long-term rise in the skills of the workforce.

It was in the second half of the 1960s that Britain became for the first time a society in which a majority of the workforce was employed in the service industries. The trend continued apace in the following decades, with service-sector employment rising from 52 per cent in 1971 to 67 per cent of all people in employment by 1991. This reflected sharp rises in the numbers employed in the welfare services (for instance, education and medicine), but even more dramatic increases in commercial services, in particular finance and recreation, where the workforce doubled between the mid-1960s and 1991. The reverse side of the coin was the sharp decline in manufacturing, where over the same period the numbers employed fell by 43 per cent. It was a far from smooth transition. There had been a high degree of regional specialisation of the traditional industries. The successive collapses of textiles, shipbuilding, steel and coal mining left whole communities bereft of their major employers and facing levels of unemployment unprecedented since the inter-war period. Sectoral transformation involved a crucial change in the nature of work. The skills required in the growing service industries were quite different in type from those in manufacturing: physical and manual skills were displaced by general educational and social skills (the ability to communicate with and deal with people as clients, customers, pupils and patients).

A second development that had a major impact on the nature of work was the new wave of automation brought about by the diffusion of micro-electronic technology. In the early post-war period, there was already considerable speculation about the way in which the automation of factories through continuous-process production would transform the nature of industrial work. Studies of chemical factories and oil refineries suggested that such technologies reversed the previous tendency towards an ever-greater division of labour and instead gave a renewed importance both to individual decision-making skills and to team work (Blauner, 1964). However, the general assumption that such processes would be applied rapidly to a much wider spectrum of industry proved to be incorrect. Their capital-intensive nature and the relatively inflexible nature of the technology restricted their use to large-scale establishments involved in the mass production of liquid or crystalline products. It was only with the spread of microprocessor technology from the 1980s that a sufficiently general and flexible means of automation emerged to transform systems of work across both manufacturing and service industries. It was a development that affected not only workers on the shop floor, but all other categories of employee. Personal computers and the growth of networks transformed activities as diverse as secretarial work, stock management, customer sales, design, financial administration and personnel management. The pace of change was remarkable: whereas 39 per cent of employees were working with computerised or automated equipment in 1986, the figure had risen to 56 per cent by 1992.

Finally, partly as a result of these sectoral and technological developments, the nature of work changed in terms of the skill levels required of the workforce. The evidence on the trends in skill in the period between 1945 to the early 1980s is rather tentative. There was a clear upward shift in terms of the occupational classification. Taking the data from the censuses, the proportion of the workforce in professional and managerial jobs rose from 12.1 per cent in 1951 to 34.3 per cent in 1991. At the same time the proportion of semi and non-skilled manual workers fell from 39.2 per cent to 23.3 per cent. But case-study evidence pointed to contradictory trends in skill development, and in some cases suggested that substantial deskilling was occurring among skilled manual, clerical and even technical workers (Braverman, 1974; Crompton and Jones, 1984; Smith, 1987). It is difficult for this period to know how far such findings reflected general processes or developments that were specific to the workplaces studied.

However, from the mid-1980s, a much clearer picture is available from na-tional data that is representative of the workforce. Comparable data on the skill requirements of jobs for 1986, 1992 and 1997 provides very consistent evidence of a general trend towards rising levels of skill (Gallie et al., 1998; Green et al., 1998). There was a marked rise in the qualifications required for jobs, and also in the length of on-the-job experience needed to do the job properly. It is notable that, in the mid-1980s, 52 per cent of all employees reported that the skill requirements of their jobs had increased over the previous five years. By the early 1990s, however, the figure had risen to 63 per cent. Deskilling, in contrast, was a relatively rare experience: in both periods only 9 per cent had experienced a reduction in the level of skill they used at work. The increase in skills was very pervasive across the occupational structure, but it is notable that the low-skilled benefited less than other categories. Whereas 79 per cent of professionals and technicians had experienced skill development between the late 1980s and early 1990s, this was the case for only 50 per cent of semi- and non-skilled workers. These broad trends are confirmed by the figures for the proportion of employees receiving training. The proportion of employees who had received training in the previous three years rose from 33 per cent in 1986/ 7 to 54 per cent in 1992, but people without qualifications had training less than half as frequently as those who did have them (Gallie and White, 1993, p. 134).

Part of the rise in skill requirements reflected the fact that there was a grow-ing proportion of higher-level jobs. But there was also evidence of substantial upskilling of existing posts. A majority even of people who had remained in the same job and with the same employer had experienced an increase in their skills. The process of upskilling affected not only manufacturing and the utilities but equally the service industries. It was most marked in energy and water, telecommunications, financial services, central and local government and med-ical services. The pressures for higher skill levels were partly related to the rapid technological change discussed above. People who worked with computerised or automated equipment were much more likely to have seen the skill require-ments of their jobs increase. For instance, in 1992, whereas 73 per cent of those in jobs involving the use of new technology had experienced an increase in their skills, this was the case for only 49 per cent of others (Gallie et al., 1998). But the growth of services for people also contributed to the trend, with skill demands increasing for 67 per cent of those whose job tasks primarily involved dealing with people. This was in sharp contrast with work in traditional assem-bly-line manufacturing industry, where only 40 per cent reported an increase in their skills, while as many as 22 per cent considered that their work had been deskilled.

The rise in skill levels had major, but quite ambivalent, implications for the quality of work life. On the one hand, it was associated with more intrinsically interesting work. People who had experienced an increase in the skill require-ments of their jobs were more likely to report increased variety in their work, they had greater discretion and responsibility in how they carried out their work tasks, they were more likely to be able to make full use of their skills, and they were more likely to feel absorbed by the work. On the other hand, the upward shift in skills was linked to a considerable intensification of work effort. Overall, 62 per cent of employees in 1992 reported that the effort they had to put into their job had increased over the previous five years. However, this was the case for more than three-quarters of those whose skills had increased (77 per cent), compared with only 16 per cent of those for whom skill requirements at work had remained unchanged (Gallie et al., 1998). This intensification of effort translated into greater stress from work. Those who had experienced a skill increase were very much more likely to feel exhausted and to find it difficult to unwind at the end of the working day.

Women in the Labour Market

The jobs generated by the expansion of the service sector were very largely taken by women, leading to major changes in the sexual division of employment. Whereas in 1951 only 33 per cent of women were economically active, the proportion had risen to 54 per cent in 1991. In contrast, over the same period men's participation rates fell from 88 per cent to 73 per cent. Taking the population of working age, men's participation declined from 96 per cent in 1951 to 87 per cent in 1991, while women's rose from 43 per cent to 71 per cent (Hakim, 1996, p. 62). The increase was particularly striking among married women aged between 35 and 54 with children (Brannen et al., 1994; Harrop and Moss, 1995). In the early post-war decades the pattern of women's labour market participation took a distinct 'M' shape, with the proportions in work rising to a relatively high level in early adulthood, followed by a sharp decline in the child-rearing years and a return to higher levels when the children grew older. In the decades since the mid-century, this has progressively given way to a relatively flat pattern of participation across the prime age ranges. Women have been increasingly likely to return to the labour market after a period of domestic absence and they have returned after shorter spells away from work (Martin and Roberts, 1984, p. 11; McRae, 1991, 1995).

These trends reflected a marked shift in the value women attached to employment, with their commitment to longer-term employment converging by the early 1990s to a very similar level to that of men (Gallie et al., 1998). Whereas in 1981 women were significantly less likely than men to say that they would want a job irrespective of financial need (60 per cent compared with 69 per cent), by 1992 there was little difference (68 and 67 per cent respectively). They were also very similar to men in terms of the importance they attached to the intrinsic quality of jobs: the variety of the work, the chance to use their abilities and the availability of training. There remained, however, some differences in the type of job that men and women wanted. Women were less likely to emphasise promotion and pay and more likely to stress the importance of the quality of human relationships (both with colleagues and supervisors), the convenience of the hours they worked and the need for good physical work conditions. Over the period 1980 to 1992, however, the importance attached to convenient work hours declined markedly: 75 per cent considered it an essential or very important aspect of a job in 1980, whereas in 1992 this was the case for only 48 per cent. In contrast, there was a rise in the importance given to the opportunity to use one's abilities (79 per cent compared to 71 per cent).[1] Overall, the evidence suggests a growing centrality of employment to women's lives. This was reflected in a tendency for the average duration of their jobs to increase while those of men were declining (Dex and McCulloch, 1997, pp. 100–1).

The increase in women's employment was heavily concentrated in the service sector. By 1998 women constituted 54 per cent of all people working in services, compared to only 27 per cent of those working in manufacturing. The concentration was particularly marked in public administration, education and health where they constituted 69 per cent of the workforce. Hence, despite the growing numbers of women employed, the level of gender segregation in the labour market was still very marked. While there was an erosion of the jobs that were virtually exclusively female (as there was of jobs that were virtually exclusively male), there was no decline since the mid-century in the likelihood that women would be working predominantly with other women. Indeed, the proportion of women working in occupations in which women constituted 70 per cent or more of those employed rose from 50 per cent in 1951 to 63 per cent in 1991. If measures of workplace rather than occupational segregation are used, the pervasiveness of sex segregation in employment emerges even more strongly (Martin and Roberts, 1984).

Despite the growing integration of women into the permanent workforce, progress with respect to equality of occupational status and terms of employment remained slow. In terms of occupational position, women were still heavily over-represented in clerical work and the lower professions, while they were much less likely than men to be in higher professional or managerial jobs. The census data show that women's share of higher professional jobs certainly increased over the period, from 8 per cent in 1951 to 18 per cent in 1991. As Crompton and Sanderson (1990) argued, this is likely to have reflected the efficacy of the 'qualification' lever in opening up opportunities for women. But even allowing for differences in participation rates, it is clear that women were very far from achieving equality of occupational position.

There has also been persisting inequality in pay, although the sex differential in earnings has declined since the 1970s. Whereas in 1970 women in full-time work earned 64 per cent of the earnings of men (excluding overtime), the proportion rose to 74 per cent in 1976 and (after a further period of relative stability in the 1980s) to 80 per cent by 1995 (Hakim, 1996, p. 175). However, the survival of such pay differentials at a time when women's qualifications have become very similar to men's, and in the context of substantially stronger legal safeguards for equal pay, has become a major focus of concern. While part of the remaining differential can be accounted for in terms of differences in work experience (for instance, in the career continuity of employment and tenure with particular employers), it has been estimated that such 'human capital' characteristics can only account for approximately one-third of the pay gap between male and female full-timers (Joshi and Paci, 1998, p. 63). There is no clear effect of the tendency for women to be segregated into jobs largely occupied by other women, although their under-representation in higher level jobs does play a role. But even when job characteristics are taken into account, there is still a significant unexplained gap, with women full-timers in a given occupation being paid 12 per cent less than equivalent men (ibid., pp. 85, 94–5).

The growth of female employment has also differed strongly from the traditional pattern for male employment in that it virtually entirely took the form of an expansion of part-time jobs. Whereas in 1951 only 11 per cent of female employees were working part-time, by 1971 this had increased to 33.5 per cent and by 1998 to 45.6 per cent. The growth in number of women in jobs was then accompanied by little change in the overall number of hours worked by women (Joshi, Layard and Owen, 1985). This raises the issue of how far part-time work has been associated with disadvantage for women in the labour market.

The growth of part-time work fitted well with the need for more flexible-hour schedules in the service sector. Part-timers were disproportionately concentrated in the service industries. In the private services they were to be found above all in retail and finance. In the public services, they were principally in education, medical services and welfare. A survey of employers found that it was above all the fact that the work tasks themselves required shorter periods of time, and the need to extend opening or production hours, that led to the preference to recruit part-timers.[2] Taken together, these two reasons accounted for 76 per cent of the main reasons given by employers (McGregor and Sproull, 1991, p. 26). This suggests that part-timers were being used for services that slotted round the standard working day, providing high levels of coverage over lunchtimes, evenings and weekends.

The fact that most of the new jobs were part-time was an important factor, accounting for the persistence of high levels of gender segregation. Over 80 per cent of part-time jobs were in female-dominated occupations (Hakim, 1998, pp. 134–5). Part-time work is also associated with a number of disadvantages in terms of employment conditions. Even when account is taken of occupational class and age, women in part-time work tend to have jobs with lower skill requirements, fewer opportunities for the use of initiative, less variety, fewer opportunities for skill development and poorer promotion opportunities than women in full-time jobs (Tam, 1997). The earnings penalty attached to part-time work is more questionable. Female part-time workers do less well in terms of gross hourly pay than their full-time equivalents, but when allowance is made for qualifications, work experience, training, firm and job characteristics, there is either only a relatively small (Joshi and Paci 1998) or no independent effect (Lissenburgh, 1996) of part-time work on pay. However, part-time workers are systematically disadvantaged in terms of a range of non-wage benefits.

While there are marked differences in employment conditions between part-time workers and full-timers, there is little evidence of an ongoing process of polarisation. Between the mid-1980s and the early 1990s, there was a clear convergence in the skill requirements of full-time and part-time female jobs, and there is also some evidence of an improvement in perceived career chances (Gallie et al. 1998, pp. 156–9, 165). In part this is due to the fact that an increased proportion of part-time jobs are at higher levels in the occupational structure. It seems likely that such convergence will continue under the pressures for greater uniformity of employment conditions deriving from the directives of the European Union (EU). For instance, during the early 1990s, as a result of European initiatives, female part-timers secured the right both to participate in employers' pension schemes and to be covered by unfair dismissal procedures.

There has been a lively debate about how far women have been constrained into the disadvantageous conditions of part-time work and how far they have chosen it in the context of essentially home-centred values. Hakim (1996), for instance, has strongly advocated a voluntaristic interpretation, pointing to evidence about the distinctiveness of part-timers in terms of their job preferences and attitudes to the domestic division of labour. Those emphasising the constrained nature of part-time work (for instance Dex, 1988; Tam, 1997) have pointed to limited opportunities for choice in a country where childcare provision remained highly inadequate. It is clear that a major factor influencing women in taking part-time work is the importance they attach to convenient hours of work for balancing their work and domestic responsibilities (Martin and Roberts, 1984, p. 72). Nearly three-quarters of female part-timers (72 per cent) report that the reason why they left their previous job to take up part-time work was for family care (Dex and McCulloch, 1997, p. 125). What is still unknown is whether the same pattern of job preferences would prevail if reliable and affordable childcare were available. It is notable, however, that at least between the 1980s and the early 1990s, there was a marked convergence in the level of employment commitment of full-time and part-time women. In 1981, 65 per cent of female full-timers reported that would want a job even if they did not need the money, whereas this was the case for only 54 per cent of part-timers. The identical question asked in 1992 showed a much narrower gap between the two categories of worker, with 69 per cent for full timers and 64 per cent for part-timers (Gallie et al., 1998).

The Polarisation of the Workforce?

From the 1980s, there were accumulating signs that, in the face of greater competitive pressure, employers were placing a new emphasis on the restructuring both of work and of the workforce. An important aspect of this was the introduction of technological change and the reskilling of the workforce. But there was also a new emphasis on the importance of increasing flexibility, both of work practices and of staffing. An influential version of this argument (Atkinson, 1984) depicted a scenario in which the workforce was becoming increasingly divided between a secure core of employees on permanent full-time contracts and a periphery of workers on non-standard contracts who could be relatively easily disposed of in times of economic downturn. This peripheral workforce was constituted primarily by temporary, part-time and self-employed workers. Estimates suggested that the flexible or peripheral workforce had expanded from 30 per cent to 38 per cent of the overall workforce from 1980 to 1993 (Hakim, 1987; Watson, 1994).

This argument assumed that employers typically had clearly conceived and relatively long-range workforce strategies. But there are grounds for doubting whether this is the case. A survey of employers who made use of workers on non-standard contracts found that just over a third said that their decisions on labour use were guided by a strategy or plan (Hunter et al., 1993). Moreover, of these only a third characterised that strategy in terms of some type of core/periphery model. Case-study evidence provided a very similar picture, suggesting that managerial decisions about the use of such workers was guided far more by temporary cost-cutting considerations than by any longer-term strategy.

The very diversity of the employment conditions of different types of non-standard worker also calls into question any simple theory of core/periphery polarisation. The employment situation of people on temporary work contracts comes closest to that held to characterise the peripheral workforce. But, while there was some increase from the 1980s in the proportion of employees on such contracts, it was much smaller than would have been expected in the light of the more apocalyptic visions of the development of the labour market. Taking the Labour Force Survey estimates, 5.3 per cent of all employees were temporary workers in 1984, whereas the proportion had risen to 7.1 per cent by 1998. The figure was consistently somewhat higher for women than for men. In 1998, 8.3 per cent of female employees were on temporary contracts compared with 6 per cent of male employees.[3] In comparative perspective, the striking point about the British labour market in the final quarter of the century was not the rapidity of the growth of temporary work, but rather the low proportion of the workforce in temporary work compared to other European countries. In 1996, at a time when temporary workers constituted 6.9 per cent of the workforce in the UK, they were on average 11.7 per cent of the workforce of the EU, while, at the extreme, the proportion rose to 33.5 per cent in Spain.

There can be little doubt that temporary workers suffered substantially from job insecurity, and a significant and growing proportion reported that they had taken a temporary job only because they had been unable to find a permanent one (Beatson, 1995, p. 17). Whereas this was the case for 35 per cent in 1984, the proportion had risen to 43 per cent by 1994. However, the employment conditions of temporary workers vary considerably by type of contract. Temporary workers on short-term contracts (lasting less than year) did experience systematically worse employment conditions than their full-time equivalents. Quite apart from particularly acute job insecurity, they were in jobs that offered more limited opportunities for developing their skills, less responsibility and lower intrinsic job interest (Gallie et al., 1998, pp. 176–8). However, temporary workers on longer contracts (1–3 years) were in a rather different position. They tended to have a skill profile that was broadly similar to that of the workforce as a whole, and their jobs were at least as good as those of permanent workers in terms of opportunities for skill development, training and intrinsic job interest. While they had a high level of anxiety about job security, a substantial proportion (43 per cent) felt that they had a reasonable chance of getting a better job within their current organisations. In short, while some temporary workers could be regarded as trapped in a 'peripheral' labour market, others were most likely to be in entry positions in preparation for careers within the permanent workforce.

Numerically, the most important type of non-standard contract has been that of part-time work, particularly female part-time work. However, the growth of women's part-time employment appeared to have reached a plateau by the early 1990s. As was seen earlier, there were many respects in which the employment conditions of part-timers are highly disadvantageous. This is not, however, sufficient to consider part-time workers to be part of a peripheral or flexible workforce. The essential characteristic of the peripheral worker is the lack of job security. But there is little evidence that part-timers have suffered from higher levels of job insecurity than women with permanent full-time jobs. They did tend to have somewhat shorter spells of employment, but this was more due to personal decision than to the action of the employer. There is little evidence that part-time work was either a reflection of or a cause of involuntary job loss. The great majority of part-timers had taken such work because they did not want a full-time job: overall this accounted for 74 per cent of part-timers in 1994 (Beatson, 1995, p. 16). Involuntary part-time work was higher among men than women, but even in the group that felt most constrained (married men) only 33 per cent wanted a full-time job. Women in part-time work were very unlikely to have experienced unemployment before moving into part-time work, with 93 per cent never having experienced unemployment (Dex and McCulloch, 1997, p. 124). They were no more likely than full-timers to move into unemployment after leaving their jobs (Gallie et al., 1998, p. 171).

Whereas the major growth in non-standard contract jobs for women was in part-time work, for men it was predominantly in self-employment. Overall, the proportion of the workforce in self-employment rose from 7.3 per cent in 1979 to 12 per cent in 1998. Over the same period, the proportion of self-employed men increased from 9.8 per cent to 16.1 per cent, and of women from 3.3 per cent to 7.2 per cent. However, the growth of self-employment appeared to have peaked for both men and women by the end of the 1980s; in the 1990s it declined slightly for men, while staying stable for women. Even more than in the case of part-time work, it is difficult to consider self-employment as unambiguously peripheral labour. The most important reason that people give for entering self-employment is their preference for autonomy, scarcely suggesting that they are coerced into a particularly undesirable form of work. There is little evidence from their past work histories that they were people trapped in a particularly unstable sector of the labour market. Whether one considers self-employed men or women, they were less likely to have had an experience of unemployment than full-time permanent employees (Dex and McCulloch, 1997, p. 81).

Overall, then, the evidence does not suggest that there has been a sharp trend towards labour market polarisation of a core/periphery type. It is the case that full-time permanent employment has declined as a proportion of the workforce and there has been a corresponding fragmentation of contract status, although these trends largely levelled off in the 1990s. Those on 'non-standard' contracts, however, represent a very diverse set of groups and they are far from sharing a high level of job insecurity. While a section of temporary workers do suffer from multiple deprivation in their employment conditions, self-employed and part-time workers are involved in a complex trade-off between advantageous and disadvantageous aspects of their job. It is significant that, if the different groups are compared on a measure of psychological well-being, it is only temporary workers that show consistently higher levels of psychological distress than permanent full-time workers (Dex and McCulloch, 1997, p. 75).

Job Insecurity and Unemployment

The more fundamental deterioration in the labour market since the mid-1970s has been the general growth in job insecurity and in the risk of unemployment. The last quarter of the century saw the re-emergence of mass unemployment on a scale unprecedented since the great depression of the inter-war years. Throughout the period between 1945 and 1970, the unemployment rate was less than three per cent of the workforce. It started rising in the second half of the 1970s, reaching 5.7 per cent by 1979, and then escalated in the early 1980s, rising as high as 12.2 per cent of the workforce in 1983. After an improvement in the second half of the 1980s, it rose again sharply to in the early 1990s, peaking at over 10 per cent of the workforce in 1993, before once more declining.

It was, then, a period of very sharp and unpredictable changes in the labour market that were likely to have major consequences for people's underlying sense of security in work. An analysis of British longitudinal data indicated that whereas 62 per cent of employees were concerned about their job security in 1991, the proportion rose to 78 per cent in 1993, a level at which it remained stable through to 1995. While women were less likely to report dissatisfaction with job security than men, the same basic upward trend was evident for both sexes (OECD, 1997, p. 136). While there is little evidence of major changes in job tenure between the mid-1980s and the mid-1990s, the likelihood of experiencing a spell of unemployment between jobs rose sharply from the 1970s (ibid., p. 140). Unemployment also fell particularly on those with low or no qualifications and on manual workers, reflecting the shifts in the occupational structure described earlier. Despite the common belief that the 1990s saw an increase in the vulnerability of those in higher class positions, the evidence indicates that there was virtually no change between the early 1980s and the early 1990s in the relative risks of manual workers compared to those in professional and managerial work, with non-skilled manual workers remaining three times more likely to become unemployed in any five-year period. While those in professional and managerial work certainly came to constitute a larger proportion of the unemployed, this just reflected the fact that they represented a growing share of employment (Gallie et al., 1998, pp. 142–3).

A distinctive feature of the situation in Britain was that the burden of unemployment fell particularly heavily on men. This might have been expected with respect to the official unemployment figures which were based on registration for benefit, since men were more likely to meet the eligibility requirement for receiving benefit. But the greater vulnerability of men also emerges when an International Labour Organization (ILO) definition of unemployment is used, which is much more comprehensive in its coverage of women's unemployment.

In every year for which such figures were available (1984–98), the unemployment rate for men was higher than that for women and, indeed, the sex differential was greater in the 1990s than had been the case in the 1980s. For instance in 1993, the peak point of unemployment in the 1990s, the female unemployment rate was 7.6 per cent, compared to 12.3 per cent for men. In part this reflected the fact that recession affected particularly severely manufacturing industry (where men were disproportionately employed). But women also escaped from unemployment more quickly, possibly because so many of the new job opportunities were in part-time work.

A controversial issue has been whether the emergence of stronger welfare provision in the post-war period has had a significant impact on either the work attitudes of the unemployed or on the experience of unemployment. In seeking to reduce the high levels of unemployment that prevailed after the early 1980s, a major preoccupation of government policy has been the alteration of the rules governing eligibility for unemployment benefit. Following the assumption that markets have a natural tendency to clear unless there are important institutional rigidities, the benefit system was considered a significant cause of persisting high unemployment. It was argued that it was necessary to make benefits less generous in order to enhance incentives for the unemployed to find work. In practice there is remarkably little empirical evidence that there has been any widespread 'motivational deficit' among the unemployed. It might be considered inherently implausible that the sharp oscillations in levels of unemployment in the 1980s and 1990s were explicable in terms of the motivational characteristics of the unemployed themselves. Certainly, analyses of the work histories of unemployed people showed that these were typically people who had demonstrated a high level of employability in the past. Moreover, evidence on work attitudes both in the 1980s and in the 1990s consistently showed that the great majority of the unemployed were committed to employment. Indeed, a higher proportion of the unemployed (men and women) would have wanted to work irrespective of pay than was the case among people who were in jobs (Gallie, Marsh and Vogler, 1993; Gallie et al., 1994).

The nature of the British benefit system, however, did have major implications for the level of deprivation that accompanied unemployment. Already in the 1980s, before the benefit system had been 'tightened', research showed that people typically experienced a very sharp drop in living standards when they became unemployed. For instance, a major study carried out in 1983–4 (Heady and Smyth, 1989) reported that, after three months of unemployment, the average disposable income of families whose head had previously been in full-time work was 59 per cent of the level it had been before signing on. Most families experienced a rapid and substantial reduction in their material living standards, with particularly sharp cuts in food, clothing and entertainment. In the 1990s comparative analyses of the extent to which unemployment benefit replaced the typical income of industrial workers showed that Britain was distinctive in its very low replacement rate. It has been estimated that in 1996 compensation rates for an unemployed 'average production worker' were 56 per cent in Denmark, 72 per cent in Sweden, 60 per cent in Germany and 70 per cent in the Netherlands, but only 16 per cent in Great Britain (Hansen, 1998).

This general impression of the particular severity of the British system is reinforced by analyses of poverty rates among unemployed people. A comparison between Denmark, Germany, France, Ireland, Italy, the Netherlands, Sweden and the UK showed that Britain stood out in the 1990s as the country which had the highest proportion of unemployed below the poverty threshold (Hauser and Nolan, 2000). In Denmark, where the unemployed were best protected, only 7 per cent of the unemployed were in poverty, whereas in Britain this was the case for 49 per cent.[4] It was also notable that, when the poverty figures for the 1990s were compared with those for the 1980s, Britain stood out as the country which had experienced the sharpest increase in poverty over the decade.

It is clear that the high level of financial deprivation experienced by the British unemployed was very closely linked to the minimalist nature of the benefit system. In the 1990s, the British transfer system was particularly ineffective as a mechanism for protecting the unemployed from poverty (Nolan Hauser and Zoyem, 2000). Only 19 per cent of those unemployed who were in poverty in terms of their non-transfer income were lifted out of poverty by social transfers. This compared with 32 per cent in Germany, over 50 per cent in France, Sweden and Ireland and 89 per cent in Denmark. Comparison with the 1980s shows that Britain was also characterised by a particularly sharp drop in the effectiveness of the welfare system in protecting the unemployed from poverty over the decade.

The evidence has been consistent that unemployment in Britain has led to significant psychological distress (Warr, 1987). This could not be accounted for by a process of self-selection in which more distressed people became unemployed. Longitudinal studies have shown that unemployment leads to a deterioration in psychological well-being and that distress is reduced again when people find work (Warr and Jackson, 1985; Warr, 1987). The effects on psychological well-being are as strong for middle-class as for working-class people (Payne, Warr and Hartley, 1984). While the level of social support available to people does reduce distress, the unemployed had lower access to such support than people in employment (ibid., pp. 253–7). In part, this was due to the tendency for the unemployed to socialise with other unemployed people, who lack the emotional or material resources to offer substantial support. Finally, it is notable that comparative research shows that, together with Ireland, it is in Britain that the severity of the psychological effects of unemployment has been greatest over the two decades (Gallie and Russell, 1998).

Overall, then, the re-emergence of high levels of unemployment in last quarter of the century resulted in very sharp personal deprivation for the many millions of people affected. Moreover, its ramifications go further than those who directly experience unemployment. Unemployment also leads to higher psychological stress for the partner of the unemployed person (Heady and Smyth, 1989, pp. 63, 66). A number of qualitative studies have emphasised the high risk of family conflict that arises as a result of unemployment, particularly as a result of the financial pressures it involves (Fagin and Little, 1984; McKee and Bell, 1985, 1986). A longitudinal analysis of the relationship of unemployment and family stability found that even when a wide range of personal characteristics have been taken into account, people who become unemployed have over twice the risk of marital dissolution in the following year of those who do not (Lampard, 1993).

Labour Regulation and Deregulation

Until the end of the 1970s Britain had a system of employment regulation that was largely based on voluntary collective bargaining and in which legal controls played a very limited role (Clegg, 1979). The 1950s and 1960s saw the culmination of this system, with the expansion of the role of shop-steward organisations which acquired substantial *de facto* powers of joint regulation, not only over pay, but over many aspects of work organisation (Batstone, Boraston and Frenkel, 1977). The informal and decentralised nature of the growth of shop-floor power led to a highly fragmented system of regulation, in which the relationship between different levels of bargaining (industry, workplace, shop floor) was weakly defined and wider industry norms increasingly gave way to a patchwork of local agreements.

It was a system that inevitably led to a rather uneven system of regulation, in which protection accrued primarily to those in larger, more strongly unionised workplaces. Many of the studies that pointed to an expansion of shop-floor control were based on manufacturing industry, in particular the automobile industry. But when, in the 1980s, surveys provided for the first time an overview of the pattern of union recognition and shop-steward presence across industry as a whole, it became clear that there were many sectors of the economy where employees had relatively little protection from arbitrary management authority. Even although small establishments with less than 25 employees were excluded from the enquiry, a third of all establishments did not recognise any union (Daniel and Millward, 1983, p. 18). While the proportions recognising manual unions rose to as high as 72 per cent in vehicle manufacture, they fell to only 30 per cent in miscellaneous services (ibid., p. 26). Taking the presence of shop stewards as a crucial indicator of significant shop-floor control, only 44 per cent of establishments had manual stewards or representatives, although the proportion rose to over three-quarters of establishments with more than 100 employees (ibid., p. 34). Given the under-representation of women in manufacturing and their high concentration in small establishments, it was a system of regulation that primarily protected male workers in the traditional manual worker industries.

The first serious attempts to restructure the system were mainly stimulated by a concern about the proliferation of unofficial strikes (which had come to represent some 95 per cent of all strikes in the 1960s) and the impact of strong workgroup power on the rate of technical change and economic growth (Royal Commission, 1968, pp. 261–2). The Donovan Commission's recommendations for the construction of a more orderly system of collective bargaining around 'factory-wide agreements' (*sic*), in which shop-steward negotiating rights would be more formally recognised, may have contributed to the increasing institutionalisation of shop-floor trade union organisation in the 1970s, but it did little to halt the escalating level of strike action. The number of officially recorded strikes in the period 1969–78 was 21 per cent higher than it had been in the pre-Donovan period 1963–8, while the number of 'days lost' as a result of strikes increased nearly threefold (Batstone, 1988, pp. 174–5). The 'winter of discontent' of 1978, which has often been seen as the turning point in which public support for the traditional voluntary system of industrial relations was severely eroded, was a culmination of a decade of exceptionally high levels of industrial conflict. While much of the blame was placed on the unregulated nature of British industrial relations institutions, the international character of the rising level of strikes in the 1970s suggests that this can be only a partial explanation (Crouch and Pizzorno, 1978).

The industrial relations legislation of the Thatcher governments in the 1980s represented a major break with traditional conceptions of the (relatively passive) role of the state in regulating the relationship between employers and the unions. It involved the imposition of a series of constraints on union capacity for the initiation of strikes, it made recruitment more difficult through the abolition of the closed shop, and it introduced measures to increase accountability to the membership within trade unions. Employer reactions to the governments, programme were initially remarkable mainly for their extreme caution. Surveys carried out in the mid-1980s, whether of employers or employees, indicated that there had been few attempts by employers to reduce the powers of unions where they were already recognised (Batstone, 1984; Millward and Stevens, 1986). Doubtless few thought that it was wise to tamper with long-standing institutional arrangements, when there might be an abrupt change in government policy with new elections.

However, the cataclysmic defeat of the strike by the miner's union, the renewed electoral success of the Conservatives in 1987, and the apparent trend towards the disintegration of the Labour Party provided a context in which employers proved far more willing, in the second half of the 1980s, to cut back the influence of the trade unions in collective bargaining. The proportion of establishments which recognised a union fell from 66 per cent in 1984 to 42 per cent in 1998 (Millward, Bryson and Forth, 2000, p. 96). The combination of declining recognition of unions in new establishments and more aggressive policies in already unionised establishments produced a marked decline in shop-steward coverage. In 1984 there was a shop steward in 53 per cent of all establishments; by 1998 this was the case in only 33 per cent (ibid., p. 115). This was paralleled by a decline in the influence that the stewards were able to wield over decision-making in the workplace (Terry, 1995, pp. 215–17).

Declining union influence was paralleled by a sharp drop in trade union membership. Whereas the 1970s had witnessed a major increase in membership, particularly as a result of the expansion of white-collar trade unionism, most of this increase was lost between 1980 and 1987. Membership peaked in 1979 at 12,639,000 but fell to 7,682,000 by 1993 (Waddington and Whitston, 1995, p. 160). Trade union density had reached 54 per cent in 1979, but was only 33 per cent by 1995. The decline was much sharper among men than among women, leading to a significant feminisation of trade union membership. The fall in membership was not due to the growth of anti-union sentiment in the workforce. The available evidence suggests that people's attitudes to trade unionism became, if anything, more favourable to the unions in the 1980s (Gallie, 1996, pp. 145–6). The causes of membership decline must be located in the structural constraints facing recruitment. The timing of the onset of decline makes it unlikely that the legal changes themselves played the crucial role in this, although they have made it more difficult for the unions to pick up new membership when economic conditions became more favourable in the late 1980s. While there was a marked decline in management support for trade union membership in the 1990s (Millward, Bryson and Forth, 2000, p. 147), explicit anti-union policies on the part of employers were also too rare to account for a drop of this magnitude. The more powerful factors leading to the decline of union membership were the very sharp rise in unemployment in the first half of the 1980s, and the ongoing shift in the composition of employment away from the large-scale establishments of manufacturing industry to the smaller and more dispersed work sites in the service industry, where it was considerably more difficult for the unions to organise. An analysis of the reasons why former union members had ceased membership showed the overwhelming importance people gave to the fact that they had become unemployed or had moved into a job where there were no unions present (ibid., pp. 168–72).

The informal nature of the regulation of the British labour market that had developed in the period up to 1979 left the British workforce particularly vulnerable when trade union power was undermined. There was little in the way of legislative protection of employment conditions on which employees could fall back. Unlike other European countries, there were no statutory controls of working hours or of holiday entitlements, formal provisions protecting people from redundancy were relatively weak and there was no general minimum threshold for wages. In the course of the 1980s even this existing low level of protection was further weakened by a series of government measures. Between 1980 and 1985, the length of time that a person had to be employed before they were eligible to take action for unfair dismissal was progressively lengthened from six months to two years. The 1989 Employment Act reduced restrictions on the working hours of young people and women. Regulative controls were also reduced over pay. The Fair Wages Resolution, which obliged public contractors to offer the terms and conditions negotiated in the industry by the trade unions, was abolished in 1983 and the powers of the wages councils to set minimum pay in industries where there was little or no union control were first weakened in 1986 and then abolished in 1993. By the end of the 1980s, there was little question that Britain represented a country with exceptionally low levels of protection of employment conditions. Indeed, a comparative study of employment regulations within the EU concluded that these were weakest of all in the UK (Grubb and Wells, 1993).

While the dominant tendency from the early 1980s was the deregulation of the labour market through the reduction of trade union and statutory controls, there were some developments that worked in the opposite direction, largely reflecting the growing concern about sex inequalities at work. Already in the 1970s, there had been a notable departure from the traditional abstentionist conception of the role of the state in matters of employment conditions with the passage first of the Equal Pay Act of 1970 (implemented in 1975) and then of the Sex Discrimination Act, measures which had a significant effect in improving women's relative pay position (Tzannatos and Zabalza, 1984; Zabalza and Tzannatos, 1985). An important dynamic behind such measures was pressure from the European Community, after Britain joined in 1973. This brought about, in 1983, a strengthening of the original equal pay provisions to allow for equal, value claims and, in 1986, an extension to the provisions of the Sex Discrimination Act to cover small businesses. In 1994 a potentially far-reaching decision by the House of Lords opened the way to the pro rata extension of employment rights hitherto denied to part-time workers on the grounds that current provisions were incompatible with European non-discrimination law. Finally, the last year of the century saw both the first general minimum wage legislation and new legislation to facilitate union recognition.

Overall, the period since the 1980s saw the deterioration of protection in a mainly informally regulated system, which had provided rather uneven coverage of different types of employee. This largely reflected the decline of trade union controls in the workplace, but it was given additional impetus by government legislation. However, there were clear signs by the end of the century that the trend towards deregulation had reached its limit. Triggered initially by issues of sex equality and given a further impetus by membership of the EU, a new element of statutory regulation had begun to develop, which in time could lead to a significant re-regulation of the British employment system.

Conclusion

At the close of the century the nature of employment and the characteristics of the workforce were strikingly different from those of mid-century. Employment had shifted away from manufacturing to predominantly service-sector work, leading to a new emphasis on conceptual and social skills. The period had seen the development of a much more skilled workforce, in which the proportion of people in professional and managerial jobs had become even greater than that in semi- and non-skilled manual work. At the same time, the growth of the service sector had drawn women into the labour force on a much larger scale, reducing (although far from abolishing) sex inequalities in employment.

The changed landscape of employment brought new issues into sharp focus. The implications of changes in the nature of jobs for the quality of working life were ambivalent: the intrinsic interest of work tasks increased, but so did the level of pressure and strain in work. How far could the intensification of work be taken without serious implications for people's health and for their commitment to employment? The growing centrality of employment for women's careers raised in a more pressing way the problem of the interface between work and family life. How were dual careers to be managed in a society that was still attached to individual meritocratic selection and that had increasing concerns about the quality of parental care of young children? The rise in employment insecurity, both in terms of the reduction of regulation of the conditions of work and the increased risk of job loss, raised fundamental issues about whether there could be meaningful citizenship at work and whether it would be possible to motivate people without any clear perspectives for the future. The problematic nature of the relationship between the developing structure of employment and the quality of life had changed in form over the decades, but remained as fundamental a challenge as it had been at mid-century.

Notes

1   The 1980 data are drawn from Martin and Roberts (1984, p. 72); that from 1992 from special runs by the author from the Employment in Britain survey.
2   The data are from the Employers Labour Use Strategies (ELUS) survey of a subsample of 740 establishments drawn from the Workplace Industrial Relations survey. The interviews were carried out in 1987.
3   Figures are drawn from the Labour Force Survey. Other surveys using a different set of indicators come out with somewhat higher proportions of temporary workers (11 per cent in 1992), but the trend across time is virtually identical (Gallie et al. 1986, p. 173).
4   The poverty threshold taken was 50 per cent of mean equivalised household income, using the new Organization for Economic Cooperation and Development (OECD) equivalence scale. Data were standardised from national household surveys.

References and Further Reading

Atkinson, J. (1984) 'Manpower Strategies for Flexible Organisations.' *Personnel Management* 15: 28–31.
Batstone, E. (1984) *Working Order*. Oxford.
Batstone, E. (1988) *The Reform of Workplace Industrial Relations. Theory, Myth and Evidence*. Oxford.
Batstone, E., Boraston, I. and Frenkel, S. (1977) *Shop Stewards in Action. The Organization of Workplace Conflict and Accommodation*. Oxford.
Beatson, M. (1995) *Labour Market Flexibility*. Employment Department Research Series, No. 48. London.
Blauner, R. (1964) *Alienation and Freedom. The Factory Worker and his Industry*. Chicago.
Brannen, J., Meszaros, G., Moss, P. and Poland, G. (1994) *Employment and Family Life: A Review of Research in the UK (1980–1994)*. London: Department for Education and Employment.
Braverman, H. (1974) *Labor and Monopoly Capital. The Degradation of Work in the Twentieth Century*. New York.
Clegg, H. A. (1979) *The Changing System of Industrial Relations in Great Britain*. Oxford.
Crompton, R. and Jones, G. (1984) *White-Collar Proletariat*. London.
Crompton, R. and Sanderson, K. (1990) *Gendered Jobs and Social Change*. London.
Crouch, C. and Pizzorno, A. (1978) *The Resurgence of Class Conflict in Western Europe since 1968. Vol 2. Comparative Analyses*. London.

Cully, M., Woodland, S., O'Reilly, A and Dix, G. (1999) *Britain at Work*. London.

Daniel, W. W. and Millward, N. (1983) *Workplace Industrial Relations in Britain*. London.

Dex, S. (1988) *Women's Attitudes Towards Work*. London.

Dex, S. and McCulloch, A. (1997) *Flexible Employment. The Future of Britain's Jobs*. London.

Dex, S. and Shaw, L. (1986) *A Comparison of British and American Women's Work Histories*. London.

Edwards, P. K. (ed.) (1995) *Industrial Relations. Theory and Practice in Britain*. Oxford.

Fagin, L. and Little, M. (1984) *The Forsaken Families. The Effects of Unemployment on Family Life*. Harmondsworth.

Gallie, D. (1996) 'Trade Union Allegiance and Decline in British Urban Labour Markets.' In D. Gallie, R. Penn and M. Rose (eds), *Trade Unionism in Recession*, pp. 140–74. Oxford.

Gallie, D., Cheng, Y., Tomlinson, M. and White, M. (1994) 'The Employment Commitment of Unemployed People.' In M. White (ed.), *Unemployment and Public Policy in a Changing Labour Market*, pp. 178–90. London.

Gallie, D., Marsh, C. and Vogler, C. (eds) (1993) *Social Change and the Experience of Unemployment*. Oxford.

Gallie, D. and Paugam, S. (eds) (2000) *Welfare Regimes and the Experience of Unemployment in Europe*. Oxford.

Gallie, D. and White, M. (1993) *Employee Commitment and the Skills Revolution*. London.

Gallie, D. and Russell, H. (1998) 'Unemployment and Life Satisfaction.' *Archives Européennes de sociologie* XXXIX: 3–35.

Gallie, D., White, M., Cheng, Y. and Tomlinson, M. (1998) *Restructuring the Employment Relationship*. Oxford.

Green, F., Ashton, D., Burchell, B., Davies, B. and Felstead, A. (1998) 'Are British Workers Getting More Skilled?' In A. B. Atkinson and J. Hills (eds), *Exclusion, Employment and Opportunity*, pp. 89–131. London.

Green, F. (1999) 'Training the Workers.' In P. Gregg and J. Wadsworth (eds), *The State of Working Britain*, pp. 127–46. Manchester.

Gregg, P. and Wadsworth, J. (eds) (1999) *The State of Working Britain*. Manchester.

Grubb, D. and Wells, W. (1993) 'Employment Regulation and Patterns of Work in EC Countries.' *OECD Economic Studies* 21: 7–56.

Hakim, C. (1987) 'Trends in the Flexible Workforce.' *Employment Gazette* (November): 549–60.

Hakim, C. (1990) 'Core and Periphery in Employers' Workforce Strategies: Evidence from the 1987 ELUS Survey.' *Work, Employment and Society* 4: 157–88.

Hakim, C. (1996) *Key Issues in Women's Work*. London.

Hakim, C. (1998) *Social Innovation and the Labour Market*. Oxford.

Hansen, H. (1998) *Elements of Social Security. A Comparison Covering: Denmark, Sweden, Finland, Germany, Great Britain, The Netherlands and Canada*. Copenhagen.

Harrop, A. and Moss, P. (1995) 'Trends in Parental Employment.' *Work, Employment and Society* 9: 421–44.

Hauser, R. and Nolan, B. (2000) *Unemployment and Poverty : Change over Time*. In D. Gallie and S. Paugam (eds), *Welfare Regimes and the Experience of Unemployment in Europe*, pp. 25–46. Oxford.

Heady, P. and Smyth M. (1989) *Living Standards during Unemployment, Vol. 1*. London.

Hunter, L. and McInnes, J. (1991) *Employer Use Strategies – Case Studies*. Department of Employment Research Paper No. 87. Sheffield.

Hunter, L., McGregor, A., MacInnes, J. and Sproull, A. (1993) 'The "Flexible Firm": Strategy and Segmentation.' *British Journal of Industrial Relations* 31: 383–407.

Joshi, H. E., Layard, P. R. G. and Owen, S. J. (1985), 'Why Are More Women Working in Britain?' *Journal of Labour Economics* 3: S147–S176.

Joshi, H. and Paci, P. (1998) *Unequal Pay for Men and Women. Evidence from the British Birth Cohort Studies*. Cambridge, MA.

Lampard, R. (1993) 'An Examination of the Relationship between Marital Dissolution and Unemployment', in D. Gallie, C. Marsh and C. Vogler (eds), *Social Change and the Experience of Unemployment*, pp. 264–98. Oxford.

Lissenburgh, S. (1996) *Value for Money:The Costs and Benefits of Giving Part-Time Workers Equal Rights*. London.

Martin, J. and Roberts, C. (1984) *Women and Employment: A Lifetime Perspective*. London.

McGregor, A. and Sproull, A. (1991) *Employer Labour Use Strategies: Analysis of a National Survey*. Sheffield, Department of Employment Research Paper, No. 83.

McKee, L. and Bell, C. (1985) 'Marital and Family Relations in Times of Male Unemployment.' In B. Roberts, R. Finnegan and D. Gallie (eds), *New Approaches to Economic Life*, pp. 387–99. Manchester.

McKee, L. and Bell, C. (1986) 'His Unemployment, Her Problem: The Domestic and Marital Consequences of Male Unemployment.' In S. Allen, A. Waton, K. Purcell and S. Wood (eds), *The Experience of Unemployment*. London.

McRae, S. (1991) *Maternity Rights in Britain*. London.

McRae, S. (1995) *Women's Employment during Family Formation*. London.

Millward, N. (1994) *The New Industrial Relations?* London.

Millward, N. , Bryson, A. and Forth, J. (2000) *All Change at Work? British Employment Relations 1980–1998, as Portrayed by the Workplace Industrial Relations Surveys*, pp. 87–106. London.

Millward, N. and Stevens, M. (1986) *British Workplace Industrial Relations 1980–1984: The DE/ESRC/PSI/ACAS Surveys*, Aldershot.

Nolan, B., Hauser, R. and Zoyem, J. P. (2000) 'The Changing Effects of Social Protection on Poverty.' In D. Gallie and S. Paugam (eds), *Welfare Regimes and the Experience of Unemployment in Europe*. Oxford.

OECD (1997) *Employment Outlook July 1997*. Paris.

Payne, R. L., Warr, P. B. and Hartley, J. (1984) 'Social Class and Psychological Ill-health during Unemployment'. *Sociology of Health and Illness* 6: 152–7.

Royal Commission on Trade Unions and Employers' Associations 1965–8. Chairman: Lord Donovan (1968). *Report*. London.

Smith, C. (1987) *Technical Workers: Class, Labour and Trade Unionism*. London.

Tam, M. (1997) *Part-Time Employment: A Bridge or a Trap?* Aldershot.

Terry, M. (1995) 'Trade Unions: Shop Stewards and the Workplace.' In P. Edwards (ed.), *Industrial Relations: Theory and Practice in Britain*. Oxford.

Tzannatos, Z. and Zabalza, A. (1984) 'The Anatomy of the Rise of British Female Relative Wages in the 1970s: Evidence from the New Earnings Survey.' *British Journal of Industrial Relations* 22: 174–94.

Waddington, J. and Whitston, C. (1995) 'Trade Unions: Growth, Structure and Policy.' In P. Edwards (ed.), *Industrial Relations: Theory and Practice in Britain*. Oxford.

Warr, P. (1987) *Work, Unemployment and Mental Health*. Oxford.

Warr, P. B. and Jackson, P. R. (1985) 'Factors Influencing the Psychological Impact of Prolonged Unemployment and Re-employment.' *Psychological Medicine* 15: 795–807.

Watson, G. (1994) 'The Flexible Workforce and Patterns of Working Hours in the UK.' *Employment Gazette* 239–48.

Zabalza, A. and Tzannatos, Z. (1985) 'The Effects of Britain's Anti-discriminatory Legislation on Relative Pay and Employment.' *Economic Journal*, 98: 839–43.

Chronology

1945	Election of Attlee government.
1945–70	Unemployment remains below 3 per cent.
1946	Abolition of marriage bar for women in the civil service.
1947	Nationalisation of coal industry.
1948	Nationalisation of railways.
1948	National Insurance Act extends unemployment benefit to all employees aged 15 or over.
1955	Equal pay for women in the civil service (non-industrial grades).
1958	Inauguration of the EEC without the UK.
1965	Donovan Commission.
1965	Redundancy Payments Act.
1965–70	National Board for Prices and Incomes.
1969	Withdrawal of Labour government's *In Place of Strife* proposals for legal restraints on unofficial strikes.
1970	Equal Pay Act – equal pay for 'like work' (implemented 1975).
1971	Industrial Relations Act – a Conservative government's first (abortive) attempt at legal regulation of the unions.
1973	UK joins the EEC.
1973	First oil shock.
1974	Miners' strike precipitates general election.
1974	Creation of the Advisory, Conciliation and Arbitration Service (ACAS).
1975	Employment Protection Act.
1975	Sex Discrimination Act.
1975	EC Directive 75/117/EEC – equal pay for work of equal value.
1976	Race Relations Act.
1975–9	'Social Contract' Incomes Policy.
1978	The 'winter of discontent'.
1979	Election of Thatcher government.
1980	Unemployment rises to 7.4 per cent of the workforce.
1982	Employment Act – unions exposed to damages in cases of unlawful industrial action.
1983	Equal Pay Act (Amended) – equal pay for work of equal value.
1983	Unemployment peaks at 12.2 per cent of the workforce.
1984	Privatisation of British Telecom.
1984	Trade Union Act – secret ballots required for strike action and election of higher union officers.
1984–5	Miners' strike.
1985	Unfair Dismissal (Variation of Qualifying Period) Order – qualifying period increased from 1 to 2 years.
1986	Wages Act – reduction of scope and function of wages councils in protection of low-paid.

1986   Sex Discrimination Act – restrictions on women's working hours and other conditions removed.

1988   Employment Act – prevents dismissal of employee for non-membership of union.

1988   Social Security Act – makes 16- and 17-year-olds ineligible for unemployment benefit.

1989   Employment Act – protective restrictions on employment of women and young people repealed.

1990   Employment Act – final abolition of 'closed shop'.

1992   UK opts out of 'Social Chapter' of Maastricht Treaty.

1993   Unemployment rises again to 10 per cent of workforce.

1993   EC Directive 93/104/EC – Working time directive.

1993   Trade Union Reform and Employment Rights Act – Wage Councils protecting low-paid abolished.

1994   Privatisation of railways.

1996   Unemployment benefit cut from 12 months to 6 months.

1996   Job Seekers' Allowance replaces income support and unemployment benefit.

1996   EC Directive 96/34/EC – Parental leave directive.

1997   Election of Blair government.

1997   Treaty of Amsterdam – sets objective of 'coordinated strategy for employment'.

1997   Luxembourg Employment Summit – introduction of monitored 'National Action Plans'.

1997   EC Directive 97/81/EC – Part-time work directive.

1998   New Deal 'Welfare to Work' Programme for the unemployed.

1999   Introduction of Minimum Wage.

1999   Employment Relations Act – improves protection for unfair dismissal, maternity/parental leave rights and rights of union recognition.

22 Industrial and Labour Relations

Chris Wrigley

Introduction

British industrial relations were often a controversial political area in the half-century after the Second World War. High levels of strikes, widespread restrictive practices and general bloody-mindedness in industry were frequently alleged to be peculiarly 'British diseases', regardless, for instance, of comparative strike statistics which suggested otherwise. Yet if poor industrial relations in some important sectors of the British economy were not peculiarly a British problem, they contributed to Britain's relatively poor economic performance. Bad industrial relations were rarely monocausal – other matters such as managerial policies and poor institutional frameworks played their part, as well as trade union failings.

The 'overmighty trade union' (a link as common as 'horse and carriage') was a subject of hostility among the well-to-do from at least the early nineteenth century. With the Labour Party, founded by the trade union movement, as one of the two major alternative parties of government, the Conservative Party had added political reasons for pressing for restrictions on trade union activity. This it frequently did in the twentieth century, with the most notable exception being the decade after the Second World War. Then, after the trade union involvement in organising the Home Front during the war and the Conservative Party's crushing defeat in the 1945 general election, Winston Churchill spoke of the trade unions as 'a long-established and essential part of our national life' when trying to make the Conservative Party appeal to larger numbers of working-class voters.[1] However, by the mid-1950s, the Conservatives in government were becoming increasingly concerned about rising inflation and were looking for ways of keeping wage and salary rises low, so were subsequently mostly hostile in their attitude to the trade unions.

After the Second World War there continued to be a strong strand of anti-trade unionism in popular culture. The bloody-minded, strike-happy trade unionist became a stereotype on television and in films. These included such substantial British films as *Chance of a Lifetime* (1950), with its theme of the need for both sides of industry to work together, *I'm All Right Jack* (1960), which satirised both sides of industry, and the more chilling *The Angry Silence* (1960), about a worker being shunned ('sent to Coventry') in his workplace. Such negative images of trade unionists were common also in a range of comedies, including *The Rag Trade* on television, and films in the very popular 'Carry On' series such as *Carry On Cabby* (1963) and *Carry On At Your Convenience* (1971).

Among the general public trade unions appear to have been least popular in the period from the early 1960s until the mid-1980s, by which time there was a growing feeling that the Thatcher government's incessant anti-trade union legislation had gone too far. In 1963 opinion polls found 63.5 per cent of all respondents believed that the trade unions had too much power, yet 70 per cent felt business had too much power. However, by 1970 those feeling that the unions were too powerful had reached 73.1 per cent, and rose to 81.1 per cent in 1979, while those feeling business had too much power had dropped to 54.7 per cent in the 1970s, rising to 60.3 per cent in 1979. It was notable that such critical perceptions of the unions were held by manual workers: 52.8 per cent in 1963, 66.4 per cent in 1970 and 75.2 per cent in 1979. However, by 1987 those feeling the trade unions had too much power had fallen back to 45.4 per cent (which included manual workers' 40.9 per cent).[2] In the 1970s, the period of most critical views, there were often ambiguous attitudes among trade union members and their families: the strikes in their own industries were almost sacred causes of securing justice, whereas strikes elsewhere – especially in the public services – were an intolerable nuisance.

Voluntaryism and Statutory Regulation: Incomes Policies

British industrial relations were based on a voluntary willingness of both sides to settle their differences. The two world wars had helped spread collective bargaining more widely and had seen more of such bargaining carried out at a national level. Since the 1896 Conciliation Act (plus, from 1919, the Industrial Courts Act) Whitehall had had the legal authority to intervene, where both parties were agreeable, to offer suggested solutions to disputes. In wartime, with attempts to forbid strikes or lockouts, the state had brought in compulsory arbitration to resolve industrial clashes. The Second World War measure – the July 1940 Conditions of Employment and National Arbitration Order (better known as Order 1305) – was maintained through the period of post-war reconstruction, being replaced only in August 1951.

The Trades Union Congress (TUC) and the Labour movement generally favoured the continuance of an interventionist state role in the economy. They believed the state should play its part in planning for economic growth as it had for victory in the war and for reconstructing and reviving the British economy in 1945–51. The TUC, for a decade after the Second World War, pressed Labour and Conservative ministers alike to take measures to secure higher productivity in British industry. In the immediate post-war period resistance to changes which could enhance productivity came primarily from employers. The state, under the Conservatives – who returned to office in 1951 committed to 'a bonfire of controls' – declined to breach voluntaryist principles and intervene in the workings of private industry.

While the TUC favoured state planning in the economy, it opposed state intervention which limited free collective bargaining. However, during the period of post-war reconstruction the General Council of the TUC did support the Attlee government's 1948 voluntary incomes policy. That pay policy did meet with some success until the government's devaluation of the pound in September 1949 led to a 6 per cent rise in the cost of living index and a subsequent erosion of willingness to agree to wage restraint.

In contrast, the Conservatives generally advocated minimum state intervention in the market economy, with the notable exceptions of measures to restrain pay rises and legislation to curb what they deemed to be over-powerful trade unions. By the mid-1950s the Eden government was concerned about slowly but steadily rising inflation and its effect on the competitiveness of British exports. It spelt out the problems of maintaining stable prices when labour was in a strong bargaining position in conditions of near-full employment in the White Paper, *The Economic Implications of Full Employment*, in March 1956. Thereafter, the Conservatives embarked on intermittent attempts to secure incomes policies, beginning with the December 1956 talks to secure a 'price and wage plateau' and culminating in Selwyn Lloyd's 'pay pause' of July 1961. In 1962 the Macmillan government moved strongly in a corporatist direction when it set up a tripartite forum (government, employers and trade unions), the National Economic Development Council (NEDC, nicknamed 'Neddy' from its acronym), to advise the government on long-term economic planning. It also set up, in the face of TUC hostility, the National Incomes Commission (NIC, nicknamed 'Nicky') 'to provide impartial and authoritative advice' on the government's incomes policy after the end of the 'pay pause'.

Pay freezes and formal incomes policies were a feature of 1961–79 under both Conservative and Labour governments. Selwyn Lloyd's 'pay pause' had been applied to the public sector, with the private sector invited to follow suit. When this did not occur the government set a pay norm of 2.5 per cent. Harold Wilson's Labour governments (1964–70) began with a voluntary policy (with a 3.5 per cent norm). After the 1966 sterling crisis there was a statutory prices and incomes policy, beginning with a six-month standstill followed by six months of 'severe restraint', with pay settlements to be made at a minimum of twelve-monthly intervals, ending with a 3.5 per cent norm from mid-1968 to mid-1969 (with higher exceptions for genuine productivity deals).

The incomes policies of the 1970s attempted to be more sophisticated than those of the 1970s. Edward Heath's Conservative government (1970–4) attempted to be fairer to public sector and low-paid workers in going beyond percentage figure norms. After the failure of an informal incomes policy (during which the government set an example by negotiating progressively lower pay settlements in the public sector), in November 1972 Heath's government brought in a statutory three-month standstill on wages, prices, rents and dividends. This was followed by stage two of its policy, which set an upper limit for pay increases of a flat-rate of £1 a week plus 4 per cent of the current pay bill for a group of employees, excluding overtime, with an upper limit of £250 per annum for any individual. Stage three increased the upper limit for pay settlement to 7 per cent (or £2.25 average for a group), with an individual maximum of £350, with a further 1 per cent for negotiators to use for removing anomalies or for efficiency. The Wilson and Callaghan Labour governments (1974–9) linked pay restraint to social welfare reforms ('the social wage') and income-tax concessions under what was known as 'The Social Contract'. After negotiations between the government and the TUC a voluntary flat-rate policy of £6 per week was introduced in mid-1975 (and in the ensuing year the rate of increase of earnings fell from 26.9 to 12.9 per cent). In the second year (1976–7) the TUC agreed to a 5 per cent pay limit with a maximum increase of £4 a week and a minimum of £2.50. In the third year (1977–8) the trade unions would not endorse the government's proposed 10 per cent average for pay rises, though there was restraint (overall earnings rising by 14.2 per cent). However, James Callaghan was too optimistic when he set a 5 per cent wage limit for a fourth year (1978–9).

The effectiveness, or otherwise, of incomes policies is a controversial matter. Frequently what has been gained in wage restraint during the policies has been lost thereafter in a 'catching-up' process. However, there is much to suggest that incomes policies had some success in reducing the rate of rises in pay during times of economic crisis, when not only the TUC's leaders but the general public appear to have supported them. This was so in 1948–50, in the period of postwar reconstruction and also in 1975–8, when the rate of inflation had been over 25 per cent per annum. While it is difficult to quantify what did not happen (i.e. what the pattern of pay increases would have been without the incomes policies), it has been estimated that in 1948–50 wage rises were some 2 per cent lower than they would otherwise have been. In 1975–7, increases in average earnings were reduced from 26 to 9 per cent per annum (though TUC support for the continuation of the policy was undermined as the rise in the cost of living fell only from 26 to 17.6 per cent per annum).[3]

Incomes policies were strongly attacked by both the Labour Left and the Conservative monetarist Right. Those on the left criticised incomes policies as serious interferences with free collective bargaining and as attempts to solve the problems of British capitalism by squeezing working-class incomes. Margaret Thatcher and her supporters were opposed to such state intervention, believing that inflation would be squeezed out of the economy by the government maintaining tight controls of the money supply and of public expenditure while allowing unemployment to rise to its 'natural' market level. The Thatcher government's policies were applied during internationally adverse economic conditions, when high levels of unemployment were experienced by many industrial nations and competition in export markets was very strong. Neither the Major governments (1990–7) nor the Blair government (from 1997) reverted to using formal incomes policies of the kind operated in the 1961–79 era.

Voluntaryism and Statutory Regulation: Trade Union Legislation

In the post-war era of near-full employment (1950 to the early 1960s), there was growing criticism of trade union activities in some sectors of the economy. In the aftermath of the Conservatives' substantial electoral defeat, Churchill and his party were cautious of appearing vehemently anti-trade union. Hence Churchill made no commitment to reinstate the hostile trade union legislation of 1927, passed after the ending of the 1926 General Strike, when it was repealed by the Attlee government in May 1946.

However, as inflation became more marked during the 1950s, there was more vocal criticism of the trade unions within the Conservative Party. In June 1958 the Inns of Court Conservative and Unionist Society published an influential study, *A Giant's Strength*, in which it was argued that there was a need for various restrictions on trade unions to be placed on the statute book, thereby undercutting trade union power in a period of near-full employment. Many of these proposals were adopted by Edward Heath's government in its 1971 Industrial Relations Act.

In 1964 and 1965 there were legal decisions against the trade unions which undermined the immunity they (and most others) had assumed that they possessed from legal action arising from industrial disputes under the 1906 Trades Disputes Act. In the 1964 *Rookes* v. *Barnard* case a former union member successfully sued his union when he lost his job after the union threatened strike action over his non-membership. A further case, *Stratford* v. *Lindley* in 1965, related to secondary boycotting. Harold Wilson and the Labour Party returned to office in 1964, pledged to restore trade union law to what was believed to be the intentions of the 1906 Trades Disputes Act, and to set up a Royal Commission to report on trade unions and employers' organisations. These intentions were carried out with the Trade Disputes Act, 1965 and by setting up, also in 1965, the Royal Commission chaired by Lord Donovan which reported in 1968.

The Donovan Report urged the maintenance of voluntarism in British industrial relations, calling for government action to help make it work but not for a new framework of law. The Donovan Commission's proposal for an administrative body, a Commission on Industrial Relations (CIR), was taken up by the Wilson government. This proved helpful in resolving industrial disputes, and the CIR was succeeded from 1974 by the Advisory, Conciliation and Arbitration Service (ACAS). However, the Wilson government did propose some legislative action to curtail voluntaryism in its 1969 White Paper, *In Place of Strife*: compulsory ballots before certain major strikes, the power to call conciliation pauses before unofficial strikes and to intervene to settle inter-union disputes. The other 22 of *In Place of Strife's* 25 proposals would have directly strengthened trade unionism. The three proposed limitations on voluntary collective bargaining caused uproar in the trade union movement and the Labour Party and, in the face of probable defeat in the House of Commons, the Wilson government withdrew the proposals.

Harold Wilson had taken up the thorny issue of industrial relations because of growing public concern about strikes. The Donovan Report had highlighted the very high level of unofficial disputes in the total of strikes (see later), while *In Place of Strife* noted of the typical unofficial strike, 'Although it is often soon over, it comes with little warning and the disruptive effect can be serious.' Wilson's failure to press ahead with industrial relations legislation in 1969 was widely felt to be one of the contributory reasons for Labour's surprise defeat in the 1970 general election.

Edward Heath's Conservative government (1970–4) did not hesitate in introducing a detailed and complicated legal framework for industrial relations. The Industrial Relations Act, 1971 had 170 sections and 9 schedules (with a later Code). Its major target was strikes, both unofficial and inter-union. It intended to cut out any inter-union disputes and strikes over trade union recognition by giving registered trade unions sole and legally enforceable negotiating rights in certain circumstances. Legally binding agreements were anticipated to strengthen centralised trade unionism by deterring shop stewards or other activists from overturning them locally. The CIR could intervene in workplaces deemed strike-prone by either the government, employers or unions and, should it fail to find voluntary solutions to problems, it could refer the matter to the National Industrial Relations Court, which could impose a legally binding procedure. As with *In Place of Strife*, there were provisions for the calling of a cooling-off period (in the 1971 Act, by the National Industrial Relations Court, and for 60, not 28 days) and for the ordering of a ballot before a strike. The trade union movement had been angered by *In Place of Strife*; with the 1971 Act, it was nearly apoplectic. The TUC's campaign to ensure unions did not register under the 1971 Act (whereby there were benefits for them) was very successful, thereby undermining the Act. Many employers were lukewarm, few wishing to take their employees to court and often willing to negotiate contracts that were specifically not legally enforceable.

The 1971 Industrial Relations Act failed in its objectives in the face of vehement trade union opposition and widespread employer apathy. It had been intended to reduce strikes, but the numbers of working days lost went up (with many days lost through political strikes against the Act). It had been seen as an alternative to an incomes policy to help keep down levels of pay – but very soon the Heath government felt it necessary to introduce a very substantial incomes policy.

With the Labour governments of Harold Wilson (1974–6) and James Callaghan (1976–9), there was a return to the voluntaryist approach to industrial relations. The 1971 Industrial Relations Act was repealed and with the Trade Union and Labour Relations Acts, 1974 and 1976 the earlier legal framework (based on 1875 and 1906 Acts) was reinstated. There was also a strengthening of employee and trade union rights with clauses following Donovan Report recommendations on such matters as 'unfair dismissals'.

The Conservative governments of Margaret Thatcher (1979–90) and John Major (1990–7) turned to legislation to 'tame' or 'attack' (according to the viewpoint) the trade unions, while rejecting state intervention in the form of prices and incomes policies. The Thatcher government developed a version of free-market and monetarist economics which was hostile to trade unions. According to this and similar views, trade union bargaining power distorted the working of free labour markets, adding to labour costs and, as goods and services became uncompetitive, to unemployment. Added to such economic views, Margaret Thatcher, Norman Tebbitt and others of the Tory Right made it clear that they strongly disliked trade unions and trade union leaders collectively. Under Margaret Thatcher and John Major there was a series of measures passed which severely curtailed trade union activities, and being passed piecemeal in eight statutes between 1980 and 1993 did not facilitate the mobilisation of opposition on the scale that had occurred against Edward Heath's one big measure (the 1971 Industrial Relations Act). Moreover, the 1980–93 legislation avoided making martyrs of individual trade unionists, with financial penalties hitting the unions as collective entities; but then the 1971 legislation had been aimed primarily at reducing strikes and encouraging higher output, whereas the 1980–93 legislation had assumed that shackling or even demolishing trade unions would lead automatically to favourable economic results.[4]

Before the serious industrial unrest of early 1979 (the so-called 'winter of discontent'), Margaret Thatcher had been cautious in her comments concerning trade unions. In December 1978 she had spoken of inviting 'the unions to join with us in building the new and prosperous Britain', adding that she would neither 'bash the unions' nor 'bow to them'. After her election, her government proceeded to fund union ballots, limit union powers within the closed shop, remove the burden of proof from the employer in unfair dismissal cases and remove legal immunity from secondary picketing under the Employment Act, 1980. Subsequent legislation removed trade union powers to discipline members who ignored majority votes for industrial action, set up a Commissioner for the Rights of Trade Union Members to assist them take legal action against their unions (Employment Act, 1988), made it illegal to refuse to employ someone because they were not in a trade union, made all secondary action illegal, made any dismissal during unofficial strikes or other action not allowable as 'unfair dismissal' (Employment Act, 1990), permitted employers legal protection if they paid non-trade unionists lower wages than trade unionists, required employers to be given at least seven days' warning of industrial action and this to specify which workers would be involved, and abolished wages councils (Trade Union Reform and Employment Rights Act, 1993). The legislation of 1980–93 took trade union law back beyond the reforms of Gladstone and Disraeli in 1871–5.

By the time Tony Blair became Prime Minister in May 1997 the Labour Party had long dropped its earlier pledges to repeal all the post-1979 Conservative trade union legislation. Labour did restore a range of employment rights and also introduced a statutory national minimum wage, which came into effect in 1999. Its Employment Relations Act, 1999 provided a complex, multi-stage procedure for trade unions to secure recognition, new rights for part-time workers and improved maternity and parental leave rights.

Trade Union Membership and Collective Bargaining

Trade union membership in the United Kingdom grew to its greatest size of 13.3 million in 1979 (see table 22.1). Thereafter, membership fell steadily until

Table 22.1   Membership of trade unions in the UK, selected years, 1945–1995 (000s)

Year	Union membership	Male membership	Female membership	Number of trade unions
1945	7,875	6,237	1,638	781
1952	9,588	7,797	1,792	723
1955	9,741	7,874	1,967	704
1965	10,325	8,084	2,241	630
1968	10,200	7,836	2,364	586
1975	12,193	8,729	3,464	501
1979	13,289	9,544	3,902	453
1985	10,821	n.a.	n.a.	370
1995	8,089	4,606	3,483	238

n.a. = not available
Source: Department of Employment, *British Labour Statistics: Historical Abstract* 1868–1968, London, HMSO, 1971, p. 395. B. R. Mitchell, *British Historical Statistics*, Cambridge, Cambridge University Press, 1988, p. 137. *Labour Market Trends*, February 1997, pp. 39–40.

1997, with the fall stopping in 1998. Alongside this decline in trade union membership, the extent of collective bargaining between management and unions dwindled in the 1980s and 1990s, but not as markedly as in the USA, where anti-trade union attitudes were more widespread and stronger in business and society.

Trade unionism in the UK grew in numbers from 1934, after the world recession, until 1979. The Second World War boosted trade union membership. The unions made a major contribution to the organisation of the wartime economy in conditions of labour scarcity on the home front. During the period of post-war reconstruction, mostly under Clement Attlee's Labour governments (1945–51), trade union membership grew from 8.8 million at an average rate of 1.5 per cent per annum over 1946–52. This rate of growth slowed to 0.4 per cent per annum over 1952–68, during the Conservative years (1951–64), then grew rapidly at 2.8 per cent per annum in 1968–79, a period of high inflation and mostly Labour governments (1964–70 and 1974–9).

From 1979 until 1997 the membership of trade unions fell. This was partly due to adverse economic conditions internationally, with a widespread pattern of trade union memberships falling in industrialised countries. It was also partly due to the hostile political climate during the Thatcher and Major governments (1979–97), marked by restrictive trade union laws and monetarist economic policies. Between 1979 and 1995 (the last year with comparable statistics) UK trade union membership fell from its all-time peak of 13.3 million to 8.1 million, an annual average rate of decline of 1.9 per cent. By 1995 trade union membership had returned to a little more than its 1945 level.

As in earlier centuries, the pattern of trade union membership changed over time. Even with the post-war growth, there had been a notable decline in the relative importance within trade unionism of such earlier strongholds as the railways, coal mines, cotton and man-made fibres. In 1948 these sectors collectively had amounted to 8.4 per cent of the civil labour force and 15.9 per cent of British trade unionists; by 1979 they had dwindled to 2.6 of the labour force and 4.6 per cent of trade unionists. In contrast, there was a continuing growth in the importance of white-collar trade unionism. In 1945 white-collar workers constituted 32.5 per cent of the civil labour force and 23.8 per cent of British trade unionists; by 1979 they made up 49.6 per cent of the labour force and 40.5 per cent of trade unionists. In terms of trade union density (the proportion of trade union members among the workforce eligible to join), this rose for white-collar workers from 31.3 per cent in 1951 to 43.6 per cent in 1979.[5]

Another major growth area for the unions was among women workers, and after 1979 these members became a notably higher proportion of all trade unionists. The unions had to adapt the meet changing working patterns of women (see Duncan Gallie's chapter 21 in this volume). By the late 1990s they were succeeding in attracting many part-time women workers to union membership; in autumn 1997, 22 per cent of those in permanent and 15 per cent of those in temporary jobs. In 1945 a fifth of British trade unionists were female; by 1979 this had risen to three-tenths, and by 1998 women constituted between two-fifths and a half of trade unionists. Consequently, it was not surprising that in 1995 half the largest ten trade unions had majorities of female members: UNISON (public service), the largest union with 1,355,000 members (72 per cent female); the Royal College of Nursing, sixth largest with 300,000 members (92 per cent); the Union of Shop, Distributive and Allied Workers (USDAW), seventh largest with 283,000 members (58 per cent); the National Union of Teachers, ninth largest with 248,000 members (75 per cent); and the National Association of Schoolmasters and Union of Women Teachers, tenth largest with 234,000 members (53 per cent).

Even before the adverse conditions of 1979–97, the trade unions, albeit slowly, had begun to readjust to the need to appeal to more than white males in full-time jobs. Even in unions which had a majority of female members, most officials were men. For example, in 1968 USDAW had only two women among its 120 officials. John Kelly and Edmund Heery, who studied trade union organisation, still found in 1991 that in 62 unions, employing 2,564 full-time staff, only 302 were female.[6] However, by the late 1980s there were unions such as the National Union of Public Employees (NUPE) and the General, Municipal and Boilermakers Union (GMB) where the leadership did take vigorous measures to increase the numbers of females in important roles.

From the 1980s the trade unions also made greater efforts to try to ensure that ethnicity did not disadvantage members. In the late 1990s there were similar proportions of non-white as white people as members of trade unions: the density of white employees as trade unionists was 30 per cent in autumn 1997, of non-white 28 per cent. However, within the non-white total the black female figure was 38 per cent (34 for black males), while the Pakistani–Bangladeshi figures were 15 and 16 per cent for women and men.

The number of people in Great Britain in workplaces where trade unions were recognised was 10.4 million in 1993 and 10 million in 1997. The proportion of employees in workplaces where unions were recognised fell from 48.9 to 44.3 per cent in the same period. As for the number of employees covered

Table 22.2 Change in trade union density,
selected countries, 1985–1995 (%)

Australia	−29.6
Austria	−19.2
Denmark	2.3
Finland	16.1
France	−37.2
Germany	−17.6
Greece	−33.8
Italy	−7.4
Japan	−16.7
Netherlands	−11.0
New Zealand	−55.1
Norway	3.6
Sweden	8.7
Switzerland	−21.7
United Kingdom	−27.7
United States	−21.1
(Average)	(−16.7)

Source: *Labour Research*, 87 (5), May 1998, p. 19.

by collective bargaining, in 1997 this amounted to 8.1 million of 10.1 million employees working where unions were recognised, 36 per cent of all employees.

By the late 1990s collective bargaining was strongest in the public sector. In 1997, 79 per cent of public-sector employees in workplaces with 25 or more employees were covered by collective bargaining (60 per cent where there were less than 25 employees), compared with 32 per cent in workplaces with 25 or more employees in the private sector (and only 7 per cent in workplaces with less than 25 employees). In the private sector collective bargaining was most extensive in electricity, gas and water supply, transport and communication, financial, manufacturing, and mining and quarrying, and weakest in such areas as catering, estate agents and business services.[7]

The decline in trade union membership in Britain in the 1980s and 1990s was not unique to the UK. In the decade 1985–95 the fall in trade union density in the UK was greater than in most comparable economies but less than in France and Greece, for instance (see table 22.2).

Strikes

The level of strike activity, like the size of trade union membership, has risen and fallen according to international economic circumstances. Generally, the scale of strikes has not been peculiarly British, a symptom of a unique 'British demise'. Apart from the early 1970s, when trade union strike issues were notably politicised, the broad pattern of British industrial unrest has been similar to that of many other industrialised economies.

While the British economy performed relatively less well than its industrial-ised rivals during the 'Golden Age' (1950–73) of the international economy, nevertheless, for much of the period, there was near-full employment and rising real standards of living for most people. These conditions strengthened trade unions' bargaining positions, and the slow but steady rise of inflation during the 1950s onwards hit hard low-paid workers and generally raised expectations of annual pay rises. The number of strikes rose markedly from 1953, and there were several periods with notably large increases in the number of days lost through strikes: 1953–62, 1968–72, 1978–81 and 1984–5 (the last being largely due to the huge mining dispute).

From the mid-1950s and during the 1960s there was considerable concern about the number of unofficial strikes. In sectors such as engineering and motor-car manufacturing there was strong shop-floor organisation and much bargain-ing carried out at plant level, often by shop stewards. There were also many short, local strikes in coal mining. The Donovan Report (1968) concluded,

> Official strikes tend to be much more serious individually than unofficial strikes in terms of working days lost, but they are relatively infrequent and their number shows no consistent tendency to grow.
>
> Some 95 per cent of stoppages are unofficial, and unofficial strikes are becoming more common. About half concern wages and over 40 per cent concern 'working arrangements, rules and discipline' and 'redundancy, dismissal, suspension etc.', matters usually dealt with at the workplace rather than at industry level.

Concern at such levels of unofficial strikes contributed to both the Labour Party under Harold Wilson, with the 1969 White Paper *In Place Of Strife*, and the Conservative Party under Edward Heath, with the 1971 Industrial Relations Act, trying to reduce the number and the impact of strikes by legislation. These efforts led to the greatest politicising of industrial relations since the period of the General Strike, 1926, with the propensity to strike becoming relatively greater in Britain during 1969–72.[8]

In the 1970s, by all the main indicators, there was a substantial rise in indus-trial unrest (see table 22.3). While there continued to be a large number of small disputes there were also a return of large national strikes (which had not been common since before the Second World War). In 1971 and 1972 there was a notable increase in the average length of disputes; the average number of working days lost per involved worker rose to 11.6 and 13.9, compared with an average of 3.4 for 1962–70. Such average lengths of dispute were only exceeded during 1980 and 1984 (14.2 and 19.5), when there were massive strikes in steel and coal.

The early 1980s were marked by major conflicts between the Thatcher gov-ernment and the trade unions. In 1980–5 the days lost during the steel and coal disputes alone amounted to 42 per cent of the total. From the mid-1980s there were less strikes in the private sector of the economy, where trade unionism declined in strength.

Mrs Thatcher and the Conservative Party claimed to have 'tamed the trade unions'. By economic policies, by legislation, by ending any important corporatist

Table 22.3   Industrial disputes in the UK: averages for 1945–1998

Period	Number of disputes	Numbers of workers (000s)	Total working days (000s)
1945–53	1,769	556	2,026
1954–64	2,472	1,055	3,760
1965–9	2,380	1,208	3,929
1970–4	2,885	1,564	14,077
1975–9	2,310	1,639	11,663
1980–4	1,350	1,443	10,486
1984–9	1,136	783	3,940
1990–8	281	208	737

Source: Calculated from statistics in *Ministry of Labour Gazette, Employment and Productivity Gazette, Department of Employment Gazette* and *Labour Market Trends*.

decision-making and by a tough line in major industrial disputes the Thatcher governments of 1979–90 helped change the climate of industrial relations – 'helped change' as it was changing anyway in the adverse international economic climate of the 1980s. Trade unions and industry generally faced a harsher economic climate in other industrial countries as well.

In terms of industrial disputes, Britain's record was not dissimilar from that of other industrialised economies. In terms of strikes during the Thatcher years, Britain did not improve relative to the other major industrial nations in terms of working days lost per 1,000 workers. There are substantial problems in making international statistical comparisons, such as variations in what are recorded as strikes, whether others laid off due to a strike are counted and the nature of the labour forces (e.g. whether or not there is a prevalence of small units employing family labour). Nevertheless, the consistency of Britain's position is notable: table 22.4 provides details of the eight most strike-prone of 15 industrial countries, plus, for contrast, Japan and West Germany. For the 1980s (but not earlier) there are statistics for all industries. This series of figures lessens the prominence of the huge steel strike (1980) and mining strike (1984–5) in the British statistics, thereby making Britain fifth in rank order (but still higher in rank order than in the 1960s or 1970s). Even when taking the average for 1987–91, i.e. after the big confrontations of 1980 and 1984–5, Britain still remains fourth (behind Canada, Australia and Italy). So, relative to other industrialised countries, Britain's levels of strikes went up and down with the others, in spite of any particular 'taming' of unions by the Thatcher governments.

Industrial Relations and Trade Unions, 1945–1999

The strong tradition of voluntaryism in British industrial relations was substantially eroded from the 1960s. It was limited by the series of incomes policies from the early 1960s until 1979. It was then altered by legislation, first the

Table 22.4 Working days lost per 1,000 workers in mining, manufacturing, construction and transport and communication, selected countries, 1961–1989 (annual averages)

	1961–9 (rank order)	1970–9 (rank order)	1980–9 (rank order)
Australia	424 (5)	1,298 (3)	770 (2)
Canada	1,026 (3)	1,840 (1)	960 (1)
France	321 (6)	312 (7)	150
Ireland	1,114 (2)	1,163 (5)	530 (3)
Italy	1,438 (1)	1,778 (2)	290 (7)
Japan	239	215	20
Sweden	18	42	330 (5=)
United Kingdom	274 (7)	1,088 (6)	740 (3)
United States	1,001 (4)	1,211 (4)	330 (5=)
West Germany	24	92	50

From the mid-1980s the French figures have a significantly different coverage. The 1961–9 figures omit 1968, so are artificially low.
Sources: Calculated from statistics in *Employment Gazette*, December 1971, October 1973, January 1981 and December 1991.

Industrial Relations Act, 1971 and then by the series of statutes passed by the Thatcher and Major governments between 1980 and 1993.

The legal framework for industrial relations which was set up by the 1980–93 legislation shifted the balance of bargaining power strongly in favour of employers. It removed the individual right to strike, with employers able to dismiss striking individual employees without risk of actions for unfair dismissal. It also weakened unskilled unions in particular, through banning secondary action (i.e. supportive action from other unions). The legislation contributed to 'a climate of opinion' in which trade union membership in many sectors of the economy was likely to weaken, not enhance, an employee's job prospects. The likelihood that trade unions were less able to deliver benefits to their members than in inflationary times or times politically more favourable to union membership contributed to the downward spiral of trade union membership.

However, the main direct impact of the wider role of the law in industrial relations from the 1980s was the impact of the requirement of ballots before strikes. The requirement to ballot may well have contributed to a smaller number of strikes. However, once under way, the desirability to ballot to conclude a dispute may well lengthen some disputes. Also, the ballots have been effectively used by some unions to rally support and maintain the momentum of a campaign.[9]

The political concern with post-war industrial relations centred on its role in Britain's relatively poor economic performance. Considerable anxieties about British industry's productivity compared to its rivals were expressed from the early years of the Attlee governments (1945–51). In the early 1960s there had been high hopes that substantial gains in productivity could be brought about through collective bargaining, as appeared to have been achieved at the Esso oil refinery at Fawley.[10] However, while large numbers of productivity agreements were negotiated in the 1960s and 1970s, writers such as David Metcalf have suggested that, overall, British productivity was nevertheless increasing at a slower rate in the period than was that of Britain's economic rivals. In contrast, he argued that higher labour productivity, which grew at a faster rate than the average of other major industrial countries, occurred in 1979–86 due to 'legislation to constrain union power, high unemployment, heightened product market competition and emphasis on numerical and functional flexibility in the labour market'.[11]

Obstructive industrial relations have been one of several prominent explanations for the relatively poor productivity growth in Britain. Professor N. F. R. Crafts has concluded,

> The important obstacles to faster productivity growth lay on the supply side of the economy and brought about a relatively slow reduction of overmanning and reduced the benefits from new technical possibilities in production. Growth was hampered by weak management, poor industrial relations, ineffective research and development, and low levels of vocational training.

He added that 'the post-war settlement together with much more powerful trade unions brought new obstacles to productivity improvements as governments sought to avoid confrontation with organised labour'; and judged 'the most persistent weaknesses' to have been in 'education and training (including the quality of industrial management) and in industrial relations'. As Professor Crafts observed, the fear of unemployment in the highly competitive international economic conditions of the late 1970s and 1980s was the major cause of the improved British industrial productivity, not industrial relations legislation.[12] Perhaps, also, Britain, like the USA, benefited from a catching-up process with regard to Japan and West Germany as they emulated some elements of their success.[13]

By the end of the twentieth century industrial relations in Britain were much less matters of controversy than they had been in the 1960s, 1970s and 1980s. The level of strikes had been relatively low for some fifteen years. The trade unions' political role had diminished not only under the Thatcher and Major Conservative governments but also under Tony Blair's New Labour. After a run of trade union legislation (1980–93) which had severely restricted them, plus a substantial drop in their membership, there was little credibility in blaming them for Britain's relatively poor economic performance. Moreover, the fall in unemployment, substantial economic growth and restrained growth in earnings in the 1980s and after were a combination which undercut some major presumptions of monetarist economists whose views were revered in government in the 1980s to mid-1990s. At the end of the twentieth century, whatever the legal framework for industrial relations, in much of the British economy collective bargaining remained common, even if not as widespread as in 1945–79.

Notes

1 *Conservative Party Conference Report*, 1947; 4 October.
2 Ivor Crewe, Neil Day and Anthony Fox, *The British Electorate 1963–1987: A Compendium of Data from the British Election Studies*, Cambridge, Cambridge University Press, 1991, pp. 251–94.
3 For incomes policies see W. J. Fishbein, *Wage Restraint by Consensus*, London, Routledge, 1984; R. Jones, *Wages and Employment Policy 1936–1985*, London, Allen and Unwin, 1987; R. J. Flanagan, D. W. Soskice and L. Ulman, *Unionism, Economic Stability and Incomes Policies*, Washington, Brookings Institute, 1983; and J. L. Fallick and R. F. Elliott (eds), *Incomes Policies, Inflation and Relative Pay*, London, George Allen and Unwin, 1981.
4 For legislation see Simon Auerbach, *Legislating for Conflict*, Oxford, Clarendon Press, 1990; Paul Davies and Mark Freedland, *Labour Legislation and Public Policy*, Oxford, Clarendon Press, 1993; and John McIlroy, *The Permanent Revolution? Conservative Law and the Trade Unions*, Nottingham, Spokesman, 1991.
5 For a more detailed survey, see Chris Wrigley, 'Trade Union Development 1945–79', in Chris Wrigley (ed.), *A History of British Industrial Relations 1939–79*, Cheltenham, Edward Elgar, 1996, pp. 62–83.
6 J. Kelly and E. Heery, *Working For The Union*, Cambridge, Cambridge University Press, 1994, pp. 34–41.
7 'Trade Union Membership and Recognition 1996–97', *Labour Market Trends*, July 1998: 353–62.
8 David Gilbert, 'Strikes in Post-war Britain', in Wrigley, *History of British Industrial Relations*, pp. 128–61.
9 Jane Elgar and Bob Simpson, 'The Impact of the Law on Industrial Disputes in the 1980s', in David Metcalf and Simon Milner (eds), *New Perspectives on Industrial Disputes*, London, Routledge, 1993, pp. 70–114.
10 Alan Flanders, *The Fawley Productivity Agreement*, London, Faber, 1964. The achievements appeared less in time; see B. Ahlstrand, *The Quest for Productivity: A Study of Fawley after Flanders*, Cambridge, Cambridge University Press, 1991.
11 David Metcalf, 'Water Notes Dry Up: The Impact of the Donovan Reform Proposals and Thatcherism at Work on Labour Productivity in British Manufacturing Industry', *British Journal of Industrial Relations* 27 (1989): 1–31.
12 N. F. R. Crafts, 'Economic Growth', in N. F. R. Crafts and N. Woodward (eds), *The British Economy Since 1945*, Oxford, Clarendon Press, 1991, pp. 261–90.
13 For some of the difficulties of emulating Japanese labour practices in motor-car manufacturing see U. Jürgens, T. Malsch and K. Dohse, *Breaking From Taylorism*, Cambridge, Cambridge University Press, 1993.

Further Reading

General accounts of modern industrial relations

Edwards, Paul (ed.), *Industrial Relations: Theory and Practice in Britain*, Oxford, Basil Blackwell, 1995.
Gospel, Howard and Palmer, Gill, *British Industrial Relations*, London, 1995.
Kessler, Sid and Bayliss, Fred, *Contemporary British Industrial Relations*, London, 1995.
Sisson, Keith (ed.), *Personnel Management*, Oxford, Basil Blackwell, 1994.

Wrigley, Chris (ed.), *A History of British Industrial Relations 1939–79*, Cheltenham, Edward Elgar, 1996.

Trade union documents (with the emphasis on trade unions and the state)

Wrigley, Chris, *British Trade Unions 1945–95*, Manchester, Manchester University Press, 1997.

The trade unions since 1945

A valuable detailed study:
Taylor, Robert, *The Trade Union Question in British Politics*, Oxford, Basil Blackwell, 1993.
A brief study:
Wrigley, Chris, *British Trade Unions since 1933*, Cambridge, Cambridge University Press, 2002.

Brief introductions to the trade union history of the post-1945 period

Fraser, W. Hamish, *A History of British Trade Unionism 1700–1998*, London, Macmillan, 1999.
Laybourn, Keith, *A History of British Trade Unionism, c.1770–1990*, Stroud, Alan Sutton, 1992.
Pelling, Henry, *A History of British Trade Unions*, London, Penguin, 1992.
Pimlott, Ben and Cook, Chris (eds), *Trade Unions in British Politics*, London, Macmillan, 1991.

Strikes

David Gilbert in Chris Wrigley (ed.), *History of British Industrial Relations 1939–79*.
Charlesworth, Andrew et al., *An Atlas of Industrial Protest in Britain 1750–1990*, London, Macmillan, 1996.
Cronin, James, *Industrial Conflict in Modern Britain*, London, Croom Helm, 1979.
Durcan, W., McCarthy, W. E. J. and Redman, G. P., *Strikes In Post-war Britain: A Study of Stoppages of Work due to Industrial Disputes, 1946–73*, London, Allen and Unwin, 1983.

Employers

Gospel, Howard, *Markets, Firms and the Management of Labour in Modern Britain*, Cambridge, Cambridge University Press, 1992.

Labour law

Davies, Paul and Freedland, Mark, *Labour Legislation and Public Policy*, Oxford, Oxford University Press, 1993.

Chronology

1948   Attlee governments (1945–51) call for voluntary wage restraint.

1956   White Paper: *The Economic Implications of Full Employment* (Mar.). Attempts by government to secure a 'price and wage plateau'.

1957   Engineering and shipbuilding strikes.

1962   Selwyn Lloyd (Chancellor of the Exchequer) introduces a 'pay pause'. NEDC established (government, employers and unions). NIC established.

1965   National Prices and Incomes Board. Trade Disputes Act.

1966   State of Emergency declared in May over seamen's strike.

1968   Report of Royal Commission on Trade Unions and Employers' Organisations (Donovan Report).

1969   *In Place of Strife* published (Jan.)

1970   National dock strike – State of Emergency declared.

1971   Industrial Relations Act.

1972   Three dockers sent to gaol for contempt of court. 90-day wage freeze (from Nov.).

1973   Miners start national overtime ban (Nov.). State of Emergency declared.

1974   Three day working week (from 1 Jan.).
National coal strike. General election, with defeat of Conservatives (Feb.). Trade Union and Labour Relations Act (1974).

1975   'Social Contract' with incomes policy as part of it.

1976   Government cuts (December) to secure IMF loan. Trade Union and Labour Relations Act (1976).

1979   Lorry drivers and public service workers' strikes ('winter of discontent').
Labour loses May general election.

1980   National steel strike. Employment Act, 1980.

1982   Employment Act, 1982.

1984   National coal strike (Mar. 1984–Feb. 1985). Trade Union Act, 1984.

1988   Employment Act, 1988.

1990   Employment Act, 1990.

1993   Trade Union Reform and Employment Rights Act.

1998   National Minimum Wage Act (with statutory minimum wage coming into operation in April 1999).

1999   Employment Relations Act.

23 The Welfare State Since 1945

Helen Fawcett

Introduction

When Prime Minister Tony Blair came to power in 1997, he announced his intention to 'modernise' the British welfare state. No other post-war Labour government since that led by Clement Attlee in 1945 has placed such a strong emphasis on social welfare. Ironically, many of the legislative achievements of the post-1945 Labour administration have been the focus of 'New Labour''s reforming zeal. In the 1999 Beveridge Memorial Lecture, Blair described the welfare state constructed after the war as being ineffective in the modern age.[1] His speech might have led his audience to believe that contemporary welfare arrangements are more or less the same as those put in place by the legislation of 1945–51. However, the welfare state has evolved over the course of the last fifty years or so, and, although its framework owes a great deal to the post-war legislation, much has changed. In this chapter, I will focus on a key aspect of the British welfare state – income maintenance policy. Income maintenance policy refers to anti-poverty measures that protect those who are unable to work: typically, the unemployed, the old, the sick and the disabled. In addition, some policies are designed to assist those who are in work, but who have insufficient income to meet their needs. Support does not only come from the social security system: the taxation system can be used to provide aid for the low-paid. Expenditure on the welfare state is one of the biggest activities of government, but aside from public spending on the National Health Service and education, the social security system constitutes one of the largest and most important core activities of the modern welfare state.

The argument presented in this chapter is that throughout the post-war years, both Labour and Conservative administrations have struggled to design a welfare system which meets the objectives of preventing poverty and low pay. More specifically, the history of the post-war era is concerned with the attempts to come to terms with the legacy of the welfare state as constructed in the late 1940s. The structure of British welfare arrangements owed much to the Beveridge Report (Cmnd 6404), *Social Insurance and Allied Services*, published in 1942. The report's author, William Beveridge, claimed that the system of social insurance he proposed would end poverty. However, within only a decade of his report being implemented, it became apparent that his system of social insurance was failing to meet this objective. The policy-makers of the 1940s designed a system of social security to meet existing social conditions. Their assumptions were based on a world of near-full employment, where most people had 'a job for life', and in which there was a stable family structure. They did not envisage conditions of long-term, large-scale unemployment as was experienced in the 1980s the restructuring of the labour force and the massive increase in divorce and lone parenthood. Consequently, during the post-war years British welfare arrangements have been forced to adapt to both economic and demographic pressures and changing social conditions. Equally, they have faced ideological challenges. 'The Golden Age' of welfare state development took place during the 1950s and 1960s, during a period of economic prosperity. Thereafter, both the cost and the effectiveness of the welfare state have been challenged, at first by conservative thinkers and politicians linked to the 'New Right', and most recently by their counterparts on the left. This reversal is reflected in the reshaping of national welfare states which has taken place throughout the world. By the end of the twentieth century, there was a new consensus that large social security systems are unsustainable and need to be retrenched: that the pressures of an ageing population will be an imperative for reform; and that forces of global economic competition demand that the tax burden and the level of public expenditure be kept at the lowest possible level. Although we can see these general trends from a cross-national perspective, this chapter will show that the particular way in which the British welfare state has evolved also influences the legitimacy of the welfare state and the policy choices available in the 1980s and 1990s. The basic structure of the welfare state was put in place after the war, and is the obvious starting point from which to understand the evolution of contemporary arrangements.

The Beveridge Report: Social Security from the Cradle to the Grave

> The 'moment of 1945' is profoundly wrapped up in what might be called the myths of recent British history which make it difficult to discern the precise character of the welfare regime which was created. On one side, '1945' is a triumphal moment – the point at which British society was transformed and a peculiarly British variety of 'socialism' was installed. Here, the welfare state, nationalisation and the managed economy are seen as a decisive break with the bad old days for pre-war Britain.[2]

The social and economic conditions of the 1920s and 1930s formed the background to the construction of the British welfare state after the war. Unemployment insurance was first introduced by the Liberal government of 1906–14,[3] and subsequently reformed on a number of occasions. However, it was not adequate to deal with the scale of mass unemployment witnessed in the 1930s.

During this period households faced a test of means to establish whether they were entitled to support when their unemployment benefit had expired. The memory of the humiliations of the means test was to play a role in the vision of a new social insurance system devised during the war. 'A wave of popular radicalisation throughout the west insisted on "no return to the thirties" as the price to be paid for the sacrifices of the war years. Social, as well as economic, reconstruction were central issue for post-war governments.'[4] An interplay of factors influenced post-war reconstruction. The politicians of the 1930s, associated with the appeasement of Hitler, were discredited and held responsible for Britain's unpreparedness for war, and military setbacks such as the defeat at Dunkirk.[5] At the same time, it has been argued that the acceptability of state intervention was increased by the popular experience of wartime conditions: mass evacuation; rationing; centralized state control and planning.[6] The Second World War has also been seen as the midwife of social change because of a swing to the left in popular opinion, and because of the need on the part of the Coalition government to develop and advocate a vision of 'reconstruction' after the war which would maintain popular morale during difficult times, such as the German bombing offensive against major cities and, particularly, the Blitz on the city of London.[7] However, one of the 'myths' that emerged in the post-war period was that the creation of the welfare state translated these dreams of post-war reconstruction into reality, which has frequently obscured the characteristics of the welfare system developed during the war.

In 1941, William Beveridge, an academic, former Permanent Secretary, and expert in the area of unemployment insurance (he helped frame the Liberal legislation of 1911) was given the task of chairing the Inter-Departmental Committee on Social Insurance and Allied Services. Beveridge seized the opportunity to devise a new scheme of social insurance based on the ideas he had developed over the years.[8] He envisaged a social security system in which all the various schemes would come together in a unitary national system. Support would be given to individuals for the full duration of the problem, whether it be unemployment, disability or retirement. The scheme was not funded from general taxation. It was to be based on the principle of insurance, comprising contributions from employers, employees and the Exchequer. Individuals would 'insure' themselves against the 'risks' or contingencies of certain life-events such as unemployment, sickness and old age, by paying contributions into a national insurance scheme which would pay them benefits in return. The collective insurance established entitlement to benefit as of right for those who had contributed. As a result there would be no means test. The hope was that most of the population would be included, but for those who were not covered by the new insurance scheme, there would be a new unitary national social assistance scheme which would act as a safety net. Thus the key principle underlying the Beveridge Report was that entitlement was to be based on labour market participation.

Beveridge spoke of 'five giants on the road to reconstruction': Want, Disease, Ignorance, Squalor and Idleness. His plan for social security was directed towards eliminating want, but his original paper was underpinned by three assumptions: the introduction of family allowances; a free national health service and full employment. Beveridge had come to believe that family allowances were essential to prevent the income of the low-paid falling below the poverty line when they had children. Family allowances addressed the issue of child poverty and a falling birth rate and was regarded as less expensive than a minimum wage. A free health service was needed to prevent medical bills eroding the value of benefits, and full employment was essential to guarantee and preserve the insurance basis of the scheme.

The first major proposal advanced by the Beveridge Report was the administrative rationalisation of social security. Since 1911, national insurance had expanded its coverage, but was administered by numerous different agencies. Beveridge wanted a single Ministry of Social Security and a unification of social insurance, so that a single weekly contribution would cover all benefits. The proposal for a unified social insurance would allow for a pooling of risks amongst all members of society. Beveridge wanted everyone to pay the same contributions and receive the same benefits. In short, he claimed that his new unified scheme would provide benefits which were sufficient to eliminate want.

The most important recommendation was that both benefits and contributions should be flat-rate (i.e. all contributors would pay the same sum of money in contributions and receive the same sum in benefits). The International Labour Office suggested the alternative that contributions and benefits should be related to earnings (in which case individuals would pay a percentage of their income as contributions). However, Beveridge was adamant in his support of the flat-rate principle. He believed that the earnings-related mechanism would damage personal saving. Some suggested that contributions should be related to earnings in return for flat-rate benefits. Again, Beveridge rejected this suggestion on the basis it would weaken the link between benefits and contributions. From Beveridge's perspective as a Liberal he wanted to make the insurance basis of the scheme as strong as possible in order to emphasise the notion of a contract between the individual and the state. His thinking represented a way of maintaining the incentive to work and enhance labour-market discipline. In addition, he rejected these options because he wanted to leave room in the market for private provision. It was not his intention to produce a social insurance scheme that was so generous that other forms of private provision would be unnecessary – in fact, he wished to encourage other forms of saving. His scheme aimed to establish a basic minimum below which no individual should fall.

Beveridge's objective was to marry the principle of social insurance with the establishment of a basic national minimum. He wished to base this on the principle of subsistence, which would serve two purposes. The first was that it set a minimum standard for adequacy and therefore benefits could not be reasonably set below subsistence. Secondly, it legitimated the range and the scope of the scheme because only a state scheme of the magnitude he envisaged could provide subsistence. It also satisfied the voluntary lobby as well, who wanted the state to provide the basic minimum and therefore enable them to maintain their role.

However, his use of a subsistence definition of poverty has been called into question. As Howard Glennester writes, Beveridge became convinced that the major causes of poverty were unemployment and old age, rather than low pay.[9] He adapted Rowntree's measures of the amount necessary to cover basic minimum needs without appreciating that these measures could not take account of unexpected expenses, and the difficulty in utilising income efficiently. Moreover, flat-rate subsistence benefits were always likely to be sabotaged by the problems associated with national and regional variations in rent levels. Thus, there was no way to take account of the variations in rents without introducing some means-tested element into the scheme. In addition, the principle of subsistence was always likely to be vulnerable when future governments attempted to reallocate, control or reduce public expenditure. There was no way of binding future governments to accept the principle and increase benefits accordingly.

The second difficult issue which emerged was how to offer cover to most of the population when it was based on insurance. There was a fundamental inconsistency between the notion of entitlement which was to be absolutely dependent on paid work and citizenship rights. A person was to have an absolute right and entitlement to benefit if they had a full contribution record. However, to achieve a full contribution record the individual had to be in paid employment. The result was that all those groups in society who were either excluded from the labour market or whose participation was erratic, were disenfranchised. In particular, what status would be given to married women under these proposals? Beveridge did not recommend that married women should have the same rights and entitlements: he assumed the vast majority would rely on their husbands, and be insured via their husbands, not in their own right. Beveridge used the family as the social unit around which the social security system would be based. After a woman married she would lose her entitlement to full sickness and unemployment benefit and would receive a lower rate of benefit. If she married, her pension would also be reduced.

For the old there would be a retirement pension paid at the ages of 60 for women and 65 for men. However, the cost of retirement pensions was bound to be heavy. Those approaching retirement when the scheme was introduced would not have a full record of contributions and would therefore not have paid enough to qualify for the new benefit. So Beveridge proposed a transition – there would be a 20-year period during which time pensions would build up to their full value.

The Beveridge Report (Cmnd. 6404), *Social Insurance and Allied Services*, was published in December 1942, and was received in an unprecedented manner. People queued outside government bookshops to buy the report and over one million copies were sold. The press greeted the report with great enthusiasm, coining the phrase, 'social security from the cradle to the grave'. Beveridge became a national hero, 'the people's William' and was surrounded by crowds wherever he went. As Paul Addison writes, his report had caught the popular mood because it came just at the right time. After the battle of El Alamein, the war seemed to be turning in the Allies' favour, and it was possible for people to look to the future and consider how society should be reconstructed in peacetime.[10]

The Coalition government was not in tune with the popular mood and the strength of feeling the Beveridge Plan had produced. The Cabinet decided not to support full subsistence or to agree to implement the scheme during the war. After the report was published a committee of civil servants began to study it in order to make recommendations to the government. This committee proposed to cut the level of family allowances by 37.5 per cent and thus there would be no relationship to subsistence. The committee also pointed out that a universal scheme involved giving benefits to those who did not need them. It rejected the idea of subsistence pensions because it argued pensioners had time to save for their retirement during their working lives. In addition, it was opposed to the idea of unemployment benefit continuing while the period of unemployment lasted. However, the government's report to Parliament appeared so negative that there was a division, with 121 MPs voting against the government and many more abstaining – the only serious pressure on the Coalition during the war.

However, the Labour Party endorsed the Beveridge Plan and committed itself to its implementation when it won the election of 1945. In this sense, the outburst of popular feeling in favour of reform greatly enhanced the chances of the report being implemented because politicians understood the political conse- quences of challenging the reform agenda. From another perspective, the en- dorsement of Beveridge may have been too uncritical. As Brian Abel Smith has written, the Labour Party became convinced by the rhetoric of the report and did not subject it to critical evaluation. It was only later that it became apparent that the social insurance scheme proposed might not be capable of delivering an end to poverty.[11]

The Implementation of the Beveridge Plan

As Rodney Lowe has pointed out, it is a mistake to think that the Beveridge Plan was fully implemented by the 1945 Labour government. Many aspects of the report did enter the statute books, but others were ignored or adjusted.[12] The central ideal of a single national social insurance scheme run by central government became law, but no Ministry of Social Security was instituted. Instead, there was to be a Ministry of National Insurance and a Ministry of National Assistance. The rates for unemployment benefit and pensions were set higher than had been proposed by the Coalition – but the rates selected were 31 per cent greater than those used by Beveridge, which had been based on 1938 prices. However, it is not clear whether either one of these indices were accur- ate. By the time the scheme was introduced in 1948 wages had risen by 76 per cent and prices had risen by 72 per cent, which meant that benefits were a third below what Beveridge had recommended for subsistence.[13]

Under the 1948 scheme benefits were to be indexed every five years, set only slightly above National Assistance, and those who received Assistance would usually have their rent paid on top. As a result, the numbers claiming National Assistance – the safety net – grew. In summary, there were many issues in the design of the social insurance system which raised questions. First of all, the notion of linking entitlement to work and insurance has been questioned be- cause it immediately created divisions between those in work and the rest. 'The rest' were a significant group: in particular, the structure of the system under-mined the citizenship rights of women. Secondly, attempting to provide subsist-ence benefits via flat-rate insurance proved impossible, as will be discussed in the next section.

The Beveridge Plan is often described as the blueprint for the modern British welfare state. From the point of view of political scientists and policy analysts, this term has deeper meaning in that the history of British social security is a history of the policy legacies which emerge from the Beveridge Report. In the decades after the 1940s, the report and the way in which it was implemented had a fundamental influence on the problems which confront policy-makers, and often created the very crises that confronted them.

The Aftermath of the Beveridge Plan

The first major issue to arise in the 1950s was the crisis of the National Insur-ance scheme. The Philips Committee discovered that there had been an increase in the numbers claiming means-tested National Assistance.[14] This was com-pletely at odds with Beveridge's vision of the scheme and the aspirations of the Labour Party policy-makers. The intention was a system of social security where most people relied on National Insurance benefits. For policy-makers on the left of the political spectrum, who supported the Beveridge scheme precisely because of the promised abolition of the stigmatizing means tests associated with the mass unemployment of the 1930s, it was a grave disappointment. The reason for the growth in the numbers claiming National Assistance was the simple fact that National Insurance was not adequate, and in particular, could not take account of housing costs. The second unpalatable fact to emerge from the review was that many of those claiming National Assistance were pension-ers. This dealt another blow to the system's credibility, because pensioners are frequently regarded as the most deserving social group, having 'worked hard all their lives' and entitled to a retirement free from financial worries.

The greatest obstacle to attaining adequacy in benefit levels was the nature of the insurance scheme that Beveridge had designed. A system of flat-rate benefits financed by flat-rate contributions was necessarily, tied to what the poorest wage-earner could afford to pay in weekly contributions. This was the disad-vantage of the scheme in comparison to those continental models of superannu-ation which were based on the principle of earnings-related benefits and contributions: in these schemes contributions were based on a percentage of the individual's income rather than a flat-rate amount.[15] The flat-rate basis of the contributions limited the amount of revenue coming in to the National Insurance fund. The difficulties this created were highlighted in 1957 when further demands were made on the social security system. The previous Labour government had deemed it politically unacceptable to exclude the elderly from the benefits of the new social security system, and had decided that those retir-ing after 1957 would receive full retirement pensions. However, this age cohort had not contributed to the scheme during their working lives – at best they had made ten years'-worth of contributions.

A second feature of the 1950s was the Conservative commitment to privatisation, particularly in the field of pensions, which destroyed the principle of universalism and comprehensiveness elaborated in the Beveridge Plan. This aspect of policy was a crucial difference between the Labour and Conservative parties and contradicts the notion that there was a post-war consensus in social policy. The Conservatives deliberately fostered the growth of private-sector occupational schemes by maintaining a modest state pension. The 1959 National Insurance Act instituted a graduated pension scheme which was very largely used to finance the basic state pension scheme rather than to provide a proper earnings-related one. The scheme was very poor value for the contributor and has frequently been dismissed as a political gimmick. However, its importance lay in allowing the private sector to 'contract out' on relatively easy terms. By 1961, the number of contracted-out employees was 4.1 million. The result was a substantial growth in the size of the occupational pension sector: by the 1960s around half the working population were contributing to private occupational pension schemes'.[16]

Social Policy in the 1960s

When the Labour Party returned to power in 1964 it had to address the failure of the social security system to provide adequate living standards. This was reflected in the groundbreaking report *The Poor and the Poorest*, written by Brian Abel Smith and Peter Townsend. They found that a large number of families with children were living on incomes below that of National Assistance. In 1953–4 the number of people living in poverty had been 600,000, but this appeared to have risen to 2 million by 1964.[17] In this sense, the 1960s became the decade in which poverty was rediscovered. In order to ameliorate this situation the Labour government introduced a number of measures. During the 1950s, it had adopted a policy of earnings-related benefits and contributions, very similar to the social security systems operating elsewhere in Europe. It began with a state superannuation scheme, but when the Labour Party came to office it was successful in extending the principle of earnings-related benefits to unemployment, sickness and disability in 1965. The rationale was that for a short period, families would not experience a huge reduction in income. The government also made an initial large increase in the value of the basic pension. Towards the end of its term of office it attempted to launch its proposal for National Superannuation. The White Paper reflected a change in Labour Party thinking, largely brought about by the need to adapt the growth in private occupational pensions. Its initial idea was to launch a national scheme which would, in all probability, have halted the growth of private pensions. By the late 1960s it proposed an accommodation with the private sector, allowing them to operate alongside the state scheme. In the event, the proposals never reached the statute book because the 1970 general election was called before they could become law.

The persistent inadequacy of National Insurance benefits led to a mushrooming of means-tested benefits to add a variety of income supplements. One of the most important was rate rebates, which were introduced in 1966, and those on National Assistance (Supplementary Benefit) increased to 7.7 per cent of the population. The government made some attempt to increase family allowances, but the financial pressures facing the government meant that this attempt to combat child poverty was far from adequate.

The government attempted to minimize the stigmatizing effects of means-testing benefits and to give better publicity to the benefits on offer (in order to combat the problem of low take-up). The ministries of National Insurance and National Assistance were merged into the Department of Health and Social Security, and National Assistance was renamed Supplementary Benefit.

The 1970s: The Welfare State in Crisis

The themes of the 1960s continued to be pursued in the 1970s. In particular, both the Conservative and Labour parties elaborated measures to tackle family poverty and the problem of low pay. In 1970 the Conservatives introduced the Family Income Supplement Act, targeted towards the low-paid with children. However, this type of benefit encouraged a 'poverty trap' in that families lost benefit as their incomes rose. After the difficulties in finding a satisfactory way to increase family allowances in the 1960s, the Labour government introduced universal Child Benefit in 1975.

The final significant piece of social legislation was the introduction of the State Earnings-Related Pension Scheme (SERPs) in 1975. It reached the statute books with cross-party support, after both parties had unsuccessfully attempted to develop such a scheme since the 1950s. The scheme offered a two-tier state pension scheme, operating in partnership with private-sector occupational schemes.[18]

However, from the mid-1970s academic and public debate became concerned with the notion of 'welfare state crisis'. The beginning of the 1970s witnessed the economic phenomenon of 'stagflation' – the condition of low growth and high inflation. The oil crisis of 1973 fuelled inflation and by the end of the 1970s Western industrial nations were experiencing high unemployment. Anthony Crosland, the Labour Cabinet minister, coined the phrase, 'the party's over' to describe the difficulties low economic growth was going to impose on public spending. In parallel, there was increasing concern about the long-term affordability of the welfare state.

The conjunction of these factors helped to produce or exacerbate a crisis of legitimacy. To a certain degree this crisis was implicit in the structure of the British welfare state, which fostered a 'social division of welfare'. The low level of benefits provided by the state encouraged those with spare resources to make alternative provision. In areas of provision, such as health, which were relied upon by most social groups, there was a high level of support and legitimacy. By contrast, unemployment benefit did not enjoy popular support. Indeed, those in receipt of unemployment benefit were often accused of being feckless and workshy. The 1970s also saw the beginnings of a serious political challenge to the welfare state. The development of the 'New Right' in the 1970s reflected a new and distinctive stance towards the welfare state.

The Advent of the New Right

It should be emphasised that 'the New Right' is a generic term for a number of different strands of economic and political thinking. The first characteristic of the New Right was the belief that the welfare state was economically inefficient. The welfare state consumes a large proportion of public expenditure financed by direct and indirect taxation. This was seen as inhibiting entrepreneurial culture because high taxation acted as a disincentive to business and individual effort. High public expenditure also encouraged inflation. The welfare state was perceived as encouraging a culture of dependency. The benefit system was seen as a disincentive to finding work, and some thinkers regarded it as encouraging a 'moral degeneration' among the poor. Theorists from the public choice school argued that bureaucrats act in their own self-interest, and those in charge of the welfare system had no incentive to be efficient; on the contrary, in order to increase their power and influence, it was in their interest to allow welfare bureaucracy to grow.

These ideas came to be accepted by a large section of the Conservative Party in the 1980s. However, it should not be assumed that the Thatcher administrations represent the complete translation of these ideas into law. Indeed, one of the lessons of the 1980s is that it is difficult to rein back spending on state welfare. In many areas there is a gap between the rhetoric and the actions of New Right administrations.

The Conservative Administrations, 1979–1997

Although there has been much scholarly debate exploring the degree to which Thatcherism marked a radical break with the past, there can be little doubt that the Conservatives did have a considerable impact on the British welfare state. As Paul Wilding argues:

> what we have seen is a gradualist but sustained attempt to extend private provision and market principles. There has been no large-scale attempt to re-commodify welfare goods – apart from housing, which has always been a very mixed economy – but private provision is now much more firmly established within all major areas of welfare and market values and mechanisms have thrust deep into the former collectivist strongholds of health and education.[19]

Wilding proceeds to describe how the gradual erosion of social rights in terms of their generosity, the introduction of quasi-markets, and shifts from the public-sector to private-sector provision meant that certain welfare sectors were progressively residualised, paving the way for more radical change. Most importantly, many of the policies that were pursued in the 1980s and 1990s produced certain structural changes which would be hard for an incoming government with a different ideological outlook to reverse.

In the field of social security we need to evaluate a combination of structural reform with a number of measures to limit the generosity of state provision. The Conservatives moved swiftly to abolish short-term earnings-related sickness and unemployment benefit. The Conservatives believed that these benefits, which reduced the financial hardship of losing full-time employment for a period, acted as a disincentive to find work. By the same token, they were believed to encourage people to stay on sick pay for longer than strictly necessary. Thus in 1982 these supplements were abolished and unemployment and supplementary benefit were made taxable.

The administration of sick pay was reformed. Until 1983 it had been paid by local Social Security offices. From 1983 it was to be administered by employers. At first employers were repaid for the costs of sick pay. But from 1992, employers became responsible for bearing the costs of sick pay and thus, in the view of the government, they had an incentive to police levels of absence for sickness amongst employees.

The most important change in the Thatcher years was to change the basis on which benefits were uprated or increased on a regular basis. As Glennester points out, it had been standard practice to increase benefits in line with increases in average earnings. The result of this policy was that the basic pension had doubled from 1948. From 1982 the government announced that pensions would be increased in line with prices. This meant that the basic pension progressively lost value – 23 per cent of average earnings in 1981 to 15 per cent in 1993, and assumed to fall to 10 per cent in 2010.[20]

The Fowler Review

A Green Paper on social security was published in 1985 aimed to reduce costs and restructure the British welfare state. The Conservatives were attracted to the idea of ending the wasteful nature of the so-called universal nature of the British welfare state, and replace it with a system targeted to those most in need. However, as the review demonstrated, the British welfare state was already one of the most highly targeted welfare systems in Europe.

The other major attempt to save money was the proposal to abolish SERPS and retain the basic state pension. In order to ensure an adequate standard of living in their old age, individuals would be compelled to contribute 4 per cent of their income to some kind of pension scheme. Financial incentives would be available to encourage contributions to private pension schemes. However, the attempt to save money would be offset by the cost of the financial incentives to join private pension scheme. Glennester reports that the Treasury calculated that abolishing SERPS would actually cost money and employer costs would also rise.[21] The abolition of SERPS was met with opposition from a variety of quarters, including the Confederation of British Industry (CBI) and the pensions industry, who were wary of having to take responsibility for poorer wage earners. As a profit-making concern, the insurance industry was reluctant to enter into less profitable sectors of the pension market.

Thus the attempt to abolish SERPS was abandoned. However, the structure of social security was radically changed. The value of the SERPS pension was reduced, while the Conservatives introduced subsidies to encourage the growth of the private sector. The Social Security Act of 1986 introduced another tier of private pension provision. From 1988, the contributor was given the choice of whether to replace their occupational pension or SERPS pension with a personal pension. The government offered financial incentives for individuals to purchase these, demonstrating that this reform was ideologically rather than economically motivated. The overall result of the package of reform measures, including the change in the method of indexing the basic state pension, led to an important shift in the balance between the public and the private sector – those covered by the private sector expanded from one-half of the working population to two-thirds.[22]

Another target of the Fowler Green Paper was the range of discretionary benefits available in the social security system. These benefits covered unusual items of expenditure which could not be met from the claimant's weekly benefit. Items covered included such things as bedding, furniture and special dietary requirements. These costs seemed out of control. The government's solution to this problem was to set annual limits on the budget available to fund these requirements. The Social Fund replaced the system of discretionary payments. Local social security offices were encouraged to make loans from the fund, which would be repaid from weekly benefit. The Social Fund reduced the cost of emergency payments but more was spent on Family Credit. Family Credit replaced Family Income Supplement and was directed towards the families of the low-paid. Income Support replaced Supplementary Benefit. However, the overall impact of government policy was that spending on means-tested benefit remained about the same, although it was distributed differently. More was given to the elderly, the sick and children – less to the unemployed and their families.

An important theme of government policy was its advocacy of measures which have an impact of social behaviour. Although we have to exercise caution in evaluating whether the primary intention was cost reduction rather than moral rehabilitation, these types of measures were a distinctive feature of government policy. The moral basis of Conservative social policy was underlined by the tests that the government placed on the unemployed. The Conservatives abolished contributory unemployment benefit (available for one year to those with an appropriate contribution record) in 1996 and replaced it with the Job Seeker's Allowance (available for six months), which included an agreement on the initiatives that the individual should take to take to find work.[23] It reduced the level of unemployment benefit by 20 per cent for 18–25-year-olds. In 1988, income support was withdrawn for 16–18-year-olds – the rationale being that they should be supported by their families.

During the 1990s the government became concerned with the growth in the number of lone mothers claiming Income Support. In 1993 there were one million lone parents, or 14 per cent of all families with dependent children – 66 per cent were dependent on income support (330,00 in 1980 and 779,000 in 1989). Of these, 66 per cent were divorced, 33 per cent never married and 7 per cent were widowed. The government wanted to reduce the burden on the Exchequer. However, certain elements within the Conservative Party wanted to halt the rise in lone parenthood, and were influenced by ideas which linked the disintegration of traditional family structure to the rise of crime and an increase in welfare dependency among a new social 'underclass'. The number of lone mothers claiming Income Support was 320,000 in 1979, but had risen to one million in 1991.[24] This was the background to the Child Support Act of 1991 which stipulated that lone mothers must authorise the state to recover maintenance from the absent father. The formula used to decide how income was distributed between first and second families created much criticism and the legislation provoked a great deal of hostility against the government.

New Labour, New Welfare

Prior to the 1997 election, the Labour leadership were determined to shed the party's image of 'tax and spend' which it believed alienated middle-class voters. As a result, the election was fought on the promise not to increase income taxes, and to maintain the Conservative government's public expenditure limits for two years after the election. Such a policy suggested that Labour's programme would evolve under extremely tight spending limits. However, large increases in expenditure were made in the popular areas of health and education. Thus, commentators have characterised government policy as 'selective universalism' or 'patchwork redistribution'.

The Prime Minister, Tony Blair, advocated a 'Third Way' between Old Labour and the New Right with the objective of modernising an allegedly outmoded and underperforming welfare state. However, it is clear that the government redefined the British social democratic approach to the welfare state. In doing so it produced a programme which combines both elements of Left and Right, abandoning many traditional features of social democracy whilst retaining others. A degree of income redistribution has taken place 'by stealth', and poverty has re-emerged as an issue on the government's agenda. In this sense, it appears that jettisoning the strategies of 'Old Labour' and the construction of a unique policy which owes little to post-war social democracy proved more difficult than imagined.

Re-casting Social Democracy: The Development of the 'Third Way'

During the 1980s, the Labour opposition responded to Conservative policy by promising to reverse the government's reforms and to restore cuts in public expenditure when it returned to office. Essentially, the Opposition followed the same type of agenda it had pursued since the Second World War, depicting themselves as the architects and defenders of the British welfare state established under the post-war Labour administration led by Clement Attlee. At first this policy of 'root-and-branch' opposition seemed viable. However, in the aftermath of the party's fourth election defeat in 1992, a process of re-evaluation and reflection began.

The change in Labour Party thinking on social welfare dates from the Report of the Commission on Social Justice (the Borrie Commission, 1994).[25] Established by John Smith in 1992, the report contained key themes, which were developed later under 'New Labour', namely that social welfare should be concerned with both social justice and economic efficiency. The report marks an important break with post-war social democracy, speaking of individual opportunity and life chances. The central concern is the need to provide individuals with the skills needed for a modern global economy.

The development of these ideas was strongly influenced by predictions about the likely effects of globalisation on social life. It no longer seemed credible to base the funding of the welfare state on the assumption that individuals would be in full-time employment for most of their working lives, or indeed that there would be a male breadwinner in every household. Equally, changes in patterns of employment were likely to have an impact on social cohesion, possibly leading to the disintegration of old communities and generating an increase in crime and deprivation.

The central themes of the 'Third Way' were twofold. First of all, it was argued that the traditional welfare state was no longer affordable because of demographic pressures such as the ageing population. However, it was also asserted that there was public resistance to high levels of taxation which set limits on the revenues available to fund social welfare.[26] Secondly, the welfare state was perceived to be the source of social problems rather than the cure. Blair and his followers adopted ideas from the outgoing Conservative administration, and American proponents of welfare reform, which suggested that state welfare fosters a 'culture of dependency' and plays a role in creating and maintaining a social underclass isolated from the economic benefits of employment. Moreover, dependency on state support was also viewed as producing social isolation. Welfare claimants were viewed as losing the self-esteem and self-discipline associated with regular employment and were excluded from participation in normal social life.

The philosophy underpinning the social democratic welfare state was that of collective insurance against the risk of ill health, unemployment or disability. The discourse of the 'Third Way' moved away from one of rights and entitlements to social protection, in favour of the welfare state's role in social investment, facilitating a return to work, and thereby creating economic security and social participation.

The New Deal

The centrepiece of government policy was the New Deal for the Unemployed and exemplifies the priority the government accorded to paid employment, and restoring the work ethic to the welfare system. The welfare-to-work strategy focused on the young unemployed (18 to 24 years of age), the long-term unemployed and lone parents. Young people who were unemployed for more than six months were offered four options:

- the possibility of full-time study or training in an approved programme for six months
- subsidised employment with a private-sector employer. Firms would receive a subsidy of £60 per week for six months as long as they provide one day's training each week
- work in the voluntary sector
- work with the Environmental Task Force.

The unemployed would undergo four months of counselling or training prior to taking up one of these options. Older workers who were unemployed for more than two years would have access to subsidised employment. Lone parents with school-age children were offered advice on training careers and childcare. Participation in the New Deal was compulsory – and as such constituted a type of American-style workfare. This demonstrates how far the Labour Party redefined the relationship between the individual and the state. Under the system of social insurance established after the Second World War, entitlement to benefit was based on the individual's participation in the labour market. During their working life, individuals made contributions to the national insurance fund, thus insuring themselves against the risk of unemployment, sickness and disability. The notion of an entitlement to benefit has now been weakened. Refusal to accept any of the options offered under the New Deal without good reason leads to a suspension of benefit for two weeks and for a further four weeks if the unemployed person continues to refuse. Thus receipt of benefit has become conditional on meeting a new set of contractual obligations specified by the government.

However, the New Deal for the Unemployed must be viewed in the overall context of government policy, which was based on a system of reciprocal obligations. The 1998 Green Paper on welfare reform summarised the government's position: it is the state's duty to provide opportunities, it is the individual's to take them up.[27] In addition, the government committed itself 'to making work pay', acknowledging that the unemployed often face financial disincentives in taking up paid work, as well as other barriers such as transport and access to childcare. Thus the government introduced a national minimum wage in April 1999 in order to reduce low pay. The government has been particularly concerned to remove the disincentives to employment created by the loss of benefit entitlements when the unemployed return to work. The main focus was assisting the low-paid with family responsibilities by introducing the Working Families' Tax Credit in place of Family Credit and the new Children's Tax Credit. In addition, universal Child Benefit was increased. When these measures were combined with the increases in allowances for dependent children in Income Support, the Treasury estimated that the number of children in poverty should fall by 800,000 by the end of the Parliament.

However, measures to assist working families were not applicable to all those who rely on social security in one form or another. Levels of income support increased substantially for families with children, and pensioners, but for other groups and for those claiming the Job Seeker's Allowance, benefit levels have been frozen in real terms. The overall impact of government policy probably reduced the numbers in poverty by about two million. As David Piachaud comments: 'Most of the likely reduction in poverty is the result of old-style redistribution, even if it is achieved with new-style tax credits. This is ironic – though no less welcome – since "redistribution" is a term rarely used by members of the Government.'[28]

However, the government's claim to promote work for those who can and security for those who cannot was open to dispute because many of those dependent on social security will continue to be so. Welfare-to-work programmes did not change the fact that most of those requiring social security are pensioners and the disabled. The fear was that the focus on in-work benefits may residualise benefits for those unable to work. Moreover, Piachaud points out that the erosion of social insurance threatens the long-run political support for the social security system: Britain risks being the only major Organization for Economic Cooperation and Development (OECD) country without a secure social insurance foundation to tackle poverty. In summary we see a rather mixed picture, in which the government focused its efforts towards certain groups but neglected others.

Summary

My discussion in this chapter has given an overview of the developments in income maintenance policy from Beveridge to Blair. As we have seen, the Beveridge system failed to produce benefits which would eliminate poverty, and although it aimed at providing a system which provided adequate universal benefits, it evolved into a system in which means testing proliferated and market alternatives grew. The idea of a post-war consensus in support of social welfare broke down in the 1980s. However, by the end of the century we have seen the formation of elements of a new consensus, critical of the post-war welfare state and aiming to achieve its transformation.

The decision to provide flat-rate benefits in return for flat-rate contributions threatened the viability of the Beveridge model of social security. First of all, it meant that contributions could only be increased according to what the poorest wage-earners could be reasonably expected to pay. Secondly, it provide a universal benefit which provided a low level of basic income security. This meant that the better-off were likely to turn to private-sector alternatives, as we can see in the case of private pension provision in the 1960s. In this sense, a social divide developed which undermined the legitimacy of the scheme. This was not the case in health, where most people relied on the National Health Service for health care. The social division in social security increased the stigma associated with claiming benefits – something Beveridge had hoped to eradicate.

Although earnings-related benefits were adopted in the 1960s, the economic crisis that followed swiftly in the 1970s began to undermine the philosophy that underpinned the post-war welfare state. Fears grew that the welfare state had become unaffordable, and a new brand of Conservative politics, associated with the thinkers of the 'New Right' was hostile to state welfare provision. The 1980s and 1990s saw the Conservative government attempting to retrench levels of social spending. Benefits became less generous in amount and shorter in duration. The government also sought to increase private provision, particularly in the case of pensions.

Throughout most of this period the Labour opposition was committed to reversing Conservative policies. However, by 1997, when 'New Labour' returned to power, its stance had changed. The government committed itself to an ambitious programme of welfare reform which built on the legacy of the previous Conservative administration. It committed itself to using the social security system as a way of providing the individual with incentives to enter or return to the labour market. It rejected many of the ideas of rights and entitlements associated with the welfare state instituted after the Second World War and advocated a programme of 'modernisation'. However, although the post-war consensus may have been superseded, the welfare state has proved to be a durable and well-established feature of British society.

Notes

1   A. Blair, Beveridge Memorial Lecture, Toynbee Hall, London, March 1999.
2   A. Cochrane and J. Clarke (eds), *Comparing Welfare States: Britain in International Context*, London, Sage, 1993, p. 29.
3   J. R. Hay, *The Origins of the Liberal Reforms. 1906–1914*, London, Macmillan, 1975.
4   Cochrane and Clarke, *Welfare States*, p. 20.
5   P. Addison, *The Road to 1945*, London, Jonathan Cape, 1975, p. 111.
6   Ibid., pp. 116–17, discusses this perspective, which was advanced by the social policy expert Richard Titmuss.
7   Ibid., pp. 125–63.
8   H. Glennester, *British Social Policy Since 1945*, Oxford, Blackwell, 1996, pp. 24–6.
9   Ibid., pp. 31–2.
10 Addison, *Road to 1945*, pp. 211–28.
11 B. Abel-Smith, 'Assessing the Balance Sheet', in H. Glennester (ed.), *The Future of Welfare*, London, Heinemann, 1983.
12 R. Lowe, *The Welfare State in Britain since 1945*, London, Macmillan, 1999.
13 B. Abel-Smith, 'The Beveridge Report: Its Origins and Outcomes', in J. Hills et al. (eds), *Beveridge and Social Security: An International Retrospective*, Oxford: Clarendon Press, 1994, p. 20.
14 Cmnd 9333, *Report of the Committee on the Economic and Financial Problems of Old Age*, London, HMSO, 1954.
15 H. Heclo, *Modern Social Policies in Britain and Sweden*, New Haven, Yale University Press, 1974.
16 H. Fawcett, 'The Beveridge Straight-Jacket: Policy Formation and the Problem of Poverty in Old Age', *Contemporary British History* 10, Spring 1996: 20–42.
17 Lowe, *Welfare State in Britain since 1945*, p. 140.
18 H. Fawcett, 'The Privatisation of Welfare: The Impact of Parties on the Private/ Public Mix in Pension Provision', *West European Politics* 18 (4), 1995: 150–69.

19   P. Wilding, 'The British Welfare State: Thatcherism's Enduring Legacy', *Policy and Politics* 20 (3), 1992, p. 203.

20   Glennester, *British Social Policy*, pp. 181–2.

21   Ibid., p. 184.

22   Fawcett, 'Privatisation of Welfare'.

23   D. King, *In the Name of Liberalism: Illiberal Social Policy in the United States and Britain*, Oxford, Oxford University Press, 1999, pp. 247–8.

24   Department of Social Security, *The Growth of Social Security*, 1993.

25   N. Ellison, 'The Changing Politics of Social Policy', in N. Ellison and C. Pierson (eds), *Developments in British Social Policy*, London, Macmillan, 1998, pp. 38–42.

26   A. Blair and G. Schroeder, 'Europe: The Third Way/Die Neue Mitte', Labour Party website, 1999.

27   New Ambitions for Our Country: A New Contract for Welfare, Cm 3805, London: HMSO, 1998.

28   D. Piachaud, 'The Prospects for Poverty', *New Economy*, 5 (1), 1998, pp. 8–13.

Further Reading

Howard Glennester's *British Social Policy Since 1945* (Oxford, Blackwell, 1996) offers an accessible and reliable textbook on this period. This can be read in conjunction with Rodney Lowe's *The Welfare State in Britain since 1945* (London, Macmillan, 1999), which presents a clear and analytical account. *Comparing Welfare States: Britain in International Context*, edited by Allan Cochrane and John Clarke (London: Sage), is another good introduction, which deals with some important theoretical issues and which looks at Britain in comparative perspective. For a more detailed consideration of the 1980s, Nicholas Deakin's *The Politics of Welfare* (Hemel Hempstead, Harvester Wheatsheaf, 1994) is an excellent and detailed account. New Labour's programme of welfare reform is assessed in Polly Toynbee and David Walker's *Did Things Get Better?: An Audit of Labour's Successes and Failures?* (Harmondsworth, Penguin 2001).

Chronology

1942   *Social Insurance and Allied Services* (Beveridge Report), Cmnd 6404.
1946   National Insurance Act.
1948   National Assistance Act.
1964   National Insurance Act.
1964   Family Allowances and National Insurance Act.
1970   National Insurance (Old Persons' and Widows' Pensions) Act.
1970   Family Income Supplement Acts.
1973   Social Security Act.
1975   Social Security Benefits Act.
1975   Social Security Pensions Act.
1975   Child Benefit Act. SERPs introduced.
1985   *The Reform of Social Security*, DSS Cmnd 9517.
1986   Social Security Act introduces personal pensions.
1988   Income support withdrawn for 16–18-year-olds.
1991   Child Support Act.

1992   Borrie Commission established.
1996   Job Seeker's Allowance introduced.
1998   *New Ambitions for our Country: A New Contract for Welfare*, Cm 3805.
1999   National Minimum Wage introduced.

Index